American Private International Law

Kluwer Law International

American Private International Law

Prof. Symeon C. Symeonides

This book was originally published as a monograph in the International Encyclopaedia of Laws/Private International Law.

Wolters Kluwer
Law & Business

AUSTIN BOSTON CHICAGO NEW YORK THE NETHERLANDS

Published by
Kluwer Law International
PO Box 316
2400 AH Alphen aan den Rijn
The Netherlands
Website: www.kluwerlaw.com

Sold and distributed in North, Central and South America by
Aspen Publishers, Inc.
7201 McKinney Circle
Frederick, MD 21704
United States of America
E-mail: customer.care@aspenpubl.com

Sold and distributed in all other countries by
Turpin Distribution Services Ltd
Stratton Business Park
Pegasus Drive, Biggleswade
Bedfordshire SG18 8TQ
United Kingdom
E-mail: kluwerlaw@turpin-distribution.com

Printed on acid-free paper.

ISBN 978-90-411-2742-6

The Author

Symeon C. Symeonides was born in 1949, in Lythrodontas, Cyprus. He received his first two law degrees *summa cum laude* (in private and public law) from the Aristotelian University of Thessaloniki in Greece, and the next two (an LL.M. and an S.J.D.) from the Harvard Law School. He began his law teaching career at Thessaloniki, and then continued at Louisiana State University, where he became the Judge Albert Tate Professor of Law and Vice Chancellor. Since 1999, he has served as Dean and Professor of Law at Willamette University in Salem, Oregon. In the interim, he has also taught and lectured widely at several American and European universities, including the Hague Academy of International Law.

Symeonides has drafted three private international law codifications and provided legislative advice to several governments. Among his publications are 20 books and more than 80 articles, including the widely read annual surveys of American choice-of-law cases now in their 20th year. He is President of the American Society of Comparative Law and the recipient of the first Friedrich K. Juenger Prize in Private International Law.

The Author

Table of Contents

General Introduction

Chapter 1. Introduction

§1. Scope and Coverage

1. This volume is a brief presentation of the law of private international law (PIL) in the United States of America. Given the nature of the series of which it is a part, this volume is intended for readers outside the United States who are generally familiar with basic PIL methodology, concepts, and norms, though not necessarily with the American peculiarities. One of the consequences of the volume's required brevity is that the discussion is infrequently footnoted and may often appear conclusory. It is hoped that these deficiencies can be cured by consulting the treatises and monographs listed at the end of this chapter, some of which are written by the undersigned author.

2. First, a couple of points regarding nomenclature. For historical reasons, the term 'private international law', although coined by an American writer (Joseph Story), has not prevailed in the United States. Instead, this subject is known as 'conflict of laws', a term first used by a European writer (Ulrich Huber). Neither term is perfect. The term 'private international law' is accurate in describing the cases that fall within the scope of the subject, namely private-law disputes that have a significant international (or interstate) dimension. However, this term can also be misleading to the extent it allows the uninitiated to infer that this branch of the law emanates from a supranational source. Needless to say, reality is much different. Besides the few international conventions that avoid or resolve conflicts cases through substantive or choice-of-law rules, international law provides little guidance on the subject. Thus, for the most part, the task of resolving conflicts cases is left to individual states or countries, subject to certain mild restraints imposed by international law. Accordingly, conflicts law is essentially national law. Moreover, as noted later, within the United States, conflicts law is, *de facto* and primarily, state rather than federal law.

The term 'conflict of laws' is not much better. It seems to assume that, in all multistate cases, each involved state[1] has an active or passive desire, claim, or 'interest' to apply its own law, and suggesting that these claims 'conflict' in the sense of always pushing in opposite directions. Both of these assumptions are questionable. For example, even accepting the propriety of using anthropomorphic terms to describe state objectives, one can question whether or why a state would be 'interested' in the outcome of disputes between private persons. Similarly, one can question whether such a state 'interest' is implicated in each case connected with that state, or whether the application of that state's law indeed effectuates that interest. Nevertheless, for better or worse, the term 'conflict of laws' has prevailed in the United States and a few other common law jurisdictions, and is used throughout this volume.

1. Hereafter the word 'state' is used to denote any country or a territorial subdivision of a country, such as a state or province, that has its own system of private law. Thus, the United States, a state of the United States, a Canadian province, or France, are 'states' within the meaning of this definition. Cases involving the laws of more than one state are referred to hereafter as 'multistate' cases.

3. Conflicts law consists of three parts: (1) jurisdiction, which deals with the question of which of the involved states' courts may adjudicate the dispute; (2) choice of law, which deals with the question of whether the merits of the dispute will be resolved under the substantive law of the state of adjudication (*lex fori*) or under the law of another involved state; and (3) judgment-recognition, which deals with the requirements under which the courts of one state will recognize and enforce a judgment rendered in another state.

This volume focuses primarily on choice of law. Jurisdiction is covered extensively in civil procedure treatises, including a volume in this Encyclopaedia.[1] For this reason, and due to space limitations, this volume discusses adjudicatory jurisdiction only to the extent necessary to facilitate the understanding of choice of law.[2] The space saved from this limitation is used to discuss the multifaceted role of federalism, which is even more essential to the foreign reader's understanding of American conflicts law. This includes the federal-state allocation of lawmaking[3] and judicial powers,[4] the constitutional limitations on state choice of law[5] and the resolution of conflicts between federal and foreign law.[6] The volume concludes with discussion of recognition of sister-state[7] and foreign-country judgments.[8]

1. *See*, e.g., J. Oakley & V. Amar, *Civil Procedure*, Volume 5, *International Encyclopaedia of Laws* (The Netherlands, Kluwer Law International, 2001).
2. *See* Chapter 2, *infra*.
3. *See infra* 17–23. Unless otherwise indicated, all cross-references are to paragraph numbers.
4. *See infra* 46–63, 64–75.
5. *See infra* 76–105.
6. *See* Part II, Chapter 9, *infra*.
7. *See* Part III, Chapter 1, *infra*.
8. *See* Part III, Chapter 2, *infra*.

§2. The American Framework

4. The fact that the United States is a federal, multistate, plurilegal system entails certain challenges and limitations to this volume. Strictly speaking, the term 'American conflicts law' is a misnomer – there is no single American conflicts law.[1] Rather, there are as many conflicts laws in the United States as there are states or 'jurisdictions' that constitute the United States. Today, this includes 50 states, the District of Columbia[2] and the United States itself as a separate sovereign with its own system of federal laws.

1. To be sure, the use of the term 'American' when referring to only one of the countries of the American continent is also a misnomer. Nevertheless, it is used solely for the sake of brevity and in full awareness of its technical inaccuracy.
2. The Commonwealth of Puerto Rico, which enjoys a special relationship described as free association (*estado libre associado*) with the United States, is also included in this study. For a discussion of this status and Puerto Rico conflicts law, *see* S. Symeonides, 'Revising Puerto Rico's Conflicts Law: A Preview', 28 *Colum J. Transnat'l L.* 601 (1990).

5. The United States Constitution allocates lawmaking powers between the federal government and the constituent states by granting to the federal government enumerated powers on matters of national concern[1] and reserving to the states the remaining powers, including the great bulk of private law.[2] By establishing and preserving a plurilegal federal union, the Constitution creates the conditions for the occurrence of four different categories of conflicts of laws, namely, conflicts between:

1. US federal law and state law ('vertical' conflicts);
2. US federal law and foreign law (federal-international conflicts);
3. the laws of states of the United States (interstate or intra-national conflicts); and
4. the law of a US state and the law of a foreign country (state-international conflicts).

1. *See* US Const. Art. I §8, discussed *infra* at 17.
2. *See* US Const. Amend. X, reproduced *infra* 18.

6. The first category of conflicts is called 'vertical' because the potentially conflicting laws do not stand on an equal level. For this reason, the process of resolving these conflicts is not one of choosing between state and federal law, but rather one of delineating the scope of federal law. Under the Supremacy clause of the federal Constitution,[1] once a case is determined to fall within the scope of federal law, that law governs and displaces state law. This volume touches on vertical conflicts only to a limited degree.[2]

The last three categories of conflicts may be characterized as 'horizontal' because the conflicting laws stand on equal footing. This includes federal law when it conflicts with foreign law. Nevertheless, as explained in Part II, Chapter 9, *infra*, the process of resolving conflicts between federal law and foreign law is guided less by ordinary choice-of-law principles and more by canons of construction unilaterally delineating the reach of federal statutes.

1. *See* US Const. Art. VI, reproduced *infra* 18.
2. *See infra* 17–21, 95–105.

7. In theory, the resolution of all four categories of conflicts is a matter of federal law. In practise, this is true only with regard to the first two of the above categories ('vertical' and 'federal-international'). The Constitution addresses horizontal interstate conflicts by enunciating the obligation of each state to give 'Full Faith and Credit' to the laws and judgments of sister states, and by granting Congress the power to enact laws governing the manner in which each state will discharge

this obligation.[1] However, Congress has exercised this power sparingly – indeed, only four times.[2] Thus, by default, the power and the initiative of resolving interstate conflicts remains with the states, subject only to mild restraints imposed by the Constitution as interpreted by the United States Supreme Court. These restraints are discussed in Part I, Chapter 2.

1. *See* US Const. Art. IV §1 (providing that 'Full Faith and Credit shall be given in each State' to the 'laws and judgments of every other State' and authorizing Congress to enact laws prescribing 'the Effect' of such laws and judgments). This clause is discussed *infra* at 21, 76–92, 712–724.
2. All four statutes are relatively short, all are found in 28 U.S.C. §1738, and three of them deal with matters of family law. Section 1738 is a general and brief implementing statute, Section 1738A (the Parental Kidnaping Prevention Act) provides for recognition of custody decrees, Section 1738B (the Full Faith and Credit for Child Support Orders Act) provides for enforcement of child support orders, and Section 1738C (the Defense of Marriage Act ['DOMA']) deals with same sex marriages. These statutes are discussed *infra* 514–522, 526–529, 543–547.

8. The states possess the same power with regard to international conflicts between state and foreign law, subject to some, but not all, of the same constitutional restraints as interstate conflicts. For example, the Full Faith and Credit clause does not apply to foreign laws or judgments, and the Privileges and Immunities clause does not apply to non-US citizens. Moreover, in addressing conflicts with foreign law, state or federal courts are admonished to not interfere with the federal government's conduct of foreign affairs.[1] Despite the constitutional restraints, which are few and far between, the resolution of most interstate and international conflicts in the United States is a matter of state rather than federal law.

1. *See Am. Ins. Ass'n* v. *Garamendi*, 539 US 396 (2003), discussed *infra* 96–99.

9. Although each state legislature has the inherent power to enact choice-of-law legislation, very few states have done so. Only one state has a comprehensive conflicts codification[1] and, although many other states have piecemeal, narrowly drawn statutes, the great bulk of American conflicts law is found in the case reporters, not in the statute books. It has been judicially created through the pronouncements of courts adjudicating conflicts cases, and through the operation of the doctrine of *stare decisis*.

1. This state is Louisiana. *See* Book IV of the Louisiana Civil Code, enacted in 1991 (hereinafter referred to as the 'Louisiana Codification'). For a discussion of this codification by its drafter, *see*, e.g., S. Symeonides, 'Private International Law Codification in a Mixed Jurisdiction: The Louisiana Experience', 57 *RabelsZ* 460 (1993). *See also infra* 253–254, 572–574, 585, 624–627. For Puerto Rico and Oregon, *see infra* 255, 625.

10. Under the American system of dual sovereignty, conflicts cases can be adjudicated by either state or federal courts. The applicable choice-of-law principles do not depend on whether the adjudicating court is state or federal, but rather on the category to which the particular conflict belongs. If, as described above, state choice-of-law principles govern a particular case, then those principles govern even if a federal court adjudicates the case.[1] Likewise, when a state court encounters conflicts that are governed by federal choice-of-law principles, such as a conflict between federal maritime law and foreign law, the state court must follow the federal principles.

1. *See Klaxon Co.* v. *Stentor Elec. Mfg. Co. Inc.*, 313 US 487 (1941) (discussed *infra* 73) (holding that when a federal court's jurisdiction is based on the parties' diversity of citizenship and the conflict in question is of the type that is governed by state choice-of-law principles, the court must follow the choice-of-law rules of the state in which the court sits).

11. This volume focuses on horizontal interstate and international conflicts. Interstate conflicts are by far the more numerous. Because, as said above, state rather than federal law governs these conflicts, and because each state has its own body of law for these conflicts, it should follow that one should not be speaking of 'American' conflicts law, but rather of 50 or more state conflicts laws, in addition to federal conflicts law. Although this would be technically accurate, the practical question is whether and to what extent the various American conflicts laws share sufficient common denominators and similarities as to constitute – at least for certain purposes – a single law susceptible to meaningful treatment as such. On balance, the answer to this question is affirmative.

§3. The Relative Insignificance of Interstate Boundaries and the High Number of Conflicts Cases

12. In an oft-quoted statement written more than four decades ago, the Supreme Court of Illinois observed that '[a]dvanced methods of distribution and other commercial activity . . . [and] modern methods of doing business . . . have largely effaced the economic significance of State lines'.[1] What was beginning to be true then is unquestionably true today, not only in the United States, but around the world. The internet is simply the latest manifestation of this reality.

State boundaries are less important within the United States than international boundaries are in the rest of the world. The lines that divide the United States into more than 50 jurisdictions each with its own system of law have little effect on the economic, political, and cultural unity of the country. It is not simply that people and goods circulate freely and constantly throughout the country, that many people live in one state and work in another, or that, as in the movies, a police car chase may begin in one state and end abruptly in another. It is also that, in their everyday lives, people cross state lines with very little awareness of doing so. Many large population centres spread across state boundaries. City names like Texarkana, or Kansas City, Missouri and Kansas City, Kansas amply illustrate this American phenomenon of 'economically and socially integrated greater metropolitan area[s]'[2] that defy state boundaries. Indeed, in retrospect, many state boundaries seem to have been drawn fortuitously.

1. *Gray* v. *Am. Radiator & Standard Sanitary Corp.*, 176 N.E.2d 761, 766 (Ill. 1961).
2. *Gaither* v. *Myers*, 404 F.2d 216, 223 (D.C. Cir. 1968) ('It is a commonplace that residents of Maryland [and Virginia] are part of the Washington metropolitan trading area, and that District residents and businesses have an interest in the well-being of the [ ] citizens of [those] State[s]'.).

13. This phenomenon is particularly relevant in tort conflicts. While cross-border torts are quite common around the world, it is doubtful that courts in other countries encounter cases in which the tort occurs literally at the boundary line. Yet one finds numerous such cases in the United States.[1] Their frequent occurrence raises the question whether strict adherence to territorial notions makes less sense in the United States than in the rest of the world.

1. For a collection and brief discussion of such cases, *see* S. Symeonides, *The American Choice-of-Law Revolution: Past, Present, and Future* 6–8 (Boston, Leiden, 2006).

14. Beyond tort conflicts, the relative insignificance of interstate boundaries in the United States explains why American courts encounter many more interstate conflicts than international conflicts and, together, many more conflicts than the courts of any other country. As a recent study documents, in the last fifteen years American courts have decided more than 2,000 conflicts cases per year.[1] These are significant numbers that have led to the accumulation of vast judicial experience in resolving conflicts cases. Despite the inevitable differences from country to country, the wealth of the American experience can be useful to other countries, even if one were to assume that the American courts get it wrong as often as they get it right.

1. *See* S. Symeonides, 'A Choice of Law in the American Courts in 2004: Eighteenth Annual Survey', 53 *Am. J. Comp. L.* 919, 921–923 (2005). These numbers are based on cases posted on Westlaw's electronic data banks, which include all federal cases, and all state cases, except those decided by state courts of first instance. In part because of the latter omission, federal cases outnumber state cases by a ratio of 7:3. Altogether, conflicts cases amount to less than 2 per cent of all cases posted on Westlaw.

Selected Bibliography

American Law Institute, *Restatement of the Law: Conflict of Laws*, St. Paul, Minn., 1934.

American Law Institute, *Restatement of the Law Second: Conflict of Laws 2d*, St. Paul, Minn., 1971.

American Law Institute, *Restatement (Third) of Foreign Relations Law of the United States*, St. Paul, Minn., 1986.

American Law Institute, *Complex Litigation: Statutory Recommendations and Analysis*, Philadelphia, Pa., 1994.

American Law Institute, *Recognition and Enforcement of Foreign Judgments: Analysis and Proposed Federal Statute* (Prop. Final Draft, 4/11/2005), Philadelphia, Pa., 2005.

Beale, J., *A Treatise on the Conflict of Laws*, Vols. 1–3, New York, 1935.

Born, G. & Rutledge, P., *International Civil Litigation in United States Courts*, Austin, 4th edn, 2006.

Brilmayer, L. & Goldsmith, J., *Conflict of Laws: Cases and Materials*, 5th edn, New York, 2002.

Brilmayer, L., *Conflict of Laws*, 2nd edn, Boston, 1995.

Casad, R. & Richman, R., *Jurisdiction in Civil Actions: Territorial Basis and Process Limitations on Jurisdiction of State and Federal Courts*, 3rd edn, Charlottes-ville, Va., 1998.

Cavers, D., *The Choice-of-Law Process*, Ann Arbor, Mich., 1965.

Cavers, D., *The Choice of Law: Selected Essays*, 1933–1983, Durham, NC, 1985.

Chemerinsky, E., *Federal Jurisdiction*, 5th edn, New York, 2007.

Cook, W., *The Logical and Legal Bases of the Conflict of Laws*, Cambridge, Mass., 1942.

Currie, B., *Selected Essays on the Conflict of Laws*, Durham, NC, 1963.

Currie, D., Kay, H., Kramer, L. & Roosevelt, K., *Conflict of Laws: Cases-Comments-Questions*, 7th edn, St. Paul, Minn., 2006.

Ehrenzweig, A., *Private International Law*, Vol. 1, 1967, Vol. II, 1973, Vol. III (with Jayme, E.), 1977, Leyden, Dobbs Ferry, NY.

Epstein, D., Snyder, J. & Baldwin, C., *International Litigation: A Guide to Jurisdiction, Practice, and Strategy*, 3rd edn, Ardsley, 1998.

Hay, P., Weintraub, R. & Borchers, P., *Conflict of Laws: Cases and Materials*, 12th edn, New York, 2004.

Juenger, F., *Choice of Law and Multistate Justice*, Special Edition, Ardsley, NY, 2005.

Juenger, F., *Selected Essays on the Conflict of Laws*, Ardsley, NY, 2001.

Low, P. & Jeffries, J., *Federal Courts and the Law of Federal-State Relations*, 5th edn, New York, 2004.
Lowenfeld, A., *International Litigation and Arbitration*, 3d edn, St. Paul, Minn., 2006.
McDougal, L., Felix, R. & Whitten, R., *American Conflicts Law*, 5th edn, Ardsley, NY, 2001.
Nanda, V. & Pansius, D., *Litigation of International Disputes in United States Courts*, 2nd edn, 2005.
Pfander, J., *Principles of Federal Jurisdiction*, St. Paul, Minn., 2006.
Reynolds, W. & Richman, W., *The Full Faith and Credit Clause: A Reference Guide to the United States Constitution*, Westport, Conn., 2005.
Richman, W. & Reynolds, W., *Understanding Conflict of Laws*, 3rd edn, Newark, NJ, 2002.
Scoles, E., Hay, P., Borchers, P. & Symeonides, S., *Conflict of Laws*, 4th edn, St. Paul, Minn., 2004.
Shreve, G., *A Conflict-of-Laws Anthology*, Cincinnati, Ohio, 1997.
Siegel, D. & Borchers, P., *Conflicts in a Nutshell*, 3rd edn, Eagan, Minn., 2005.
Simson, G., *Issues and Perspectives in Conflict of Laws*, 4th edn, 2005.
Story, J., *Commentaries on the Conflict of Laws, Foreign and Domestic*, 5th edn, Boston, 1857.
Symeonides, S., *The American Choice-of-Law Revolution: Past, Present, and Future*, Leiden, Boston, 2006.
Symeonides, S., *Private International Law at the End of the 20th Century: Progress or Regress?*, The Hague, London, Boston, 2000.
Symeonides, S., Perdue, W. & von Mehren, A., *Conflict of Laws: American, Comparative, International*, 2nd edn, St. Paul, Minn., 2003.
Varady, T., Barcelo, J. & Von Mehren, A., *International Commercial Arbitration*, 3rd edn, 2006.
von Mehren, A., *Adjudicatory Authority in Private International Law*. Leiden, Boston, 2007.
Weintraub, R., *Commentary on the Conflict of Laws*, 5th edn, New York, 2006.
Weintraub, R., *International Litigation and Arbitration: Practice and Planning* (2006).
Wright, C. & Kane, M.K., *Law of Federal Courts*, 6th edn, St. Paul, Minn., 2002.

Part I. Federalism and Conflicts Law

15. The fact that the United States is a federal system affects American conflicts law in several ways. For example, unlike other federations, the constituent states of the United States retain the majority of lawmaking and judicial powers. Conversely, and also unlike many other countries, a large and powerful system of federal courts operates side-by-side with state courts in the 50 states. These and other features of American federalism make American conflicts law to some extent peculiar. For the benefit of the foreign reader, this Part focuses on those aspects of American conflicts law that are most affected by federalism. Among them are: the division of lawmaking and adjudicatory competence between the federal and state authorities, the territorial jurisdiction of the state and federal courts, the law applied in federal courts, the federal constitutional limitations on state choice of law, and the recognition of sister-state and foreign-country judgments. A basic familiarity with these aspects will facilitate the understanding of choice of law, which is the focus of the rest of this volume.

Chapter 1. Jurisdiction

16. In the most general all-encompassing sense, jurisdiction is the power of a public organ to: (1) prescribe norms of conduct; (2) apply these norms in resolving a dispute; or (3) enforce these norms when they are not complied with. The first type of jurisdiction is called *prescriptive* jurisdiction or, when the prescribing organ is a legislative body, *legislative* jurisdiction. The second type of jurisdiction is called *adjudicatory* jurisdiction or, when the deciding organ is a court, *judicial* jurisdiction. Finally, the third type of jurisdiction is called *enforcement* jurisdiction. This chapter provides a brief overview of the first two types of jurisdiction under the American federal system. Chapters 1 and 2 of Part III, *infra*, review one aspect of enforcement jurisdiction, the recognition and enforcement of sister-state and foreign-country judgments, respectively.

§1. Legislative Jurisdiction

I. The Division of Lawmaking Competence between the Federal and State Governments

17. The United States Constitution establishes the federal government as one of superior but limited competence and retains the states as the holders of general residual competence. The first three articles of the Constitution establish the three branches of the federal government – legislative (Article I), executive (Article II), and judicial (Article III) – and 'vests' in them their respective powers. Article I delineates the lawmaking competence of Congress by vesting it, not with general lawmaking powers, but rather with the 'legislative Powers herein granted'.[1] Section 8 of the article provides a list of specific legislative powers in 17 clauses, including the following:

> To lay and collect taxes . . . and provide for the common defence and general welfare of the United States . . . ; To regulate commerce with foreign nations, and among the several states and with the Indian tribes; To establish an uniform rule of naturalization, and uniform laws on the subject of bankruptcies . . . ; To coin money . . . ; To promote the progress of science and useful arts, by securing for limited times to authors and inventors the exclusive right to their respective writings and discoveries; To constitute tribunals inferior to the supreme court; To define and punish piracies and felonies committed on the high seas, and offences against the law of nations; To declare war, grant letters of marque and reprisal, and make rules concerning captures on land and water; To raise and support armies.[2]

Section 8 concludes with the 'Necessary and Proper' clause, which vests Congress with the power to 'make all Laws which shall be necessary and proper for carrying into Execution the foregoing Powers, and all other Powers vested by this Constitution in the Government of the United States'.[3]

1. US Const. Art. I, §1.
2. US Const. Art. I, §8, cls. 1–12.
3. US Const. Art. I, §8, cl. 18.

18. Article VI of the Constitution establishes the supremacy of federal law over state law by providing:

> This Constitution, and the Laws of the United States . . . and all Treaties made . . . under the Authority of the United States, shall be the supreme Law of the Land; and the Judges in every State shall be bound thereby, any Thing in the Constitution or Laws of any State to the Contrary notwithstanding.[1]

Finally, the Tenth Amendment of the Constitution confirms the residual lawmaking competence of the states by providing that 'The powers not delegated to the United States by the Constitution, nor prohibited by it to the States, are reserved to the States respectively, or to the people'.[2]

1. US Const. Art. VI, cl. 2.
2. US Const. Amd. X.

19. As the above scheme indicates, the lawmaking competence of the federal government, although superior, is much more limited than that of the states. The states retain the authority to enact or judicially create laws on any subject, including the bulk of private law, except those subjects that the Constitution assigns to the federal government. In some respects, the powers of the states are even greater than the above division indicates. This is because, in interpreting the Constitution, the Supreme Court has, in many cases,[1] adopted the principle that only the actual *exercise*, not the availability, of a constitutionally granted federal power can displace the residual competence of states to regulate the same subject.[2] Two examples, both relating to conflicts law, illustrate this proposition.

1. *See* e.g., *infra* 96–99 (discussing 'field pre-emption').
2. *See Fla. Lime & Avocado Growers, Inc.* v. *Paul*, 373 US 132, 142 (1963).

20. The first example involves the Commerce Clause, which grants Congress the power to 'regulate commerce with foreign nations, and among the several states and with the Indian tribes'.[1] On its face, this clause grants Congress plenary powers to regulate interstate and international commerce, thereby displacing any state laws on the same subject. However, the Supreme Court has adopted a more restrictive reading, first by defining 'interstate commerce' more restrictively than in the past, and, second, by ruling that, when Congress has not exercised its power to regulate a particular commercial activity ('dormant Commerce Clause'), states are free to regulate that activity if they do not discriminate against, adversely affect, or unduly burden interstate commerce.[2]

1. US Const. Art. I, §8, cl. 3.
2. *See*, e.g., *Pike* v. *Bruce Church, Inc.*, 397 US 137, 142 (1970); *Bibb* v. *Navajo Freight Lines, Inc.*, 359 US 520 (1959); *Kassel* v. *Consol. Freightways Corp.*, 450 US 662 (1981); *Bendix Autolite Corp.* v. *Midwesco Enterprise, Inc.*, 486 US 888 (1988); *Quill Corp.* v. *N.D.*, 504 US 298 (1992).

21. The second example involves the Full Faith and Credit clause found in Article IV of the Constitution, which provides:

> Full Faith and Credit shall be given in each State to the public Acts, Records, and judicial Proceedings of every other State. And the Congress may by general Laws prescribe the Manner in which such Acts, Records and Proceedings shall be proved, and the Effect thereof.[1]

By authorizing Congress to enact laws prescribing the 'effect' in one state of the laws and judgments of another state, the second sentence of this clause grants Congress broad power to enact comprehensive statutes occupying the entire field of conflicts law. However, since the adoption of the Constitution, Congress has exercised this power only four times and the statutes it enacted have been fairly brief and narrow.[2] Because of Congress's inertia, and the Supreme Court's relative unassertiveness in requiring states to give full faith and credit to the *laws* (as opposed to the judgments) of sister states,[3] conflicts law remains by default a matter of state law, even in cases adjudicated in federal courts.

1. US Const. Art. IV. This clause is discussed *infra* at 76–92, 712–724.
2. *See supra* 7.
3. *See infra* 76–92, 712–724.

II. Constitutional Limitations on Federal and State Powers

22. Article I also imposes certain direct limitations on the legislative powers of the federal[1] and state[2] governments, such as by prohibiting the enactment of *ex post facto* laws, or laws impairing the obligation of contracts. As noted earlier, the Full Faith and Credit clause of Article IV also limits the states in how they deal with sister state laws and judgments. Article IV also contains the 'Privileges and Immunities' clause, which prohibits a state from withholding from citizens of sister states certain 'privileges and immunities' it accords to its own citizens.[3]

1. Section 9 of Art. I prohibits Congress from, *inter alia*, suspending the writ of Habeas Corpus, enacting *ex post facto* laws, taxing goods exported from any state, discriminating among state ports, or according nobility titles.
2. Section 10 of Art. I prohibits states from, *inter alia*, entering into treaty, alliance, confederation, or agreement or compact with another state or a foreign power, coining money, enacting *ex post facto* laws, or law impairing the obligation of contracts, or granting nobility titles.
3. *See* US Const., Art. IV, §2. This clause is discussed *infra* at 93–94. Another Privileges and Immunities clause found in the Fourteenth Amendment prohibits states from adopting laws 'abridg[ing] the privileges or immunities of citizens of the United States'. US Const., Amend. XIV.

23. The most far-reaching limitations on governmental powers are found in the several amendments of the Constitution, especially the first ten (the 'Bill of Rights') and the Fourteenth Amendment. Of these limitations, the ones having a bearing on conflicts law are: the Due Process clauses of the Fifth Amendment, which binds the federal government,[1] and the Due Process[2] and Equal Protection[3] clauses of the Fourteenth Amendment, which bind the states. These limitations, and the way in which the Supreme Court has interpreted them, are discussed *infra*.[4]

1. *See* US Const., Amd. IV ('No person shall be . . . deprived of life, liberty, or property, without due process of law'.).
2. *See* US Const., Amd. XIV ('No State shall . . . deprive any person of life, liberty, or property, without due process of law'.).
3. *See* US Const., Amd. XIV ('No State shall . . . deny to any person within its jurisdiction the equal protection of the laws'.).
4. *See infra* 76–94.

§2. Adjudicatory Jurisdiction

I. Federal and State Courts

24. In contrast to legislative or prescriptive jurisdiction, judicial or adjudicatory jurisdiction is the power of courts or other adjudicatory organs to decide disputes in a binding manner. This Section provides an overview of the latter type of jurisdiction as understood in the United States. The discussion is confined to those aspects of judicial jurisdiction that are relevant to private international law, namely the power of American courts to decide cases with non-forum elements. Within these confines, the discussion is further limited to providing a sketch of basic terms, concepts, and principles.[1]

1. Basic bibliography for judicial jurisdiction includes: R. Casad & W. Richman, *Jurisdiction in Civil Actions: Territorial Basis and Process Limitations on Jurisdiction of State and Federal Courts* (3rd edn, Charlottesville, Va., 1998); D. Epstein, J. Snyder & C. Baldwin, *International Litigation: A Guide to Jurisdiction, Practice, and Strategy* (3rd edn, Ardsley, 1998); E. Scoles, P. Hay, P. Borchers & S. Symeonides, *Conflict of Laws* 284–517 (4th edn, St. Paul, Minn., 2004); A. von Mehren, *Adjudicatory Authority in Private International Law* (Boston, Leiden, 2007).

25. Because a court derives its jurisdiction from the law that constitutes that court, the law of jurisdiction is national rather than international law. In the United States, national (i.e., federal) courts coexist side-by-side with state courts in each state. Article III of the Constitution which, like the rest of the Constitution, presupposes the existence of states and their own court systems, establishes the federal judiciary as a separate branch of the federal government and vests the 'judicial power' of the United States 'in one supreme Court, and in such inferior Courts as the Congress may from time to time ordain and establish'.[1]

1. US Const. Art. III, §1, Art. III, §3, grants to the Supreme Court original jurisdiction in certain cases (those 'affecting Ambassadors, other public Ministers and Consuls, and those in which a State shall be Party') and final appellate jurisdiction in all other cases 'with such Exceptions, and under such Regulations as the Congress shall make'.

26. Following this authorization, Congress has established a system of federal trial courts ('district courts')[1] spread throughout the states and territories of the United States, as well as regional and national intermediate appellate courts ('circuit courts').[2] The Constitution and federal law establish the line separating the jurisdiction of the federal courts from that of state courts by defining the jurisdiction of the former. This line is discussed later in this Section. Suffice it to say for now that, in principle, the federal courts possess only enumerated, specifically granted powers, while state courts possess residual 'general' jurisdiction to hear all cases not assigned to the federal courts. Although the jurisdiction of state courts is defined by state law, it must conform to certain restraints and requirements imposed by federal law, primarily by the Due Process clause of the Fourteenth Amendment.

1. In 2006, there were 94 federal judicial districts, with at least one district in each state, the District of Columbia, and Puerto Rico. These courts were staffed by 645 active judges, 311 senior (part-time) judges, and 505 magistrates. Source <www.uscourts.gov/judicialfactsfigures/_2006/Table101.pdf> (last visited 26 May 2007). In addition, in exercising its lawmaking powers under Article I of the Constitution, Congress has established several other courts, such as Bankruptcy courts (one in each district), the Court of International Trade, the Court of Federal Claims, and district courts for the District of Columbia and the territories of the Virgin Islands, Guam, and the Northern Mariana Islands.
2. In 2006, the 94 federal judicial districts were grouped into eleven regional circuits (each with a court of appeals empowered to hear appeals from the district courts of that circuit and from decisions of federal administrative agencies) and one for the District of Columbia. In addition, the Court of Appeals for the Federal Circuit has nationwide jurisdiction to hear appeals in specialized cases, such as those involving patent laws, and cases decided by the Court of International Trade and the Court of Federal Claims. *See* 28 USC §41. The above courts were staffed by 165 active judges and 103 senior judges. Source <www.uscourts.gov/judicialfacts figures/2006/Table101.pdf> (last visited 26 May 2007).

II. Terminology and Other Basics

27. The aforementioned division of adjudicatory authority between federal and state courts is an example of delineating the 'competence' or '*subject matter*' *jurisdiction* of courts within the same country. Each state within the United States delineates for itself the subject matter jurisdiction of its own courts, or other adjudicatory organs. For example, many states divide subject matter jurisdiction among: (a) courts of general jurisdiction, which are empowered to hear most civil cases; (b) specialized courts, which are authorized to hear certain kinds of cases, such as domestic relations disputes or probate matters; and (c) other inferior courts, such as municipal courts, which can hear certain cases in which the amount in dispute does not exceed a certain level.

28. Likewise, each state allocates adjudicatory jurisdiction among the various geographical subdivisions or judicial districts within that state ('local jurisdiction' or *venue*). For example, depending on the nature of the action, a venue rule may authorize or require that the action be brought in the judicial district in which the defendant resides, the property is located, or the critical event occurred.

29. Finally, and most importantly for multistate cases, each state delineates the power of its courts to adjudicate cases with foreign elements, especially those involving foreign defendants, provided it remains within the constraints of the federal law and the constitution as interpreted by the Supreme Court. This allocation of adjudicatory authority or 'jurisdiction in the interstate or international sense' is referred to hereafter as *territorial* jurisdiction, although in some cases it may amount to *extra*territorial jurisdiction.[1]

1. In the United State, the prevailing term for this type of jurisdiction is 'personal jurisdiction'. However, this term is not used here because it can be confused with *in personam* jurisdiction, which is a subcategory of territorial jurisdiction as defined in the text.

30. To render a valid judgment, a court must possess all three types of jurisdiction. Generally, a court must affirmatively ascertain the existence of subject-matter jurisdiction, even if the parties have not questioned it or have waived objections to it. In contrast, both the lack of territorial jurisdiction and the lack of venue can be waived.

Logically, in multistate cases, the jurisdictional inquiry begins by asking whether the chosen forum state has territorial jurisdiction. If the answer is affirmative, the second question is which court within that state has subject matter jurisdiction and, when that court is identified, the final question is whether that court is one of proper venue. The discussion below focuses primarily on the first question by discussing the territorial jurisdiction of state courts. It touches on subject matter jurisdiction only in the context of the division between state and federal courts.

III. The Territorial Jurisdiction of State Courts

A. *Some History and Basic Concepts*

31. Unlike American choice of law which owes its origins to continental sources,[1] the American law of jurisdiction owes its origin to English common law sources. Unlike continental law, the English common law based the assertion of jurisdiction, not on the defendant's forum contacts as such, but rather on a formal, if not ceremonial, act that symbolized the sovereign's power over the defendant at the time of the act – the service of summons on the defendant within the realm. This transient or 'tag jurisdiction' survives today in much of the common law world, although its propriety and constitutionality in the United States is now questionable.

When the US Supreme Court rendered its first major formative decision on jurisdiction, *Pennoyer* v. *Neff*,[2] territoriality was the favourite principle in explaining the spatial operation of laws. It is therefore not surprising that, from its inception, American jurisdictional law was territoriality oriented. Although subsequent decisions have shifted the focus from territorial power to personal liberty and fairness, the territorial infrastructure remains visible, if not largely intact.

1. *See infra* 107–108.
2. 95 US 714 (1878).

32. Under *Pennoyer* and its progeny, a state could only assert jurisdiction over persons who were domiciled, or were served with summons, in the forum state (*in personam* jurisdiction) or over property situated there (*in rem* jurisdiction). *In personam* jurisdiction empowered a court to adjudicate any personal claims against the defendant (even claims unrelated to his domicile or presence in the forum state) and to render a judgment that could be satisfied form any of the defendant's non-exempt assets, wherever situated. *In rem* jurisdiction empowered a court to adjudicate claims in the specific property (the *res*) and to render a judgment that could be satisfied only out of that property. A hybrid of this jurisdictional basis known as *quasi in rem* jurisdiction allowed a court to adjudicate personal claims against a non-resident defendant who owned tangible or intangible property situated in the forum state, even if the claims were unrelated to the property's presence in the forum, and to render a judgment that could be satisfied out of that property.

33. In many cases, the assertion of *quasi in rem* jurisdiction could be overbroad, especially when the attached property was a debt owed to the defendant by a third party.[1] The same was true of tag jurisdiction in cases in which the defendant's presence in the forum state was transient and unrelated to the cause of action. Although often overbroad, the *Pennoyer* regime was also too narrow in some respects. For example, it did not allow for the assertion of jurisdiction over foreign corporations, which lack physical existence, or over certain foreign defendants like motorists who committed an offence within the forum state but were not served with process while there. To fill these gaps, American courts developed several legal fictions, such as corporate 'presence' or 'implied consent'. A foreign corporation that 'transacted' business in the forum state was deemed to have consented to jurisdiction regarding claims arising from that business. Likewise, a foreign motorist who drove into the forum state and caused an accident there was deemed to have impliedly consented to that state's jurisdiction for claims arising from that accident.[2]

1. *See Harris* v. *Balk*, 198 US 215 (1905).
2. *See Hess* v. *Pawloski*, 274 US 352 (1927).

34. In 1945, the Supreme Court rendered a critical decision making these fictions unnecessary, although not demolishing the *Pennoyer* regime entirely. In *International Shoe Co.* v. *Washington*,[1] the Court held that a state could assert *in personam* jurisdiction whenever the defendant had sufficient 'minimum contacts' with the forum so that adjudicating a claim against that defendant 'does not offend traditional notions of fair play and substantial justice'.[2] More important than this principle is its corollary that a judgment rendered by a court that *lacks* these 'minimum contacts' violates the Due Process clause of the Fourteenth Amendment. Hence, the judgment is invalid in the forum state and unenforceable in any other state under the Full Faith and Credit clause.

1. 326 US 310 (1945).
2. *Id.* at 316.

35. The obvious question, however, is how to determine when these 'minimum contacts' are sufficient. This is a fact-intensive, case-specific inquiry guided by less than definitive Supreme Court precedents. For example, in *World-Wide Volkswagen Corp.* v. *Woodson*[1] and *Asahi Metal Industry Co.* v. *Superior Court*,[2] the Court made it clear that these contacts must result from some deliberate conduct of the non-resident defendant. The defendant must have engaged in conduct 'purposefully directed' at the forum state, or must have 'purposefully availed himself of the benefits and protection of forum law'.

1. 444 US 286 (1980).
2. 480 US 102 (1987).

36. In *Shaffer* v. *Heitner*,[1] the Court continued the reformation of jurisdictional law by holding that *all* assertions of jurisdiction must comply with the 'minimum contacts' standard of *International Shoe*. *Shaffer* concluded that one sub-category of *quasi in rem* jurisdiction was unconstitutional, holding that, in the absence of other contacts, the mere presence of the defendant's property in the forum state does not provide a jurisdictional basis for adjudicating claims unrelated to that property.[2] Thus, the attachment of the defendants' corporate stock in the forum state of Delaware (the state of incorporation) did not confer *quasi in rem* jurisdiction to adjudicate a derivative suit against the corporation's non-resident officers.

1. 433 US 186 (1977).
2. *Shaffer* did not outlaw other types of *quasi in rem* jurisdiction, such as when the unrelated claim is reduced to a valid judgment rendered outside the forum, or is embodied into a security interest that can be enforced against the debtor's property. *See Rush* v. *Savchuck*, 444 US 320 (1980).

37. The principle underlying *Shaffer could* also mean that tag jurisdiction is no longer constitutional. However, in *Burnham* v. *Superior Court*,[1] the Court upheld tag jurisdiction in the case of a New Jersey defendant who was served with process in California while visiting his children there in a suit by his wife seeking divorce and incidental relief. The eight justices who participated in the decision split evenly on the reasoning, with half of them finding tag jurisdiction in and of itself constitutional and the other half finding that, in the particular circumstances, including the defendant's voluntary and planned visit to California, the assertion of jurisdiction by California passed muster under *International Shoe*.

1. 495 US 604 (1990).

38. Finally, in *Helicopteros Nacionales de Colombia, S.A.* v. *Hall*,[1] the Court adopted a distinction first proposed by Professors von Mehren and Trautman between general and specific jurisdiction.[2] When a court has general jurisdiction, it may adjudicate any claims against the defendant, even claims unrelated to the defendant's contacts with, or activity in, the forum state. In contrast, when a court has only specific jurisdiction, it may only adjudicate claims against the defendant that arise from the defendant's specific contacts with, or activity in, the forum state. This distinction, which is familiar to civil law lawyers, is a good vehicle for providing a sketch of the basics of American law on territorial jurisdiction.

1. 466 US 408 (1984).
2. *See* A. von Mehren & D. Trautman, 'Jurisdiction to Adjudicate: A Suggested Analysis', 79 *Harv. Law Rev.* 1121 (1966).

B. General Jurisdiction

39. Despite its dubious constitutionality, tag jurisdiction remains a basis for general jurisdiction. In fact, in recent years, this jurisdictional basis has enjoyed a certain resurgence in the lower courts in suits filed against foreign defendants involved in human rights abuses in foreign countries.

Another traditional basis of general jurisdiction is the defendant's domicile at the time of the lawsuit.[1] For corporations, the state of incorporation and the state of the corporation's principal place of business, are treated as analogous to domicile. In addition, a corporation may be subject to general jurisdiction in any state in which it conducts 'continuous and systematic' business activity.[2]

1. *Milliken* v. *Meyer*, 311 US 457 (1940). US citizenship is also a basis for personal jurisdiction in the federal courts when a statute so provides. *See Backer* v. *United States*, 284 US 421 (1932).
2. *See Perkins* v. *Benguet Consol. Mining Co.*, 342 US 437 (1952). In contrast, non-continuous or isolated business activities may give rise only to specific jurisdiction, which means that the corporation may only be sued for claims 'arising from' that activity. *See Helicopteros Nacionales de Colombia, S.A.* v. *Hall*, 466 US 408 (1984).

C. Specific Jurisdiction

40. All other jurisdictional bases provide only specific jurisdiction, that is, they empower the court to render a judgment arising only from the particular basis. For example, the traditional *in rem* and the permissible subcategory of *quasi in rem* jurisdiction empower the court to render a judgment arising from and binding on the particular *res* that is the subject of the lawsuit. The following is a list of the other bases for specific *in personam* jurisdiction.

1. Appearance and Consent

41. Because *in personam* jurisdiction is waivable, a defendant who appears and fails to raise jurisdictional objections is deemed to have consented to the court's jurisdiction. Similarly, by filing a lawsuit, a plaintiff impliedly consents to jurisdiction with regard to all counterclaims and cross-actions by the defendant.

A defendant may consent in advance to the jurisdiction of a court by agreeing to a choice-of-forum clause. Although American courts were initially hostile to such clauses on the ground that the parties could not oust or confer jurisdiction, these clauses are in principle enforceable and quite common today.[1]

Many states require foreign corporations, as a condition for doing business in the forum state to appoint a local agent for the receipt of service of process. By appointing such an agent, a corporation is deemed to consent to specific jurisdiction for claims arising out of the corporation's business within that state.

1. *See infra* 54–57.

2. Long-Arm Statutes: Torts and Contracts

42. In American legal jargon, the enactments authorizing the assertion of jurisdiction over non-forum residents or cases with other foreign elements are known as 'long-arm statutes'. Although these statutes vary from state to state, they can be divided into two main types. The first type authorizes the assertion of jurisdiction on any basis permitted by the federal Due Process clause. For example, the Utah long-arm statute grants Utah courts jurisdiction to the 'fullest extent permitted by the Due Process Clause of the Fourteenth Amendment',[1] while the California statute authorizes jurisdiction 'on any basis not inconsistent with the constitution of this state or of the United States'.[2] Under these statutes, the whole jurisdictional inquiry is a question of constitutional law and is answered under the Supreme Court's jurisprudence.

1. Utah Code Ann. §78-27-22 (2007).
2. Cal. Civ. Proc. Code §410.10 (2007).

43. The second type of long arm statute limits jurisdiction to certain specifically enumerated bases. Under these statutes, a court must first determine whether, as a matter of statutory construction, the case satisfies one of the enumerated bases, and only then, whether the statutorily authorized basis is constitutionally permissible under the federal Due Process clause. The following New York statute, CPLR §302, is representative of these types of statutes. It authorizes jurisdiction as to a cause of action 'arising from' any of the enumerated acts over any non-domiciliary who:

1. transacts any business within the state or contracts anywhere to supply goods or services in the state; or
2. commits a tortious act within the state . . . ; or
3. commits a tortious act without the state causing injury to person or property within the state, . . . , if he
   (i) regularly does or solicits business, or engages in any other persistent course of conduct, or derives substantial revenue from goods used or consumed or services rendered, in the state, or
   (ii) expects or should reasonably expect the act to have consequences in the state and derives substantial revenue from interstate or international commerce;[1]

The phrase 'transacts any business within the state' in Paragraph 1 applies not only to corporations, as noted above, but also to natural persons. However, this phrase, which authorizes only *specific* jurisdiction, differs significantly from the phrase 'doing business'. The latter phrase is typically used to denote the conduct of continuous and systematic business activity of the type that subjects a foreign corporation to *general* jurisdiction.[2] In contrast, the phrase 'transacts business' is used to denote contacts that are not as pervasive as those supporting general jurisdiction, but must still satisfy a certain 'minimum' and be of the type making it foreseeable that the defendant would be subject to litigation in the forum state and reasonable for that state to do so.

A person who 'contracts anywhere to supply goods or services in the state' is subject to specific jurisdiction in that state, even if she did not transact any other business in that state and the contract was negotiated and concluded outside that state. Taken literally, the quoted phrase would authorize jurisdiction even if that person did not know that the goods would end up in the forum state. In all likelihood, however, such a literal construction would run afoul of the Due Process clause.

1. N.Y. C.P.L.R., 302 (McKinney 2007).
2. *See supra* 39.

44. Paragraphs 2 and 3 of the above New York statute deal with jurisdiction in tort cases. The commission of a 'tortious act within the state' is a basis for specific jurisdiction under a straight territorial approach. As the phrasing of Paragraph 2 makes clear, especially in juxtaposition with Paragraph 3, it suffices if only the tortious act (i.e., the conduct) occurs within the forum state, even if the injury materializes in another state.

In contrast, when only the injury occurs within the forum state, then the defendant must have the additional forum contacts described in either of the two parts of Paragraph 3, which render more concrete the 'purposeful availment' or 'purposeful direction' requirements mandated by Supreme Court precedents. The first part describes contacts which, although less systematic and continuous than those that confer general jurisdiction, are nevertheless sufficient for specific jurisdiction for actions arising from the injury: the defendant must either regularly transact or solicit business, or engage in any other persistent course of conduct, or derive substantial revenue from goods used or consumed or services rendered, in the forum state. The second part of Paragraph 3 addresses foreseeability as a predicate for jurisdiction. The defendant's tortious act must be such that a person in the defendant's position should reasonably have expected the act to cause consequences in the forum state. In addition, however, the defendant must derive 'substantial revenue from interstate or international commerce', though not necessarily from commerce with the forum state.

3. Status and Domestic Relations

45. Jurisdiction to grant a divorce or to annul a marriage is a special species which is closer to *in rem* rather than *in personam* jurisdiction. It is based on the notion that the status of marriage is a kind of *res* and that, as long as the *res* rests within the territory of the forum state, that state has adjudicatory jurisdiction over it, even in the absence of *in personam* jurisdiction over the defendant. Initially, the *res* was supposed to rest in the state of the matrimonial domicile, and thus that state had jurisdiction to grant a divorce, even if the defendant had abandoned the plaintiff and moved to another state. In *Williams* v. *North Carolina [I]*,[1] the Supreme Court held that a state that was not the matrimonial domicile but subsequently became the domicile of only the *plaintiff* spouse had jurisdiction to grant a divorce, even in the absence of *in personam* jurisdiction over the defendant spouse ('*ex parte* divorce').[2] However, subsequent decisions made it clear that this jurisdiction was confined to the narrow question of dissolving the status of marriage and did not extend to adjudicating its incidents, such as marital property or alimony ('divisible divorce').[3] In order to adjudicate these incidents of divorce, a court must have *in personam* jurisdiction over both parties.[4]

1. 317 US 287 (1942), discussed *infra* 534–535.
2. An *ex parte* divorce is contrasted to a 'bilateral divorce', namely, a divorce granted in a proceeding in which both spouses participate. In *Sherrer* v. *Sherrer*, 334 US 343 (1948), discussed *infra* 536), the Supreme Court held that when the defendant appears in the divorce proceeding and fails to object to the court's jurisdiction, the defendant may not collaterally attack the resulting final judgment in another state.
3. *See*, e.g., *Estin* v. *Estin*, 334 US 541 (1948); *Vanderbilt* v. *Vanderbilt*, 354 US 416 (1957); *Simons* v. *Miami Beach First Nat'l Bank*, 381 US 81 (1965).
4. Status jurisdiction, as well as child support and custody jurisdiction are discussed in Part II, Chapter 6, *infra*.

IV. Federal Court Jurisdiction

A. *Introduction*

46. Article III of the Constitution prescribes the outer perimeters of the federal judicial power and relegates to Congress the authority to enact laws defining its exact contours. Pursuant to this authority, Congress defined the subject matter jurisdiction of the federal courts more restrictively than Article III permits. This is why, in determining the existence of subject matter jurisdiction in a particular case, the court must affirmatively establish both a statutory and a constitutional authorization for it.[1] The Constitutional grants federal court jurisdiction in two categories depending on the content of the dispute, or the identity of the disputants.

1. Unlike *in personam* jurisdiction, which can be conferred by the defendant's express or implied consent, such as when the defendant fails to raise jurisdictional objections at the beginning of the trial, the subject matter jurisdiction of federal courts may not be conferred by consent and objections to it may be raised at any time before the final appellate judgment. For comprehensive discussions of federal jurisdiction, *see*, e.g., E. Chemerinsky, *Federal Jurisdiction* (5th edn, New York, 2007); J. Pfander, *Principles of Federal Jurisdiction* (St. Paul, Minn., 2006).

47. The first category encompasses (1) 'all Cases of admiralty and maritime Jurisdiction';[1] and (2) all cases 'arising under' the Constitution, laws or treaties of the United States.[2] The latter is known as *federal question* jurisdiction. Although the federal statute authorizing this jurisdiction uses identical language to that of the Constitution ('arising under'),[3] the Supreme Court has interpreted the statute restrictively, thus narrowing the cases covered by federal question jurisdiction.[4]

1. US Const. Art. III, §2. For the statutory grant, *see* 28 USC §1333 (vesting district courts with exclusive jurisdiction over '[a]ny civil case of admiralty or maritime jurisdiction, saving to suitors in all cases all other remedies to which they are otherwise entitled'.).
2. US Const. Art. III, §2.
3. *See* 28 USC §1331.
4. *See*, e.g., *Cully* v. *First Nat'l. Bank*, 299 US 109 (1936).

48. The second category of federal court jurisdiction encompasses: (1) cases 'affecting Ambassadors, other public Ministers and Consuls'; (2) cases in which one of the parties is the United States, a state of the United States, or a foreign country; and (3) cases in which the parties are citizens of different states or citizens of such states and of foreign countries.[1] Of these cases, the Constitution assigns to the Supreme Court original jurisdiction over those 'affecting Ambassadors, other public Ministers and Consuls, and those in which a State shall be Party'.[2] The Constitution authorizes Congress to assign the remaining categories of cases to the lower courts. Congress has done this by, *inter alia*, granting federal district courts jurisdiction to hear cases in which the amount in controversy exceeds $75,000 and the dispute is between or among: (1) citizens of different states (2) citizens of a state and citizens of a foreign state; and (3) 'a foreign state . . . as plaintiff and citizens of a State or of different States'.[3] This is referred to hereinafter as *diversity jurisdiction*.[4] By its very nature, diversity jurisdiction includes many, many conflicts cases and hence it is of special interest to this volume.

1. US Const. Art. III, §2.
2. US Const. Art. III, §3.
3. 28 USC §1332(a). For actions in which the foreign state is a defendant, *see* 28 USC §1330 (authorizing federal court jurisdiction regardless of the amount in controversy); 28 USC §1602 *et seq*. (Foreign Sovereign Immunities Act, discussed *infra* 105).
4. When the dispute is between state citizens and foreign citizens, this jurisdiction is also referred to as *alienage jurisdiction*.

49. A comparison of the constitutional and statutory grants of diversity jurisdiction reveals several differences, the most conspicuous of which is that, unlike the constitutional grant, the statutory grant is limited to cases in which the amount in dispute exceeds $75,000. This is a perfectly valid exercise of congressional power because Congress is not mandated to vest *all* the constitutionally authorized judicial power in the lower courts. Consequently, diversity cases involving amounts less than $75,000 fall within the subject matter jurisdiction of the state courts. This is because, as courts of general and residual jurisdiction, state courts are empowered to hear any cases that federal statutes do not assign to the federal district courts even if the Constitution does.

Another difference between the constitutional and the congressional grant is that, while the constitutional grant requires only 'minimal diversity', (which is satisfied even when only *one* plaintiff is diverse from at least *one* defendant), the statutory grant has been interpreted as requiring 'complete diversity, i.e., *all* plaintiffs must be diverse from *all* defendants.[1]

1. *See Strawbridge* v. *Curtiss*, 7 US (3 Cranch) 267 (1806).

B. Exclusive or Concurrent Jurisdiction

50. The subject matter jurisdiction of the federal courts is exclusive in some cases and concurrent with that of state courts in other cases. For example, federal courts have exclusive jurisdiction in bankruptcy cases,[1] cases relating to patents, copyrights, and trademarks,[2] or arising under federal securities laws,[3] and some cases of admiralty or maritime jurisdiction.[4]

1. *See* 28 USCA §1334.
2. *See* 28 USCA §1338.
3. *See* 15 USCA §§77(1)(2) and 78(a)(a).
4. Although 28 USC §1333 vests federal courts with exclusive jurisdiction in maritime cases, it also contains a cryptic clause 'saving to suitors in all cases all other remedies to which they are otherwise entitled'. This clause has been interpreted as giving plaintiffs the option to sue in state court in all cases except *in rem* actions against vessels or other maritime property.

51. In most other cases, the jurisdiction of the federal courts is, or can be, concurrent with that of state courts. Although a federal statute provides for the removal of cases from state to federal court when the case falls within the jurisdiction of the latter court, the statute is subject to several exceptions. For example, in cases of maritime personal injury and cases arising under the Federal Employers Liability Act that are filed in state court, the defendant may not remove the case to federal court.[1] Secondly, in diversity cases, removal is precluded if *any* defendant is a citizen of the forum state.[2] Thirdly, in all cases, the removal must be sought by *all* defendants. Finally, removal is a right, not an obligation, of the defendants. When a defendant does not exercise this right, the case remains with the state court, even though it would normally belong to the jurisdiction of the federal courts.[3]

1. For maritime cases, *see supra* 50, footnote 4. For employment cases, *see* 28 USC §1445(a).
2. *See* 28 USC §1441(b). In federal question cases, removal is available 'without regard to the citizenship or residence of the parties'. *Id.*
3. *See* 28 USC §1441(a).

C. Territorial Jurisdiction

52. In many cases, the territorial jurisdiction of a federal court is coextensive with that of the state in which the court sits, and when that state comprises more than one federal district, such jurisdiction is allocated between or among the districts by the federal venue statute.[1] Rule 4(k)(1)(A) of the Federal Rules of Civil Procedure essentially incorporates state jurisdictional law by providing that federal service of process 'is effective to establish jurisdiction over the person of a defendant . . . who could be subjected to the jurisdiction of a court of general jurisdiction in the state in which the district court is located'.[2] When a federal court exercises territorial jurisdiction under a state long-arm statute, the constitutionality of that assertion is judged under the Due Process clause of the Fourteenth Amendment which binds the state and contemplates contacts with that state, as opposed to national contacts. This is clear when the court's subject matter jurisdiction is based on diversity, and less clear when it is based on federal question.

1. *See* 28 USC §1391.
2. Fed. R. Civ. P. 4(k)(1)(A).

53. However, Rule 4(k)(1)(D) also authorizes jurisdiction over any defendant 'when authorized by a statute of the United States',[1] and Rule 4(k)(2) does likewise with regard to 'any defendant who is not subject to the jurisdiction of the courts of general jurisdiction of any state', provided that the exercise of jurisdiction is 'consistent with the Constitution and laws of the United States'.[2] Indeed, several federal statutes provide for wider territorial jurisdiction than that of the states by authorizing nationwide[3] or worldwide[4] service of process. The prevailing view among the lower courts is that, in these cases, a federal court's assertion of jurisdiction over an alien defendant is subject to the restraints of the Due Process clause of the Fifth Amendment, which binds the federal government and contem-plates contacts with the entire United States.[5]

1. Fed. R. Civ. P. 4(k)(1)(D).
2. Fed. R. Civ. P. 4(k)(2).
3. *See*, e.g., 18 USC §1965 (RICO); 42 USC §9613(e) (environmental cleanup).
4. *See*, e.g., 15 USC §22 (antitrust); 15 USC §§77(v) and 78(a)(a) (securities).
5. For cases so holding and pertinent discussion *see* G. Born & P. Rutledge, *International Civil Litigation in United States Courts* 195–204 (Austin, 4th edn, 2000).

V. Forum Selection Clauses

54. Forum-selection or choice-of-forum clauses are a means of establishing *in personam* jurisdiction by consent. When a lawsuit is filed in the designated and otherwise competent forum, the clause has the effect of depriving the defendant of *in personam* jurisdictional objections the defendant could raise in the absence of the clause. When the lawsuit is filed in a forum other than the one designated in the clause, the plaintiff is in breach of the clause, thus entitling the defendant to object to the forum's jurisdiction. However, the effectiveness of this objection depends, not only on the validity *per se* of the forum selection clause (namely, the absence of contractual defects), but also on whether the clause purports to confer exclusive (derogation) or non-exclusive (prorogation) jurisdiction in the designated forum. When the wording of the clause is ambiguous, American courts tend to interpret the clause as exclusive, but such interpretation is not uniform. In fact, while they accepted non-exclusive clauses relatively early and easily,[1] American courts initially rejected exclusive clauses on the ground that they illegally ousted a court's jurisdiction.[2] A similar hostility existed towards arbitration clauses but was eliminated by the enactment in 1925 of the Federal Arbitration Act.[3]

1. *See Nat'l Equip. Rental, Ltd.* v. *Szukhent*, 375 US 311 (1964).
2. *See*, e.g., *Nute* v. *Hamilton Mut. Ins. Co.*, 72 Mass. (6 Gray) 174 (1856).
3. *See infra* 481–483.

55. The attitude toward choice-of-forum clauses began changing in 1972, when the Supreme Court upheld an exclusive English choice-of-forum clause in *The Bremen* v. *Zapata Off-Shore Co.*,[1] a case involving an international maritime towing contract between two large and sophisticated corporations. Two decades later, in *Carnival Cruise Lines, Inc.* v. *Shute*,[2] the Court moved to the farthest extreme by upholding an exclusive Florida choice-of-forum clause printed on the back of a cruise ticket for a voyage in the Pacific Ocean. The Court was unmoved by the fact that this clause was part of a consumer contract in which the parties' bargaining power was clearly unequal, the clause was not bargained for, and Florida was quite remote from the passenger's home state of Washington. Although universally criticized by commentators, *Shute* illustrates the dramatic move of American courts from initial hostility to enthusiastic, and often uncritical, acceptance of choice-of-forum clauses.

1. 407 US 1 (1972).
2. 499 US 1522 (1991).

56. Both *Bremen* and *Shute* are admiralty cases and thus they are binding authority only in such cases. In the meantime, other decisions have also upheld exclusive forum selection clauses in other federal question cases, such as securities[1] and antitrust cases.[2] Technically, these authorities are not binding when the federal court's jurisdiction is based solely on diversity, because, in these cases, state rather than federal law governs substantive legal questions.[3] In *Stewart Organization, Inc.* v. *Ricoh Corp.*,[4] the only diversity case to reach the Supreme Court in which enforcement of an exclusive forum selection clause was a key issue, the Court upheld the clause and rejected the argument that state law (which held the clause unenforceable) should govern this question. However, *Stewart* was decided in the special context of a federal statute that allows the transfer of cases between federal district courts[5] Thus, *Stewart* did not address the question of whether state or federal law governs the enforceability of exclusive forum selection clauses when this statute is inapplicable, such as when the clause designates a state court or a foreign court. Lower courts are split on this question, with some courts applying state law and others applying federal law.

1. *See Scherk* v. *Alberto-Culver Co.* 417 US 506 (1974).
2. *See Mitsubishi Motors Corp.* v. *Soler Chrysler–Plymouth, Inc.*, 473 US 614 (1985). *See also Vimar Seguros y Reaseguros, S.A.* v. *M/V Sky Reefer*, 515 US 528 (1995), discussed *infra* 476–478.

3. *See infra* 68–75.
4. 487 US 22 (1988).
5. *See* 28 USCA §1404(a), discussed *infra* 61–63.

57. *The Bremen* and other aforementioned federal cases are not binding on state courts, at least when dealing with questions of state law. Nevertheless, most state courts have chosen to adopt *Bremen*'s reasoning and philosophy and have overcome their initial hostility toward exclusive forum selection clauses. However, most courts probably would not go to the extreme of enforcing *Shute*-type clauses.[1] In a similar vein, some states have enacted statutes that invalidate foreign choice-of-forum clauses in consumer, employment, an insurance contracts under certain conditions.

1. For example, on remand from the Supreme Court in *Shute*, the California court held the clause unenforceable as to cruise passengers who did not have sufficient advance notice of the clause. *See Carnival Cruise Lines, Inc.* v. *Super. Ct.*, 286 Cal.Rptr. 323 (Cal. App. 1991). The Supreme Court had not addressed this issue. *See also Schaff* v. *Sun Line Cruises, Inc.*, 999 F.Supp. 924 (S.D. Tex. 1998); *Casavant* v. *Norwegian Cruise Line, Ltd.*, 829 N.E.2d 1171 (Mass. App. 2005), *review denied*, 834 N.E.2d 256 (Mass. 2005), *cert. denied*, 126 S.Ct. 1337 (US 2006); *Mack* v. *Royal Caribbean Cruises*, Ltd., 838 N.E.2d 80 (Ill. App. 2005), *appeal denied* 850 N.E.2d 808 (Ill. 2006), *cert. denied* 127 S.Ct. 350 (US 2006).

VI. *Forum Non Conveniens*

58. In the Anglo-American world, the fact that a court has jurisdiction over the parties does not obligate the court to exercise it. Under the doctrine of *forum non conveniens*, the court has discretion to decline to adjudicate the merits if litigation in the forum state would be seriously inconvenient and burdensome, and if another, more convenient, forum is available to the plaintiff. *Forum non conveniens* is an antidote to forum shopping, which is made possible by the fact that in many cases jurisdiction is available in several states, from which the plaintiff is entitled to choose. This doctrine is designed to protect the defendant from hardship[1] and to relieve courts from the burden of hearing cases which, but for the existence of jurisdiction, have little connection to the forum state.

1. *See Gulf Oil Corp.* v. *Gilbert*, 330 US 501, 508 (1947) ('[T]he plaintiff may not, by choice of an inconvenient forum, "vex", "harass" or "oppress" the defendant by inflicting upon him expense or trouble not necessary to his own right to pursue his remedy'.).

59. The leading US case on *forum non conveniens* is *Gulf Oil Corp.* v. *Gilbert*,[1] in which the Supreme Court articulated the factors that should guide the courts' discretion in applying the doctrine. The Court divided these factors into private-interest factors, and public-interest factors. The private factors include:

> [A]vailability of compulsory process for attendance of unwilling, and the cost of obtaining attendance of willing, witnesses; possibility of view of premises, if view would be appropriate to the action; and all other practical problems that make trial of a case easy, expeditious and inexpensive[;] . . . the enforceability of a judgment if one is obtained[;] . . . [and the] relative advantages and obstacles to fair trial.[2]

The public interest factors include the forum's interest in avoiding congested judicial dockets and other similar logistical burdens such as jury duty, as well as the difficulties in 'untangl[ing] problems in conflict of laws' and foreign law, and the interest of the alternative forum 'in having localized controversies decided at home'.[3]

The Court made it clear that the defendant bears the burden of showing that another forum is available and that the above factors '*strongly*' favour the other forum. In the absence of such a showing, the plaintiff's choice of forum 'should rarely be disturbed'.[4]

1. 330 US 501 (1947).
2. *Id.* at 508.
3. *Id.*
4. *Id.* (emphasis added) ('[U]nless the balance is strongly in favor of the defendant, the plaintiff's choice of forum should rarely be disturbed'.).

60. In the next major Supreme Court case, *Piper Aircraft Co.* v. *Reyno*,[1] the Court accepted the assumption that, when the plaintiff is an alien, his or her choice of forum 'deserves less deference'[2] than that of an American plaintiff. The converse of this premise is that, when the plaintiff is a domiciliary of the initial forum, the doctrine should be inoperable. Many lower courts have so held, and some state statutes have adopted this principle as well.

To be truly available, the alternative forum must provide a remedy that is roughly comparable to that of the initial forum, even if it is less generous to the plaintiff. Although not determinative, a preliminary showing that the case will be governed by the law of the initial forum generally favours retaining the case, while a showing that the case will be governed by the law of the alternative forum generally favours *forum non* dismissal.

When a court decides that the *forum non conveniens* doctrine is applicable, the court may dismiss the case outright, dismiss it on condition or stipulation that the defendant submit to the jurisdiction of the court in the alternative forum and waive certain defences such as the statute of limitations, or stay the action while the action is pending in the alternative forum.

State *forum non conveniens* practise is generally similar to the federal practise described above, although some states have enacted statutes that preclude the doctrine's operation in certain narrowly defined circumstances.

1. 454 US 235 (1981).
2. *Id.* at 256.

VII. Federal Transfers

61. A federal venue statute, 28 USCA §1404(a), provides that a federal district court may transfer any civil action to any other federal district court 'where it might have been brought', if such transfer would serve 'the convenience of parties and witnesses . . . and the interest of justice'.[1] This laconic provision supplants the *forum non conveniens* doctrine in all cases in which *both* the initial forum and the alternative forum are *federal* district courts and both have jurisdiction. In applying this statute, courts have relied heavily on the factors articulated in *Gulf Oil Co.* v.

Gilbert, supra, although the Supreme Court has held that this statute allows a transfer on a lesser showing of inconvenience than the *forum non conveniens* doctrine.[1]

1. 28 USCA §1404(a).
2. *See Norwood* v. *Kirkpatrick*, 349 US 29 (1955).

62. There is one important difference between the consequences of a *forum non conveniens* dismissal and a transfer granted under §1404(a). When the dismissed lawsuit is re-filed in the alternative forum, that court that will apply its own choice-of-law rule to determine which substantive law will govern the case. In contrast, when a case is transferred to another federal court under §1404(a), the transferee court is required to apply to same choice-of-law rule that would have been applied by the transferor court. The Supreme Court held to this effect in *Van Dusen* v. *Barrack*,[1] reasoning that the purpose of §1404(a) was simply to authorize a change of courtrooms, not a change of results. In *Van Dusen*, the transfer was sought and obtained by the defendant. In *Ferens* v. *John Deere Co.*,[2] the Court held that the same principle applies in cases in which the transfer is sought by the plaintiff.

1. 376 US 612 (1964).
2. 494 US 516 (1990), discussed *infra* 631–634.

63. When the initially chosen forum is a federal court that lacks jurisdiction or is a court of improper venue, two other statutes allow that court to either dismiss the action or transfer it to another federal court 'in which it could have been brought', if such transfer is 'in the interest of justice'.[1] However, in these transfers – unlike those under §1404(a) – the transferee court will apply its own choice-of-law rules. In other words, a plaintiff who (unlike the *Ferens* plaintiff) files in the wrong court (and is lucky enough to have his suit transferred rather than dismissed), may not carry with it the choice-of-law rules of the transferor court.

1. 28 USCA §1406(a) (jurisdiction); 28 USCA §1631 (venue).

Chapter 2. Federalism and Choice of Law

§1. Introduction

64. This chapter discusses some of the ways in which American federalism affects choice-of-law decisions. Because these decisions are made by both state and federal courts, the chapter begins with a brief review of the law that governs federal courts and the law they apply. After explaining why federal courts do not always, perhaps not even primarily, apply federal law, the discussion moves to the state level and examines the extent to which federal law affects state choice-of-law decisions, in both the interstate and the international arena.

§2. Law Applied in Federal Courts

I. In General

65. The foreign reader should not be blamed for assuming that federal courts apply federal law and state courts apply state law. However, as the discussion in the preceding chapter indicates, this assumption is inaccurate – state courts routinely apply federal law, and federal courts routinely apply state law. While the supremacy of federal law may suffice to explain why state (and federal) courts must apply federal law in a certain case, nothing intuitive explains why federal courts must apply state law. The reasons for this phenomenon are partly historical, partly practical and partly constitutional.[1]

1. For in-depth discussion of the law governing federal courts, *see*, e.g., C. Wright & M.K. Kane, *Law of Federal Courts* (6th edn, St. Paul, Minn., 2002) and P. Low & J. Jeffries, *Federal Courts and the Law of Federal-State Relations* (5th edn, New York, 2004).

66. To begin with, many cases involve inextricably interrelated issues of both federal and state law. For example, a federal question case filed in federal court may involve interrelated claims or counterclaims arising under state law. In such a case, the federal court may adjudicate the state claims (relying on 'supplemental jurisdiction')[1] and will apply state law to them. Conversely, a case filed in state court and arising under state law may involve interrelated claims or defences arising under federal law. Again, the state court will have to apply federal law to those claims or defences.

1. *See* 28 USCA §1367.

67. In other cases, federal law expressly requires federal courts to apply state law. One general example is the Rules of Decision Act, a kind of 'basic law' that is discussed *infra*. Another example is the Federal Tort Claims Act, which authorizes suits against the United States for injuries caused by its employees. The Act requires the application of the law of the 'the place where the act or omission occurred'.[1] If that place is in a state of the United States, the court will apply that state's law, *including* its conflicts law.[2] Finally, one major category of cases in which federal courts routinely apply state substantive and conflicts law, and which calls for more detailed explanation, are cases in which the court's subject matter jurisdiction rests solely on diversity. This category is discussed in the next section.

1. 28 USCA §1346.
2. *See Richards* v. *United States*, 369 US 1 (1962), discussed *infra* 691–692.

II. Law Applied in Diversity Cases

A. Substantive Law

68. The first Judiciary Act of 1789 provided:

> The laws of the several states, except where the Constitution or treaties of the United States or Acts of Congress otherwise require or provide, shall be regarded as rules of decision in civil actions in the courts of the United States, in cases where they apply.[1]

Through the 'except clause', the Act distinguished between: (1) cases that the Constitution or federal laws 'require or provide' to be governed by federal law; and (2) other cases for which the Constitution or federal laws do not so provide. Federal question cases are an example of the former category, while diversity cases are an example of the latter, but only when they are not otherwise governed by federal law. For these cases, the Act provides that '[t]he *laws* of the several states . . . shall be regarded as rules of decision in civil actions in the courts of the United States, in cases where they apply'. Leaving aside the circularity of the concluding phrase, this provision expressly requires the application of state statutes. During the formative era, the question was raised whether the word 'laws' also included the common law of the several states. In *Swift* v. *Tyson*,[2] the Supreme Court answered this question in the negative, thus allowing federal courts in sitting in diversity to ignore state common law and to begin creating their own common law.

1. Judiciary Act of 1879 §34, 1 Stat. 92. This Act, now codified in 28 USCA §1652, is also known as the Rules of Decision Act.
2. 41 US (16 Pet.) 1 (1842).

69. Almost a century later, the Court overruled *Swift* in *Erie Railroad Co.* v. *Tompkins*,[1] holding that when sitting in diversity and adjudicating a matter not covered by applicable federal law, a federal court must follow the common law of the forum state. The Court based its overturning of *Swift* partly on constitutional grounds, and partly on policy grounds. The constitutional ground was that *Swift* had put federal courts in the position of usurping the lawmaking powers reserved to the states by the Tenth Amendment because it allowed these courts to create federal common law on subjects that the Constitution did not assign to the federal government. The policy ground was that, by allowing a federal court to create a common law different from that of the forum state, *Swift* undermined intrastate uniformity and favoured non-resident plaintiffs by providing forum-shopping opportunities that were unavailable to resident plaintiffs. Thus, the *Erie* decision opted for *intra*state uniformity at the expense of *inter*state uniformity.

1. 304 US 64 (1938).

70. Although *Erie* pronounced that '[t]here is no federal *general* common law',[1] that statement must be limited to diversity cases that do not involve a subject falling within the lawmaking competence of the federal government. Federal courts may, and do, create federal common law when they decide a matter which is within the lawmaking competence of the federal government but on which Congress has not legislated, or its legislation contains gaps. In such cases, federal courts are free to create federal common law, provided that the subject in question involves a 'uniquely federal interest' that requires uniform national treatment.[2] Invoking this authority, federal courts have created common law on several subjects, including foreign relations.[3] Federal common law preempts contrary state law, as does federal statutory law.

1. *Id.* at 78 (emphasis added).
2. *See Boyle* v. *United Techs. Corp.*, 487 US 500 (1988).
3. *See infra* 95–105.

B. Procedural Law

71. The Conformity Act of 1872 required federal courts to follow 'as near as may be, . . . the practice, pleadings, and forms and modes of proceeding' of the courts of the state in which the federal court sits.[1] This provision was intended to enable attorneys to practise in both federal and state courts without having to learn two procedural systems. This regime remained in place until 1938 (which was also the year *Erie* was decided), when the Supreme Court promulgated the Federal Rules of Civil Procedure[2] which, as subsequently amended, apply in federal courts to date.

Thus, 1938 was the year of a fairly dramatic flip-flop. Federal courts ceased applying state procedural law and began applying federal procedural law. They also stopped creating their own common law and began applying state common law.

1. Act of 1 June 1872, ch. 255, 17 stat. 196, 197.
2. The promulgation was authorized by the Rules Enabling Act of 1934.

72. The one thing that did not change in 1938 was the practical need for a clear line separating 'substantive' and 'procedural' law. In a series of decisions, the Supreme Court attempted to draw such a line 'for *Erie* purposes',[1] as have state courts for general choice-of-law purposes.[2] Neither set of decisions can be recounted here.[3] Suffice it to say, the line separating substance from procedure for *Erie* purposes is not necessarily the same as the line separating these categories for choice-of-law purposes. For example, as discussed later, a statute of limitation is considered substantive for *Erie* purposes,[4] although most states consider it procedural for choice-of-law purposes.[5]

1. *See*, e.g., *Ragan* v. *Merchs. Transfer & Warehouse Co.*, 337 US 530 (1949); *Byrd* v. *Blue Ridge Rural Elec. Coop., Inc.*, 356 US 525 (1958); *Hanna* v. *Plumer*, 380 US 460 (1965); *Walker* v. *Armco Steel Corp.*, 446 US 740 (1980).
2. *See infra* 134–140.
3. For discussion, *see* E. Scoles, P. Hay, P. Borchers & S. Symeonides, *Conflict of Laws* 180–208 (4th edn, St. Paul, Minn., 2004).
4. *See Guaranty Trust Co.* v. *York*, 326 US 99 (1945).
5. *See infra* 593–604.

C. Choice of Law

73. Three years after *Erie*, the Supreme Court extended *Erie's* reasoning to choice of law. In *Klaxon Co.* v. *Stentor Electric Manufacturing Co.*,[1] the Court held that, when a federal court sits in diversity and the case is not otherwise governed by federal law, the court must apply the choice-of-law rules of the state in which it sits.[2] This is a significant development considering that, as noted in the Introduction, federal courts decide the majority of conflicts cases.[3]

The *Klaxon* decision has been criticized as being neither constitutionally mandated nor resting on solid policy grounds.[4] Indeed, from a constitutional perspective, it is clear that, although federal courts lack the power to create new rules of, say, tort law, they certainly have the authority under the Full Faith and Credit clause to determine which of the conflicting state tort rules should govern in a multistate case. As noted earlier, under this clause, conflicts law is a matter of federal law, and only by default has it become a matter of state law. From a policy perspective, the reasons that might have supported *Erie*'s choice of *intra*state over *inter*state uniformity arguably point to the opposite choice in *Klaxon*. This is because *inter*state forum shopping is more likely in multistate cases and thus *inter*state uniformity should receive higher billing than *intra*state uniformity.

1. 313 US 487 (1941).
2. When the federal court's jurisdiction is based on federal question, *Klaxon* is inapplicable and the court is free to fashion its own choice-of-law rules. Many federal courts choose to follow the choice-of-law rules of the forum state, while other courts follow other options, such as applying the *Restatement (Second)*.
3. *See supra* 14.
4. *See* E. Scoles, P. Hay, P. Borchers & S. Symeonides, *Conflict of Laws* 177–180 (4th edn, St. Paul, Minn., 2004).

74. Notwithstanding these and other criticisms, the Supreme Court reaffirmed *Klaxon* in *Day & Zimmermann, Inc.* v. *Challoner*.[1] *Challoner* was a products liability action filed in Texas by the survivors of an American soldier who was killed in Cambodia during the Vietnam war when a mortar shell manufactured by an American defendant exploded prematurely. Applying a modern choice-of-law analysis, the Texas federal court ignored Texas's *lex loci delicti* rule, which pointed to Cambodian law, instead applying American law. The Supreme Court reversed in a brief *per curiam* opinion making it clear that federal courts were not free to exercise independent judgment in choice-of-law decisions. 'A federal court in a diversity case is not free to engraft onto those state rules exceptions or modifications which may commend themselves to the federal court but which have not commended themselves to the State in which the federal court sits'.[2]

1. 423 US 3 (1975).
2. *Id.* at 4.

75. Thus, a federal court is not free to ignore a state choice-of-law rule, even when it leads to an absurd result. The court may adopt a new rule only when it can credibly claim that the rule would 'commend itself' to the state courts. In turn, such a claim is plausible when state choice of law is ambiguous, or when the case involves a novel issue or an issue that the state courts have not considered in recent years.[1] Even then, the court must be careful to couch its ruling not as its own conclusion, but rather as a 'prediction' of what the state court would rule if confronted with the same case.

1. Many states provide for a process known as 'certification' under which a federal court can request an opinion from the state's highest court on novel questions of law pending before the federal court.

§3. Federal Limitations on State Choice of Law

I. The Four Principal Constitutional Clauses

76. As noted earlier, choice of law is *de facto* and by default a matter of state law, because Congress has not exercised its constitutional power to federalize it. Thus, the states are, in principle, free to legislatively or judicially enunciate their choice-of-law rules or approaches, and to resolve interstate or international conflicts of laws without federal approval. However, in so doing, the states must remain within the outer restraints imposed by the federal Constitution as interpreted by the United States Supreme Court. These restraints are found primarily in four constitutional clauses: the Full Faith and Credit and Privileges and Immunities clauses of Article IV, and the Due Process and Equal Protection clauses of the Fourteenth Amendment.[1] The first clause applies to the laws or judgments of sister states, the second to 'citizens' of sister states (i.e., natural persons domiciled in such states, but not corporations or aliens) and the last two clauses apply to 'persons', natural or juridical, domestic or foreign.

1. For the text of these clauses, *see supra* 22–23. The first three clauses are discussed *infra* 77–94. The equal protection clause is not discussed here because it has not, as yet, being employed to scrutinize choice-of-law decisions. Basic bibliography on this subject includes: L. McDougal, R. Felix & R. Whitten, *American Conflicts Law* 189–216 (5th edn, New York, Ardsley, 2001); W. Reynolds & W. Richman, *The Full Faith and Credit Clause: A Reference Guide to the United States Constitution* (Westport, Conn., 2005); E. Scoles, P. Hay, P. Borchers & S. Symeonides, *Conflict of Laws* 149–176 (4th edn, St. Paul, Minn., 2004) and R. Weintraub, *Commentary on the Conflict of Laws* 620–686 (5th edn, New York, 2006).

77. The first two clauses are phrased as affirmative commands directing states to behave in a certain way toward sister states: States 'shall' accord 'Full Faith and Credit' to the laws and judgments of sister states and 'shall' accord certain 'privileges and immunities' to the citizens of sister states.[1] Thus, these clauses are highly relevant to conflicts law, having been designed to directly address issues affecting the horizontal relationship or coexistence of the several states within the federal union.

In contrast, the Due Process and Equal Protection clauses of the Fourteenth Amendment (which are phrased as negative commands) appear, at least facially, as less relevant to conflicts law, having been designed to address the vertical, government-to-person relationship in each state: 'No State shall . . . deprive any person,' *including its own citizens*, 'of life, liberty, or property, without due process of law; nor deny to any person within its jurisdiction the equal protection of the laws'.[2]

Nevertheless, for reasons explained *infra*, the Supreme Court recently has relied more on the Due Process clause as the main vehicle for policing state choice-of-law decisions.

1. US Const., Art. IV.
2. US Const., Amd. XIV.

II. The Full Faith and Credit and Due Process Clauses

A. *From Interventionism to Laissez Faire*

78. In the early part of the 20th century, the Supreme Court took a fairly interventionist stance in using both the Full Faith and Credit and Due Process clauses in policing state choice-of-law decisions. For example, in *New York Life Ins. Co.* v. *Dodge*,[1] the Court held that the Due Process clause prohibited Missouri from applying its law to a contract between a Missouri insured and a New York insurer, because the contract was technically 'made' in New York.[2] The fact that the insurer had ample contacts with Missouri and had knowingly dealt with a Missouri insured, or that Missouri had a legitimate interest in protecting insureds domiciled and acting there, were not considered relevant. Influenced by the then prevalent vested rights dogma, the Court thought that the *lex loci contractus* was not merely a good choice-of-law rule, but also a constitutionally compelled one.

Similarly, in *Bradford Electric Light Co., Inc.* v. *Clapper*,[3] the Court held that the Full Faith and Credit clause required New Hampshire to apply Vermont law in a workers' compensation dispute between a Vermont employer and the survivors of a Vermont employee, even though the actual dispute arose out of the employee's fatal injury that occurred in New Hampshire. Again, neither New Hampshire's contacts, nor its potential interest in protecting workers injured on its territory, were relevant considerations for the Court.

1. 246 US 357 (1918).
2. For a similar decision to the same effect, *see N.Y. Life Ins. Co.* v. *Head*, 234 US 149 (1914).
3. 286 US 145 (1932).

79. Gradually, the Court lost enthusiasm for the vested rights doctrine and began backing away from its interventionist reading of the two clauses and giving increasing consideration to the contacts and interests of states other than those in which the contract was made, or the injury occurred. Initially, the Court weighed the contacts and interests of the involved states, but later on abandoned any weighing. The cases discussed below illustrate this movement.

80. In *Clay* v. *Sun Office, Ltd.*,[1] the Court held that the Due Process clause did not prohibit Florida from applying its law to protect an insured who was domiciled and suffered the loss in Florida, even though Florida was neither the place of contracting nor the insured's domicile at the time of the contract. Because the insurance policy provided 'world wide coverage' to an insured who was free to move his domicile to any state other than the contract state, the insurer could have anticipated the move to Florida and the occurrence of the loss there. Hence, the application of Florida law was not arbitrary or unfair to the insurer.

1. 377 US 179 (1964).

81. Similarly, in two workers' compensation cases, *Alaska Packers Association* v. *Industrial Accident Commission*[1] and *Pacific Employers Insurance Co.* v. *Industrial Accident Commission*,[2] the Court compared the contacts and interests of the state of the employment relationship, on the one hand, and the state of the worker's injury, on the other. After finding that the contacts and interests of the two states were comparably strong, the Court held that the Full Faith and Credit clause did not require either state to apply the law of the other state. Thus, in the first case, California, the state of the employment relationship, was free to apply its workers' compensation law to the action of a California employee injured in Alaska. In the second case, California, the state of the injury, was also free to apply its workers' compensation law to the action of a Massachusetts worker injured in California. The Court explained its reasoning, while revealing a certain frustration with the Full Faith and Credit clause:

> To the extent that California is required to give full faith and credit to the conflicting Massachusetts statute it must be denied the right to apply in its own courts its own statute, constitutionally enacted in pursuance of its policy to provide compensation for employees injured in their employment within the state. . . . We cannot say that the full faith and credit clause goes so far.
>
> . . . [T]he very nature of the federal union of states, to which are reserved some of the attributes of sovereignty, precludes resort to the full faith and credit clause as the means for compelling a state to substitute the statutes of other states for its own statutes dealing with a subject matter concerning which it is competent to legislate. . . .
>
> Full faith and credit does not here enable one state to legislate for the other or to project its laws across state lines so as to preclude the other from prescribing for itself the legal consequences of acts within it.[3]

1. 294 US 532 (1935).
2. 306 US 493 (1939).
3. *Id.* at 501–505.

82. By the middle of the 20th century, the Court abandoned any effort to weigh the contacts and interests of the involved states and instead asked whether the state that applied its law had *sufficient* contacts and interests.[1] This movement culminated in the all-important, though not necessarily commendable, decision in *Allstate Insurance Co.* v. *Hague*.[2] *Hague* involved an insurance dispute between Allstate, a nationwide insurer doing business in Minnesota, and the wife of a Wisconsin insured, Mr Hague, who was killed in Wisconsin while driving the insured vehicle. The wife subsequently moved to Minnesota and sued the insurer there, seeking to take advantage of Minnesota 'stacking rule', which provided more coverage than Wisconsin's anti-stacking rule. Following Minnesota's 'better law approach',[3] the Minnesota Supreme Court applied Minnesota law. Without approving of that approach, the US Supreme Court affirmed, holding that the application of Minnesota law was constitutionally permissible.

In so holding, the Court: (1) re-affirmed its previous inclination to abandon the weighing of contacts and interests; (2) merged the Full Faith and Credit test into the Due Process test; and (3) enunciated a new combined test for determining the constitutionality of a state's choice of its own law to multistate cases: According to this test,

> [F]or a State's substantive law to be selected in a constitutionally permissible manner, that State must have a significant contact or significant aggregation of contacts, creating state interests, such that choice of its law is neither arbitrary nor fundamentally unfair.[4]

1. *See*, e.g., *Carroll* v. *Lanza*, 349 US 408 (1955); *Wells* v. *Simonds Abrasive Co.*, 345 US 514 (1953).
2. 449 US 302 (1981).
3. This approach is discussed *infra* at 193–194, 242–251.
4. 449 US at 313.

83. Seven justices agreed with this conflated test, but only a four-member plurality agreed that it was satisfied in this case.[1] The plurality found that Minnesota had three contacts which, 'in the aggregate', satisfied this test.

The first contact was that the deceased insured had worked in Minnesota on a commuting basis for 15 years and Minnesota had an 'interest' in protecting a 'member of its work force'. The plurality thought that the fact that the accident did *not* occur in Minnesota, or during this commuting, but rather during a weekend trip inside Wisconsin was irrelevant. The plurality noted, however, that '[b]ecause Allstate . . . was undoubtedly aware that Mr. Hague was a Minnesota employee, it had to have anticipated that Minnesota law might apply to an accident in which Mr. Hague was involved',[2] apparently even to an accident occurring outside Minnesota.

The second contact was that Allstate was doing business in Minnesota and thus it could 'hardly claim unfamiliarity with the laws of the host jurisdiction and surprise that the state courts might apply forum law to litigation in which the company is involved.'[3] Moreover, 'Allstate's presence in Minnesota gave Minnesota an interest in regulating the company's insurance obligations insofar as they affected both a Minnesota resident [Mrs. Hague] . . . and a longstanding member of Minnesota's work force – Mr. Hague'.[4]

The third contact was that Mrs Hague moved to Minnesota after the accident but before filing the lawsuit, and there was 'no suggestion' that she did so 'for the purpose of finding a legal climate especially hospitable to her claim'.[5] This move gave Minnesota 'an interest in [Mrs. Hague's] recovery, an interest which the lower court identified as full compensation for "resident accident victims" to keep them "off welfare rolls"'.[6]

While 'express[ing] no view [on] whether the first two contacts, either together or separately, would have sufficed to sustain the choice of Minnesota law',[7] the plurality concluded that Minnesota had 'a significant *aggregation* of contacts with the parties and the occurrence, creating state interests, such that application of its law was neither arbitrary nor fundamentally unfair'.[8] Therefore, the choice of Minnesota law 'did not violate the Due Process Clause or the Full Faith and Credit Clause'.[9]

1. Justice Stevens concurred in the result, but disagreed with the reasoning, and Justice Stewart did not participate.
2. 449 US at 318, fn. 24.
3. *Id.* at 317–318.
4. *Id.* at 318.
5. *Id.* at 319.
6. *Id.*
7. *Id.* at 320, fn. 29.
8. *Id.* at 320 (emphasis added).
9. *Id.* at 320.

84. The three dissenting justices agreed with the plurality's conflating of the Full Faith and Credit and Due Process clauses and its articulation of the particular test. However, they pointedly noted that '[a] contact . . . satisfies the Constitution when it protects the litigants from being unfairly surprised . . . and when the application of the forum's law reasonably . . . further[s] a legitimate public policy of the forum State'.[1] The dissenters concluded that whether taken separately or in the aggregate, Minnesota's contacts were 'trivial or irrelevant to the furthering of any public policy of Minnesota'.[2]

1. *Id.* at 335–336.
2. *Id.* at 339.

85. Holding the middle ground, concurring Justice Stevens disagreed with the merging of the Full Faith and Credit clause into the Due Process clause. In his view, the constitutional limitations to state choice of law involve two separate questions: 'First, does the Full Faith and Credit Clause *require* Minnesota, the forum State, to apply Wisconsin law? Second, does the Due Process Clause of the Fourteenth Amendment *prevent* Minnesota from applying its own law?'[1] The first question implicates the 'federal interest in ensuring that Minnesota respect the sovereignty of the State of Wisconsin', while the second question implicates 'the litigants' interest in a fair adjudication of their rights'.[2] Justice Stevens concluded that the Full Faith and Credit clause did not require Minnesota to apply Wisconsin law because the defendant failed to show that Minnesota's refusal to apply Wisconsin law 'poses any direct or indirect threat to Wisconsin's sovereignty'[3] or 'any threat to national unity.[4] He also concluded that the Due Process clause did not prevent Minnesota from choosing its own law because that choice was not 'totally arbitrary or . . . fundamentally unfair'.[5]

1. *Id.* at 320.
2. *Id.*
3. *Id.* at 325.
4. *Id.* at 323.
5. *Id.* at 325.

86. Justice Stevens correctly underscored the need to separate the full faith and credit question from the due process question, although he posed a rather high threshold for both clauses ('threat to . . . sovereignty' and 'totally arbitrary'). The Court's merging of the two clauses – or actually the absorption of the Full Faith and Credit clause into the Due Process clause – is problematical, although it is understandable in light of the Court's difficulty in reconciling the positive command of the Full Faith and Credit clause with the negative command of the Due Process clause. The consequence of the merging is to compress the whole constitutional inquiry into one of fairness to the defendant. When the defendant is a big multistate corporation named 'Allstate' and the court chooses the law that favours the plaintiff widow, the defendant's arguments about unfairness tend to fall on unsympathetic ears. However, even if such a result is affirmatively fair (as opposed to 'not unfair'), the inclusion of the Full Faith and Credit clause in the Constitution is evidence that there is more to federalism than the pursuit of fairness, as laudable as that goal is. By mothballing the Full Faith and Credit clause, the Court deprived itself of a far more appropriate and effective instrument in ensuring respect for sister states' laws. The loss of such an instrument would be more visible in cases in which the choice of the forum's law, though not unfair, is improper for other reasons, such as when it undermines a national policy of uniformity.[1]

1. For example, the application of the law of the state of incorporation to the internal affairs of corporations might serve such a national policy, although the choice of another state's law may not violate the Due Process clause. *Cf. Order of United Commercial Travelers* v. *Wolfe*, 331 US 586 (1947).

87. The *laissez faire* attitude exhibited in *Hague* left the impression that the Court would reverse a state choice-of-law decision only in extreme circumstances. However, in *Phillips Petroleum Co.* v. *Shutts*,[1] the Court reversed a Kansas decision to apply Kansas law in a case in which Kansas arguably had no fewer contacts than Minnesota had in *Hague*. *Shutts* was a class action in which 97 per cent of the plaintiffs were domiciled outside Kansas and 99 per cent of the mineral leases giving rise to their claims for interest on delayed royalty payments were on lands located in other states. However, the defendant oil company did 'substantial business' in Kansas, and the Court recognized Kansas's 'interest in regulating [defendant's] *conduct in Kansas*.'[2] Nevertheless, the Court held that Kansas could not constitutionally apply its law to the claims of non-Kansan plaintiffs arising from non-Kansas leases.

1. 472 US 797 (1985).
2. *Id.* at 819 (emphasis added).

88. *Sun Oil Co.* v. *Wortman*[1] is the third case of the *Hague* trilogy, and the last on the topic of full faith and credit and due process limitations on choice of law. *Wortman* involved essentially the same facts as *Shutts*, in which the Court held that

Kansas did not have enough contacts to apply its *substantive* law. However, the issue in *Wortman* was whether Kansas could apply its own statute of limitation, which allowed an action that would have been barred in the other involved states.[2] In a somewhat surprising decision, the Court invoked the traditional mechanical characterization of statutes of limitations as procedural and answered the question in the affirmative. Writing for the Court, Justice Scalia found that 'the society which adopted the Constitution did not regard statutes of limitations as substantive provisions . . . but rather as procedural restrictions fashioned by each jurisdiction for its own courts'.[3] He reasoned that '[s]ince the procedural rules of its courts are surely matters on which a State is competent to legislate, it follows that a State may apply its own procedural rules to actions litigated in its courts,'[4] even if it lacks the contacts necessary for applying its substantive law to the merits.

1. 486 US 717 (1988).
2. For the converse situation, namely, when the forum has a shorter statute of limitations barring an action that is not barred in the other state, the Court had earlier approved the application of the forum's shorter statute. *See Wells* v. *Simonds Abrasive Co.*, 345 US 514 (1953). The result in *Wells* is not problematical because, even when it lacks sufficient contacts, the forum always has genuine procedural interest in applying its *shorter* statute of limitation because such a shorter statute relieves the forum's courts from the burden of hearing old claims.
3. *Wortman*, 486 US at 726.
4. *Id. Wortman* is discussed again *infra* at 628–630.

89. Despite its conclusory reasoning, *Wortman* reaffirms the proposition that, on *truly* procedural issues, a state is free to apply its own law. This freedom, however, is not unlimited. For example, a state may not, through procedural laws or otherwise, refuse to provide a forum to causes of action *solely* on the ground that they arise under the laws of sister states, nor may it interpose undue procedural obstacles to the filing or prosecution of such actions in its courts.[1] Such action would be an indirect violation of the Full Faith and Credit clause, and, depending on the specifics, of other constitutional limitations as well. Also, a state may not keep litigation at home by preventing other states from providing a forum for otherwise transitory actions arising under it laws.[2]

1. *See Hughes* v. *Fetter*, 341 US 609 (1951); *Broderick* v. *Rosner*, 294 US 629 (1935).
2. *See Tenn. Coal, Iron & R.R. Co.* v. *George*, 233 US 354 (1914); *Crider* v. *Zurich Ins. Co.*, 380 US 39 (1965).

B. Overview and Comparison with Jurisdiction and Choice of Law

90. As the above review of the cases indicates, the Supreme Court has moved from an interventionist stance at the beginning of the 20th century to a *laissez faire* stance at the end of the century. Perhaps it is not coincidental that (wrongly or rightly) at the beginning of the century there was a universal consensus around the vested rights doctrine and, by the end of the century, that consensus disappeared, primarily because of the conflicts revolution of the 1960s.[1] At the beginning of the century, a state that deviated from the vested right doctrine stood out as doing something out of the ordinary, thus evoking the Supreme Court's attention and intervention. In contrast, toward the end of the century, the wide divergence of opinion brought by the revolution made it difficult for the Court to pick any one opinion as 'the right' one, much less to accord it constitutional sanction.

1. *See infra* Part II, Chapter 3.

91. The Court may have also concluded that, in light of its limited resources, it would be more efficient to police state action in the interstate arena by tightening the jurisdictional rules, as it has done through cases such as *Shaffer* v. *Heitner*,[1] than by closely scrutinizing choice-of-law decisions. Through rulings like *Shaffer*, the Court sought to ensure that a state will not assert jurisdiction unless it had the requisite 'minimum contacts' with the case. After *Shaffer*, the Court could expect that in the majority of cases, these same contacts will also suffice to constitutionally sustain the application of the forum's substantive law.

Admittedly, in many cases, the same contacts will satisfy both the 'minimum contacts' test of *International Shoe* and the 'significant contacts' test of *Hague*. However, this does not mean that the two tests are identical. In fact, even setting aside the Full Faith and Credit clause and looking at the *Hague* test as one based exclusively on the Due Process clause and its preoccupation with protecting the *defendant* from unfair surprise,[2] the *Hague* test is still analytically separate from the jurisdictional test. The jurisdictional test asks whether the defendant's contacts with the forum were such that subjecting him to *litigation* in that state would not be unfair. The *Hague* test asks whether the defendant's contacts with the forum were such that the application of the forum's *substantive law* would be 'neither arbitrary nor fundamentally unfair'.[3] In many cases, the same contacts would meet both tests, but not in all. For example, the defendant's consent to jurisdiction satisfies the jurisdictional test but, in the absence of other contacts, it does not satisfy the *Hague* test. Similarly, if tag jurisdiction still empowers a court to hear a case, this basis alone does not empower, much less justify, the court to apply its own law. In a few cases, the converse may also be true. For example, a valid choice-of-law clause satisfies the *Hague* test and, *together with other contacts*, it contributes to satisfying the jurisdictional test.[4] However, a choice-of-law clause *alone* may not satisfy the jurisdictional test.

1. 433 US 186 (1977), discussed *supra* 36.
2. Of course, the *Hague* test does not focus exclusively on the defendant. In fact, two of the three contacts the Court found significant, were plaintiff-affiliating contacts.
3. *Hague*, *supra* at 82.
4. *See Burger King Corp.* v. *Rudzewicz*, 471 US 462 (1985).

92. Similarly, the *Hague* test is different from the choice-of-law inquiry. The *Hague* test determines whether the application of a state's law is constitutionally *permissible*, *not* whether it is *appropriate* from a choice-of-law perspective. The *Hague* case itself is a good example of this difference. The Minnesota Supreme Court employed Professor Leflar's 'better-law approach' in choosing Minnesota law.[1] The US Supreme Court held that the choice of that law was constitutionally permissible, even if it was otherwise ill-advised. As the plurality opinion noted,

> It is not for this Court to say whether the choice-of-law analysis suggested by Professor Leflar is to be preferred or whether we would make the same choice-

of-law decision if sitting as the Minnesota Supreme Court. Our sole function is to determine whether the Minnesota Supreme Court's choice of its own substantive law in this case exceeded federal constitutional limitations.[2]

1. Leflar's approach is discussed at 193–194, *infra*.
2. *Allstate Ins. Co.* v. *Hague*, 449 US 302 at 307. Justice Stevens concurred:

> Although I regard the Minnesota courts' decision to apply forum law as unsound as a matter of conflicts law, . . . I concur in the plurality's judgment. It is not this Court's function to establish and impose upon state courts a federal choice-of-law rule, nor is it our function to ensure that state courts correctly apply whatever choice-of-law rules they have themselves adopted. Our authority may be exercised in the choice-of-law area only to prevent a violation of the Full Faith and Credit or the Due Process Clause.

Id. at 331–332 (Stevens, J., concurring). *See also id.* at 323 ('[T]he fact that a choice-of-law decision may be unsound as a matter of conflicts law does not necessarily implicate the federal concerns embodied in the Full Faith and Credit Clause'.).

III. Privileges and Immunities

93. The Privileges and Immunities Clause of Article IV provides that a state of the United States must grant to citizens of sister states all the 'Privileges and Immunities' it grants to its own citizens. The clause applies to 'citizens' (i.e., domiciliaries of sister states) but does not apply to aliens or to corporations.[1] Also, the clause does not protect all rights, but only so-called 'fundamental' rights. The Court determines whether a right is 'fundamental' by assessing not its importance to the individual but rather its importance to the federal union, specifically in light of the purpose of this clause, which was to 'fuse into one Nation a collection of independent, sovereign States'.[2] The Court held that 'it is "[only] with respect to those 'privileges' and 'immunities' bearing on the vitality of the Nation as a single entity" that a State must accord residents and nonresidents equal treatment'.[3] As another court put it, this clause protects 'those privileges and immunities which are, in their nature, fundamental; which belong, of right, to the citizens of all free governments; and which have, at all times, been enjoyed by the citizens of the several states which compose this Union'.[4]

1. *See Hemphill* v. *Orloff*, 277 US 537, 548–550 (1928); *Blake* v. *McClung*, 172 US 239 (1898). However, discrimination against out-of-state corporations may violate the Equal Protection Clause, *see Metropolitan Life Ins. Co.* v. *Ward*, 470 US 869 (1985) or the Commerce Clause, *see Bendix Autolite Corp.* v. *Midwesco Enterprises, Inc.*, 486 US 888 (1988). Indeed, the Court has held that discrimination against interstate commerce is 'virtually per se invalid'. *Brown-Forman Distillers Corp.* v. *N.Y. State Liquor Auth.*, 476 US 573, 579 (1986).
2. *Sup. Ct. of N.H.* v. *Piper*, 470 US 274, 279 (1985).
3. *Id.*
4. *Corfield* v. *Coryell*, 6 F. Cas. 546, 551 (E.D.Pa. 1823).

94. Moreover, even when the right in question qualifies as fundamental, the clause does not prohibit all differences in the treatment afforded residents and nonresidents. As the Court explained:

> The Clause does not preclude discrimination against nonresidents where (i) there is a substantial reason for the difference in treatment; and (ii) the dis-

> crimination practiced against nonresidents bears a substantial relationship to the State's objective.[1]

The Supreme Court has held that access to the state's courts, the right to own private property and the right to engage in private employment or commercial activity are protected by the clause. However, recreational activity, such as sport hunting, is not protected.[2] The Court has struck down under the Privileges and Immunities clause the following: a New Hampshire law limiting admission to the bar to New Hampshire residents;[3] the 'Alaska Hire' Act which gave employment preference to Alaska residents over non-residents for jobs arising out of oil and gas leases;[4] a South Carolina law that required a licence fee of 25 US dollars (USD) for shrimp boats owned by residents and 2,500 USD for such boats owned by non-residents;[5] a Georgia statute permitting only residents to secure abortions;[6] and a New Hampshire provision imposing an income tax on New Hampshire derived income of non-residents but exempting similar income of residents.[7]

1. *Piper*, 470 US 274, 284 (1985).
2. *See Baldwin* v. *Fish & Game Comm'n of Mont.*, 436 US 371, 388 (1978).
3. *Piper*, 470 US 274 (1985).
4. *Hicklin* v. *Orbeck*, 437 US 518 (1978).
5. *Toomer* v. *Witsell*, 334 US 385 (1948).
6. *Doe* v. *Bolton*, 410 US 179 (1973).
7. *Austin* v. *N.H.*, 420 US 656 (1975).

IV. Foreign Affairs

95. The Constitution designates the president as commander-in-chief, places within his executive power the conduct of diplomacy, including the power to negotiate treaties,[1] and grants Congress power 'to regulate Commerce with foreign Nations' as well as a panoply of financial and war powers to support the conduct of foreign policy.[2] The Constitution also expressly prohibits states from 'enter[ing] into any Treaty, Alliance, or Confederation . . . Agreement or Compact with . . . another Power or engag[ing] in War'.[3] Thus, there is no question that the conduct of foreign affairs is a federal rather than a state function, and primarily an executive rather than a judicial function. This division of competence means, *inter alia*, that: (1) states may not – by executive, legislative or judicial action – intrude into the federal government's conduct of foreign affairs; and (2) courts – state or federal – may not interfere with the federal executive's conduct of foreign affairs.

1. US Const. Art. II, §2. The same provision also vests the Senate with the power of advice and consent to treaties and the appointment of ambassadors.
2. US Const. Art. I, §8.
3. US Const. Art. I, §10.

A. Federal vs. State Competence

96. The two major Supreme Court cases involving the federal vs. state division are *Zschernig* v. *Miller*[1] and *American Insurance Ass'n* v. *Garamendi*.[2] In *Zschernig*, the Court struck down an Oregon statute on a subject (inheritance) that was entirely within the states' legislative competence[3] because of the possibility that in the process of applying it, the state could 'intrude' 'into the field of foreign affairs which the Constitution entrusts to the President and the Congress'.[4] The statute was one of several 'reciprocity' statutes enacted during the Cold War. It provided that nonresident aliens could not inherit Oregon property unless their own country permitted Americans to inherit property in that country on equal footing with its own citizens and to export the money, and permitted its citizens to inherit Oregon property without confiscating the proceeds. In the Court's view, the problem with the statute was not so much its substance,[5] but rather the possibility that in its application judges might employ undiplomatic rhetoric that could affect foreign relations. The Court wrote that, 'as applied', the statute could 'make unavoidable judicial criticism of nations established on a more authoritarian basis than our own . . . [and could] affect the power of the central government to deal with those problems'.[6]

In reaching this result, the *Zschernig* majority employed a test known as 'field preemption'. This test provides that federal foreign policy preempts state action that has a more than incidental effect on foreign affairs, even in the absence of any affirmative federal activity on the same subject, and hence without any showing of conflict. Concurring Justice Harlan found this test too broad and instead employed the narrower test of 'conflict preemption'. According to this test, in the absence of federal action, states may legislate in areas of their traditional competence even if their statutes have an incidental effect on foreign relations, provided that they do not 'impair the effective exercise of the Nation's foreign policy'.[7]

1. 389 US 429 (1968).
2. 539 US 396 (2003). Other important cases include, *United States* v. *Belmont*, 301 US 324 (1937); *Hines* v. *Davidowitz*, 312 US 52 (1941); *United States* v. *Pink*, 315 US 203 (1942); *Dames & Moore* v. *Regan*, 453 US 654 (1981); and *Crosby* v. *Nat'l. Foreign Trade Council*, 530 US 363 (2000).
3. In other cases, the Court has held that the federal government's treaty power may extend into matters that the Tenth Amendment reserves to the lawmaking competence of states. *See Missouri* v. *Holland*, 252 US 416 (1920). For example, in *Hauenstein* v. *Lynham*, 100 US (10 Otto) 483 (1879), the Court upheld against a Tenth Amendment challenge a 1850 Swiss–US treaty on inheritance. Although the states can be said to have an indirect voice – through the Senate's advice and consent – in the treaty making process, the Senate has no voice when the president signs executive agreements, which recently are more common than treaties.
4. *Zschernig*, 389 US at 432.
5. Two decades earlier, in *Clark* v. *Allen*, 331 US 503 (1947), the Court upheld a similar California reciprocity statute.
6. *Zschernig*, 389 US at 440. It is worth noting that the federal government had formally stated that the statute did not interfere with its conduct of foreign affairs. In a concurring opinion, Justice Stewart opined that it should be immaterial whether the federal government had articulated a position on the subject:

   > We deal here with the basic allocation of power between the States and the Nation. Resolution of so fundamental a constitutional issue cannot vary from day to day with the shifting winds at the State Department. . . . [T]he fact remains that the conduct of our foreign affairs is entrusted under the Constitution to the National Government, not to the probate courts of the several States.

   Zschernig, 389 US at 443 (Stewart, J., concurring).
7. *Id.* at 458–459 (Harlan, J., concurring).

97. In *American Insurance Ass'n* v. *Garamendi*,[1] the Court acknowledged both tests[2] but did not choose between them because it held that the state statute in question failed even Harlan's more lenient test. The basis of the *Garamendi* dispute were life insurance policies that European insurers sold before and during World War II to European domiciliaries, many of whom perished in the Holocaust, and the insurers' subsequent intransigence and failure to honour those policies. To address this problem and the potential friction with European governments, the United States government negotiated certain mechanisms of voluntary compliance and dispute resolution, including the establishment of a compensation fund. The negotiations culminated in the signing of an Executive Agreement with Germany in 2000, and later parallel agreements with Austria and France.

In the meantime, California enacted its Holocaust Victim Insurance Relief Act (HVIRA) in 1999, despite contrary admonitions from the federal government. HVIRA required any insurer doing business in California to disclose (upon penalty of losing its licence) all the details of all insurance policies the insurer, or any company 'related' to it, sold 'to persons in Europe' (not only Holocaust victims) between 1920 and 1945. The plaintiffs (who were insurers affiliated with two German insurers who had issued Holocaust-era policies in Germany, but were not parents, subsidiaries, or corporate alter-egos of the German companies) challenged HVIRA's constitutionality on several grounds. In a five-to-four decision, the Supreme Court held that HVIRA was unconstitutional because it interfered with the federal government's conduct of foreign relations.

1. 539 US 396 (2003).
2. The Court suggested that the two tests 'can be seen as complementary'. *Id.* at 420 note 11, with field preemption to be employed when a state is acting outside 'a traditional state responsibility', and conflict preemption to be employed when a state acts within such competence 'but in a way that affects foreign relations'. In the latter case 'it might make good sense to require a conflict, of a clarity or substantiality that would vary with the strength or the traditional importance of the state concern asserted'. *Id.*

98. The majority opinion began by stating the obvious, that '*at some point* an exercise of state power that touches on foreign relations must yield to the National Government's policy'.[1] The question here was whether California had reached the forbidden point. Because the executive agreements at issue did not contain preemptive language (which would make the issue 'straightforward'), the Court had to answer the question under the tests enunciated in *Zschernig*. Without repudiating the field-preemption test, *Garamendi* employed the conflict-preemption test to hold that HVIRA was unconstitutional because it produced 'more than an incidental effect in conflict with express foreign policy.'[2] Because the authority of the federal government to negotiate and settle claims like the ones involved in this case was unquestioned, the only question was whether there was a 'clear conflict'[3] between HVIRA and the exercise of federal policy. The Court found 'a sufficiently clear conflict to require finding preemption'.[4]

The Court characterized HVIRA as 'an obstacle to the success of the National Government's chosen "calibration of force" in dealing with the Europeans using a voluntary approach'.[5] California's indiscriminate disclosure provisions diminished the effectiveness of the President's chosen approach 'by undercutting European privacy protections'. Although California and the President had the same laudable goals, 'a common end hardly neutralizes conflicting means'.[6] While the President 'has consistently chosen kid gloves', California used 'an iron fist'[7] by making exclusion from a large sector of the American insurance market the automatic sanction for non-compliance with its policies. Regardless of which approach was wiser, California's approach had to give way because it 'undercut[ ] the President's diplomatic discretion and the choice he ha[d] made exercising it' and 'compromise[d] the very capacity of the President to speak for the Nation with one voice in dealing with other governments'.[8]

1. *Id.* at 413 (emphasis added).
2. *Id.* at 420.
3. *Id.* at 421.
4. *Id.* at 420.
5. *Id.* at 425.
6. *Id.*
7. *Id.* at 427.
8. *Id.* at 424. The Court stated that, since the federal policy on the matter was 'express' and the conflict with the state law was 'clear', this alone was 'enough to require state law to yield'. However, the Court stated that, had there been a doubt about the clarity of the conflict, it would have to be resolved in favour of the federal policy 'given the weakness of the State's interest'. *Id.* at 425. The Court found California's interest to be weak because HVIRA's highly targeted disclosure requirements undercut California's claim of pursuing general consumer protection interests and, in any event, the insureds or their descendants residing in California represented only a small fraction of the national total.

99. At least seven other states enacted statutes similar to California's HVIRA. In *Gerling Global Reinsurance Corp. of America* v. *Gallagher*,[1] the 11th Circuit struck down the Florida statute under the Due Process clause. Florida argued that, because the insurers did business in Florida, they had sufficient contacts with Florida to permit regulation by Florida. The court rejected this argument, pointing out that what is needed is not only sufficient contacts with the affected party, but also sufficient contacts with the *subject* of the state's regulation. In this case, the subject was the foreign practises of foreign insurers (the insurers' German affiliates) who had no connection with Florida. The court concluded that the Florida statute 'violate[d] Due Process to that extent, *regardless* of whether there are minimum contacts'[2] between Florida and the insurers.[3]

1. 267 F.3d 1228 (11th Cir. 2001).
2. *Id.* at 1238 (emphasis in original).
3. In *Garamendi*, the Supreme Court did not consider the due process challenge (which the lower court had rejected), because the Court reversed the lower court on other grounds.

B. Executive vs. Judicial Function

100. The principle that courts, federal or state, should refrain from interfering with the federal executive's conduct of foreign affairs finds expression in several interrelated and sometimes overlapping doctrines, including the 'act of state' doctrine, the now codified doctrine of foreign sovereign immunity, and the 'political question' doctrine.[1]

1. The political question doctrine is a subcategory of the doctrine of non-justiciability, a self-imposed judicial limitation on the powers of judicial review. The doctrine of non-justiciability is not limited to political questions, and the political question doctrine is not limited to foreign affairs. The latter doctrine stands for the proposition that courts will not review the 'political' acts of the other two branches of government. *See Baker* v. *Carr*, 444 US 996 (1979). As one would expect, however, there is little consensus on what constitutes a political question, so much so that this 'doctrine' is more of a conclusion than a true doctrine. In any event, this doctrine is invoked, but not necessarily applied, in many cases involving foreign affairs. For a review of cases applying the doctrine, *see* G. Born & P. Rutledge, *International Civil Litigation in United States Courts* 54–55 (4th edn, Austin, 2006); C. Wright, A. Miller, E. Cooper & R. Freer, *Federal Practice & Procedure* §3534.2.

101. The act of state doctrine is a judicially created doctrine derived from federal powers over foreign affairs. It provides that American courts, state or federal, 'will generally refrain from examining the validity of a taking by a foreign state of property within its own territory, or from sitting in judgment on other acts of a governmental character done by a foreign state within its own territory and applicable there'.[1] The Supreme Court enunciated this doctrine in *Underhill* v. *Hernandez*,[2] a case that affirmed a dismissal of a suit for damages brought by a US citizen against a former Venezuelan military commander who was responsible for the plaintiff's wrongful detention during a coup in Venezuela. Relying mostly on notions of international comity, the Court declared:

> Every sovereign State is bound to respect the independence of every other sovereign State, and the courts of one country will not sit in judgment on the acts of the government of another done within its own territory. Redress of grievances by reason of such acts must be obtained through the means open to be availed of by sovereign powers as between themselves.[3]

1. American Law Institute, *Restatement (Third) of Foreign Relations Law* §443 (1987).
2. 168 US 250 (1897).
3. *Id.* at 252.

102. Building on *Underhill* and subsequent cases, the Supreme Court explained the act of state doctrine in terms of domestic separation-of-powers principles in *Banco Nacional de Cuba* v. *Sabbatino*.[1] The Court declared that 'the Judicial Branch will not examine the validity of a taking of property within its own territory by a foreign sovereign government, extant and recognized by this country at the time of suit . . . even if the complaint alleges that the taking violates customary international law'.[2] The Court explained further that the act of state doctrine is a matter of federal common law because the problems surrounding the doctrine are 'intrinsically federal'.[3] Thus, the doctrine is binding on state courts, as well as on federal courts, even in diversity cases.

This doctrine has been described as a 'limitation on the exercise of . . . adjudicatory jurisdiction . . . [as] a mechanism of judicial abstention to allow the judiciary prudentially to avoid litigating a foreign sovereign's public conduct committed within its territory . . . [and thus] avoid being enmeshed in matters of foreign affairs which could risk embarrassment to the executive'.[4] However, the doctrine has also been described as 'a special rule of conflict of laws' that functions in a way that displaces the *ordre public* reservation.[5]

1. 376 US 398 (1964).
2. *Id.* at 428.
3. *Id.* at 427.
4. C. Oliver, E. Firmage, C. Blakesley, R. Scott & S. Williams, *The International Legal System*, 624 (4th edn, 1995).
5. American Law Institute, *Restatement (Third) Foreign Relations* §443, Reporter's Note 1 (1986).

103. The Supreme Court's latest pronouncement on the doctrine in *W.S. Kirkpatrick & Co.* v. *Environmental Tectonics Corp.*[1] seems to lend support to the above view. Although the Court held the doctrine inapplicable because this case did not require passing judgment on the validity of the acts of a foreign government, the Court found it necessary to explain that 'the act of state is not some vague doctrine of abstention but [rather] a "*principle of decision* binding on federal and state courts alike"'.[2] After reiterating the obligation of American courts to decide cases properly presented to them, the Court said:

> The act of state doctrine does not establish an exception [from the above obligation] for cases and controversies that may embarrass foreign governments, but merely requires that, in the process of deciding, the acts of foreign sovereigns taken within their own jurisdiction shall be deemed valid.[3]

The precise scope of this 'principle of decision' is defined by a series of Supreme Court decisions, and unreviewed lower court decisions, suggesting that this principle may not be as broad as the above formulation implies. For example, although the Supreme Court has not produced a majority opinion defining the exceptions to the act of state doctrine, it has been assumed that the doctrine does not apply to 'commercial acts' of foreign states, or to cases in which the executive branch informs the court that adjudication of the case will not impede the conduct of foreign affairs.[4]

1. 493 US 400 (1990).
2. *Id.* at 406 (quoting from *Sabbatino*, emphasis in original).
3. *Id.* at 408.
4. For an in-depth discussion of the scope of, and exceptions to, the act of state doctrine, *see* G. Born & P. Rutledge, *International Civil Litigation in United States Courts*, pp. 751–806 (4th edn, Austin, 2006).

104. The doctrine of foreign sovereign immunity is broader than the act of state doctrine in that, in its absolute expression, the former doctrine exempts from judicial jurisdiction the foreign sovereign as such, regardless of the nature or location of its acts. The United States initially followed the 'absolute theory' of foreign sovereign immunity but later followed a modified practise that allowed the US State Department to request immunity in actions against friendly sovereigns. In 1952, the State Department began to apply the 'restrictive theory', whereby immunity was recognized with regard to a foreign state's sovereign or public acts, but not its private acts.

105. In 1976, Congress enacted the Foreign Sovereign Immunities Act (FSIA),[1] which codified the general principle that foreign states and their instrumentalities are immune from the jurisdiction of federal and state courts in the United States. However, the Act also provides several exceptions from this general principle. The exceptions grant to federal courts subject-matter and *in personam* jurisdiction with regard to certain acts of the foreign state.[2] Among the cases covered by these exceptions are cases in which the action is based on a commercial activity with a US nexus,[3] taking of property in violation of international law,[4] certain non-commercial torts occurring in the United States,[5] and acts of torture, extrajudicial killing, aircraft sabotage and hostage taking, wherever committed.[6]

1. 28 USCA §1602 *et seq.* (2007).
2. For a comprehensive discussion of the FSIA, accompanied by all pertinent authorities, *see* G. Born, *International Civil Litigation in United States Courts*, pp. 219–344.
3. *See* 28 USCA §1605(a)(2) (authorizing jurisdiction over actions 'based upon a commercial activity carried on in the United States by the foreign state; or upon an act performed in the United States in connection with a commercial activity of the foreign state elsewhere; or upon an act outside the territory of the United States in connection with a commercial activity of the foreign state elsewhere and that act causes a direct effect in the United States'.).
4. The exception applies only if the taken property or any property exchanged for it 'is present in the United States in connection with a commercial activity carried on in the United States by the foreign state or . . . is owned or operated by an agency or instrumentality of the foreign state and that agency or instrumentality is engaged in a commercial activity in the United States'. 28 USCA §1605(a)(3).
5. The exception applies if the injury occurred in the United States, even if the tortious act or omission of the foreign state occurred elsewhere, but not if the act was in the exercise of a 'discretionary function'. *See* 28 USCA §1605(a)(5).
6. *See* 28 USCA §1605(a)(7).

Part II. Choice of Law

Chapter 1. The Traditional Choice-of-Law System

§1. Introduction

106. This chapter focuses on the traditional American choice-of-law approach, as exemplified in the first conflicts Restatement.[1] The word 'traditional' usually has negative connotations, especially when used in juxtaposition with 'modern'. Nevertheless, the study of the traditional approach is necessary and valuable, for a couple of reasons. First, as explained later, the traditional approach remains in force in most states in areas other than torts and contracts where it has given way to other 'modern' approaches. Thus, 'traditional' in this context does not necessarily mean *passé*, especially because, even in torts and contracts, this approach retains its following in about a dozen states.[2] Second, regardless of its current viability, the traditional approach remains the best vehicle for introducing the elementary questions, basic syllogism, and fundamental objectives of the choice-of-law process. Because the modern approaches grew out of a reaction to the traditional approach, the study of the traditional approach provides a valuable frame of reference within which to compare, contrast, understand and critique the modern approaches.

1. *See* American Law Institute, *Restatement of the Law, Conflict of Laws* §1 (1934) (hereinafter '*Restatement*').
2. *See infra* 123.

107. Conflicts law is one of the few branches of American law that owes its origin to the continental civil law, rather than the English common law. In large part, this is due to the fact that, during the formative period of American conflicts law, English private international law was virtually undeveloped compared to its continental counterpart. The first conflicts book published on American soil was authored by a civil law lawyer from Louisiana, Samuel Livermore.[1] His book was a concerted effort to import to the United States the doctrine of the continental statutists. Although this effort failed, Livermore indirectly influenced the course of American conflicts law by making available the otherwise inaccessible continental conflicts literature to Joseph Story. In addition to providing a thorough English summary of this literature in his own book, Livermore donated his entire library of continental writings to the Harvard Law School (his alma mater) where Justice Joseph Story, then a professor, was teaching.

1. *See* S. Livermore, *Dissertations on the Questions Which Arise from the Contrariety of the Positive Laws of Different States and Nations* (1828).

§2. Joseph Story

108. Joseph Story is the progenitor of American conflicts law. His *Commentaries on the Conflict of Laws*[1] was the first comprehensive conflicts treatise in the English language. Indeed, Story made something out of nothing. Faced with the dearth of American conflicts cases, Story drew heavily from the rich continental literature of the previous two centuries. He synthesized and recast in a systematic fashion the writings of dozens of continental authors, as well as several judicial decisions from England and especially Scotland. He was decidedly influenced by the work of the Frisian commentator Ulrich Huber (1635–1694), known for his comity theory.[2] Story reformulated Huber's axioms as follows:

> [E]very nation possesses an exclusive sovereignty and jurisdiction within its territory . . . [and its laws] affect, and bind directly all property, whether real or personal, within its territory and all persons, who are residents within it, . . . and also all contracts made, and acts done within it. . . .
>
> [N]o state or nation can, by its laws, directly affect, or bind property out of its own territory, or bind persons not resident therein . . . .
>
> [W]hatever force and obligation the laws of one country have in another, depend solely upon the laws . . . of the latter . . . and upon its own express or tacit consent. A state may prohibit the operation of all [or of some] foreign laws, and the rights growing out of them, within its own territories. . . . When [its law is] silent, then, and then only, can the question properly arise, what law is to govern in the absence of a clear declaration of the sovereign will. . . .
>
> [T]he phrase 'comity of nations' . . . is the most appropriate phrase to express the true foundation and extent of the obligation of the laws of one nation within the territories of another. It is derived altogether from the voluntary consent of the latter; and is inadmissible, when it is contrary to its known policy, or prejudicial to its interests.[3]

1. *See* J. Story, *Commentaries on the Conflict of Laws, Foreign and Domestic* (1834)
2. Huber's brief essay on conflict of laws entitled 'De conflictu legum diversarum in diversis imperiis' was published in *Ulrich Huber, Praelectiones Juris Romani et Hodierni* (1689).
3. J. Story, *Commentaries on the Conflict of Laws*, 19, 21, 24–25, 37 (1834).

109. Story's *Commentaries* exercised considerable influence, not only in the United States, but also in Europe.[1] The *Commentaries*, however, were no more than a broad outline of aspirational principles, albeit well-written. Although these principles helped American courts in the early years, more guidance was needed. By the end of the 19th century, the case law began developing in different directions and no writer attempted to collect or systematize it. Francis Wharton's one-volume treatise published in 1872[2] was rich in its discussion of foreign authorities, especially continental writers, but thin in discussion of American cases. A course on conflicts law was not taught in any American law school until 1893, when Joseph H. Beale first introduced it at Harvard.[3]

1. For this influence, *see* E. Scoles, P. Hay, P. Borchers & S. Symeonides, *Conflict of Laws* 19 (4th edn, St. Paul, Minn., 2004).
2. *See* F. Wharton, *A Treatise on the Conflict of Laws, or Private International Law: A Comparative View of Anglo-American, Roman, German, and French Jurisprudence* (1872).
3. *See* S. Symeonides, 'The First Conflicts Restatement Through the Eyes of Old: As Bad as Its Reputation?', 32 *S. Ill. U. L. J.* (2007).

§3. Joseph H. Beale

110. While Joseph Story established the broad principles of American conflicts law, it was Joseph Beale who erected a system of conflicts law, albeit one that did not always conform to Story's principles. Beale was a prolific and energetic scholar who dominated the American conflicts landscape for 50 years.[1] Not only did he establish the first conflicts course, but he also published the first conflicts casebook, a three-volume collection of 400 American and English cases and seventy foreign cases translated into English.[2] This casebook was adopted far and wide for teaching conflicts law in most other American law schools. The third volume included a summary of Beale's conception of conflicts law, which was the foundation of his three-volume *Treatise* published in 1935, a year after the promulgation of the Conflicts Restatement and generally following its structure and sequence.[3] By the 1920s, most American law schools introduced conflicts courses in their curricula, and, largely because of Beale's stature, conflicts law was chosen as one of the four subjects that the American Law Institute (ALI) decided to restate. In the end, the first Conflicts Restatement was more of a pre-statement of Beale's views than a restatement of the case law.

Beale's view of conflicts law was founded on two overarching principles: territoriality and vested rights. The first principle identified the state whose law created a substantive right, and the second explained why other states were mandated to enforce that right.

1. For a recent assessment of his work, *see* Symeonides, *supra* 109.
2. *See* J.H. Beale, *Collection of Cases on the Conflict of Laws*, 3 vols (1900–1902). Another casebook published in 1899 contained only 40 cases. *See* J.W. Dwyer, *Cases on Private International Law* (1899).
3. *See* J.H. Beale, *A Treatise on the Conflict of Laws*, vols 1–3 (1935).

I. Territoriality

111. Beale believed that 'the law is territorial'; and he really meant all law. '[T]here can be no law in a particular state except the law of that state, and therefore . . . a foreigner coming into that state can by no means bring with him his personal law . . . ; [he] is subject to the law of the state as much as the nationals of the state'.[1] For Beale, this was an incontrovertible proposition, an axiom. On this axiom he built his entire theory.

> Law operates by extending its power over acts done throughout the territory within its jurisdiction and creating out of those acts new rights and obligations. . . . It follows . . . that not only must the law extend over the whole territory subject to it and apply to every act done there, but only one law can so apply. . . . By its very nature law must apply to everything and must exclusively apply to everything within the boundary of its jurisdiction.[2]

1. J.H. Beale, *A Treatise on the Conflict of Laws* (vol. 1, 1935), p. 52.
2. *Id.* at 45–46.

112. This premise became the cornerstone of the Conflicts Restatement, the first section of which declared:

> No state can make a law which by its own force is operative in another state; the only law in force in the sovereign state is its own law, but by the law of each state rights or other interests in that state may, in certain cases, depend upon the law in force in some other state or states.[1]

The same principle was then reiterated in other Restatement sections covering torts (the *lex loci delicti* rule),[2] contracts (the *lex loci contractus* rule),[3] property (the *lex rei sitae* rule),[4] and virtually every other subject.

1. American Law Institute, *Restatement of the Law, Conflict of Laws* §1 (1934).
2. *See id.* §378 ('The law of the place of wrong determines whether a person has sustained a legal injury'.).
3. *See id.* at §332 ('The law of the place of contracting determines the validity and effect of a [contract]'.).
4. *See id.* at §§208–254.

113. In Beale's time, territoriality was by no means a new principle (although it was newer than the opposite principle of personality of the laws); indeed it was the favourite, if not the prevailing, principle in the Anglo-American world. Until Beale, however, neither the case law nor the doctrinal writers had accepted this principle wholesale, nor did anyone regard it as the exclusive foundation on which to build the entire system of conflicts law. Beale's territorialist system allowed for much fewer 'personal' exceptions than most continental systems, which had adopted the personality principle for most matters of capacity, personal status, and succession at death.

In the abstract, the principle of territoriality begged two important questions. First, which territorial state should supply the applicable law? Second, if it is a state other than the forum, why would or should the forum apply that law? If, as Beale argued, '[n]o law is administered as such by the courts except [its] territorial law',[1] why should the forum apply another state's territorial law? Beale answered the first question by choosing *a priori*, and fairly arbitrarily, a state that had a particular designated territorial contact, such as the occurrence of the injury in torts, or the dispatch of the acceptance in contracts.[2]

1. *See* J.H. Beale, *A Treatise on the Conflict of Laws* (1935), p. 52.
2. *See Restatement* at §§377 and 326.

II. Vested Rights

114. Regarding the second question, Beale rejected Story's answer, which was based on the principle of comity, and adopted instead the vested rights theory proposed earlier by the English author Arthur V. Dicey.[1] Focussing on the designated contact or event, Beale reasoned:

> The [territorial] law annexes to the event a certain consequence, namely, the creation of a legal right. . . . When a right has been created by law, this right itself becomes a fact; . . . [T]he existing right should everywhere be recognized; since to do so is merely to recognize the existence of a fact. A right having been created by the appropriate [i.e., territorial] law, the recognition of its existence should follow everywhere. Thus an act valid where done cannot be called in question anywhere'.[2]

This theory provided the philosophical rationalization for the entire Restatement. For example, in statements premised on the assumed inevitability of this theory, the Restatement proclaimed:

1. If a cause of action in tort is created at the place of wrong, a cause of action will be recognized in other states.
2. If no cause of action is created at the place of wrong, no recovery in tort can be had in any other state.[3]

1. *See* A.V. Dicey, *A Digest of the Law of England With Reference to the Conflict of Laws* (1896), p. 22.
2. Beale, *Treatise* (vol. 3), p. 1969.
3. *Restatement* §384.

115. By separating rights from the law that created them, Beale could declare that the forum does not really apply foreign law. Rather the forum takes cognizance of the fact that a foreign law created a right and then recognizes it under the forum's own law.[1] Despite its many flaws,[2] the vested rights theory was in some respects a modest advancement from Story's comity theory. Rather than relegating the choice-of-law decision to the courts' potentially unfettered discretion, the vested rights theory turned this choice into a legal obligation. In this sense, the vested rights theory was more deferential to foreign law than was Story's 'quasi-legal, quasi-diplomatic, quasi-policy-oriented concept of comity'.[3] The irony is that Beale was clearly not an internationalist and, in fact, he was far less cosmopolitan than Story.

The problem was that, while the comity theory may have given courts too much discretion in refusing to apply foreign law, the vested rights theory gave them no discretion at all. Worse yet, it often mandated the application of the wrong law, such as the law of a state that had only a tenuous or fortuitous contact with the case, or of a state that had no true interest in the outcome (i.e., what is known today as a 'false conflict').

1. *See* Beale, *Treatise* (vol. 1), p. 53.
2. Beale's artificial construct was full of holes, but it was no more artificial than the 'local law theory' proposed by Walter W. Cook, one of Beale's arch-critics at the time, who argued that

the forum 'enforces not a foreign right but a right created by its own law', though modelled after the applicable foreign law. *See* W. Cook, *The Logical and Legal Bases of the Conflict of Laws* (Mass., Cambridge, 1942), pp. 20–21. Thus, while Beale's theory separated foreign law from the rights it created and then treated them as facts, Cook's theory simply re-created the foreign rights under the law of the forum.

3. A. Riles, 'A New Agenda for the Cultural Study of Law: Taking on the Technicalities', 53 *Buff. L. Rev.* 973, 992 (2005).

§4. The First Conflicts Restatement

I. Some of the Restatement's Flaws

116. Beale's view of conflicts law did not remain unchallenged during his own time, especially from the then popular legal realist school.[1] However, Beale's views prevailed where it mattered most – in the American Law Institute, which adopted his draft Restatement with virtually no amendments.[2] The academic criticisms continued after the Restatement's promulgation in 1934 and have intensified ever since. Gradually, the Restatement became the favourite punching bag of virtually every conflicts teacher and writer. Indeed, the Restatement was an easy target, with too many flaws. The following are some of the most general and serious.

1. The Restatement was a Prussian-like system of detailed, mechanical and rigid rules that: (a) completely sacrificed flexibility on the altar of ostensible certainty and predictability, which eventually proved illusory; (b) ignored the lessons of experience in favour of the pursuit of an ill-conceived theoretical purity; and (c) completely eliminated judicial discretion, even as they purported to be a distillation of the courts' experience.
2. Like Beale, the Restatement relied exclusively and excessively on two principles – territoriality and vested rights – deducing virtually all of its rules from these principles while disregarding contrary case law. Beale and his fellow drafters saw the world as a neatly laid out, black and white chessboard in which the critical event would always occur entirely in either a black or a white square. Needless to say, reality is never so simple. Beale never accepted the proposition that in some cases, for some issues, the law of a person's home state may have a legitimate claim of application (personality principle), even if the dispute is triggered by events occurring in another state. Beale thought that territoriality was the 'modern' and personality the medieval principle. Had he been a better student of history or a better comparatist, he would have realized that any system that completely banishes either one of these two grand principles will inevitably run into an impasse, and that the key is to know when and how to compromise them.[3]
3. The Restatement's choice-of-law rules – despite their name – were not designed to choose among conflicting laws but instead *a priori* assigned 'legislative jurisdiction' to a particular state.[4] The assignment was based solely on a single, predesignated, territorial contact. Subject only to limited post-choice exceptions, the law of the designated state applied almost automatically, regardless of its content, its underlying policy, or the substantive quality of the solution it

would bring to the case at hand. All that mattered was whether that state had the specified contact, even if its presence there was entirely fortuitous, and even if that state had no real interest in the outcome. As David Cavers observed as early as 1933, the Restatement was not much different from a slot machine programmed to find the 'right' state in a 'blindfold' and random fashion.[5] Indeed, the Restatement's goal was to find what it considered the spatially-appropriate law ('conflicts justice'), rather than to ensure a substantively-appropriate result in the particular case (material justice).[6] It did not occur to Beale and his fellow drafters that to intelligently resolve any conflict, one must first ascertain what the conflict is about, and what the conflicting objectives and claims are. In the field of conflicts law, this requires looking into the content of the potentially conflicting laws, identifying their purposes or policies, and then proceeding from there.

1. Beale's main critics were three well-known legal realists: Walter W. Cook (1873–1943), Ernest G. Lorenzen (1876–1951), and Hessel E. Yntema (1891–1966), as well as David F. Cavers (1903–1988), who was one of Beale's students. For a summary and assessment of their criticisms, *see* Symeonides, 'The First Conflicts Restatement Through the Eyes of Old: As Bad as Its Reputation?', 32 *S. Ill. U. L. J.* (2007).
2. For a discussion of the ALI meetings and the whole process and background of adopting the First Restatement, *see* Symeonides, *supra* note 1.
3. For a discussion of this point, *see* S. Symeonides, 'Territoriality and Personality in Tort Conflicts', in: T. Einhorn & K. Siehr, (eds), *Intercontinental Cooperation Through Private International Law: Essays in Memory of Peter Nygh* (2004), p. 401.
4. For a thorough discussion of this 'jurisdiction-selecting' feature of the Restatement, *see* D. Cavers, 'A Critique of the Choice-of-Law Problem', 47 *Harv. L. Rev.* 173 (1933).
5. *See id.* at 191–192.
6. *See* S. Symeonides, 'Material Justice and Conflicts Justice in Choice of Law' in: P. Borchers & J. Zekoll, (eds.), *International Conflict of Laws for the Third Millennium: Essays in Honor of Friedrich K. Juenger* (2000), p. 125.

II. The Restatement's Contributions

117. Nevertheless, despite its many flaws, the Restatement did make some positive, albeit modest, contributions, including the following:

1. The Restatement raised the level of awareness about, and knowledge of, conflicts law among the members of the bar and the bench. There is little doubt that, had it not been for Beale's stature in the 1920s, conflicts law would not have been included among the first Restatements. Because of Beale and the Restatement, the then prevailing 'pedagogical neglect'[1] of conflicts law gave way to a renewed interest in the subject. Conflicts law gained its rightful place in the curriculum of all American law schools, which, in turn, made possible the renaissance of American conflicts law during the next generation.
2. The Restatement unified American conflicts law, which until then had been scattered in the law reports, some of which were not widely available. For the first time, it was possible to speak of a single American conflicts law, despite variations from state to state. This unification, as well as the Restatement's content, both caused and facilitated the conflicts revolution.

3. The Restatement was a comprehensive and complete system. It provided a complete, organized, and disciplined network of bilateral, fixed, neutral, and detailed choice-of-law rules designed to provide solutions for all possible conflicts situations. This was the first time such a comprehensive and complete work on conflicts law had been produced on American soil. According to one contemporary commentator, the Restatement was 'a system, something tangible out of the chaos of cases, a point of departure, a beginning, systematic, rational, and withal not inconsistent with what is implicit in most American precedents and explicit in many of the decisions of the last twenty years'.[2]
4. The Restatement was non-parochial, even if it was not particularly internationalist. It was non-parochial in that, unlike most of the American approaches proposed since then (but not before), the Restatement did not give preference to the forum state *qua forum*. The Restatement purported to be, and in many respects was, impartial *vis-à-vis* forum and foreign law. Its explicit aspiration was to eliminate or curtail forum shopping and to foster international or interstate uniformity of result by ensuring that a case would be resolved in the same way regardless of where it was litigated. That this aspiration has never been fully realized is another matter.

1. *See* W.D. Lewis, 'Introduction to the Restatement', in: American Law Institute, *Restatement of the Law: Conflict of Laws*, xiii–xiv (1934).
2. F.L. de Sloovère, 'On Looking into Mr Beale's Conflict of Laws', 13 *N.Y.U. L.Q.* 333, 345 (1936).

III. Some of the Restatement's Specific Rules

A. Torts and Contracts

118. As noted earlier, the Restatement categorically and inexorably assigned all tort conflicts to the exclusive legislative jurisdiction of the law of 'the place of wrong' (*lex loci delicti*).[1] The Restatement was equally categorical in defining the 'place of the wrong' as the place where the 'last event necessary to make an actor liable for an alleged tort takes place'.[2] In characteristic detail, this was further defined as the place in which the harmful force or 'deleterious' substance 'takes effect upon the body' and, in cases of harm to the reputation, the place where the defamatory statement is 'communicated'.[3]

For contracts, the Restatement's provided an equally sweeping rule. The law of the place where the contract was 'made' (*lex loci contractus*) – which was defined as the place 'where the second promise is made in consideration of the first promise'[4] or the place from which the acceptance of an offer was sent[5] – governed virtually all issues, i.e., not only issues of form, but also contractual capacity, mutual assent or consideration, fraud, illegality and any other circumstances that make a promise voidable.[6] Thus, the Restatement's version of the *lex loci contractus* rule had a much broader scope than its civil law counterpart. Only matters of performance, such as the manner, time, place, and sufficiency of performance, and the permissible excuses for non-performance, were assigned to the law of the place of performance (*lex loci solutionis*).[7]

1. *Restatement* §384.
2. *Id.* at §377.
3. *Id.* at Note.
4. *Id.* at §325.
5. *Id.* at §326.
6. *Id.* at §332.
7. *Id.* at §358.

B. Property, Marital Property and Successions

119. In areas other than torts and contracts, the Restatement was equally dominated by 'jurisdiction-selecting', territorially-based, and usually inexorable choice-of-law rules. Chapter 7 of the Restatement, covering matters of property, marital property, and successions, is typical in this respect. The chapter adopts the civil-law division into movables and immovables and provides that most issues pertaining to immovables are governed by the law of the place where the immovable is situated (*lex rei sitae*), virtually without any exceptions.[1] Again, a perusal of the chapter reveals that the Restatement's version of the *situs* rule had a vastly broader scope than the corresponding rule of other countries.[2]

1. Thus, the law of the *situs* applied to: (a) the substantive and formal validity of a conveyance of an interest in land (*id.* at §§215, 217), the effect and interpretation of the conveyance (§§220, 214), and the capacity of the grantor and the grantee (§§216, 219); (b) to transfers by operation of law and acquisition through adverse possession or prescription (§§223–224); (c) to the validity, effect, and enforcement of mortgages (§§225–231); (d) to the effect of marriage upon immovables owned by a spouse at the time of marriage (§237) or acquired by either or both spouses during the marriage (§238); and the effect of a divorce or the death of either spouse upon such immovables (§248); (e) to all issues of intestate succession to land (§245), including the right of illegitimate and adopted children to inherit and the extent of their share (§§246–247); and (f) to most issues of testate succession to land, including the validity, effect, and revocation of a will (§§249–250).
2. *See infra* Part II, Chapter 7.

120. Under the Restatement, the *situs* rule also applied to movables, but only with regard to *inter vivos* transactions. Thus, the formal and substantive validity of a conveyance of an interest in a chattel was governed by 'the law of the state where the chattel is at the time of the conveyance'.[1] In the area of marital property and successions, the Restatement shifted gears and resorted to the law of the domicile. Thus, the law of the husband's domicile at the time of marriage determined the rights of both spouses to movables then owned by either spouse, while the law of the spouses' common domicile determined their respective rights in movables acquired during marriage.[2] In successions, both testate and intestate, the pertinent domicile was the decedent's domicile at the time of death.[3] This rule was thought to be consistent with the decedent's expectations by allowing all of her movables to be treated as a single unit, regardless of where situated. However, this otherwise sound principle was not extended to immovables.[4]

1. Restatement at §§255–257.
2. *See id.* at §§289–290.
3. *See id.* at §§300–310.
4. *See infra* 578–584.

IV. The Restatement's Following

121. Despite its many flaws, the Restatement was adopted with varying degrees of enthusiasm in virtually all states in the United States. Such a consensus is a rare phenomenon (at least in conflicts law) and is unlikely to be repeated. The Restatement dominated American conflicts law for more than a generation and continued to command a majority of states as late as 1979 in tort conflicts, and as late as 1984 in contract conflicts.[1]

Although one might interpret this widespread acceptance as a validation of the Restatement's quality, other explanations are more plausible. American courts accepted the Restatement because it was the only option available and because it was comprehensive and complete. Most courts encounter conflicts cases only infrequently and thus do not have the opportunity or the incentive to develop the necessary expertise in this subject. 'Judicial experience with any given choice-of-law problem is usually more episodic than with analogous domestic-law problems'.[2] As one commentator noted, '[j]udges are not stupid, just busy'.[3] They do not have the time to read and evaluate the numerous conflicting academic commentaries. In their busy minds, the availability of an authoritative-sounding document like the Restatement, which bears the prestigious imprimatur of the ALI, obviates the need to look elsewhere.

1. *See* S. Symeonides, *The American Choice-of-Law Revolution: Past, Present and Future* (Leiden, Boston, 2006), pp. 10–11, 37 *et seq.*
2. A.T. von Mehren, 'Recent Trend in Choice-of-Law Methodology', 60 *Cornell L. Rev.* 927, 966 (1975).
3. R. Weintraub, 'Courts Flailing in the Waters of the Louisiana Conflicts Code: Not Waving but Drowning', 60 *La. L. Rev.* 1365, 1366 (2000).

122. In any event, the courts' allegiance to the Restatement did not run as deep as the numbers might suggest. In relatively short time, courts began deviating from the Restatement's dictates by employing various 'escape devices', such as characterization, *renvoi*, and the public policy exception.[1] As Cavers predicted, 'neither [Beale's] Treatise nor [his] Restatement can mechanize judgment'.[2] The first overt departures from the Restatement occurred in 1954, when the New York Court of Appeals rejected the *lex loci contractus* rule,[3] and in 1963 when the same court rejected the rule of *lex loci delicti*.[4] This was the beginning of the American conflicts revolution, which is discussed in Part II, Chapter 3.

1. *See infra*, 133–155.
2. D. Cavers, 'Restatement of the Law of Conflict of Laws', 44 *Yale L.J.* 1478, 1482 (1935).
3. *See Auten* v. *Auten*, 124 N.E.2d 99 (N.Y. 1954). For an earlier case refusing to follow the *lex loci contractus* rule, *see W.H. Barber Co.* v. *Hughes* 63 N.E.2d 417 (Ind. 1945).
4. *See Babcock* v. *Jackson*, 191 N.E.2d 279 (N.Y. 1963), discussed *infra* 206–214.

123. At the time of this writing (2007), ten states continued to follow the traditional theory in tort conflicts,[1] and twelve states do so in contract conflicts.[2] The two groups are not identical. For example, Florida, Oklahoma, Rhode Island, and Tennessee have abandoned the traditional theory in tort conflicts but not in contract conflicts, while North Carolina and West Virginia have done the reverse.

In any event, it would be a mistake to assume that either these or the other states are equally committed to the status quo, or that they will remain so for the same length of time.[3]

1. These states are: Georgia, Kansas, Maryland, New Mexico, North Carolina, South Carolina, Virginia, West Virginia and Wyoming
2. These states are: Alabama, Florida, Georgia, Kansas, Maryland, New Mexico, Oklahoma, Rhode Island, South Carolina, Tennessee, Virginia and Wyoming. In areas other than torts and contracts, the traditional approach continues to be followed in many more, if not most, states.
3. For discussion of recent precedents from each of these states, *see* S. Symeonides, *The American Choice-of-Law Revolution: Past, Present, and Future* (Leiden, Boston, 2006), pp. 51–62.

Chapter 2. The Mechanics of Choice of Law: The Structure and Operation of the Choice-of-Law Syllogism

§1. The Choice-of-Law Rule and its Components

124. In designating the law that governs multistate cases, traditional systems that subscribe to multilateralism employ choice-of-law rules formulated around broad categories borrowed from domestic law, such as torts, contracts, conveyances, successions, status, etc. These rules differ in their specifics, but they all consist of three basic components: (1) the legal category that is the object of the rule (e.g., tort, contract, etc.); (2) the applicable law (e.g., *lex loci delicti, lex loci contractus*); and (3) the connecting factor (*locus delicti, locus contractus*) which 'connects' the legal category or problem with the state that supplies the applicable law.

125. Modern systems, such as the Restatement (Second) (to be discussed later), as well as recent PIL codifications, employ rules or approaches that are more flexible than the traditional rules. Most of the modern rules are constructed around narrower categories or 'issues', they use multiple or soft connecting factors, and generally are far less categorical in designating the applicable law. Nevertheless, the basic choice-of-law syllogism is fundamentally the same in both the traditional systems like the First Restatement and modern rule-based multilateralist systems. This chapter explores the constituent steps of this syllogism, first under the First Restatement as representative of the traditional approach, and then under the Restatement (Second) as the approach followed in the majority of states today.[1]

1. Basic bibliography for the topics discussed in this chapter includes: L. McDougal, R. Felix & R. Whitten, *American Conflicts Law* 403–446 (5th edn, Ardsley, New York, 2001); E. Scoles, P. Hay, P. Borchers & S. Symeonides, *Conflict of Laws* 119–149 (4th edn, St. Paul, Minn., 2004); R. Weintraub, *Commentary on the Conflict of Laws* (5th edn, New York, 2006), pp. 52–116.

126. The choice-of-law syllogism typically proceeds in the following three distinct mental steps, corresponding to the three components of the choice-of-law rule.

1. *Characterization.* The first step is to determine which choice-of-law rule is principally applicable to the case at hand by fitting the case into the legal category of tort, contract, and so forth, employed by the rule.
2. *Localization.* The second step is to 'localize' the connecting factor, to place it on the map, by determining where the tort occurred or the contract was made. Although this is largely a factual inquiry, it is aided by certain localization subrules, such as that a contract is deemed made at the place of acceptance, or that a tort occurs at the place of the injury rather than the place of conduct.
3. *Application.* The third step consists of several smaller steps: ascertaining the content of the law of the state in which the connecting factor is located; determining 'how much' of that law is applicable to the case; and examining whether any exceptions to its application are operable, and, if they are not, apply that law to the case at hand.

4. '*Escapes*'. Each of these three steps offers different opportunities for exceptions, 'escapes', or manipulations. Judges who disagree with the results dictated by a particular rule tend to seek ways to avoid it. This was particularly true with the rules of the First Restatement; so much so, that the above three steps of the choice-of-law syllogism continue to be taught in many American law schools under the heading of 'escapes devices'. This phraseology represents an unnecessarily negative and narrow conception. The fact that American judges have occasionally (or even often) manipulated the characterization step under the First Restatement does not mean that characterization is an escape. Rather, it means that characterization is a process that does not guarantee unanimity.

There is, however, a close correlation between the quality of a choice-of-law rule and the frequency with which judges seek to escape from it. In this sense, the frequent use of escapes by courts following the First Restatement may be seen as an indication of the poor quality of its rules. The problem is that the use of escapes, as opposed to a more direct and candid analysis, is at best a short-term solution because it simply prolongs the life of bad choice-of-law rules.

§2. Characterization

127. The characterization process is not peculiar to conflicts law. It is encountered in applying any legal rule, foreign or domestic. In domestic cases, characterization is easier because it is conducted exclusively under a single law and usually is facilitated by readily available precedent. In multistate cases, characterization is more difficult due to the involvement of foreign law or laws and the relative paucity of precedent. Under the First Restatement – as with any system that depends on rigid rules leading to different results – characterization played a crucial role in determining the outcome of a case. Deciding whether the dispute at hand was one of tort, contract or something else, determined which choice-of-law rule was applicable, and hence, which state's law governed the case. For this reason, many American courts used characterization as a tool for avoiding the results dictated by an orthodox application of the Restatement's rules.

128. One can find numerous examples of such manipulative uses of the characterization process, especially in the second half of the 20th century. An earlier example that pre-dates the Restatement is *Levy* v. *Daniels' U-Drive Auto Renting Co.*[1] In *Levy*, a Connecticut court applied Connecticut's pro-recovery law to a dispute between Connecticut parties but arising from a Massachusetts accident, after characterizing the plaintiff's action as one of contract rather than tort. The contract in question was a lease by which the defendant car owner leased the accident car to another Connecticut domiciliary, the driver. A Connecticut statute, if applicable, would have made the lessor liable under such circumstances. The court's decision was partly based on an examination of the 'purpose of the statute', a factor that was not supposed to be relevant under the traditional methodology. Another example is *Haumschild* v. *Continental Cas. Co.*,[2] which involved an action by a Wisconsin plaintiff against her husband and his insurer for injuries she suffered in a California traffic accident caused by the husband. Wisconsin law allowed the action, while California's interspousal immunity rule would bar it. Reasoning that the purpose of the California rule was to preserve interspousal harmony, the Wisconsin court characterized the 'issue' in question as one involving family law. This characterization allowed the court to apply the law of the parties' common domicile, Wisconsin, which preserved the wife's action.

1. 143 A. 163 (Conn., 1928).
2. 95 N.W.2d 814 (Wis. 1959).

129. The long-term importance of these cases was not that they manipulated the characterization process but, rather that, in doing so, they moved the choice-of-law inquiry in more fruitful directions by: (1) narrowing the focus of the choice-of-law inquiry from the whole case to the precise 'issue' with regard to which the involved laws conflicted; and (2) examining the purposes or policies of the conflicting laws. In time, this led to two of the important hallmarks of the modern choice-of-law approaches – issue-by-issue analysis and content-oriented law selection (as opposed to jurisdiction-selection).

130. Under the Restatement (Second), characterization remains a necessary step because one still needs to determine, for example, whether the case falls under the torts or the contracts chapter of the Restatement. The difference is that this step is far less crucial because most of the Restatement (Second)'s rules are quite equivocal and do not inexorably point to a particular law. For this reason, there is little temptation to manipulate the characterization process under the Restatement (Second).

Even so, uniformity of outcome remains elusive. For example, Connecticut cases involving the same statute as the one in *Levy* and decided after Connecticut abandoned the *lex loci delicti* in favour of the Restatement (Second) have uniformly characterized the issue as one of tort but nevertheless reached irreconcilable results.[1] Also, courts confronting cases involving similar statutes in other states have uniformly characterized these statutes as tort statutes but have encountered a new characterization question – whether the purpose of those statutes is to regulate the car owner's conduct ('conduct-regulating' rules) or rather to ensure compensation for the victim ('loss-allocating' rules).[2] This new distinction of tort rules (which is discussed later)[3] and the difficulty in applying it serve as a reminder that characterization problems have not disappeared with the advent of the modern approaches.

1. *See* S. Symeonides, W.C. Perdue & A.T. von Mehren, *Conflict of Laws: American, Comparative, International* (2nd edn, St. Paul, Minn., 2003), pp. 46–48.
2. *See* S. Symeonides, *The American Choice-of-Law Revolution: Past, Present, and Future* (Leiden, Boston, 2006), pp. 134, 202–203, 221–222, 224–226.
3. *See infra* 211–213, 263–270.

§3. LOCALIZATION

131. Most of the First Restatement's rules utilized a single connecting factor, such as the place of injury for torts, or the place of the making for contracts. The applicable law depended exclusively on the location of that factor, thus raising the temptation for manipulation. For example, determining where a contract was made depended on which promise was deemed to be the offer and which the acceptance, and then where the latter was made. It is unnecessary to recite here the numerous cases that either struggled with, or manipulated, the localization process. Suffice it to say that sometimes localization is a genuinely difficult inquiry. This is particularly true when the connecting factor is peripatetic. Examples from recent experience include product liability cases involving pharmaceuticals or other products with latent defects that were used by the victims over a long period time while residing in several states.[1]

1. *See*, e.g., *Braune* v. *Abbott Labs.*, 895 F.Supp. 530 (E.D.N.Y. 1995) and *Millar-Mintz* v. *Abbott Labs.*, 645 N.E.2d 278 (Ill. App. 1994) (involving a pharmaceutical known as DES which was prescribed to pregnant women in the 1950s and caused injuries to those women and then to their adult daughters while the victims were domiciled in different states). *See also Philip Morris, Inc.* v. *Angeletti*, 752 A.2d 200 (Md. 2000) and *Tune* v. *Philip Morris, Inc.*, 766 So.2d 350 (Fla. App. 2000) (actions against tobacco manufacturer brought by plaintiffs who used tobacco products for many years while domiciled in different states).

132. The Restatement (Second) avoids most of these difficulties by using multiple and softer connecting factors. For example, for torts, the place of injury remains a connecting factor, but it is only one on a non-exclusive list that includes the place of conduct, the domicile, residence, or principal place of business of the parties, and the place of their relationship, if any.[1] Similarly, for contracts, the place of contracting is simply one connecting factor on a non-exclusive list that includes the places of negotiation and performance of the contract, the location of the subject matter, and the domicile, residence, or place of business of the parties.[2] Moreover, the phrasing of the Restatement permits the choice-of-law inquiry to go forward even if some of these factors cannot be precisely localized. Under these circumstances, there is little temptation to manipulate the localization process under the Restatement (Second).

1. *See Restatement (Second)* §145.
2. *See id.* at §188.

§4. THE APPLICATION OF THE DESIGNATED LAW AND ITS EXCEPTIONS

133. While the characterization step identifies the applicable choice-of-law rule, the localization step identifies the state whose law will govern the case or issue. If that state is one other than the forum, then the court is allowed to (for the first time) examine the content of that state's law and ask certain questions before applying it. For example, should the court apply the 'whole' law of the identified state, including its procedural and conflicts law? What if the applicable foreign law is penal, or its application would offend the forum's public policy? This section explores the questions encountered in this third step of the choice-of-law process.

I. Substance vs. Procedure

134. The first question involves the basic dichotomy between substantive and procedural law.[1] As the First Restatement stated, '[a]ll matters of procedure are governed by the law of the forum'.[2] Thus, the forum will not apply the procedural rules of the otherwise applicable foreign law. The Restatement explains that, because the application of those rules would be impractical, inconvenient and costly, '[a] limitation upon the scope of the reference to the foreign law is . . . necessary'. This limitation excludes 'those phases of the case which make administration of the foreign law by the local tribunal impracticable, inconvenient, or violative of local policy'.[3]

Professor Beale offered a balancing test that might have been implicit in the Restatement: 'If the practical convenience to the court in adopting the local rule of law is great, and the effect of so doing upon the rights of the parties is negligible, the law of the forum will be held to be controlling'.[4] The test may be plausible, but applying it in practise was far from simple. Drawing a bright line between substance and procedure is a difficult exercise in domestic, federal and conflicts law because, more often than not, 'the substantive shades off by imperceptible degrees into the procedural'.[5]

1. Methodologically, this question may also be asked in the characterization step of the process. Characterizing certain issues as procedural in the first step of the process ends the choice-of-law inquiry before even the localization step because all procedural issues are automatically governed by the law of the forum.
2. *Restatement* §585.
3. *Restatement*, Intro. Note to Chapter 12, at 700–701.
4. J.H. Beale, *A Treatise on the Conflict of Laws* (vol. 3, 1935), pp. 1599–1600.
5. W. Cook, *The Logical and Legal Bases of the Conflict of Laws* (Cambridge, Mass., 1942), p. 166.

135. Undaunted, the Restatement offered what purported to be an exhaustive list of subjects classified as procedural. Among them were: which court can entertain the action (§586); the form of the action (§587); who may and who must be sued (§588); methods of serving process (§589); methods of securing obedience to the court (§590); at what moment the action began (§591); all matters of pleading and the conduct of proceedings in court (§592); whether a claim of a defendant may be pleaded by way of setoff or counterclaim (§593); whether an issue of fact shall be tried by the court or by a jury (§594); the proof in court of a fact alleged as well as presumptions and inferences to be drawn from evidence (§595); the competency and credibility of witnesses (§596); admissibility of a particular piece of evidence (§597); matters pertaining to the execution of judgments (§600); whether the plaintiff must be free of fault in order to maintain an action (§601); whether compliance with a certain form is a prerequisite for filing an action (statute of frauds) (§602); statutes of limitation (§§603–605); limitations by forum law on the amount of recovery (§606); and access to courts (§§607–620).

136. Opinions differ as to whether all of the above issues are actually procedural, and many of the cases applying the First Restatement have indeed disagreed by either contracting or expanding this list. A notorious example from the latter group is *Kilberg* v. *Northeast Airlines, Inc.*,[1] in which the New York Court of Appeals characterized the amount of damages as a procedural matter. The court thus felt free to ignore the law of the state of injury, which limited the amount of damages, and to allow unlimited damages under New York law. Another example is *Grant* v. *McAuliffe*,[2] in which the California Supreme Court characterized as procedural an Arizona rule that barred a tort action against a tortfeasor who died before the filing of the suit. The court thus held that rule inapplicable in a California action involving California parties but arising from an Arizona accident.

1. 172 N.E.2d 526 (N.Y. 1961).
2. 264 P.2d 944 (Cal. 1953).

137. The Restatement (Second) states that a court 'usually' applies its own local rules 'prescribing how litigation shall be conducted',[1] and then provides several examples of issues that fall within this category. However, the Restatement wisely avoids any attempt to supply an exclusive or even comprehensive list of procedural issues or rules. Instead, the Restatement calls for an examination of the policies embodied in each rule of law claimed to be applicable to a particular issue.[2] This examination allows a court to take account of the procedural character of a particular rule, but without tying the court to a particular result. Nevertheless, as the following discussion illustrates, this flexible scheme has not eliminated all of the difficulties.

1. *Restatement (Second)* §122.
2. *See*, e.g., *id.* at §6(2)(a)(b).

138. For example, the Restatement (Second) provides that, subject to some exceptions, 'the local law of the forum determines the admissibility of evidence',[1] (apparently assuming that this is a procedural question). Many cases apply the law of the forum, either because they agree with this characterization, or because they conclude that the forum's substantive interests are predominant.[2] One example is *State* v. *Lynch*.[3] *Lynch* involved the admissibility of wiretap evidence obtained in Nevada and used to prosecute a Nevada domiciliary in Montana, for a crime committed in Montana. The evidence would have been admissible in Nevada, but not in Montana. The Montana Supreme Court characterized this as a procedural question and held that the evidence was inadmissible under Montana's exclusionary rule. However, the court noted that the objective of the exclusionary rule was 'to punish illegal police conduct'[4] (which is clearly a substantive policy), and that Montana had no control over police conduct in another state. Nevertheless, the court concluded, 'Montana's paramount interest in affording defendants the fullest protection of Montana law when appearing in its courts and this State's clear prohibition against non-consensual electronic surveillance of oral and wire communications, must prevail'.[5]

Other cases involving the same scenario have reached the opposite result and applied the law of the foreign state. One such case is *Commonwealth* v. *Sanchez*.[6] In this case, the evidence was collected in California during a 'canine sniff' that was lawful in California, but unlawful under the law of Pennsylvania, the forum state. Characterizing the question as substantive, the Pennsylvania Supreme Court held that California law should govern because California 'possessed the greater interest in the validity of [a] canine sniff' that took place there and involved California police officers.[7]

1. *Id.* at §138. Section 138 excepts from its scope privileged communications, parol evidence rule, and the statute of frauds.
2. *See*, e.g., *State* v. *Briggs*, 756 A.2d 731 (R.I. 2000) (holding that the law of the forum governed the voluntariness and thus admissibility of statements made to police in another state, as well as the admissibility of evidence collected there; that state's law was more favourable to defendant than the law of the forum); *Davidson* v. *State*, 25 S.W.3d 183 (Tex. Crim. App. 2000), *on remand* 42 S.W.3d 165 (Tex. App. 2001) (holding that incriminating oral statement made by defendant in Montana and admissible there was inadmissible in Texas because it was not electronically recorded as required by Texas law.); *Vega* v. *State*, 32 S.W.3d 897 (Tex. App. 2000) (holding that evidence obtained in Illinois and admissible there, was not admissible in Texas).
3. 969 P.2d 920 (Mont. 1998).
4. *Id.* at 924.
5. *Id.*
6. 716 A.2d 1221 (Pa. 1998).
7. *Id.* at 1223. The court stated that '[w]hile [Pennsylvania] has an interest in protecting its citizens from police misconduct and searches that are not supported by probable cause, the courts of [Pennsylvania] have no power to control the activities of a sister state or to punish conduct occurring within that sister state'.

139. *Larrison* v. *Larrison*,[1] a child custody case, involved the admissibility of a taped telephone call made from Pennsylvania and taped by the recipient in New York. Pennsylvania law required consent of both parties before recording the conversation, while New York did not require such consent. The court characterized the question as substantive and resolved the conflict by applying New York law, holding the recording admissible. The court reasoned that New York had the greater interest in allowing its citizens to lawfully record telephone conversations within its borders and that, while Pennsylvania also had an interest in protecting its citizens, Pennsylvania courts had 'no power to control the activities that occur within a sister state'.[1]

1. 750 A.2d 895 (Pa. Super. 2000).
2. *Id.* at 898. *See Washington* v. *Brown*, 940 P.2d 546 (Wash. 1997), *cert. denied*, 503 US 1007 (1998) (holding that defendant's statements recorded by California police without defendant's knowledge, as permitted by California law, were admissible in a Washington murder trial, even though such recording in Washington might have violated Washington law). For cases presenting the converse scenario and finding admissible, under forum law, evidence that was unlawfully collected in another state, *see Commonwealth* v. *Dennis*, 618 A.2d 972 (Pa. Super. 1992) (applying Pennsylvania standards for determining sufficiency of application for New Jersey search warrant); *People* v. *Benson*, 454 N.Y.S.2d 155 (N.Y.A.D. 1982) (confession obtained in Texas was admitted in New York, although it would be inadmissible in Texas; however, the confession was obtained by a New York police officer and complied with New York standards).

140. The Restatement (Second) considers as substantive the issue of admissibility of 'privileged communications', such as those between spouses, patient and doctor, penitent and confessor, and client and attorney. Indeed, unlike many other rules of evidence, the rules that establish these privileges subordinate the goal of truth-seeking to the broader societal interests of protecting certain relationships and encouraging socially desirable confidences. For this reason, the Restatement

(Second) assigns this question to the law of the state that has 'the most significant relationship' to the communication – usually the state in which the communication occurred. It provides that a communication that is not privileged under the law of that state, but is privileged under the law of the forum, is admissible unless admission would be 'contrary to the strong public policy of the forum'.[1] For the converse scenario in which a communication is not privileged under forum law but is privileged under the law of the state of the most significant relationship, the Restatement provides that the communication is admissible 'unless there is some special reason why the forum policy favouring admission should not be given effect'.[2]

1. *Restatement (Second)* §139(1). *Gonzalez* v. *State*, 45 S.W.3d 1001 (Tex.Crim.App. 2001), involved this scenario. The defendant confided to a pastor in California for a crime committed in Texas. This communication would be privileged under the law of Texas, but not California. The Texas court held that California had the most significant relationship to the communication and allowed the evidence, after finding that Texas did not have a strong public policy against admission. *See also State* v. *Donahue*, 18 P.3d 608 (Wash. App. 2001) (reaching the same result in a similar case involving physician-patient privilege).
2. *Restatement (Second)* §139(2). For a case applying this provision, *see Kos* v. *State*, 15 S.W.3d 633 (Tex.App. 2000) (holding that statements made by defendant to a physician in New Mexico, which would be privileged under the law of New Mexico law but not Texas, were admissible in Texas).

II. *Renvoi*

141. When the choice-of-law rule refers to the law of another state, a question arises whether the reference is to that state's 'whole' law (i.e., including its conflicts law), or instead to its 'substantive' or 'internal' law. This is the famous *renvoi* question, and it is answered by the forum's choice-of-law rule. If the reference is to include the whole law of the other state, then it is said that the forum adheres to the doctrine of *renvoi*. In such a case, the foreign conflict rule may point back to the law of the forum state (remission) or to the law of a third state (transmission) with further questions and possibilities depending on whether the remitting or transmitting state itself adheres to the *renvoi* doctrine.

142. Obviously, things can get quite complex, but this potential complexity should not obscure the important philosophical question that the *renvoi* debate seeks to answer. Should the forum resolve conflicts problems based exclusively on its own view about which is the proper law, or should the forum consult the corresponding views of other states? The First Restatement took the former position by categorically rejecting *renvoi* (§7) except in cases involving title to land or matters of divorce (§8). A more lenient explanation is that the Restatement's drafters thought that the complexities associated with *renvoi* would disrupt the simplicity of the system they attempted to establish. Nevertheless, courts following the Restatement have ignored its proscription of *renvoi* in order to avoid the results that the Restatement's rules dictated. This is why in the United States *renvoi* came to be viewed as an 'escape device', rather than as a useful tool for attaining rational and uniform results.

143. One example of a case that used *renvoi* as a vehicle for avoiding the results dictated by the traditional system is *American Motorists Ins. Co.* v. *ARTRA Group, Inc.*,[1] which was decided by the Supreme Court of Maryland, a state that continues to adhere to the *lex loci contractus* rule. The *locus contractus* was in Illinois, the home state of both contracting parties, which had abandoned this rule in favour of the Restatement (Second). The court managed to avoid the *lex loci* rule by assuming, albeit erroneously, that an Illinois court would have concluded that 'Maryland ha[d] the most significant relationship'[2] apparently because the contract insured property located in Maryland. Adopting a 'limited *renvoi* exception' the court held that 'Maryland's adherence to *lex loci contractus* must yield to a test such as Restatement (Second) Conflict of Laws §188 when the place of contracting would apply Maryland law pursuant to that test'.[3]

1. 659 A.2d 1295 (Md. 1995).
2. *Id.* at 1304.
3. *Id.*

144. The drafters of the Restatement (Second) understood the potential held by *renvoi* for attaining uniformity and they put it to good use, albeit in hortatory language. Section 8 of the Restatement (Second) provides in part:

1. When the objective of the particular choice-of-law rule is that the forum reach the same result on the very facts involved as would the courts of another state, the forum will apply the choice-of-law rules of the other state, subject to considerations of practicability and feasibility.
2. When the state of the forum has no substantial relationship to the particular issue or the parties and the courts of all interested states would concur in selecting the local [substantive] law rule applicable to this issue, the forum will usually apply this rule.

The Restatement (Second) implements the uniformity *desideratum* in the area of successions by providing that succession to land is governed by 'the law that would be applied by the courts of the *situs*',[1] and that succession to movables is governed by 'the law that would be applied by the courts of the state where the decedent was domiciled at the time of death'.[2]

1. *See*, e.g., *Restatement (Second)* §236, 239–242.
2. *See*, e.g., *Restatement (Second)* §260, 261, 263–265.

145. Modern conflicts codifications in countries such as Germany, Italy and Portugal employ *renvoi* in a way that is designed to attain certain substantive results considered *a priori* as desirable, such as favouring the validity of juridical acts or according a person the status of legitimacy.[1] In the United States, the Louisiana conflicts codification utilizes *renvoi* in certain cases (involving foreign immovables, status, and limitations), prohibits *renvoi* in all cases in which the forum legislature provides dispositive choice-of-law rules, and permits *renvoi* in all cases in which the legislature relegates the choice to the courts.[2] As these examples illustrate, *renvoi* need not be an all-or-nothing proposition. Furthermore, acceptance of *renvoi* in principle does not entail the surrender of the choice-of-law process to the wishes of other states. The forum retains full control of this process and the freedom to decide which and how much of *renvoi* to accept.

1. *See*, e.g., German EGBGB, Art. 4; Swiss PIL codification, Art. 14; Italian PIL codification, Art. 13(3); Portuguese Civ. Code, Arts 17–19.
2. *See* La. Civ. Code Art. 3517 (1992), and pertinent discussion in S. Symeonides, 'Private International Law Codification in a Mixed Jurisdiction: The Louisiana Experience', 57 *RabelsZ* 460, 477–478 (1993).

III. The Public Policy Exception

146. Buried towards the end of the First Restatement (in Section 612 of 625), is the statement: 'No Action can be maintained upon a cause of action created in another state the enforcement of which is contrary to the strong public policy of the forum'.[1]

The location of the public policy exception perhaps symbolized the traditional system's view of it as almost an afterthought in the choice-of-law process. In principle, the choice of the applicable law was to be made without regard to its content, flowing automatically from the application of the Restatement's territorially focussed, jurisdiction-selecting rules. Once the choice was made, however, the court was permitted to examine the content of the chosen law and to entertain certain limited defences or exceptions to its application.

One such exception was the public policy exception (stated in Section 612) which was intended to serve as a corrective mechanism in extraordinary cases.[2] According to Justice Cardozo's classic statement in *Loucks* v. *Standard Oil Co. of New York*,[3] the public policy exception applies only if the foreign law 'offends our sense of justice or menaces the public welfare', 'shock[s] our sense of justice' or 'violate[s] some fundamental principle of justice, some prevalent conception of good morals, some deep-rooted tradition of the common weal'. A mere difference between the two laws 'is not enough to show that public policy forbids us to enforce the foreign right'.[4]

1. *Restatement* §612.
2. Two other exceptions, the penal and the tax exceptions, are discussed *infra* 150–155.
3. 120 N.E. 198 (N.Y. 1918).
4. *Id.* at 202.

147. The First Restatement did not endorse this particular phraseology (which the Restatement (Second) endorses) although it enunciated a similar test:

> The application of this [exception] . . . is *extremely limited*. . . . There is a strong public policy favouring the enforcement of duties validly created by the law governing their creation. . . . The desirability of uniform enforcement of rights acquired in other states is especially strong among the states of the United States. Differences in policy among them are of minor nature . . . The social interest in uniform enforcement regardless of state lines is particularly great.[1]

Thus, a mere difference between forum and foreign law should not trigger deployment of the public policy exception. Only a clear conflict in fundamental policy can do so. As one judge observed, 'The test is a matter of degree. The public policy exception . . . necessarily refers to a high degree of public policy; otherwise, differences between the laws of sister states would always result in applying the law of the forum[.]'[2]

1. *Restatement* §612 cmt. (c), (emphasis added).
2. *Bethlehem Steel Corp.* v. *G.C. Zarnas & Co., Inc.*, 498 A.2d 605, 613 (Md. 1985) (Rodowski, J., dissenting). In *Cooney* v. *Osgood Mach., Inc.*, 612 N.E.2d 277 (N.Y. 1993), the New York Court of Appeals, reiterated Cardozo's classic test and stated: '[N]ot every difference between foreign and New York law threatens our public policy. Indeed, if New York statutes or court opinions were routinely read to express fundamental policy, choice of law principles would be meaningless. Courts invariably would be forced to prefer New York law over conflicting foreign law on public policy grounds'. *Id.* at 284.

148. Despite these tests, many courts applying the traditional approach have used a much lower threshold in employing the public policy exception. For example, recent cases have used this exception as the reason for refusing to apply the foreign state's interspousal immunity rule;[1] guest statute;[2] contributory negligence rule (compared to the forum's comparative negligence);[3] and a rule requiring proof of negligence in product liability actions (compared to the forum's strict liability rule).[4] All of these cases applied forum law in place of the rejected foreign law. Had these courts been prepared to abandon the *lex loci* rule, they could easily justify the application of forum law because the forum state had multiple contacts and interests. Instead, these courts chose to keep the rule but avoid its results.[5] While this is typical of many courts that continue to adhere to the traditional approach, the fact remains that this loose employment of the public policy exception violates the basic prescriptions of that approach.

1. *See Boone* v. *Boone*, 546 S.E.2d 191 (S.C. 2001).
2. *See Owen* v. *Owen*, 444 N.W.2d 710 (S.D. 1989); *Paul* v. *Nat'l. Life*, 352 S.E.2d 550 (W.Va. 1986).
3. *See Mills* v. *Quality Supplier Trucking, Inc.*, 510 S.E.2d 280 (W.Va. 1998).
4. *See Alexander* v. *Gen'l Motors Corp.*, 478 S.E.2d 123 (Ga. 1996).
5. *See* e.g., *Dowis* v. *Mud Slingers, Inc.*, 621 S.E.2d 413, 416 (Ga. 2005) (refusing to abandon the *lex loci delicti* rule, partly because 'the courts of this State have the power to ameliorate the sometimes seeming harshness of the rule' through the public policy exception).

149. Equally unorthodox is the affirmative use of the forum's public policy, which has become increasingly common in recent years.[1] Under the traditional approach, public policy was not a rule of choice of law but rather it was an exception to all choice-of-law rules. As such, it was supposed to function only negatively, by repelling obnoxious foreign laws, rather than affirmatively, as a justification for the application of forum law. Yet, many cases from the *lex loci* states routinely use the forum's public policy offensively rather than defensively. For example, the Supreme Court of New Mexico applied the law of the forum without even looking at the law of the state of injury because, the court reasoned, the *lex loci* rule 'is not utilized if [its] application would violate New Mexico public policy'.[2]

This use of public policy differs little from its use by modern approaches under which the forum's public policy is an integral affirmative factor in the court's decision to apply or not to apply the law of the forum. Indeed, one of the differences between the First Restatement and modern approaches such as interest analysis is that, in Brainerd Currie's words, interest analysis 'summon[s] public policy from the reserves and place[s] it in the front lines where it belongs'.[3] Currie's statement also describes other modern approaches, such as the Restatement (Second) under which an examination of the polices of the conflicting laws is one of the primary criteria for choosing between or among them.[4]

1. *See* S. Symeonides, *The American Choice-of-Law Revolution: Past, Present, and Future* (Leiden, Boston, 2006), pp. 52–58.
2. *Torres* v. *State*, 894 P.2d 386, 390 (N.M. 1995).
3. B. Currie, *Selected Essays on the Conflict of Laws* (Durham, N.C., 1963), p. 88.
4. *See Restatement (Second)* §6(2)(a)(b).

IV. The Penal-Law Exception

150. 'The courts of no country execute the penal laws of another',[1] proclaimed the United States Supreme Court in 1825. Before the end of the 19th century, the Court explained that this principle also applied to judgments that were 'penal in the international sense'.[2] This principle holds true today, even as among the states of the United States. Strictly speaking, in the area of criminal law there is not a choice-of-law question; it is merged into the jurisdictional question. A state either has jurisdiction, in which case it applies its own law, or it lacks jurisdiction, in which case it would ordinarily extradite the defendant to a state with proper jurisdiction.

1. *The Antelope*, 23 US (10 Wheat) 66 (1825) (emphasis added).
2. *Huntington* v. *Attrill*, 146 US 657 (1892).

151. However, the penal-law exception sounds broader than it is. First, to fall within the exception (and thus outside the scope of the choice-of-law process), the foreign statute must be 'penal in the international sense'. This means that the statute must be designed primarily for the 'vindication of the public justice', rather than the 'vindicat[ion of] a private right'.[1]

1. *Loucks* v. *Standard Oil Co. of N.Y.*, 120 N.E. 198, 198–199 (N.Y. 1918).

152. Second, the exception means only that the forum does not directly apply ('*execute*') foreign penal laws or enforce foreign penal judgments. The forum may choose to rely on foreign penal laws or judgments for its own purposes as it deems appropriate. For example, a state may choose to recognize a foreign conviction for purposes other than enforcement, such as determining whether the convicted person is a multiple offender or a felon ineligible for public office. Likewise, in applying the forum's 'three-strikes' law, a court may include in the count the defendant's prior convictions in another state.[1]

In *Small* v. *United States*,[2] the Supreme Court faced the question whether a provision of the US Criminal Code that prohibited the possession of firearms by persons convicted 'in any court'[3] and sentenced to more than a year of imprisonment included convictions by a foreign court.[4] The Court answered this question in the negative, but only because it found that, in enacting the Code, Congress did not intend it to include foreign convictions. These convictions 'differ from domestic convictions in important ways',[5] either because they may be based on laws that prohibit conduct that US law permits or punishes much less severely, or because they may result from proceeding that are 'inconsistent with an American understanding of fairness'.[6] The Court reasoned that, although these differences alone were not determinative, they tipped the scales in favour of concluding that Congress intended the phrase 'convicted in any court' to apply 'domestically, not extraterritorially'.[7]

1. 'Three-strikes' laws impose higher penalties on persons with two previous convictions for certain offences. For cases involving such laws, *see*, e.g., *State* v. *Berry*, 5 P.3d 658 (Wash. 2000); *Berry* v. *Morgan*, 137 Fed.Appx. 952 (9th Cir. 2005), *cert. denied*, 126 S.Ct. 1364 (2006); *State* v. *Keller*, 19 P.3d 1030 (Wash. 2001).
2. 544 US 385 (US 2005).
3. 18 USC §922(g)(1) (2005).
4. The defendant in *Small* was convicted by a Japanese court for smuggling firearms into Japan and was sentenced to five years' imprisonment. Two years later, he was paroled and returned to the United States where he was arrested in possession of two other firearms.
5. *Small*, 544 US at 388.
6. *Id.*
7. *Id.* In *State* v. *Menard*, 888 A.2d 57 (R.I. 2005), the court reached the same conclusion in a case involving a prior conviction in another state, again because the court interpreted the pertinent forum statute as excluding consideration of foreign convictions. The defendant was previously convicted in Arizona of 'class 4 felony arson' in a judgment that characterized the offense as 'not of a dangerous nature' and was later arrested in the forum state in possession of a firearm. A forum statute prohibited persons convicted 'in this state or elsewhere of a crime of violence' from possessing firearms and defined 'crime of violence' as including 'first and second degree arson'. The court affirmed the defendant's indictment under this statute, reasoning that forum law governed whether a foreign conviction can qualify as a predicate 'crime of violence' under the statute, and that another state's characterization was 'wholly irrelevant'. *Id.* at 62. It would be 'absurd', said the court, 'to accord another state's lawmakers the ability to determine the propriety of firearm prosecutions in Rhode Island . . . [and] allow out-of-state law to steer prosecutorial discretion in Rhode Island'. *Id* at 61. However, the court compared the elements of a class 4 felony arson under Arizona law to second degree arson under Rhode Island law and found them to be similar, despite differences in terminology.

V. The Foreign Tax-Law Exception

153. Although the obligation to pay taxes is not penal, the foreign tax-law exception (also known as 'the revenue rule') resembles the penal-law exception in the sense that: (1) they both function as effective defences to the application of otherwise governing foreign law; and (2) both involve foreign laws enacted in *jure imperii*, that is, in the exercise of direct sovereign authority. The revenue rule stands for the proposition that, in the absence of a treaty, the courts of one country do not directly enforce the tax judgments or laws of another country.[1] At a minimum, this means that American courts will not entertain a suit by a foreign government seeking to directly enforce its tax laws or judgments.

1. *See* American Law Institute, *Restatement (Third) of Foreign Relations* §483 (1987) ('Courts in the United States are not required to recognize or to enforce judgments for the collection of taxes, fines, or penalties rendered by the courts of other states'.); E. Scoles, P. Hay, P. Borchers & S. Symeonides, *Conflict of Laws*, (4th edn, St. Paul, Minn., 2004), pp. 1290, 1296–1298.

With regard to sister states, most American states have statutes that expressly authorize the application of the tax laws of sister states on the condition of reciprocity. Sister-state tax judgments have always been enforceable under the Constitution's Full Faith and Credit clause.

154. Recently, lower courts have extended this practise to situations in which the foreign government's lawsuit would amount to indirect enforcement of its tax laws. For example, in *Attorney General of Canada* v. *R.J. Reynolds Tobacco Holdings, Inc.*,[1] the Second Circuit held that the revenue rule barred a civil action brought under the RICO statute[2] by the Government of Canada. The action sought damages for lost taxes and law enforcement costs resulting from defendants' evasion of Canadian taxes by smuggling cigarettes across the US–Canadian border. In a similar case, *Republic of Honduras* v. *Philip Morris Companies, Inc.*,[3] brought by Central American countries, the Eleventh Circuit reached the same result. Both courts distinguished these cases from those in which the United States government initiates criminal prosecutions premised on violations of foreign tax laws. Until 2005, the lower courts were split as to whether the revenue rule barred such prosecutions.

1. 268 F.3d 103 (2nd Cir. 2001), *cert. denied*, 537 US 1000 (2002).
2. *See* 18 USCA §1965 (Racketeering Influenced and Corrupt Organizations).
3. 341 F.3d 1253 (11th Cir. 2003), *cert. denied*, 540 US 1109 (2004).

155. In *Pasquantino* v. *United States*,[1] the Supreme Court resolved the split, holding that the revenue rule does not bar prosecutions by the US government, but 'express[ed] no view'[2] on whether the rule bars civil RICO actions by foreign governments. In *Pasquantino*, the defendants were convicted under the federal wire fraud statute for smuggling liquor into Canada and evading Canadian excise duties and other taxes. The defendants argued, *inter alia*, that their prosecution violated the revenue rule because it was premised solely on violations of Canadian tax laws. The Court rejected the argument, holding that the revenue rule did not bar the prosecution. The Court conceded that 'this criminal prosecution 'enforces' Canadian revenue law in an attenuated sense', but concluded that the connection was too attenuated to 'contravene the revenue rule'.[3] The Court reasoned that, unlike cases in which a foreign government seeks to recover taxes, this was a criminal prosecution brought by the United States in its sovereign capacity to punish domestic criminal conduct. Such a prosecution, the Court reasoned, does not implicate any of the traditional rationales for the revenue rule, such as the avoidance of judicial evaluation of foreign tax policies or giving domestic effect to politically sensitive foreign policy decisions. Noting that the defendants were convicted for their conduct in the United States and not for the effects of that conduct in Canada, the Court also rejected the argument that this decision gave extraterritorial effect to the wire fraud statute.[4]

1. 544 US 349 (2005).
2. *Id.* at 365 note 11.
3. *Id.* at 366.
4. In *European Cmty* v. *RJR Nabisco, Inc.*, 424 F.3d 175 (2nd Cir. 2005), *cert. denied*, 126 S.Ct. 1045 (US 2006), the Second Circuit held that the revenue rule barred civil RICO actions brought by the European Community and other countries against tobacco product manufacturers seeking damages for lost taxes and related costs caused by the smuggling of contraband

cigarettes into the plaintiffs' territories. The court distinguished *Pasquantino* on the ground that 'the involvement of the United States government [which] was a key factor in determining the outcome of *Pasquantino*' was absent in this action, which was a lawsuit 'brought by foreign governments, not by the United States' and in which 'the executive branch ha[d] given us no signal that it consent[ed] to this litigation'. 424 F.3d at 181.

§5. Domicile

156. Domicile is a concept that performs a variety of services in American conflicts law. For example, it is the basis of: (1) general *in personam* judicial jurisdiction and diversity jurisdiction; (2) prescriptive jurisdiction for tax and similar regulatory purposes; and (3) entitlement to certain benefits, such as welfare or tuition. Moreover, domicile is one of the most important connecting factors under both the traditional and modern choice-of-law approaches.[1] As noted earlier, the First Restatement called for the application of the law of a person's domicile to all succession and matrimonial property matters involving movables.[2]

1. Basic bibliography on domicile includes L. McDougal, R. Felix & R. Whitten, *American Conflicts Law* 17–40 (5th edn 2001); E. Scoles, P. Hay, P. Borchers & S. Symeonides, *Conflict of Laws* 232–283 (4th edn 2004); R. Weintraub, *Commentary on the Conflict of Laws* 13–51 (5th edn 2006).
2. *See supra* 120.

157. The Restatement (Second) relies on the same connecting factor, albeit not exclusively. More importantly, under all modern American approaches, domicile has become an important factor (although non-exclusive) even in the area of tort conflicts where territoriality used to be the dominant principle. For example, as documented in Chapter 4 of this part, *infra*, when both the tortfeasor and the victim are domiciled in the same state and the tort occurred in another state, most courts apply the law of the common domicile to resolve loss-distribution conflicts.[1]

1. *See infra* 278–288.

158. The basic principles regarding domicile are the same as in most other countries, namely: (1) every natural person has a domicile at all times; (2) no person has more than one domicile at a time, at least for the same purpose; (3) once established, a domicile continues until another one is acquired; and (4) in order to acquire a new domicile, a person must establish a dwelling-place with the intention of making it his or her home for an indefinite period of time. Thus, domicile presupposes physical residence but requires in addition the concurrent mental element of intending to make it one's permanent or at least indefinite home.[1]

1. Special rules govern the acquisition of domicile by persons of limited capacity, such as minor children or adults under guardianship, or persons whose freedom of choice is limited by other factors, such as prisoners, soldiers or government employees. For these rules as well as a fuller discussion and documentation of the principles governing domicile, *see* the sources cited *supra* at 156.

159. 'Habitual residence', which is a concept used in several international conventions and is something closer to domicile than to residence, is not in vogue in the United States. Also, the term 'citizenship', rather than 'nationality', is used in the United States. National citizenship is defined by federal law, while state citizenship depends on domicile. The federal Constitution provides that persons who are US citizens are also citizens of the state in which they 'reside',[1] which in this context means 'domiciled'. Many constitutional or statutory provisions use the term residence when contemplating domicile. The mixed usage is also common in judicial decisions. Indeed, because the two terms often are used interchangeably, it is often difficult to ascertain what was intended without examining the specific context.

1. US Const. Amd. XIV.

160. With regard to corporations, a federal statute provides that, for purposes of federal-court diversity jurisdiction, a corporation is a citizen of the state in which it is incorporated, as well as the state in which it has its principal place of business.[1] Each of these contacts is also a basis of state-court general jurisdiction over a corporation. In addition, the place of incorporation is the critical connecting factor for choice-of-law purposes for matters involving the corporation's internal affairs, while its principal place of business is a connecting factor equivalent to domicile for other choice-of-law matters.

1. 18 USC §13312(c).

§6. Judicial Notice and Proof of Foreign Law

161. *Jus novit curia* ('the court knows the law') is an ancient and widely accepted maxim in both the civil-law world and the common-law world. Theoretically, a litigant does not need to prove to the court the existence of the law on which her remedy is based. If such a law exists, the court ought to know about it, take judicial notice of it *sua sponte*, and apply it to the case, regardless of whether that litigant pleaded it or proved its content.

However, whether this maxim also applies to foreign law is something on which various systems disagree. While civil-law systems have always answered this question affirmatively, common-law systems began with a negative answer, moving gradually toward the middle.[1] They began by treating foreign law as a question of fact, with all the resulting consequences regarding pleading, proof, and appellate review. For example, when the content of foreign law was not proven but the action was based upon it, the court would either dismiss the action or apply the *lex fori*, on the basis of varying rationales or fictions. One such rationale was that the *lex fori* is the basic or residual law that applies in all cases unless a litigant demonstrates a good reason for its displacement. Such reason is absent when the content of the competing foreign law is not proven. Another rationale was the often fictitious assumption that the unproven foreign law was the same as the law of the forum.

1. Basic American bibliography on this topic includes: L. McDougal, R. Felix & R. Whitten, *American Conflicts Law* (5th edn, Ardsley, New York, 2001), pp. 440–445; E. Scoles, P. Hay, P. Borchers & S. Symeonides, *Conflict of Laws* (4th edn, St. Paul, Minn., 2004), pp. 543–556; R. Weintraub, *Commentary on the Conflict of Laws* (5th edn, New York, 2006), pp. 112–116.

162. Eventually, common law courts, and later legislatures, began moving in the direction of treating at least sister-state law as a question of law. By the middle of the 20th century, most states enacted statutes on judicial notice of foreign law, which were based on the Uniform Judicial Notice of Foreign Law Act of 1936.[1] Most of those statutes differentiate between sister-state law and foreign-country law. Judicial notice is compulsory with regard to the former ('shall'), and discretionary with regard to the latter ('may').

1. *See* Scoles, Hay, Borchers & Symeonides, *supra* 161 at 547–549.

163. More recent statutes are modelled after the Act's successor, the Uniform Interstate and International Procedure Act of 1962, which blurred the distinction between sister-state and foreign-country law. The Act provides in part:

> *§4.01 [Notice].* A party who intends to raise an issue concerning the law of any jurisdiction or governmental unit thereof outside this state shall give reasonable notice in his pleadings or other reasonable notice.
>
> *§4.02 [Materials to be considered].* In determining the law of any jurisdiction or governmental unit thereof outside this state, the court may consider any relevant material or source, including testimony, whether or not submitted by a party or admissible under the rules of evidence.
>
> *§4.03 [Court Decision and Review].* The court, not jury, shall determine the law of any governmental unit outside this state and its determination shall be subject to review on appeal as a ruling on a question of law.[1]

1. Uniform Interstate and International Procedure Act, 13 U.L.A. 355 (1986). In 1977, the National Conference of Commissioners on Uniform State Laws withdrew this Act as obsolete because in the meantime many states enacted laws modeled after Federal Rule of Civil Procedure 44.1, *infra* at 164.

164. Since 1966, federal courts follow Federal Rule of Civil Procedure 44.1, which provides:

> *Determination of foreign law.* A party who intends to raise an issue concerning the law of a foreign country shall give notice by pleadings or other reasonable written notice. The court, in determining foreign law, may consider any relevant material or source, including testimony, whether or not submitted by a party or admissible under the federal rules of evidence. The court's determination shall be treated as a question of law.[1]

1. 28 USCA Rule 44.1.

165. Despite these or similar statutes, when neither party raises the question of foreign law or provides proof of its content, most American courts will adjudicate the case under the law of the forum, even though under the forum's choice-of-law rules the case would be governed by foreign law. An amazingly high number of conflicts cases thus goes undetected.[1] Here the fiction is that the parties tacitly acquiesce to the application of forum law. This fiction may be economical for the court and convenient for one side's attorneys, but only rarely does it serve the interests of both sides.

1. *See* S. Symeonides, *Private International Law at the End of the 20th Century: Progress or Regress?* (The Hague, London, Boston, 2000), pp. 6–7.

Chapter 3. The Choice-of-Law Revolution

§1. Introduction

166. The traditional choice-of-law regime had its critics, at least among academics, even before it was 'codified' in the First Restatement. These criticisms gradually increased in frequence and intensity, and began appearing in judicial decisions. Beginning in the 1960s, the academic and judicial dissent took on the appearance, and eventually the dimensions and intensity of, a figurative rebellion against the established system. This movement came to be known as the American choice-of-law 'revolution'. This chapter discusses this movement, beginning with academic theory, and then turning to its following among courts.[1]

1. For a comprehensive discussion and documentation of this movement, *see* S. Symeonides, *The American Choice-of-Law Revolution: Past, Present, and Future* (Leiden, Boston, 2006), pp. 9–121 (hereafter Symeonides, *Choice-of-Law Revolution*, from which this chapter draws heavily).

§2. The Scholastic Revolution

167. American conflicts law, and choice of law in particular, is one of the few branches of American law that has been heavily influenced by academic writers. Whether this is due to the perceived esoteric nature of the subject matter, the dearth of English precedent or doctrine during the formative period of American conflicts law, or the relatively infrequent occurrence of conflicts cases in general – which slows the accumulation of judicial expertise on the subject – is beside the point. The fact remains that it was academic writers like Story, Wharton, and later Beale, who provided the theoretical underpinnings of the traditional choice-of-law system that lasted for more than a century. It is also academic writers like Cook, Cavers, and Currie who pinpointed and articulated the deficiencies of the traditional system and instigated dissension from it. This part of the chapter focuses on their writings,[1] which have served both as the motor and the compass of the judicial revolution during its early years.

1. Space limitations prevent discussion of the writings of other scholars, such as Albert Ehrenzweig (*see* A. Ehrenzweig, *A Treatise on the Conflict of Laws* (1962)), von Mehren and Trautman (*see* A. von Mehren & D. Trautman, *The Law of Multistate Problems*, (1965)), and Russell J. Weintraub (*see* R. Weintraub, *Commentary on the Conflict of Laws* (4th edn 2001)).

I. The First Critics

A. Walter W. Cook

168. One of the earliest and most outspoken critics of the established choice-of-law system was Professor Walter W. Cook (1873–1943).[1] Together with Judge Learned Hand, Cook is usually described as the author of the 'local law' theory. This theory – which is no more memorable than the vested right theory Cook intended to displace – was Cook's attempt to explain the seemingly paradoxical application of foreign law and reconcile it with the forum's sovereignty. Cook argued that, in adjudicating cases that otherwise would be 'governed' by foreign law, the forum neither applies foreign law, nor enforces a foreign vested right. Instead, it recreates the foreign right by fashioning a local-law remedy that approximates the result provided by the pertinent foreign law. Besides being of dubious explanatory value, this theory had the potentially regressive effect of overemphasizing the role of the *lex fori*. Cook's subliminal message was that the function of conflicts law is not to preserve the international order, but rather to carry out local law and policy. This message was a drastic departure from the universalistic conception of PIL that characterized earlier generations of American scholars, including Story and even Beale.

1. Cook's critiques of the then prevailing approach are found in W.W. Cook, *The Logical and Legal Bases of the Conflict of Laws* (Mass., Cambridge, 1942), a collection of 18 previously published in various law reviews. For the writings of other early critics like Ernest G. Lorenzen (1876–1951) and Hessel E. Yntema (1891–1966), *see* S. Symeonides, 'The First Conflicts Restatement Through the Eyes of Old: As Bad as Its Reputation?', 32 *S. Ill. U. L. J.* (2007).

169. Cook was a de-constructionist well before that term became fashionable. His main contribution to American conflicts law was not in proposing a new theory, but rather in deconstructing the traditional theory and freeing the 'intellectual garden' of conflicts law of 'rank weeds' to facilitate the planting and growth of 'useful vegetables'.[1] Cook argued that the Restatement's professed goals of predictability and uniformity were illusory because of the multiple escape devices that judges could and did use. He posited that the Restatement's seemingly simple, but excessively broad, principles were inadequate for describing what courts were doing or directing them what to do. Finally, Cook argued that a simplistic, static system based on prefabricated rules could not provide workable solutions to complex problems. He advocated for a set of guiding principles that would provide not only a modicum of certainty and, more importantly, 'continuity of growth'.[2] This concept was the harbinger of the notion that later prevailed in American conflicts thought – that an 'approach' is superior to a rule system.

1. W.W. Cook, *Logical Bases*, *supra* p. x.
2. *See* W.W. Cook, 'An Unpublished Chapter of the Logical and Legal Bases of the Conflict of Laws', 37 *U. Ill. L. Rev.*, 1943, 418. The quoted phrase is from John Dewey, *Human Nature and Conduct* (1922), p. 244 ('Continuity of growth not atomism is the alternative to fixity of principles and aims'.).

170. Although Cook fell short of articulating an affirmative approach of his own, his writings contained seeds of the modern theories. For example, in response to the basic question of how the forum court should choose the foreign law on which to 'model' its rule of decision, Cook simply pointed to 'the same method actually used in deciding cases involving purely domestic torts, contracts, property, etc.'[1] His resort to the 'domestic method' for handling conflicts cases anticipated Brainerd Currie's conception of the choice-of-law process as being based on the 'ordinary process of construction and interpretation'.[2] Cook's instrumentalist reference to 'socially useful' solutions to conflicts problems also anticipated the result-selectivity of many judicial decisions and academic commentators, and the notion that courts should not sacrifice material justice in the pursuit of 'conflicts justice'. Moreover, Cook's admonition that one should consider legislative purposes and policies 'before a wise choice between conflicting rules can be made'[3] suggests that, like many modern American scholars, Cook thought of the choice-of-law problem as one of choosing between competing rules, not competing states or 'jurisdictions' in the abstract.

1. W.W. Cook, *Logical Bases*, *supra* 43.
2. *See* B. Currie, *Selected Essays on the Conflict of Laws* (Durham, NC., 1963), pp. 183–184, discussed *infra* 177.
3. W.W. Cook, *Logical Bases* at 46 (emphasis added).

B. David F. Cavers

171. Professor David F. Cavers, who at the time shared many of Cook's legal-realist convictions, continued the attack on the traditional system. In a pioneering law review article, Cavers further exposed the mechanical nature of the traditional methodology. He compared it to a slot machine, programmed to select the applicable law in a 'blindfold' fashion, based solely on territorial contacts, regardless of the content of the implicated laws.[1] In his view, this exclusive reliance on territorial contacts and the insistence on using 'jurisdiction-selecting' rules not only prevented a more individualized treatment of conflicts cases, but also prevented intelligent choices. After all, Cavers observed, '[t]he court is not idly choosing a law; it is deciding a controversy. How can it choose wisely without considering how that choice will affect that controversy?'[2]

1. *See* D. Cavers, 'A Critique of the Choice-of-Law Problem', 47 *Harv. L. Rev.* 173, 1933, 178.
2. *Id.* at 189.

172. Cavers proposed a drastic rearrangement of the priorities of the choice-of-law process. He contented that rather than choosing between states or 'jurisdictions' without regard to how their laws would regulate the case at hand, the court should choose between the conflicting legal rules based, in large part, on the result each rule would produce in the particular case. Rather than choosing on the basis of territorial contacts, the court should focus directly on the content of the competing rules and their underlying policies, the peculiarities of the particular case, and the need to ensure justice for the involved parties. Although this proposal fell short of articulating a comprehensive alternative to the First Restatement, it did provide direction to the search for alternative methodologies.

173. In 1965, Cavers returned to the conflicts scene with his seminal book *The Choice of Law Process.*[1] This book set forth his position regarding many of the new ideas that revolution had generated. Although for the most part Cavers remained sympathetic to some basic tenets of Professor Currie's interest analysis (discussed below), he disassociated himself from Currie's 'solution' of true conflicts and his insistence that conflicts should be resolved on an entirely *ad hoc* basis. The judicial applications of interest analysis convinced Cavers that Currie's rejection of all choice-of-law rules was bound to lead to an impasse. Cavers saw the need for providing judges with sufficiently specific directives that would facilitate principled choice-of-law decisions.

1. D. Cavers, *The Choice of Law Process* (Ann Arbor, Mich., 1965).

174. To that end, Cavers formulated seven 'principles of preference', five for tort and two for contract conflicts. Cavers conceded, 'without apology', a 'territorial bias' in his torts principles.[1] The fact that he was one of the first and most effective critics of the blind and mechanical territorialism of the traditional theory, enabled Cavers to credibly urge a return to what he termed a 'principled' territorialism. Its difference from traditional territorialism was that Cavers's version did not base the choice of law solely on a state's territorial contacts, but rather on the presence of the 'right' combination of contacts and laws. For example, his first principle for torts covered situations in which the injury is in one state and either the conduct or the tortfeasor's domicile are in another state. The principle calls for the application of the law of the state of injury, but only if that law 'set[s] a higher standard of conduct or of financial protection against injury than do the laws of the [other] state'.[2] His second principle covered situations in which the conduct and the injury are in one state and the victim's domicile is in another. The principle called for the application of the law of the former state, if that law provides for 'a lower standard of conduct or of financial protection than the victim's domicile'.[3] Thus, Cavers was the first to implement the concept of content-oriented law-selection as opposed to content-blind 'jurisdiction-selection'.

1. D. Cavers, *The Choice of Law Process*, *supra* 173 at 134, 139.
2. *Id.* at 139 (emphasis added).
3. *Id.* at 146 (emphasis added).

II. An Open Revolution: Brainerd Currie

175. While Cook and Cavers demonstrated the deficiencies of the traditional system, it was Professor Brainerd Currie who inflicted the decisive blow. Currie built on the foundations they and others provided and enunciated a new approach in a series of law review articles published in the 1950s and early 1960s.[1] His approach consists of the following basic components, which are discussed below: (1) his rejection of choice-of-law rules in favour of the 'domestic method' of statutory construction and interpretation; (2) the notion that states have a 'governmental interest' in the outcome of conflicts cases; (3) his narrow conception of those interests; (4) the concepts of 'true' and 'false' conflicts and 'unprovided-for' cases; and (5) a *de facto* and *de jure* forum favouritism.

1. These articles are collected in B. Currie, *Selected Essays*, *supra*.

A. *Anti-rulism*

176. Currie issued a categorical indictment of not only the particular choice-of-law rules of the First Restatement – which 'have not worked and cannot be made to work',[1] but also of all choice-of-law rules in general. Assuming that all such rules were not only bad but also harmful, he proclaimed that '[w]e would be better off without choice-of-law rules'.[2] Although this is the least noticed and criticized of Currie's postulates, it is the one directly responsible for why American conflicts law rejected the route of reform in favour of revolution.

1. *Id.* at 180.
2. *Id.* at 183. *See also id.* at 180 ('The [traditional] rules . . . have not worked and cannot be made to work . . . But the root of the trouble goes deeper. In attempting to use rules we encounter difficulties that stem not from the fact that the particular rules are bad, . . . but rather from the fact that we have such rules at all'.).

B. The 'Domestic Method'

177. To fill the void left by his rejection of choice-of-law rules, Currie resorted to the method of statutory 'construction and interpretation' that courts employ in fully domestic cases. In Currie's words, '[j]ust as we determine by that process how a statute applies in time, and how it applies to marginal cases, so we may determine how it should be applied to cases involving foreign elements'.[1] Although this was not a new idea, it entailed several interrelated consequences, including the following:

1. a rejection of the theretofore prevailing assumption that conflicts cases are so different from wholly domestic cases as to require a distinctive mode of refereeing that draws from principles superior, or at least external, to the involved states. Indeed, Currie rejected the existence of an overarching legal order delineating *a priori* the legislative jurisdiction of each state. He believed that, in searching for choice-of-law solutions, the forum should look inward rather than upward;
2. the rejection of pre-established choices in favour of an *ad hoc* judicial choice of the applicable law;
3. the rejection of multilateralism in favour of unilateralism; and
4. a rejection of the notion that the choice of the applicable law could be made on the basis of territorial contacts alone, regardless of the content of the substantive laws of the contact states.

In sum, rather than choosing the applicable law through preordained choice-rules that were oblivious to the content of the conflicting laws, Currie's approach – like Cavers's – focuses directly on the content of the involved states' laws and, through the 'ordinary process of construction and interpretation' identifies their respective policies and, depending on those policies, delineates their spatial reach.

1. *Id.* at 184.

C. The Concept of Governmental Interests

178. According to Currie, whenever a case falls within a law's spatial reach as delineated by the interpretative process, the state from which that law emanates has a 'governmental interest' in applying it in order to effectuate its underlying policy. In Currie's words, an 'interest . . . is the product of (1) a governmental policy and (2) the concurrent existence of an appropriate relationship between the state having the policy and the transaction, the parties, or the litigation'.[1] In this way, Currie projected his legal-realist conception of law as 'an instrument of social control'[2] at the interstate level by postulating that states have an interest in the outcome of litigation between private parties.

1. *Id.* at 621.
2. *Id.* at 64.

D. Currie's Assumptions about State Interests

179. The notion that a state may have an interest in private-law disputes between private parties was not a novel one in American law, domestic or interstate. For example, this idea had figured prominently in a cluster of US Supreme Court decisions in the 1930s interpreting the Full Faith and Credit clause of the Constitution. What was new was Currie's partisan articulation of this concept. He thought and wrote in terms of a state's yearning to maximize its gains at the expense of other states' policies, rather than in terms of a state's need to avoid impairment of its own strongly held policies. Indeed, the main problem with Currie's interest-theory was not so much the core concept of state interests, but rather his narrow assumptions about the nature and scope of those interests.

180. In particular, Currie refused to consider a state's 'multistate' interests, namely, interests which, though not reflected directly in a state's domestic law, stem from the state's membership in a broader community of states.[1] Second, Currie assumed that, in the vast majority of cases, a state has an interest in applying its law only when it would benefit its domiciliaries, but not when it would benefit similarly situated non-domiciliaries[2] (a notion referred to hereafter as Currie's 'personal-law principle'). Finally, Currie specifically downplayed the interests of the individuals involved in the conflict, as opposed to the interests of their respective home states.[3] Because of these postulates, some critics charged that Currie's approach was constitutionally infirm.[4] However, the real problem with these postulates was not their constitutional permissibility in the abstract, but rather their appropriateness, especially in interstate conflicts.

1. For example, Currie specifically dismissed the view that a state should be guided in its choice-of-law decisions by the 'needs of the interstate and international system'. *Id.* at 614. He thought that, because of its international origins, the traditional system was overtaken by 'the compulsion of internationalist and altruist ideals'; it had 'guiltily suppressed the natural instincts of community self-interest . . . [and] enforce[d] a purposeless self-denial'. *Id.* at 525. To compensate for this, Currie championed 'the rational, moderate and controlled pursuit of self-interest'. *Id.* These adjectives offered some reassurance, as did his statements that '[t]he short-sighted, selfish state is nothing more than an experimental model', and that '[n]o such state exists, at least in this country'. *Id.* at 616. Nevertheless, both the whole tenor and many of the specifics of his theory were far less moderate.
2. Currie argued that a state has an interest in applying its pro-plaintiff rules only for the benefit of local plaintiffs and its pro-defendant rules only for the benefit of local defendants. *See id.* at 691–721 (arguing that New York's unlimited compensatory-damages law 'is not for the

protection of all who buy tickets in New York, or board planes there. It is for the protection of New York people'.) and *id.* at 724, and 85–86 (arguing that a state that has a guest statute or a pro-defendant contract rule has an interest in applying them only if the defendants are domiciled in that state).

3. *See* B. Currie, *Selected Essays*, *supra* at 610 (stating that Currie found 'no place in conflict-of-laws analysis for a calculus of private interests [because] [b]y the time the interstate plane is reached the resolution of conflicting private interests has been achieved; it is subsumed in the statement of the laws of the respective states'.).
4. *See* J. Ely, 'Choice of Law and the State's Interest in Protecting its Own', 23 *Wm. & Mary L. Rev.*, 1981, 173. Anticipating these criticisms, Currie argued, in essence, that his theory was not unconstitutional because the Constitution would not allow it to be. *See* B. Currie, *Selected Essays* at 123–126, 185, 191, 280, 285 (stating that the Equal Protection and Privileges and Immunities clauses of the Constitution would help control undue protectionism), and at 271, 280–281, 191 (stating that the Due Process and Full Faith and Credit clauses would help control excessive forum favouritism). Ironically, Currie was correct in the sense that: (1) the Supreme Court does not judge the constitutionality of theories in the abstract, but rather limits itself to deciding whether the application of a theory in the particular case produces an unconstitutional result (*see supra* 92); and (2) knowing this, reasonable courts will be careful not to apply Currie's theory in an unconstitutional manner, and thus the theory will not be found unconstitutional.

E. False, True and In-Between Conflicts

181. In Currie's view, when a litigant argues that the court should apply foreign law to a multistate case, the court should first inquire into the policies embodied in the laws of the involved states, asking whether it is reasonable for each state to assert an interest in applying its respective law to effectuate its policies. This inquiry may lead to three possibilities, which in turn correspond to the three well-known (if not well-accepted) categories of conflicts:

1. only one of the involved states is interested in applying its law (the 'false conflict' pattern);
2. more than one state is interested (the 'true conflict' pattern); or
3. none of the states are interested (the 'no-interest' pattern or 'unprovided-for case').[1]

To be sure, whether a conflict falls into one or the other categories is a question that different analysts often answer differently. Even accepting the concept of state interests in the abstract, there is plenty of room for disagreement on whether a state has an interest in the particular case, to say nothing of measuring the strength of that interest. Nevertheless, the above three categories are useful in providing a common vocabulary and a framework for analysis and they have been accepted in the literature beyond interest analysis.

1. In his later work, Currie recognized a fourth category, what he called an 'apparent conflict', which is something between a false and a true conflict. In his words, an apparent conflict is a case in which 'each state would be constitutionally justified in asserting an interest, but on reflection the conflict is avoided by a moderate definition of the policy or interest of one state or the other', or 'a case in which reasonable men may disagree on whether a conflicting interest should be asserted', B. Currie, 'The Disinterested Third State', 28 *Law & Contemp. Probs.*, 1963, 754, 763, 764.

182. As explained below, Currie argued that, subject only to constitutional restraints, the forum is entitled to, and should, apply its law to all of the above cases, except those false and apparent conflicts in which the forum has no real interest in applying its law.

183. In false conflicts, Currie would apply the law of the only interested state, which in the majority of cases is likely to be the forum state. This part of Currie's analysis is neither controversial nor controvertible, at least for those who subscribe to the view that consideration of state interests is a proper starting point for resolving conflicts of laws. In contrast to the traditional theory which, by failing to inquire into state interests, had the propensity to randomly sacrifice the interests of one state without promoting the interests of another state, Currie's solution to an admittedly false conflict can effectuate the policies of an interested state without sacrificing any policies of an uninterested state. In this sense, the concept of a false conflict was an important breakthrough in American choice-of-law thinking, and has become an integral part of all modern policy-based analyses.

184. However, Currie's solutions to the other categories of conflicts are questionable. Under Currie's analysis, true conflicts are to be resolved by the application of the law of the forum, because a court may not subordinate the forum's interests to those of another state.[1] Indeed, the very possibility of such a subordination impelled Currie to insist that judges should not even attempt to weigh the interests of the two states. His explanation was that judges do not have the constitutional power or the requisite resources to weigh conflicting governmental interests, and should not be put in the position of potentially subordinating the forum's interests. Currie thought that interest-weighing is a 'political function of a very high order . . . that should not be committed to courts in a democracy'.[2]

1. *See* B. Currie, 'Comments on *Babcock* v. *Jackson* – A Recent Development in Conflict of Laws', 63 *Colum. L. Rev.*, 1963, 1233, 1237–1238.
2. B. Currie, *Selected Essays* at 182. In one of his last writings, Currie advised that in some cases the judge should subject the laws of the involved states to a more moderate and restrained interpretation, which could lead to the conclusion that one of those states is not as interested as it might appear at first blush. If so, this would be an 'apparent conflict' to which the judge should apply the law of the other state. Currie contended that this process of re-evaluating the two states' interests is qualitatively different from weighing those interests. *Id.* at 759.

185. In light of Currie's proud adherence to the common law tradition, the above explanation is surprising in that it assumes a conception of the judicial process that does not reflect the realities of the American common law tradition, in which judges routinely evaluate and weigh conflicting social policies. Currie's explanation also contradicts the basic tenets of his theory, which all other respects assumes an activist judge. For example, according to Currie's own analysis, in order to determine whether the conflict is false or true, the judge must identify and articulate the interests of the involved states. The judicial application of this part of Currie's analysis suggests that this task is no less subjective or politically sensitive than the weighing of interests. The two tasks differ only in degree. If judges are empowered and qualified to articulate a governmental interest, they can also weigh it. Stated another way, the distance between articulating an interest and evaluating it is very short, at least when the evaluator is also the articulator.

186. Finally, under Currie's analysis, the law of the forum applies to his third category of conflicts – the 'unprovided-for' or 'no-interest' cases – even though in these cases the forum is, *ex hypothesi*, a disinterested state. Currie's explanation for applying the law of the forum is that 'no good purpose will be served by putting the parties to the expense and the court to the trouble of ascertaining the foreign law'.[1] This is a practical explanation. Unfortunately, it overlooks the problem grammarians call *prothysteron*: one cannot know whether the case is a no-interest case without first knowing whether the foreign state is uninterested; and one cannot know whether that state is uninterested without first ascertaining the content of its law and identifying the policies underlying it.

1. *Id.* at 152–156.

F. Forum Favouritism

187. In sum, under Currie's analysis, almost all roads lead to the *lex fori*. Currie would apply foreign law in only two situations, both of which are fairly infrequent: *(a)* false conflicts in which the forum is an uninterested state; and *(b)* apparent conflicts in which the judge chooses to subject the law of the forum, rather than that of the foreign state, to a restrained interpretation. In all other cases, Currie would apply the *lex fori*, to wit: *(1)* in a false conflict in which the forum is the interested state; *(2)* in a true conflict in which the forum is one of the interested states; *(3)* in the no-interest or unprovided-for case; and *(4)* even in a true conflict before a disinterested forum, if the court cannot dismiss on grounds of *forum non conveniens*.

188. Currie defended his forum favouritism with arguments ranging from the practical to the philosophical.[1] Many commentators remained unpersuaded. As one of them noted, 'Currie's analysis, which compels him to give to the forum's law such broad effects, would tend to fasten upon the international and the inter-state communities . . . a legal order characterized by chaos and retaliation'.[2]

1. *See*, e.g., *id.* at 89, 93–94, 191, 197, 278–280, 323, 447, 489–490, 592, 627, 697.
2. A. von Mehren, 'Book Review', 17 *J. Legal Edu.* 91, 1964, 97 note 2.

G. Currie's Contribution

189. Currie's theory dominated choice-of-law thinking in the United States for almost three decades. His 'seductive style' of writing 'hypnotized a whole generation of American lawyers',[1] perhaps in the same way that Beale's teachings had indoctrinated the previous generation. Currie's judicial following has decreased dramatically in recent years. However, his analysis 'still controls the academic conflicts agenda',[2] perhaps because this analysis remains the most popular pedagogical vehicle for teaching conflicts law in American law schools and 'interest analysis is the very language of contemporary conflicts theory'.[3]

1. H. Korn, 'The Choice-of-Law Revolution: A Critique', 83 *Colum. L. Rev.* 772, 1983, 812.
2. F. Juenger, 'Conflict of Laws: A Critique of Interest Analysis', 32 *Am. J. Comp. L.* 1, 1984, 4.
3. L. Weinberg, 'Theory Wars in the Conflict of Laws', 103 *Mich. L. Rev.* 1631, 2005, 1649.

190. In recent years, Currie's critics clearly outnumber his allies, old and new. Although there is much to criticize in Currie's theory, there is also much that deserves praise. Some of Currie's critics have focussed more on debunking his theory than on separating its tenable elements from the untenable. Even if the latter elements outnumber the former, Currie's overall contribution to the advancement of American conflicts law is a decidedly positive one, if only because he stirred the stagnant waters of the 'dismal swamp' of American conflicts law. In fact Currie did much more. His analysis was intentionally provocative and unintentionally extreme. However, in its basic core of making state interests the basis for resolving conflict of laws, Currie's analysis was both new to American conflicts law and fundamentally correct.

III. Comparative Impairment

191. Professor William F. Baxter's 'comparative impairment' theory took interest analysis to the next step, or perhaps in a different direction.[1] Baxter agreed with Currie on two points, on the process of identifying and resolving false conflicts, and on the impropriety of weighing interests as a means of resolving true conflicts.[2] Baxter did not, however, accept Currie's view that the application of the *lex fori* is the only possible solution for true conflicts. Baxter argued that a 'normative resolution of real conflicts cases is possible', and that an examination of the basic premises underlying the federal system would reveal 'normative principles which could and should serve as a foundation for choice-of-law rules'.[3] To this end, Baxter proposed his 'comparative impairment' formula.

Baxter distinguished between two types of governmental interests or objectives – the 'internal' and the 'external'. Internal objectives are those underlying each state's resolution of conflicting private interests in wholly domestic situations. The external objectives embody each state's goal 'to make effective in all situations involving persons as to whom it has responsibility for legal ordering, the resolution of contending private interests the state has made for local purposes'.[4] In a true conflict, *ex hypothesi*, this external objective conflicts with the corresponding external objective of a foreign state. Rather than subordinating the external objective of the foreign state to that of the forum (as would Currie), Baxter suggests 'subordinat[ing] . . . the external objective of the state whose internal objective will be least impaired in general scope and impact by subordination in cases like the one at hand'.[5] Put simply, Baxter would apply the law of that state whose interests would be most impaired if its law were not applied.

1. *See* W. Baxter, 'Choice of Law and the Federal System', 16 *Stan. L. Rev.* 1, 1963.
2. *See id.* at 8, 5–6, 18–19. Echoing Currie, Baxter stated that weighing of interests involves super-value judgments that are incompatible with the judge's 'non-political status'.

3. *Id.* at 8–9.
4. *Id.* at 18.
5. *Id.*

192. In essence, rather than weighing the interests, comparative impairment weighs the loss that would result from subordinating the interests of one state to those of another state. However, inasmuch as the gravity of the loss depends on the strength and importance of each state's interest, one cannot avoid the conclusion that comparative impairment does weigh the interests. This statement is not a criticism of comparative impairment. Weighing of state interests is an appropriate, if not inevitable, means of resolving conflicts in any approach that acknowledges the existence of state interests. The question is not whether courts can or should weigh state interests, but rather how to weigh them, and how to resolve the resulting conflicts.

IV. Leflar and the 'Better Law' Approach

193. Despite their criticism of the traditional theory in other respects, Cook, Currie, and to a lesser extent Cavers, remained within the confines of the classical view of PIL in one core respect – they subscribed to the same basic premise that the goal of conflicts law is to achieve 'the spatially best solution'[1] ('conflicts justice'), rather than 'the *materially* best solution'[2] ('material justice'). In contrast, Professor Robert A. Leflar was among the first proponents of the material-justice view in the United States. In two successive law review articles,[3] Leflar proposed a non-hierarchical list of five choice-influencing considerations to guide courts in resolving conflicts problems. The list consisted of: (1) predictability of results; (2) maintenance of interstate and international order; (3) simplification of the judicial task; (4) advancement of the forum's governmental interest; and (5) the application of the 'better rule of law'. Leflar argued that, by using these considerations, 'courts can replace with statements of real reasons the mechanical rules and circuitously devised approaches which have appeared in the language of conflicts opinions, too often as cover-ups for the real reason that underlay the decisions'.[4]

1. G. Kegel, 'Paternal Home and Dream Home: Traditional Conflict of Laws and the American Reformers', 27 *Am. J. Comp. L.* 615, 1979, 616–617.
2. *Id.*
3. *See* R. Leflar, 'Choice-Influencing Considerations in Conflicts Law', 41 *N.Y.U. L. Rev.* 367, 1966; R. Leflar, 'Conflicts of Law: More on Choice Influencing Considerations', 54 *Cal. L. Rev.* 1584, 1966.
4. R. Leflar, 54 *Cal. L. Rev.* at 1585.

194. As the above list indicates, there is much more to Leflar's approach than the 'better-law' criterion, which in his words 'is only one of five, more important in some types of cases than in others, almost controlling in some but irrelevant in others'.[1] Even so, nothing prevents the better-law criterion from becoming decisive in all those cases (and they are many) in which the other four considerations are not dispositive. This is precisely how courts employed this criterion (at least in the early years), while paying lip service to the other four. Moreover, but for the better-law criterion, Leflar's list differs little from the lists proposed by others or from the list of Section 6 of the Restatement (Second). Consequently, Leflar's approach is deservedly known as 'the better-law approach' and may be criticized or praised on that basis. The main criticisms are that a better-law approach can become a euphemism for a *lex fori* approach and that it provides convenient cover for judicial subjectivism. Although Leflar admonished against subjective choices, arguing that judges are capable of recognizing when foreign law is better than forum law,[2] there is considerable evidence to support the conclusion that these risks are real.[3]

1. R. Leflar, L. McDougal & R. Felix, *American Conflicts Law* (4th edn 1986), p. 300.
2. *See id.* at 298–299 ('Judges can appreciate . . . the fact that their forum law in some areas is anachronistic . . . or that the law of another state has these benighted characteristics').
3. *See infra* 243–247.

V. The First Synthesis: The Second Conflicts Restatement

195. In 1953, the American Law Institute (ALI) began drafting the Restatement (Second), partly in response to the challenge of the conflicts revolution. The task of Reporter was assigned to Professor Willis L. Reese, who was a member of the new school of conflicts thought, although not of its revolutionary branch. Reese agreed with many of the criticisms levelled against the First Restatement, but more importantly, he was receptive to the criticisms of his own drafts of the Restatement (Second). A cursory look at the successive versions of what eventually became Section 6 of the Restatement (Second) reveals an evolution in the Reporter's own thinking, as well as the gradual gains of the new school over the old. The final version of the Restatement (Second), promulgated in 1969, did not join the revolution, but was a conscious compromise and synthesis between the old and new schools (and among the various branches of the new schools).

A. *Section Six*

196. The cornerstone of the Restatement (Second) is Section 6. It instructs the court to consider the following factors in searching for the applicable law: *(a)* the needs of the interstate and international systems; *(b)* the relevant policies of the forum; *(c)* the relevant policies of other interested states and their interests in applying their law to the particular issue; *(d)* the protection of justified party expectations; *(e)* the basic policies underlying the particular field of law; *(f)* the objectives of certainty, predictability, and uniformity of result; and *(g)* the ease in determining and applying the governing law.[1]

1. American Law Institute, *Restatement (Second) of Conflict of Laws* §6(2).

197. From a philosophical perspective, Section 6 is important in that it enunciates the Restatement's ideology, distinguishing it from other modern theories such as that of Leflar or Currie. For example, the 'better-law' criterion is noticeably absent from the factors listed in Section 6. Moreover, the list of Section 6 is broader and qualitatively different from the policies relied upon by Currie, whose analysis disregards, de-emphasizes, or expressly rejects most of the Section 6 factors, except the policies of the forum and other involved states. The contrast between interest analysis and the Restatement is most apparent in the varying degrees of sensitivity towards 'the needs of the interstate and international systems' and the need for 'uniformity of result'. To Currie's ethnocentric attitude toward both of these goals, the Restatement juxtaposes a universalistic conception of private international law reflected in the statement that 'the most important function of choice-of-law rules is to make the interstate and international systems work well[,] . . . to further harmonious relations between states and to facilitate commercial intercourse between them'.[1] The contrast is hardly surprising. Unlike interest analysis – which Currie conceived from the perspective of the forum judge confined to the role of the 'handmaiden' of the forum legislature – the Restatement was drafted from the perspective of a neutral forum under the auspices of the American Law Institute, a body that strives for national uniformity.

1. *Restatement (Second)* §6, cmt. d.

198. From a methodological viewpoint, Section 6 is important in that it provides a guiding, as well as a validating, test for applying almost all other sections of the Restatement, most of which incorporate Section 6 by reference.[1] Because the Section 6 factors are not listed in a hierarchical order, and in fact they may point in different directions in a given case,[2] they fall short of providing an actual choice of law for the court. Nevertheless, these factors can help steer courts away from a jurisdiction-selecting choice based solely on factual contacts. Although the specific sections of the Restatement call for the application of the law of the state with the 'most significant relationship' – a term that evokes jurisdiction-selecting notions – the choice of that state is to be made 'under the principles stated in §6',[3] and by taking into account the contacts listed in the specific sections. By constantly repeating this cross-reference to Section 6, the Restatement supplements the multilateral approach used in most other Restatement sections with elements from a unilateral approach.

1. *See*, e.g., *id.* at §145 (providing that a tort issue is governed by the law of the state that, with respect to that issue, has the most significant relationship to the occurrence and the parties 'under the principles stated in §6'.).
2. *Id.* at §6, cmt. (c).
3. *Id.* at §145.

B. The 'Most Significant Relationship'

199. The 'most-significant-relationship' formula is the other cornerstone of the Restatement (Second). While Section 6 articulates the principles and policies that should guide the choice-of-law process, the ubiquitous most-significant-relationship formula describes the objective of that process – to apply the law of the state that, with regard to the particular issue, has the most significant relationship with the parties and the dispute. This catch phrase resembles both Savigny's 'seat' of a legal relationship, and more recent European catch phrases, such as the state with the 'closest' or 'strongest' connection. However, the similarities are only terminological. The Restatement is built around narrowly defined 'issues' rather than entire legal relationships, and requires an individualized issue-by-issue analysis with the concomitant un-Savignian possibility of *dépeçage*. Furthermore, as noted above, the Restatement's approach is a blend of multilateralism and unilateralism. Finally, although acoustically the Restatement's catch phrase may suggest otherwise, the state of the most significant relationship is not to be chosen by the quantity or even the closeness of its factual contacts, but rather 'under the principles stated in §6', which include consideration of the policies and interests of the contact states. Herein lies an essential difference between the Restatement and one of its precursor movements, the 'center of gravity' or 'significant-contacts' approach.

C. Rules

200. In relatively few cases, primarily in the areas of property and successions, the Restatement identifies *a priori* the state of the most significant relationship through black-letter rules.[1] In cases involving land, the applicable law is almost invariably the 'law that would be applied by the courts of the *situs*'.[2] This is as close as the Restatement comes to prescribing black-letter choice-of-law rules. These rules are subject to the traditional generic escape mechanisms, such as *ordre public* and *renvoi*. For example, the above-quoted phrase regarding land is an explicit authorization for *renvoi*, which contains the potential for applying, in appropriate cases, a law other than that of the *situs* state.

1. *See id.* §§260–265 (succession to movables); §§245–255 (*inter vivos* transactions involving movables). *See also* the unilateral choice-of-law rules contained in §§285 (divorce), 286 (nullity of marriage), and 289 (adoption).
2. *See id.* §§223, 225–232 (*inter vivos* transactions involving land); §§236, 239–242 (succession to land). This phrase is often accompanied by the prediction that these courts 'usually' will apply their own law.

D. Presumptive Rules

201. In other cases, the Restatement identifies the state of the most significant relationship only tentatively through presumptive rules that instruct the judge to apply the law of a certain state, unless it appears that in the particular case another state has a more significant relationship. For example, all ten of the Restatement sections that designate the law applicable to different types of torts conclude with the escape clause: 'unless, with respect to the particular issue, some other state has a more significant relationship under the principles stated in §6 to the occurrence and the parties, in which event the local law of the other state will be applied'.[1] This clause is repeated throughout the entire Restatement.[2]

1. *See*, e.g., *id.* §152 which provides that, in an action for an invasion of privacy, the applicable law is the local law of the state where the invasion occurred, 'unless, with respect to the particular issue, some other state has a more significant relationship'.
2. *See*, e.g., *id.* §§146–151, 153–155, 175. In the area of contract conflicts, the 'unless' clause appears in most of the sections devoted to particular contracts. *See*, e.g., §§189–193, 196.

E. Pointers

202. In some instances, the presumptive rules are even more equivocal, and amount to no more than mere 'pointers' directing to the presumptively applicable law. The pertinent sections provide that the state with the most significant relationship will 'usually' be one particular state.

For example, in tort conflicts, eleven of the nineteen sections devoted to specific tort issues conclude with the adage that the applicable law will 'usually be the local law of the state where the injury occurred';[1] one section provides that for intra-family immunity the applicable law 'will usually be the local law of the state of the parties' domicil';[2] and only the remaining seven sections are unaided by such a presumption.[3]

In contract conflicts, the Restatement provides that, subject to some exceptions, 'if the place of negotiating the contract and the place of performance are in the same state, its local law will 'usually be applied';[4] that the capacity of a party to contract will 'usually be upheld if he has such capacity under the local law of the state of his domicil';[5] and that contractual formalities that meet the requirements of *locus contractus* will 'usually be acceptable'.[6] Similar language is found in other sections of the Restatement.

1. *See id.* §156 (tortious character of conduct); §157 (standard of care); §158 (interest entitled to legal protection); §159 (duty owed to plaintiff); §160 (legal cause); §162 (specific conditions of liability); §164 (contributory fault); §165 (assumption of risk); §166 (imputed negligence); and §172 (joint torts) (Emphasis added).
2. *Id.* §169.
3. *Id.* §§161, 163, 168, 170–171, and 173–174.
4. *Id.* §188.
5. *Id.* §198.
6. *Id.* §199.

F. Ad Hoc Analysis

203. In the remaining and most difficult cases, the Restatement (Second) does not even attempt to enunciate presumptive rules. It simply provides a non-exclusive, non-hierarchical list of the factual contacts or connecting factors that should be 'taken into account' by the judge in choosing the applicable law. This choice is to be made 'under the principles stated in §6' by 'taking into account' the above factual contacts 'according to their relative importance with respect to the particular issue'.[1] This language suggests that the policy part of this analysis should carry more weight than the evaluation of the factual contacts.

Yet, courts tend to do the opposite. They first focus on the factual contacts listed in the pertinent section of the Restatement, and then, if at all, on the policies of Section 6. When the contacts of one state are clearly more numerous than those of another state, some courts tend to assume that the first state has the more significant relationship without testing that assumption under the principles of Section 6. In contrast, when the factual contacts are split evenly between the two states, courts look to the policies of Section 6, but many courts consider only two of the policies listed in that section – 'the relative policies of the forum' and of 'other interested states'.[2] It seems that the first type of practise differs little from a 'grouping of contacts' approach, while the latter type of practise differs little from interest analysis.

1. *See*, e.g., *id.* §§145, 188.
2. *Id.* §6.

§3. The Judicial Revolution in Torts and Contracts

I. Introduction

204. The scholastic dissent from the established conflicts system described above is interesting, but it would have been inconsequential had it not been followed by a similar dissent in the judicial ranks. Indeed, inspired in part by these academic commentators, many judges gradually questioned the premises of the established system and began to openly depart from it. This judicial movement away from the traditional approach is demonstrated by the initially gradual, and later not so gradual, erosion of two typical and important traditional choice-of-law rules – the *lex loci delicti* and the *lex loci contractus*.[1] This section chronicles this movement.

1. At the same time, it should be pointed out that most other traditional choice-of-law rules have survived the conflicts revolution virtually unscathed.

II. The Erosion of the *Lex Loci Delicti* Rule

205. Although revolutions often appear to erupt overnight, discerning eyes can see the harbingers long before the actual eruption. The same was true of the conflicts revolution. Conflicts casebooks are replete with cases in which courts created exceptions to, or openly manipulated, the *lex loci delicti* rule. Many of these cases spoke in language that was indicative of later developments.

As noted in Part II, Chapter 2,[1] *Levy* v. *Daniels' U-Drive Auto Renting Co.*, and *Haumschild* v. *Continental Cas. Co.* are correctly cited as examples of manipulative characterization, but they were also harbingers of things to come. Each of these cases spoke of the policies or purposes of the substantive rules involved in the conflict. Similarly, *Grant* v. *McAuliffe* and *Kilberg* v. *Northeast Airlines, Inc.* are correctly cited as examples of a misuse of the substance versus procedure dichotomy, but they also exemplified the courts' increasing impatience with the fortuitous way in which the *lex loci delicti* rule operated. Finally, although seemingly unrelated, *Lauritzen* v. *Larsen*[2] was a cue from the US Supreme Court that reliance on multiple factors was not only acceptable, but also preferable to reliance on a single connecting factor for selecting the law applicable to tort conflicts.

1. *See supra* 128.
2. 345 US 571 (1953) (discussed *infra* 675–676; enunciating a multifactor test for delineating the extraterritorial application of the Jones Act and selecting the law governing certain maritime torts).

A. *Babcock* v. *Jackson*

206. For all practical purposes, the revolution began in 1963 with the seminal New York case of *Babcock* v. *Jackson*,[1] the first case to openly abandon the traditional *lex loci delicti* rule. *Babcock* arose out of a single-car accident in Ontario, Canada, which resulted in injury to a New York domiciliary who was a guest-passenger in a car driven by a New York host-driver, and insured and garaged in New York. New York law allowed the passenger to bring a tort action against the host-driver, whereas Ontario's 'guest statute' immunized the driver and his insurer from suits brought by a gratuitous guest-passenger.

The *Babcock* court resolved the resulting conflict by enunciating a new approach for tort conflicts that drew from the 'center of gravity' approach, but also went much farther. The court described the new approach as one based on a '[c]omparison of the relative "contacts" and "interests"'[2] of the involved states. The court asked the rhetorical question of whether 'the place of the tort [should] invariably govern the availability of relief for the tort or [whether] the applicable choice of law rule [should] also reflect a consideration of other factors which are relevant to the purposes served by the enforcement or denial of the remedy'.[3] The court ultimately answered the question by deciding to apply the law of the state which, 'because of its *relationship* or contact with the occurrence of the parties, has the *greatest concern* with the *specific issue* raised in the litigation'.[4] The italicized phrases illuminate the four important elements of the court's approach, discussed below.

1. 191 N.E.2d 279 (N.Y. 1963).
2. *Id.* at 284.
3. *Id.* at 280–281 (first emphasis in original, second emphasis added).
4. *Id.* at 283 (emphasis added).

1. Issue-by-Issue Analysis

207. First, the word 'invariably' suggests that the court did not seek a wholesale abandonment of the *lex loci* rule, but rather a narrowing of its scope depending on the particular issue on which the laws of the involved states actually conflicted. Here the conflict was confined to a single issue – the driver's immunity from suit because of the Ontario guest-statute, and the absence of such a statute in New York. The court was no longer thinking in broad global terms, such as whether the problem at hand should be characterized as one of tort or contract, or which law should apply to the tort as a whole. Rather, the court isolated the particular issue and focussed its analysis on the actually conflicting laws.

208. This 'issue-by-issue analysis' was a return to the familiar schemes of common-law decision making – temporarily submerged by Bealian systematics – which is characterized by small, cautious steps of inductive reasoning. At least in the abstract, this method of analysis is more conducive to a nuanced, individualized, and thus more rational, resolution of conflicts problems. This is why this analysis has become an integral feature of all modern policy-based approaches.

2. *Dépeçage*

209. One of the reasons *Babcock* was an easy case was because it involved a conflict with regard to only one issue. When a case, or more precisely a cause of action, involves conflicts with regard to more than one issue, then the court is to analyze each conflict separately. Depending on the circumstances, this analysis may lead to the conclusion that: (a) one state is interested in applying its law to all issues; or (b) one state is interested in one issue, while another state is interested in another issue. In the latter situation, if the court applies the laws of the each state to the issue in which each state is respectively interested, the resulting phenomenon is called *dépeçage*.

210. Today, *dépeçage* is widely practised by American courts. It is neither a choice-of-law 'doctrine' nor a goal of the choice-of-law process. Rather, it is the often unintended result of the abandonment of the traditional theory's broad categories and the adoption of issue-by-issue analysis. It is also a natural consequence, and an appropriate recognition, of the fact that the states involved in the case may be interested in different aspects or in varying degrees. As such, *dépeçage* is, *per se*, neither good nor bad. However, in some cases the application of the law of two different states to different issues in the same case may unintentionally defeat the policies of both states. In such cases, *dépeçage* is inappropriate and must be avoided.

3. The Distinction between Loss-Distribution and Conduct-Regulation Issues

211. Because *Babcock* was a single-issue conflict, the court did not need to engage in *dépeçage* in the sense of actually applying the laws of two different states. However, the *Babcock* court clearly signalled its willingness to engage in *dépeçage* by stating in dictum that it would have reached a different conclusion with regard to Ontario's interest 'had the issue related to the manner in which the defendant had been driving his car at the time of the accident . . . [or to] the defendant's exercise of due care'.[1]

1. *Id.* at 284.

212. At the same time, through this dictum, the court enunciated a distinction between, on the one hand, issues of regulation of conduct, such as 'whether the defendant offended against a rule of the road prescribed by Ontario for motorists generally or whether he violated some standard of conduct imposed by that jurisdiction and, on the other hand, issues like those actually involved in *Babcock*, namely, 'whether the plaintiff, because she was a guest in the defendant's automobile, is barred from recovering damages for a wrong concededly committed'.[1] The latter issues are hereinafter referred to as 'issues of loss distribution'. They include guest-statutes such as Ontario's in *Babcock*, as well as New York's opposite common-law rule which provided recovery to the victim despite her status as a gratuitous guest, rules eliminating or limiting the defendant's liability, such as rules of intrafamily or charitable immunity, or rules imposing a ceiling on the amount of recovery. With regard to conduct-regulation issues, the court stated that the state in which the conduct occurred 'will usually have a predominant, if not exclusive, concern' and that 'it would be almost unthinkable to seek the applicable rule in the law of some other place'.[2] Thus, according to *Babcock*, rules that regulate conduct operate territorially. In contrast, rules that regulate loss distribution, do not necessarily operate territorially.

1. *Id.*
2. *Id.*

213. As we shall see later, the distinction between conduct-regulating rules and loss-distributing rules is conceptually easy, but often it is difficult to apply in practise. Not only do reasonable people disagree about whether a particular rule falls within the one category or the other, but they often agree that a given rule of law may both regulate conduct and effect or affect loss distribution. *Babcock* assumed that a guest statute does not affect a driver's conduct in that a driver does not drive differently depending on whether the state in which she drives has a guest statute. If this assumption is correct, then this is another reason for which *Babcock* was an easy case.

4. Policy Analysis

214. According to *Babcock*, the search for the applicable law should take account of more factors and contacts than the place of the tort and should include the overall relationship of each involved state with the occurrence and the parties. More importantly, the search should seek to identify the state that, because of this relationship and the 'purposes' sought to be served by its laws, has the 'greatest concern' with regard to the specific issue in dispute. Thus, *Babcock* introduced a policy-based analysis going beyond the 'center-of-gravity' approach enunciated earlier in *Auten*.

The *Babcock* court identified the policies underlying the respective rules of Ontario and New York, and then examined whether the application of each rule would further its underlying purpose or policy. Assuming that the purpose of the Ontario guest statute was to protect insurers – and only Ontario insurers – from collusion between drivers and their gratuitous guests, the court concluded that the application of the statute would not further its purpose in this case, which did not involve an Ontario insurer. Thus, Ontario was 'not interested' in applying that statute.

Conversely, assuming that the policy underlying New York's refusal to enact a guest-statute was to compensate traffic-accident victims regardless of their status as gratuitous guests, the court concluded that the application of New York law to this case, which involved a New York victim injured by a New York driver, would further this policy by allowing a New York victim to recover damages. Hence, New York was interested in applying its law, and since Ontario was not, this was a false conflict which the court resolved by applying the law of the only interested state – New York.

B. After Babcock

215. Since *Babcock*, 41 other jurisdictions have followed New York's lead and abandoned the *lex loci delicti* rule in the following chronological order: Pennsylvania (1964); Wisconsin (1965); Minnesota, New Hampshire, and Puerto Rico (1966); California, District of Columbia, Kentucky, New Jersey, and Oregon (1967); Alaska, Arizona, Iowa, Mississippi, and Rhode Island (1968); Missouri (1969); Illinois, Maine (1970); North Dakota (1972); Colorado and Louisiana (1973); Oklahoma, and Washington (1974); Massachusetts (1976); Arkansas (1977); Texas (1979); Florida (1980); Hawaii (1981); Michigan (1982); Ohio (1984); Idaho (1985); Connecticut (1986); Indiana, and Nebraska (1987); Utah (1989); Delaware (1991); South Dakota, and Tennessee (1992); Nevada (1996); Vermont (1997); and Montana (2000).[1] Sixteen of those states made this move during the 1960s, thus establishing that decade as the decade of the conflicts revolution. The equipoise point was 1977, at which time as many jurisdictions (26) adhered to the *lex loci* rule as had abandoned it.

By the time of this writing (in 2007), a total of 42 jurisdictions had abandoned the *lex loci delicti* rule, while ten states appeared to adhere to it.[2]

1. For citations and details, *see* S. Symeonides, *The Choice-of-Law Revolution* 39–43.
2. The latter states are listed *supra* 123.

III. The Erosion of the *Lex Loci Contractus* Rule

216. In contract conflicts, the first abandonment of the *lex loci contractus* rule occurred as early as 1945, in the Indiana case of *W. H. Barber Co.* v. *Hughes*.[1] *Barber* employed 'a method used by modern teachers of Conflict of Laws in rationalizing the results obtained by the courts in decided cases' called the 'center of gravity'[2] approach. Nine years later, the New York Court of Appeals employed the same approach in *Auten* v. *Auten*.[3]

Although *Auten* is generally considered as the beginning of the revolution in contract conflicts, it did not garner a following until the 1960s. Even then, dissension from the *lex loci contractus* rule was slow. Since *Auten* the following jurisdictions abandoned this rule in the years indicated: New York (1945); Puerto Rico (1961); Oregon (1964); California, Washington (1967); Idaho, New Hampshire, Vermont, Wisconsin (1968); District of Columbia (1969); Arizona, Delaware (1970); Iowa, Kentucky (1977); Missouri (1978); Arkansas, Colorado, Illinois, Minnesota (1979); Mississippi, New Jersey (1980); Maine, Pennsylvania (1983); Ohio, Texas (1984); Massachusetts (1985); North Dakota (1986); Hawaii, North Carolina, West Virginia (1988); Louisiana (1992); Connecticut, Montana, Nebraska, Nevada, South Dakota (1994); Alaska, Michigan (1995) and Utah (1996).[4] The equipoise point was in 1985, when 27 jurisdictions had abandoned the *lex loci contractus* rule. By the time of this writing (in 2007), a total of forty jurisdictions had abandoned this rule, while twelve continued to adhere to it.[5]

1. 63 N.E.2d 417 (Ind. 1945).
2. *Id.* at 423.

3. 124 N.E.2d 99 (NY 1954).
4. For citations and other specifics, *see* S. Symeonides, *The Choice-of-Law Revolution* 43–48.
5. The latter states are listed *supra* 123.

§4. The Choice-of-Law Revolution Today

I. Introduction

217. The fact that the vast majority of states have abandoned the traditional system does not mean that they all follow the same approach to tort and contract conflicts. Indeed, the revolution did not consist of a single movement, but rather encompassed several parallel movements united only in their opposition to the old order. Therefore it is not surprising that the revolution did not produce a new choice-of-law system but rather several alternative approaches that continue to vie for judicial following. Among them, the Restatement (Second) attracts a slight majority of the states that abandoned the traditional system, but its application from state to state is by no means uniform. This section groups states by the approach or approaches they follow,[1] and discusses or cites a few representative cases from each group.

1. For caveats and qualifications regarding these groupings, *see* S. Symeonides, *The Choice-of-Law Revolution* 66–70.

II. The Restatement (Second)

218. The Restatement (Second) is by far the most popular among the modern methodologies. It is followed in 22 states for tort conflicts[1] and 24 states for contract conflicts.[2] The two lists are not identical in that a few states have adopted the Restatement for torts but not contracts, and *vice versa*. Florida and Tennessee follow the Restatement only in tort conflicts, whereas Kentucky, Michigan, New Hampshire, and West Virginia follow the Restatement only in contract conflicts. These divided loyalties are the result of deliberate choice in some instances and lack of a good opportunity in others.

1. These states are: Alaska, Arizona, Colorado, Connecticut, Delaware, Florida, Idaho, Illinois, Iowa, Maine, Mississippi, Missouri, Montana, Nebraska, Ohio, Oklahoma, South Dakota, Tennessee, Texas, Utah, Vermont, and Washington. For citations, *see* S. Symeonides, *The Choice-of-Law Revolution* 88–89.
2. These states are: Alaska, Arizona, Colorado, Connecticut, Delaware, Idaho, Illinois, Iowa, Kentucky, Maine, Michigan, Mississippi, Missouri, Montana, Nebraska, New Hampshire, Ohio, Oklahoma, South Dakota, Texas, Utah, Vermont, Washington, and West Virginia. For citations, *see* S. Symeonides, *The Choice-of-Law Revolution* 89–90.

219. In addition to the above states, many federal courts follow the Restatement (Second) in federal question cases.[1] Furthermore, on the issue of choice-of-law clauses, many states follow Section 187 of the Restatement, even if on other issues they follow other approaches, including the traditional approach.[2] Thus, three decades after its promulgation, the Restatement (Second) appears close to dominating the American methodological landscape. However, as explained elsewhere,[3] this high numerical following does not necessarily entail a deep-seated commitment to the Restatement. In many cases the Restatement simply offers the most convenient, and authoritative-sounding, rationalization for results that the court would have reached under any other modern methodology.[4] The Restatement's relative popularity can be attributed to varied reasons (some of which are not necessarily complimentary), including the following. The Restatement: (a) provides judges with virtually unlimited discretion and, as applied by some judges, it does not require hard thinking; (b) is not ideologically 'loaded'; (c) is a complete 'system'; (d) carries the prestige of the American Law Institute; and (e) has 'momentum'.[5]

1. For citations, *see* S. Symeonides, *The Choice-of-Law Revolution* 90.
2. *Id.*
3. *See* S. Symeonides, 'The Judicial Acceptance of the Second Conflicts Restatement: A Mixed Blessing', 56 *Md. L. Rev.* 1248, 1997, 1261–1263 (describing the various 'gradations of commitment' to the Restatement and suggesting several other qualifications for such classifications).
4. *See id.* at 1261–1273.
5. For explanation and discussion of these reasons, *see* S. Symeonides, *The Choice-of-Law Revolution* 91–96.

220. The Restatement's dominance of the American conflicts landscape is a mixed blessing for American conflicts law. Its contribution has been positive to the extent that it facilitated the abandonment of the traditional rules of *lex loci delicti* and *lex loci contractus* and of all the accompanying artificial and mechanical logic. It is true that persistent academic attacks had undermined the traditional theory even before the drafting of the Restatement's began (in 1953) and certainly before its official promulgation (in 1969). However, before 1953, these academic attacks had made only marginal inroads in judicial opinions. From 1953 on, these inroads began to increase and by 1966 five states had abandoned the traditional theory in tort conflicts. Although none of these states adopted the Restatement, its influence helped move the courts in that direction, as the *Babcock* court acknowledged.[1] More importantly, between 1967 and 1969, the years during which the ALI publicized the Proposed Official Drafts of the Restatement (Second), eleven more states abandoned the traditional theory and eight of them adopted these drafts.[2] Thus, although it did not cause the conflicts revolution, the Restatement (Second) was a major contributing factor in the cascading decisions of the courts in the 1960s and 1970s to abandon the traditional theory.

1. *See Babcock*, 12 N.Y.2d at 479, relying in part on the Restatement (Second) (Tentative Draft) (1960).
2. These states were: Kentucky, Oregon and the District of Columbia in 1967, Alaska, Arizona, Idaho and Mississippi in 1968, and Missouri in 1969. The first three states later abandoned the Restatement in favour of other approaches.

221. Naturally, whether the decision of these states to adopt the Restatement, rather than other modern approaches, is a positive development depends on one's opinion of the Restatement. Nevertheless, one positive contribution of the Restatement is that it has helped avoid polarization among American courts, and has laid the foundation for a new synthesis to grow out of competing choice-of-law theories.

Contrary to the First Restatement's rigidity and dogmatism, which caused the revolution, the Second Restatement's lack of dogmatism and flexible and compromissory content have helped spawn a benign, albeit uncertain, evolution. Had the Restatement (Second) aspired for ideological purity rather than philosophical pluralism, it would have pleased a few of its academic critics but it would have been far less attractive to judges. Its followers would have been more devoted but fewer in number, and the polarization among American courts would have been inevitable.

To date, this polarization has been avoided. As the majority of American courts abandoned the old dogma, they moved not in a single direction, but in parallel and in their view fungible directions, including the Restatement (Second). Unlike academics who focus on the differences between these directions, judges tend to overlook or ignore the differences and merge competing approaches. Although academic critics tend to vilify this eclecticism, it is a fact of life. One can continue to decry this phenomenon, or one can exploit its positive aspects. Perhaps this eclecticism can become the basis for a productive synthesis of the American conflicts experience and help prepare the ground for a third Restatement.[1]

1. *See* S. Symeonides, 'The Need for a Third Conflicts Restatement (and a Proposal for Tort Conflicts)', 75 *Ind. L.J.* 437, 2000. For different viewpoints, *see* 'Symposium: Preparing for the Next Century-A New Restatement of Conflicts', 75 *Ind. L.J.*, 2000, 399–686 (containing articles by Shreve, Juenger, Richman, Reynolds, Symeonides and Weinberg, and comments by Borchers, Dane, Gottesman, Hill, Maier, Peterson, Posnak, Reimann, Reppy, Sedler, Silberman, Lowenfeld, Simson, Singer, Twerski and Weintraub).

III. Significant-Contacts Approaches

222. The approach known as 'significant-contacts', 'grouping of contacts', or 'center of gravity' is followed by three jurisdictions in tort conflicts and by five in contract conflicts.[1] The above quoted terms are interchangeable and descriptive of this approach's reliance on physical contacts, rather than on state policies or interests. The state that has the 'most significant contacts' is the 'center of gravity' of the dispute, and thus its law governs, essentially regardless of its content or underlying policy.

When this approach first appeared in the 1950s,[2] it was a hopeful step in the right direction. By abandoning the traditional system's reliance on a single connecting factor and relying instead on multiple contacts, this approach opened the door to new and promising ways of thinking and began the transition from the traditional system to modern approaches. However, some states have chosen not to complete this transition, not even by switching to the Restatement (Second) which, although itself a transitional document, was the next logical step.

1. For torts, the three jurisdictions are: Indiana, North Dakota, and Puerto Rico. For contracts, the five jurisdictions are: Arkansas, Indiana, Nevada, Puerto Rico, and arguably North Carolina. Also, after many years of employing a policy-based approach, New York has partly reverted to the 'center of gravity' approach in contract conflicts. *See infra* 229.
2. The first case to employ this approach was *W. H. Barber Co.* v. *Hughes*, 63 N.E.2d 417, 423 (Ind. 1945), but *Auten* v. *Auten*, 124 N.E.2d 99 (N.Y. 1954) is the case that brought it to prominence.

223. One of the differences between these two approaches is that, although they both tend to consider the same contacts, the Restatement also requires a policy analysis by providing that the contacts must be evaluated 'in light of the policies of §6', which include the policies of the contact states, as well as multistate policies. In contrast, the significant-contacts approach does not require, and according to some courts does not even contemplate, examination of these policies, confining itself to a comparison of contacts alone. More troublesome still, it is rarely clear whether the court is looking for the most contacts or rather the most significant contacts. The comparison is supposed to be qualitative rather than quantitative, but even assuming that this is a meaningful exercise, few courts discharge it convincingly.

IV. The New York Experience

A. Tort Conflicts

224. In the years following *Babcock* v. *Jackson*, New York courts encountered several guest statute conflicts which they resolved in a less than consistent manner. To remedy this problem, the New York Court of Appeals took the next step, of pro-nouncing in a quasi-legislative fashion a new set of choice-of-law rules for guest-statute conflicts in the 1973 case *Neumeier* v. *Kuehner*.[1] These rules provide as follows:

> [Rule 1]. When the guest-passenger and the host-driver are domiciled in the same state, and the car is registered there, the law of that state should control and determine the standard of care which the host owes to his guest.
>
> [Rule 2a]. When the driver's conduct occurred in the state of his domicile and that state does not cast him in liability for that conduct, he should not be held liable by reason of the fact that liability would be imposed upon him under the tort law of the state of the victim's domicile. [Rule 2b]. Conversely, when the guest was injured in the state of his own domicile and its law permits recovery, the driver who has come into that state should not – in the absence of special circumstances – be permitted to interpose the law of his state as a defence.
>
> [Rule 3]. In other situations, when the passenger and the driver are domiciled in different states, the rule is necessarily less categorical. Normally, the applicable rule of decision will be that of the state where the accident occurred but not if it can be shown that displacing the normally applicable rule will advance the relevant substantive law purposes without impairing the smooth workings of the multi-state system or producing great uncertainty for litigants.[2]

1. 286 N.E.2d 454 (N.Y. 1972), *appeal after remand* 43 A.D.2d 109, 349 N.Y.S.2d 866 (1973).
2. *Neumeier*, 286 N.E.2d at 457–458.

225. *Neumeier*, like *Babcock*, arose out of a single-car accident in Ontario, Canada, involving a New York host-driver and a car insured and garaged in New York. The difference was that in *Neumeier* the guest-passenger was an Ontario domiciliary. Because of this difference, Rule 1 was inapplicable and the case fell within the scope of Rule 3, which calls for the application of Ontario law, subject to the escape provided in the rule. The court refused to apply the escape, reasoning that to displace the *lex loci* would not advance New York's 'substantive law purposes', and would impair the smooth functioning of the multi-state system by sanctioning forum shopping.

226. The next major case was *Schultz* v. *Boy Scouts of America, Inc.*[1] *Schultz* involved a fact pattern that was the reverse of *Babcock*. The plaintiffs and one of the defendants (Boy Scouts) were domiciled in New Jersey, the law of which accorded the Boy Scouts charitable immunity, whereas the injury was deemed to have occurred in New York, which did not accord such immunity. The court characterized the immunity rules as loss-distributing rather than as conduct-regulating, and concluded that the law of the parties' common domicile should govern this conflict.[2] Thus *Schultz* confirmed the applicability of the first *Neumeier* rule to cases of the reverse-*Babcock* pattern which, as we shall see later, are more difficult than the *Babcock*-pattern cases.

The second defendant, the Franciscan Brothers, had its domicile in Ohio. Because the parties were domiciled in different states, *Neumeier* Rule 1 was inapplicable. Rule 2 was also inapplicable because neither party was domiciled in a state whose law favoured that party. Thus, this case fell within the residual provisions of Rule 3, which calls for the application of the law of the state 'where the accident occurred', subject to an escape contained in that rule. The court chose to apply the escape, displacing the *lex loci* in favour of New Jersey law. The court reasoned that application of the law of New Jersey 'would further that State's interest in enforcing the decision of its domiciliaries to accept the burdens as well as the benefits of that State's loss-distributing tort rules and its interest in promoting the continuation and expansion of defendant's charitable activities in that State'.[3]

1. 480 N.E.2d 679 (N.Y. 1985).
2. *Id.* at 687. The court reasoned that application of the law of the parties' common domicile 'reduces forum-shopping opportunities . . . , rebuts charges that the forum-locus is biased in favor of its own law . . . , [furthers] mutuality and reciprocity [through] consistent application of the common-domicile law [and] produces a rule that is easy to apply and brings a modicum of predictability and certainty to an area of the law needing both'.
3. *Id.*

227. Although the substantive fairness of the *Schultz* result is open to intense debate, *Schultz* is important from a methodological perspective, for at least two reasons. It reaffirmed and solidified the *Babcock* distinction between conduct-regulating rules and loss-distributing rules,[1] and it expanded the scope of the *Neumeier* rules to encompass conflicts between loss-distribution rules other than the now obsolete guest statutes.

The latter development, however, created some new technical problems arising from the fact that the *Neumeier* rules did not differentiate between the place of injurious conduct and the place of the resulting injury. Indeed, such differentiation was unnecessary because the *Neumeier* rules were devised for guest-statute conflicts in which the driver's conduct and the guest's injury coincide in the same state. Thus, when the first sentence of *Neumeier* Rule 2 (hereafter 'Rule 2a') speaks of the 'driver's conduct', it presupposes that any injury resulting from that conduct will also occur in the same state. Likewise, when the second sentence of the same rule (hereafter 'Rule 2b') speaks of a 'guest [being] injured in the state of his own domicile', it assumes that the injury is the result of the host-driver's conduct and that this conduct also must have occurred in the same state. These assumptions are both natural and logical.

However, in many other torts, the conduct may occur in one state and the injury in another. By extending the scope of the *Neumeier* rules beyond guest-statute conflicts, the *Schultz* court made the rules applicable to cross-border torts. Besides other complications, these cases also raise the old question of 'localizing' the tort. Depending on which side of the border the 'locus of the tort' is placed determines which of the *Neumeier* rules is applicable and ultimately the outcome of the case. Unfortunately, the *Schultz* court did not elaborate on this question, apparently because the answer would not have affected the outcome in that case.

1. The importance of this distinction, both for New York and American conflicts law is discussed *infra* 263–270.

228. Eight years after *Schultz*, the localization problem reappeared in *Cooney* v. *Osgood Machinery, Inc.*,[1] a cross-border tort in which the disputants were joint tortfeasors domiciled in different states, with each state's law favouring that state's domiciliary.[2] The court found that the case 'presented a true conflict in the mold of Neumeier's second rule'[3] and concluded that '[u]nder that rule, the place of injury governs'.[4] This conclusory statement suggests that either the court did not recognize that, in cross-border torts, the two sentences of that rule conflict with each other or the court chose to resolve this conflict by arbitrarily opting for the state of injury. Even with this simplification, however, the second *Neumeier* rule could not easily resolve the *Cooney* conflict because it involved a dispute between joint tortfeasors and it was unclear which tortfeasor's conduct injured the other tortfeasor, and in which state.[5]

Indeed, without further refinement or modification, the *Neumeier* rules are ill-suited for cross-border torts, or for cases in which the dispute is not between the injured victim and the tortfeasor, but rather between joint tortfeasors.[6] The *Cooney* court may have recognized this deficiency, because it proceeded to resolve the conflict under a full-fledged policy analysis. After finding that the interests of the two states were 'irreconcilable', the court concluded that the place of the injury 'tips the balance'[7] and that the application of the law of the injury state 'is consistent with the result reached historically, and reflects application of a neutral factor that favours neither the forum's law nor its domiciliaries'.[8]

1. 612 N.E.2d 277 (N.Y. 1993).
2. *Cooney* arose out of an employment accident in Missouri in which a Missouri employee of a Missouri employer was injured by a machine owned by the latter. The employer bought the machine from a New York company which, ten years earlier, had bought the machine from its manufacturer through defendant, a New York sales agent. The employee received workers'

compensation through his employer under Missouri law, and then brought a product liability action in New York against the sales agent who then third-partied the employer, seeking contribution. Only this third-party action was at stake in *Cooney*. The Missouri employer would be liable for contribution under New York law, but not under Missouri law. The *Cooney* court reiterated the *Babcock-Schultz* distinction between conduct-regulating and loss-allocating rules, classified contribution rules into the latter category, and reaffirmed the applicability of the *Neumeier* rules to loss-allocating conflicts other than guest-statute conflicts.

3. *Id.* at 283 (emphasis added). The words 'in the mold of' may signify the court's understanding that the case did not fall precisely within the scope of Rule 2, first because the conduct and the injury occurred in different states and, second, because the dispute was one between joint-tortfeasors rather than between a victim and a tortfeasor. *See infra* at text.
4. *Id.*
5. For an extensive discussion of these difficulties, *see* S. Symeonides, *The Choice-of-Law Revolution* 109–114.
6. The Louisiana codification avoids both of these pitfalls. The pertinent article (La. Civ. Code Ann. Art. 3544) which, like the *Neumeier* rules, applies to conflicts between loss-distribution rules, differentiates between cases in which the conduct and the injury occurred in different states. Furthermore, the article is confined to disputes 'between a person injured by an offense or quasi-offense and the person who caused the injury'. Disputes between joint tortfeasors, or between a tortfeasor and a person vicariously liable for his acts, are relegated to the flexible choice-of-law approach of Art. 3542, the residual article. For an explanation of the rationale of these two features by the codification's drafter, *see* S. Symeonides, 'Louisiana's New Law of Choice of Law for Tort Conflicts: An Exegesis', 66 *Tul. L. Rev.* 677, 1992, 715–731.
7. *Cooney*, 612 N.E.2d at 283.
8. *Id.*

B. Contract Conflicts

229. As noted earlier, in the 1954 case *Auten* v. *Auten*,[1] the New York Court of Appeals abandoned the traditional *lex loci contractus* rule and adopted the 'center of gravity' approach for resolving contract conflicts. Since then, the court has moved to a full-fledged policy analysis (if not interest analysis) relying more on policies and less on contacts.

However, in the 1993 case *In re Allstate Ins. Co.* v. *Stolarz*,[2] involving the interpretation of an insurance contract, the court made a partial return to the 'center-of-gravity' approach. After stating that interest analysis is the court's 'preferred analytical tool in tort cases'[3] because 'in a typical tort case . . . strong governmental interests may underlie the choice of law issue',[4] the court stated the following:

By contrast, contract cases often involve only the private economic interests of the parties, and analysis of the public policy underlying the conflicting contract laws may be inappropriate to resolution of the dispute. It may even be difficult to identify the competing 'policies' at stake, because the laws may differ only slightly. . . . The 'center of gravity' or 'grouping of contacts' choice of law theory applied in contract cases . . . enables the court to identify which law to apply without entering into the difficult, and sometimes inappropriate, policy thicket.[5]

This statement, coupled with other statements in *Stolarz*, suggests a dichotomy in the court's approach to contract conflicts. Interest analysis remains the 'preferred approach' when 'the policies underlying conflicting laws . . . are readily identifiable and reflect strong governmental interests'. However, 'center of gravity' is the preferred approach when the policies are not readily identifiable, when the policies do not reflect strong governmental interests, or when they 'involve only the private economic interest of the parties'.

1. 124 N.E.2d 99 (N.Y. 1954).
2. 613 N.E.2d 936 (N.Y. 1993).
3. *Id.* at 938.
4. *Id.* at 939.
5. *Id.*

V. Currie-Based Approaches

230. Although several states had adopted Currie's interest analysis during the early years of the revolution, today only three states follow that analysis in tort conflicts (California, the District of Columbia, and New Jersey),[1] and no state does so in contract conflicts.[2] In light of the pivotal role that interest analysis played in the conflicts revolution, this development is nothing short of astonishing. Moreover, a more literal classification might place even these three states elsewhere, insofar as they engage in the very weighing of state interests that Currie proscribed. As discussed below, New Jersey and the District of Columbia weigh interests openly and unapologetically, while California prefers to weigh not the interests themselves but rather the impairment that would result from subordinating them. Thus, a more technical classification might move these states to different columns, leaving completely blank the interest-analysis column.

1. Initially, Pennsylvania and Wisconsin also had adopted interest analysis for tort conflicts, but Pennsylvania later switched to a 'combined modern' approach, and Wisconsin to Leflar's approach. New York is not considered an interest-analysis state because of its adherence to the *Neumeier* rules, which in some instances deviate significantly from interest analysis. Similarly, with regard to contracts, New York is not an interest-analysis state, at least since 1993, when it switched to a mixed approach.
2. Three states had initially adopted interest analysis for contract conflicts: Oregon (*see Lilienthal* v. *Kaufman*, 395 P.2d 543 (Or. 1964)); California (*see Travelers Ins. Co.* v. *Workmen's Comp. Appeals Bd.*, 434 P.2d 992 (Cal. 1967)); and the District of Columbia (*see McCrossin* v. *Hicks Chevrolet, Inc.*, 248 A.2d 917 (DC 1969)). However, all three states eventually switched to a mixed approach.

231. However, this should not suggest that Currie's influence has disappeared. First, an interest analysis traceable to Currie forms the core of most of the 'combined modern' approaches followed in other states. Second, interest analysis is often heavily employed in states that follow the Restatement (Second), especially in cases in which the factual contacts are evenly divided between the involved states.[1] Thus, in the same manner that the high numerical following of the Restatement (Second) tends to inflate its importance in deciding actual cases, the low numerical following of Currie's original approach tends to undervalue the importance of his approach in influencing judicial decisions.

1. *See* S. Symeonides, 'The Judicial Acceptance of the Second Conflicts Restatement: A Mixed Blessing', 56 *Md. L. Rev.* 1248, 1997, 1262–1263.

232. Be that as it may, the three states named above remain closer to the core of Currie's approach than all other states that follow a modern methodology.

Similarly, for entirely different reasons, two other states that follow the *lex fori* approach – Kentucky and Michigan – are also in the close periphery of Currie's camp. Although they do not overtly speak in terms of interests, these states are statistically if not ideologically in tune with Currie's approach because they tend to produce the very results he advocated for in the majority of cases – the application of the *lex fori*.

A. *Modified Interest Analysis*

233. New Jersey and the District of Columbia remain close to Currie's original analysis in that they resolve conflicts on the basis of state interests. However, neither jurisdiction appears constrained by Currie's proscription of interest-weighing, and both jurisdictions appear to have emancipated themselves from his parochial reading of such interests.

A good example of both interest-weighing and a non-parochial one is *Eger* v. *E.I. Du Pont De Nemours Co.*,[1] a tort and workers' compensation case. *Eger* was a true conflict between the laws of New Jersey, the forum state, and South Carolina. New Jersey law favoured the injured employee who was domiciled and hired in New Jersey, while South Carolina law favoured a defendant employer operating in South Carolina.[2] Without the slightest hesitation, the New Jersey court put the interests of the two states on the scale and concluded, over a strong dissent, that 'New Jersey's interest in protecting New Jersey employees and sub-contractors was 'not strong enough to outweigh South Carolina's interest'[3] in protecting its employers. The court applied South Carolina law.

1. 539 A.2d 1213 (N.J. 1988).
2. The defendant was a general contractor who subcontracted with plaintiff's employer. The plaintiff was exposed to radioactivity while working for his employer in defendant's South Carolina plant. South Carolina, but not New Jersey, accorded defendant immunity from a tort action.
3. *Eger*, 539 A.2d at 1218.

234. Another example of identifying state interests in a way that seems to liberate interest analysis from some of its congenital biases is *Gantes* v. *Kason Corporation*,[1] a products liability case. Pursuant to Currie's assumptions, *Gantes* would be classified as a no-interest case because New Jersey law favoured the Georgia plaintiff injured in Georgia, while Georgia law favoured the New Jersey defendant who manufactured the product in New Jersey.[2] After concluding that Georgia did not have an interest in protecting a New Jersey manufacturer, the New Jersey court took a broader view in identifying New Jersey's interests. The court concluded that, in addition to protecting plaintiffs (domestic or foreign), New Jersey law was intended to deter the manufacture of unsafe products in New Jersey. Because the product had been 'manufactured in, and placed into the stream of commerce from, [New Jersey]',[3] that state had a 'cognizable and substantial interest in deterrence that would be furthered by the application of its . . . law'.[4] Thus, by reading the forum's interests in a non-protectionist way, the court was able to conclude that this was a false conflict in which only New Jersey had an interest. The court applied

New Jersey law, which benefited a foreign plaintiff at the expense of a forum defendant.

1. 679 A.2d 106 (N.J. 1996).
2. The plaintiff's action was timely under New Jersey's two-year statute of limitations, but was barred by Georgia's ten-year statute of repose for products liability claims.
3. *Gantes*, 679 A.2d at 111–112.
4. *Id.* at 113.

235. Finally, another example of articulating the forum's interests in a non-protectionist way is *Kaiser-Georgetown Comm. Health Plan, Inc.* v. *Stutsman*,[1] a medical malpractise case. Under Currie's assumptions, this would also qualify as a no-interest case because the law of the forum, the District of Columbia, favoured a Virginia plaintiff by providing unlimited tort damages but the law of Virginia favoured a forum defendant by limiting the amount of damages. Nevertheless, the court found that the forum had a 'significant interest . . . in holding its [defendants] liable for the full extent of the negligence attributable to them'.[2] Thus, the court applied forum law, even though that law favoured a foreign plaintiff at the expense of a forum defendant.

1. 491 A.2d 502 (D.C. App. 1985).
2. *Id.* at 509–510.

B. Comparative Impairment

236. As noted earlier, California's comparative impairment approach also entails interest-weighing, albeit with a different name. Two well-known California cases, *Bernhard* v. *Harrah's Club*,[1] and *Offshore Rental Co.* v. *Continental Oil Co.*,[2] illustrate this phenomenon.

Bernhard was a true conflict between the laws of California and Nevada. California law favoured the plaintiff who was domiciled and injured in California, while Nevada law favoured the defendant, a Nevada tavern owner who acted in Nevada. The defendant had served alcohol to an apparently intoxicated California patron, who then drove to California and caused the accident that resulted in plaintiff's injury. California, but not Nevada, imposed civil liability on the tavern owner for injuries caused by the patron. Following Professor Baxter's comparative impairment approach, the court applied California law. The court found that California's interest in imposing civil liability on tavern owners 'would be very significantly impaired if its policy were not applied to defendant', whereas 'Nevada's interest in protecting its tavern keepers from civil liability . . . will not be significantly impaired'[3] by imposing on them civil liability under California law.[4]

The court reiterated Baxter's statements to the effect that the process of comparative impairment 'is very different from a weighing process'.[5] However, the court apparently misunderstood the meaning of 'weighing' by assuming it to be a process of 'determining which conflicting law manifest[s] the "better" or the "worthier" social policy on the specific issue'.[6] Neither Currie nor Baxter ever advocated such a value-laden weighing.[7] All in all, when one looks beyond the confusion created by misused nomenclature, there remains little doubt that *Bernhard* is simply another example of interest-weighing by another name. 'Rather than weighing interests as such, comparative impairment weighs the loss that would result from subordinating the interest of one state to those of the other . . . [and that] the gravity of the loss depend[s] on the strength and importance of the state interest at issue'.[8]

1. 546 P.2d 719 (Cal. 1976), *cert. denied*, 429 US 859 (1976).
2. 583 P.2d 721 (Cal. 1978).
3. *Id.* at 725.
4. *Id.* This was so because 'such liability involves an increased economic exposure, which, at least for businesses which actively solicit extensive California patronage, is a foreseeable and coverable business expense', and because, 'as in the instant case liability is imposed only on those tavern keepers who actively solicit California business'.
5. *Id.* at 723.
6. *Id.*
7. *Id.* The court was closer to the mark when it described this process as one of 'accommodation of conflicting state policies . . . in multi-state contexts'.
8. S. Symeonides, W. Perdue, A. von Mehren, *Conflict of Laws; American Comparative International*, 220 (2nd edn, St. Paul, Minn., 2003).

237. In *Offshore Rental Co.* v. *Continental Oil Co.*,[1] another (potentially) true conflict, the California court applied the law of the other state, Louisiana. A California statute favoured a California plaintiff, and a Louisiana rule favoured a defendant operating in Louisiana.[2] The court found that Louisiana's interest in applying the rule was 'stronger, [and] more current'[3] than California's corresponding interest, and that the application of California law 'would strike at the essence of a compelling Louisiana law'.[4] In contrast, California was not really committed to its statute, which was 'archaic and isolated in the context of the federal union'. Hence, California's interest in applying its 'unusual and outmoded statute [was] comparatively less strong'.[5] Thus, *Offshore* appeared to repudiate not only Currie's proscription of interest-weighing, but also Baxter's more subtle formulation that the court should only weigh the effects of the application or non-application of a state's law. Indeed, in a very real sense, *Offshore* engaged in a comparative evaluation of the conflicting laws themselves, thus coming perilously close to a better-law approach.

1. 583 P.2d 721 (Cal. 1978).
2. *Offshore* was an action by a California employer for the loss of the services of a key employee who was injured in Louisiana by defendant's employees. California, but not Louisiana, provided employers with an action for the loss of services of a key employee.
3. 583 P.2d at 729.
4. *Id.* at 728.
5. *Id.*

C. The Lex Fori Variant

238. As explained earlier, Currie's interest analysis was heavily biased in favour of the *lex fori*, in both true conflicts and in unprovided-for cases. The courts of Kentucky and Michigan seem to have turned this bias into a doctrine.[1]

Foster v. *Leggett*[2] illustrates Kentucky's *lex fori* approach. Most casebooks classify *Foster* as an interest-analysis case, even though the majority opinion contains no reference to Currie's writings or, for that matter, any academic commentary.

This classification is correct in the sense that the court reached the precise result Currie advocated. However, the court's heavy reliance on the forum's contacts and the absence of any discussion of policies suggest a contacts-based *lex fori* approach that is potentially more parochial than Currie's. According to this approach: *(a)* '[t]he basic law is the law of the forum which should not be displaced without valid reasons'; and *(b)* such reasons are not present whenever the forum has 'significant contacts – not necessarily the most significant contacts'.[3]

Foster arose out of an accident in Ohio, which resulted in the death of a Kentucky domiciliary who was a guest-passenger in a car driven by the defendant, an Ohio domiciliary.[4] Ohio, but not Kentucky, had a guest-statute shielding the driver and his insurer from a suit brought on behalf of the guest-passenger. Thus, based on the assumptions of interest analysis, this was a true conflict in which each state had an interest in applying its law to protect its own domiciliary. The court spoke of neither policies nor interests, nor did it cite any of Currie's writings. However, the court did echo Currie's views when it stated that the court's 'primary responsibility is to follow its own substantive law', and that '[t]he basic law is the law of the forum, which should not be displaced without valid reasons'.[5] Whether such a valid reason existed in this case is not free from doubts, but the court did not appear to entertain any. In a fashion that replicates Currie's solution to true conflicts, the court concluded that 'if there are significant contacts – not necessarily the most significant contacts – with Kentucky, then Kentucky law should be applied'.[6] The court acknowledged that its decisions could justify the inference that 'we have accepted the rule of "most significant contacts" . . . to apply to Kentucky residents involved in another state and the rule of "enough contacts" for residents of other states involved in Kentucky'. Nevertheless, the court stated, '[s]uch is not the holding or policy of this court'.[7]

1. The Nevada Supreme Court also adopted a *lex fori* approach for tort conflicts in 1996 in *Motenko* v. *MGM Dist., Inc.*, 921 P.2d 933 (Nev. 1996), but later abandoned it in favour of the *Restatement (Second)*. *See Gen. Motors Corp.* v. *Eighth Jud. Dist.*, 134 P.3d 111 (Nev. 2006).
2. 484 S.W.2d 827 (Ky. 1972).
3. *Id.* at 829.
4. The defendant worked in Kentucky, where he rented a room and had his social relationships, including a dating relationship with the deceased. Because of these Kentucky contacts, one could argue that *Foster* was sufficiently analogous to the common-domicile pattern as to justify the application of Kentucky law on this basis. However, as explained in the text, this was not the basis of the court's decision.
5. *Foster*, 484 S.W.2d at 829.
6. *Id.*
7. *Id.*

239. While the court's interpretation of its holdings is entitled to respect, the court's failure to explain the absence of 'valid reasons' for displacing forum law (other than reciting forum contacts) makes its analysis vulnerable to the same criticism for parochialism as Currie's own theory.

240. *Sutherland* v. *Kennington Truck Service, Ltd.*,[1] illustrates Michigan's *lex fori* approach. *Sutherland* arose out of a traffic accident in Michigan involving an Ohio plaintiff and an Ontario defendant. The plaintiff's action was timely under

Michigan's three-year statute of limitation, but was barred by the two-year statutes of Ohio and Ontario.[2] Relying on its own perception that most courts following the modern approaches tend to prefer forum law, the court opined that this phenomenon was 'hardly surprising [because] the tendency toward forum law promotes judicial economy: judges and attorneys are experts in their state's law, but have to expend considerable time and resources to learn another state's law'.[3] Turning preference into virtue, the court elevated this 'tendency' into a choice-of-law method according to which a Michigan court should apply Michigan law, unless a 'rational reason'[4] exists to do otherwise. In determining whether such a reason exists, the court first decides whether any foreign state has an interest in applying its law. If not, the analysis ends, and forum law applies. If a foreign state has an interest, then the court determines 'if Michigan's interests mandate that Michigan law be applied, despite the foreign interests',[5] in which case Michigan law again applies.

Applying this method, the court concluded that neither Ohio nor Ontario had an interest in applying their respective statutes of limitation. Thus, 'the *lex fori* presumption [was] not overcome, and [the court] need not evaluate Michigan's interests'.[6] The court found that Ohio did not have an interest because the application of Ohio law would 'violat[e] the defendants' due process rights.[7] The court did not explain how the application of a law that favours the defendant would somehow violate that defendant's due process rights. The court also concluded that Ontario did not have an interest in applying its two-year statute (which favoured the Ontario defendant), because, 'according to Canadian and Ontario law, Ontario has an interest in having Michigan's statute of limitations applied in this case'.[8] The basis for this conclusion was a decision of the Supreme Court of Canada that had adopted the *lex loci delicti* rule for both substantive tort matters and statutes of limitation. The *Sutherland* court did not explain how the *lex loci* rule, which the court had earlier discarded as mechanical and oblivious to state interests, suddenly had become an accurate barometer of another state's 'interest' in the modern sense of that word.

1. 562 N.W.2d 466 (Mich. 1997).
2. To its credit, the court refused to resolve the conflict through the traditional mechanical characterization of statutes of limitations as procedural, which, in the absence of a borrowing statute, would have led to the application of the *lex fori*. *See infra* 593–604. Rather, the court employed a full-fledged choice-of-law analysis, leading to the same result.
3. *Sutherland*, 562 N.W.2d at 470.
4. *Id.* at 471.
5. *Id.*
6. *Id.* at 473.
7. *Id.* at 472.
8. *Id.*

241. The two versions of the *lex fori* approach appear to differ in phraseology and nuance regarding the burden for rebutting the *lex fori* presumption. Both versions, however, remain statistically, if not ideologically, attuned with Currie's approach in that they tend to produce the very results he advocated for in the majority of cases – the application of the *lex fori*. In this sense both versions entail the risk of encouraging or legitimizing (especially in the lower courts) the very parochialism that private international law strives to minimize.

VI. The Better-Law Approach

242. The first state to adopt Professor Leflar's choice-influencing considerations, including the better-law criterion, was New Hampshire in 1966. Since then, Wisconsin (1967), Rhode Island (1968), Minnesota (1973), and Arkansas (1977) have adopted this approach for tort conflicts, although, by the turn of the century, they began combining it with other approaches. In contract conflicts, only Minnesota and Wisconsin follow Leflar's approach.

A. Early Cases: The Biases

243. The early cases that followed Leflar's approach provided ample vindication for most of the philosophical and methodological criticisms levelled against this approach. Indeed, it is not surprising that an approach that authorizes an *ad hoc*, unguided, and *ex post* choice of the 'better' law produces choices reflective of the subjective predilections of the judges making them. To the extent that judges tend to prefer domestic over foreign law, plaintiffs over defendants (foreign or domestic), or domestic over foreign litigants (plaintiffs or defendants), such preferences are bound to be reflected in judicial decisions. The early cases from the five states following Leflar's approach exhibit all three of these tendencies to a higher degree than usual. Although these tendencies are not parallel, they all stem from the same source – the judicial subjectivism that the better-law approach legitimizes.

1. Pro-Forum Law Bias

244. A preference for forum law is a by-product of the human tendency to gravitate to the familiar. With human nature being what it is, it is not surprising that judges tend to consider the forum's law, with which they are most familiar, to be the better law. More often that not, this is precisely what judges applying the better-law approach have concluded. In this sense the Wisconsin Supreme Court was refreshingly forthright in essentially equating its adherence to Leflar's approach with a strong presumption in favour of the *lex fori.*[1]

1. *See State Farm Mut. Auto. Ins. Co.* v. *Gillette*, 641 N.W.2d 662, 676 (Wis. 2002) (prefacing its application of the five Leflar factors with a statement that the primary choice-of-law rule in Wisconsin is that 'the law of the forum should presumptively apply unless it becomes clear that nonforum contacts are of the greater significance').

245. Indeed, as documented elsewhere,[1] in the five states that followed Leflar's approach for tort conflicts, there are only four Supreme Court cases in which the court admitted that the foreign law was better than the forum's. In three of those cases, the court applied the foreign law, but – perhaps not coincidentally – in two of these cases that law favoured a forum plaintiff. In the third case, a legislative change prior to trial had eliminated the difference between the forum and foreign law. In the fourth case, the court did not apply the 'better' foreign law, perhaps because that law disfavoured a forum defendant. Finally, in the only other tort conflict in which the court applied foreign law, that law produced the same result as a forum statute that was inapplicable on technical grounds.

The bias in favour of forum law is more visible in lower court cases, many of which never reach the state supreme court. For example, some lower Minnesota courts have applied a Minnesota rule after proclaiming it 'better' than the conflicting foreign rule, even after the Minnesota legislature repealed the Minnesota rule and replaced it with a rule identical to the rejected foreign rule.[2]

1. *See* S. Symeonides, *The Choice-of-Law Revolution* 82–83.
2. *Id.* at 83.

2. Pro-Plaintiff, Pro-Recovery Bias

246. A preference for forum law often, though not always, translates into a preference for plaintiffs. This is true because of the wide latitude plaintiffs generally enjoy in choosing a forum and the strong likelihood that they will choose a forum whose conflicts law and substantive law favour recovery. For example, as documented in detail elsewhere,[1] in four out of the five post-*lex loci* tort conflicts that reached the Rhode Island Supreme Court in which the plaintiff's recovery depended on the applicable law, the court applied the pro-recovery law of the forum for the benefit of a foreign plaintiff. Similarly, of the six tort conflicts cases decided by the New Hampshire Supreme Court, two cases applied forum law for the benefit of a forum plaintiff, three cases applied forum law for the benefit of a foreign plaintiff, and the sixth case applied forum law for the benefit of a forum defendant.

1. *Id.* at 83–84.

3. Pro-Forum-Litigant Bias

247. Sometimes the preference for a forum litigant (plaintiff or defendant) prevails over other preferences, including the preference for forum law. For example, in two of the three cases in which the Minnesota Supreme Court applied foreign law (in both tort and contract conflicts), that law benefited a forum plaintiff.[1] If this is not coincidental, it suggests that, when forced to choose between forum law and protecting forum litigants, courts tend to choose the latter. Lower court cases present clearer evidence of this trend.[2]

1. *Id.* at 84–85.
2. *See, e.g.*, *Boatwright* v. *Budak*, 625 N.W.2d 483, 489 (Minn. Ct. App. 2001) (applying Iowa law, because 'Iowa law best serve[d] Minnesota's interests in compensating tort victims' domiciled in Minnesota, even though Minnesota law favoured the defendant by limiting the amount of damages); *Lommen* v. *The City of East Grand Forks*, 522 N.W.2d 148 (Minn. Ct. App. 1994) (applying Minnesota's pro-defendant law to protect a Minnesota defendant in an action brought by a North Dakota plaintiff injured in North Dakota).

B. Recent Cases: Eclecticism and Watering-Down

248. The above-described biases became less pronounced in the cases decided around and since the end of the 20th century. Most likely, this change is related to the fact that, by that time, most of the states that initially adopted Leflar's approach had begun to combine it with other approaches and to de-emphasize the better-law factor.

1. Eclecticism

249. The trend towards an eclectic approach is most prominent in Rhode Island and Minnesota. By its own statements, the Rhode Island Supreme Court combines Leflar's approach with an 'interest-weighing approach' (namely, governmental interest analysis, but one that engages in the very weighing of interests that Currie proscribed), and the approach of the Restatement (Second).[1] Even more eclectic, if not confusing, is the latest articulation of the Minnesota Supreme Court's approach. In *Nodak Mutual Insurance Co.* v. *American Family Mutual Insurance Co.*,[2] this court twice described its approach as 'the significant contacts test'[3] and noted that 'this court has not placed any emphasis on [the better-law] factor in nearly 20 years'.[4] The court dutifully listed the five Leflar choice-influencing factors but, after quickly finding four of them to be unhelpful, the court spent the balance of the opinion discussing the fifth factor – 'advancement of the forum's governmental interest'.[5] Ultimately, the court concluded that it was not the forum's, but the other state's interests that needed advancement because, all other factors being equal, 'the state where the accident occurred has the strongest governmental interest . . . [and its law] should be applied'.[6]

1. *See Cribb* v. *Augustin*, 696 A.2d 285, 288 (R.I. 1997). In its most recent decision, *Oyola* v. *Burgos*, 864 A.2d 624 (R.I. 2005), the Rhode Island Supreme Court followed this combination but without mentioning the better-law criterion or any of the other Leflar factors.
2. 604 N.W.2d 91 (Minn. 2000).
3. *Id.* at 94, 96.
4. *Id.* at 96.
5. *Id.*
6. *Id.* That law was more favourable to the Minnesota party than was Minnesota law.

250. Thus, by its own statements, the Minnesota Supreme Court follows a 'significant contacts' approach. However, on closer examination, this approach relies not on contacts, but on five choice-influencing factors, which are not really five, but rather one, because the first three factors (being no more than hortatory statements) are inconclusive in the vast majority of cases, while the fifth factor (the better-law) has not been employed 'in nearly 20 years'. Thus, Minnesota's approach boils down to the remaining factor – the '[a]dvancement of *the forum's* governmental interest'. However, this does not mean that Minnesota is parochially bent on advancing the forum's governmental interests because, on appropriate occasions, Minnesota may choose to advance the interests of a non-forum state.[1] In fact, Minnesota may have advanced beyond thinking in terms of forum versus non-forum interests in that it presumes *a priori* that the accident state, be it the forum or not, 'has the strongest governmental interest'.

1. At least when the law of that state would benefit a forum litigant. *See supra* 249 footnote 6.

2. De-emphasis of Better-Law Factor

251. As *Nodak* indicates, the better-law criterion seems to play a far less significant role in recent decisions than it did 30 years ago. In recent years, some courts have expressed misgivings about their ability to determine which law is better, or have tried to dispel the notion that better law and forum law are synonymous terms, while other courts have employed the better-law criterion only as a tie-breaker, or ignored it altogether.[1] If this trend persists, then perhaps the better-law approach should resume its original name of [many] 'choice-influencing considerations'.

1. *See* S. Symeonides, *The Choice-of-Law Revolution* 87.

VII. Other 'Combined Modern' Approaches

252. The following states follow a combination of approaches other than the traditional one: New Jersey and the District of Columbia combine interest analysis with the Restatement (Second) in contract conflicts; Massachusetts does likewise in both tort and contract conflicts; Oregon follows the same combination in tort conflicts, but coupled with a fairly strong *lex fori* presumption; Hawaii follows a combination of interest analysis, the Restatement (Second), and Leflar's choice-influencing considerations for both tort and contract conflicts; North Dakota follows the same combination in contract conflicts, but perhaps in different dosages; and Pennsylvania combines interest analysis and the Restatement (Second) in contract conflicts but also draws from Cavers's principles of preference in tort conflicts.[1]

1. *Id.* at 115–116.

VIII. Modern Codifications

A. Louisiana

253. In 1991, Louisiana became the first state of the United States to enact a comprehensive choice-of-law codification.[1] The civil law heritage of that state explains why codification was a viable option there, but it does not mean that the resulting product is peculiarly civilian. The codification uses civilian drafting technique and draws elements from many European approaches but, more than anything, it draws from the general American conflicts experience.

The codification, which now forms Book IV of the Louisiana Civil Code, employs comparative-impairment terminology. Article 3515, which is the general and the residual article of the entire codification, calls for the application of the law of the state 'whose policies would be most seriously impaired if its law were not applied to that issue'.[2] The codification's drafter has explained the intended meaning of this terminology both in the legislatively approved 'Revision Comments' and in subsequent publications. He has stated that the negative phrasing of the above article was 'intended to disassociate its approach from Currie's governmental interest analysis, and other modern American approaches that seem to perceive the choice-of-law problem as a problem of interstate competition rather than as a problem of interstate cooperation in conflict avoidance'.[3] Although this negative phraseology, as well as the use of the key word 'impaired', is bound to evoke comparison with California's comparative impairment approach, the similarity is only phraseological. An examination of the specifics reveals much fewer similarities. The drafter has stated that the Louisiana codification 'is based on the premise that the choice-of-law process should strive for ways to minimize the impairment of the interests of the involved states, rather than to maximize the interests of one state at the expense of the interests of the other states'. This is accomplished by identifying the state that 'in light of its relationship to the parties and the dispute and its policies rendered pertinent by that relationship, would bear the most serious legal, social, economic, and other consequences if its law were not applied to that issue'.[4]

Article 3515 provides that the state of the least impairment is to be determined

> ... by evaluating the strength and pertinence of the relevant policies of all involved states in the light of: (1) the relationship of each state to the parties and the dispute; and (2) the policies and needs of the interstate and international systems, including the policies of upholding the justified expectations of parties and of minimizing the adverse consequences that might follow from subjecting a party to the law of more than one state.[5]

1. For discussion of this codification by its drafter, *See, inter alia*, S. Symeonides, 'Private International Law Codification in a Mixed Jurisdiction: The Louisiana Experience', 57 *RabelsZ* 460, 1993; S. Symeonides, 'Les grands problèmes de droit international privé et la nouvelle codification de Louisiane', 81 *Revue critique* 223 (1992); S. Symeonides, 'Louisiana's New Law of Choice of Law for Tort Conflicts: An Exegesis', 66 *Tul. L. Rev.* 677, 1992, 690.
2. La. Civ. Code Ann. Art. 3515. The phrase quoted in the text is prefaced by a qualifier giving precedence to more specific articles contained in the same codification and to other special conflicts statutes of the forum state.
3. *Id.* S. Symeonides, 'Louisiana's New Law of Choice of Law for Tort Conflicts: An Exegesis', 66 *Tul. L. Rev.* 677, 1992, 690.
4. *Id.* at 690.
5. La. Civ. Code Ann. Art. 3515. Similar phraseology is contained in Arts 3519, 3537 and 3542, which are the residual articles for status, contracts and torts, respectively.

254. With regard to tort conflicts, Article 3542, the general and residual article for such conflicts, provides that, except as otherwise provided by the more specific articles, these conflicts are governed by the law of the state whose policies would be most seriously impaired if its law is not applied to the particular issue. In turn this state is determined by evaluating the strength and pertinence of the relevant policies of the involved states in the light of:

> (1) the pertinent contacts of each state to the parties and the events giving rise to the dispute, including the place of conduct and injury, the domicile, habitual residence, or place of business of the parties, and the state in which the relationship, if any, between the parties was centred; and (2) the policies referred to in Article 3515, as well as the policies of deterring wrongful conduct and of repairing the consequences of injurious acts.[1]

1. La. Civ. Code Ann. Art. 3542.

B. Puerto Rico

255. Another attempt at a comprehensive choice-of-law codification has been undertaken in the Commonwealth of Puerto Rico under the auspices of the Puerto Rican Academy of Jurisprudence and Legislation. A Draft Code of Private International Law[1] was completed in 1991 and was to be submitted to the Puerto Rican Legislature that year. However, for extraneous reasons unrelated to the merits of the project, the introduction to the Legislature was delayed for more than a decade, at which time the Draft Code became part of a broader project for the Revision of the Puerto Rican Civil Code. At the time of this writing, the Draft Code is pending before the Puerto Rico Legislature. This Code is more comprehensive and more civilian than the Louisiana code, but it also draws from the general American conflicts experience.

1. *See* Academia Puertorriqueña de Jurisprudencia y Legislacion, *Proyecto para la Codificación del Derecho internacional privado de Puerto Rico* (S. Symeonides & A. von Mehren, *Rapporteurs*, 1991). For discussion, *see* S. Symeonides, 'Revising Puerto Rico's Conflicts Law: A Preview', 28 *Columbia J. Transnat'l L.* 601, 1990; S. Symeonides, 'Codifying Puerto Rico's Choice-of-Law for Contracts', in: S. Symeonides & J. Nafziger (eds), *Law and Justice in a Multistate World: Essays in Honor of Arthur T. von Mehren* (Ardsley, N.Y. 2002), p. 419.

C. Oregon

256. In 2001, Oregon became the second state to begin a comprehensive choice-of-law codification effort, under the auspices of the Oregon Law Commission. The first installment of this effort was the 2001 enactment of a new choice-of-law statute for contract conflicts, which relied heavily on the Puerto Rico Draft Code.[1]

The statute's first operative provision contains an unilateral rule providing that forum law governs four types of contracts having certain enumerated forum contacts, notwithstanding a choice-of-law clause to the contrary, or any other factors.[2] These are contracts in which the forum state's contacts and interests predominate, and in which the law of the forum would govern under almost any choice-of-law theory. In the interest of judicial economy, the statute singles out these contracts and essentially exempts them from the judicial choice-of-law process.

1. *See* Or. Rev. Stat. §81.100–135 (2001). For a discussion, *see* J. Nafziger, 'Oregon's Conflicts Law Applicable to Contracts', 38 *Willamette L. Rev.* 397, 2002; S. Symeonides, 'Codifying Choice of Law for Contracts: The Oregon Experience', 67 *RabelsZ* 726, 2003.
2. *See* Or. Rev. Stat. §81.105 (providing for certain contracts involving a state entity, as well as construction, employment, and consumer contracts that have certain enumerated close connections with Oregon).

257. The following three provisions of the statute deal with form, capacity, and consent. In general, these provisions facilitate upholding the contract through alternative references to certain validating laws, while also providing exceptions in favour of incapable parties,[1] consumers, and employees. Also, in order to avoid the bootstrapping phenomenon, the statute removes issues of capacity and consent from the scope of party autonomy.

1. Even so, *Lilienthal* v. *Kaufman*, 395 P.2d 543 (Or. 1964), the infamous Oregon spendthrift case, is overruled by Or. Rev. Stat. §81.110–115(2), which provides in part that '[a] party that lacks capacity to enter into a contract under the law of the state in which the party resides may assert that incapacity against a party that knew or should have known of the incapacity at the time the parties entered into the contract'.

258. The next provision enunciates the principle of party autonomy, delineates its scope, and defines its modalities. Section 81.125 defines the limitations to party autonomy. It provides that the chosen law will not be applied to the extent its application would: *(a)* require a party to perform an act prohibited by the law of the state where the act is to be performed; *(b)* prohibit a party from performing an act required by the law of the state where it is to be performed; or *(c)* contravene an established fundamental policy of the law that would otherwise govern the issue in dispute.

259. Section 81.130 (the statute's general and residual rule), enunciates the general approach for issues other than those covered by the specific sections and in contracts that do not contain an effective choice-of-law clause. The aim of this approach is to find the law that, in light of the multistate elements of the contract, is 'the most appropriate' for the resolution of the particular issue in dispute. This law is determined by:

1. identifying the states that have a relevant connection with the transaction or the parties, . . . ;
2. identifying the policies underlying any apparently conflicting laws of these states that are relevant to the issue; and
3. evaluating the relative strength and pertinence of these policies in: *(a)* Meeting the needs and giving effect to the policies of the interstate and international systems; and *(b)* Facilitating the planning of transactions, protecting a party from undue imposition by another party, giving effect to justified expectations of the parties concerning which state's law applies to the issue, and minimizing adverse effects on strong legal policies of other states.[1]

1. Or. Rev. Stat. §81.130.

260. Recognizing that the choice-of-law process contemplated by the above provision can be both labourious and uncertain, the statute's next provision introduces presumptive rules for certain types of contracts. The court is to apply the law designated by these rules, unless the opposing party demonstrates that the application of that law would be 'clearly inappropriate'[1] under the principles of the general rule.

1. *Id.* at §81.131.

Chapter 4. Torts and Products Liability

§1. Introduction

261. The previous chapter chronicled the movement of American conflicts law from the rigid territorial system of the First Restatement, to the choice-of-law revolution, and to the new approaches that followed it. Because much of this movement has occurred in the arena of tort conflicts, this chapter concentrates on those conflicts. It focuses on cases decided by American courts since the abandonment of the *lex loci delicti* rule and seeks to identify the emerging trends. However, the sheer number of these cases combined with the space limitations of this volume make it impossible to discuss or even cite these cases here. Instead, this chapter is confined to reporting the findings of a comprehensive study published in another volume.[1]

1. *See* S. Symeonides, *The Choice-of-Law Revolution: Past, Present, and Future* (Martinus Nijhoff Pubs., copyright by Koninklijke Brill NV, Leiden, Boston, 2006) (hereafter Symeonides, *The Choice-of-Law Revolution*), from which this chapter extensively draws. Basic bibliography on the subjects discussed in this chapter includes: L. McDougal, R. Felix & R. Whitten, *American Conflicts Law* (5th edn, New York, Ardsley, 2001), pp. 447–487; E. Scoles, P. Hay, P. Borchers & S. Symeonides, *Conflict of Laws* (4th edn, St. Paul, Minn., 2004), pp. 709–945; R. Weintraub, *Commentary on the Conflict of Laws* (5th edn, New York, 2006), pp. 371–474.

262. One of the major developments of this period has been the emergence of a distinction between tort rules that are designed primarily to regulate conduct and those designed primarily to allocate between parties the losses caused by admittedly tortious conduct. This chapter begins by briefly describing this distinction (Part II) and then discusses loss-distribution conflicts, which are more numerous (Part III). Part IV discusses conduct-regulation conflicts, and Part V discusses products liability conflicts, which deserve separate consideration because of their complexity and other factors.

§2. The Distinction between Conduct-Regulation and Loss-Distribution

263. As previously noted, this distinction originated in the seminal 1963 New York case *Babcock* v. *Jackson*[1] and was reiterated in other New York cases. Since then, courts in many states have also adopted this distinction, explicitly or implicitly.[2] As one recent study concluded, '[w]hile not every state has decided the issue, there are no states that have rejected [it]'.[3]

1. 191 N.E.2d 279 (N.Y. 1963), discussed *supra* 206–214.
2. For documentation, *see* Symeonides, *The Choice-of-Law Revolution* 125–127. The 1991 Louisiana codification also adopted a similar distinction, although it used terminology that was intended to narrow down the category of conduct-regulating rules. For a similar provisions, *see* Arts 46 and 47 of the Puerto Rico Draft Code. In the meantime, a parallel, but not identical, distinction also emerged in Europe. For example, the Swiss codification provides in Art. 142.2 that, regardless of which law governs a tort case, '[r]ules of safety and conduct in force at the place of the act are [to be] taken into consideration'. The Belgian, Dutch, Portuguese, Hungarian, and Tunisian codifications contain similar provisions as do the Hague conventions on

traffic accidents and products liability, and the Rome II Regulation. *See* Symeonides, *The Choice-of-Law Revolution* 128–129.

3. Cross, 'The Conduct-Regulating Exception in Modern United States Choice-of-Law', 36 *Creighton L. Rev.* 425, 2003, 441.

264. Implicit in this development are certain assumptions about state interests and the spatial operation of laws. One assumption is that a state's policy of deterring substandard conduct is implicated whenever such conduct occurs in, or causes injury within, that state's territory, regardless of whether the involved parties are domiciled there. Another assumption is that, while a state's loss-distribution policy may or may not extend to non-domiciliaries acting within its territory, the policy does extend to state domiciliaries even when they act outside the state. In simpler words, conduct-regulating rules are territorially oriented, whereas loss-distribution rules are *usually* not territorially oriented.

265. While the above assumptions may or may not be questionable, what is questionable is the precision with which one can expect to classify conflicting tort rules into one or the other of the two categories. Indeed, the line between conduct-regulating and loss-distributing rules is not always bright. While some tort rules are clearly conduct-regulating and some are clearly loss-distributing, there are many tort rules that do not fit easily into either category. There are even rules that appear to fit in both categories. Indeed, in many instances, loss-allocative and conduct-regulative motives or even purposes can co-exist in the same rule. Examples include dram shop acts,[1] strict liability rules, contributory negligence rules, and 'car-owner statutes', namely statutes that impose vicarious liability on car owners for injuries caused by a driver using the car with the owner's consent.

1. A dram shop act is a statutory or judicial rule imposing civil liability on a tavern owner for serving alcohol to an apparently intoxicated patron for injury to another person. In enacting a dram shop act, a state may be motivated by both conduct-regulating and loss-allocating objectives, namely: (1) providing additional incentives for tavern owners to act more carefully and refrain from serving apparently intoxicated patrons; and (2) facilitating financial recovery for victims by making available to them an additional defendant, the tavern owner, and placing on the latter the economic loss of accidents caused by his drunk patrons. In contrast, in refusing to enact a dram shop act – or in enacting an anti-dram shop act – a state may be motivated by loss-allocating rather than conduct-regulating considerations, namely, to shield tavern owners or social hosts from financial responsibility, rather than to encourage them to act carelessly.

266. Another well known example is provided by a series of New York cases involving Section 240 of New York's Labour Law, which imposes on the owner of an immovable absolute liability for injury caused by defective scaffolding to a construction worker working on the premises. Six lower court cases had characterized these provisions in three different ways before the New York Court of Appeals had the opportunity to consider the matter in *Padula* v. *Lilarn Props. Corp.*[1] After defining as conduct-regulating those rules that 'have the prophylactic effect of governing conduct to prevent injuries from occurring' and as loss-distributive those rules that 'prohibit, assign, or limit liability after the tort occurs, such as charitable immunity statutes',[2] the *Padula* court acknowledged that Section 240 'embod[ied] both conduct-regulating and loss-allocating functions'.[3] However, the court concluded that the primary function of Section 240 was to regulate conduct.[4] Thus, the court provided a simple answer to a complex question: whenever a particular rule embodies both conduct-regulating and loss-distributing functions, one should focus on the rule's primary function and proceed accordingly.

1. 644 N.E.2d 1001 (N.Y. 1994). In this case, a New York worker invoked Section 240 in an action filed against a New York defendant for injuries the plaintiff sustained in Massachusetts, when he fell from scaffolding while working on defendant's building.
2. *Id.* at 1002.
3. *Id.* at 1003. The conduct-regulating function was 'requiring worksites be made safe', while the loss-distributing function was the imposition of vicarious liability on the owner of the property for failure to provide a safe worksite.
4. *See id.* (characterizing §240 and its companion §241 as 'primarily conduct-regulating rules, requiring that adequate safety measures be instituted at the work site' and holding them inapplicable to the Massachusetts accident).

267. While the answer of the *Padula* court is not profound, it is sensible and practical. It enunciates a criterion for distinguishing between the two categories and invites the parties and their experts to present their best arguments. The criterion may appear vague, but it is no more vague than the criteria courts employ in so many other situations in resolving conflicts in interstate or domestic law. Despite contrary opinion, the process of determining the purpose, function, or 'policy' underlying a rule of law is neither futile nor unworthy of the effort. The process of teleological interpretation, so integral to most modern American choice-of-law approaches, is admittedly difficult at times, but attorneys and their tort experts can certainly handle this difficulty, and many of them would prefer it over the old mechanical rules that lead inexorably to a pre-ordained result. While opinions differ, recent cases suggest that the following are relatively clear examples of rules that belong primarily in one category or the other.

268. As *Babcock* stated, 'rules of the road' are a classic example of conduct-regulating rules, or 'rules of conduct and safety'. They are designed to ensure the safety of the public by defining permissible and impermissible conduct and by imposing sanctions on violators. This category is not as small as most commentators assume. It includes not only speed limits and traffic-light rules, but also rules that prescribe the civil sanctions for violating traffic rules, including presumptions and inferences attached to those violations. For example, a rule providing that drivers involved in collisions while driving intoxicated or in excess of the speed limit are presumed negligent, is primarily a conduct-regulating rule, as is a rule providing that, in a rear-end vehicular collision, the driver of the rear car is presumed to be at fault.

Other examples are rules that prescribe safety standards for work sites, buildings, and other premises. These rules are primarily conduct-regulating, although they may have an impact on loss-allocation. As Judge Posner noted in a case involving safety standards in a foreign hotel, it would be both nonsensical and dangerous to impose on the hotel operator a duty to follow the safety standards in force in the home-states of the hotel guests. This would subject the operator 'to a hundred different bodies of tort law',[1] each imposing potentially inconsistent duties of care. 'A resort might have a system of firewalls that under the law of some states or nations might be considered essential to safety and in others might be considered a safety hazard'.[2]

Finally, other examples of conduct-regulating rules are those that impose punitive damages. As the word 'punitive' suggests, the purpose of these rules is to punish the individual tortfeasor, as well as to deter other potential tortfeasors, rather than to compensate the victim who is, *ex hypothesi*, made whole through compensatory damages. Do punitive damages have an impact on loss-allocation? Absolutely! Large punitive damages awards can drive a whole industry to the ground and may effect a massive transfer of wealth from the insurance industry to the plaintiffs' bar. However, this transfer of wealth is simply an effect of the punitive damage rule, not its purpose, which is to deter egregious conduct.

1. *Spinozzi* v. *ITT Sheraton Corp.*, 174 F.3d 842, 845 (7th Cir. 1999).
2. *Id.*

269. On the loss-distributive side, the following are examples of rules that are primarily loss-distributive, even if they do have a bearing on conduct: guest statutes; rules providing intrafamily or charitable immunity; rules imposing ceilings on the amount of damages or excluding certain types of damages, such as for pain and suffering; rules defining the beneficiaries of wrongful death actions, survival actions, and loss of consortium actions; the old rules providing that a tort action does not survive the tortfeasor's death; rules dealing with contribution or indemnification among joint tortfeasors; rules providing for no-fault automobile insurance, statutes of repose, which protect manufactures from suits filed after a designated number of years from the product's first use, corporate-successor liability or non-liability rules, and direct action statutes, namely statutes that allow the victim to directly sue the tortfeasor's insurer.

270. Even if some of the above examples are questionable, the remaining ones comprise a long enough list to support the usefulness of the basic distinction between conduct-regulating and loss-distributing rules. The fact that opinions may differ in classifying some of these rules illustrates the difficulties of this distinction, but it does not negate its usefulness. These difficulties are inherent in any teleological approach and are a fair price to pay in return for the rational resolution of conflicts that such an approach promises. Moreover, these difficulties should not be overestimated. They are no more insurmountable than, for example, the difficulties of distinguishing between substance and procedure or, in some close cases, distinguishing between tort and contract actions.[1] In any event, as Judge Weinstein observed, this distinction, far from being a rigid one, is no more than 'a proxy for the ultimate question of which state has the greater interest in having its law applied to the litigation at hand'.[2]

Indeed, at least in a judicial choice of law, the above distinction does no more than focus the parties' and the court's attention on the right questions and to draw the lines along which the battle will be fought. It stands for the simple proposition that in conflicts between conduct-regulation rules, one should focus on the place or places of conduct and injury, whereas in conflicts between loss-distribution rules, one should also focus on the parties' connections, if any, with other states. Surely, in hard cases or cases in which the distinction is unworkable, the lines may be adjusted or even stepped-over. However, it is still preferable to have soft or adjustable lines than no lines at all. Thus, one can conclude that, despite the difficulties in its application, the distinction between conduct-regulating and loss-distributing rules provides a useful framework for resolving many tort conflicts.

1. While this comparison may evoke the difficulties encountered in the characterization process under the traditional theory, the similarity is only superficial. The traditional theory sought to ascribe labels to rules without regard to their underlying purposes. In contrast, the process of distinguishing between conduct-regulating and loss-distributing rules seeks to ascertain the rule's purpose, and does so in a much more nuanced and focused manner. It asks the right questions and, more importantly, it is expected to provide reasons for the answers to which it arrives.
2. *Hamilton* v. *Accu-Tek*, 47 F.Supp. 330, 337 (E.D.N.Y. 1999).

§3. Loss-Distribution Tort Conflicts

I. Introduction

271. This Part focuses on the major loss-distribution conflicts cases decided since the abandonment of the *lex loci delicti* rule.[1] It classifies the cases into eight typical, primary, fact-law patterns based on the most common combinations of the pertinent factual contacts (territorial and personal) and substantive laws of the contact-states, and then summarizes and recasts the results of the cases into descriptive choice-of-law rules.

1. Logically one should discuss conflicts between loss-distributing rules after examining conflicts between conduct-regulating rules, for the same reasons that one should discuss reparation only after establishing culpability or at least liability. The fact is, however, that almost all the major cases that constitute the American conflicts revolution involved loss-distribution conflicts, precisely because it is with regard to these conflicts that the territorially based traditional system proved most deficient. Moreover, even today, loss-distribution conflicts are more common than conduct-regulation conflicts, apparently because the laws of the various states are more likely to differ on loss-distribution than on conduct-regulation issues.

II. Defining the Typical Patterns

A. The Pertinent Connecting Factors

272. Unlike conduct-regulating rules which operate territorially, loss-distributing rules operate in a more complex mode that focuses more on the individuals involved in the conflict rather than on the physical location of the events that caused the conflict. Because of its fixation with territoriality and its one-size-fits-all mentality, the traditional system was unable to recognize or accommodate this basic reality and thus precipitated the revolution in tort conflicts. It is therefore not surprising that one of the common points of reference among all branches of the revolution has been the acceptance of the parties' domicile[1] as the focal point around which to resolve conflicts between loss-distribution rules. In the span of a few years, the parties' domicile, which was an irrelevant factor under the *lex loci delicti* rule, became a primary factor in loss-distribution conflicts.

However, the new importance of domicile does not mean that the traditional contact of *locus delicti* has become irrelevant. Rather it means that domicile now shares the stage with the *locus delicti*, which remains an important, albeit not an exclusive factor. From a more general perspective, this development also signifies that territoriality is no longer the exclusive governing principle in the resolution of tort conflicts.

1. As used hereafter, the term domicile includes other equivalent concepts, such as habitual residence, 'home state', or, in the case of juridical persons like corporations, the principal place of business.

273. Because many torts are committed across state boundaries, the *locus delicti* can be in more than one state. Rather than artificially place the *locus delicti* at the place of the 'last event', proper analysis should consider both the place of the last event, the injury, *and* the place in which the injurious conduct occurred.[1]

1. Of course, in some cases the conduct may have occurred in more than one state, as in products liability cases in which the product was designed in one state, tested in another, and manufactured in another state. Similarly, in some cases the injury may be in more than one state, as in multi-state defamation cases. Nevertheless, in order to keep things relatively simple, the following discussion focuses on typical cases which do not present these factual complexities.

274. To summarize, the pertinent contacts for resolving loss-distribution conflicts are: (1) the parties' domiciles; (2) the place of the injurious conduct; and (3) the place of the resulting injury.[1] Thus, if one were to classify loss-distribution conflicts on the basis of factual contacts only, one would arrange them into: (1) common-domicile cases arising from torts in another case; (2) split-domicile cases involving intrastate torts; and (3) split-domicile cases involving cross-border torts.

1. Naturally, the list of contacts could be longer so as to include, for example, the place of the parties' pre-existing relationship, if any. However, for the purposes of this discussion, which is to categorize cases into primary patterns rather than to resolve them in a judicial fashion, the list is confined to the primary contacts.

B. The Content of the Involved Laws

275. An important lesson of the modern American conflicts experience is that one cannot resolve conflicts intelligently and rationally without considering the substantive content of the laws of each involved state, and without making that content an integral part of the whole choice-of-law process. Loss-distribution laws may be grouped into two major categories, depending on whether their application benefits the injured party (hereafter 'victim' or 'plaintiff'), or the party whose conduct is claimed to have caused the injury (hereafter 'tortfeasor' or 'defendant'). Based on these categories, loss-distribution conflicts can be grouped into cases in which: (1) both states' laws favour the same party ('false' conflicts); (2) each involved state has a law that favours its own domiciliary (hereafter 'direct' conflicts);

and (3) each state's law favours the domiciliary of the other state (hereafter 'inverse' conflicts).

276. In the prevailing conflicts jargon introduced by Brainerd Currie, direct conflicts would be called 'true' conflicts and inverse conflicts would be called 'no-interest' or 'unprovided-for' cases. However, even if one agrees with Currie's assumptions, his labels for these categories are problematic because they prejudge the answer to the basic question – whether in fact a state has an interest in applying its law to the particular case – a question that reasonable minds often answer differently.[1] For this reason, this chapter employs categorizations that are descriptive but non-prescriptive. Rather than being dependent on largely subjective assumptions about each state's ostensible or real interests, the terms 'direct' and 'inverse' describe objectively the content of each state's substantive laws. Direct conflicts are those in which the application of each state's law would favour the party affiliated with that state ('each for its own'). Inverse conflicts are those in which the application of each state's law favours the party affiliated with the other state ('each for the other'). These terms are also non-prescriptive, because they do not prejudge the court's own categorization of the conflict nor its ultimate outcome.

1. Indeed, most courts do not subscribe to Currie's assumptions; many courts do not employ his labels; and courts that employ these labels reach different conclusions regarding each state's interests than Currie would have reached. For example, in many inverse conflicts – which Currie would label as no-interest cases – the courts concluded that one of the involved states did in fact have an interest, and this conclusion would move these cases from the no-interest category to the false conflict category.

C. The Typical Fact-Law Patterns in Conflicts Involving Two States

277. Placing the pertinent factual contacts and substantive laws in the mix produces multiple fact-law patterns, depending on how many states are involved in the conflict. In the most common cases which involve only two states, the combination of contacts and laws produces eight typical patterns of loss-distribution conflicts, which are described below.

1. *Common-domicile cases.* These are cases in which the parties are domiciled in the same state and are involved as tortfeasor and victim in a tort committed entirely in another state. Depending on the content of each state's law, these cases can be subdivided into cases in which the law of the common domicile:
   (a) favours the plaintiff (while the law of the state of the tort favours the defendant) (*Pattern 1*); or
   (b) favours the defendant (while the law of the state of the tort favours the plaintiff) (*Pattern 2*);
2. *Split-domicile intra-state tort cases.* These are cases in which the tortfeasor and the victim are domiciled in different states but in which both the conduct and the injury occur in the home state of one of the parties. Depending on which of the two parties is domiciled in that state and which party its law favours, these cases can be divided into four patterns, as follows:

(a) cases in which the conduct and the injury occur in the defendant's home state, and in which that state's law:
   (i) favours the defendant (while the law of the plaintiff's home state favours the plaintiff) (*Pattern 3*); or
   (ii) favours the plaintiff (while the law of the plaintiff's home state favours the defendant) (*Pattern 6*); and

(b) cases in which the conduct and the injury occur in the plaintiff's home state, and in which that state's law:
   (i) favours the plaintiff (while the law of the defendant's home state favours the defendant) (*Pattern 4*); or
   (ii) favours the defendant (while the law of the defendant's home state favours the plaintiff) (*Pattern 5*);

3. *Split-domicile cross-border tort cases.* These are cases in which the parties are domiciled in different states and in which the conduct and the injury also occur in different states. The most common of this broad category of cases are those in which the conduct occurs in the tortfeasor's home state and the injury occurs in the plaintiff's home state. Depending on the content of the two states' laws, these cases can be subdivided into cases in which:
   (a) the law of each home-state favours the domiciliary of that state (*Pattern 7*); or
   (b) the law of each home-state favours the domiciliary of the other state (*Pattern 8*).

Obviously, there are several additional variations, especially when one adds a third state to the mix. Nevertheless, the aforementioned eight patterns are the most common, and the following review is confined to them.

III. Common-Domicile Cases Arising from Torts in Another State

278. Of the 42 states that have abandoned the *lex loci delicti* rule, the vast majority (32 cases or 76 per cent) did so in cases involving intra-state torts of the common-domicile pattern, namely cases in which parties domiciled in the same state were involved in a tort that was committed entirely in another state. All but one (or 98 per cent) of the 32 cases applied the law of the common domicile.[1]

As explained above, common-domicile cases can be divided into two permutations, depending on the content of the law of the common domicile:

1. Pattern 1 (the *Babcock* pattern), in which the law of the state of the common domicile favours recovery more than the law of the state of conduct and injury; and
2. Pattern 2 (the converse-*Babcock* pattern), in which the law of the common domicile is less favourable to recovery than the law of the state of conduct and injury.

1. For citations and discussion, *see* Symeonides, *The Choice-of-Law Revolution* 145 *et. seq.*

A. Pattern 1: The Babcock Pattern

279. The majority of the above cases (26 out of 32) involved Pattern 1 (the *Babcock* pattern), in which the law of the state of the common domicile favours recovery more than the law of the state of conduct and injury. The same pattern appeared in at least nine more state supreme court cases decided after the particular court had abandoned that rule, thus raising the total number of *Babcock*-pattern cases to 35. Thirty-three of the 35 cases (or 94 per cent) applied the law of the parties common domicile in conflicts involving guest statutes, interspousal or intra-family immunity, compensatory damages, and other similar conflicts between the loss-distribution rules of the common domicile and the state of the tort.[1]

1. *See id.* 146–150. The two cases that did not apply the law of the common domicile were factually distinguishable, and one of them was subsequently overruled.

280. In the most recent of the 35 cases, *Miller* v. *White*,[1] the court concluded that the application of the law of the common domicile 'correspond[s] with international norms and promote[s] consistent treatment of accident victims across borders'.[2] The court applied Vermont law to an action between Vermont parties arising out of a single-car accident in Quebec. Vermont's law allowed a tort action, but Quebec's no-fault law confined the plaintiff to an administrative remedy and a much lower recovery. The court characterized the issue as one that 'raises competing policies that allocate postevent losses'[3] and concluded that, with regard to such an issue, 'the domicile of the parties is the most significant contact bearing on the determination of the relevant law'.[4] The court found that Quebec's no-fault law was designed to 'expedite compensation to victims of automobile accidents, reduce the amount of tort litigation in Quebec courts, and guarantee relatively low automobile-insurance rates'.[5] The court reasoned that Quebec had 'little interest in . . . the rights of action of an United States citizen against another United States citizen in an United States court'.[6] In contrast, said the court, Vermont, as the domicile of both parties and the place of their relationship, as well as the place where the 'social and economic repercussions of personal injury will occur', had a 'strong interest in applying its law'.[7]

1. 702 A.2d 392 (Vt. 1997).
2. *Id.* at 397.
3. *Id.* at 394.
4. *Id.* at 394–395.
5. *Id.*
6. *Id.* at 395.
7. *Id.* at 396.

281. The above cases indicate that, in common-domicile cases of the *Babcock* pattern, American courts that have abandoned the *lex loci* rule are virtually unanimous in applying the law of the parties' common domicile.

B. Pattern 2: The Converse-Babcock Pattern

282. In cases of the converse-*Babcock* pattern (namely cases in which the law of the common domicile is less favourable to recovery than the law of the state of conduct and injury), there is also strong, though not unanimous, support for applying the law of the common domicile. This pattern appeared in six cases in which a court of last resort abandoned the *lex loci* rule, and in nine other state supreme court cases decided after the particular court had abandoned that rule. Eleven of the 15 cases (or 73 per cent) applied the pro-defendant law of the common domicile, rather than the pro-recovery law of the accident state, while four cases reached the opposite result.[1]

1. For citations and discussion, *see* Symeonides, *The Choice-of-Law Revolution* 150–155.

283. Of the four cases that did not apply the law of the common domicile, the only one that is relatively recent is also factually atypical,[1] while the remaining three cases are old and discredited. They applied the (pro-plaintiff) law of the accident state, but in all of them the accident state was also the forum state. This fact can explain the outcome much better than any other factor, especially because two of these cases, *Conklin* v. *Horner*[2] and *Milkovich* v. *Saari*,[3] were decided under the usually pro-plaintiff and pro-forum better-law approach which now appears to be losing both steam and luster, while the third case, *Arnett* v. *Thompson*,[4] was decided under Kentucky's unapologetically parochial *lex fori* approach.

Despite their limited contemporary persuasive value, these cases deserve attention to the extent that they articulate the interest of the accident state, when it has a pro-recovery law, to ensure recovery of medical costs resulting from the tort and, to a lesser extent, to deter wrongful conduct within that state. Although the New York Court of Appeals dismissed this interest in *Schultz*,[5] other courts may be more hesitant to reject it, especially when the accident state is also the forum state. This interest does not necessarily trump, but it does rival to some extent the interest of the parties' common-domicile in denying or reducing recovery. Thus, the very presence of an interest, even a weak one, on the part of the accident state prevents the easy classification of reverse-*Babcock* cases into the classic false conflict paradigm and suggests the need for an appropriate escape clause.

1. This case is *Martineau* v. *Guertin*, 157 N.W.2d 579 (Wis. 1968). Although the parties in this case were domiciled in the same state, they resided together in another state, and the accident occurred in a third state, the law of which was identical to the residence state. This factor tipped the scales in favour of the accident state.
2. 157 N.W.2d 579 (Wis. 1968).
3. 203 N.W.2d 408 (Minn. 1973).
4. 433 S.W.2d 109 (Ky. 1968).
5. *See supra* 226.

284. The majority of cases involving the converse-*Babcock* pattern, including the most recent ones, have applied the law of the common domicile with little hesitation. For example, in *Collins* v. *Trius, Inc.*,[1] the supreme court of Maine refused to apply Maine's pro-recovery law to the actions of Canadian passengers of a Canadian bus that was involved in an accident in Maine. The court noted that, '[a]lthough Maine ha[d] a significant interest in regulating conduct on its highways', the issue at stake, recovery for non-economic loss, was 'primarily loss-allocating rather than conduct-regulating'.[2] The court continued as follows:

'[O]ne incontestably valuable contribution of the choice-of-law revolution in the tort conflict field is the line of decisions applying common-domicile law . . . The superiority of the common domicile as the source of law governing loss-distribution issues is evident. At its core is the notion of a social contract, whereby a resident assents to casting her lot with others in accepting burdens as well as benefits of identification with a particular community, and ceding to its lawmaking agencies the authority to make judgments striking the balance between her private substantive interests and competing ones of other members of the community'.[3]

1. 663 A.2d 570 (Me. 1995).
2. *Id.* at 573.
3. *Id.* The court concluded that, in light of the parties' common domicile in Canada and its other contact with the case, 'Canada has the most significant interest with respect to the issue of damages for non-pecuniary harm in this case'.

C. A Common-Domicile Rule

285. The above review indicates that, when both the tortfeasor and the injured party are domiciled in the same state, judicial opinions converge on the proposition that the state of the common domicile has a better claim to apply its law to loss-distribution issues than the state of conduct and/or injury. As the *Schultz* court stated, in these cases, 'the locus jurisdiction has at best a minimal interest in determining the right of recovery or the extent of the remedy', and proper analysis favours the jurisdiction of common domicile 'because of its interest in enforcing the decisions of both parties to accept both the benefits and the burdens of identifying with that [state] and to submit themselves to its authority'.[1]

1. *Schultz*, 491 N.Y.S.2d at 96.

286. Based on sheer numbers, one can safely conclude that, regardless of which modern choice-of-law methodology or philosophy they follow, American courts that have abandoned the *lex loci* rule have adopted the above thesis in cases of both the *Babcock* and the converse-*Babcock* patterns. All together, a total of 50 common-domicile cases have reached 34 state supreme courts with, and since, the abandonment of the *lex loci delicti* rule. Forty-four of these cases (or 88 per cent) applied the law of the common domicile and six cases (12 per cent) did not. Of the latter cases, two were factually exceptional, one was overruled, and the remaining three are probably discredited.

287. These numbers are convincing, especially because they come from courts of all modern methodological and philosophical persuasions. Indeed, based on these numbers one may accurately speak of the emergence of a *de facto* common-domicile *rule*. This rule can be phrased in terms that are both content- and forum-neutral, as follows:

RULE I. When the injured party (victim) and the party whose conduct caused the injury (tortfeasor) are domiciled in the same state, the law of that state governs [whether it favours the victim (Pattern 1) or the tortfeasor (Pattern 2)].[1]

1. For a comparison with similar statutory rules in other countries, *see* Symeonides, *The Choice-of-Law Revolution* 157–159.

288. This rule is phrased in bilateral terms that are not only forum-neutral, but also party-neutral and content-neutral. The rule authorizes the application of the law of the common domicile, not only when it favours the plaintiff (as in the *Babcock* pattern) but also when it favours the defendant (as in the converse-*Babcock* pattern). Although, in cases of the latter pattern, this result is less than unanimous, on balance it is supported by 'concepts of mutuality and reciprocity',[1] as well as 'a social contract notion' whereby domiciliaries of the same state agree to 'accept[ ] burdens as well as benefits of identification with a particular community'.[2] For these reasons, a common-domicile rule that cuts both ways, is superior to a unilateral rule. Nevertheless, when such a rule is cast in statutory language, one must exercise caution not to completely deprive courts of the necessary flexibility to deviate from the rule in exceptional cases.[3]

1. *Schultz*, 491 N.Y.S.2d at 98.
2. *Collins* v. *Trius, Inc.*, 663 A.2d 570, 573 (Me. 1995).
3. At the same time, a common-domicile rule can go too far if it is phrased so broadly as to extend beyond loss-distribution issues. This appears to be the case with some civilian formulations, such as those in the Italian (Art. 61.2), Quebec (Art. 3126.2), and Polish (Art. 31.2) codifications, which provide for the application of the law of the parties' common domicile or nationality without any differentiation on whether the issue involved is a loss-distribution or conduct-regulation issue, and without allowing any escape.

D. Cases Analogous to Common-Domicile Cases

289. A variation of Patterns 1 and 2 appear when the tortfeasor and the victim are domiciled in different states whose loss-distribution rules produce the same result.[1] For example, in a case like *Babcock*, if the defendant had been domiciled in New Jersey (rather than in New York) and if New Jersey (like New York) did not have a guest statute, there would be little argument that the resulting conflict would be as false as *Babcock* itself, and that it should be resolved by allowing the action to proceed. Similarly, in a converse-*Babcock* case, if the two parties had been domiciled in Ontario and Quebec, respectively, and both of these provinces had a guest statute, the resulting conflict would not differ in any material way from the cases of Pattern 2. Most courts encountering such cases have expressly or implicitly accepted this line of reasoning and have treated them as functionally analogous to common-domicile cases.[2]

1. A somewhat similar pattern appears when the parties, though not domiciled in the same state, are nevertheless parties to a pre-existing relationship that is centred in a state other than the state of injury. European codifications have adopted the notion that the law that governs the parties' pre-existing relationship displaces the law that would otherwise govern the tort. For citations, *see* E. Scoles, P. Hay, P. Borchers & S. Symeonides, *Conflict of Laws*, (4th edn, St. Paul, Minn., 2004), pp. 808–809. In the United States, neither the literature nor the case law have sufficiently explored this notion. However, the place in which the parties' relationship, if

any, is centred is one of the contacts that courts consider under the Restatement (Second), or other modern approaches, in selecting the applicable law.

2. *See* Symeonides, *The Choice-of-Law Revolution* 160–162.

IV. Split-Domicile Cases – Intrastate Torts

290. This Section focuses on split-domicile cases involving intrastate torts, namely cases in which the tortfeasor and the victim are not domiciled in the same state, but are involved in a tort that occurs entirely in the home state of either the tortfeasor or the victim. Obviously, some of these cases present the false conflict paradigm, such as when the laws of the two states produce the same outcome. Such cases need not occupy us here. Instead, the following review focuses on cases in which the two states have different loss-distribution laws that produce different outcomes. If the law of each state favours the domiciliary of that state, the case presents a *direct* conflict or what interests analysts call a true conflict. If the law of each state favours the domiciliary of the other state, the case presents an inverse conflict or what interest analysts call the unprovided-for, or no-interest paradigm.

A. *Direct or True Conflicts*

291. Depending on which domiciliary state has the additional contacts of conduct and injury, direct conflicts can be further subdivided into two primary patterns: *(a)* Pattern 3: Split-domicile cases in which both the conduct and the injury occur in the tortfeasor's home state, which has a law that favours the tortfeasor; and *(b)* Pattern 4: Split-domicile cases in which both the conduct and the injury occur in the victim's home state, which has a law that favours the victim.

1. Pattern 3: Split-Domicile Cases in Which the Conduct, the Injury and the Tortfeasor's Domicile Are in a State Whose Law Favours the Tortfeasor

292. *Foster* v. *Leggett*[1] and *Cipolla* v. *Shaposka*[2] are both well known, old illustrations of split domicile cases falling within Pattern 3. In both cases, the conduct and injury (traffic accident) occurred in the defendant's home state, which had a guest statute favouring the defendant and his insurer. *Foster* applied the pro-plaintiff law of the victim's domicile (which was also the forum state), whereas *Cipolla* applied the pro-defendant law of the defendant's domicile, which was the accident and non-forum state.

In *Foster*, the Kentucky court acknowledged that its decision was based exclusively on the presence of contacts with the forum state *qua* forum, rather than on any other considerations. The court stated bluntly that its 'primary responsibility is to follow its own substantive law', that '[t]he basic law is the law of the forum, which should not be displaced without valid reasons', and that 'if there are significant contacts – not necessarily the most significant contacts – with [the forum], then [forum] law should be applied'.[3] For reasons explained earlier, such a self-centred approach has little to contribute to the rational resolution of interstate or international conflicts and should be ignored for this reason.

1. 484 S.W.2d 827 (Ky. 1972) (discussed *supra* 68; refusing to apply Ohio's guest state and allowing under Kentucky law an action arising from an Ohio accident involving an Ohio host-driver and a Kentucky guest-passenger).
2. 267 A.2d 854 (Pa. 1970) (applying Delaware's guest-statute and thus denying recovery to a Pennsylvania plaintiff injured in Delaware while riding as a guest-passenger in a car owned and driven by a Delaware host-driver).
3. *Foster*, 484 S.W.2d at 829 (emphasis added).

293. In *Cipolla*, a Pennsylvania court took a non-parochial approach resulting in the application of the Delaware guest statute favouring a Delaware host-driver at the expense of a Pennsylvania guest-passenger. The court found that Delaware's contacts were 'qualitatively greater' than Pennsylvania's and that Delaware's policies – protecting host-drivers and ensuring stability of insurance rates – were more pertinent because this case involved a Delaware host-driver and a car insured in that state. Hence, Delaware had 'the greater interest in having its law applied'.[1]

More meaningful than this questionable comparison of contacts was the court's reasoning regarding the parties' expectations or at least reliance, which was influenced by Professor Cavers. 'It seems only fair', said the court, 'to permit a defendant to rely on his home state's law when he is acting within that state'. Inhabitants of a state 'should not be put in jeopardy of liability exceeding that created by their state's law just because a visitor from a state offering higher protection decides to visit there'. Conversely, '[b]y entering the state . . . the visitor has exposed himself to the risk of the territory and should not subject persons living there to a financial hazard that their law had not created'[2] As the old saying goes, 'when in Rome do as Romans do'.[3] Not because of Roman imperialism but rather because this is more in line with both party expectations and state polices.

1. *Cipolla*, 267 A.2d at 856.
2. *Id.* (*quoting* D. Cavers, *The Choice-of-Law Process*, (1965), pp. 146–147).
3. *Bledsoe* v. *Crowley*, 849 F.2d 639, 647 (D.C. Cir. 1988) (Williams, J., concurring).

294. Without explicitly subscribing to this maxim but following a similar rationale, 30 of the 31 cases falling within Pattern 3 (*Foster* being the lone exception) have reached the same result as *Cipolla*. They resisted the temptation of applying the pro-plaintiff law of the plaintiff's home state (which in many of these cases was also the forum state) and instead applied the pro-defendant law of the defendant's home state, which was also the place of both the conduct and the injury.[1] If one were to restate these results in the form of a rule, this rule would provide as follows:

> RULE II. When the conduct and the injury occur in the tortfeasor's home state and that state's law favours the tortfeasor, that law governs (even if the law of the victim's home state favours the victim).

It is important to note that this rule is stated in forum-neutral terms despite the fact that it is designed to cover only direct or true conflicts. Indeed, although all 31 cases presented the direct or true conflict paradigm, only 11 of them applied forum law, and, except for *Foster* (which was decided under an explicit *lex fori* approach more than three decades ago), they based this result on the forum state's other contacts and interests. Thus, these cases suggest lack of support for Currie's automatic *lex fori* prescription, as well as his proscription of weighing state interests in true conflicts. Moreover, these cases suggest that courts are not as parochial as Currie's personal-law principle assumes or instructs them to be. In fact, in 20 out of 21 cases in which the plaintiff was a forum domiciliary, the courts applied the pro-defendant law of the non-forum state for the benefit of a non-forum defendant and at the expense of a forum plaintiff. *Foster* was the exception.

1. While some of these cases have been decided under the same 'mixed' approach as *Cipolla*, more numerous are the cases decided under other approaches, such as the Restatement (Second), interest analysis, New York's *Neumeier* Rule 2a, and even the *lex-fori* and the better-law approaches. For documentation, *see* Symeonides, *The Choice-of-Law Revolution* 165–171.

2. Pattern 4: Split-Domicile Cases in Which the Conduct, the Injury and the Victim's Domicile Are in a State Whose Law Favours the Victim

295. Pattern 4 is the converse of Pattern 3. Here the conduct and the injury are both in the victim's home state, which has a law that favours the victim, while the defendant's home state has a law that favours the defendant. One category of cases involving this pattern are cases in which a governmental entity enjoying immunity from suit under the law of its home state engages in conduct in another state that does not accord such immunity, and causes injury there.

Nevada v. *Hall*[1] is the most well known of these cases. In *Hall*, an employee of the University of Nevada, an entity that enjoyed sovereign immunity under Nevada law, drove to California on official university business and caused an accident there, injuring a California domiciliary. The California court refused to recognize Nevada's immunity, or Nevada's 25,000-dollar (USD) limitation on damages. The court recognized Nevada's interest in protecting the financial well-being of Nevada entities, but found this interest to be much weaker than California's interest 'in providing full protection to those who are injured on its highways through the negligence of both residents and non residents'.[2] The court contrasted this case with *Bernhard* v. *Harrah's Club*[3] and concluded that California had an even stronger interest in applying its law because, unlike *Bernhard* in which the defendant's conduct had occurred in Nevada, in *Hall* both 'the State of Nevada's activities and the [victim's] injuries took place in California'. The court continued: 'By thus utilizing the public highways within our state to conduct its business, Nevada should fully expect to be held accountable under California laws'.[4]

1. 44 US 410 (1979).
2. *Hall* v. *Nevada*, 141 Cal.Rptr. 439 at 442 (Cal.App. 1977).
3. 546 P.2d 719 (1976). *Bernhard* is discussed *supra* 236 and *infra* 349.
4. *Hall*, 141 Cal.Rptr. at 442. The US Supreme Court upheld the constitutionality of this decision after noting, *inter alia*, California's 'substantial' interest in 'providing full protection to those who are injured on its highways'. *Hall*, 440 US at 423. Many years later, in *Franchise Tax Bd. of California* v. *Hyatt*, 538 US 488 (2003), the shoe was on the other foot. The Supreme Court

affirmed the constitutionality of Nevada's refusal to accord sovereign immunity to a California tax assessing agency that was claimed to have caused injury to a Nevada domiciliary in Nevada through acts committed in both Nevada and California.

296. Many other state courts have also refused to recognize another state's immunity under similar circumstances.[1] Some of those cases involved police car chases that began in one state and ended in another, causing injury in the latter state. In one such case, *Biscoe* v. *Arlington County*,[2] a policeman employed by the defendant, a Virginia county, began chasing a suspected bank robber in that county. The chase continued into the District of Columbia where it ended in an accident injuring plaintiff, an unsuspecting bystander.[3] Under the law of Virginia, but not D.C., the Virginia county would be immune from liability. The D.C. court held that D.C. law governed because 'the District's policies would be substantially more seriously thwarted by nonapplication of its law . . . than would those of Virginia'.[4] The court found that 'Virginia's concern for the economic well-being of its counties . . . [was] not an especially compelling one'. In contrast, the District's 'interests in deterrence of potential tortfeasors and compensation of injured parties' were 'strongly implicated' because the District was 'the site of the most relevant conduct and all the injury', and the 'defendants' acts created . . . danger to District life and property'.[5]

1. For documentation, *see* Symeonides, *The Choice-of-Law Revolution* 173–177.
2. 738 F.2d 1352 (D.C. Cir. 1984).
3. The victim, though a Maryland domiciliary, was working in the District of Columbia and the court treated him as a D.C. domiciliary, because of the 'special and largely unique interest of the District in protecting persons who live in the surrounding suburbs and work in the District'. *Id.* at 1361.
4. *Id.* at 1362.
5. *Id.* at 1361.

297. Even cross-border tort cases in which the tortfeasor's conduct occurred outside the victim's home state and injured the victim in the latter state have applied the pro-plaintiff law of that state. Although these cases fall within Pattern 7 (discussed *infra*), they suggest that, *a fortiori*, the same result is appropriate in Pattern 4 cases in which the tortfeasor's conduct takes place within the victim's home state. A person injured in her home state by conduct in that state should be able to rely on the protection of that state's law, regardless of whether the tortfeasor is from that state or from another state whose law protects the tortfeasor.

As Cavers explained, 'the system of physical and financial protection [of the victim's domicile] would be impaired if a person who enters the territory of [that] state were not subject to its laws'.[1] That state's domiciliaries 'should not be put in jeopardy in [that state] simply because [an out-of-stater] . . . had come into [that state] from a state whose law provides a lower standard of financial protection'.[2] The out-of-state defendant who is held to the higher standard of the state of injury 'is not an apt subject for judicial solicitude. He cannot fairly claim to enjoy whatever benefits a state may offer those who enter its bounds and at the same time claim exemption from the burdens'.[3] Again, '[t]he maxim 'When in Rome do as Romans do' bespeaks the common sense view that it is the traveler who must adjust'.[4]

1. D. Cavers, *The Choice-of-Law Process*, (1965), p. 140.
2. *Id.* at 142.

3. *Id.* at 141.
4. *Bledsoe* v. *Crowley*, 849 F.2d 639, 647 (D.C. Cir. 1988) (Williams, J., concurring).

298. If one were to restate the results of Pattern 4 cases in the form of a rule, this rule would provide as follows:

> RULE III. When the conduct and injury occur in the victim's home state and that state's law favours the victim, that law applies (even if the law of the tortfeasor's home state favours the tortfeasor).

B. Inverse Conflicts or No-Interest Cases

299. The converse of Patterns 3 and 4 cases are those cases in which the conduct, the injury, and one party's domicile are in a state whose law favours the other party. These 'inverse' conflicts can be subdivided into two patterns:

1. *Pattern 5*: Cases like *Neumeier* v. *Kuehner*[1] and *Erwin* v. *Thomas*[2] in which the conduct and the injury occur in the victim's home state, which has a law that favours the tortfeasor who is domiciled in another state; and
2. *Pattern 6*: Cases like *Hurtado* v. *Superior Court*[3] in which the conduct and the injury occur in the tortfeasor's home state, which has a law that favours the victim who is domiciled in another state.

Under Currie's assumptions, especially his 'personal-law' principle, both patterns present the no-interest paradigm on the theory that neither state would have an interest in protecting the domiciliary of the other state. Currie argued that in these cases the court should apply the law of the forum *qua* forum. Yet, only *Erwin* v. *Thomas* followed Currie's prescription as such, although other cases applied the law of the forum on other grounds.

1. 286 N.E.2d 454 (N.Y. 1972), discussed *supra* 224–225.
2. 506 P.2d 494 (Or. 1973), discussed *infra* 300.
3. 522 P.2d 666 (Cal. 1974), discussed *infra* 304.

1. Pattern 5: The *Neumeier* Pattern

300. *Erwin* was an action for loss of consortium filed by a Washington woman whose husband was injured in Washington by the conduct of an Oregon defendant. Oregon law favoured the Washington plaintiff by allowing such an action, whereas Washington law favoured the Oregon defendant by denying it. The court concluded that 'neither state ha[d] a vital interest in the outcome of this litigation'.[1] Washington's defendant-favouring policy was not implicated because this case did not involve a Washington defendant, and Oregon's plaintiff-favouring policy also was not implicated because this case did not involve an Oregon plaintiff.[2] Thus, as Currie said, 'neither state cares what happens',[3] and hence, said the court, 'an Oregon court does what comes naturally and applies Oregon law'.[4]

1. *Erwin* v. *Thomas*, 506 P.2d 494, 496 (Or. 1973).
2. *See id.* ('[I]t is stretching the imagination more than a trifle to conceive that the Oregon Legislature was concerned about the rights of all the nonresident married women in the nation whose husbands would be injured outside of the state of Oregon'.).
3. B. Currie, *Selected Essays*, 152.
4. *Erwin*, 506 P.2d at 496–497. The court also noted that Washington would not object to the application of Oregon law because 'Washington has little concern whether other states require non-Washingtonians to respond to such claims . . . afford[ing] rights to a Washington woman which Washington does not afford, so long as a Washington defendant is not required to respond'. *Id.* at 496.

301. In contrast to *Erwin*, the majority of cases falling within Pattern 5 have reached the opposite result by doing what *Neumeier* did, even without following its precise rationale.[1] These cases applied the pro-defendant law of the state that, besides being the plaintiff's home state, was also the state in which both the conduct and the injury occurred. They did so on a variety of rationales, ranging from a territorial presumption, with or without reliance on the Restatement Second, to a different reading of the respective interests of the involved states.

In one of these cases, *Miller* v. *Gay*[2] (a guest-statute conflict presenting the converse pattern from *Cipolla*),[3] the court concluded that neither state's relationship was more significant, and that reliance on state interests could not resolve the conflict. The court quoted *Cipolla*'s statement that defendants acting in their home state 'should not be put in jeopardy of liability exceeding that created by their state's laws just because a visitor from a state offering higher protection decides to visit there'.[4] The *Miller* court turned this statement around by concluding that 'inhabitants of a state (here Delaware) should not be accorded rights not given by their home states, just because a visitor from a state offering higher protection decides to visit there'.[5]

1. For documentation, *see* Symeonides, *The Choice-of-Law Revolution* 179–184. *Labree* v. *Major*, 306 A.2d 808 (R.I. 1973), another old case involving the same pattern, also reached the same result, but under a different theory. *Labree* refused to apply the Massachusetts guest statute to an action arising from a Massachusetts accident involving a Massachusetts guest-passenger, the plaintiff, and a Rhode Island host-driver, the defendant. Instead the court applied Rhode Island's pro-plaintiff law on the theory that, when the defendant driver is domiciled in a state whose law provides recovery, 'the plaintiff should recover no matter what the law of his residence or the place of the accident'. *Id.* at 818.
2. 470 A.2d 1353 (Pa. Super. Ct. 1984).
3. *See supra* 293. *Miller* arose out of a Delaware accident involving a Pennsylvania host-driver and a Delaware guest-passenger. Delaware, but not Pennsylvania, had a guest statute. The court applied the Delaware guest statute, barring the action.
4. *See supra* 293, text at footnote 2.
5. *Miller*, 470 A.2d at 1356.

302. In *Boomsma* v. *Star Transport, Inc.*,[6] the court reached a similar result by applying Wisconsin's pro-defendant law, rather than Illinois' pro-plaintiff law, to a wrongful death action arising from a Wisconsin accident involving Wisconsin victims and an Illinois driver. The court acknowledged that Wisconsin's cap on wrongful death damages was not intended to protect foreign defendants, but concluded that on balance Wisconsin law should govern because the plaintiffs failed to rebut the Second Restatement's *lex loci* presumption. After noting that 'plaintiffs had no "justified expectation" that Illinois law would apply to their claims', the court observed that the application of Illinois law would endorse 'a kind of lottery system' for Wisconsin plaintiffs injured in Wisconsin in which '[t]he "winners" . . . would be those injured by states that do not cap wrongful death damages [and] [t]he "losers" would be those injured by fellow Wisconsinites'.[2]

1. 202 F.Supp.2d 869 (E.D. Wis. 2002) (decided under Illinois conflicts law).
2. *Id.* at 879.

2. Pattern 6: The *Hurtado* Pattern

303. As said above, cases falling within Pattern 6 also qualify as inverse conflicts, insofar as each state's law favours a litigant not domiciled in that state. However, whether they also qualify as 'no interest' cases is more debatable here than in Pattern 5 because in Pattern 6 cases the law of the state of the conduct and injury favours recovery. If the court interprets that law as motivated by a policy of deterrence, then the pro-recovery state becomes interested in applying its law in order to deter that conduct. Such an interpretation converts a potential no-interest case into a false conflict. Right or wrong, this was precisely the interpretation of the California court in *Hurtado* v. *Superior Court.*[1]

1. 522 P.2d 666 (Cal. 1974).

304. *Hurtado* was a wrongful death action filed by the survivors of a Mexico domiciliary who was killed in a California accident caused by the negligence of a California driver. Mexico, but not California, limited the amount of wrongful-death damages. Under Currie's personal-law principle, this would have been a no-interest case. The court followed this principle when it concluded that Mexico did not have an interest in applying its defendant-protecting limited-damages rule to non-Mexican defendants at the expense of Mexican plaintiffs.[1] Based on the same principle, the court could have concluded that California also did not have an interest in applying its pro-plaintiff rule for the benefit of non-California plaintiffs at the expense of California defendants. However, the court found that the California rule was designed to deter negligent conduct in California. The court stated that California's 'primary purpose' in creating a cause of action for wrongful death was not so much to compensate the victim as 'to deter the kind of conduct within its borders which wrongfully takes life', and that the unlimited-damages aspect of the rule simply 'strengthen[ed] the deterrent aspect of the civil sanction'.[2]

Thus, the court essentially reclassified the California rule as conduct-regulating. Having done so, the court could not avoid the conclusion that California had an interest in applying the rule. As the court stated, 'when the defendant is a resident of California and the tortious conduct . . . occurs here, California's deterrent policy of full compensation is clearly advanced by application of its own law. . . . California has a decided interest in applying its own law to California defendants who allegedly caused wrongful death within its borders'.[3] Thus, what might have been a no-interest case, became a false conflict.

1. That law was designed to protect only Mexican defendants 'from excessive financial burdens or exaggerated claims'. *Id.* at 670.
2. *Id.* at 671.
3. *Id.* at 671–672.

305. The same was true in *Jett* v. *Coletta*,[1] a medical malpractise action filed by an Idaho domiciliary and arising out of medical services rendered in a New Jersey hospital. The New Jersey court found that, although Idaho had no interest in applying its limited-damages rule to protect New Jersey defendants, New Jersey had a 'strong interest' in applying its unlimited-damages law so as to: (1) 'deter[ ] negligent conduct in the medical profession'; (2) 'promot[e] the competence of its medical practitioners'; and (3) 'ensur[e] that visitors to the state receive full compensation for their injuries', particularly when the visitors' 'presence is nonfortuitous'.[2]

1. 2003 WL 22171862 (D.N.J. 2003).
2. *Id.* at *3. The plaintiff was spending the summer in New Jersey when she was taken to the New Jersey hospital. The court also found that New Jersey's contacts were 'more substantial' than Idaho's, and thus New Jersey had a 'much stronger relationship' and 'a much greater incentive than Idaho to apply its law'. *Id.* at 4.

306. Finally, in *Arcila* v. *Christopher Trucking*,[1] an action filed by New Jersey plaintiffs against Pennsylvania defendants arising out of a Pennsylvania accident, a Pennsylvania court applied Pennsylvania's pro-plaintiff compensatory damages law rather than New Jersey's pro-defendant law. The court reasoned that the application of New Jersey law would not promote New Jersey's interest in protecting defendants, but would 'impair Pennsylvania's interest . . . in deterring tortious conduct within its borders'.[2] The court also noted that, because the defendants were Pennsylvania domiciliaries and had acted in Pennsylvania, they were 'on notice – at least constructively – of Pennsylvania's law governing remedies for injuries caused by negligent conduct'.[3]

1. 195 F.Supp.2d 690 (E.D.Pa. 2002).
2. *Id.* at 694.
3. *Id.* at 695.

3. Summary and Rule

307. The majority of cases falling within Patterns 5 and 6 applied the law of the state that had three of the four pertinent contacts, namely the conduct and the injury and: (a) in Pattern 5, the plaintiff's domicile; and (b) in Pattern 6, the defendant's domicile.[1] If one were to restate these results in the form of a rule, that rule would provide as follows:

> RULE IV. When both the conduct and the injury occur in the home state of one of the parties, that state's law applies (even if it does not favour that party).

This is a forum-neutral, jurisdiction-selecting rule that is bound to encounter criticism, especially in cases falling within the *Neumeier* pattern (Pattern 5). Interest analysts would be particularly critical, if only because this rule does not follow

Currie's prescription that so-called 'no-interests' cases should be resolved by resorting to the *lex fori*. However, by and large, the courts have already rejected that prescription. For example, most of the cases that chose forum law based the choice on the existence of affirmative forum interests, forum contacts, or factors other than Curie's rationale of either the primacy or the residuality of the *lex fori*.

1. *See* Symeonides, *The Choice-of-Law Revolution* 187–188.

308. In any event, there is no denying that the 'no-interest' cases are more problematic for interests analysts than are true conflicts. It is perfectly logical and consistent to resolve a true conflict by applying the law of the state that has the greatest or strongest interest, or whose interests would otherwise suffer the most serious impairment. However, this logic falls short in the no-interest cases. Looking for the 'least uninterested' state is certainly not a promising route. This is just another way of saying that interest analysis, being built around the notion of state interests, runs into an impasse when neither state has an interest. Consequently, to resolve the conflict, one must look for options outside the framework of interest analysis rather than simply re-calibrating state interests and searching for phantom common policies. In this sense, Currie's solution of applying the *lex fori* as the residual law is a solution that lies outside the framework of interest analysis.

Once it is understood that the solution to the no-interest conundrum must be sought outside the framework of interest analysis, then other options become more palatable. One option is to fall back on territorialism, which was the established system before the advent of interest analysis. In light of this long tradition, it is not unreasonable to apply to these particular inverse conflicts the law of the state in which both the conduct and the injury occurred and where one of the parties is domiciled.

V. Split-Domicile Cases – Cross-Border Torts

309. This Section reviews split-domicile cases in which the conduct occurs in one state and the injury in another. Examples of such cross-border torts are products liability cases (discussed *infra*) as well as cases involving wrongful emissions, defamation, fraud, or other torts that may be committed from a distance. The most likely scenaria involving two states are those in which the conduct occurs in the tortfeasor's home state and the injury in the victim's home state. Depending on the content of each state's law, these cases can be divided into two patterns: (1) cases in which each state favours its own domiciliary (Pattern 7); and (2) cases in which each state favours the domiciliary of the other state (Pattern 8).

A. *Pattern 7: Cases in Which the Conduct and the Tortfeasor's Domicile Are in a State Whose Law Favours the Tortfeasor, while the Injury and the Victim's Domicile Are in a State Whose Law Favours the Victim*

310. Pattern 7 is similar to Patterns 3 and 4, inasmuch as that in all three patterns each state's law favours its own domiciliary. This similarity explains why Pattern 7 poses at least as much of a true conflict as do Patterns 3 or 4. The difference is that in Patterns 3 and 4 both the conduct and the injury occur in one of the domiciliary states, whereas in Pattern 7 the conduct occurs in the tortfeasor's domicile and the injury occurs in the victim's domicile. In other words, both the personal contacts (domiciles) and the territorial contacts (conduct and injury) are now evenly split, with a concomitant bearing on both state policies and party expectations.

This difference makes Pattern 7 cases more difficult than those of Patterns 3 or 4. In Pattern 3, both the conduct and the injury occur in the tortfeasor's home state, and this explains why most courts apply the law of that state. In Pattern 4, both the conduct and the injury occur in the victim's home state, and this explains why most courts apply the law of that state. Pattern 7 is the exact middle point between Patterns 3 and 4, which suggests that Pattern 7 cases could go in either direction, i.e., apply the law of either the tortfeasor's home state and place of conduct, or the victim's home state and place of injury.

311. Nevertheless, American courts have generally shown little hesitation before applying the law of the victim's home state,[1] thus equating Pattern 7 cases with Pattern 4 cases. This includes cases involving professional malpractise, fraud and deceptive practises, or defamation, as well as products liability cases. On balance, this result is appropriate, provided that the circumstances are such that the defendant should have foreseen the application of the law of the victim's home state and place of injury. In product liability cases, the foreseeability proviso can be easily satisfied when the product is marketed through ordinary commercial channels. In other cases, the foreseeability inquiry must be undertaken on a case-by-case basis.

1. For documentation, *see* Symeonides, *The Choice-of-Law Revolution* 192–197.

312. One representative case from Pattern 7 is *Kuehn* v. *Children's Hospital, Los Angeles*,[1] which was decided under Wisconsin's choice-influencing considerations. *Kuehn* was an action filed by the parents of a Wisconsin child who died in Wisconsin as a result of the negligence of a California hospital in improperly shipping to Wisconsin a package containing the child's bone marrow. Under the law of Wisconsin, but not California, the action survived the victim's death. In an opinion authored by Judge Posner, the court held that Wisconsin law governed based in part on Wisconsin's interest 'in obtaining for its residents the measure of relief that the state believes appropriate in tort cases'.[2] However, the court also took care to explain why the California hospital should have foreseen the occurrence of the injury in Wisconsin, and thus the possibility of having to account under Wisconsin law – the hospital had shipped the package to Wisconsin based on a contractual arrangement with a Wisconsin hospital.[3]

1. 119 F.3d 1296 (7th Cir. 1997).
2. *Id.* at 1302.
3. Moreover, said the court, the only difference between California and Wisconsin law was 'in the scope of liability for negligence, not in the standard of care. It [was] not as if California had required one method of packing and shipping bone marrow and Wisconsin another'. *Id.*

313. In contrast, in *Troxel* v. *A.I. duPont Institute*,[1] a medical malpractise case, the foreseeability element was less clear, and this may partly explain why the court reached the opposite result. A Delaware hospital treated a Pennsylvania patient who then returned to Pennsylvania and, unaware that she was suffering from a contagious disease, communicated that disease to her pregnant friend, the plaintiff. The plaintiff's *in utero* child died as a result of the disease and she sued the hospital for failure to inform its patient of the contagious nature of her disease and of the risk to pregnant women who might come into contact with her. The Pennsylvania court recognized Pennsylvania's interest in protecting its citizens, but concluded that this interest was 'superseded by Delaware's interest in regulating the delivery of health care services in Delaware'[2] and in protecting defendants who acted in that state. The court said that, when acting in Delaware, the defendant was 'entitled to rely on the duties and protections provided by Delaware law'.[3]

1. 636 A.2d 1179 (Pa.Super. 1994), *appeal denied*, 647 A.2d 903 (Pa. 1994).
2. *Id.* at 1181.
3. *Id.* at 1181.

314. This discussion of state interests simply confirms that Pattern 7 cases are veritable true conflicts, which in turn suggests that the two states' interests are more or less equally strong and pertinent. One element that can tip the scales is the actor's ability to reasonably foresee where the act will manifest its direct consequences. In *Kuehn*, the California hospital clearly should have foreseen that the consequences of its negligence in sending a package to Wisconsin would have been felt in Wisconsin. Arguably, the same was true in *Troxel*. The Delaware doctors should have foreseen that, when they send an uncured and uniformed contagious patient back to her home in Pennsylvania, the consequences of that negligence would have been felt in Pennsylvania. The fact that the *Troxel* court did not accept this argument suggests that the court strongly believed that, from a systemic perspective, medical malpractise conflicts should be resolved invariably under the law of the place where the medical services are rendered, regardless of any other factors. Indeed, the *Troxel* court stated that any rule that would allow patients to carry with them the protective law of their domicile when they travel to another state for medical care 'would be wholly unreasonable, for it would require hospitals and physicians to be aware of and be bound by the laws of all states from which patients came to them for treatment'.[1] However, although this reasoning is entirely defensible in typical medical malpractise cases in which the plaintiff is the patient who chooses in-patient treatment in an out-of-state hospital, *Troxel* was an atypical case insofar as it involved a plaintiff who was not treated at the out-of-state hospital and had no relation to it.

1. *Id.*

315. Subject to the above caveat regarding foreseeability, the results reached in the majority of Pattern 7 cases can be summarized as follows:

> RULE V. When conduct originating in one state injures, in another state, a person domiciled in the latter state, the law of the latter state applies if it is more favourable to the injured person and if the occurrence of the injury in that state was objectively foreseeable.[1]

1. For a comparison of this rule with the *Neumeier* rules, as well as similar statutory rules, *see* Symeonides, *The Choice-of-Law Revolution* 198–200.

B. Pattern 8: Cases in Which the Conduct and the Tortfeasor's Domicile Are in a State Whose Law Favours the Victim, while the Injury and the Victim's Domicile Are in a State Whose Law Favours the Tortfeasor

316. Pattern 8 is similar to Patterns 5 and 6, inasmuch as in all three patterns the tortfeasor is domiciled in a state whose law favours the victim, while the victim is domiciled in a state whose law favours the tortfeasor. Thus all three patterns present the inverse conflict or, in Currie's terms, the no-interest paradigm. However, in Patterns 5 and 6 both the conduct and the injury occur in the home state of one of the parties, whereas in Pattern 8 these two contacts are divided, with the conduct occurring in the tortfeasor's home state and the injury in the victim's home state. This division makes Pattern 8 cases more difficult than the cases of Pattern 5 or 6.

To be sure, as in the cases of Pattern 6 (the *Hurtado* pattern), a court may choose to characterize the pro-recovery law of the tortfeasor's home state and place of conduct as partly conduct-regulating. If so, the no-interest case becomes a 'false' conflict. Several products liability cases discussed later have done precisely that. They applied the pro-plaintiff law of the manufacturer's home state and place of manufacture, rather than the pro-defendant law of the plaintiff's home state and injury.

Similarly, as *Ardoyno* v. *Kyzar*[1] illustrates, a court may articulate a state's interests in a way that dissociates them from the parties' domiciles. *Ardoyno* was an action for interference with contract filed by a Louisiana plaintiff against a Mississippi defendant whose conduct in Mississippi caused injury to plaintiff in both states. Mississippi, but not Louisiana, allowed such an action. The court reasoned that the Louisiana rule, which prohibited the action, was geared not toward protecting defendants as such, but rather toward fostering competition with regard to employment contracts. Since the contract in question was entered into in Louisiana, the court concluded that Louisiana had an interest in applying this rule, even though a Louisiana plaintiff resisted, and a Mississippi defendant benefited from, the rule's application.

1. 426 F.Supp. 78 (E.D.La. 1976).

317. In many Pattern 8 cases the above avenues may be unavailable. If so, these will remain 'no-interest' cases which, by definition, cannot be resolved on the basis of state interests. One option is to fall back on territorial factors or to a presumptive *lex loci* rule (with its 'last event' sub-rule) as other no-interest cases have done. The majority of product liability cases that fall within Pattern 8 applied the pro-defendant law of the plaintiff's domicile and place of injury under a variety of rationales.[1] However, in most of those cases, that state was also the state of the product's acquisition. For courts that tend to think in quantitative terms even when proclaiming otherwise, this additional contact tips the scale in the direction of the state with the most contacts.

Currie's solution to Pattern 8 cases was to apply the law of the forum *qua* forum. This is no doubt an efficient solution. It is also a solution that more often than not favours plaintiffs, because they can choose to sue in the defendant's home state whenever it has a pro-plaintiff law. On balance, a better option is to concede that Pattern 8 cases are not susceptible to *a priori* solutions. A court that has the opportunity to consider the totality of the circumstances of the particular case, including factors such as the parties' relationship, if any, is likely to reach a better result than a result preformulated *ex ante*.

1. *See* Symeonides, *The Choice-of-Law Revolution* 200–201, 298–300.

VI. Split-Domicile Conflicts Involving Three States

318. When the tortfeasor and the victim are domiciled in different states and the tort is committed in whole or in part in a third state, the resulting conflict can be quite complex. Depending on the content of the laws of the three states, these cases can present the false, direct, or inverse conflict paradigms. The involvement of the third state usually adds to the difficulty of resolving the conflict.

Budget Rent-A-Car System, Inc. v. *Chappell*[1] is a recent example of a tri-state conflict in which the laws of each state would produce a different outcome. Joseph, a domiciliary of Michigan rented in that state a car from the defendant company and, one day before Valentine's day, drove it to New York to deliver roses and a bracelet to Nicole, a New York domiciliary. He was driving back to Michigan through Pennsylvania with Nicole as his passenger when he fell asleep at the wheel. The resulting accident left Nicole a paraplegic. The rental-car company brought an action in Pennsylvania, seeking a declaratory judgment freeing it from vicarious liability arising from its ownership of the rented car. The company would be entitled to such a declaration under the law of Pennsylvania but not of Michigan or New York, both of which had statutes imposing on car owners civil liability for injuries caused by persons using the car with the owner's consent. However, unlike the New York statute, the Michigan statute limited the owner's liability to USD 20,000.

The court found that Pennsylvania had no interest in limiting the company's liability, while Michigan's interest was 'uncertain and tenuous'[2] under the circumstances of this case. In contrast, the court found that New York's interest was 'clear, direct and compelling', because all of the reasons for which New York enacted the pertinent statute were directly implicated in this case. New York had an interest in '(1) [Nicole's] full recovery from a financially responsible party, (2) the compensation of New York vendors who furnish medical and hospital care to [Nicole], and (3) recouping the State's welfare expenses'.[3]

1. 407 F.3d 166 (3d Cir. 2005) (decided under Pennsylvania conflicts law).
2. *Id.* at 178.
3. *Id.* at 177.

319. In characteristic simplicity, *Neumeier* Rule 3 submits all tri-state conflicts to a presumptive *lex loci delicti* rule accompanied by an escape that authorizes displacement of the *lex loci*, if this would 'advance the relevant substantive law purposes without impairing the smooth working of the multi-state system or producing great uncertainty for litigants'.[1] This escape came in handy in the part of the *Schultz* case[2] involving the second defendant, the Franciscan Brothers, which had its principal place of business in Ohio. Through this escape, the court managed to avoid the application of the pro-plaintiff law of the 'locus of the tort' (New York) and thus to treat this defendant as favourably as the other defendant, Boy Scouts.

1. *Neumeier* Rule 3, *supra* 93.
2. *Schultz* v. *Boy Scouts of America*, 480 N.E.2d 679 (N.Y. 1985), discussed *supra* 226–227.

320. In *Gilbert* v. *Seton Hall University*,[1] another tri-state conflict involving the same New Jersey charitable immunity rule and a New York injury, the court again avoided the *lex loci*, but through a different route. The defendant Seton Hall was a non-profit New Jersey corporation protected by New Jersey's charitable immunity rule. The plaintiff was a Seton Hall student who was severely injured during a school rugby game held in New York. He was domiciled in Connecticut which, like New York, had abolished charitable immunity. The court noted that the case fell within the scope of *Neumeier* Rule 3, but, barely mentioning this rule again, proceeded to conduct a full-fledged interest analysis ending with the conclusion that New Jersey law should govern because, unlike New York, New Jersey had a strong interest in applying its law. The court discounted the plaintiff's Connecticut domicile and treated his decision to attend a New Jersey school as equivalent to a choice of a domicile in New Jersey. This made the case functionally analogous to a common-domicile case, which *Neumeier* Rule 1 subjects to the law of the common domicile.

1. 332 F.3d 105 (2d Cir. 2003) (decided under New York conflicts law).

321. In *Bodea* v. *Trans Nat Express, Inc.*,[1] New York was again the locus of the tort and its law favoured the plaintiff more than both of the other involved states. The case arose out of a New York traffic accident involving an Ontario plaintiff and a Quebec defendant, driving in separate cars. The conflict involved the issue of damages for non-economic losses. Quebec did not allow such damages, Ontario allowed them but limited the amount, and New York allowed them without limits. The defendant invoked the Rule 3 escape and, apparently realizing that his chances of convincing the court to apply Quebec law were limited, made a more modest argument in favour of Ontario law. The court rejected the argument because it found 'no reason why' a Quebec resident 'would expect that the laws of the Province of Ontario would apply to an accident that occurred in New York'.[2] The court noted that the analysis would differ if Ontario and Quebec had the same law but, because they did not, 'the *situs* of the accident (New York) is appropriate as a tie breaker'.[3]

1. 731 N.Y.S.2d 113 (N.Y.App.Div. 2001).
2. *Id.* at 118.
3. *Id.* The court also noted that 'both plaintiffs and defendants have purposefully associated themselves with the laws of New York', *id.*, and that their presence there was not fortuitous. The plaintiff traveled regularly through New York on his way to his apartment and job in Maryland, while the defendant, who was a truck driver, drove frequently through New York.

322. Whether the *lex loci* should be the tie breaker in these tri-state conflicts is a question on which reasonable minds can differ. The judicial experience accumulated thus far in cases of this pattern does not permit the articulation of even presumptive rules derived from that experience. The *Neumeier* court took a different route, which was both bold and more conservative at the same time. It subjected these cases to a presumptive *lex loci* rule qualified by an open-ended escape, the phrasing of which was left deliberately vague. For that time, this was a sensible combination of certainty and flexibility. However, more than three decades after *Neumeier*, it is still not possible to identify any clear patterns emerging from the application of the Rule 3 escape.

In *Gould Electronics Inc.* v. *United States*,[1] a federal court attempted to summarize the circumstances under which New York courts displace the *lex loci* under *Neumeier* Rule 3. According to this summary, displacement is more likely when one or more of the following factors are present: (1) when the parties' contacts with the locus state are a matter of fortuity rather than voluntary action; (2) when the tort does not occur in the domicile of either party; (3) when displacement will not encourage forum-shopping nor create the appearance of favouring local litigants; (4) when the parties are domiciled in states with similar laws; or (5) when the other state has a stronger interest than the locus state in applying its law.[2]

1. 220 F.3d 169 (3d Cir. 2000) (decided under New York conflicts law).
2. *Id.* at 187.

323. This summary is eminently plausible. Whether it is also entirely accurate is another question. For example, one need not be facetious to suggest that, all other factors being equal, the *lex loci* is less likely to be displaced when it favours recovery than when it does not. Indeed, cases involving this tri-state pattern and decided by lower New York courts after *Schultz* suggest a certain pro-recovery bent. With the notable exception of *Gilbert*, and unlike the *Schultz* and *Neumeier* cases (both of which denied recovery in a two-state conflict of the no-interest paradigm), most of these lower-court cases have allowed recovery either by following the *lex loci* part of Rule 3, or by utilizing the escape contained in that rule.[1] It remains to be seen whether this trend will continue, and whether it will meet the approval of New York's highest court.

1. *See* Symeonides, *The Choice-of-Law Revolution* 206–207.

VII. Summary and Rules for Loss-Distribution Conflicts

324. This chapter reports the findings of a fairly comprehensive study of cases involving loss-distribution conflicts and decided by state and federal courts throughout the United States during the last three decades, under all modern choice-of-law methodologies. If one looks beyond the diversity of methodology and focuses on the actual results reached by the cases, one can discern a surprising degree of consistency, if not uniformity, so much so that, for most patterns of cases, these results can be compressed into a few sentences of descriptive rules. If one were to assemble these rules and integrate them into a single rule, this rule would provide as follows:

When, in a tort case that has pertinent contacts with more than one state, the loss-distribution laws of these states would produce a different outcome, the applicable law is determined as designated below, in the following order:

1. (Common-Domicile Cases). If the injured party and the party whose conduct caused the injury (tortfeasor) are domiciled in the same state,[1] the law of that state governs [whether it favours the victim (Pattern 1) or the tortfeasor (Pattern 2)];
2. (Split-Domicile Cases). If the injured party and the tortfeasor are domiciled in different states and both the tortfeasor's conduct and the victim's injury occurred in one of those states, the law of that state governs [whether it favours the victim (Patterns 4 and 6) or the tortfeasor (Patterns 3 and 5)];
3. (Split-Domicile Cross-Border Cases). If conduct originat-ing in one state has injured in another state a party domiciled in the other state, the law of the latter state governs if it is more favourable to the injured party and if the occurrence of the injury in that state was objectively foreseeable. [(Pattern 7)].

1. When the victim and the tortfeasor are domiciled in different states the laws of which produce the same result, the law of either state may be applied. *See supra* 289.

325. As the bracketed phrases indicate, the above three rules cover seven of the eight typical patterns reviewed in this section. In turn, these patterns represent the majority of loss-distribution conflicts. Each rule reflects the results reached by the majority of cases falling within the patterns covered by the rule. In some instances, this majority approaches unanimity (as in Pattern 1), in others it is overwhelming (as in Patterns 2–4 and 6–7), and in others it is simply a majority (as in Pattern 5). In this sense, all of the above rules are 'restatements' of the case law.

326. Although these rules cover many cases, they do not cover all cases. They are deliberately elliptical. For example, the rules do not cover: (1) the cases falling within Pattern 8; (2) all cases involving three states; and (3) all disputes between joint tortfeasors in all patterns. Judicial experience thus far has not produced clear solutions for any of these categories. Although one can detect certain weak trends, it would be premature to give them the status of either a descriptive, or especially a prescriptive, rule.

327. The above rules are not phrased with the precision and the degree of detail that is necessary or customary for statutory rules. Furthermore, because they are descriptive rather than prescriptive, the above rules are not accompanied by any escape clause authorizing judicial deviations in exceptional cases. Such a clause would be necessary, however, if one were to put these rules in statutory language.[1]

1. The similarly phrased rules of the Louisiana codification are accompanied by escapes.

328. All three of the above rules are forum-neutral. Rules 1 and 2 are also content-neutral, that is, they are phrased in terms that, on their surface, do not take account of the content of the involved states' laws. They provide for the application of the law of the designated state, regardless of whether that law favours the victim or the tortfeasor. In this sense, Rules 1 and 2 are 'jurisdiction-selecting' rules. In contrast, Rule 3 is a content-dependent or content-oriented rule, because it provides for the application of the law of the designated state only if that law has a certain content (i.e., it favours the victim).

The reason for the difference is not an *a priori* preference, but rather the judicial experience accumulated during the revolution, and a careful study and analysis of that experience. For example, as the reader will recall, the above review divided the common-domicile cases covered by Rule 1 into two patterns (1 and 2), based precisely on the content of the involved states' laws. However, after collecting and analyzing the cases of each pattern, the conclusion emerged that this content did not affect the outcome of the cases. Similarly, the cases covered by Rule 2 were divided into four patterns (3–6), again based on the content of the involved states' laws. Again, in the majority of cases that content proved to be immaterial in affecting the outcome.

In contrast, in the remaining two patterns (Patterns 7 and 8), the content of the involved states' laws did make a difference. The majority of cases applied the law of the victim's home state when that law favoured the victim (Pattern 7), but not when it favoured the tortfeasor (Pattern 8). For this reason, Rule 3 has been phrased narrowly so as to encompass Pattern 7, but not Pattern 8, cases.

§4. Conduct-Regulation Conflicts

I. Introduction

329. This section discusses conflicts between conduct-regulating rules, namely rules which, in the words of the New York Court of Appeals, 'have the prophylactic effect of governing conduct to prevent injuries from occurring'.[1] As explained earlier, whether a particular rule falls within this category depends on the rule's primary purpose or function as determined by the court through the interpretative process. 'Rules of the road', as well as those rules that prescribe the civil sanctions for violating rules of the road, and rules that prescribe safety standards for work sites, buildings, and other premises are examples of rules whose primary function is to regulate conduct, even if they ultimately also have an impact on loss-distribution.

One peculiarly American example of conduct-regulating rules are those that impose punitive or exemplary damages for egregious conduct. These rules go beyond the normative goal of deterrence that characterizes all conduct-regulating rules in that they seek to civilly punish the individual wrongdoer, setting an example for others. In the words of one American court, these rules aim for 'deterrence through public condemnation'.[2] Because of these special features, punitive-damages conflicts are reserved for separate discussion at the end of this section. Part II of this section discusses cases involving other conduct-regulating rules or, at least, rules that the courts classified as conduct-regulating rules.

1. *Padula* v. *Lilarn Props. Corp.*, 644 N.E.2d 1001, 1002 (N.Y. 1994), discussed *supra* 266–267.
2. *Horowitz* v. *Schneider Nat'l Inc.*, 708 F.Supp. 1573, 1577 (D.Wyo. 1989).

II. Generic Conduct-Regulation Conflicts

A. The Pertinent Contacts and Typical Patterns

330. Unlike loss-distributing rules which focus both on people and territory, conduct-regulating rules are primarily territorial. For example, a state has an interest in enforcing its traffic rules, without regard to who violates them and who suffers from the violation. A foreigner who enters the territory may not claim exemption from these rules and, when injured by conduct that violates them, the foreigner may not be denied the benefit of their protection. This suggests that, as a general proposition, the parties' domiciles are a far less significant factor in conduct-regulation conflicts than in loss-distribution conflicts.[1] For this reason, conduct-regulating conflicts should be analyzed and resolved by focussing more on the spatial aspects of the conduct and the injury, and less on the parties' domiciles.

1. This is not to say that domicile is an irrelevant contact. For example, if the violator of a conduct-regulating rule is a domiciliary of the enacting state, this state has an additional reason to insist on the rule's application. Similarly, if the victim of the violation is a domiciliary of the enacting state, this state has an additional reason to insist on the rule's application. The point is, however, that a state has a general interest in enforcing its conduct-regulating rules even if neither the violator nor the victim resides in that state.

331. The reference to both the conduct and the injury underscores the possibility that these two events may occur in different states. Indeed, cross-border torts are more common today than ever before. In such torts, the old phrase '*locus* of the tort' becomes ambiguous. When conduct in one state produces injury in another, either state may qualify as the locus of the tort. Rather than retreating to outmoded and artificial 'last-event' notions, one should be prepared to accept the premise that, when the conduct and the injury are not in the same state, both of these contacts deserve due consideration.

332. With this premise in mind, as well as the idea that the parties' domiciles are not a significant *a priori* factor in conduct-regulation conflicts, these conflicts can be classified into the following four patterns:

1. cases in which the conduct and the injury occur in the same state (*Pattern 1*); and
2. cases in which the conduct and the injury occur in different states, and in which:
   (a) the two states prescribe the same standards of conduct (*Pattern 2*); or
   (b) the two states prescribe different standards (designated with the adjectives 'high' and 'low'), and in which the particular conduct:
      (i) violates the ('higher') standards of the state of conduct, but not the ('lower') standards of the state of injury (*Pattern 3*); or
      (ii) does not violate the ('lower') standards of the state of conduct, but does violate the ('higher') standards of the state of injury (*Pattern 4*).

B. Pattern 1: Conduct and Injury in Same State

333. Ordinarily, the cases of Pattern 1 are so obviously false conflicts that they should not occupy us here. If the issue in question clearly qualifies as one of conduct-regulation, then the state in which both the injurious conduct and the resulting injury occurred has the exclusive claim to apply its law. As the *Babcock* court stated, in these cases, 'it would be almost unthinkable to seek the applicable rule in the law of some other place'.[1] Indeed, even the Restatement Second abandons its characteristic equivocation and declares that, '[w]ith respect to issues relating to the standards of conduct, the local law of the state of conduct and injury has been invariably applied'.[2]

1. *Babcock* v. *Jackson*, 191 N.E.2d at 280. *See also supra* 212.
2. *Restatement (Second)* §146 cmt. d., Reporters Note (emphasis added).

334. Yet, perhaps because of the increased importance of the parties' domiciles in loss-distribution conflicts, it is easy to forget that the parties' domiciles are simply irrelevant in conduct-regulation conflicts. It therefore bears repeating that the principle that the state of conduct and injury has the 'dominant interest' to apply its law holds true even when one *or both* of the parties are domiciled in such 'other place'. Cases confirming this proposition are countless. They involve issues of not only traffic safety and work site safety, but also premises liability, contributory negligence, interference with contract, misappropriation of trade secrets, and many other issues. In all of these cases, the courts applied the law of the state in which both the conduct and the injury occurred, without considering the parties' domiciles. Conversely, some cases have held that the forum's conduct-regulating rule was inapplicable to an out-of-state accident involving exclusively forum domiciliaries.[1]

1. For documentation, *see* Symeonides, *The Choice-of-Law Revolution* 214–220.

335. *Bertram* v. *Norden*[1] is a recent example of the controlling interest of the state of conduct and injury to apply its law, even when the tortfeasor and the victim have a joint domicile and a preexisting relationship in another state. *Bertram* arose from a snowmobiling collision in Michigan between two young Ohio domiciliaries who had travelled together to Michigan for a weekend of snowmobiling activities. A Michigan statute barred the plaintiff's action, providing that '[e]ach person who participates in the sport of snowmobiling accepts the risks associated with that sport insofar as the dangers are obvious and inherent'.[2] Ohio permitted the action.

The Ohio court applied the Michigan statute, holding for the defendant. The court reasoned that the parties' common domicile and relationship in Ohio did not overcome the presumption in favour of Michigan law, because Michigan had a special interest in applying its snowmobiling statute to snowmobiling activity within its borders. Noting that Michigan is a well known snowmobiling destination, the court found it 'important that Michigan has created a law specifically regulating the operation of snowmobiles . . . and . . . recogniz[ing] a rider's own assumption of risk'.[3] The court concluded that Michigan law should govern '[b]ecause . . . the place where the conduct causing . . . injury occurred in Michigan and Michigan has enacted specific legislation involving the risks of snowmobiling'.[4]

1. 823 N.E.2d 478 (Ohio App. 2004), *appeal not allowed*, 824 N.E.2d 541 (Ohio 2005).
2. Mich. Comp. Laws §324.82126(6) (2004).
3. *Bertram*, 823 N.E.2d at 484.
4. *Id.*

336. *Spinozzi* v. *ITT Sheraton Corporation*,[1] a case involving the issue of premises liability, is another good illustration of how irrelevant the parties' domicile is in conduct-regulation conflicts. *Spinozzi* was an action by an Illinois domiciliary who was injured in an American-owned hotel while on vacation in Mexico. The plaintiff, who was contributorily negligent, could recover under Illinois' comparative negligence rule, but not under Mexico's contributory negligence rule. The plaintiff argued that, because defendant had solicited the plaintiff in Illinois, the defendant should be deemed to have caused the injury in Illinois, and that this 'contact', together with the plaintiff's Illinois domicile, made Illinois the state with the most significant relationship.

Writing for the court, Judge Posner considered this argument as tantamount to saying that 'each guest be permitted to carry with him the tort law of his state or country, provided that he is staying in a hotel that had advertised there'.[2] Acceptance of the plaintiff's argument, said Posner, would subject a hotel operator like Sheraton 'to a hundred different bodies of tort law',[3] each imposing potentially inconsistent duties of care. 'A resort might have a system of firewalls that under the law of some states or nations might be considered essential to safety and in others might be considered a safety hazard'.[4] These dangers are avoided, said Posner, by the application of the *lex loci delicti*, which is 'the only choice of law that won't impose potentially debilitating legal uncertainties on businesses that cater to a multinational clientele while selecting the rule of decision most likely to optimize safety'.[5] Posner concluded that, in the absence of unusual circumstances, the state where the tort occurred is the state that has 'the greatest interest in striking a reasonable balance among safety, cost, and other factors pertinent to the design and administration of a system of tort law'.[6]

Posner's witty statements are correct, provided they are confined to issues of conduct regulation. For these issues, the cases have consistently, if not invariably, applied the law of the state in which the hotel or other building is situated, which is the state of both the conduct and the injury.[7]

1. 174 F.3d 842 (7th Cir. 1999) (decided under Illinois conflicts law).
2. *Id.* at 845.
3. *Id.* at 845.
4. *Id.* ('Illinois residents may want a higher standard of care than the average hotel guest in Mexico, but to supplant Mexican by Illinois tort law would disserve the general welfare because it would mean that Mexican safety standards (insofar as they are influenced by tort suits) were being set by people having little stake in those standards'.)
5. *Id.* at 846.
6. *Id.* at 845.
7. For documentation, *see* Symeonides, *The Choice-of-Law Revolution* 218–219.

337. Finally, like *Bertram* and *Spinozzi*, countless other cases involving issues of road safety ignore the parties' domiciles and focus instead on the state of conduct and injury. As noted earlier, this category of issues is much broader than commonly assumed. It includes not only traffic rules, but also the presumptions, inferences, and other legal consequences and sanctions that states impose on violators of those rules. For example, although all states of the United States require car drivers and passengers to wear seat belts, many states differ on some of the legal consequences of violating this requirement. Some states allow evidence of failure to use a seatbelt to establish the parties' relative fault and mitigate civil damages, while other states prohibit such evidence. Depending on their specific language and history, these seatbelt rules can be procedural or substantive, and, if the latter, they can be either loss-distributing or conduct-regulating. If they fall into the latter category, then they apply to all persons driving or riding in the enacting state, regardless of their domicile.[1]

1. For cases so holding, *see id.* at 219–220.

C. Pattern 2: Conduct and Injury in Different States that Prescribe the Same Standards of Conduct

338. Cases in which the conduct and the injury occur in different states also present the false conflict paradigm if the two states prescribe the same standard of conduct. In policy terms, these cases are virtually indistinguishable from Pattern 1 cases. Whether the court applies the law of the one state or the other state, the outcome will be the same. Hence, applying the law of the conduct state is both sensible and non-controversial.

For example, in *Pardey* v. *Boulevard Billiard Club*,[1] both the conduct state, Rhode Island, and the injury state, Massachusetts, had dram shop acts imposing civil liability on a tavern owner whose intoxicated patrons caused injury to another. A Massachusetts patron caused such injury in Massachusetts after becoming intoxicated in defendant's Rhode Island tavern. The court noted Rhode Island's 'substantial governmental interest'[2] in applying the Rhode Island act to violations occurring in that state, even when the resulting injury occurs in another state. The court also noted that Massachusetts would not be 'offended' by the application of the Rhode Island dram shop act because Massachusetts also had a dram shop act. Thus, the court concluded, '[a]pplication of Rhode Island law . . . effectuates, rather than frustrates, the policies of both states'.[3] Other dram shop act cases have recognized this elementary principle and have reached the same result under similar circumstances.[4]

1. 518 A.2d 1349 (R.I. 1986).
2. *Id.* at 1352.
3. *Id.* (emphasis added).
4. *See* Symeonides, *The Choice-of-Law Revolution* 221.

339. Another group of Pattern 2 cases involves statutes that impose vicarious liability on car owners for injuries caused by a driver using the car with the owner's consent (hereafter referred to as 'car-owner statutes'). Although some courts have characterized these statutes as loss-distributing, others have characterized them as conduct-regulating. Accepting for now the latter characterization, Pattern 2 appears when both the state of the critical conduct (i.e., the state in which the owner consented to the use of the car by another) and the state in which the driver caused the injury have such statutes. In such cases, the court can apply the statute of either state without altering the outcome.

In *Elson* v. *Defren*,[1] two of the involved states, Idaho and New York, had similar car-owner liability statutes. The only difference was that the text of the New York statute limited its application to cars with certain New York connections that were absent in this case. The court found that, because of this territorial limitation, the New York statute was inapplicable. However, the outcome remained the same because 'under the law of both Idaho and New York, when a vehicle is involved in an accident within their respective borders, the owner of the vehicle is vicariously liable'. Accordingly, said the court, 'without further inquiry, we apply Idaho law to effectuate the public policy reflected in the statutes of both jurisdictions'.[2]

1. 726 N.Y.S.2d 407 (N.Y.A.D. 2001).
2. *Id.* at 412.

D. Pattern 3: Conduct in State with Higher Standard and Injury in State with Lower Standard of Conduct

340. The false conflict paradigm is also present in the cross-border torts falling within Pattern 3, *supra*, namely cases in which the tortfeasor's conduct violates the 'higher' standard of the conduct-state but not the 'lower' standard of the injury-state. *Schmidt* v. *Driscoll Hotel*,[1] and *Rong Yao Zhou* v. *Jennifer Mall Restaurant, Inc.*,[2] are two well known dram shop act cases exemplifying this pattern. In both cases the tortious conduct (serving alcohol to an intoxicated patron) occurred in a state that had a dram shop act that imposed civil liability on tavern owners for this conduct, while the resulting injury occurred in a state that did not impose such liability. Both cases properly applied the dram shop act of the conduct-state, after concluding that only that state had an interest in deterring this conduct, while the injury state did not have a countervailing interest in protecting the conduct.[3] As the *Rong Yao Zhou* court stated, it, any interest the injury-state might have in protecting tavern owners from civil liability is 'not implicated where the [tavern] is situated in [another state] and the unlawful conduct occurred therein'.[4]

1. 82 N.W.2d 365 (Minn. 1957) (applying Minnesota's dram shop act to impose civil liability on a Minnesota tavern owner whose intoxicated customer caused an accident in Wisconsin injuring plaintiff, also a Minnesota resident. Wisconsin did not have a dram shop act).
2. 534 A.2d 1268 (App. D.C. 1987) (applying the District of Columbia's dram shop act to impose civil liability on a DC tavern owner whose intoxicated customer caused an accident in Maryland. Maryland did not have a dram shop act).
3. In both cases, the victim was also a domiciliary of the conduct state. Thus the application of that state's law could have also been based on that state's compensatory interests. However, even in the absence of such interests, the application of the law of the conduct state would be justified for reasons stated in the text.
4. 534 A.2d at 1271.

341. Indeed, the application of the dram shop act of the conduct-state promotes that state's policy of policing conduct within its borders, without subordinating the policies of the state of injury. The effectiveness of the conduct-regulating rule of the conduct-state would be seriously impaired if exceptions were made for cross-border torts in which the injury occurs in another state.[1] Such exceptions are not warranted by the fact that the injury-state adheres to a lower standard, because the lower standard is designed to protect conduct within, not outside, that state. Moreover, there is nothing unfair in subjecting a tortfeasor to the law of the state in which he acted. Having violated the standards of that state, the tortfeasor should bear the consequences of such violation and should not be allowed to invoke the lower standards of another state.

1. *See*, e.g., *Patton* v. *Carnrike*, 510 F.Supp. 625 (N.D.N.Y. 1981) (involving a Pennsylvania accident caused by Pennsylvania minors who purchased alcohol in New York in violation of a New York statute prohibiting alcohol sales to minors; finding that 'New York ha[d] a compelling interest in maintaining the integrity of the [statute's] deterrent effect', and that the 'goal of deterring unlawful [alcohol] sales [was] well served by preserving the vendor's complete liability irrespective of where the injury occurred' and irrespective of the 'fortuity that the purchasers were residents of Pennsylvania'.) *Id.* at 629–630.

342. Many cases involving car-owner liability statutes have reached similar results by applying the statute of the state in which the owner consented to the use of the car, even though the accident occurred in a state that did not have such a statute.[1] For example, in *Veasley* v. *CRST International, Inc.*,[2] the court applied Iowa's car-owner statute to a case arising from an accident in Arizona, which did not have such a statute. The plaintiff was an Iowa domiciliary who was injured in the accident while riding in a truck driven by his co-employee and owned by an Iowa company. The court found that one of the purposes of the Iowa statute was 'to make vehicle owners responsible for the actions of others to whom they have entrusted their motor vehicle', and that the non-application of this statute to out-of-state accidents 'would undermine [its] effectiveness'.[3] Following the Restatement (Second), the court held that the Iowa statute should govern because, 'based on the deterrence policy underlying [the statute,] . . . Iowa ha[d] a substantial connection regarding the responsibility of all persons or corporations with a local nexus that loan or lease motor vehicles to other entities'.[4]

1. *See* Symeonides, *The Choice-of-Law Revolution* 224–226.
2. 553 N.W.2d 896 (Iowa 1996).
3. *Id.* at 899.
4. *Id.*

343. *Gaither* v. *Myers*[1] involved a different type of car-owner's liability statute. The place of conduct, the District of Columbia, imposed civil liability on owners who leave their cars unattended without locking them and removing the keys. The state of injury, Maryland, would not impose liability under the circumstances of this case. The plaintiff, a Maryland domiciliary, was injured in a Maryland accident caused by a car owned by the defendant, a D.C. resident. The defendant had left the ignition key in his car in D.C., where it was presumably stolen and driven into Maryland. The court concluded that this was a false conflict in which only D.C. was interested and its law should govern.

The court reasoned that the main purpose of the D.C. rule was not to protect theft for the sake of car owners, but rather 'to promote the safety of the public in the streets . . . [and] to make streets safer by discouraging the hazardous conduct [the rule] forbids'.[2] Thus, D.C. had a 'significant', indeed 'powerful', interest in applying the rule 'to an actor who leaves his car keys to a thief in the District',[3] setting in motion the chain of events likely to lead to injury. The fact that this injury occurred in Maryland did not diminish D.C.'s interests, nor did it generate a countervailing Maryland interest in applying its defendant-protecting rule.[4]

1. 404 F.2d 216 (D.C. Cir. 1968).
2. *Id.* at 222.
3. *Id.* at 223.
4. *See id.* at 224 (Whatever interest Maryland had in protecting car owners, it 'would not seem to extend to an owner like our defendant, who is not a citizen of Maryland . . . especially . . . where it is a Maryland citizen who is being compensated for his injuries'.).

344. *Pittman* v. *Maldania, Inc.*[1] is illustrative of cases involving other conduct-regulation issues. In this case, the defendant operated a water-ski rental office located on the Delaware side of the Delaware-Maryland border, with the boundary line running exactly in front of the office door. Both states prohibited renting to persons under age sixteen, but (unlike Maryland) Delaware also required the showing of a valid driver's licence. After misrepresenting their ages, two under-age Pennsylvanians rented skis from defendant's Delaware office, and, while riding the skis in Maryland, collided with each other resulting in injury to one of them, the plaintiff. The plaintiff invoked Delaware law, while the defendant store-owner invoked Maryland law.

Following the Restatement (Second), the Delaware court held that Delaware law should govern, despite the presumption of Restatement Section 146 in favour of the place of injury. The court found that: (1) this presumption was rebutted because the precise issue in this case was the defendant's conduct in renting the skis in Delaware to an underage person; (2) the Delaware statute reflected 'a clear policy against renting jet skis to people who are unable to produce a valid driver's licence'; (3) this policy was 'part of a comprehensive statute on boating safety'; and (4) a 'statute regulating conduct should be enforced throughout the state'. The court also found that: (1) 'Maryland ha[d] no conflicting policy'; (2) Delaware's law '[did] not interfere in any way with Maryland's regulation of water safety in its state', and (3) the defendant, having acted in Delaware, could not complain about the application of Delaware law.[2]

1. 2001 WL 1221704 (Del. Super. Ct. 2001).
2. *Id.* at *4. The court also noted that this holding was confined to the narrow issue of renting the skis, and that if other issues were present in this case, a different conclusion might have followed.

345. Finally, *D'Agostino* v. *Johnson & Johnson, Inc.*[1] is another illustration that a state's interest in deterring substandard conduct within its territory is not diminished by the fact that the conduct produces its effects in another state. In *D'Agostino*, the wrongful conduct occurred in New Jersey and had its impact in Switzerland. Executives of a New Jersey corporation allegedly 'orchestrated' the retaliatory firing of an American citizen (who was employed by their wholly-owned Swiss subsidiary) for refusing to bribe Swiss officials in charge of regulating the licensing of pharmaceuticals in Switzerland. If proven, this conduct would violate the Federal Corrupt Practices Act, which New Jersey cases had incorporated into New Jersey law. Under Swiss law, the alleged bribes would be considered 'consulting fees' and would be lawful, as would be the employee's firing.

In a unanimous opinion applying interest analysis, the New Jersey Supreme Court held that New Jersey's interests in deterring wrongful conduct in New Jersey 'outweigh the Swiss interest in the at-will employment relationship that would not seek to deter such conduct through its civil law'.[2] The court emphasized that this case was 'not about regulating just Swiss employment relationships . . . [but rather] about regulating the conduct of parent companies in New Jersey that engage in corrupt practices through subsidiary employees'.[3] The court concluded that the strength of New Jersey's commitment to deterring commercial bribery, coupled with the 'extensive New Jersey contacts',[4] suggested a 'strong public interest' in applying New Jersey law, and that '[a]ny opposing interest involving extraterritoriality' did not outweigh New Jersey's 'interests in preventing bribery, which could have a negative impact on public health and safety in New Jersey'.[5]

1. 628 A.2d 305 (N.J. 1993).
2. *Id.* at 307. The court noted that, although the fired employee was at all times a resident of Switzerland, and had signed an at-will employment contract in that country containing a Swiss choice-of-law clause, and although Switzerland had an interest in regulating the employment relationship between a Swiss company and a Swiss resident, Switzerland did 'not have an interest in condoning corporate bribery orchestrated beyond its boundaries'. *Id.* at 316.
3. *Id.* at 311.
4. *Id.* at 316.
5. *Id.* at 315.

E. Pattern 4: Conduct in State with Lower Standard and Injury in State with High Standard

346. Pattern 4 involves the most difficult cross-border torts. In this pattern the conduct in question does not violate the 'lower' standard of the state of conduct, but violates the 'higher' standard of the state of injury. In interest analysis terminology, these cases usually present the true conflict paradigm because each state has an interest in applying its own law. The first state has an interest in protecting conduct that is lawful there, while the second state has an interest in ensuring reparation for injuries that occurred there and preventing future injuries.

347. As in all true conflicts, the choice of either law is bound to encounter disagreement. However, the argument for applying the higher standard of the state of injury is stronger in cases involving intentional torts than in negligence cases. Indeed, not many people would question the right of a state to punish conduct that is intended to produce, and does produce, detrimental effects within its territory, even when that conduct takes place outside the state. As Justice Holmes stated almost a century ago, '[a]cts done outside the jurisdiction, but intended to produce and producing detrimental effects within it, justify a state in punishing the cause of the harm'.[1]

1. *Strassheim* v. *Daily*, 221 US 280, 284 (1911).

348. To this end, federal courts have developed the so-called 'effects doctrine', at least for acts committed abroad and producing intended injuries in the United States. For example, in *Hartford Fire Ins. Co.* v. *California*,[1] the United States Supreme Court held that federal antitrust legislation, the 'Sherman Act', applied to 'foreign conduct that was meant to produce, and did in fact produce, some substantial effects in the United States'.[2] The Court applied the Act to British insurance underwriters who, while in London, engaged in conduct designed to affect the California insurance market. Several lower court cases have applied the Sherman Act in the same fashion.[3] One case went as far as to uphold under the Act a criminal prosecution of a Japanese defendant for conduct in Japan (price-fixing) that was intended to, and did, produce detrimental effects in the United States.[4]

1. 509 US 764 (1993), discussed *infra* 685–687.
2. *Id.* at 795–796.
3. *See* Symeonides, *The Choice-of-Law Revolution* 229; *see also* Restatement (Third) of Foreign Relations §402.
4. *See United States* v. *Nippon Paper Indus.*, 109 F.3d 1 (1st Cir. 1997).

349. In cases involving negligent conduct, the argument for applying the higher standard of the state of injury may be less powerful psychologically, but it is still a fairly strong one, provided that the actor could have foreseen that his conduct in one state would produce injury in the other state. *Bernhard* v. *Harrah's Club*,[1] is a well known example of such a case.

Bernhard applied California law imposing civil liability on a Nevada tavern owner for conduct in Nevada that caused injury in California. Nevada law did not impose such liability. An important factor in justifying the choice of California law was that the defendant should have foreseen that its conduct in Nevada would produce detrimental effects in California. The geographic proximity of the defendant's operation to the California-Nevada border, the defendant's active solicitation of California patrons, and the composition of defendant's clientele made it foreseeable that tavern patrons might drive into California and cause an accident there. It is this foreseeability factor that tips the scales and makes the application of the law of the injury-state an appropriate solution to these otherwise difficult true conflicts.

1. 546 P.2d 719 (Cal. 1976), discussed *supra* 236.

350. Similarly, in *Hoeller* v. *Riverside Resort Hotel*,[1] a case decided under the Restatement (Second), the court applied Arizona's common law which imposed civil liability on a Nevada casino owner under circumstances identical to those in *Bernhard*.[2] The court compared Nevada's interest in 'free[ing] tavern owners, and other alcohol purveyors such as casinos, from the cost and inconvenience of incurring either civil or criminal liability' with Arizona's 'strong interest in providing an opportunity for its residents to recover full compensation from persons and business that contribute to automobile accidents on Arizona highways . . . [and] in holding tortfeasors responsible for their actions' foreseeable effects in Arizona'.[3] The court also noted the casino's proximity to the Nevada-Arizona border and pointed out that the casino had gone to great lengths to attract Arizona clientele. The court concluded that, under these circumstances, the casino should have known that 'many of the patrons it seeks, many of those who sit at its tables and drink its [free] liquor, have come to the casino from Arizona and will return to Arizona . . . in an intoxicated condition and . . . may cause accidents that injure third persons in Arizona'.[4]

1. 820 P.2d 316 (Ariz. Ct. App. 1991).
2. An Arizona domiciliary became intoxicated in the Nevada casino and on his return to Arizona caused an accident injuring plaintiff, another Arizona domiciliary.
3. 820 P.2d at 320.
4. *Id.* at 321.

351. Other dram shop act cases have reached the same result under similar circumstances.[1] In one such case, *Young* v. *Players Lake Charles, L.L.C.*,[2] the conduct-state, Louisiana, had enacted an 'anti-dram shop act' that expressly insulated liquor servers from liability. A patron who became intoxicated in the defendant's riverboat casino in Louisiana, drove into Texas and caused injury there. The court noted that Louisiana's 'appalling insulation of casino boats who use free or discounted liquor as the bait to entice gamblers, while ignoring the consequences when those predictably intoxicated gamblers hit the streets in lethal vehicles',[3] was within Louisiana's prerogatives, but only as long as the consequences of that decision were felt exclusively in Louisiana. In this case, the consequences were felt in other states. Louisiana casino-owners 'entice[d] residents of Texas and other states to flock in huge numbers to their casinos to drink too much and return home in a murderous condition'.[4] The court applied Texas law, which imposed liability on the casino owner.

1. *See* Symeonides, *The Choice-of-Law Revolution* 230–232.
2. 47 F.Supp.2d 832 (S.D. Tex. 1999).
3. *Id.* at 834.
4. *Id.* at 837. *Blamey* v. *Brown*, 270 N.W.2d 884 (Minn. 1978), *cert. denied*, 444 US 1070 (1980) (decided under Minnesota's better-law approach), was a closer case, if only because it was not an 'enticement' case. The defendant, who operated a small tavern on the Wisconsin side of the Wisconsin-Minnesota border, did not advertise in Minnesota nor attempt to attract Minnesota customers. However, he occasionally sold alcohol to Minnesota residents and in this case he sold alcohol to a Minnesota minor who drove back to Minnesota and caused an accident there, injuring another Minnesota domiciliary. The court concluded that the bar's proximity to the border and the defendant's knowledge that some of his customers were Minnesotans allowed Minnesota courts to assume jurisdiction and to apply Minnesota's 'better' law, which imposed liability on the bar owner.

F. Summary and Rule for Conduct-Regulation Conflicts

352. The results of the cases involving conflicts between conduct-regulating rules (other than punitive damages) can be compressed into the following one-sentence rule:

> Conflicts between conduct-regulating rules are governed by the law of the state of conduct, except when the injury foreseeably occurs in another state that imposes a higher standard of conduct, in which case the law of the latter state governs.[1]

This rule is simple, predictable, and balanced. It resolves the false conflicts cases of Patterns 1–3 in the only logical and non-controversial way possible. The fact that the rule resolves the true conflicts of Pattern 4 in a way that favours plaintiffs may appear to negate the claim that it is balanced. This claim is valid, however, because the rule subjects the application of the plaintiff-protecting law of the state of injury to the foreseeability proviso. Because of this proviso, this result can be defended not so much on the basis of that state's interest or on the basis of the *favour laesi* principle, but on the basis of basic principles of accountability. One who predictably causes harm in a state whose law considers that harm tortious should be held accountable under that law.

1. For a comparison of this rule with similar statutory rules, *see* Symeonides, *The Choice-of-Law Revolution* 236.

III. Punitive-Damages Conflicts

A. *Introduction*

353. Punitive or exemplary damages are money damages assessed against a defendant in a civil action for misconduct that the legal system regards as heinous or egregious. They have been part of American law since at least the 19th century, when many states began introducing them for certain cases of aggravated or egregious misconduct. Today, all but one state allow punitive damages, at least in some cases.[1]

1. *See* D. Owen, M. Madden & M. Davis, *Madden & Owen on Products Liability*, (3d edn 2002), v. 2, §18:1 note 41. Only Nebraska prohibits punitive damages in *all* cases. Even the mixed jurisdiction of Louisiana allows punitive damages for injury caused by drunk drivers, and for sexual abuse of minors. *See* La. Civ. Code Ann. Arts 2315.4 and 2315.7. Although most American states allow punitive damages in general, these states often disagree on the specific cases, causes of action, or other circumstances in which punitive damages are available. When such disagreements exist, the resulting conflicts are as intense as they come, if only because they involve large sums of money.

354. The adjectives 'punitive' and 'exemplary' are often used interchangeably and express the two purposes of punitive damages: punishment and deterrence. Punishment or retribution is individual but backward looking, in that it focuses on the individual wrongdoer and his or her specific misconduct. The degree of punishment depends on both the egregiousness of the specific misconduct, and the wrongdoer's financial capacity to bear and internalize the punishment. Deterrence or prevention is more general and forward looking, in that it focuses not only on the individual wrongdoer, but on others who might consider engaging in similar misconduct in the future. Deterrence is achieved by attaching to certain conduct a price tag that is much higher than the gains one might expect from engaging in that conduct. Thus, punitive damages differ in important respects from compensatory damages, which are designed to compensate the victim, and hence are proportional to the victim's harm or loss.

355. The fact that compensatory damages are proportional to the victim's loss explains why they often cannot effectively punish or deter economically powerful wrongdoers, especially corporate offenders who have the ability to pass this additional cost to the consumers. The fact that punitive damages are awarded to a private plaintiff in a civil trial indicates their differences from criminal and civil fines, both of which inure to a public fund.[1] At the same time, the fact that, in a civil trial, the defendant does not enjoy certain procedural protections of the criminal law (such as proof beyond a reasonable doubt, the right against self-incrimination, and the protection from double jeopardy and excessive fines) is one of the reasons for which punitive damages are often controversial,[2] although they are subject to continuous scrutiny by the US Supreme Court. In any event, the function of PIL is not to gauge the wisdom of a state's substantive law, but rather to delineate the multistate cases to which this law should properly apply. This Part attempts to do so by reviewing the experience of American courts in resolving punitive-damages conflicts.

1. Although a recent movement to direct a portion of punitive damages to a public fund tends to blur this distinction, that movement has had only limited success so far. *See* S. Symeonides, 'Resolving Punitive Damages Conflicts', 5 *Y.B. of Priv. Int'l L.* 1, 2003, 2–3.
2. Yet, precisely because punitive damages are sought, and their prerequisites proven, by private plaintiffs rather than by the state, one could argue that the above procedural protections of the criminal law are largely unnecessary and perhaps inappropriate; for private plaintiffs possess neither the coercive power of the state nor its superior investigatory resources. Moreover, while punitive damages can carry severe economic consequences, they do not endanger the defendant's life or liberty. In any event, many states have recently raised the burden of proof for punitive damages from 'preponderance of the evidence' (which is the typical standard in civil cases) to 'clear and convincing evidence'. *See* Symeonides, 'Punitive Damages' *supra*. note 1 at 3. One state, Colorado, has further raised the standard to 'beyond reasonable doubt', which is the criminal law standard.

B. The Pertinent Contacts and Typical Patterns

356. Because rules imposing punitive damages are *par excellence* conduct-regulating rules, the place or places of the conduct and injury are contacts that are as pertinent in punitive-damages conflicts as in generic conduct-regulation conflicts. The state of the conduct has the right to regulate (police, punish, deter, or protect) conduct within its borders, and the state where this conduct produces its effects – the injury – has a right to determine what sanctions are appropriate for such conduct.

However, as the word 'punitive' suggests, these rules have a greater sting than generic conduct-regulation rules, in that they seek to punish the individual tortfeasor, as well as to deter other potential tortfeasors. Thus, the tortfeasor's domicile is a pertinent contact in punitive-damages conflicts. When the law of the tortfeasor's home state imposes punitive damages, the application of that law serves its underlying purpose of punishing that tortfeasor and deterring him and other potential tortfeasors from engaging in similar conduct in the future. Similarly, when that law prohibits punitive damages, then its application would serve its underlying purpose of protecting that tortfeasor from excessive financial exposure.

This then leaves the domicile of the victim. If it is true that punitive damages are designed to punish and deter tortfeasors rather than to compensate victims (and their attorneys) who, *ex hypothesi*, are made whole through compensatory damages, then the victim's domicile should, in principle, be irrelevant in punitive-damages conflicts.

Thus, the contacts pertinent in identifying the concerned states in punitive damages conflicts are: (1) the place of conduct; (2) the place of injury; and (3) the tortfeasor's domicile, habitual residence, or principal place of business.

357. Putting factual contacts and substantive laws[1] in the mix produces eight typical patterns of potential or actual punitive-damages conflicts, which can be grouped into four groups, namely cases in which punitive damages are imposed by a state or states that have:

1. all three pertinent contacts (one pattern);
2. two pertinent contacts (three patterns);
3. one pertinent contact (three patterns); and
4. none of the pertinent contacts (one pattern).

The remainder of this Section reports the results of studying the cases in each group.

1. The following review assumes that a state either imposes or does not impose punitive damages for the particular conduct. It is true that in some cases, states that impose punitive damages may differ on the available or permissible amounts. For example, one state may limit the amount, either through an absolute cap or in proportion to compensatory damages. These cases present a choice-of-law problem only if the claimant requests, and the court is prepared to grant, an amount exceeding this limit. Similarly, two states that allow punitive damages may differ on the applicable burden of proof. Even so, these cases are few and far between. For the sake of simplicity, this Section does not discuss these issues.

C. Group 1: All Three Contacts

358. In cases falling within Group 1, a state that has all three pertinent contacts (or three states with each having a pertinent contact) imposes punitive damages. For example, a defendant acts in his home state and causes injury there to a domiciliary of another state. If the law of the former state imposes punitive damages for this conduct, that state has every interest in applying its law to punish that defendant and to deter other defendants from engaging in similar conduct in the future. Even if the victim's home state prohibits punitive damages, such a prohibition need not be heeded, because it is designed to protect tortfeasors acting or domiciled in that state, rather than to prevent victims domiciled there from recovering punitive damages. In the United States, this solution is widely accepted, even in states like Louisiana which prohibits punitive damages in the vast majority of cases.[1]

The same rationale should apply if the state that denies punitive damages is the forum state, whether or not it is also the victim's home state. In most cases, the forum's denial of punitive damages is designed to protect either forum defendants or forum conduct, or both, and in this case the forum has neither of these contacts. Thus, the award of punitive damages under the law of the other state does not undermine the forum's policies.

1. *See* La. Civ. Code Ann. Art. 3546, which provides that punitive damages may be awarded if such damages are available under the law of a state or states that have any two or all of the following contacts: place of conduct, place of injury, or defendant's domicile. Most civil law systems take exactly the opposite position. For a discussion of the Swiss position, *see* Symeonides, 'Punitive Damages', *supra* note 355 at 3–4, 31–33.

D. Group 2: Two-Contact Patterns

1. State(s) of Defendant's Domicile and Conduct Impose(s) Punitive Damages

359. In this pattern, the tortfeasor is domiciled in a state that imposes punitive damages and, while in that state, engages in conduct that causes injury in another state that does not impose punitive damages.[1] This case presents the false conflict paradigm. The first state has an interest in applying its punitive-damages law so as to punish the tortfeasor who engaged in egregious conduct in that state, and to deter similarly situated potential tortfeasors. That state has 'an obvious and substantial . . . interest in ensuring that it does not become either a base or a haven for law breakers to wreak injury [elsewhere]'.[2] In contrast, the state of injury does not have an interest in applying its non-punitive damages law, because that law is designed to protect tortfeasors who are either domiciled in, or act in that state, neither of which is the case here. Thus, the application of the law of the first state promotes the deterrence policies of that state without impairing the defendant-protecting policies of the state of injury.

1. A functionally analogous variation of this pattern appears when the tortfeasor acts outside his home state, but in a state that also imposes punitive damage.
2. *In re Simon II Litig.*, 2002 WL 31323751 at *95 (E.D.N.Y. 2002), vacated and remanded on grounds not relevant here, 407 F.3d 125 (2nd Cir. 2003).

360. Many cases involving this pattern have reached this precise result.[1] One example is *In re Air Crash Disaster at Stapleton Int'l Airport, Denver*,[2] a case arising from the crash of a passenger plane in Colorado. In this case, Texas was both the airline's principal place of business and the place of the conduct most likely responsible for the crash. Texas, but not Colorado, provided for punitive damages in wrongful death actions. The court reiterated a principle first articulated in *In re Air Crash Disaster Near Chicago, Illinois*[3] and since followed in most air disaster cases to the effect that,

> Because the place of injury is much more fortuitous than the place of misconduct or the principal place of business, its interest in and ability to control behaviour by deterrence or punishment, or to protect defendants from liability is lower than that of the place of misconduct or the principal place of business.[4]

The *Stapleton* court concluded that, because Texas was both the site of the critical conduct and the defendants' principal place of business, 'its relationship to this litigation is most significant' and thus its law should govern. The court acknowledged that Colorado might have an interest in regulating the conduct of corporations entering its territory to do business but concluded that this interest was 'somewhat lessened when a foreign corporation attempts to shield itself from the more onerous laws of its home state'.[5]

1. *See* Symeonides, *The Choice-of-Law Revolution* 245–247.
2. 720 F.Supp. 1445 (D. Colo. 1988).
3. 644 F.2d 594 (7th Cir.), *cert. denied*, 454 US 878 (1981).
4. 720 F.Supp. at 1453.
5. *Id.* Conversely, said the court, the knowledge that the law of a corporation's principal place of business will be applied in the event of litigation was 'not likely to discourage corporations like [the defendant airline] from doing business in Colorado'. *Id.*

361. Another example is *Jackson* v. *Travelers Ins. Co.*,[1] a case involving an action for bad faith insurance practises. In this case, the court held that Iowa's punitive-damages law applied to the insurer's conduct in that state, even though the resulting injury to the Nebraska plaintiff had occurred in Nebraska, which did not allow for such damages. The court found that 'it [was] not in the interest of the Nebraska legislature to extend protection to all insurance companies nationwide regardless of whether they are Nebraska businesses',[2] and that Nebraska 'ha[d] no interest in preventing punitive damages awards from other states to Nebraska citizens'.[3] On the other hand, said the court, because Iowa 'was the location of the *cause* of the injuries[,] . . . Iowa ha[d] a significant interest in using punitive damages to punish bad faith conduct that occurs in Iowa',[4] and 'failure to apply Iowa law . . . would wholly frustrate Iowa's interest in deterring outrageous conduct'.[5]

1. 26 F.Supp.2d 1153 (S.D. Iowa 1998).
2. *Id.* at 1162.
3. *Id.* at 1165.
4. *Id.* (emphasis added).
5. *Id.* at 1164.

2. State(s) of Conduct and Injury Impose(s) Punitive Damages

362. In this pattern, a tortfeasor domiciled in a state that does not impose punitive damages, engages in conduct in another state that does impose such damages, and causes injury in the latter state.[1] This pattern presents the direct or true conflict paradigm because both states have an interest in applying their laws. The first state has an interest in protecting its domiciliary tortfeasor from punitive damages, whereas the second state has an interest in deterring conduct in that state that causes injury there. On balance, the application of the law of the latter state is entirely justified. The fact that the defendant acted outside his home state weakens any argument that he relied on that state's law, and the fact that he acted in the other state destroys any argument of unfair surprise from the application of the latter state's law.

1. A functionally analogous variation of this pattern is when the injury occurs in a third state that also imposes punitive damages.

363. Cases involving this pattern have reached the result suggested above by applying the punitive-damages law of the state of conduct and injury.[1] For example, in *Horowitz* v. *Schneider Nat'l Inc.*,[2] the court applied Wyoming's punitive-damages law to an action arising from a Wyoming traffic accident, even though none of the parties were Wyoming domiciliaries. The court found that Wyoming had a 'paramount interest "in the manner in which its highways are used and the care exercised by drivers"'.[3] The court reiterated that '[t]he policy behind . . . punitive damages is not compensation of the victim . . . [but rather] deterrence through public condemnation'.[4]

Likewise, in *Isley* v. *Capuchin Province*,[5] an action for sexual abuse arising out of events in Wisconsin and filed against an out-of-state religious order, a Michigan court applied Wisconsin law, which imposed punitive damages. The court concluded that 'Wisconsin's interest outweigh[ed] Michigan's interest',[6] because Wisconsin had a 'strong interest in protecting minors in Wisconsin from sexual abuse and in punishing those found guilty'.[7]

1. *See* Symeonides, *The Choice-of-Law Revolution* 247–249.
2. 708 F.Supp. 1573 (D. Wyo. 1989).
3. *Id.* at 1577 (quoting *Brown* v. *Riner*, 500 P.2d 524, 526 (Wyo. 1972)).
4. *Id.*
5. 878 F.Supp. 1021 (E.D.Mich. 1995).
6. *Id.* at 1023.
7. *Id.* at 1024.

364. Finally, in *Schoeberle* v. *United States*,[1] the court held that the law of Iowa, which was the state of both the pertinent conduct and the injury, should govern the question of punitive damages, even though the plaintiffs and some of the defendants were domiciled in Wisconsin, which did not allow such damages. The court concluded that Wisconsin's interest in protecting its resident corporate defendant from excessive liability was 'outweighed by Iowa's interest in applying its punitive damages law to conduct within its borders'.[2] The court reasoned that, '[w]hen a balance between punishment and deterrence on the one hand and protection from excessive liability on the other must be struck, "it is fitting that the state whose interests are more deeply affected should have its local law applied"'.[3] That state was Iowa, because, as the place of both the conduct and the injury, Iowa had an 'obvious interest . . . in punish[ing] those responsible for [the] misconduct . . . [and] in deterring such misconduct and occurrences in the future'.[4]

1. 2000 WL 1868130 (N.D.Ill. 2000).
2. *Id.* at *14.
3. *Id.* at *13 (quoting *In Re Air Crash Disaster Near Chicago*, 644 F.2d 594, at 613 (7th Cir. 1981)).
4. *Id.*

3. State(s) of Injury and Defendant's Domicile Impose(s) Punitive Damages

365. In this pattern, a defendant domiciled in a state that imposes punitive damages engages in conduct in another state that does not impose punitive damages, and causes injury in the defendant's home state. This scenario is factually uncommon, but a variation of it is not as unlikely – when, in the same case, the defendant's conduct causes injury in a third state that also imposes punitive damages.

In re Air Crash Disaster at Washington D.C.[1] involved the latter pattern. The defendant, a Florida-based airline, engaged in conduct in Virginia that caused its air plane to crash in the District of Columbia. Both Florida and D.C., but not Virginia, imposed punitive damages. The court applied D.C. law, allowing punitive damages. It is true that, when the conduct occurs in a state that does not allow punitive damages, that state has a certain interest to apply its law so as to protect that conduct. However, the fact that the consequences of that conduct are felt in another state, and are caused by a tortfeasor domiciled in a third state that also imposes punitive damages, suggests that on balance the interests of the conduct state must give way to the interests of the other two states.

1. 559 F.Supp. 333 (D.D.C. 1983).

E. Group 3: Single-Contact Patterns

366. Several cases have applied the punitive-damages law of a state that had only one of the above three contacts, even though the other two contacts were in a state or states disallowing punitive damages. However, for every case that did so, there is at least one other case that reached the opposite result.

1. Only the Defendant's Home State Imposes Punitive Damages

367. In this pattern, the defendant's home state imposes punitive damages and thus has an interest in punishing the defendant and deterring others from engaging in similar conduct. However, both the defendant's conduct and the resulting injury occur in another state (or states) that does not impose punitive damages. In such a case, one could argue that the latter state has an interest in protecting, if not the defendant as such, at least the defendant's activity within its territory, which may be beneficial in other ways, such as by providing jobs for the local population. The resulting conflict is not easy to resolve, and this explains why courts encountering such conflicts have reached different results. While most courts deny punitive damages, a few courts have allowed them by applying the law of the defendant's domicile.[1]

1. *See* Symeonides, *The Choice-of-Law Revolution* 250–251.

2. Only the State of Conduct Imposes Punitive Damages

368. In this pattern, the state of conduct imposes punitive damages (and thus has an interest in punishing and deterring the particular conduct), while the defendant's domicile and the place of injury are in a state, or states, that do not impose punitive damages (and thus have an interest in protecting the defendant). This results in a true conflict between the laws of the state of conduct and the state of the defendant's domicile, with the state of injury playing a secondary role. Cases involving this pattern have applied the law of any one of these three states.[1] For example, in *Long* v. *Sears Roebuck & Co.*,[2] a products liability case, the court imposed punitive damages under the law of the place of wrongful conduct, which the court assumed to be the sale of a defective mower and a misrepresentation of its safety features. In contrast, in *Harlan Feeders* v. *Grand Laboratories, Inc.*,[3] another product liability case, the court applied the law of the state of injury, which prohibited punitive damages, rather than the law of the state of conduct (manufacture), which allowed them.

1. *See id.* at 251–253.
2. 877 F.Supp. 8 (D.D.C. 1995).
3. 881 F.Supp. 1400 (N.D. Iowa 1995).

3. Only the State of Injury Imposes Punitive Damages

369. In this pattern, the state of the injury imposes punitive damages, but the state (or states) of the defendant's conduct and domicile prohibits such damages. Again, there is little doubt that this pattern presents the true conflict paradigm. The first state has an interest in punishing and deterring conduct and actors that cause injury within its territory, while the latter state has an interest in protecting its domiciliary actor from paying the heavy financial price of punitive damages. On balance, the application of the law of the state of injury (and the award of punitive damages under that law) is a perfectly sensible resolution to these conflicts, provided it meets two conditions.

370. The first condition is constitutionally mandated and is specific to punitive damages. It has been enunciated by the United States Supreme Court in *BMW of North America, Inc.* v. *Gore*,[1] which held that, in assessing the amount of punitive damages, the court should consider only the conduct that caused detrimental effects in the state of injury, and not the conduct that caused such effects in other states.

1. 517 US 559 (1996) (holding that, although in assessing the degree of reprehensibility of the defendant's conduct, Alabama may consider evidence of the defendant's non-Alabama conduct, nevertheless, in fixing the amount of punitive damages, Alabama may not punish the defendant for non-Alabama conduct that produced injuries outside of Alabama). For a discussion of this case and the test it articulated, *see* S. Symeonides, 'Resolving Punitive Damages Conflicts', 5 *Y.B. of Priv. Int'l L.* 1, 2003, 9–11.

371. The second condition is the general proviso for objective foreseeability that should be kept in mind in all cross-border torts, namely the requirement of avoiding unfair surprise to the party adversely affected by the application of the law of the state of injury, here the defendant. A court should not apply the law of that state if the defendant demonstrates that one could not reasonably have foreseen the occurrence of the injury in that state. This is a fact-intensive, case-by-case inquiry. In the most common cross-border torts – products liability – this condition is satisfied unless the manufacturer demonstrates that its products were not available in the state of injury through ordinary commercial channels. Judging by how rarely manufacturers even choose to raise this argument,[1] one can conclude that this condition is easily met. Indeed, in all the product liability cases that allowed punitive damages under the law of the state of injury, this condition has been met.[2]

For example, in *Kramer* v. *Showa Denko K.K.*,[3] the court awarded punitive damages under the law of the state of injury (New York) against a Japanese defendant who manufactured a car in Japan, a country that does not allow punitive damages. However, the car had reached the New York market through ordinary commercial channels, and the victim bought and used it in that state. Thus, the imposition of the financial burden of punitive damages under New York law was a foreseeable and insurable risk, which the manufacturer should expect to bear in exchange for deriving financial benefits from the New York market.

1. *See* Symeonides, *The Choice-of-Law Revolution* 357.
2. *See id.* at 254–256.
3. 929 F.Supp. 733 (S.D.N.Y. 1996).

F. Group 4: None of the Above (Victim's Nationality or Domicile)

372. In this group of cases, the three pertinent contacts are in a state (or states) that does not impose punitive damages for the conduct in question. In these cases, there is little justification for awarding punitive damages, even if, for example, the victim's home state imposes such damages, and even if that state is also the forum state. Most cases in this group have followed this logic.[1]

1. *See* Symeonides, *The Choice-of-Law Revolution* 257.

373. Nevertheless, one finds a few cases reaching the opposite result. For example in *Phillips* v. *General Motors Corp.*,[1] the Montana Supreme Court awarded punitive damages to a Montana plaintiff under Montana law, even though Montana did not have any other pertinent contacts and the other involved states did not allow or limited such damages. Similar to *Phillips*, but more defensible, are certain cases decided under federal 'antiterrorist' statutes, such as the Antiterrorist and Effective Death Penalty Act of 1996.[2] This Act imposes punitive damages against certain defendants for death or personal injury of United States citizens who are victims of attacks sponsored or aided by states designated as sponsors of terrorism. These cases are more defensible than *Phillips*, not only because they are dictated by statute, but also because they involve deliberate conduct that targets victims because of their US citizenship.

1. 995 P.2d 1002 (Mont. 2000).
2. 28 USC §1605(a)(7). This Act lifts the sovereign immunity of foreign states designated by the US State Department as sponsors of terrorism and provides a cause of action for US citizens killed or injured by acts of terrorism sponsored or aided by these states. For cases awarding punitive damages under this Act, *see* Symeonides, *The Choice-of-Law Revolution* 258–259.

G. Summary and Rule

374. As the above review indicates, American courts have awarded punitive damages in cases involving each of the four groups defined above. If one were to compress these results into a descriptive choice-of-law rule, the rule would provide as follows:

> Subject to some exceptions, American courts award punitive damages if such damages are imposed by one or more of the following states: (1) the state of

the defendant's domicile or principal place of business; (2) the state of the defendant's conduct; or (3) the state of the injury.[1]

This rule does not include cases falling within group 4, because the cases that awarded punitive damages in such cases are both uncommon and extreme. It does include the cases falling within group 3 (one contact), which are more common and more defensible.

1. If punitive damages are available only in the state of injury, the application of that state's punitive damages law is subject to the proviso that the occurrence of the injury in that state must have been objectively foreseeable. *See supra* 371.

375. However, while being 'defensible' is an acceptable attribute of *de facto* practise, it is not a sufficient attribute of a prescriptive rule, namely a rule that seeks to guide future practises. One who attempts to draft a prescriptive rule should aspire to a higher standard – a rule that has a solid foundation in judicial practise and takes a more even-handed position towards these sharp conflicts, while keeping in mind the severity of punitive damages when compared to other conduct-regulating rules. For this reason, a less liberal rule might be more appropriate for punitive damages than for other conduct-regulating issues. The view of this author is that such a rule must be grounded on the cases of groups 1 and 2, which are both more numerous and better-reasoned.

376. Such a rule can be modelled after the rule adopted by the Louisiana codification of 1991[1] and later by the ALI's Complex Litigation Project of 1994.[2] Although phrased differently, both of these rules are based upon the three contacts discussed above: the place of conduct, the place of the defendant's domicile, and the place of injury. These rules provide that: Punitive damages may be awarded if all three, or any two, of the above contacts are located in a state or states that allow such damages. These rules steer a middle course between outright hostility and undue liberality toward punitive damages. For this reason, they can be challenged from both the left and the right, i.e., to the effect that the two-contacts requirement is either too restrictive or not restrictive enough.[3]

1. *See* La. Civ. Code Ann. Art. 3546. For discussion of the rationale of this article by its drafter, *see* S. Symeonides, 'Louisiana's New Law of Choice of Law for Tort Conflicts: An Exegesis', 66 *Tul. L. Rev* 677, 71992, 35 749.
2. *See* American Law Institute, *Complex Litigation: Statutory Recommendations and Analysis* §6.06 (1994).
3. For a discussion of these criticisms, *see* Symeonides, *The Choice-of-Law Revolution* 261–263.

§5. Products Liability

I. Introduction

A. Scope of This Section

377. This section reviews products liability conflicts cases decided between 1990 and 2005, inclusive. Because of space limitations, it is confined to simply reporting the findings of a comprehensive study published in another volume.[1] The study excluded: (1) class actions; (2) cases decided as contract conflicts; (3) cases in which both the plaintiff and the defendant were affiliated with the same state or with states whose laws of which produced the same outcome; and (4) cases in which the choice-of-law question remained undetected or uncontested or the court's discussion of it was cursory or inconsequential.[2] These limitations reduce the total number of cases to exactly 100,[3] a manageable number that is also high enough to permit the drawing of some general conclusions.

1. *See id.* at 265–364.
2. Also excluded are cases disposed on *forum non conveniens* grounds, and cases in which the choice-of-law discussion, though substantial, is not related to the manufacturer's liability, e.g., whether the proceeds of a survival action belong to the estate or to the heirs or other beneficiaries.
3. For a tabular presentation of these cases, *see* Symeonides, *The Choice-of-Law Revolution* 274–277. The number 100 is too round and convenient not to be suspect. However, no cases have been excluded or included in order to round up or down the number. It is also worth noting that the findings and conclusions from the 100 cases reported here do not differ, except in minor measure, from those drawn from the 70 and 80 cases, respectively, discussed in two earlier studies by the same author. *See* S. Symeonides, 'The American Choice-of-Law Revolution in the Courts: Today and Tomorrow', 298 *Recueil des Cours* 1, 2003, 278–356; S. Symeonides 'Choice of Law for Products Liability: The 1990s and Beyond', 78 *Tul. L. Rev.* 1247, 2004.

B. The Pertinent Contacts

1. The List

378. The abandonment of the *lex loci delicti* rule has allowed courts to consider multiple factual contacts, or connecting factors, in the process of identifying the concerned jurisdictions. In product liability conflicts, these contacts are:

1. the domicile, habitual residence, or 'home state' of the party injured by the product (hereafter interchangeably referred to as 'plaintiff' or 'victim');
2. the place where the injury occurred;
3. the place where the product was sold as such, either to the eventual victim (as in the case of most consumer products) or to a third party who owned the product at the time of the injury (as in the case of industrial machinery or public transportation means). This place is referred to hereafter as the 'place of acquisition';
4. the place where the product was manufactured or designed (even though these two contacts do not always coincide in the same state); and
5. the principal place of business of the manufacturer (hereinafter referred to as 'defendant').[1]

1. In some cases, parties other than the manufacturer, such as a distributor or retailer, may be defendants. Nevertheless, all but six of the cases discussed in this Part involve lawsuits against manufacturers and in two of those cases, the retailer had also serviced the product.

2. Qualifications

379. The above list calls for explanation and qualification. First, the list should not lead to the inference that all of these contacts are taken into account in all cases.

For example, cases decided under the *lex loci delicti* rule do not consider, and often do not mention, the other contacts.

Second, in some cases, one or more of these contacts may be located in more than one state. Thus, in the case of certain products used over long periods in several states, the injury may be peripatetic. Examples from recent experience include pharmaceuticals, breast implants, and tobacco products that the victims used over long periods of time while residing in several states. Similarly, in many cases, the manufacturing process takes place in different states for different phases. The product is designed in one state, tested in another, approved in another, and manufactured and assembled in yet another state.

Third, each of the above contacts may be fortuitous in a given case, such as the place of injury in an air plane crash, or the place of acquisition in the case of a product purchased by a tourist in a distant state.

Fourth, the above contacts are not necessarily of equal weight or pertinence. For example, the place of the product's acquisition is generally less pertinent when a party other than the victim acquired the product, or when the victim was not the original acquirer. Likewise, in today's world of multi-state corporate mobility, the manufacturer's principal place of business is justifiably given less weight, and in some cases – though not as many as one might expect – the defendant is not the manufacturer but rather the seller of the product.

A final qualification affecting the relative pertinence of some of the above contacts has to do with the inherent breadth of the very term 'product' in encompassing things of widely diverse qualities and uses. For example, certain products, such as industrial or similar production-equipment, are intended for use in one state, while other products, such as air planes or other means of public transportation, are intended for use in more than one state. In-between the two categories are consumer products, such as pharmaceuticals, appliances, foods, cosmetics, and personal vehicles that are used primarily, but not exclusively, in one state. While products of the last category are usually purchased directly by the user and eventual victim of the product, the products of the first two categories are purchased by someone other than the victim, and are usually not subject to the victim's control. The nature of the product often determines the relative pertinence of each of the above contacts. For example, the place of injury is given significant weight in cases of industrial machinery, especially one attached to a building, and much less weight in the case of an air plane crash. Similarly, as said above, the place of acquisition is given more weight when the acquirer is the victim than when it is not.

380. Despite these qualifications, the above list of contacts remains a useful vehicle through which to catalogue and analyze products liability conflicts. The analysis, or at least the description of it, can be further facilitated by grouping these contacts into plaintiff-affiliating and defendant-affiliating contacts. Thus, the plaintiff's domicile and the place of injury are plaintiff-affiliating contacts, while the defendant's principal place of business and the place of the manufacture are defendant-affiliating contacts. The remaining contact, the place of the product's acquisition, is where, figuratively speaking, the two sides meet each other. However, at least when the product is acquired by the victim rather than by a third party (as in the case of an air plane acquired by an airline company), this contact can be considered as a victim-affiliated contact and is treated as such in the discussion below.

3. Dispersement of Contacts

381. Although today's products travel great distances both before and after the time of purchase, it appears that most of the individual product-liability lawsuits involve cases that have contacts with only two or three states. For example, in 36 of the 100 cases, the five contacts were grouped in two states, and in 34 cases in three states in 34 cases. In 51 cases, three of the five contacts were in the same state, and in 42 of those both the acquisition of the product and the eventual injury occurred in the plaintiff's home state. In 16 of the 100 cases, the injury occurred in the plaintiff's home state, but the product was acquired outside that state. In 14 of the 100 cases, the product was acquired in the plaintiff's home state, but the injury occurred elsewhere. In 16 of the 100 cases, the injury and the place of the product's acquisition were in the same state, but not the plaintiff's home state. In the remaining 12 cases, the three plaintiff-affiliating contacts were located in three different states, although in five of those cases the defendant-affiliating contacts were located in the same state.[1]

1. *See* Symeonides, *The Choice-of-Law Revolution* 320–322.

C. The Content of the Contact-States' Laws

382. One important lesson of the modern American conflicts experience is that one cannot intelligently and rationally resolve conflicts without giving considerable weight to the substantive content of the laws of each involved state. Product-liability laws may be categorized in many different ways, but at the most basic level these laws favour either the manufacturer or the injured person. This Part refers to the former laws as pro-defendant laws and to the latter as pro-plaintiff laws.

The most common examples of pro-defendant laws are statutes of repose that bar lawsuits against manufacturers when filed after a specified number of years from the date the product entered the stream of commerce ('first use'), regardless of when the injury occurs. Other examples are rules that prohibit punitive damages, require the plaintiff to prove the manufacturer's negligence, or accord manufacturers' special defences such as 'state-of-the-art', or shield a manufacturer's successor from liability for the predecessor's products.

Conversely, among the clearest examples of pro-plaintiff laws are the absence of a statute of repose protecting manufacturers, and rules that impose strict liability, punitive damages, unlimited compensatory damages, or corporate successor liability on manufacturers.

D. Typical Patterns of Product Conflicts

383. The combination of pertinent contacts and product-liability laws produces three typical patterns of product-liability conflicts, depending on the laws of the involved states and on whether each state has contacts affiliating it only with the plaintiff, only with the defendant, or with both parties.

1. The first pattern (hereafter called '*direct* conflicts') encompasses cases in which all three plaintiff-affiliating contacts (namely, the plaintiff's domicile, injury, and place of the product's acquisition) are located in a state or states that have pro-plaintiff laws, while both defendant-affiliating contacts (namely, the defendant's principal place of business and the product's manufacture) are located in a state or states that have pro-defendant laws.
2. The second pattern (hereafter called 'inverse conflicts') encompasses cases in which all three plaintiff-affiliating contacts are located in a state or states that have pro-defendant laws, while both defendant-affiliating contacts are located in a state or states that have pro-plaintiff laws.
3. The third pattern is the residual pattern. It encompasses all the remaining combinations, such as situations in which the three plaintiff-affiliating contacts (domicile, injury, and product acquisition) are located in different states the laws of which favour a different party. Hereafter, these cases are called mixed conflicts.

II. Cases in Which the Three Plaintiff-Affiliating Contacts Were in the Same State

384. The review of cases begins with those that fall within the most frequent pattern: cases in which three of the five pertinent contacts – the ones affiliated with the plaintiff – were situated in the same state. Forty-two of the 100 cases fall within this category, that is, they involved situations in which the plaintiff's injury and the acquisition of the product were in the plaintiff's home state.[1]

1. *See id.* at 277–295. In 14 of these cases, that state was also the forum state. In 33 (or 79 per cent) of the 42 cases, the court applied the law of the state that had the three plaintiff-affiliating contacts. In 13 (or 39 per cent) of the 33 cases, that state was also the forum state.

A. *Direct Conflicts*

385. Nine of the 42 cases presented the direct or true conflict pattern, because the state with the three plaintiff-affiliating contacts had a pro-plaintiff law, while the state with the defendant-affiliating contacts had a pro-defendant law.[1] Under the assumptions of interest analysis, the fact that each of the three plaintiff-affiliating contacts is in a state that has a pro-plaintiff law generates an interest on the part of that state to apply its law: the injured plaintiff's domicile in a state brings into play that state's interest in financially repairing the consequences of the injury for the victim and the victim's dependents; the occurrence of the injury within a state brings into play that state's interest in determining the legal consequences of the injury and minimizing similar injuries in the future; and the sale of the product in a state implicates that state's interest in ensuring that products marketed there conform with certain minimum standards of safety. By the same token, the fact that the state defendant-affiliating contacts has a pro-defendant law also generates an interest in applying its law to protect its manufacturers and through them its own economic welfare.

1. *See id.* at 278–282.

386. According to Currie's interest analysis, all nine of these true conflicts should be resolved by applying the law of the forum if the forum state is one of the interested states. Indeed, six of these cases applied the law of the forum state.[1] However, the fact that in all six cases the forum state also had all three plaintiff-affiliating contacts may have been more determinative than the fact that it was the forum. Indeed, a review of many other cases suggests that, whenever the three plaintiff-affiliated contacts are in the same state, courts tend to apply the law of that state, regardless of methodology and regardless of whether that state is also the forum state or its law favours the plaintiff or the defendant.[2]

1. *See id.* at 278–279.
2. *See id.* at 279, 323.

B. Inverse Conflicts

387. In 33 of the 100 cases, the state with the three plaintiff-affiliating contacts had a pro-defendant law, while the state with the defendant-affiliating contacts had a pro-plaintiff law.[1] Thus, these cases presented the inverse conflict pattern because each state's law favoured the party affiliated with the other state. According to Currie, these are 'no-interest' cases because neither state has an interest in applying its law to protect non-domiciliaries at the expense of local domiciliaries. Thus, according to Currie, all of these cases should be resolved by applying the law of the forum in its role as the residual law.

1. *See id.* at 282–295.

388. Yet, slightly more than half of the cases (18 of 33) did not apply forum law, including three cases decided in states that officially follow the *lex fori* approach.[1] The remaining 15 cases applied forum law, but, except for one case, none of them based that application on Currie's advocacy of the dominant role of the forum *qua* forum. Rather, they based that application on the forum state's contacts with the case and, in some instances, its affirmative interest – rather than its lack of interest – in applying its law. Moreover, in all 15 cases, the application of the law of the forum benefited a foreign litigant, and in 13 of those cases it worked to the detriment of a local litigant. In short, none of these cases followed Currie's 'personal-law principle' that a state whose law favours the non-local litigant or disfavours the local litigant necessarily has no interest in applying it.

1. *See id.* at 282.

389. Three-fourths (or 25) of the 33 inverse conflicts applied the pro-defendant law of a state that had all three plaintiff-affiliating contacts (domicile, injury, and acquisition). In seven of those cases, that state was also the forum state. In the remaining 18 cases, the state with the three plaintiff-affiliating contacts had a pro-defendant law, but the forum state had a pro-plaintiff law. All of these cases applied the law of the former state and none applied the law of the forum.[1]

1. Three of these cases were transparent attempts at forum-shopping, which, however, did not pay off. In all but one of the remaining 15 cases, the defendant had significant contacts with the forum state, such as maintaining its principal place of business or manufacturing the product there, in whole or in part. Even if these cases involved forum-shopping, it did not pay off because they applied the pro-defendant law of the non-forum state that had the plaintiff-affiliating contacts.

390. Six of the 33 inverse conflicts reached the opposite result by applying the pro-plaintiff law of a state that was both the manufacturer's principal place of business and the place of manufacture.[1] The fact that, in all six cases, that state was also the forum state means that these cases applied the forum's pro-plaintiff law for the benefit of a foreign plaintiff and at the expense of a forum manufacturer defendant. They did so not so much for the sake of protecting the foreign victim, but rather in pursuance of the forum's own policy of deterring the manufacture of substandard products within its territory.

1. The two remaining cases applied the pro-plaintiff law of the forum state, which did not have any of the five pertinent contacts. The first state did so on procedural grounds, and the other because the products liability action was interconnected with a medical malpractise action that was governed by forum law.

III. Cases in Which Two Plaintiff-Affiliating Contacts Were in the Same State

391. In 47 of the 100 cases, two plaintiff-affiliating contacts were in one state, while the other three pertinent contacts where in one or more other states. Thirty of the 47 cases applied the law of the first state. Lest one mistakes this for a pro-plaintiff bent, it should be noted that in more than half of the 30 cases (17), that state had a pro-defendant law.[1]

1. *See* Symeonides, *The Choice-of-Law Revolution* 296–312.

A. *Plaintiff's Domicile and Injury*

392. In 16 of the 47 cases, the plaintiff's domicile and injury were in the same state, while the other three contacts were in another state or states.[1] Ten of those cases applied the law of the state with the two plaintiff-affiliating contacts while the remaining six cases applied another state's law. Five of the ten cases presented the direct conflict pattern in that the state with the plaintiff-affiliating contacts had a pro-plaintiff law, while the state with the defendant-affiliating contacts had a pro-defendant law. All five cases applied the pro-plaintiff law of the former state.

In four of those cases, the product was commercially available in that state, thus negating any argument of unfair surprise on defendant's part. Eleven of the 16 cases presented the inverse conflict pattern, in that the state with the plaintiff-affiliating contacts had a pro-defendant law, while the state with the defendant-affiliating contacts had a pro-plaintiff law. Five of these cases applied the pro-defendant law of the plaintiff-affiliated state.

1. *See id.* at 296–302.

393. Of the remaining six cases, four cases applied the pro-plaintiff law of the state with the defendant-affiliating contacts.[1] In only one of those cases did that state have the additional contact of being the forum, but this was not the basis for the court's decision. Rather the court based its decision on that state's affirmative and 'strong' interest in 'deterring the design, manufacture and sale of unsafe products within its borders' and the lack of a countervailing interest on the part of the state of the victim's domicile and injury to 'merely limit [the victim's] ability to recover'.[2] As other courts have noted, the state of manufacture had a greater interest in providing deterrence than the other state had 'in preventing a windfall to its citizens',[3] while the defendant could not complain against the application of the laws of its home state.[4]

1. Two cases applied the pro-plaintiff law of the state in which the victim acquired the product, even though that state had no other contacts with the case.
2. *Zenaida-Garcia* v. *Recovery Sys. Tech., Inc.*, 2005 WL 1560279 at *4 (Wash. Ct. App. 2005).
3. *Lewis-DeBoer* v. *Mooney Aircraft Corp.*, 728 F.Supp. 642, 645 (D.Colo. 1990).
4. *See Magnant* v. *Medtronic, Inc.*, 818 F.Supp. 204 (W.D. Mich. 1993).

B. Victim's Domicile and Product Acquisition

394. In 14 of the 100 cases, the product was acquired in the victim's home state but the injury occurred in another state.[1] In these cases, the parties did not plead the law of the state with the defendant-affiliating contacts. Thus the choice was confined to the laws of the victim's home state and place of acquisition on the one hand, and the state of injury on the other. Ten of the 14 cases applied the law of the former state, and four applied the law of the latter state.

In six of the 14 cases, the state of the victim's domicile and product acquisition was also the forum state and had a pro-plaintiff law, while the state of injury had a pro-defendant law. Five of the six cases applied the law of the former state.

In the other eight cases, the law of the plaintiff's home state and place of acquisition favoured the defendant, while the law of the state of injury favoured the plaintiff. Five of these cases applied the law of the former state, although in four of them, that law favoured a foreign defendant at the expense of a forum victim. Three cases applied the pro-plaintiff law of the state of injury, which was also the forum state. In all three cases, that law benefited a non-forum victim at the expense of a non-forum defendant.

1. *See* Symeonides, *The Choice-of-Law Revolution* 302–306.

C. Injury and Product Acquisition

395. In 16 of the 100 cases, the injury occurred outside the plaintiff's home state but the product was acquired in the state of injury, either by the victim's employer or by the victim while temporarily in that state.[1] In most of these cases, the parties did not plead the laws of the states of manufacture or the manufacturers' principal place of business. Thus, the courts' choice was confined to the laws of the victim's home state on the one hand, and the state of injury and the product's acquisition on the other.

Ten of the 16 cases applied the law of the latter state. That law favoured the plaintiff in two cases and the defendant in eight cases. In all but one of the latter cases, that law favoured a non-forum defendant at the expense of a forum victim.

Six of the 16 cases went the other way by applying the law of the victim's home state rather than that of the state of injury and acquisition. In four of those cases, the defendant had its principal place of business in, or similar affiliation, with the victim's home state making these cases analogous to common-domicile cases. The remaining two cases applied the pro-plaintiff law of the plaintiff's home state despite that state's lack of any other contacts.

1. *See id.* at 307–312.

IV. The Rest of the Cases

396. Of the remaining 12 of the 100 cases, no two cases are alike. Most of these cases present the mixed conflict pattern in that the plaintiff-affiliating contacts were located in different states, some of which had a pro-plaintiff law while others had a pro-defendant law.[1]

In four cases, the parties did not plead the laws of the plaintiffs' domiciles, instead confining their arguments to the laws of the state of injury on the one hand and the defendant-affiliated states on the other. The courts applied the laws of the latter states in all four cases, but in three of them those laws favoured the plaintiffs.

Six cases applied the pro-plaintiff law of the plaintiff's home state, even though that state did not have any other contacts with the case. However, in all but one of these cases, the five pertinent contacts were dispersed in four or five different states. In one case, except for the defendant's principal place of business, all other involved states had a pro-plaintiff law. In three cases the defendants pleaded only the laws of states with plaintiff-affiliating contacts, confining the court's choice between the laws of the victim's home state and the state of injury, or between the victim's home state and the state of the product's acquisition.

1. *See id.* at 312–319.

V. General Observations

A. The Role of State Policies and Interests

397. The 100 cases reviewed in this section have been decided under a variety of contemporary choice-of-law methodologies. The majority of these cases subscribe, explicitly or implicitly, to two basic premises: (1) that states do have an interest in the outcome of multi-state product-liability disputes between private parties; and (2) to properly resolve these disputes, one should take account of these interests, albeit not to the exclusion of other factors, such as factual contacts and party expectations. Because of this, a casual observer might conclude that Brainerd Currie's interest analysis is still alive and well among the courts. However, such a conclusion would be inaccurate because the courts do not subscribe to two essential ingredients of Currie's analysis: his 'personal-law' principle, and the primacy of the *lex fori*.

398. As noted earlier, the first principle denotes Currie's assertion that a state always has an interest in protecting its own domiciliaries but is never interested in protecting similarly situated out-of-staters. As the preceding review documents, very few cases subscribe to this proposition. For example, several cases: (1) applied the forum's pro-plaintiff law even when it favoured a plaintiff who was not a forum domiciliary and disfavoured a defendant affiliated with the forum state; or (2) applied the forum's pro-defendant law for the benefit of a non-forum defendant and at the expense of a forum plaintiff.[1]

Currie's approach assigned a primary role to the *lex fori*, because he argued that the law of the forum should govern, *inter alia*, in all true conflicts before an interested forum, and in all no-interest cases. The vast majority of the 100 cases fall into one or the other of these two categories (called direct and inverse conflicts, respectively), yet only a slight majority of them (56 per cent) applied the law of the forum.

1. *See id.* at 319–320.

399. For this reason, it is safe to conclude that, although many cases speak the language of interest analysis – or more accurately policy analysis – most cases do not subscribe to the most controversial specifics of the particular approach that Currie advocated. If anything, most courts seem to be more impressed with the number of factual contacts a state has with the case than with an advocate's sophisticated analysis of state interests.

B. A Contacts Analysis

400. The vast majority (83 per cent) of the 100 cases applied the law of a state that had two or more of the five pertinent contacts.[1] Specifically: (a) 41 of the 100 cases applied the law of a state that had three of the five contacts;[2] and (b) 42 of the 100 cases applied the law of a state that had two contacts.[3]

1. *See id.* at 323–324. Only 15 of the 100 cases applied the law of a state that had only one contact. In all but one of those cases, that state had a pro-plaintiff law. In eight of those cases, the five pertinent contacts were dispersed in four or five states. In eight of the 15 cases, that state was the plaintiff's home state and had a pro-plaintiff law, and in seven cases it was also the forum state.
2. In 33 of those cases, that state was the plaintiff's domicile, the place of injury, and the place of the product's acquisition; in 13 of these cases, that state was also the forum state. It had a pro-plaintiff law in eight cases and a pro-defendant law in 25 cases.

In four of the 41 cases, the three contacts were the place of the product's acquisition, the place of manufacture, and the defendant's principal place of business. In all four cases, that state had a pro-plaintiff law, and in two of them it was also the forum state. In the remaining four cases, the three contacts were aggregated in different ways.

3. The two contacts were aggregated as follows: (a) the plaintiff's domicile and the place of injury in ten cases (b) the plaintiff's domicile and the place of the product's acquisition in 10 cases; (c) the place of injury and the product's acquisition in nine cases; (d) the defendant's principal place of business and the place of manufacture in ten cases; (e) the plaintiff's and the defendant's domiciles in two cases; and (f) the places of manufacture and acquisition in one case.

401. More than two-thirds (77 per cent) of the 100 cases applied the law of a state that had only plaintiff-affiliating contacts, but in 43 (or 56 per cent) of those cases that state had a pro-defendant law.[1] In 10 of the 100 cases, the court applied the law of a state that had only defendant-affiliating contacts, but in eight of those cases that state had a pro-plaintiff law.[2]

1. In 33 cases, the court applied the law of a state that had all three plaintiff-affiliating contacts, but in 25 (or 76 per cent) of those cases that state had a pro-defendant law. In 29 cases, the court applied the law of a state that had two plaintiff-affiliating contacts, but in 17 (or 59 per cent) of those cases that state had a pro-defendant law. Fifteen cases applied the law of a state that had only one plaintiff-affiliating contact, and in 14 of those cases that state had a pro-plaintiff law. Eight of the 15 cases applied the pro-plaintiff law of the plaintiff's home state, which in seven of those cases was also the forum state. Two cases applied the pro-plaintiff law of the state of the product's acquisition, one case applied the pro-plaintiff law of the state of injury and another state applied the pro-defendant law of the state of injury.
2. In 11 of the 100 cases, the court applied the law of a state that had both plaintiff- and defendant-affiliating contacts, and in nine of those cases that state had a pro-plaintiff law. In the remaining two cases, the court applied the law of the forum state which had none of the contacts considered pertinent in this Part, although it did have the contacts necessary for the court's jurisdiction.

1. Plaintiff's Domicile

402. In 65 of the 100 cases, the court applied the law of the plaintiff's home state.[1] However, in all but eight of those cases, that state had one or two additional contacts.[2] This is not a bent towards the plaintiff because, in more than half of those cases (36 cases out of 65 [or 55 per cent]), that state had a pro-defendant law. In any event, the plaintiff's domicile, especially when coupled with another contact, appears to be an important contact in product liability conflicts.

1. *See* Symeonides, *The Choice-of-Law Revolution* 325.
2. It had two additional contacts in 35 cases, and one additional contact in 22 cases.

2. Place of Injury

403. In 58 of the 100 cases, the court applied the law of the state of injury, but in all but four of them that state had one or two additional contacts.[1] This does not entail a return to the *lex loci* rule, although it is a reminder that the place of the injury continues to be a relevant contact. In any event, the application of the law of the state of injury favoured defendants by a wide margin (40 of the 58 cases [or 69 per cent]).

1. The state of injury had two additional contacts in 35 cases, and one additional contact in 19 cases.

3. Place of the Product's Acquisition

404. In 61 of the 100 cases, the court applied the law of a state in which the product was acquired, but in all but three of those cases that state had one or two additional contacts.[1] Again, this is not a tilt toward the plaintiff because, in 38 (or 62 per cent) of the 61 cases, that state's law favoured the defendant. In any event, the place of acquisition has gradually gained in significance, although this significance varies considerably from case to case. As noted earlier, this contact is more important in cases involving consumer goods and other similar products acquired by the victim. It is less important in cases involving other products, such as transportation means or machinery acquired by a third party.

1. *See* Symeonides, *The Choice-of-Law Revolution* 326. The state of acquisition had two additional contacts in 38 cases, and one additional contact in 20 cases.

405. In 65 of the 100 cases, the two defendant-affiliating contacts – the place of manufacture and the defendant's principal place of business – were in the same state. Yet, only ten of those cases applied the law of a state that had only those contacts and no others.[1] One reason for this low number is the fact that in most cases the defendants did not plead the law of that state (apparently because it was unfavourable) and instead relied on the more favourable law of a state with a plaintiff-affiliating contact. In many cases, it was the plaintiffs who invoked the law of the defendants' state and in some cases the plaintiffs prevailed – in eight of the ten cases, that state had a pro-plaintiff law.

1. Ten additional cases applied the law of a state that had one or both of those contacts *and* a plaintiff-affiliating contact.

4. State of Manufacture

406. Only 18 of the 100 cases applied the law of the state of manufacture, but in all of them that state had either two additional contacts (seven cases) or one additional contact (11 cases). In 14 of the 18 cases, that state had a pro-plaintiff law.[1]

1. *See* Symeonides, *The Choice-of-Law Revolution* 327.

5. Defendant's Principal Place of Business

407. Only 20 of the 100 cases applied the law of the state of the defendant's principal place of business, but in all of them that state had either two additional contacts (eight cases) or one additional contact (12 cases).[1] Stated another way, no case applied the law of the manufacturer's principal place of business as such. Of the five pertinent contacts, this one appears to be the least significant, and appropriately so. In 15 of the 20 cases, the state of the defendant's principal place of business had a pro-plaintiff law.

1. *See id.*

C. Forum-Shopping is Neither Common nor Rewarding

408. The 100 cases reviewed here do not confirm the widespread impression that product-liability plaintiffs engage in rampant forum-shopping. Obviously, the validity of this observation depends on one's definition of forum-shopping, as well as the size and nature of the sample examined.[1] If one defines forum-shopping as to include all cases in which the plaintiff sues in a state that has a favourable substantive law, then one could conclude that plaintiffs do engage in forum-shopping because in 79 of the 100 cases the forum state had a pro-plaintiff substantive law.

1. This review is confined to cases that resulted in a choice-of-law decision that is either published or reported in Westlaw. One could argue that, insofar as courts dispose of many forum-shopping suits without issuing such a decision, this review is not representative enough with regard to this specific issue.

409. However, a more precise definition of forum-shopping should encompass only those cases in which a plaintiff unfairly exploits the jurisdictional rules to sue in a state that does not have relevant contacts other than the jurisdictional nexus with the defendant (e.g., 'doing business' and nothing else). Under this definition, only five of the 100 cases involved forum-shopping.[1] Two additional cases might qualify as 'borderline' forum-shopping cases in that the forum's contacts were somewhat tenuous. Even if one adds these cases, the percentage of forum-shopping cases rises to only 7 per cent. In any event, in six of the seven cases, the plaintiff's forum-shopping attempt did not succeed because the courts applied the pro-defendant law of a state other than the forum.

1. *See* Symeonides, *The Choice-of-Law Revolution* 328. Two of these cases were filed in Mississippi in order to take advantage of that state's long statute of limitations, two cases were filed in Minnesota to take advantage of that state's better-law approach, and one case was filed in Pennsylvania to take advantage of that state's substantive law.

410. On the other hand, when a plaintiff sues a defendant in a state with defendant-affiliating contacts (e.g., a state that is the manufacturer's principal place of business or the place of manufacture), the plaintiff does not unfairly exploit the jurisdictional rules since the defendant can hardly complain for being forced to litigate at home. More than one fourth of the cases (29 out of 100) were filed in states with defendant-affiliating contacts. Although in 23 of the 29 cases the forum had a pro-plaintiff law, the court applied that law in only 11 cases.

411. Conversely, when the plaintiff sues in a state with plaintiff-affiliating contacts (i.e., places of domicile, injury, or acquisition), the defendant may be subject to a certain degree of inconvenience depending on remoteness and other factors. However, this inconvenience is a fair price to pay in exchange for selling products in the forum's market. When a consumer injured by one of these products sues in that state, the consumer is not necessarily engaging in inappropriate forum-shopping, especially if that state has more than one of the above five contacts. In this context, one should note that, except for the seven aforementioned cases of actual or border-line forum-shopping, in all the other cases in which the forum had a pro-plaintiff law, that state had at least one additional contact – three such contacts in 12 cases, two contacts in 29 cases, and one contact in 29 cases.

412. More importantly, even if one adopts the broadest definition of forum-shopping to include all cases in which plaintiffs sue in states that have pro-plaintiff laws, this strategy does not succeed as frequently as one might think. Of the 79 cases in which the forum had a pro-plaintiff law, the court applied that law in only 42 cases (or 53 per cent). In contrast, of the 20 cases in which the forum had a pro-defendant law, the court applied that law in 13 cases (or 65 per cent). Thus, defendants have had a better chance in persuading a court to apply its pro-defendant law than plaintiffs had in persuading the court to apply its pro-plaintiff law.

D. Plaintiffs Tend to Sue at or Close to Home

413. The assumption that American courts are a magnet for foreign products-liability plaintiffs is both widespread and plausible. Nevertheless, of the 100 cases of this period, only seven cases were filed by foreign plaintiffs and in all seven cases the plaintiffs were domiciliaries of neighbouring countries – Mexico or Canada. On the whole, these 100 cases suggest that most product-liability plaintiffs tend to sue close to home. Only 29 of the 100 cases were filed in defendant-affiliated states.[1] This may be because of distance and inconvenience (more likely for the attorneys) because the manufacturer-affiliated states do not seem to have pro-defendant laws. In fact, in 63 per cent of the cases that reveal the law of the state of manufacture (37 out of 59 cases), that state had a pro-plaintiff law.

1. *See id.* at 331–332. In 22 cases, the forum state was both the defendant's principal place of business and the place of manufacture. In 6 cases, the forum was the defendant's principal place of business, and in one case the place of manufacture. In all but five of the 29 cases, the forum state had a pro-plaintiff law, which the court applied in 11 cases.

414. In 53 of the 100 cases, the plaintiffs sued in their home states. In more than one-half of those cases (29 out of 53) that state had either one additional contact (16 cases) or two additional contacts (13 cases). In 38 (or 72 per cent) of the 53 cases in which the plaintiffs sued in their home state, that state had a pro-plaintiff law. The court applied that law in 26 (or 68 per cent) of the 38 cases. Perhaps more noteworthy are the remaining 15 of the 53 cases in which the plaintiffs sued in their home states, even though their laws favoured the defendants. Not surprisingly, 12 of those cases applied that state's law.

415. In 12 of the 100 cases, the action was filed in states with other plaintiff-affiliating contacts, such as the place of injury.[1] The remaining seven cases are the forum-shopping cases described earlier, which were filed in states that did not have any of the five contacts identified as pertinent in this part.

1. Seven cases were filed in the state of injury and three of them applied the law of that state. Four cases were filed in the state of the product's acquisition. In all four cases, that state had a pro-plaintiff law, which the court applied in three cases. One case was filed in a state that was both the place of injury and the product's acquisition.

E. No Pro-Plaintiff Bias

416. The 100 cases do not support the widely-held assumption that, in their choice-of-law decisions, American courts favour plaintiffs as a class. Plaintiffs continue to fare better in state courts,[1] while defendants fare slightly better in federal courts,[2] but on the whole the number of cases that applied a pro-plaintiff law (52 cases) barely exceeded the number of cases that applied a pro-defendant law (48 cases).[3] Whether this is the outgrowth of the 'tort reform' movement of the 1980s, or a series of conservative appointments to the federal bench during the same period, or a combination of these and other factors is unclear. What is clear is that, at the beginning of the twenty-first century, products liability plaintiffs encounter more difficulties in recovering from manufacturers than in previous decades.

1. Forty-three of the 100 cases were decided by state courts and 25 (or 58 per cent) of them applied a pro-plaintiff law.
2. Fifty-seven of the 100 cases were decided by federal courts and 29 (or 51 per cent) of them applied a pro-defendant law.
3. *See* Symeonides, *The Choice-of-Law Revolution* 332–333.

417. Plaintiffs do enjoy a significant advantage in direct or true conflicts. Of the 18 conflicts that fall within this category, 16 applied a pro-plaintiff law.[1] However, the inverse conflicts, which are more numerous, close the gap. Of the 44 cases that fall in this category, 30 cases applied a pro-defendant law.[2]

Even if one focuses only on the cases in which the forum had a pro-plaintiff law (78 out of 100 cases), the plaintiffs' successes were short of spectacular. Only 42 (or 54 per cent) of the 78 cases applied that law. The remaining 46 per cent applied the law of another state that favoured the defendant.

1. Plaintiffs also enjoyed an advantage in mixed conflicts. Of the 38 cases that fall in this category, 22 cases applied a pro-plaintiff law.
2. In 21 (or 64 per cent) of the 33 inverse conflicts in which the forum had a pro-plaintiff law, the court applied the law of another state that favoured the defendant.

418. Thus, it is more accurate to say that most courts apply the law of a state or states that have plaintiff-affiliating contacts (domicile, injury, and acquisition), whether or not that law favours the plaintiff. Indeed, as noted earlier, 77 of the 100 cases applied the law of a state with the plaintiff-affiliating contacts, but in 43 (or 56 per cent) of those cases that state had a pro-defendant law.

F. No Favouritism toward Forum Domiciliaries

419. Another surprising finding is the apparent lack of favouritism towards the local litigant (plaintiff or defendant). Only 41 of the 100 cases applied a law that favoured the local litigant. Of these cases, 28 favoured a local plaintiff and 13 favoured a local defendant. Even more surprising, a comparable number of cases, 35 out of 100, applied a law that disfavoured the local litigant. Of these cases, 24 cases applied a law that disfavoured a local plaintiff, and 11 cases applied a law that disfavoured a local defendant.[1]

1. *See* Symeonides, *The Choice-of-Law Revolution* 333–334. Of the remaining 24 cases, 20 cases applied a law that neither favoured nor disfavoured a local litigant and four cases applied a law that was common to both litigants.

G. No Pro-Forum Law Bias

420. Another widely held assumption is that 'courts employing the new [choice-of-law] theories have a very strong preference for forum law that frequently causes them to manipulate the theories so that they end up applying forum law'.[1]

The 100 cases of this period do not support this assumption. Although the cases that applied forum law outnumber the cases that applied foreign law, the margin is too narrow to justify the above assumption. Of the 100 cases, 56 applied forum law, and 44 applied foreign law.[2] The margin is even narrower if one excludes the three federal-transfer cases that applied the law of the transferee forum. Moreover, in most of these cases, the forum state had significant aggregations of contacts that could justify the application of its law, even if it was not the forum, and regardless of the choice-of-law theory the court followed. The forum state had three additional contacts in 17 cases, two additional contacts in 22 cases, and one additional contact in 15 cases.

1. *Sutherland* v. *Kennington Truck Serv., Ltd.*, 562 N.W.2d 466, 469–470 (Mich. 1997).
2. *See* Symeonides, *The Choice-of-Law Revolution* 334–337. Federal courts applied forum law less frequently (49 per cent) than state courts (67 per cent). Of the 57 cases decided by federal courts, 28 cases applied forum law. Of the 43 cases decided by state courts, 29 cases applied forum law.

421. These numbers also exhibit a lack of judicial support for Brainerd Currie's strong advocacy of the law of the forum. As noted earlier, Currie argued that the law of the forum should govern in all true conflicts in which the forum was one of the interested states and in all no-interest cases. According to Currie's assumptions about state interests, 62 of the 100 cases fall within one or the other of these categories and thus all 62 cases should be governed by the law of the forum. Instead only about half of those cases (32 out of 62 [or 52 per cent]) applied forum law. Specifically, only 12 of the 18 true conflicts and only 20 of the 44 inverse conflicts applied forum law.[1] Thus, the cases as a whole do not support the impressionistic assertion that courts manipulate all modern choice-of-law approaches looking for excuses to apply the law of the forum.

1. The remaining 38 cases were classified as mixed conflicts because at least one of the plaintiff-affiliating contacts was located in a state that had a pro-plaintiff law and at least one such contact was located in a state with a pro-defendant law. However, under Currie's scheme, these cases would fall in either the true conflict category or the no-interest category and thus all of them should be governed by the law of the forum. In fact only 24 of the 38 cases applied forum law.

H. No Surprise to Manufacturers

422. As noted earlier, several cases applied the pro-plaintiff law of a state with plaintiff-affiliating contacts, and in a few of those cases that state had only one such contact (e.g., the plaintiff's domicile). Yet in none of these cases, including the nine cases involving non-US manufacturers, nor in any of the other cases, did the defendants assert that the product was unavailable in that state through ordinary commercial channels.[1]

1. *See* Symeonides, *The Choice-of-Law Revolution* 337.

I. The Cases, on the Whole

423. On the whole, the results of these cases appear pleasingly but suspiciously symmetrical: the cases that applied a pro-plaintiff law barely outnumber the cases that applied a pro-defendant law (52:48); the cases that applied the law of the forum outnumber by only a slim margin the cases that applied foreign law (56:44); and the number of cases that applied a law favouring a local litigant was not much higher than the number of cases that applied a law disfavoured a local litigant (41:35).

424. Does the symmetry of these numbers mean that the results are objectively sound? Not necessarily. Suppose for example that: (a) several cases that, by some objective standard, should have applied a pro-plaintiff law applied instead a pro-defendant law; and (b) that an equal number of cases that should have applied a pro-defendant law applied instead a pro-plaintiff law. In such a scenario, the fact that the 'wrong' cases in the one group would cancel the 'wrong' cases in the second group does not mean that the aggregate result is objectively good, especially from the perspective of the losing litigants. For this reason, this review does not contend that each and every one of the 100 cases has been 'correctly' decided, nor that all cases together have been correctly decided. The sole contention is that, on the whole, the cases do not support certain widely-held assumptions about the current state of American conflicts law, at least in product-liability conflicts. Despite impressions to the contrary, American courts do not favour plaintiffs as a class; do not favour local over non-local litigants; and do not unduly favour the law of the forum.

Chapter 5. Contracts

§1. Contractual Choice of Law (Party Autonomy)

I. The Principle

425. It is an ancient principle[1] that parties to a multi-state contract should be allowed to choose, within certain limits, the law that would govern their contract (party autonomy). However, American conflicts law was rather slow in sanctioning this principle. In 1825, the US Supreme Court referred in passing to a principle of 'universal law' that a contract is governed by the law 'with a view to which it was made',[2] thus recognizing the notion of an implied choice of law by the parties. Although this recognition should have made acceptance of an express choice of law even easier, cases involving such a choice did not begin to appear until the end of the 19th century.[3] In the 1930s, the drafters of the First Restatement rejected party autonomy on the ground that it amounted to a licence for private legislation,[4] although by that time party autonomy was taking roots in both transactional and judicial practise. Recognizing this reality, the Restatement (Second) formally sanctioned and 'codified' the principle of party autonomy in Section 187, thus bringing American law in accord with most other western legal systems. Today, choice-of-law clauses have become commonplace in multi-state contracts.[5]

1. *See* S. Symeonides, W. Perdue & A. von Mehren, *Conflict of Laws: American, Comparative, International* (2nd edn, St. Paul, Minn., 2003), p. 338. Basic bibliography on the subjects discussed in this chapter includes: L. McDougal, R. Felix & R. Whitten, *American Conflicts Law* (5th edn, New York, Ardsley, 2001), pp. 489–540; E. Scoles, P. Hay, P. Borchers & S. Symeonides, *Conflict of Laws* (4th edn, St. Paul, Minn., 2004), pp. 946–1052; R. Weintraub, *Commentary on the Conflict of Laws* (5th edn, New York, 2006), pp. 475–541.
2. *Wayman* v. *Southard*, 23 US (10 Wheat.) 1, 48 (1825). *See also Pritchard* v. *Norton*, 106 US 124 (1882).
3. *See* E. Scoles, P. Hay, P. Borchers & S. Symeonides, *Conflict of Laws* (4th edn, St. Paul, Minn., 2004), p. 860, note 1.
4. *See* J. Beale, *Treatise on the Conflicts of Laws* (New York, 1935) v. II, §332.2 (attacking party autonomy because 'at their will . . . [parties] can free themselves from the power of the law which would otherwise apply to their acts'.).
5. *See* S. Symeonides, W. Perdue & A. von Mehren, *supra* note 1 at 339 ('About twenty per cent of conflicts cases decided by intermediate courts and courts of last resort every year involve a choice-of-law clause. . . . Although this is a high percentage, it is probably even higher if one considers lower court cases that are not appealed or contracts that do not result in litigation'.).

426. As noted in Part II, Chapter 3, 23 US states follow the Restatement (Second) in contract conflicts.[1] On the issue of party autonomy, this following is much higher because Section 187 'is followed by more American courts than any other provision of the Restatement (Second), including some courts that otherwise follow the traditional theory'.[2] Clearly, the Restatement represents the prevailing American view on the issue of party autonomy, except where it is superseded by statutes, such as the Uniform Commercial Code (UCC) (discussed later).[3]

1. *See supra* 218.
2. *See supra* 219.
3. *See infra* 464–472.

427. Because of its importance, Section 187 is reproduced in full and discussed below:

1. The law of the state chosen by the parties to govern their contractual rights and duties will be applied if the particular issue is one which the parties could have resolved by an explicit provision in their agreement directed to that issue.
2. The law of the state chosen by the parties to govern their contractual rights and duties will be applied even if the particular issue is one which the parties could not have resolved by an explicit provision in their agreement directed to that issue, unless either
   (a) the chosen state has no substantial relationship to the parties or the transaction and there is no other reasonable basis for the parties' choice, or
   (b) application of the law of the chosen state would be contrary to a fundamental policy of a state which has a materially greater interest than the chosen state in the determination of the particular issue and which, under the rule of Section 188, would be the state of the applicable law in the absence of an effective choice of law by the parties.
3. In the absence of a contrary indication of intention, the reference is to the local law of the state of the chosen law.[1]

1. American Law Institute, *Restatement (Second) of Conflict of Laws (2d)* §187 (1971).

II. Its Parameters and Limitations

428. Although most legal systems recognize the principle of party autonomy, they also agree on the need for some limitations, be they geographical, substantive, or both.[1] This sub-section discusses these limitations, primarily under the Restatement (Second).

1. *See DeSantis* v. *Wackenhut Corp.*, 793 S.W.2d 670. 677 (Tex. 1990), *cert. denied*, 498 US 1048 (1991) ('[T]he parties' freedom to choose what jurisdiction's law will apply to their agreement cannot be unlimited'.).

A. The Distinction between Waivable and Non-waivable Rules

429. Section 187 of the Restatement draws a basic distinction that is familiar to civil law lawyers between *jus dispositivum* and *jus cogens*, or between 'waivable', 'suppletive', or 'default' rules of law, on the one hand, and 'non-waivable', 'mandatory', 'imperative' or 'obligatory' rules, on the other. Although the Restatement does not use any of these terms, it distinguishes between: (a) issues that the parties 'could have resolved by an explicit provision in their agreement directed to that issue',[1] such as those 'relating to construction, to conditions precedent and subsequent, to sufficiency of performance and to excuse for nonperformance, . . . frustration and impossibility',[2] and (b) issues that are beyond the parties' contractual power, such as those involving 'capacity, formalities and substantial validity'.[3]

1. *Restatement (Second)* §187(1).
2. *Id.* cmt. c.
3. *Id.* cmt. d.

430. Subsection 1 of Section 187 provides that, for issues of the first category,[1] the parties' choice of law is not subject to any geographical or substantive limitations. As the official comments to the Restatement explain, this provision recognizes the common phenomenon of 'incorporation by reference'.[2] Noting that 'most rules of contract law are designed to fill gaps in a contract which the parties could themselves have filled with express provisions', the comments state that the parties may do so, either by spelling out in detail the terms of the contract, or by 'incorporat[ing] into the contract by reference extrinsic material which may, among other things, be the provisions of some foreign law'.[3] Understandably, therefore, this incorporation is not subject to any limitations.

1. Whether an issue belongs to the first or the second category is determined by 'the local law of the state selected by application of the rule of §188', namely the state whose law would govern in the absence of a choice-of-law clause. *Id.* cmt. c.
2. *Id.*
3. *Id.*

B. Basis for the Parties' Choice: Substantial Relationship or Reasonable Basis

431. Subsection 2 of Section 187 provides that, for issues that are beyond the parties' contractual power, the parties' choice of law will be honoured, but only if it meets the requirements specified in that subsection. The first requirement is that the state of the chosen law must have a 'substantial relationship' to the parties or the transaction, or there must be an 'other reasonable basis' for the parties' choice.[1] This phrasing suggests that a 'substantial relationship' is a sub-species of a 'reasonable basis'.

1. *Restatement (Second)* §187(2)(a).

432. The 'substantial relationship' requirement is geographic and fact-specific. It is usually satisfied if the chosen state has a significant contact, such as when it is the place of making or performance of the contract, or the domicile or principal place of business of one of the parties. This requirement absorbs, but also expands the requirement of 'internationality' found in several international conventions and foreign codifications. A contract that has a substantial relationship with another state is by definition international or multi-state, but additionally the chosen state itself must have a substantial relationship. This limitation is intended to prevent parties from evading those provisions of the otherwise applicable law that do not reflect a fundamental policy. Recent international conventions and codifications, including the latest revision of the UCC, eliminate or ease this requirement, choosing instead to police party autonomy by other means.[1] Although many cases underscore the importance of this requirement in dicta, very few cases have struck down choice-of-law clauses solely on this ground.[2]

1. The UCC is discussed *infra* at 464–472. A New York statute (N.Y. Gen. Oblig. §5–1401) provides that a choice of New York law in a contract not involving a consumer or personal services will be given effect even if New York has no substantial contacts, as long as it involves a transaction exceeding $250,000 and does not contravene the specific limitations of the UCC.
2. *See Sentinel Indus. Contracting Corp.* v. *Kimmins Indus. Serv. Corp.*, 743 So.2d 954 (Miss. 1999) (disregarding a Texas choice-of-law clause in a contract for the dismantlement of a Mississippi ammonia plant and its shipment and reassembly in Pakistan); *Robinson* v. *Robinson*, 778 So.2d 1105 (La. 2001) (finding that one spouse's brief residence in the chosen state was not a sufficient connection for upholding the choice-of-law clause in a marital property contract); *Curtis 1000, Inc.* v. *Suess*, 24 F.3d 941 (7th Cir. 1994) (disregarding Delaware choice-of-law clause in an Illinois employment contract because Delaware's only connection was that it was the place of the employer's incorporation); *Curtis 1000, Inc.* v. *Youngblade*, 878 F. Supp. 1224 (N.D. Iowa 1995) (disregarding Delaware choice-of-law clause in an Iowa employment contract because Delaware had no substantial relationship to contract *and* because Delaware law would be repugnant to a fundamental policy of Iowa); *Cable Tel Services, Inc.* v. *Overland Contracting, Inc.*, 574 S.E.2d 31(N.C.App. 2002) *CCR Data Sys., Inc.* v. *Panasonic Communications & Sys. Co.*, 1995 WL 54380 (D.N.H. 1995).

433. As noted above, Section 187(2) also permits the parties to choose the law of a state that lacks a 'substantial relationship' as long as they can show any 'other reasonable basis' for that choice. A reasonable basis may be the parties' familiarity with the chosen law,[1] its completeness and maturity[2] or other similar reasons.[3]

1. *Restatement (Second)* §187, cmt. f.
2. In *Radioactive, J.V.* v. *Manson*, 153 F.Supp.2d 462 (S.D.N.Y. 2001), a case involving a music recording contract, the court noted that even if the chosen state of New York did not have sufficient contacts, the parties' choice of New York law would have been reasonable in light of the fact that New York courts 'have significant experience with music industry contracts'. *Id.* at 471.
3. In *Prows* v. *Pinpoint Retail Sys., Inc.*, 868 P.2d 809 (Utah, 1993), the court acknowledged that, although the chosen state of New York had no contacts with the contract or the parties, the New York choice-of-law clause could be upheld under the other 'reasonable basis' proviso of §187(2)(a) because it would enable one of the parties, a Canadian corporation doing business in several American states, to rely on the law of a single American state and to plan accordingly. However, the court held that this proviso does not apply 'when all the contacts are located in a single state and when as a consequence, there is only one interested state'. *Id.* at 811 (quoting from *Restatement (Second)* §187 cmt. d.). After listing Utah's numerous contacts, the court concluded that 'Utah is the only state with an interest in the action', *id.*, and disregarded the choice-of-law clause.

C. Substantive Limitations: Public Policy

1. The Public Policy Limitation in General

434. Because each state's public policy limits party autonomy in fully domestic contracts, one should not expect multi-state contracts to completely avoid these limitations. However, the fact that the limitations to party autonomy vary from one state to another raises two preliminary questions: (1) which state's limitations will be used as the standard for policing party autonomy in multi-state contracts, namely, which state's law will perform the role of the *lex limitatis*, and (2) which precise level or gradation of public policy should be employed for this function?

a. Which State's Public Policy?

435. Regarding the first question, the two main candidates for the role of the *lex limitatis* are the *lex fori* and the law that would be applicable in the absence of a choice-of-law clause (hereafter referred to as *lex causae*).[1] The *lex fori* is relevant because party autonomy operates only to the extent that the *lex fori* permits. The *lex causae* is relevant because, when party autonomy operates, it displaces the *lex causae*. If the application of the chosen law exceeds the public policy limits of both the *lex fori* and the *lex causae* (or if the two laws coincide in the same state), then the chosen law will not be applied. The difficulty arises when the two laws do not coincide in the same state and the chosen law violates the public policy limits of: (1) the *lex fori*, but not the *lex causae*; or (2) the *lex causae*, but not the *lex fori*.[2]

1. The option of policing party autonomy through the chosen law is circular and should be eliminated for this reason.
2. The Puerto Rican Draft Code (Art. 35) takes the unique position that the chosen law is not to be applied if it violates restrictions on party autonomy imposed by both the *lex fori and* the *lex causae*. For the rationale of this provision, *see* S. Symeonides, 'Codifying Choice of Law for Contracts: The Puerto Rico Project', in: J. Nafziger & S. Symeonides (eds), *Law and Justice in a Multi-state World: Essays in Honor of Arthur T. von Mehren* (Ardsley, N.Y., 2002), pp. 419, 422–424.

436. Some courts instinctively strike down choice-of-law clauses in cases of the first category.[1] This position is unduly restrictive to party autonomy, except in cases in which – coincidentally – the *lex fori* would also have been the *lex causae*. To be sure, under the traditional *ordre public* exception, the public policy of the forum *qua* forum is always relevant as the last line of defence against the application of a repugnant foreign law, whether that law is chosen by the parties or through the forum's choice-of-law rules. However, as noted in Part II, Chapter 2, the threshold for employing this exception is very high, i.e., only when the foreign law is 'shocking' to the forum's sense of justice and fairness.[2] The Restatement (Second) recognizes the difference, at least as one of degree, between the roles of the traditional *ordre public* exception on the one hand, and the public policy exception in limiting party autonomy, on the other.[3] Thus, in cases of category one, the contractually chosen law should be applied even if it violates the public policy of the forum *qua* forum, so long as it is not repugnant to the forum's *ordre public*.

1. Many of these cases end their analysis as soon as they find that the chosen law contravenes the public policy of the *lex fori*, without explaining whether the *lex fori* also would have been the *lex causae*. For citations, *see* E. Scoles, P. Hay, P. Borchers & S. Symeonides, *Conflict of Laws* (4th edn, St. Paul, Minn., 2004), p. 959, note 8.
2. *See Loucks* v. *Standard Oil Co. of New York*, 120 N.E. 198, 201–202 (1918), *supra* 146.
3. *See Restatement (Second)* §187 cmt. g (Noting that, '[t]o be 'fundamental' within the meaning of [§187], a policy need not be as strong as would be required to justify the forum in refusing to entertain suit upon a foreign cause of action under the rule of §90', which enunciates the traditional *ordre public* test.). Unfortunately, the latest revision of the UCC conflates the two concepts by stating that Cardozo's definition of public policy provides 'a helpful touchstone' in determining whether the policy is 'fundamental' under revised §1–301. *See* UCC §§1–301 cmt. 6 (2001 Revision).

437. The remaining second category of cases are those in which the application of the contractually chosen law violates the public policy limits of the *lex causae*, but not the *lex fori*. The majority of modern systems, including the Restatement (Second) and the latest revision of the UCC,[1] take the view is that in these cases the choice-of-law clause should not be upheld. Thus, for these systems, the *lex limitatis* is the *lex causae* rather than the law of the forum *qua* forum.[2] However, in contrast to the UCC,[3] the Restatement (Second) imposes the additional requirement that the public policy of the state of the *lex causae* may defeat the parties' choice only if that state has 'a materially greater interest'[4] in applying its law. Although the two requirements often overlap, they are not identical, especially for courts that do not engage in interest analysis. While a state that has a materially greater interest in applying its law will likely be the state of the *lex causae*, the reverse is not necessarily true. In any event, most cases knowingly or unknowingly merge the two requirements into one.

1. *See infra* 468–472.
2. For cases illustrating this position, *see*, e.g., *DeSantis* v. *Wackenhut Corp.*, 793 S.W.2d 670, 677 (Tex. 1990), *cert. denied*, 498 US 1048 (1991) (chosen law may not 'thwart or offend the public policy of the state the law of which ought otherwise to apply'); *Nedlloyd Lines B.V.* v. *Super. Ct*, 834 P.2d 1148, 1152 note 6. (1992) ('[In] a case in which California is the forum, and the parties have chosen the law of another state, but the law of yet a third state, rather than California's, would apply absent the parties' choice . . . a California court will look to the fundamental policy of the third state in determining whether to enforce the parties' choice of law'.); *Long* v. *Holland Am. Line Westours, Inc.*, 26 P.3d 430 (Alaska 2001) (invalidating a Washington choice-of-law clause because Washington law, which permitted contractual shortening of the limitation period, would violate the fundamental policy of Alaska law, which would be applicable in the absence of a contrary choice-of-law clause).
3. *See* UCC §§1–301(f) (2001 Revision) (providing that the contractually chosen law will not be applied if it violates a 'fundamental' policy of a state 'whose law would govern in the absence of agreement').
4. *Restatement (Second)* §187(2)(b).

b. Which Level of Public Policy?

438. After identifying the state whose law defines the limits of party autonomy (*lex limitatis*), the next step is to establish the threshold or line beyond which the parties' choice of another law will be held unenforceable. If any difference between the *lex limitatis-causae* and the chosen law would defeat the parties' choice, then party autonomy would become a specious gift. As one court said, '[t]he result would be that parties would have the right to choose the application of another state's law only when that state's law is identical to [the *lex causae*]. Such an approach would be ridiculous'.[1] Thus, there is a general consensus on the need for a higher public-policy threshold for multi-state contracts than for fully domestic contracts. Predictably however, the various systems differ in defining this threshold.

1. *Cherokee Pump & Equip., Inc.* v. *Aurora Pump*, 38 F.3d 246, 252 (5th Cir. 1994). *See also Bethlehem Steel Corp.* v. *G.C. Zarnas & Co.*, 498 A.2d 605 (Md. 1985).

439. The Restatement (Second) sets a fairly high threshold, at least in verbiage. As noted earlier, Section 187(2)(b) provides that, before invalidating a choice-of-law clause, the court must be satisfied that: (a) the chosen law is contrary to a 'fundamental policy' of the state of the *lex causae*; and (b) that state has a 'materially greater interest than the chosen state in the determination of the particular issue'.[1]

Recognizing that the qualifier 'fundamental' is not easily defined, the Restatement (Second) does not attempt to define it.[2] It does, however, provide a few examples of rules that embody a fundamental policy, such as statutes declaring certain contracts illegal or designed to protect one party from 'the oppressive use of superior bargaining power' (such as statutes protecting insureds against insurers).[3] As previously noted, the Restatement also states that, to be fundamental in the sense of Section 187(2)(b), a policy need not be as strong as the policy that justifies a refusal to apply foreign law under the traditional *ordre public* exception.[4]

1. *Restatement (Second)* §187(2)(b).
2. The 2001 Oregon codification provides that a policy is fundamental 'only if the policy reflects objectives or gives effect to essential public or societal institutions beyond the allocation of rights and obligations of parties to a contract at issue'. Or. Rev. Stat. §81.125(2). The codification also provides that the chosen law does not apply 'to the extent that its application would: (a) Require a party to perform an act prohibited by the law of the state where the act is to be performed under the contract; [or] (b) Prohibit a party from performing an act required by the law of the state where it is to be performed under the contract[.]' §81.125(1). For the background and rationale of these provisions, *see* S. Symeonides, 'Codifying Choice of Law for Contracts: The Oregon Experience', 67 *RabelsZ* 726, 2003, 739–742.
3. *Restatement (Second)* §187 cmt. g. The Restatement also provides examples of rules that do not embody a fundamental policy, such as statutes of frauds, rules 'tending to become obsolete', and 'general rules of contract law, such as those concerned with the need for consideration'. *Id.*
4. *Id.*

440. Judicial decisions do not always accept (or understand) all of the above fine distinctions, and those that do accept them often struggle to apply them in practise. One example is *Machado-Miller* v. *Mersereau & Shannon, LLP*.[1] In this case, an Oregon court had to determine whether California's policy against non-compete agreements was fundamental under Section 187(2)(b) so as to defeat an Oregon choice-of-law clause in an Oregon employment contract. The court expressed serious misgivings about the facility and exactness of such a determination:

> To announce that a policy or a right is 'fundamental' is to announce a conclusion and not a premise, and the reasoning that leads to the conclusion is almost always obscure, hopelessly subjective, or expressed in verbal formulations that are of little help. . . . Further, whether a particular interest is deemed 'fundamental' under such indeterminate formulations depends on the level of generality at which the Court chooses to identify it. To the extent the interest is described at a high level of generality, it is likely to be 'fundamental', and vice versa. Further, every piece of legislation, even the most apparently trivial, implements and therefore indicates the presence of some larger policy, which, in turn, serves an even larger one. A speed limit is not itself a fundamental policy statement, but its purpose is to promote highway safety, which is one way to protect the health, welfare and safety of citizens, which is, of course, one of the most fundamental of all public policies.[2]

Ultimately, the court concluded that California's policy was fundamental 'in the dictionary sense [of] basic, underlying and primary', because it was contained in a statute phrased 'at a high level of generality'[3] and clearly stating a policy of prohibiting non-compete agreements in order to maximize competition and minimize restraints on trade.[4]

1. 43 P.3d 1207 (Or. Ct. App. 2002).
2. *Id.* at 1211.
3. *Id.* at 1212.
4. The statute provided that 'every contract by which anyone is restrained from engaging in a lawful profession, trade, or business of any kind is to that extent *void*'. Cal. Bus. & Prof. Code §16600.

2. Examples

a. Employment Contracts

441. As *Machado-Miller* illustrates, statutes limiting the power of employers to bind their employees through non-compete covenants usually embody a fundamental policy. More often than not, courts refuse to enforce such covenants if they violate the law of the employee's home state, even if the employment contract contains a choice-of-law clause pointing to another law, on the ground that employees need protection against the superior bargaining position of employers.[1]

1. *See DeSantis* v. *Wackenhut Corp.*, 793 S.W.2d 670 (Tex. 1990), *cert. denied*, 498 US 1048 (1991); *Blalock* v. *Perfect Subscription Co.*, 458 F.Supp. 123 (S.D.Ala. 1978), *aff'd* 599 F.2d 743 (5th Cir. 1979); *Fine* v. *Property Damage Appraisers, Inc.*, 393 F.Supp. 1304 (E.D.La. 1975); *Boyer* v. *Piper, Jaffray & Hopwood, Inc.*, 391 F.Supp. 471 (D.S.D. 1975); *Forney Indus., Inc.* v. *Andre*, 246 F.Supp. 333 (D.N.D. 1965); *Nasco, Inc.* v. *Gimbert*, 238 S.E.2d 368 (Ga. 1977).

442. The more difficult cases are those in which the employee resigns from his or her employment in his or her home state and moves to another state to work for a competing employer there. If the first employment contract contains a non-compete covenant that is enforceable under the law of the first but not the second employment state, the result is a true conflict between the pro-employer law of the first state and the pro-employee law of the second state. A choice-of-law clause in the first contract choosing the law of the first state makes the case more difficult, but, if litigation takes place in the second state, the court will probably hold both the clause and the non-compete covenant unenforceable.

443. One case presenting this conflict is *Application Group, Inc.* v. *Hunter Group, Inc.*,[1] in which the employee did not even move her domicile to the second employment state. The employee was a Maryland domiciliary who, after resigning from her job with a Maryland employer, began working for a competing California employer from her home in Maryland ('telecommuting'). In the ensuing litigation in California, the court held that the non-compete clause contained in the Maryland contract was unenforceable in California, after finding that California met all three prongs of Section 187(2) of the Restatement (Second), namely, that: (1) California law would be applicable to this issue in the absence of the choice-of-law clause; (2) California had a materially greater interest in applying its law to this issue; and (3) enforcement of the non-compete clause would be contrary to a fundamental policy of California.

The court noted that, although Maryland had all the contacts relevant to the employment contract (which was not at issue), California had the contact that was most relevant to the particular issue – the enforceability of the non-compete covenant in California. As to this issue, 'the subject matter of the contract' was the employee's 'subsequent employment which was, in this case, employment by a competitor who is "located" in California'.[2] Thus, to the extent the covenant purported to restrict competition in California, California had the most pertinent contact which brought into play California's interest in protecting competing California employers and 'business opportunities in California'.[3] The court concluded that California had a strong interest in protecting both the employee and the second (California) employer. With regard to the employee, California had 'a strong interest in protecting the freedom of movement of persons whom California-based employers . . . wish to employ . . . , regardless of the person's state of residence'.[4] With regard to the second employer, California had a 'public policy which ensures that California employers will be able to compete effectively for the most talented, skilled employees in their industries, wherever they may reside',[5] and thus California had an 'interest in protecting its employers and their employees from anti-competitive conduct by out-of-state employers . . . who would interfere with or restrict these freedoms'.[6]

1. 72 Cal.Rptr.2d 73 (Cal. Ct. App. 1998).
2. *Id.* at 87.
3. *Id.* at 88.
4. *Id.* at 85.
5. *Id.*
6. *Id.* This reading of California interests drew a sharp rebuke from a California judge who dissented in a similar case in which the employee did move to California: 'Relocating to California is not a chance to walk away from valid contractual obligations, claiming California policy as a protective shield. We are not a political safe zone *vis-à-vis* our sister states, such that the mere act of setting foot on California soil somehow releases a person from the legal duties our sister states recognize'. *Advanced Bionics Corp.* v. *Medtronic, Inc.*, 59 P.3d 231 (Cal. 2002), Brown, J., dissenting. *See also id.* (speaking of California's 'political imperialism, absorbing every state into the California legal ethos'.).

444. In *Keener* v. *Convergy's Corp.*,[1] Ohio was the first employer's state and the employee's first domicile, while Georgia was the second employer's state and the employee's new domicile. A Georgia federal court refused to enforce the Ohio choice-of-law clause and non-compete covenant because the latter was contrary to the free-competition policy embodied in the Georgia constitution. The court acknowledged that '[t]his may wind up encouraging non-Georgia employees to "flee to Georgia" to shed their [non-compete covenants]'.[2] However, analogizing to 'quickie divorces', the court said, '[t]he aches and pains of federalism . . . have long formed part of the American legal fabric'.[3]

1. 205 F.Supp.2d 1374 (S.D.Ga. 2002).
2. *Id.* at 1379.
3. *Id.* On appeal the Eleventh Circuit Court of Appeals certified to the Georgia Supreme Court the question of whether Georgia would follow Section 187(2) of the Restatement (Second) and whether in this case Georgia would have a materially greater interest to apply its law. *See Keener* v. *Convergys Corp.*, 312 F.3d 1236 (11th Cir. 2002). The latter court reaffirmed its refusal to adopt the Restatement as well as its refusal to enforce non-compete agreements. *See Convergys Corp.* v. *Keener*, 582 S.E.2d 84 (Ga. 2003). The Eleventh Circuit affirmed the District Court opinion. *See* 342 F.3d 1264 (11th Cir. 2003).

445. These aches are even more serious when the case provokes litigation in both states of employment. *Advanced Bionics Corp.* v. *Medtronic, Inc.*,[1] involved this scenario. The first employer was a Minnesota corporation that hired a Minnesota domiciliary for work in Minnesota. The contract contained a Minnesota choice-of-law clause, as well as a non-compete covenant valid under Minnesota law. The employee resigned from his job with the Minnesota employer and was subsequently hired by a competing California employer for work in California. The latter employer filed in California an action for a declaratory judgment to declare the non-compete covenant unenforceable in California. Meanwhile, the Minnesota employer filed an action in Minnesota to enjoin the employee from violating the non-compete covenant. The lower courts in both states rendered conflicting judgments in favour of the domestic employer[2] before the California Supreme Court set aside the California judgment. The latter court acknowledged that California had a 'strong interest' in protecting the freedom of new California domiciliaries to seek employment in California, and that a California court 'might reasonably conclude' that the Minnesota non-compete and choice-of-law clauses were 'void in this state'.[3] However, the court specifically refused to base its decision regarding the propriety of an antisuit injunction on choice-of-law factors and instead based it on principles of judicial restraint and comity.[4]

1. 59 P.3d 231 (Cal. 2002).
2. *See Advanced Bionics Corp.* v. *Medtronic, Inc.*, 105 Cal.Rptr.2d 265 (Cal. Ct. App. 2001); *Medtronic, Inc.* v. *Advanced Bionics Corp.*, 630 N.W.2d 438 (Minn. Ct. App. 2001).
3. 59 P.3d at 237.
4. *See id.* (noting that these principles required 'that we exercise our power to enjoin parties in a foreign court sparingly'.). For a similar case, *see Holeman* v. *Nat'l. Bus. Inst.*, 94 S.W.3d 91 (Tex.App. 2002).

b. Franchise or Distributorship Contracts

446. Statutes regulating franchises or distributorships are another example of statutes that restrict party autonomy in the interest of protecting the presumed weak party – the franchisee or distributee. Typically, these statutes prohibit waivers of franchisee protections, either directly or through the contractual choice of another state's law. Most of these statutes limit the scope of their operation to franchises or distributorships operating within the enacting state or franchisees or distributees domiciled there. Thus, when a contract purports, through a choice-of-law clause, to opt out of such a statute and litigation takes place in the enacting state, the only question for the court to answer is whether the contract falls within the statute's reach.[1] If it does, the court will apply the statute, notwithstanding a contrary choice-of-law clause. Many cases have so held.[2] In fact, courts will likely disregard such clauses, even if the statute in question does not expressly prohibit them.[3]

1. For the converse phenomenon, *see Fred Briggs Distr. Co., Inc.* v. *California Cooler, Inc.*, 2 F.3d 1156 (Table) (9th Cir. 1993) (disregarding a contractual choice of California franchise law because the case did not fall within the intended territorial reach of the California statute); *Cromeens, Holloman, Sibert, Inc.* v. *AB Volvo*, 349 F.3d 376 (7th Cir. 2003) (disregarding a contractual choice of Illinois franchise statute because the case did not fall within the statute's intended reach); *Gravquick A/S* v. *Trimble Navig. Int'l. Ltd.*, 323 F.3d 1219 (9th Cir. 2003) (acknowledging that California's Dealers Act was intended for the protection of California

dealers but honouring contractual choice of the California Act in a contract between a foreign dealer and a California manufacturer).

2. *See* S. Symeonides, 'Choice of Law in the American Courts in 1994: A View From the Trenches', 43 *Am. J. Comp. L.* 1, 1994, 61–63. For later cases, *see*, e.g., *Power & Tele. Supply Co., Inc.* v. *Harmonic, Inc.*, 268 F.Supp.2d 981 (W.D.Ten. 2003); *Beatty Caribbean, Inc.* v. *Viskase Sales Corp.*, 241 F.Supp.2d 123 (D.P.R. 2003); *Stawski Distrib. Co., Inc.* v. *Browary Zywiec S.A.*, 349 F.3d 1023 (7th Cir. 2003), *cert. denied*, 541 US 1010 (2004); *Healy* v. *Carlson Travel Network Associates, Inc.*, 227 F.Supp.2d 1080 (D.Min. 2002); *Ticknor* v. *Choice Hotels Int'l, Inc.*, 265 F.3d 931 (9th Cir. 2001).
3. *See*, e.g., *Instructional Sys., Inc.* v. *Computer Curriculum Corp.*, 130 N.J. 324, 614 A.2d 124 (N.J. 1992); *Wright-Moore Corp.* v. *Ricoh Corp.*, 908 F.2d 128 (7th Cir. 1990).

447. When litigation occurs in the franchisor's state, the courts of that state tend to be less deferential to the protective statutes of the franchisee's state and more receptive to a contractual choice of the forum's law.[1] *Modern Computer Systems* v. *Modern Banking Systems*[2] is representative of these cases. In a contract for a Minnesota franchise, the Minnesota franchisee and the Nebraska franchisor had chosen the law of Nebraska which did not have a franchisee-protecting statute. In contrast, Minnesota had a non-waivable statute that accorded Minnesota franchisees more protection than traditional common law, although the statute did not specifically prohibit the choice of another state's law. Assisted by Minnesota's Attorney General as *amicus curiae*, the plaintiff franchisee argued that the application of Nebraska common law would frustrate the 'fundamental policies' embodied in the Minnesota Franchise Act. The court rejected the argument and upheld the parties' choice of Nebraska law. Noting that this was not an adhesion contract and that the territorial and personal contacts were divided almost evenly between the two states, the court held that the choice of the law of either state was reasonable and that Minnesota's policies were not sufficiently strong to override such a choice. Shortly thereafter, Minnesota amended its Franchise Act, to expressly prohibit waiver of its provisions through 'any condition, stipulation or provision, including any choice of law provision'.[3]

1. *See*, e.g., *JRT, Inc.* v. *TCBY Sys., Inc.*, 52 F.3d 734 (8th Cir. 1995) (decided under Arkansas conflicts law; franchise agreement for a Michigan franchise; contractual choice of Arkansas law upheld because Michigan anti-waiver statute 'did not specifically target choice of law provisions', and 'even if . . . Michigan has the greatest interest, . . . no fundamental Michigan policy is at stake'. *Id.* at 739).
2. 871 F.2d 734 (8th Cir. 1989) (decided under Nebraska conflicts law).
3. Minn. Stat. §80C.21 (1989) (emphasis added).

c. Insurance Contracts

448. Whether franchise agreements are typically adhesion contracts may be debatable,[1] but the Restatement takes the position that the adhesionary nature of a contract does not by itself defeat the choice-of-law clause, unless the application of the chosen law would result in 'substantial injustice'.[2] Insurance contracts are one of the most common examples of adhesion contracts and for this reason they are subject to detailed regulation by state statutes. Many statutes mandate their application to contracts having certain enumerated connections with the enacting state[3] and some of these statutes expressly prohibit choice-of-law or choice-of-forum clauses.

For example, an Oregon statute provides that, for an insurance policy 'delivered or issued for delivery in [Oregon]', any 'condition, stipulation or agreement requiring such policy to be construed according to the laws of any other state or country . . . shall be invalid'.[4] Most courts faithfully apply these statutes and refuse to enforce contrary choice-of-law clauses,[5] except when the clause chooses a law that favours the insured.[6]

1. The Restatement (Second) considers adhesionary those contracts that are 'drafted unilaterally by the dominant party and then presented on a 'take-it-or-leave-it' basis to the weaker party who has no real opportunity to bargain about its terms'. *Restatement (Second)* §187, cmt. b.
2. *Id.*
3. Likewise, a Texas statute provides that '[a]ny contract of insurance payable to any citizen or inhabitant of this State by any insurance company . . . doing business within this State shall be . . . governed by [the laws of this State] notwithstanding such . . . contract . . . may provide that the contract was executed and the premiums . . . should be payable without this State'. Tex.Ins.Code Ann. §21.42. A North Carolina statute provides that '[a]ll contracts of insurance on property, lives, or interests in this State shall be deemed to be made therein, and all contracts of insurance the applications for which are taken within the State shall be deemed to be made within this State and are subject to the laws thereof'. N.C.Gen.Stat. §58-3-1. *See also* Wis.Stat. §632.09 ('Every insurance against loss or destruction of or damage to property in this state . . . is governed by the law of this state'.); Minn. Stat. §60A.08(4) ('All contracts of insurance on property, lives, or interests in this state, shall be deemed to be made in this state'.); Colo.Rev.Stat. §10-4-711; Fla.Stat. §627.727; Okla.Stat. tit.36 §3636; La.Rev.Stat. §§22:611, 22:655 22:1406(D).
4. Or. Rev. Stat. §§742.001, 742.018.
5. *See Param Petroleum Corp.* v. *Commerce and Indus. Ins. Co.*, 686 A.2d 377 (N.J.Super. A.D. 1997); *Nelson* v. *Aetna Life Ins. Co.*, 359 F.Supp. 271, 290–292 (W.D.Mo. 1973).
6. *See Haisten* v. *Grass Valley Med. Reimbursement Fund, Ltd.*, 784 F.2d 1392 (9th Cir. 1986); *State Farm Mut. Auto. Ins. Co.* v. *Baker*, 797 P.2d 168 (Kan. Ct. App. 1990). For an additional exception in cases involving group insurance policies, *see Reger* v. *Nat'l. Ass'n of Bedding Mnfgs. Group Ins. Trust Fund*, 372 N.Y.S.2d 97 (N.Y. Sup. Ct. 975); *Davis* v. *Humble Oil & Refining Co.*, 283 So.2d 783 (La. Ct. App. 1973); *Kahn* v. *Great-West Life Assurance Co.*, 307 N.Y.S.2d 238 (N.Y. Sup. Ct. 1970).

III. Modalities of the Choice-of-Law Agreement

A. *Which Law Determines Existence and Validity*

449. A choice-of-law clause is itself an agreement that is usually contained in the contract that the clause purports to submit to the chosen law. Before one can properly speak of such an 'agreement', however, one must first verify that it came into existence. Did the parties have the capacity to make such an agreement? Was their consent to it free of vices (such as duress, error, etc.)? Was there a 'meeting of the minds'? Was the agreement clothed in the requisite form? These questions do not arise often but, when they do, they raise the preliminary question of which law will provide the answers.

Of the three possible options – the *lex fori*, the chosen law, and the *lex causae* – the Restatement (Second) employs the first two. It assigns to the *lex fori* issues of misrepresentation, duress, undue influence, or mistake,[1] and to the chosen law all other issues of formation and validity, including capacity and form.[2] Both options offer the advantage of practicality and judicial economy. In addition, the *lex fori* option can be defended on the ground that, to the extent that a choice-of-law agreement displaces some of the forum's choice-of-law rules, the forum should be free to determine under its own substantive standards whether such an agreement exists before allowing the displacement. On the other hand, the option of applying the chosen law may entail serious 'bootstrapping' which can be avoided only by employing the policing mechanism of Section 187(2)(b). The third option – applying the *lex causae* – avoids the bootstrapping problem, but it also undercuts much of the convenience and efficiency that make choice-of-law clauses attractive to courts and litigants in the first place.

1. *See Restatement (Second)* §187, cmt. b. ('Whether such consent was in fact obtained by improper means [such as misrepresentation, duress, or undue influence] or by mistake will be determined by the forum in accordance with its own legal principles'.)
2. *See id.* §198 cmt. a (capacity 'determined by the law chosen by the parties, *if they have made an effective choice*'; §199 cmt. a (same as to form), §200 cmt. a (same for validity for issues other than capacity and form). The Restatement follows the third option to the extent it assigns to the *lex causae* the question of whether the subject of the choice-of-law agreement is – or is not – one that the parties 'could have resolved by an explicit provision in their agreement'. *See id.* §187, cmt. c. The answer to this question determines whether the enforceability of the choice-of-law agreement will be determine under §187(1), which imposes no limitations, or rather §187(2), which imposes public policy limitations.

B. Written, Express and Implied Choice

450. Most choice-of-law agreements are express and written into the contract they purport to govern. Oral choice-of-law agreements are rarer than oral contracts and even rarer in written contracts.[1] The Restatement (Second) allows for an oral or an implied choice, but distinguishes the latter from a hypothetical choice by providing that it 'does not suffice to demonstrate that the parties, if they had thought about the matter, would have wished to have the law of a particular state applied'.[2]

1. The UN Convention on Contracts for the International Sale of Goods ('Vienna Sales Convention'), which is in force for the United States (15 USCA Appendix), provides that the parties may vary the applicable law (Art. 6), and that the contract (Art. 11) or its modification (Art. 29) need not be in writing. Even so, oral choice-of-law clauses remain rare.
2. *Restatement (Second)* §187, cmt. a.

C. Multiple or Partial Choice

451. The parties may choose the law of more than one state to govern different parts or issues of the contract.[1] For example, in a contract to be performed in more than one state, the parties may subject questions of performance to the laws of the states of the respective performances. Similarly, the parties may choose a law to govern only part of their contract. In that case, the rest of the contract will be governed by the *lex causae*. This partial choice of law, as well as the choice of more than one law, may result in *dépeçage*.

1. *See id.* §187 cmt. l, as revised in 1988.

D. Timing of Choice

452. Although usually the parties' agreement on the applicable law is contained in the same contract that the agreement purports to regulate, recent codifications and international conventions expressly allow the parties to choose the applicable law at a later time, or to modify a choice made earlier, so long as they do not prejudice the rights of third parties. The Restatement (Second) does not address these issues, but general contract principles should lead to the same results.

E. Choice of an Invalidating Law

453. The Restatement (Second) takes the position that, when the contractually chosen law invalidates the contract, or part of it, the choice should be disregarded because the application of the chosen law would 'defeat the expectations of the parties which it is the purpose of the [Section 187] to protect'.[1] Although some foreign systems and a few American courts have taken the opposite position,[2] the Restatement's position is defensible when the chosen law invalidates the whole contract. However, this position becomes more debatable when the chosen law invalidates only a part of the contract, such as a non-compete covenant. In such a case, the parties' general expectations of having a binding contract are satisfied and thus, in the absence of special circumstances, there is little reason to allow one party to pick the favourable and discard the unfavourable provisions of the chosen law. Several cases have adopted this reasoning and have applied the partially invalidating law.[3]

1. *Id.* cmt. e.
2. *See* E. Scoles, P. Hay, P. Borchers & S. Symeonides, *Conflict of Laws* (4th edn, St. Paul, Minn., 2004), pp. 982–983.
3. *See*, e.g., *Boatland, Inc.* v. *Brunswick Corp.*, 558 F.2d 818 (6th Cir. 1977) (invalidating under the chosen law a clause dealing with the termination of a dealership agreement); *Hardy* v. *Monsanto Enviro-Chem Sys., Inc.*, 323 N.W.2d 270 (Mich. 1982) (applying the chosen law to invalidate an indemnity clause); *Stoot* v. *Fluor Drilling Servs., Inc.*, 851 F.2d 1514 (5th Cir. 1988) (*accord*); *General Elec. Credit Corp.* v. *Beyerlein*, 286 N.Y.S.2d 351 (N.Y. Sup. 1967), *aff'd*, 292 N.Y.S.2d 32 (A.D. 4th Dept. 1968) (applying the chosen law to invalidate a clause that cut off defences against an assignee). *But see Kipin Indus.* v. *Van Deilen Int'l, Inc.*, 182 F.3d 490 (6th Cir. 1999) (disregarding the chosen law 'to the extent' it invalidated a part of the contract); *Infomax Office Sys.* v. *MBO Binder & Co.*, 976 F.Supp. 1247 (S.D. Iowa, 1997) (*accord*).

F. Choice of Non-state Norms

454. Throughout its many provisions, including Section 187, the Restatement uses the terms 'local law' and 'law' in a way that ties both terms to a 'state', which the Restatement defines as a 'a territorial unit with a distinct general body of law'.[1] This definition, combined with the repeated use of the phrase 'law of the state' in Section 187, makes it clear that the drafters of the Restatement did not contemplate the contractual choice of non-state norms, such as the Unidroit Principles.[2] This is understandable considering that the Restatement was drafted during the 1950s and early 1960s, a period in which non-state norms did not have the clarity, maturity, and status they have today. However, closer analysis reveals that the Restatement is not altogether hostile to non-state norms. To the extent it recognizes the doctrine of incorporation by reference for issues that fall within the parties' contractual power, the Restatement allows the parties to incorporate by reference into their contract the non-state norms of their choice.[3]

1. *Restatement (Second)* §3.
2. For a detailed discussion of this issue, *see* S. Symeonides, 'Contracts Subject to Non-State Norms', 53 *Am. J. Comp. L.* 209, 2006 Supp.
3. *See supra* 430. The UCC employs a similar dichotomy between variable and non-variable rules of the UCC and (implicitly in the old and explicitly in the new version) allows the contractual 'incorporation' of non-state norms with regard to matters governed by variable rules. *See* Symeonides, *supra* footnote 2 at 218–221.

G. Choice of Conflicts Law and Procedural Law

455. Like most foreign systems, the Restatement takes the position that, in the absence of clear evidence of contrary intention, the contractual choice of a state's law does not include that state's conflicts law.[1]

1. *Restatement (Second)* §187 cmt. h.

456. Whether a choice-of-law clause includes the chosen state's procedural law is a question that the Restatement does not address expressly. However, nothing in the Restatement suggests that the drafters contemplated the idea that a routine choice-of-law clause (as opposed to a choice-of-forum clause) would include the chosen state's procedural law. This question has particular practical relevance with regard to statutes of limitations, which most American states continue to characterize as procedural.[1] Most cases that have considered this issue have concluded that the clause did not include the chosen state's statute of limitation.[2]

1. *See infra* 593–604.
2. *See Long* v. *Holland Am. Line Westours, Inc.*, 26 P.3d 430 (Alaska 2001); *Belleville Toyota, Inc.* v. *Toyota Motor Sales, U.S.S., Inc.* 770 N.E.2d 177 (Ill. 2002); *Educ. Research Inst.* v. *Lipsky*, 2002 WL 1463461 (Cal. App. 2002); *Western Group Nurseries, Inc.* v. *Ergas*, 211 F.Supp.2d 1362 (S.D.Fla. 2002); *Shaw* v. *Rivers White Water Rafting Resort*, 2002 WL 31748919 (E.D.Mich. 2002); *Fin. Bancorp. Inc.* v. *Pingree & Dahle, Inc.*, 880 P.2d 14 (Ut. Ct. App. 1994); *Federal Deposit Ins. Corp.* v. *Petersen*, 770 F.2d 141, 142–143 (10th Cir. 1985); *Hambrecht & Quist Venture Partners* v. *American Medical Int'l, Inc.*, 46 Cal.Rptr.2d 33 (Cal. Ct. App. 1995); *Manion* v. *Roadway Package System, Inc.*, 938 F.Supp. 512 (C.D.Ill. 1996); *In re Western United Nurseries, Inc.* v. *Estate of Adams*, 191 B.R. 820 (Bankr.D.Ariz. 1996); *In re Fineberg*, 202 B.R. 206 (Bankr.E.D. Pa. 1996); *Springfield Oil Servs., Inc.* v. *Costello*, 941 F.Supp. 45 (E.D.Pa. 1996); *Nez* v. *Forney*, 783 P.2d 471 (N.M. 1989); *Florida State Bd. of Admin.*, v. *Eng'g & Envtl. Servs., Inc.*, 262 F.Supp.2d 1004 (D.Minn. 2003); *Hemar Ins. Corp.* v. *Ryerson*, 108 S.W.3d 90 (Mo.App. 2003); *Belleville Toyota, Inc.* v. *Toyota Motor Sales, U.S.S., Inc.*, 770 N.E.2d 177 (Ill. 2002). For other procedural issues, *see*, e.g., *Maddox* v. *American Airlines, Inc.*, 298 F.3d 694 (8th Cir. 2002) (prejudgment interest); *North Bergen Rex Transport* v. *Trailer Leasing Co.*, 730 A.2d 843 (N.J. 1999) (attorney fees); *Weatherby Associates, Inc.* v. *Ballack*, 783 So.2d 1138 (Fla. Dist. Ct. App. 2001) (same).

H. Choice-of-Forum Clauses and Floating Clauses

457. A choice-of-law clause does not, without more, operate as a selection of the chosen state's courts for jurisdictional purposes.[1] Conversely, a choice-of-forum clause does not, without more, entail a contractual choice of the chosen state's law, although, combined with other contacts, it may lead a court to conclude that the parties made an implied choice of that law.[2]

1. *See Algemene Bank Nederland, M.V.* v. *Mattox*, 611 F.Supp. 144 (N.D.Ga. 1985); *Dent-Air, Inc.* v. *Beech Mountain Air Serv.*, 332 N.W.2d 904 (Minn. 1983). Combined with other contacts, a choice-of-law clause may provide a partial basis of jurisdiction to the extent it amounts to purposeful availment of the chosen state's benefits and protections. *See Burger King Corp.* v. *Rudzewicz*, 471 US 462, 482 (1985).
2. *See* E. Scoles, P. Hay, P. Borchers & S. Symeonides, *Conflict of Laws* (4th edn, St. Paul, Minn., 2004), p. 951.

458. American case law is inconclusive on the problem of 'floating' clauses (also known as 'service or suit' (SOS) clauses), which are common in insurance contracts. Through these clauses, the insurer agrees in advance to submit to the jurisdiction of a court to be chosen by the insured, also agreeing that all disputes arising under the contract 'shall be determined in accordance with the law and practice of such Court'.[1] One question raised by such a clause is whether it constitutes a choice-of-law clause (in addition to being a choice-of-forum clause).[2] The majority of cases that have considered this question have concluded that these clauses are not choice-of-law clauses, or, if they are, then they encompass the 'whole law' of the forum state, including its conflicts law.[3]

1. *Burlington Northern R.R. Co.* v. *Allianz Underwriters Ins. Co.*, 1994 WL 637011 at *2 (Del Super. Ct. 1994), *appeal refused*, 653 A.2d 304 (Del. Super. Ct. 1994).
2. On whether such clauses are genuine choice-of-forum clauses, *see Cannelton Indus., Inc.* v. *Aetna Cas. & Sur. Co.*, 460 S.E.2d (W.Va. 1994); *Price* v. *Brown Group, Inc.*, 619 N.Y.S.2d 414 (N.Y.A.D. 1994), *appeal denied*, 1995 WL 121748 (N.Y.A.D. 4 Dept. 1995).
3. *See*, e.g., *Norfolk Southern Corp.* v. *California Union Ins. Co.*, 859 So.2d 167 (La. Ct. App. 1 Cir. 2003); *Liggett Group Inc.* v. *Affiliated FM Ins. Co.*, 788 A.2d 134 (Del. Super. Ct. 2001); *Burlington Northern R.R. Co.* v. *Allianz Underwriters Ins. Co.*, 1994 WL 637011 (Del. Super. Ct. 1994), *appeal refused* 653 A.2d 304 (Del. Super. Ct. 1994); *North Am. Philips Corp.* v. *Aetna Cas. and Sur. Co.*, 1994 WL 555399 (Del. Super. 1994); *Carrier Corp.* v. *Home Ins. Co.*, 648 A.2d 665, (Conn. 1994); *W.R. Grace & Co.* v. *Hartford Accident and Indem. Co.*, 555 N.E.2d 214 (Mass. 1990); *Chesapeake Utilities Corp.* v. *Am. Home Ass. Co.*, 704 F.Supp. 551 (D. Del. 1989); *Singer* v. *Lexington Ins. Co.*, 658 F.Supp. 341 (N.D.Tex. 1986).

IV. The Scope of the Choice-of-Law Clause

459. The above discussion touches on the issue of the scope of the choice-of-law clause. This question can arise even with regard to contractual issues,[1] but the more common question is whether the clause encompasses non-contractual issues arising from the same contractual relationship that is the object of the clause. Examples include quasi-contractual claims such as unjust enrichment, tort claims, unfair trade practises, statutes of limitation, attorney fees, and prejudgment interest. Most courts that have encountered this question assume it to be simply one of contractual intent and examine whether the phrasing of the clause is broad enough to include those issues. Analytically, however, a distinction is appropriate between contractual intent and power, that is, between the intended and the permissible scope of the choice-of-law clause.

1. *See*, e.g., *Heating & Air Specialists, Inc.* v. *Jones*, 180 F.3d 923 (8th Cir. 1999) (holding that a clause providing that 'the laws of the State of Texas shall govern [the contract's] interpretation', *id.* at 930, was confined to Texas's rules of contract construction and did not displace any other rules of the otherwise applicable Arkansas law). *But see Kipin Indus.* v. *Van Deilen Int'l, Inc.*, 182 F.3d 490 (6th Cir. 1999) (concluding that to focus on the technical distinction between 'interpret/construe' and 'govern' would 'yield an unwarranted, strained and narrow construction of the [contract's] language'. *Id.* at 494).

A. *Intended Scope*

460. Whether or not the parties intended to submit non-contractual issues to the law they chose is a relatively easy question of contractual interpretation that depends heavily (but not exclusively) on the phrasing of the choice-of-law clause. The only difficulty is determining which state's law governs the interpretation. Because contractual interpretation rarely involves issues of fundamental public policy, there is no need to interpret the clause according to the *lex causae*. Instead the choice is between the *lex fori* and the chosen law, and the Restatement (Second) seems to point to the *lex fori*.

B. *Permissible Scope*

461. A more difficult question is whether the parties have the power to select the law that will govern issues that are not purely contractual. One should not lightly assume an affirmative answer, if only because the principle of party autonomy was born and has been nurtured exclusively in the area of contract law. The Restatement appears to take this position because it speaks of the law of the state chosen by the parties to govern their 'contractual rights and duties'.[1]

1. *Restatement (Second)* §187(2).

462. Nevertheless, many cases tend to assume that contracting parties have the power to submit to the chosen law tort-like issues arising from the same contractual relationship, provided that the parties use clear language expressing such an intent. At the same time, these cases also tend to scrutinize much more closely clauses that purport to encompass tort-like issues than clauses confined to purely contractual issues,[1] and, more often than not, conclude that the clause did not include tort issues.[2]

1. *See*, e.g., *Inacom Corp.* v. *Sears, Roebuck & Co.*, 254 F.3d 683 (8th Cir. 2001); *Stagecoach Transp., Inc.* v. *Shadow*, Inc., 741 N.E.2d 862 (Mass. App. Ct. 2001); *Twinlab Corp.* v. *Paulson*, 724 N.Y.S.2d 496 (N.Y.A.D. 2001); *Florida Evergreen Foliage* v. *E.I. DuPont DeNemours & Co.*, 135 F.Supp.2d 1271 (S.D.Fla. 2001); *Krock* v. *Lipsay*, 97 F.3d 640 (2d Cir. 1996); *Valley Juice Ltd., Inc.* v. *Evian Waters of France, Inc.*, 87 F.3d 604 (2d Cir. 1996);

Precision Screen Machines, Inc. v. *Elexon, Inc.*, 1996 WL 495564 (N.D.Ill. 1996); *Shelley* v. *Trafalgar House Public Ltd. Co.*, 918 F.Supp. 515 (D.P.R. 1996); *Telemedia Partners Worldwide, Ltd.* v. *Hamelin Ltd.*, 1996 WL 41818 (S.D.N.Y. 1996); *Champlain Enters., Inc.* v. *United States*, 945 F.Supp. 468 (N.D.N.Y. 1996); *Young* v. *W.S. Badcock Corp.*, 474 S.E.2d 87 (Ga. Ct. App. 1996); *Lyons* v. *Turner Const. Co.*, 551 N.E.2d 1062 (Ill.App. 1990); *Young* v. *Mobil Oil Corp.*, 735 P.2d 654 (Or. Ct. App. 1987).

2. For recent cases holding that the clause did *not* encompass contract-related tort claims, *see*, e.g., *Benchmark Elecs., Inc.* v. *J.M. Huber Corp.*, 343 F.3d 719 (5th Cir. 2003); *Green Leaf Nursery* v. *E.I. DuPont De Nemours & Co.*, 341 F.3d 1292 (11th Cir. 2003); *Fin. Trust Co. Inc.* v. *Citibank, N.A.*, 268 F.Supp.2d 561 (D.V.I. 2003); *Gloucester Holding Corp.* v. *US Tape and Sticky Products, LLC*, 832 A.2d 116 (Del.Chan. 2003); *Owen J. Roberts Sch. Dist.* v. *HTE, Inc.*, 2003 WL 735098 (E.D.Pa. 2003); *Thomas* v. *Fidelity Brokerage Servs., Inc.* 977 F.Supp. 791 (W.D. La. 1998); *Krock* v. *Lipsay*, 97 F.3d 640 (2d Cir. 1996); *Valley Juice Ltd., Inc.* v. *Evian Waters of France, Inc.*, 87 F.3d 604 (2d Cir. 1996); *Precision Screen Machines, Inc.* v. *Elexon, Inc.*, 1996 WL 495564 (N.D.Ill. 1996); *Shelley* v. *Trafalgar House Public Ltd. Co.*, 918 F.Supp. 515 (D.P.R. 1996); *Telemedia Partners Worldwide, Ltd.* v. *Hamelin Ltd.*, 1996 WL 41818 (SD. N.Y. 1996); *Chaplain Enters., Inc.* v. *United States*, 945 F.Supp. 468 (N.D.N.Y. 1996); *Young* v. *W.S. Badcock Corp.*, 474 SE.2d 87 (Ga. App. 1996); *Ezell* v. *Hayes Oilfield Const. Co., Inc.*, 693 F.2d 489 (5th Cir. 1982), *cert. denied*, 464 US 818 (1983). For cases reaching the opposite conclusion, *see Nedlloyd Lines B.V.* v. *Superior Court*, 834 P.2d 1148 (1992); *Wireless Distribs., Inc.* v. *Sprintcom, Inc.*, 2003 WL 22175607 (N.D.Ill. 2003); *Birnberg* v. *Milk Street Residential Associated Ltd. P'ship*, 2003 WL 151929 (N.D.Ill. 2003); *Lloyd* v. *Loeffler*, 694 F.2d 489 (7th Cir. 1982); *Twohy* v. *First Nat. Bank of Chicago*, 758 F.2d 1185 (7th Cir. 1985); *Barrow* v. *ATCO Mfg. Co.*, 524 N.E.2d 1313 (Ind. Ct. App. 1988).

463. However, as *Sutton* v. *Hollywood Video Entertainment Corp.*,[1] indicates, this approach can lead to exploitation of the weak party, to say nothing of prolonging litigation. *Sutton* was a tort action for malicious prosecution and false imprisonment filed against a Maryland video store owner who had the plaintiff arrested for allegedly stealing merchandise the previous night. Besides being innocent, the plaintiff was a customer and 'member' of the defendant's video store, in that he had applied for and received a 'membership' card allowing him to rent video discs. The membership agreement provided that 'any dispute arising out of or *relating in any way* to [plaintiff's] relationship with [defendant] shall be subject to final, non-appealable, binding arbitration. . . . Exclusive venue for any dispute resolution shall be in Portland, Oregon and Oregon law shall control for all purposes'.[2]

Relying on the italicized language (which was abundantly explicit), the defendant moved to dismiss the action. The court correctly pointed out that the plaintiff's tort claims had 'nothing whatsoever to do with the video rental contracts'.[3] 'It is logically untenable' said the court, 'that the membership agreements were meant to cover . . . accusations of theft. Taken to an extreme, Defendant's reading of the arbitration clause would require arbitration of claims such as a [defendant's] store ceiling falling in on customers, or a [defendant] store employee brutally attacking a customer . . . who has signed a membership agreement'.[4]

1. 181 F.Supp.2d 504 (D.Md. 2002).
2. *Id.* at 508 (emphasis added).
3. *Id.* at 511.
4. *Id.* at 512. It may be worth noting, although it would not have affected the *Sutton* case, that the 2001 Oregon codification confines to contractual issues the parties' power to choose the applicable law. *See* S. Symeonides, 'Codifying Choice of Law for Contracts: The Oregon Experience', 67 *RabelsZ* 726, 2003, 737.

V. The Uniform Commercial Code

A. *The Present Version*

464. The Uniform Commercial Code (UCC), which has been adopted by statute in all states of the United States, prevails over the Restatement (Second) for contracts that fall within the scope of the UCC. Section 1–105(1) of the UCC provides that 'when a transaction bears a reasonable relationship to [the forum] state and also to another state or nation the parties may agree that the law of either [the forum] state or of such other state or nation shall govern their rights and duties'.[1]

1. Sections 1–105(1) provides further that 'failing such agreement this Act applies to transactions bearing an appropriate relation to this state'. The Section is silent on what law applies when the parties have not designated the applicable law and the transaction does *not* bear an 'appropriate relation' to the forum. *See United Counties Trust Co.* v. *Mac Lum, Inc.*, 643 F.2d 1140 (5th Cir. 1981), *reh'g. denied*, 647 F.2d 1123 (5th Cir. 1981).

465. This provision is not a model of good drafting. If read literally, this provision would permit a choice-of-law clause only if the transaction bears a reasonable relationship to both the chosen state and the forum state. Obviously, such a reading would defeat the very purpose of party autonomy and thus should be avoided. Secondly, unlike the Restatement, this provision does not expressly distinguish between suppletive or variable rules and mandatory or non-variable rules. Reading this provision literally would require a 'reasonable relationship' with regard to both categories of rules. Fortunately, the official comments avoid this result by suggesting that Sections 1–105 does not displace the doctrine of incorporation.[1] Moreover, another provision of the UCC, Section 1–102(3), expressly recognizes the parties' freedom to vary by agreement any UCC provision that the UCC does not designate as non-variable.[2] Because a choice-of-law clause is such an agreement, there is little doubt that, with regard to matters governed by variable or suppletive rules of the UCC, the parties may incorporate by reference the law of a state that lacks a 'reasonable relationship'.[3]

1. UCC §1–105, cmt. 1 ('But an agreement as to choice of law may sometimes take effect as a shorthand expression of the intent of the parties as to matters governed by their agreement, even though the transaction has no significant contact with the jurisdiction chosen').
2. UCC §§1–102(3). Among the non-variable provisions are those declaring the obligations of good faith, diligence, and reasonableness, but even with regard to those obligations, the parties 'may by agreement determine the standards by which the performance of such obligations is to be measured if such standards are not manifestly unreasonable'. *Id.*
3. *See* E. Scoles, P. Hay, P. Borchers & S. Symeonides, *Conflict of Laws* (4th edn, St. Paul, Minn., 2004), pp. 984–985.

466. Section 1–105 does not contain an explicit public policy limitation to party autonomy. This omission is problematical only for matters covered by non-variable rules and only in international conflicts. In interstate conflicts, this omission is practically inconsequential because all US states have adopted the UCC (albeit with variations in details).

467. Despite these interpretative difficulties, courts have applied Section 1–105 in the same manner as Section 187 of the Restatement (Second) and most view the two provisions as interchangeable.[1]

1. *See id.* at 986.

B. The Proposed Version

468. In 2001, the drafters of the UCC proposed a new version of Article 1, which replaces Sections 1–105 with proposed Sections 1–301. Like its predecessor, the new version applies only to contracts that are otherwise within the scope of the UCC, but, unlike its predecessor, it differentiates between contracts involving a consumer and other contracts ('business to business' transactions). The new version restricts party autonomy with regard to the former contracts and expands it with regard to the latter contracts.

469. For consumer contracts, Sections 1–301 provides that a choice-of-law clause is not effective unless the chosen law bears a 'reasonable relation'[1] to the transaction. Moreover, the Section provides that, even when such a relationship exists, the application of the chosen law may not deprive the consumer of the protection of certain rules of the state in which the consumer principally resides,[2] or, in certain sales contracts, the state of delivery.[3] In a fashion similar to the Rome Convention, Sections 1–301 defines these rules as those that are both 'protective of consumers and may not be varied by agreement'[4] ('mandatory rules').

1. UCC §§1–301(e)(1) (2001 Revision).
2. UCC §§1–301(e)(2)(A) (2001 Revision).
3. UCC §§1–301(e)(2)(B) (2001 Revision) provides that, if the transaction is a sale of goods and the consumer both made the contract and took delivery of the goods in a state other than that of her principal residence, then the protection described in the text encompasses only the mandatory rules of the former state (i.e., not the residence state). This provision, which is influenced in part by Art. 5 of the Rome Convention, 'enables a seller of goods engaging in face-to-face transactions to ascertain the consumer protection rules to which those sales are subject, without the necessity of determining the principal residence of each buyer'. *Id.* cmt 3.
4. UCC §§1–301(e)(2) (2001 Revision). The accompanying Comments explain that '[not all] rules that cannot be changed by agreement . . . are, for that reason alone, mandatory rules. Otherwise, contractual choice of law . . . would be illusory and redundant; the parties would be able to accomplish by choice of law no more than can be accomplished under §§1–302, which allows variation of otherwise applicable rules by agreement'. UCC §§1–301, cmt. 6 (2001 Revision).

470. For contracts not involving a consumer, Sections 1–301 allows the parties to choose the applicable law (for matters of both construction and validity), even if the choice is that of a state that bears no relation to the transaction.[1] The only requirement is that, if the transaction does not bear a reasonable relation with a country other than the United States ('domestic' transaction), the chosen law must be that of a state of the United States.[2]

1. UCC §§1–301(c) (2001 Revision).
2. *See* UCC §§1–301(a) (distinguishing between 'domestic' and 'international' transactions) and §§1–301(c)(1) and (2) (2001 Revision). For international transactions, there is no limitation, and under §§1–302, the parties may even choose non-state norms, such as those promulgated by intergovernmental organizations like UNCITRAL or UNIDROIT. *See* §§1–301 cmt. 2, §§1–302 cmt. 2 (2001 Revision).

471. Sections 1–301 contains a general public policy reservation. However, the reservation does not cover consumer contracts, apparently because of an assumption that consumers are adequately protected through the mandatory rules mentioned above. As in the Restatement (Second), the public policy reservation of the UCC becomes operative only if the application of the chosen law conflicts with a 'fundamental' policy of the state whose law would govern in the absence of a valid choice-of-law agreement.[1] The accompanying comments seem to conflate the two concepts by considering the operation of the mandatory rules an example of the fundamental policy exception.[2]

1. UCC §§1–301(f) (2001 Revision). The latter state is determined through the choice-of-law rules of the forum state. *Id.* §§1–301(d) and (f).
2. *See id.* §§1–301, cmt. 6 ('Application of the designated law may be contrary to a fundamental policy of the State or country whose law would otherwise govern *either* (i) because the substance of the designated law violates a fundamental principle of justice of that State or country or (ii) because it differs from a rule of that State or country that is 'mandatory' in that it must be applied in the courts of that State or country without regard to otherwise-applicable choice of law rules of that State or country and without regard to whether the designated law is otherwise offensive'. (emphasis added).

472. Finally, in the absence of an effective choice-of-law agreement, in both consumer and non-consumer contracts, the applicable law is the law selected through the choice-of-law rules of the forum state.[1] This is a welcome departure from Sections 1–105(1), which authorized the forum to apply its own substantive law if the transaction bore 'an appropriate relation' to the forum state.

1. UCC §§1–301(d) (2001 Revision). However, the application of the law thus chosen by the court may not deprive the consumer of the protection of the mandatory rules of the consumer's home state or of the state of sale and delivery as described *supra*. *See id.* cmt. 3.

VI. Arbitration Clauses

A. *Foreign Arbitration*

473. The United States is party to the 1958 UN Convention on the Recognition and Enforcement of Foreign Arbitral Awards ('New York Convention'),[1] as are more than 130 other countries. According to Article I, the Convention applies to 'non-domestic' awards rendered outside the United States. The implementing federal statute confines the Convention to awards arising out of 'commercial' relationships. Exempt from its scope are awards arising from 'a relationship which is entirely between citizens of the United States . . . unless that relationship involves property located abroad, envisages performance or enforcement abroad, or has some other reasonable relation with one or more foreign states'.[2]

1. *See* 21 U.S.T. 2517, 330 U.N.T.S. 3.
2. 9 USCA §202.

474. Neither the Convention nor the implementing statute addresses the question of which law will govern the merits of the dispute, or the parties' power to choose that law. Both the Convention and the statute require American courts to enforce an otherwise valid arbitration agreement without regard to whether it is accompanied by a choice-of-law clause or which law a clause chooses. Indeed, the United States Supreme Court has taken a strong pro-arbitration stance even in cases that implicate mandatory rules of public law, such as securities or antitrust laws.[1]

1. *See*, e.g., *Scherk* v. *Alberto-Culver Co.*, 417 US 506 (1974); *Mitsubishi Motors Corp.* v. *Soler Chrysler-Plymouth, Inc.*, 473 US 614 (1985).

475. *Vimar Seguros Y Reaseguros, S.A.* v. *M/V Sky Reefer*,[1] is representative of this trend. The underlying contract, a maritime bill of lading, provided for arbitration in Tokyo under Japanese law. A Moroccan supplier had sold to a New York distributor a shipload of oranges to be transported from Morocco to Massachusetts by a Panamanian-owned ship chartered to a Japanese company. When the cargo was damaged, the New York distributor and its insurer sued the ship-owner in Massachusetts. The defendant moved to stay the action and compel arbitration in Tokyo under the bill of lading and Section 3 of the Federal Arbitration Act (FAA), which requires courts to stay proceedings and enforce arbitration agreements covered by the Act.

The plaintiffs opposed the motion, arguing that the arbitration clause was unenforceable under the FAA because it violated Section 3(8) of the Carriage of Goods by Sea Act (COGSA) which prohibits the 'lessening' of the carrier's liability for fault.[2] Pursuant to this section, lower courts have routinely invalidated foreign forum-selection clauses because such clauses 'put[ ] "a high hurdle" in the way of enforcing liability, and thus . . . effective[ly enable] . . . carriers to secure settlements lower than if cargo [owners] could sue in a convenient forum'.[3] Lower courts have also expressed strong doubts as to whether foreign tribunals 'would apply [COGSA] in the same way as would an American tribunal subject to the uniform control of the Supreme Court'.[4] Because foreign arbitration clauses are only a subset of foreign forum-selection clauses in general, lower courts have also invalidated such clauses under the same rationale.[5]

1. 515 US 528 (1995).
2. That section provides: 'Any clause . . . in a contract of carriage relieving the carrier or the ship from liability for loss or damage to or in connection with the goods, arising from negligence, fault, or failure in the duties or obligations provided in this section, or lessening such liability otherwise than as provided in this chapter, shall be null and void and of no effect'. 46 USC §1303(8).
3. *Indussa Corp.* v. *S.S. Ranborg*, 377 F.2d 200, 203 (1967) (*en banc*). *See also Union Ins. Soc. of Canton, Ltd.* v. *S.S. Elikon*, 642 F.2d 721, 723–725 (4th Cir. 1981); *Conklin & Garrett, Ltd* v. *M/V Finnrose*, 826 F.2d 1441, 1442–1444 (5th Cir. 1987).
4. *Indussa*, 377 F.2d, at 203–204.

5. *See State Est. for Agric. Product Trading* v. *M/V Wesermunde*, 838 F.2d 1576, 1580–1581 (11th Cir.), *cert. denied*, 488 US 916 (1988).

476. In *Vimar Seguros*, the Supreme Court repudiated this rationale. In an opinion by Justice Kennedy, the Court read the above section of COGSA as prohibiting only the lessening of the substantive liability of the carrier, 'without addressing the separate question of the means and costs of enforcing that liability'.[1] The Court reasoned:

> If the question whether a provision lessens liability were answered by reference to the costs and inconvenience to the cargo owner, there would be no principled basis for distinguishing national from foreign arbitration clauses. Even if it were reasonable to read §3(8) to make a distinction based on travel time, airfare, and hotels bills, these factors are not susceptible of a simple and enforceable distinction between domestic and foreign forums. Requiring a Seattle cargo owner to arbitrate in New York likely imposes more costs and burdens than a foreign arbitration clause requiring it to arbitrate in Vancouver.[2]

The Court also characterized as 'parochial' the argument that foreign tribunals or arbitrators might not be able or willing to apply COGSA correctly. Quoting *The Bremen*,[3] *Scherk*,[4] *Mitsubishi Motors*,[5] and other 'internationalist' cases, the Court said:

> [T]he historical judicial resistance to foreign forum selection clauses 'has little place in an era when . . . businesses . . . now operate in world markets. . . . The expansion of American business and industry will hardly be encouraged . . . if, notwithstanding solemn contracts, we insist on a parochial concept that all disputes must be resolved under our laws and in our courts. . . . [I]f international arbitral institutions are to take a central place in the international legal order, national courts will need to shake off the old judicial hostility to arbitration, and also their customary and understandable unwillingness to cede jurisdiction of a claim arising under domestic law to a foreign or transnational tribunal' . . . A parochial refusal by the courts of one country to enforce an international arbitration agreement' would frustrate the orderliness and predictability essential to any international business transaction.[6]

The Court added that '[i]f the United States is to be able to gain the benefits of international accords and have a role as a trusted partner in multilateral endeavours, its courts should be most cautious before interpreting its domestic legislation in such manner as to violate international agreements'.[7] The Court concluded that this factor 'counsels against construing COGSA to nullify foreign arbitration clauses because of inconvenience to the plaintiff or insular distrust of the ability of foreign arbitrators to apply the law'.[8]

1. *Vimar Seguros*, 515 US at 534.
2. *Id.* at 536.
3. 407 US 1. 1907 (1972), discussed *supra* at 55–57.
4. 417 US 506 (1974).

5. 473 US 614 (1985).
6. *Vimar Seguros*, 515 US at 537–538 (internal quotation marks omitted).
7. *Id.* at 539.
8. *Id.*

477. Finally, the Court held 'premature'[1] the plaintiff's argument that the Japanese arbitrators would not apply COGSA but rather the Japanese Hague Rules, which in fact lessen the carrier's liability for the acts or omissions of stevedores hired by the shipper. Apparently forgetting the choice-of-law clause, the Court thought that it was 'mere speculation that the foreign arbitrators might apply Japanese law',[2] but noted that, because the district court had retained jurisdiction to enforce the arbitration award, that court had the traditional power to refuse enforcement if the award was 'repugnant to the public policy of the United States'.[3]

1. *Id.* at 540.
2. *Id.* at 541.
3. *Id.* at 540.

478. Justice Stevens in a strong dissent facetiously observed that, under the majority's reasoning, '[a] carrier who truly wished to relieve itself of liability might select an outpost in Antarctica as the setting for arbitration of all claims',[1] and could also 'require the consignee to pay the costs of the arbitration, or perhaps the travel expenses and fees of the expert witnesses, interpreters, and lawyers employed by both parties'.[2] Justice Stevens also criticized the majority's failure to address the issues raised by the choice-of-law clause.[3]

1. *Id.* at 551 note 12.
2. *Id.* at 551.
3. *See id.* at 548 ('The foreign-law clause leaves the shipper . . . open to the application of unfamiliar and potentially disadvantageous legal standards, until he can obtain review (perhaps years later) in a domestic forum under the high standard applicable to vacation of arbitration awards'.); *id.* at 549, note 1 ('[T]he majority is apparently willing to allow arbitration to proceed under foreign law, and to determine afterwards whether application of that law has actually lessened the carrier's formal liability'.).

479. When an arbitration clause is silent on the substantive law to be applied, the arbitrators have several options depending on the law that governs the arbitration. They may: (a) apply the substantive law designated by the choice-of-law rules of the state in which the arbitration is held, or the rules of another state chosen by the arbitrators; or (b) directly choose the substantive law they consider most appropriate for the case (*voie directe*).[1] In any case, the tribunal's choice-of-law decision may not be judicially challenged. Article V of the New York Convention, which lists the grounds for not recognizing an arbitral award, does not include among them an erroneous choice of law or, for that matter, any error or misapplication of law. As the authors of a standard treatise observed, 'whereas the effectiveness of the choice of governing law made by the parties is liable to be restricted in some respects, that of the choice made by the arbitrators is virtually unlimited'.[2] There is the possibility of the public policy defence of Article V.2(b), but this defence may succeed only upon a showing of some specific and serious defect beyond the mere fact that the tribunal chose to apply the 'wrong' law.[3]

1. *See* Art. 33.1 of the UNCITRAL Arbitration Rules of 1976, 15 *I.L.M.* 701 (1976). Several contemporary arbitration regimes expressly authorize the latter option. For example, the arbitration rules of the International Chamber of Commerce (ICC Rules Art. 17.1 (1998)), the London Court of International Arbitration (LCIA Rules, Art. 22.3 (1998)), and the Stockholm Chamber of Commerce (SCC Rules, Art. 24.1) all provide that, in the absence of a choice-of-law clause, 'the Arbitral Tribunal shall apply the law(s) or rules of law which it considers appropriate'. Art. 59(a) of the World Intellectual Property Organization (WIPO) Arbitration Rules of 1994, and Art. 10.1 of the Center for Public Resources (CPR) Arbitration Rules of 2000 contain similar language.
2. Fouchard, Gaillard, Goldman on *International Commercial Arbitration* (E. Gaillard & J. Savage, eds, 1999), p. 865.
3. *See Karaha Bodas Co., L.L.C.* v. *Perusahaan Pertambangan Minyak Dan Gas Bumi Negara*, 364 F.3d 274, 306 (5th Cir. 2004), *cert. denied*, 543 US 917 (2004) ('The public policy defense is to be construed narrowly to be applied only where enforcement would violate the forum state's most basic notions of morality and justice. The general pro-enforcement bias informing the convention . . . points to a narrow reading of the public policy defense. Erroneous legal reasoning or misapplication of law is generally not a violation of public policy within the meaning of the New York Convention'. (internal quotations omitted); *Parsons & Whittemore Overseas Co., Inc.* v. *Societé Generale De L'Industrie Du Papier (RAKTA)*, 508 F.2d 969, 973 (2nd Cir. 1974); *and Coutinho Caro & Co. U.S.A., Inc.* v. *Marcus Trading, Inc.*, 2000 WL 435566, at *12 (D.Conn. 2000)).

480. Finally, both the New York Convention and the implementing statute require American courts to recognize arbitral awards that fall within the Convention's scope, without reviewing the arbitrators' choice of law. Although Article V.2(b) of the Convention provides for a public policy defence to recognition, the defence is unlikely to succeed if it is based solely on the arbitrator's choice of law.[1]

1. Recognition of foreign arbitral awards is discussed *infra* 768–772.

B. Domestic Arbitration

481. Arbitration conducted in the United States, whether it involves international or interstate disputes, differs in many respects from international arbitration. The Federal Arbitration Act (FAA),[1] which preempts state law with respect to arbitration agreements that affect interstate or international commerce, takes a strong pro-arbitration stance. The Act provides that arbitration agreements that fall within its scope 'shall be valid, irrevocable, and enforceable, save upon such grounds as exist at law or in equity for the revocation of any contract'.[2]

1. *See* Federal Arbitration Act, 9 USC §§1–16 (2001) [hereinafter *FAA*].
2. *Id.*

482. The FAA includes within its scope '*any* . . . contract . . . involving commerce'.[1] Because in the United States just about everything 'involves' commerce,[2] the foreign reader should not be surprised to find cases enforcing pre-dispute arbitration agreements in consumer contracts and certain employment contracts.[3] Although the FAA exempts from arbitration 'contracts of employment of seamen, railroad employees, or any other class of workers engaged in foreign or interstate commerce',[4] the Supreme Court has narrowed this exception by holding that it did not encompass all employment contracts involving commerce, but rather only those involving transportation workers.[5] However, the New York Convention, which displaces the FAA for most international cases, applies to all employment contracts, including those involving transportation workers. Because the Convention pre-empts state law, states must enforce arbitration clauses in international employment contracts, such as those of maritime employment.[6]

1. *Id.* (emphasis added).
2. The United States Supreme Court has interpreted the FAA as co-extensive with Congress's broad power to regulate interstate commerce. *See Allied-Bruce Terminix Cos.* v. *Dobson*, 513 US 265 (1995).
3. *See* S. Symeonides, 'Choice of Law in the American Courts in 2006: Twentieth Annual Survey', 55 *Am. J. Comp. L.* 697, 2007, 750–752, and cases discussed therein, including a case subjecting to arbitration a claim from medical malpractise resulting in death.
4. 9 USC §1.
5. *See Circuit City Stores, Inc.* v. *Adams*, 532 US 105 (2001).
6. For cases so holding, *see Francisco* v. *M/T Stolt Achievement*, 293 F.3d 270 (5th Cir. 2002), *cert. denied*, 537 US 1030 (2002); *Bautista* v. *Star Cruises*, 396 F.3d 1289 (11th Cir. 2005) *Lim* v. *Offshore Specialty Fabricators, Inc.*, 404 F.3d 898 (5th Cir. 2005), *cert. denied*, 126 S.Ct. 365 (US 2005); *Dahiya* v. *Talmidge Int'l Ltd.*, 931 So.2d 1163 (La. App. 4th Cir. 2006), *reh'g denied* (30 June 2006).

483. The FAA contains no limitation on the power of arbitrators to choose the substantive law that will govern the merits of the dispute. The International Arbitration Rules of the American Arbitration Association[1] give arbitrators the same choice-of-law power as do the ICC and LCIA rules described above and thus raise the same possibilities as those discussed in connection with foreign arbitration. The FAA lists the grounds on which a court may vacate an arbitral award but, surprisingly, the list does not include a general public policy defence. However, the intermediate federal courts have held that a violation of public policy is a ground for vacating an arbitral award.[2] The Supreme Court has acknowledged in dicta that the public policy defence is available, provided that the arbitrator's interpretation of the contract 'would violate some explicit public policy that is well defined and dominant, and is to be ascertained by reference to the laws and legal precedents and not from general considerations of supposed public interests'.[3] The intermediate courts have also developed an additional ground for vacating an award, known as 'manifest disregard of the law'.[4] Although the Supreme Court has yet to rule on the propriety of this defence, what is clear is that the threshold for triggering it is very high.[5] An award that remains below this threshold will not be vacated solely on the ground that it made the 'wrong' choice of law.

1. *See* American Arbitration Association, *International Arbitration Rules*, Art. 28.1–3 (2000).
2. For citations and discussion, *see* S.L. Hayford, 'Law in Disarray: Judicial Standards for Vacatur of Commercial Arbitral Awards', 30 *Ga. L. Rev.* 731, 1996.
3. *United Paperworkers Int'l Union, AFL-CIO* v. *Misco, Inc.*, 484 US 29, 43 (1987) (internal quotation marks omitted).
4. For citations and discussion, *see* S.L. Hayford, 'Reigning in the Manifest Disregard of the Law Standard: The Key to Stabilizing the Law of Commercial Arbitration', 1999 *J. Disp. Resol.* 117, 1999.
5. *See*, e.g., *Twin Cities Galleries, LLC* v. *Media Arts Group, Inc.*, 415 F.Supp.2d 967, 972 (D.Minn. 2006), *stay granted*, 431 F.Supp.2d 980 (D.Minn. 2006) ('manifest disregard of the law requires more than an error of law' and comes into play only when the arbitrators 'clearly identify the applicable governing law and then proceed to ignore it'.)

§2. Contracts without Choice-of-Law Clauses

484. When a contract does not contain a choice-of-law clause, there is considerably less certainty as to which law will govern. This is because American courts follow a variety of approaches none of which are sufficiently predictable. This is certainly true of the Restatement (Second) and other modern approaches, all of which consciously subordinate the goal of predictability to other goals of the choice-of-law process. Even the traditional approach is unpredictable, despite its efforts to the contrary, because of the courts' frequent utilization of escape devices such as *ordre public* and *renvoi*.[1]

1. *See supra* 127–149.

I. The Traditional Approach

485. As noted in Part II, Chapter 1, 12 states continue to follow the traditional approach in contract conflicts. Four of these states (Alabama,[1] Florida,[2] Georgia,[3] and Virginia[4]) have recently reaffirmed their adherence to the *lex loci contractus* rule. At the other extreme are Rhode Island and Tennessee, which remain in the *lex loci contractus* camp only because their supreme courts have not had the opportunity to reconsider their adherence to that rule since 1968 and 1992, respectively, when they abandoned the *lex loci delicti* rule.[5] The remaining six states (Kansas, Maryland, New Mexico,[6] Oklahoma,[7] South Carolina,[8] and Wyoming[9]) nominally adhere to the *lex loci contractus* rule, but not without ambivalence, equivocation, and often direct avoidance. Maryland's use of *renvoi* is an example of such avoidance, as was discussed earlier.[10] Another example is Kansas's use of the *ordre public* doctrine. The supreme court of Kansas found it unnecessary to abandon the *lex loci contractus* rule and reserved consideration of the Second Restatement's approach 'for a later day', because the traditional public policy exception – which the court employed offensively rather than defensively – enabled the court to avoid the *lex loci* rule and protect '[t]he interests of Kansas'.[11]

1. *See Am. Nonwovens, Inc.* v. *Non Wovens Eng'g*, S.R.I. 648 So.2d 565 (Ala. 1994).
2. *See Sturiano* v. *Brooks*, 523 So.2d 1126 (Fla. 1988) (reaffirming the *lex loci contractus* rule and specifically refusing to extend to contract conflicts the 'most significant relationship' formula earlier adopted for tort conflicts).
3. *See Convergys Corp.* v. *Keener*, 582 S.E.2d 84 (Ga. 2003) (reaffirming adherence to the traditional, if peculiar, Georgia approach and expressly rejecting the Restatement Second in a case in which the Restatement would have produced the same outcome.) Georgia's adherence to the *lex loci contractus* rule is subject to several exceptions because Georgia courts: (1) do not apply the common law (as opposed to the statutory law) of another state, even if the *locus contractus* is in that other state; (2) do not apply the *lex loci contractus* rule: *(a)* when the contract is to be performed in a state other than the state in which it was made; or *(b)* when the contract contains a valid choice-of-law clause. However, contracts made in Georgia and not containing a choice-of-law clause to the contrary are presumed to have been tacitly submitted by the parties to the law of Georgia. *See* S. Symeonides, *The American Choice-of-Law Revolution: Past, Present, and Future* (Leiden, Boston, 2006), p. 84.
4. *See Buchanan* v. *Doe*, 431 S.E.2d 289 (Va. 1993); *Erie Ins. Exch.* v. *Shapiro*, 450 S.E.2d 144 (Va. 1994); *Lexie* v. *State Farm Mut. Auto. Ins. Co.*, 469 S.E.2d 61 (Va. 1996).
5. *See Woodward* v. *Stewart*, 243 A.2d 917, 923 (R.I. 1968); *Hataway* v. *McKinley*, 830 S.W.2d 53 (Tenn. 1992).

6. *See Reagan* v. *McGee Drilling Corp.*, 933 P.2d 867 (N.M. Ct. App. 1997), *cert. denied* (applying alternatively the Restatement (Second) and the public policy exception to the *lex loci contracts*). *But see Shope* v. *State Farm Ins. Co.*, 955 P.2d 515 (N.M. 1996) (applying the *lex loci contractus* without discussion).
7. Oklahoma follows the Restatement (Second) in auto-insurance contracts and contracts falling within the scope of the UCC, and the *lex loci contractus* rule in all other contracts. *See Harvell* v. *Goodyear Tire & Rubber Co.*, 2007 WL 1991433 (Okla.), *reh'g denied*, (3 July 2007).
8. *See Sangamo Weston, Inc.* v. *Nat'l Sur. Corp.*, 414 S.E.2d 127 (S.C. 1992) (acknowledging North Carolina's previous adherence to the *lex loci contractus* rule and noting that, with the record presently before it, the court was 'unable to address the question of whether South Carolina would adopt the more modern view of the [Second] Restatement'. *Id.* at 147–148); *Lister* v. *NationsBank of Delaware, N.A.*, 1997 WL 723056 (S.C. Ct. App. 1997) (applying alternatively the *lex loci* rule and the Restatement (Second)).
9. Wyoming has vacillated between the *lex loci contractus* and the Restatement (Second). *Cherry Creek Dodge Inc.* v. *Carter*, 733 P.2d 1024 (Wy. 1987) cited the Restatement favourably but relied mostly on the 'reasonable relationship' language of the UCC. *Amoco Rocmount Co.* v. *The Anschutz Corp.*, 7 F.3d 909 (10th Cir. 1993), interpreted *Cherry Creek* as having adopted the Restatement. *BHP Petroleum (Americas), Inc.* v. *Texaco Explor. & Prod., Inc.*, 1 P.3d 1253 (Wy. 2000) renounced the view that *Cherry Creek* had adopted the Restatement (Second).
10. *See supra* 143. For other examples from Maryland, *see Bethlehem Steel Co.* v. *G.C. Zarnas & Co., Inc.*, 498 A.2d 605 (Md. 1984) (using an expansive notion of public policy and refusing to apply Pennsylvania law to a contract made in Pennsylvania because 'Pennsylvania ha[d] no strong interest in [applying its law] . . . [because] had [this] suit . . . been brought in Pennsylvania, the Pennsylvania court would likely have decided the issue according to Maryland law [because of Maryland's "significant contacts" with the case]'. *Id.* at 609; *Nat'l Glass* v. *J.C. Penney*, 650 A.2d 246 (Md. 1994) (following Restatement Second §187 in analyzing a choice-of-law clause); *Kronovet* v. *Lipchin*, 415 A. 2d 1096 (Md. 1980) (*accord*).
11. *St. Paul Surplus Lines* v. *Int'l Playtex, Inc.*, 777 P.2d 1259 at 1267 (Kan. 1989). *See also id.* ('The interest of Kansas exceeds [that of the other states]'.). *See also Hartford Accident & Indem. Co.* v. *Am. Red Ball Transit Co.*, 938 P.2d 1281 (Kan. 1997) (*accord*); *Safeco Ins. Co.* v. *Allen*, 941 P.2d 1365 (Kan. 1997) (reaffirming both the *lex loci contractus* rule and the public policy exception enunciated in *St. Paul* but finding the exception inapplicable because in this case the *lex loci* was 'consistent with the stated policy of [Kansas law]'. *Id.* at 1372).

486. The First Restatement rejected the principle of party autonomy and subjected virtually all contractual issues to the law of the place of the contract's making – which it defined as the place 'where the second promise is made in consideration of the first promise', or the place from which the acceptance of an offer was sent.[1] Only certain issues of performance were governed by the law of the place of performance (*lex loci solutionis*).[2] Thus, the Restatement's version of the *lex loci contractus* rule had a much broader scope than its civil law counterpart, covering not only issues of form, but also contractual capacity, mutual assent or consideration, fraud, illegality, and any other circumstances that make a promise voidable.[3]

1. *See* Restatement (First) §§325, 326.
2. *See id.* §358.
3. *See id.* §332.

487. *Milliken* v. *Pratt*[1] is a classic example of the breadth of this rule, the difficulty in applying it, and its manipulation by the courts. *Milliken* involved a cross-border guaranty contract between a Maine merchant and a Massachusetts woman acting as guarantor for her husband. The contract was valid under the law of Maine, but not Massachusetts, which considered married women incapable of contracting. The court rejected the continental rule (which – subject to exceptions that the court did not appear to acknowledge – assigns contractual capacity to the *lex domicilii*) in favour of the common law view of subjecting all such issues to the *lex loci contractus*. Then, the court turned to localizing the *locus contractus*. Ordinarily, the *locus* should be in Massachusetts because that is 'where the second promise [was] made in consideration of the first promise'.[2] The merchant had prepared the guaranty promise in Maine, and the woman signed it in Massachusetts. Instead, the court found this to be a unilateral contract (i.e., one formed by an act of the promisee made in reliance upon the promise), which is deemed to be concluded when and where such act took place.[3] In this case, the promisee's act was the sale of the goods to the woman's husband. Because the goods were delivered to a carrier for the buyer in Maine, the court concluded that the contract was made in Maine. Thus, Maine law governed, and the contract was valid.[4]

Whether the court applied the right law or reached the right result is not as important methodologically as is the fact that it would be impossible to predict the court's decision. The outcome hinged on whether the contract was bilateral or unilateral, and therefore on which promise was deemed to be the offer and which the acceptance. These are question that admit varying answers, especially in cross-border oral contracts.[5]

1. 125 Mass. 374 (1878).
2. Restatement (First) §325. Of course *Milliken* predates the Restatement, but this particular sub-rule also predates the Restatement.
3. *See* Restatement (First) §§323–324.
4. In the meantime, Massachusetts removed the incapacity of married women and thus the application of Maine law did not offend Massachusetts public policy.
5. *See*, e.g., *Lin* v. *Employers Reinsurance Corp.*, 139 A.2d 638 (Pa. 1958) (contract by telephone across state lines).

II. The Restatement (Second)

488. The fact that 23 states follow the Restatement (Second) in contract conflicts[1] does not mean that one can predict with any accuracy how these states will actually resolve a particular contract conflict. The uncertainty is due to the fact that the Restatement itself is quite equivocal in designating the applicable law, and the courts that follow it are even more so. Even so, the Restatement provides a helpful starting point for the choice-of-law analysis, not only for the courts that formally follow the Restatement, but also those following other modern approaches. This sub-section describes the Restatement's approach to contracts that do not contain a choice-of-law clause.

1. *See supra* 218.

A. Section 188

489. The Second Restatement's chapter on contracts contains twenty sections for determining the governing law in the absence of an effective choice-of-law clause. The first of these sections, Section 188, is the anchor of the whole chapter, being the general and residual provision for all contracts and issues for which the chapter does not provide otherwise. Section 188 provides that the rights and duties of the parties 'with respect to an issue in contract' are governed by the law of the state which, with respect to that issue, has the 'most significant relationship'[1] to the transaction and the parties. That state is identified 'under the principles stated in §6', and by 'tak[ing] into account' certain pertinent contacts, listed in a non-exclusive, non-hierarchical order, such as '(a) the place of contracting, (b) the place of negotiation of the contract, (c) the place of performance, (d) the location of the subject matter of the contract, and (e) the domicil, residence, nationality, place of incorporation and place of business of the parties'.[2]

1. *Restatement (Second)* §188(1).
2. *Id.* §188(2). Subsection (3) provides that if the place of negotiating the contract and the place of performance are in the same state, the law of that state will 'usually' be applied. However, this subsection does not apply to the nine types contracts for which the Restatement provides specific rules (listed in the text immediately following), nor to the issues of capacity, form, and usury.

B. Particular Contracts

490. Section 188 is followed by nine sections providing presumptive rules designating the applicable law for nine different types of contracts. The designated law applies, 'unless, with respect to the particular issue, some other state has a more significant relationship under the principles stated in §6 . . . , in which event the local law of the other state will be applied'.[1] The presumptively applicable law is:

1. for contracts for the transfer of interests in land – the law of the state where the land is situated;[2]
2. for contractual duties arising from a transfer of interests in land – the law of the state where the land is situated;[3]
3. for contracts to sell an interests in chattel – the law of the state where, under the terms of the contract, the seller is to deliver the chattel;[4]
4. for life insurance contracts – the law of the state where the insured was domiciled at the time the policy was applied for;[5]
5. for contracts of fire, surety, or casualty insurance – the law of the state that the parties understood was to be the principal location of the insured risk during the term of the policy;[6]
6. for contracts of suretyship – the law governing the principal obligation that the contract of suretyship was intended to secure;[7]
7. for contracts for the repayment of money lent – the law of the state where the contract requires that repayment be made;[8]
8. for contracts for the rendition of services – the law of the state where the contract requires that the services, or a major portion of the services, be rendered;[9] and
9. for contracts of transportation – the law of the state from which the passenger departs or the goods are dispatched;[10]

In all of these sections, the Restatement refers to the 'local' law of the designated state, excluding its conflicts law. Moreover, the designated law applies 'in the absence of an effective choice of law by the parties'.[11]

1. *Id.* §§189–197.
2. *Id.* §189. A contract for the transfer of an interest in land differs from the transfer itself. The latter is governed by 'the law that would be applied by the courts of the situs[, which] . . . usually apply their own local law'. *Id.* §223. In contrast, §189 refers directly to the *local* law of the situs state, but since this reference is a displaceable presumption, the two sections potentially may lead to the law of different states.
3. *See id.* §190.
4. *See id.* §191. Sections 1–105(1) of the UCC provides that, in the absence of valid choice-of-law clause, the law of the forum applies if the transaction bears an 'appropriate relation' to the forum. For a discussion of this provision as well as §191 of the Restatement, and cases applying them, *see* E. Scoles, P. Hay, P. Borchers & S. Symeonides, *Conflict of Laws* (4th edn, St Paul, Minn., 2004), pp. 1007–1009. Since 1988, the United States has been party to the UN ('Vienna') Convention on Contracts for the International Sale of Goods. According to Art. 1, the Convention applies to contracts of sale of goods between parties who, regardless of nationality or allegiance, have their places of business in different states that are parties to the Convention, or 'when the [forum's] rules of private international law lead to the application of the law of a Contracting State'. However, the United States' ratification of the convention is subject to a reservation that excludes the application of the quoted provision, thus narrowing the Convention's sphere of application. The reasons for this reservation are explained in the United States declaration, printed in 22 *I.L.M.* 1380 (1984).
5. *See Restatement (Second)* §192. Insurance contracts are discussed *infra* at 497–503.
6. *See Restatement (Second)* §193.
7. *See id.* §194. This presumption seeks to ensure that suretyship contracts, which are accessory to the principal contract and usually are concluded contemporaneously, are treated uniformly. *See id.* §194, cmt. (b). For cases applying this Section, *see* Scoles, Hay, Borchers & Symeonides, *supra* at 1016–1017.
8. *See Restatement (Second)* §195. This place usually coincides with the place of the making of the contract and the location of the lender. *See* Scoles, Hay, Borchers & Symeonides, *supra* at 1018. This provision is often displaced by state statutes that protect domiciliary consumers in small loan transactions. *See id.* 1017–1018.
9. *See Restatement (Second)* §196. For cases applying Section 196, *see* Scoles, Hay, Borchers & Symeonides, 1019–1021. This provision does not apply to agency contracts. Section 291 of the Restatement provides that the internal relationship between principal and agent, and thus the rendition of the agent's services, is governed by the law of the state of the most significant relationship which is identified 'under the principles stated in §6' and through the 'application of the rules of §§187–188'. For conflicts cases involving agency contracts, *see* Scoles, Hay, Borchers & Symeonides, *supra* 1023–1030. For brokerage contracts, *see id.* 1022–1023.
10. *See Restatement (Second)* §197. For cases applying §197, *see* Scoles, Hay, Borchers & Symeonides, *supra* 1021. For contract claims for damages to goods in interstate or international transportation, this Section is preempted by federal statutes or international conventions. *See Restatement (Second)* §197 cmt. a.
11. *Restatement (Second)* §§189–192, 194–197. Section 193 (on casualty insurance) does not refer to choice-of-law by the parties.

C. Particular Issues

491. The remaining ten sections of the Restatement provide rules for determining the law applicable to the following issues regardless of the type of the contract: (1) capacity; (2) formalities; (3) validity for matters other than capacity and formalities; (4) misrepresentation, duress, undue influence and mistake; (5) illegality;

(6) usury; (7) construction; (8) nature and extent of contractual obligations; (9) details of performance; and (10) measure of recovery.

492. Only one of these sections designates directly the applicable law – Section 206 provides that details of performance are governed by the law of the place of performance. Eight sections simply refer back to the 'law selected by application of the rules of §§187–188'.[1] This reference means that, in the absence of a choice-of-law clause that passes the test of Section 187, the particular issue will be determined under the general test of Section 188. To assist in the application of the latter test, three sections contain pointers suggesting the 'usual' and permissible substantive result. They provide that:

1. the capacity of a party to contract will 'usually be upheld if he has such capacity under the local law of the state of his domicil' (§198(2));
2. formalities that meet the requirements of the place of making will 'usually be acceptable' (§199(2));[2] and
3. when performance is illegal in the place of performance, the contract will 'usually be denied enforcement' (§202(2)).

1. *Id.* §§198–202, 204–205, 207.
2. Section 141 provides that, '[w]hether a contract must be in writing, or evidenced by a writing, in order to be enforceable is determined by the law selected by application of the rules of §§187–188'. This Section eliminates the old debate of whether statutes of frauds are procedural or substantive by essentially characterizing them as substantive.

493. The remaining section in this group also provides a result-oriented rule. Section 203 provides that a contract will be sustained against the charge of usury if it provides for a rate of interest that is 'permissible in a state to which the contract has a substantial relationship and is not greatly in excess of the rate permitted by the general usury law of the state of the otherwise applicable law under the rule of §188'.[1]

1. *Restatement (Second)* §203.

D. Application

494. Ordinarily, a court that follows the Restatement (Second) should begin with the specific sections and then proceed to the general sections. For example, if the contested issue is one of the ten issues for which the Restatement provides pointers in Sections 198–207, the court should begin its analysis with the particular pointer, rather than with Section 188. Likewise, if the particular contract is one of those nine contracts for which the Restatement provides presumptive rules in Sections 189–197, the court should not bypass those presumptions and go straight to Section 188. Finally, the application of Section 188 should not degenerate into a numerical counting of physical contacts. Identifying the state of the 'most significant relationship' is to be done 'under the principles stated in §6'[1] which include the pertinent policies of the involved states and the general goals of the choice-of-law process. The contacts listed in Section 188 are simply to be 'taken into account'[2] in initially identifying the potentially concerned states, determining which of the Section 6 polices are actually implicated, and assessing their comparative pertinence.

1. *Id.* §188(1).
2. *Id.* §188(2).

495. In reviewing judicial decisions applying the Restatement (Second), one is left with the distinct impression that many courts either do not understand or choose to ignore the precise conceptual analysis the Restatement prescribes. Many courts by-pass the presumptions or pointers of the special sections, going directly to the general Section 188, and, once there, pay lip service to the cross reference to Section 6.[1] This type of analysis is virtually indistinguishable from the significant-contacts method.

1. *See* S. Symeonides, *The American Choice-of-Law Revolution: Past, Present, and Future* (Leiden, Boston, 2006), pp. 120–123.

III. Other Modern Approaches

496. As noted in Part II, Chapter 2, four states (Arkansas, Indiana, Nevada and North Carolina) and Puerto Rico follow a significant contacts approach; two states (Minnesota and Wisconsin) follow Leflar's better law approach and eight states and the District of Columbia follow a combination of modern approaches.[1] If these approaches designated the applicable law with any degree of specificity, it would be appropriate to discuss representative cases decided under each of these approaches. Unfortunately, this is not the case. These approaches are even more equivocal than the Restatement (Second), which may explain why some courts prefer them to the Restatement. Consequently, little could be gained by discussing such cases here. One can fairly assume that cases decided under these approaches are as likely to reach the results suggested by the Restatement (Second) as cases actually decided under the Restatement. Thus, rather than discussing these cases, the next Section focuses on one category of contracts with important practical consequences – insurance contracts.

1. New Jersey, the District of Columbia, Massachusetts, and Pennsylvania combine interest analysis with the Restatement (Second). New York combines interest analysis with the 'center of gravity' approach. Hawaii and North Dakota follow a combination of interest analysis, the Restatement (Second), and Leflar's choice-influencing considerations. Louisiana and Oregon have their own comprehensive codifications. For documentation and caveats, *see* Scoles, Hay, Borchers & Symeonides, 1002–1004.

IV. Insurance Contracts

497. As noted earlier, many state statutes mandate their application to insurance contracts having certain enumerated contacts with the enacting state, while some of these statutes take a step further and expressly prohibit the contractual choice of another state's law.[1] In some of these statutes, the enumerated contacts are significant. For example, in cases involving coverage for environmental contamination, some statutes mandate their application to cases in which the contaminated site is located in the enacting state.[2] In other statutes, the enumerated contacts may be tenuous.[3] But in either case, these statutes – which are typical examples of unilateral choice-of-law rules delineating a priori the reach of the *lex fori* – pre-empt a judicial choice-of-law analysis (including that of the Restatement) for all cases falling within their scope. Consequently, one is advised to search for such statutes before choosing a forum or researching the case law.

1. *See supra* 448.
2. For example, an Oregon statute provides that 'Oregon law shall be applied in all cases where the contaminated property to which the action relates is located within the State of Oregon'. Or. Rev. Stat. §465.480(2)(a). The statute also provides that nothing in it 'shall be interpreted to modify common law rules governing choice of law determinations for sites located outside the State of Oregon'. *Id.* Thus, the statute preserves the possibility of applying Oregon law to non-Oregon sites as well. *See also* Mich. Comp. Laws §324.1804 ('The law to be applied . . . , including what constitutes 'pollution' is the law of this state, excluding choice of law rules'.); Colo. Rev. Stat. §§13-1.5-104; Wis. Stat §299.33(4).
3. *See*, e.g., the Texas statutes reproduced *supra* at 448 note 3.

498. The most numerous among insurance conflicts are those involving automobile insurance. The majority of these cases involve the issue of uninsured or underinsured motorist (UM or UIM) coverage in actions brought by the insureds against their own insurers. The typical scenario involves a person who, in his or her home state, purchased a policy insuring a car registered and garaged in that state, is involved in an accident in another state caused by an uninsured or underinsured motorist. A conflict results when the two states have different limits of or requirements for UM coverage, or take different positions on the validity of anti-stacking or setoff clauses contained in the policy. Like other insurance conflicts, these conflicts tend to depend heavily on local statutes. Many of these statutes require the application of the law of the forum state if: (1) the insurance policy was delivered, or issued for delivery, in that state; or (2) the insured automobile is principally garaged there; or (3) the accident occurred there.

499. When the forum does not have such a statute, or when the court finds the statute inapplicable, the court resolves the conflict under the forum's judicial choice-of-law approach. Besides the few states that continue to follow the *lex loci contractus* rule, the majority of states follow approaches based on Sections 193 or 188 of the Restatement (Second), or other similar flexible approaches. Regardless of the approach, however, most recent cases exhibit a trend away from applying the law of the place of the accident as such, perhaps because most of them employ a contract choice-of-law analysis. Most recent cases apply the law of the state where the insured automobile is principally garaged, which usually is the state in which the insured is domiciled and/or the policy has been delivered.[1] However, one still finds cases that continue to apply the law of the accident state.[2]

1. *See*, e.g., *Johnson* v. *US Fidelity and Guaranty Co.*, 696 N.W.2d 431 (Neb. 2005); *State Farm Mut. Auto. Ins. Co.* v. *Gillette*, 641 N.W.2d 662 (Wis. 2002); *Howe* v. *Howe*, 625 S.E.2d 716 (W.Va. 2005); *Owens* v. *Mississippi Farm Bureau Cas. Ins. Co.*, 910 So.2d 1065 (Miss. 2005);

Champagne v. *Ward*, 893 So.2d 773 (La. 2005); *Flaherty* v. *Allstate Ins. Co.*, 822 A.2d 1159 (Me. 2003); *Ohayon* v. *Safeco Ins. Co.*, 747 N.E.2d 206 (Ohio 2001); *Cecere* v. *Aetna Ins. Co.*, 766 A.2d 696 (N.H. 2001); *Fortune Ins. Co.* v. *Owens*, 526 S.E.2d 463 (N.C. 2000); *Ryals* v. *State Farm Mut. Ins. Co.*, 1 P.3d 803 (Idaho 2000); *Great West Cas. Co.* v. *Hovaldt*, 603 N.W.2d 198 (S.D.1999); *US Fidelity & Guar. Co.* v. *Preston*, 26 S.W.3d 145 (Ky. 2000); *In re Allstate Ins. Co. (Stolarz)*, 613 N.E.2d 936 (N.Y. 1993).

2. *See*, e.g., *Mikelson* v. *United Servs. Auto. Ass'n.*, 111 P.3d 601 (Hawaii 2005); *Mitchell* v. *State Farm Ins. Co.*, 68 P.3d 703 (Mont. 2003); *State Farm Mut. Auto. Ins. Co.* v. *Ballard*, 54 P.3d 537 (N.M. 2002); *Nodak Mut. Ins. Co.* v. *Am. Family Mut. Ins. Co.*, 604 N.W.2d 91 (Mn. 2000); *Csulik* v. *Nationwide Mut. Ins. Co.*, 723 N.E.2d 90 (Ohio 2000); *Williams* v. *State Farm Mut. Auto. Ins. Co.*, 641 A.2d 783 (Conn. 1994).

500. With regard to casualty insurance, Section 193 of the Restatement (Second) calls for the application of the law of the state that the parties understood was to be the 'principal location' of the insured risk, unless, again, another state has a more significant relationship. This Section has significant following in the case law, but, when the insured risk is located in more than one state, that following is not universal.

501. In cases involving coverage for environmental contamination, courts are divided as to whether to apply a single law to all risks or instead to apply the law of each state to the risk situated in that state.[1] Some cases follow the first option, which is known as the 'uniform-contract-interpretation' approach and usually is based on Section 188 of the Restatement. This approach focuses on the insurance contract and aspires to apply the law of a single state, even when the contract covers multiple risks situated in different states.[2] It usually leads to the application of the law of a state that is either the place of the making of the contract or has other significant connections with the contract and the parties, but not necessarily the location of the risk. More numerous are the cases that follow the second option, which is called 'site-specific approach' and is based on Section 193 of the Restatement. This approach abandons the goal of applying a single law to the whole contract and focuses on the interests of the state or states where the insured risks are located. The applicable law is usually the law of that state or states (the site-states), unless another state has a more significant relationship with regard to the particular issue.[3]

1. For a discussion of these two options and the cases following them, *see* the annual choice-of-law surveys by Symeonides in 42 *Am. J. Comp. L.* 599, 1994, 645–649; 43 *Am. J. Comp. L.* 1, 75, 1995, 80–82; 44 *Am. J. Comp. L.* 181, 1996, 230–232; 45 *Am. J. Comp. L.* 447, 1998, 491–492; 47 *Am. J. Comp. L.* 327, 1999, 360–371.
2. *See*, e.g., *Maryland Cas. Co.* v. *Cont'l. Cas. Co.*, 332 F.3d 145 (2d Cir. 2003) (decided under New York conflicts law); *Lapham-Hickey Steel Corp.* v. *Protection Mut. Ins. Co.*, 655 N.E.2d 842, 845 (Ill. 1995); *Asbestos Removal Corp.* v. *Guaranty Nat. Ins. Co.*, 48 F.3d 1215 (4th Cir. 1995) (Virginia conflicts law); *Bituminous Cas. Corp.* v. *St. Clair Lime Co.*, 69 F.3d 547 (10th Cir. 1995) (Oklahoma conflicts law); *Sequa Corp.* v. *Aetna Cas. & Sur. Co.*, 1995 WL 465192 (Del. Super. Ct. 1995); *Aetna Cas. & Sur. Co.* v. *Dow Chemical Co.*, 883 F. Supp. 1101 (E.D.Mich. 1995); *Employers Ins. of Wausau* v. *Duplan Corp.*, 899 F.Supp. 1112 (S.D.N.Y. 1995); *Gould, Inc.* v. *Continental Cas. Co.*, 822 F.Supp. 1172 (E.D.Pa. 1993); *Lumbermens Mut. Cas. Co.* v. *Connecticut Bank and Trust Co.*, 806 F.2d 411, 415 (2d Cir. 1986); *Vigen Constr. Co.* v. *Millers Nat. Ins. Co.*, 436 N.W.2d 254 (N.D. 1989); *Eli Lilly & Co.* v. *Home Ins. Co.*, 764 F.2d 876 (D.C. Cir. 1985).
3. *See*, e.g., *Reichhold Chem., Inc.* v. *Hartford Acc. & Indem. Co.*, 750 A.2d 1051 (Conn. 2000); *Pfizer, Inc.* v. *Employers Ins. of Wausau*, 712 A.2d 634 (N.J. 1998); *Unisys Corp.* v. *Ins. Co.*

of North Am., 712 A.2d 649 (N.J. 1998); *HM Holdings, Inc.* v. *Aetna Cas. & Sur. Co.*, 712 A.2d 645 (N.J. 1998); *Gilbert Spruance Co.* v. *Pennsylvania Mnfgs. Ass'n Ins. Co.*, 629 A.2d 885 (N.J. 1993); *Consol. Mut. Ins. Co.* v. *Radio Foods Corp.*, 240 A.2d 47 (N.H. 1968); *Boardman Petroleum, Inc.* v. *Federated Mut. Ins. Co.*, 135 F.3d 750 (11th Cir. 1998); *LaFarge Corp.* v. *Travelers Indem. Co.*; 118 F.3d 1511 (11th Cir. 1997) (Florida conflicts law); *Millipore Corp.* v. *Travelers Indem. Co.* 115 F.3d 21 (1st Cir. 1997) (Massachusetts conflicts law); *General Ceramics Inc.* v. *Firemen's Fund Ins. Co.*, 66 F.3d 647 (3rd Cir. 1995); *CPC Int'l, Inc.* v. *Northbrook Excess & Surplus Ins. Co.*, 46 F.3d 1211 (1st Cir. 1995) (Rhode Island conflicts law); *Byers* v. *Auto-Owners Ins. Co.*, 119 S.W.3d 659 (Mo.App. 2003); *Hartford Acc. & Indem. Co.* v. *Dana Corp.*, 690 N.E.2d 285 (Ind. Ct. App. 1998); *Albert Trostel & Sons Co.* v. *Employers Ins. of Wausau*, 216 Wis.2d 381 (Wis. Ct. App. 1998); *Commercial Union Ins. Co.* v. *Port Hayden Co.* 698 A.2d 1167 (Md. App. 1997), *cert. denied* 703 A.2d 147 (Md. 1997); *W.C. Richards Co., Inc.* v. *Hartford Indem. Co.*, 682 N.E.2d 220 (Ill. App. 1997); *Morton Int'l, Inc.* v. *Aetna Cas. & Sur. Co.*, 666 N.E.2d 1163 (Ohio Ct. App. 1995); *CXY Chemicals U.S.A.* v. *Gerling Global Gen'l Ins. Co.*, 991 F.Supp.2d 770 (E.D.La. 1998); *Wysong & Miles Co.* v. *Employers of Wausau*, 4 F.Supp.2d 421 (M.D.N.C. 1998); *In re Combustion, Inc.*, 960 F.Supp. 1056 (W.D.La. 1997); *E.B. & A.C. Whiting Co.* v. *Hartford Fire Ins. Co.*, 838 F.Supp. 863 (D.Vt. 1993); *Jones Truck Lines* v. *Transport Ins. Co.*, 1989 WL 49517 (E.D. Pa. 1989).

502. A problem slightly different from that of multi-state risks appears when the principal location of a single insured risk – or in life insurance policies the domicile of the insured – moves from one state to another between the time the policy was issued and the time the insured risk materialized. In most of the litigated cases, the second state's law is more favourable to the insured than the first. From a constitutional perspective, the Supreme Court's due process precedents allow the second state to apply its pro-insured law if it has sufficient contacts with the case so that application of its law does not unfairly surprise the insurer.[1] The question of whether to apply that law is answered by the forum's choice-of-law approach or statute, and most courts tend to answer it affirmatively.[2] When the second state's law is less favourable to the insured than the law of the first state, the application of the law of the second state is subject to the same constitutional test. However, most courts tend to answer the choice-of-law question in the negative, refusing to apply the forum's pro-insurer law.[3]

1. *See Clay* v. *Sun Ins. Office, Ltd.*, 377 US 179 (1964). *Compare Home Ins. Co.* v. *Dick*, 281 US 397 (1930). For a discussion of these precedents, *see supra* 80–89.
2. Among recent cases presenting this pattern is *Heslin-Kim* v. *CIGNA Group Ins.*, 377 F.Supp.2d 527 (D.S.C. 2005). In this case, the insured bought a life insurance policy in Georgia and, 13 years later, moved to South Carolina, continuing to pay premiums from there until his death six years later. Under a clause in the policy, which was valid under Georgia (but not South Carolina) law, the insured's widow would not be entitled to a certain supplemental coverage for which the insured paid premiums for less than ten years. The court applied South Carolina law based on statute which provides that '[a]ll contracts of insurance on . . . lives . . . in this State are considered to be made in the state and . . . and are subject to the laws of this State'. S.C. Code Ann. §38-61-10.
3. A recent case presenting this pattern is *NGK Metals Corp.* v. *Nat'l. Union Fire Ins. Co.*, 2005 WL 1115925 (E.D.Tenn. 2005). In this case, the insured bought a liability insurance policy while it had its principal place of business in Pennsylvania, then moved to Tennessee, and, some years later, sued its insurer for breach of contract in Tennessee. The insurer invoked a Tennessee statute which provides that '[e]very policy of insurance, issued to or for the benefit of any citizen or resident of this state . . . by any insurance company or association doing business in this state . . . shall be held as made in this state and construed solely according to the laws of this state'. (Tenn.Code Ann. §56-7-102). The court refused to apply this statute

because it would 'effectively override Tennessee's traditional choice-of-law rules' and 'violate the parties' intention . . . to be bound by Pennsylvania law'. *Id.* at *5. The court also reasoned that the statute 'was not enacted to harm the Tennessee policy holder' and, to apply it 'to the detriment of the policy holder . . . [would violate] the very purpose of the statute'. *Id.* at *6.

503. Finally, another controversial issue in recent litigation is whether an insurer must cover punitive damages assessed against the insured.[1] About half of the states allow the insurability of punitive damages, nine states allow it only in cases of vicarious liability, eight states prohibit it, and the remaining states have not taken a definitive stance.[2] The conflicting policies on this subject are: (a) ascertaining and protecting the justified expectations of the insured and the insurer, and (b) deterring the type of misconduct that evokes punitive damages by not allowing the insured to pass on the pain of punitive damages to the insurer. A common strategy in these cases is the use of declaratory judgment actions, both offensively and defensively. Many of these cases involve the familiar race to the most hospitable forum, with the insurer bringing such an action in one state and the insured in another. Again, the basic choice-of-law options are to: (1) focus on the insurance contract; or (2) focus on the place where the risk was located and materialized. Although the courts remain divided between these two options, it is apparent that the forum's own position on the issue of the insurability of punitive damages weighs heavily in choosing between these two options.[3]

1. For discussion of recent conflicts cases, *see* the annual choice-of-law surveys by S. Symeonides in 50 *Am. J. Comp. L.* 1, 2002, 56–57; 43 *Am. J. Comp. L.* 1, 1995, 75–80; 42 *Am. J. Comp. L.* 599, 1994, 649–650; 38 *Am. J. Comp. L.* 601, 1990, 621–623.
2. *See* J. Stein, *Personal Injury Damages*, (3d edn 2003) §4:37.
3. For representative cases, *see Fluke Corp.* v. *Hartford Accident & Indem. Co.*, 34 P.3d 809 (Wash. 2001); *Hartford Accident & Indem. Co.* v. *Am. Red Ball Transit Co., Inc.*, 938 P.2d 1281 (Kan. 1997); *St. Paul Surplus Lines* v. *Int'l Playtex, Inc.*, 777 P.2d 1259 (Kan. 1989), *cert. denied*, 493 US 1036 (1990); *Zurich Ins. Co.* v. *Shearson Lehman Hutton, Inc.*, 642 N.E.2d 1065 (N.Y. 1994); *Meijer, Inc.* v. *General Star Indem. Co.*, 826 F.Supp. 241 (W.D.Mich. 1993); *United States Gypsum Co.* v. *Admiral Ins. Co.*, 643 N.E.2d 1226 (Ill. App. Ct. 1994); *Stonewall Surplus Lines Ins. Co.* v. *Johnson Controls, Inc.*, 17 Cal.Rptr.2d 713 (Cal.Ct.App. 1993); *Am. Home Assur.* v. *Safeway Steel Prod.*, 743 S.W.2d 693 (Tex. App. 1987); *Johnson Controls, Inc.* v. *Am. Motorists Inc.*, 719 F.Supp. 1459 (E.D. Wis. 1989); *Alcolac Inc.* v. *St. Paul Fire & Marine Ins. Co.*, 716 F.Supp. 1541 (D. Md. 1989).

Chapter 6. Status and Domestic Relations

§1. Introduction

504. In strict legal theory, the concept of status includes issues such as nationality or citizenship, marriage, legitimacy, filiation, parental authority, custody, and support, the capacity to enter into contracts (or other juridical acts), and the capacity to be the subject of rights and duties (referred to in civil law systems as 'personality'). In the United States, matters of citizenship are governed by federal law, while the two types of capacity are merged together and are relegated to the law that governs the contract, juridical act, or relationship in question. For example, under the traditional conflicts approach, the capacity of a person to be an heir or to make a testament were governed by the same law that governed the succession, while the capacity to enter into a contract were governed by the *lex loci contractus*. Modern approaches allow for a separate treatment of each of these issues insofar as these approaches permit an issue-by-issue analysis. This chapter focuses primarily on marriage, including its incidents and dissolution, and secondarily on some issues pertaining to children.[1]

1. Basic bibliography on these issues, includes: L. McDougal, R. Felix & R. Whitten, *American Conflicts Law* (5th edn, New York, Ardsley, 2001), pp. 711–758, 781–826; E. Scoles, P. Hay, P. Borchers & S. Symeonides, *Conflict of Laws* (4th edn, St. Paul, Minn., 2004), pp. 557–595, 627–708; R. Weintraub, *Commentary on the Conflict of Laws* (5th edn, New York, 2006), pp. 307–370.

§2. Marriage

505. Marriage and domestic relations in general are subjects that fall within the lawmaking competence of the states, not the federal government. Federal statutes routinely refer to state law for the definition of terms such as 'marriage', 'spouse', 'child', or other domestic relations terms.[1] During the first half of the 20th century, conflicts involving the validity of marriages were quite frequent because the substantive laws of the states differed widely on the requirements and conditions for a valid marriage, including interracial marriages. By the 1960s, these conflicts faded away as the differences began to disappear. However, before the end of the 20th century, the issue of same sex unions began to divide the states once again.

1. *But see* Defense of Marriage Act ('DOMA'), reproduced *infra* 514 (defining marriage for federal law purposes).

I. Validity

506. The traditional choice-of-law rule for determining the validity of marriage was the *lex loci celebrationis*. This rule was subject to public policy exceptions in favour of either the *lex fori* or the law of either party's premarital domicile.[1] Polygamous, and certain incestuous or interracial marriages were mentioned as examples falling within the public policy exception.[2]

1. *See* American Law Institute, *Restatement (First) of Conflict of Laws* §§121–122, 132, 134.
2. *See id.* §134.

507. The Restatement (Second) has softened the rule in both language and substance. Section 283 provides:

1. The validity of a marriage will be determined by the local law of the state which, with respect to the particular issue, has the most significant relationship to the spouses and the marriage under the principles stated in §6.
2. A marriage which satisfies the requirements of the state where the marriage was contracted will everywhere be recognized as valid unless it violates the strong public policy of another state which had the most significant relationship to the spouses and the marriage at the time of the marriage.[1]

1. American Law Institute, *Restatement (Second) of Conflict of Laws 2d* §283.

508. It is not a coincidence that, departing from the drafters' usual wishy-washy practise, Subsection (2) is phrased as a categorical black-letter rule that is displaced only by a contrary and 'strong' public policy of only one state – the state that had the 'most significant' relationship 'at the time of the marriage' and not later.[1] Moreover, as the accompanying Restatement comments make clear, a marriage that is invalid under the law of the state of contracting will not necessarily be treated as invalid elsewhere. Rather, the marriage will be upheld if it would be valid under the law of 'some other state having a substantial (i.e., not necessarily 'the most significant') relation to the parties and the marriage'.[2] Thus, if read literally, the Restatement (Second) adopts an alternative-reference type 'rule of validation' – a marriage is valid if it would be valid under the law of: (a) a state that had the most significant relationship, either at the time of marriage or at later time; (b) a state having a 'substantial' relation to the parties and the marriage; or (c) the state of contracting.[3] The only exception resulting in invalidity operates when the marriage is valid only in the state of contracting and its validation elsewhere would violate a 'strong' public policy of the state that had the 'most significant' relationship 'at the time of the marriage'.

1. Without expressly excluding other possibilities, the Restatement's examples suggest that 'a state where at least one of the spouses was domiciled at the time of the marriage and where both made their home immediately thereafter' (*id.* cmt. j) qualifies as the state of the most significant relationship.
2. *Restatement (Second)* §283. cmt. i (emphasis added). For recent cases involving this scenario, *see Xiong* v. *Xiong*, 648 N.W.2d 900 (Wis. App. 2002) (upholding a Laotian marriage that was formally invalid under Laotian law, partly because the parties lived for three years as husband and wife in Pennsylvania, which recognizes common law marriages, before living for 15 years in Wisconsin, which does not recognize such marriages); *Donlann* v. *Maggurn*, 55 P.3d 74 (Ariz. Ct. App. 2002), *rev. denied*, (11 February 2003) (holding that a Mexican marriage that was formally invalid under Mexican law but valid under Arizona law was valid because, as the parties' pre- and post-marriage domicile, Arizona had the most significant relationship).
3. The use of the word 'contracting' rather than 'celebrated' is deliberate so as to include informal or 'common-law' marriages formed when parties live together for a period of time and hold themselves out as husband and wife. Although the majority of states no longer allow these marriages in their own territory, they do recognize such marriages contracted in states that allow them. For recent cases to this effect, *see Fritsche* v. *Vermilion Parish Hosp. Serv Dist.*

#2, 893 So.2d 935 (La.App. 2005), *writ denied*, 899 So.2d 574 (La. 2005), and *writ denied*, 899 So.2d 576 (La. 2005); *In re Catapano*, 794 N.Y.S.2d 401 (N.Y.A.D. 2 Dept. 2005); *Xiong* v. *Xiong*, 648 N.W.2d 900 (Wis. App. 2002). For cases based on the same premise but finding no common-law marriage under the facts of the case, *see In re Estate of Gernold*, 800 N.Y.S.2d 329 (N.Y.Sur. 2005); *In the Matter of Landolfi*, 724 N.Y.S.2d 470 (N.Y.A.D. 2001); *Smith* v. *Anderson*, 821 So.2d 323 (Fla. Dist. Ct. App. 2002); *Police & Firemen's Disability & Pension Fund* v. *Redding*, 2002 WL 1767362 (Ohio Ct. App. 2002).

509. Although the case law and statutes in some states are not quite as liberal,[1] the Restatement's clear preference for validation reflects the old policy of *favour matrimonii*, which, at the time of the Restatement's drafting, was entrenched in the domestic law of all states. At the multistate level, this policy is reinforced by the desideratum of avoiding 'limping marriages'. This policy favoured upholding the validity of marriages whenever reasonably possible, precisely because the consequences of invalidity, especially on the status of children and on good-faith spouses were too grave.[2] Two intervening events may have reduced the strength of this policy. The first were the Supreme Court decisions holding unconstitutional many state laws discriminating against illegitimate children. The second was the advent of same sex marriages. These developments are discussed later.

1. For a comprehensive discussion of the case law and references to pertinent statutes, *see* E. Scoles, P. Hay, P. Borchers & S. Symeonides, *Conflict of Laws* (4th edn, St. Paul, Minn., 2004), pp. 564–583.
2. *See Restatement (Second)* §283, cmt. h (stating that 'there is a strong inclination to uphold a marriage because of the hardship that might otherwise be visited upon the parties and their children', and that 'differences among the marriage laws of various states usually involve only minor matters of debatable policy rather than fundamentals'; *id.* cmt. i ('Upholding the validity of a marriage is . . . a basic policy in all states'.).

II. Incidents

510. Marriage vests the parties with the status of 'spouse' with all the attendant legal consequences on name, the right to lawfully cohabit, the right to claim support or inheritance, or to sue for the wrongful death or injury of the other spouse. The status of marriage also produces similar effects or 'incidents' on the children born of the marriage, such as legitimacy, filiation, and presumed paternity, and their right to receive support and inheritance, or to sue for a parent's wrongful death. In the majority of cases, the dispute concerns one of these incidents, rather than the validity of the marriage for all purposes. The validity of the marriage is simply a preliminary or 'incidental' question, whose answer may – or may not – determine the answer to the principal question of whether the claimed incident exists.

511. Although some courts tend to assume that the two questions are inexorably interconnected and that an invalid marriage produces zero incidents and a valid marriage produces all incidents, in reality things are more complex, both in domestic and conflicts law. For example, the domestic law of most states provides that a party who in good faith contracts a marriage, while being reasonably unaware of an existing impediment, is entitled to certain marital benefits (such as marital property) even though the marriage itself is invalid. Hence, even under domestic law, an invalid marriage may nevertheless produce certain incidents. Stated another way, a marriage may be invalid for some purposes and valid for others.

512. The same distinction between marriage and its incidents exists in multistate cases. The Restatement (Second) makes this distinction clear by both requiring an issue-by-issue analysis in Section 283, and by devoting a separate section to the incidents of marriage. Section 284 provides that a state 'usually' gives the same incidents to a foreign marriage 'which is valid under the principles stated in Section 283, that it gives to a marriage contracted within its territory'.[1]

This statement seems redundant or innocuous because, even if the marriage would be invalid had it been contracted in the forum state, a marriage that is 'valid under the [conflicts] principles stated in §283' is treated as a valid marriage in the forum state. However, the use of the word 'usually' implies that the forum may choose to deny some incidents to such a marriage. Moreover, the accompanying comments suggest that the forum state may accord certain incidents to a foreign marriage even if the marriage would be invalid under both its domestic and its conflicts law.[2] For example, in a state that has a strong policy against polygamy, a foreign polygamous marriage will not be treated as valid under the conflicts principles of Section 283 because of the forum's contrary policy. Nevertheless, the forum may choose to, for example, accord the children of the marriage the status of legitimacy, or allow them to sue for the husband's wrongful death.[3] Likewise, nothing prevents the forum state from according some incidents, while denying others, such as the right of the husband to cohabit with all of his wives. The decision of whether or which incidents to accord depends on the strength of the forum's public policy with regard to the particular incident, the nature and context of the particular issue, and, of course, the equities of each case.[4]

1. *Restatement (Second)* §284.
2. *See Restatement (Second)* §284, cmts. b–c. The Restatement also states that, in certain cases, a state may give certain incidents to a foreign marriage that was invalid under foreign law. *See id.* cmt. d.
3. *See id.* cmt. c. *In re Dalip Singh Bir's Estate*, 188 P.2d 499 (Cal. Ct. App. 1948).
4. *Cf. Hudson Trail Outfitters* v. *D.C. Dept. of Employment Servs.*, 801 A.2d 987 (D.C. 2002) (holding that a Catholic marriage performed in Nicaragua but which the priest forgot to register in the civil registry as required by Nicaraguan law was invalid and thus the wife did not lose her eligibility for worker's compensation benefits from the death of her previous husband); *Police & Firemen's Disability &Pension Fund* v. *Redding*, 2002 WL 1767362 (Ohio Ct. App. 2002), *appeal not allowed*, 780 N.E.2d 287 (Ohio 2002) (holding that an Ohio policeman's widow who moved to Wyoming where she cohabited for thirty years with a Wyoming man with whom she had three children was entitled to continue receiving pension benefits from her previous husband because Wyoming did not recognize common-law marriages, although Ohio recognized them).

§3. Same Sex Marriages and Similar Relations

I. The Movement For and Against

513. From 1993 to 2003, the supreme courts of four states held that state laws confining the right of marriage to parties of the opposite sex were unconstitutional under their respective state constitutions.[1] Subsequent constitutional amendments overturned the rulings in two of these states – Hawaii and Alaska. In the third state, Vermont, the ruling led to the enactment in 1999 of the first 'civil union' law in the United States.[2] In the fourth state, Massachusetts, the effort to overturn the court's ruling has been unsuccessful (so far) and, as a result, Massachusetts began allowing marriages between persons of the same sex in 2004.[3] By the time of this writing (2007), no other state has followed Massachusetts's course, but six other states, Connecticut, New Jersey, California, Oregon, Washington, and Maine have followed Vermont's lead and have enacted legislation allowing formalized legal unions between persons of the same sex, although in some of these states the term used is 'registered partnership' rather than 'civil union'.

1. *See Baehr* v. *Miike*, 852 P.2d 44 (Haw. 1993); *Brause* v. *Bureau of Vital Statistics*, 1998 WL 88743 (Alaska 1998); *Baker* v. *State*, 744 A.2d 864 (Vt. 1999); *Goodridge et al.* v. *Dept. of Public Health*, 798 N.E.2d 941 (Mass. 2003). The recent conflicts literature on same-sex marriages and related issues is extensive and diverse. It includes the following symposia: Symposium, 'Interjurisdictional Recognition of Civil Unions, Domestic Partnerships, and Benefits', 3 *Ave Maria L. Rev.* 393, 2005; Symposium, 'On the Implications of *Lawrence* and *Goodridge* for the Recognition of Same-Sex Marriages and the Validity of DOMA', 38 *Creighton L. Rev.* 233, 2005; Symposium, 'Current Debates in the Conflict of Laws', 153 *U.Pa. L.Rev.* 1815, 2005. *See also*, P. Hay, 'Recognition of Same Sex Relationships in the United States', 54 *Am. J. Comp. L.* 254, 2006 Supp.; M. Rosen, 'Why the Defense of Marriage Act is Not (Yet?) Unconstitutional: *Lawrence*, Full Faith and Credit, and the Many Societal Actors That Determine What the Constitution Requires', 90 *Minn. L. Rev.* 915, 2006; J. Singer, 'Same Sex Marriage, Full Faith and Credit, and the Evasion of Obligation', 1 *Stan. J. C.R. & C.L.* 1, 2005; R. Spector, 'Same-Sex Marriages, Domestic Partnerships and Private International Law: At the Dawn of a New Jurisprudence in the United States', 8 *Y.B. of Priv. Int'l. L.* 169, 2006.
2. *See* 15 V.S.A. §1201 *et seq.* (1999). A civil union is a formalized legal relationship between two persons of the same sex which confers upon them the same rights and duties as a marriage, but it is expressly defined as something other than a marriage. It must be concluded in a specified formal way, it acts as an impediment to another civil union or marriage, and may be dissolved only in a formal way.
3. However, under an old Massachusetts statute modeled after the Uniform Marriage Evasion Act, the right to enter into a same sex marriage is limited to Massachusetts domiciliaries or to domiciliaries of states that do not prohibit same sex marriages. *See* Mass. Gen. L.Ann. 207, §11; *Cote-Whitacre* v. *Dep't of Public Health*, 844 N.E.2d 623 (Mass. 2006).

514. In the meantime, Congress enacted the Defense of Marriage Act (DOMA)[1] in 1996. DOMA consists of two parts. One part (hereafter called the 'vertical' DOMA) provides that:

> In determining the meaning of any Act of Congress, . . . the word 'marriage' means only a legal union between one man and one woman as husband and wife, and the word 'spouse' refers only to a person of the opposite sex who is a husband or a wife.[2]

It is estimated that more than one thousand provisions of federal statutes use the terms 'marriage' or 'spouse'. Vertical DOMA prevents courts from interpreting these terms as including same sex relationships.

1. *See* 1 USCA §7 and 28 USCA §1738C (1996).
2. 1 USCA §7.

515. The second part (hereafter called 'horizontal' DOMA) provides:

> No State . . . shall be required to give effect to any public act, record, or judicial proceeding of any other State . . . respecting a relationship between persons of the same sex that is treated as a marriage under the laws of such other State . . . or a right or claim arising from such relationship.[1]

Since 1996, more than forty states have enacted constitutional amendments or statutes known as 'mini DOMAs' which restrict the right of marriage to persons of the opposite sex and expressly or impliedly prohibit recognition of same sex marriages, and in some cases civil unions, entered into in another state or country.

1. 28 USCA §1738C.

II. DOMA and Its Constitutionality

516. The vertical part of DOMA means that a party to a valid same sex marriage or civil union may not be treated as a spouse under federal law.[1] For example, a party to a Massachusetts same sex marriage may file a joint tax return as a spouse under Massachusetts law, but not under federal law. This part of DOMA has been challenged under the Due Process and Equal Protection clauses of the federal Constitution. Thus far, these challenges have been unsuccessful,[2] as have similar challenges levelled against state DOMAs under state constitutions.[3]

1. *Cf.*, e.g., *In re Kandu*, 315 B.R. 123 (Bankr. W.D. Wash. 2004) (holding that parties to a Canadian same-sex marriage did no qualify as 'spouses' for purposes of the federal Bankruptcy Code); *In re Goodale*, 2003 WL 22173701 (Bankr. W.D. Wash. 2003).
2. *See*, e.g., *Wilson* v. *Ake*, 354 F.Supp.2d 1298 (M.D. Fla. 2005) (reasoning that, although the right to marry is a fundamental right, it does not include the right to marry a person of the same sex; that DOMA did not create a suspect classification; and DOMA was 'rationally related to the government's proffered legitimate interests'. *Id.* at 1308); *Smelt* v. *County of Orange*, 374 F.Supp.2d 861 (C.D. Cal. 2005), *aff'd*, 447 F.3d 673 (9th Cir. 2006), *cert. denied*, 127 S.Ct. 396 (US 2006).
3. *See*, e.g., *Andersen* v. *King County*, 138 P.3d 963 (Wash. 2006); *Hernandez* v. *Robles*, 855 N.E.2d 1 (N.Y. 2006).

517. The vertical DOMA has also withstood constitutional challenges based on federalism grounds. In *In re Kandu*,[1] the plaintiffs challenged DOMA under the Tenth Amendment, which preserves the lawmaking powers of states on subjects, such as domestic relations, that the Constitution does not assign to Congress.[2] The court rejected the argument, reasoning that, because DOMA's definition of marriage applies only for purposes of 'determining the meaning of any Act of Congress', that definition was 'not binding on states', which therefore 'retain the power to decide for themselves the proper definition of the term marriage'.[3] Hence, there was 'no federal infringement on state sovereignty' and the Tenth Amendment was 'not implicated'.[4] Indeed, although domestic relations fall within the lawmaking competence of the states, Congress has the power to define the terms used in federal statutes, such as the federal income tax or bankruptcy codes. Thus, the vertical

DOMA is not unconstitutional on this ground, although it is a conspicuous departure from a long tradition in which the federal law routinely referred or deferred to state law for definitions of terms like 'spouse' and 'marriage'.

1. 315 B.R. 123 (Bankr. W.D. Wash. 2004).
2. *See supra* 18.
3. 315 B.R. 123 at 132.
4. *Id.*

518. The constitutionality of the horizontal DOMA is a question under the Full Faith and Credit clause, under the authority of which Congress enacted this part of DOMA. As noted earlier, the second sentence of that clause grants Congress the power to enact laws 'prescrib[ing] the Manner in which . . . Acts, Records and Proceedings [of one state] shall be proved, and the Effect thereof [in another state]'.[1] To date, Congress has exercised this power only four times. The first statute, enacted in 1948 and known as the Full Faith and Credit Act (FFCA), provides for the manner of authenticating and proving the laws and judgments of sister states and requires that they 'shall have the same full faith and credit in every court within the United States . . . as they have . . . in the courts of the states . . . from which they are taken'.[2] The next two statutes, the Parental Kidnapping Prevention Act (PKPA)[3] enacted in 1980, and the Full Faith and Credit for Child Support Orders Act (FFCCSOA),[4] enacted in 1994, require states to enforce child custody and child support judgments of sister states. The fourth statute is DOMA, which was enacted in 1996.

1. US Const. Art. IV.
2. 28 USCA §1738 (emphasis added).
3. *See* 28 USCA §1738A.
4. *See* 28 USCA §1738B.

519. The fact that DOMA is the first and only statute that releases states from the obligation to enforce laws and judgments of sister states raises multiple questions of both statutory construction and constitutionality. First, as a matter of statutory construction, DOMA clearly conflicts with the FFCA, to the extent DOMA allows states to give less (indeed no) effect to a sister state judgment. One must assume that Congress was aware of this conflict and that it intended DOMA, as the later enactment, to supersede the FFCA insofar as same sex relationships are concerned.

520. However, DOMA also conflicts with both the child custody and the child support statutes mentioned above. These conflicts become apparent if a state that allows same sex unions and has jurisdiction under the standards of these two statutes renders a child custody or a child support order involving a child of the same sex relationship. In such a case, the two statutes would require other states to enforce the order while DOMA would allow them to deny enforcement. It is unclear whether Congress was aware of this conflict or whether DOMA should prevail in this case. The only case that has considered this issue has concluded that DOMA does not create an exception to the PKPA and thus does not supersede it.[1] If this conclusion is correct, it suggests that DOMA may not be as effective as its proponents might have expected because it would remove a large number of cases from the scope of DOMA.

1. *See Miller-Jenkins* v. *Miller-Jenkins*, 637 S.E.2d 330 (Va.App. 2006), discussed *infra* 527. *See also Miller-Jenkins* v. *Miller-Jenkins*, 912 A.2d 951 (Vt. 2006), *cert. denied*, 127 S.Ct. 2130 (US 2007).

521. The argument regarding unconstitutionality is limited to the extent that DOMA affects the judgments, rather than the laws, of sister states. As noted in Part I, Chapter 2, the Supreme Court has been quite lenient in defining the obligation of states to apply the laws of sister states. The Court held that a state may apply its own law (and thereby refuse to apply sister state law) if it has 'significant' (but in practise very modest) contacts with the case and a sufficient interest in doing so.[1] Under this test, a state that is the present domicile of the parties and has a public policy against same sex marriages or unions is free to invoke that policy and refuse to apply a sister state *law* that authorizes such marriages or unions. In contrast, under the Court's full faith jurisprudence regarding judgments, a state is not free to invoke its public policy as a reason for refusing to recognize an otherwise valid sister state judgment.[2] Before the enactment of horizontal DOMA, a state could not, under any circumstances, refuse to recognize an otherwise valid sister state judgment that was premised on the validity of a same sex marriage or union. DOMA changed this by releasing states from their full faith and credit obligation as previously defined in a long line of Supreme Court decisions.

1. *See supra* 82–85.
2. *See infra* 712–717.

522. The Supreme Court has not yet had an opportunity to consider the constitutionality of DOMA on this or any other ground. However, in an earlier unrelated case, at least a plurality of the Court expressed doubt about Congress's power to 'cut back on the measure of faith and credit required by a decision of this Court'.[1] The plurality noted that Congress's power to implement the Full Faith and Credit clause was 'not exclusive', and that the Court 'has given effect to the Clause beyond that required by implementing legislation'. The plurality concluded that 'while Congress clearly has the power to increase the measure of faith and credit that a State must accord to the laws or judgments of another State, there is at least some question whether Congress may cut back on the measure of faith and credit required by a decision of this Court'.[2] It remains to be seen whether this view will garner enough votes for a majority of the present Court.[3]

1. *Thomas* v. *Washington Gas Light Co.*, 448 US 261, 272 (1980).
2. *Id.*
3. In the meantime, lower courts have rejected this view. *See Wilson* v. *Ake*, 354 F.Supp.2d 1298, at 1303 (M.D. Fla. 2005) ('Congress' actions in adopting DOMA are exactly what the Framers envisioned. . . . [They are] an appropriate exercise of its power to regulate conflicts between the laws of two different States, in this case, conflicts over the validity of same-sex marriages'.).

III. Interstate Recognition of Same Sex Relationships

523. DOMA simply permits, but does not require, states to refuse recognition of sister-state same sex marriages or unions. States that have not enacted their own DOMAs or have not otherwise articulated a strong public policy against such marriages or unions are free to grant such recognition. Thus far, the majority of cases have denied such recognition.[1] Indeed, as of the time of this writing (2007), only two lawsuits by same sex partners have found a hospitable forum in another state.[2] However, both suits sought the dissolution of the respective civil unions, and one of them was filed in Massachusetts, a state whose highest court had previously held unconstitutional that state's own prohibition of same sex marriages. In contrast, two similar dissolution suits filed in Connecticut which at that time did not allow civil unions were dismissed for lack of subject matter jurisdiction.[3]

1. *See*, e.g., *Wilson* v. *Ake*, 354 F.Supp.2d 1298, at 1303 (M.D. Fla. 2005) (rejecting a DOMA challenge in a case brought by two forum domiciliaries who were parties to a Massachusetts same sex marriage); *Burns* v. *Burns*, 560 S.E.2d 47 (Ga. Ct. App. 2002) (holding that a Georgia partner in a Vermont civil union did not qualify as a spouse under a child visitation agreement between her and her former heterosexual spouse).
2. *See Salucco* v. *Alldredge*, 2004 WL 864459 (Mass. 19 March 2004) (dissolving a Vermont civil union between a Massachusetts and an Arkansas domiciliary); *Alons* v. *Iowa Dist. Ct. for Woodbury County*, 698 N.W.2d 858 (Iowa 2005) (dismissing for lack of standing a challenge against a decree dissolving a Vermont civil union between Iowa domiciliaries).
3. *See Rosengarten* v. *Downes*, 802 A.2d 170 (Conn. App. Ct. 2002), *cert. granted*, 806 A.2d 1066, *appeal dismissed as moot* (Conn. 2002) (holding that the court had no domestic-relations jurisdiction to dissolve a Vermont civil union between Connecticut domiciliaries); *Lane* v. *Albanese*, 2005 WL 896129 (Conn. 2005) (holding that the court did not have subject matter jurisdiction to annul a Massachusetts same sex marriage between two Connecticut domiciliaries).

524. *Langan* v. *St. Vincent's Hospital of N.Y.*[1] illustrates the distinction noted earlier between, on the one hand, recognizing a same-sex marriage or union as such and, on the other, according it some of the incidents of marriage. *Langan* involved a Vermont civil union, which had ended with the death of one of the partners. The sole question before the court was whether the surviving partner qualified as a spouse for purposes of a wrongful death action.[2] In a well-written opinion, the lower court answered the question affirmatively.[3] However, in a brief decision, a slight majority of New York's intermediate court reversed. The court first examined whether New York's wrongful death statute, which did not encompass same sex partners in the list of wrongful death beneficiaries, violated the equal protection clauses of the federal and state constitutions. After a brief discussion employing minimal scrutiny, the court ruled that the plaintiff did not carry his burden of showing that New York's refusal to treat same sex partners as spouses served no legitimate governmental purpose. Regarding the interstate aspect of the case, the court found that 'theories of Full Faith and Credit and comity ha[d] no application'[4] to this case because Vermont had not accorded the status of spouses to civil-union partners. In authorizing civil unions, said the court, 'the Vermont Legislature went to great pains to expressly decline to place civil unions and marriage on an identical basis . . . and refused to alter traditional concepts of marriage'.[5]

1. 802 N.Y.S.2d 476 (N.Y.A.D. 2d. Dept. 2005).
2. The parties, New York domiciliaries, had lived together in New York for 15 years before they traveled to Vermont where they entered into a civil union. A year after they returned to New York, one of the partners was injured in a New York accident and later died in defendant's New York hospital.
3. *See Langan* v. *St. Vincent's Hosp. of New York*, 765 N.Y.S.2d 411 (N.Y. Sup. Ct. 2003).
4. *Langan*, 802 N.Y.S.2d at 479.
5. *Id.*

525. A dissenting opinion agreed with the majority's interstate analysis, but disagreed with its equal protection analysis. The dissent argued that, although neither the Full Faith and Credit clause nor interstate comity required New York to accord Vermont civil-union partners a status they did not have in Vermont, the equal protection clause prevented New York from treating spouses and same sex partners unequally. The dissent concluded that, by excluding the latter from wrongful-death recovery, New York was differentiating between 'similarly-situated persons on the basis of sexual orientation without a rational relationship to any conceivable governmental purpose'.[1] The dissent reasoned that 'the wrongful death statute . . . is not intended to recompense the survivor [but] . . . is instead designed solely to make a culpable tortfeasor liable for fair and just compensation to those who, by reason of their relationship to the decedent, suffer economic injury as a result of the decedent's death'.[2] '[P]reventing the plaintiff from asserting a wrongful death claim [does not] promote the State's interest in fostering the institution of marriage . . . [but does] provide a windfall to a potential tortfeasor'.[3]

1. *Id.* at 480 (Fisher, J., dissenting).
2. *Id.* at 486.
3. *Id.* at 490. For a subsequent New York case to the same effect, *see Funderburke* v. *NYS Department of Civ. Serv.*, 822 N.Y.S.2d 393 (N.Y. Sup. Ct. 2006) (denying spousal health insurance benefits to a party to a same sex Canadian marriage). *But see Godfrey* v. *Spano*, 836 N.Y.S.2d 813 (N.Y. Sup. 2007) (upholding a local ordinance requiring recognition of same sex marriages contracted in states or countries that allow them).

526. With some modification, the *Langan* situation can illustrate the difference between the treatment of sister state judgments before and after DOMA. Suppose that, instead of suing in New York, the *Langan* plaintiff had sued in Vermont (assuming jurisdiction) and obtained a money judgment awarding him damages for the wrongful death of his partner and then sought recognition of this judgment in New York. Under the Supreme Court's pre-DOMA jurisprudence, New York would be compelled to recognize this judgment, regardless of New York's policy on civil unions. Under DOMA, New York will be free to deny recognition to the judgment to the extent it is premised on 'a relationship between persons of the same sex that is treated as a marriage under the laws of such other State . . . *or a right or claim arising* from such relationship'.[1]

1. 28 USCA §1738C (emphasis added). *But see Bishop* v. *Oklahoma ex rel. Edmondson*, 447 F.Supp.2d 1239 (N.D. Okla. 2006) (holding that DOMA was inapplicable in a case involving a Vermont civil union because Vermont does not treat a civil union as a marriage).

527. *Miller-Jenkins* v. *Miller-Jenkins*[1] did involve a sister state judgment rendered in a state that allowed civil unions, Vermont. However, it was a judgment which another federal statute, the Parental Kidnapping Prevention Act (PKPA) required other states to recognize. Lisa and Janet, two Virginia domiciliaries went to Vermont and entered into a civil union there. After they returned to Virginia, Lisa was artificially inseminated with the sperm of an anonymous donor and gave birth to a child. They then moved to Vermont where they lived together for 13 months after which they separated. Lisa returned to Virginia and Janet remained in Vermont. Two months later, Lisa filed a suit in Vermont seeking dissolution of the union and child custody. The court dissolved the union, declared the child to be the child of the union, and awarded custody to Lisa and visitation rights to Janet.

Dissatisfied with the latter aspect of the judgment, Lisa sought and obtained a Virginia judgment declaring her the sole parent of the child and denying visitation rights to Janet. Subsequently, the Vermont supreme court affirmed the lower court opinion, specifically holding that, because Vermont had continuing custody jurisdiction under the PKPA,[2] Virginia lacked jurisdiction to entertain Lisa's parentage action. Thus, Vermont did not have to recognize the Virginia judgment, which itself improperly denied recognition to the previous Vermont judgment.[3] A few months later, the Virginia Court of Appeals reversed the lower Virginia court and agreed that, under the PKPA, Virginia did not have jurisdiction to modify the Vermont custody and visitation decree or to make a new parentage determination.

However, the Virginia court had to answer a question that was not before the Vermont courts – whether the horizontal DOMA trumps the previously enacted PKPA. The court answered the question in the negative, finding that '[n]othing in the wording or the legislative history of DOMA indicates that it was designed to affect the PKPA and related custody and visitation determinations'.[4] In the court's view, this case did not involve a recognition of the Vermont civil union, but rather 'whether, considering the PKPA, Virginia can deny full faith and credit to the orders of the Vermont court regarding [the child's] custody and visitation. It cannot'.[5]

1. 637 S.E.2d 330 (Va. Ct. App. 2006).
2. The jurisdictional bases of the PKPA are discussed *infra* at 546.
3. *See Miller-Jenkins* v. *Miller-Jenkins*, 912 A.2d 951 (Vt. 2006), *cert. denied*, 127 S.Ct. 2130 (US 2007).
4. *Miller–Jenkins*, 637 S.E.2d at 102.
5. *Id.*

528. Although this was a graceful way to avoid a sharp conflict, the fact remains that the asserted basis for Janet's visitation rights was her parentage of the child, which depended on the validity of the Vermont civil union. In turn, if DOMA trumped the PKPA, DOMA would free the Virginia court from the obligation of recognizing the union. However, under a Virginia statute which expressly prohibited such recognition, the court would have no discretion to do otherwise.[1]

1. Enacted in 2004, the Virginia's Marriage Affirmation Act provides that any 'civil union, partnership contract or other arrangement between persons of the same sex purporting to bestow the privileges or obligations of marriage is prohibited' in Virginia, and that any such arrangement entered into in another state 'shall be void in all respects in Virginia and any contractual rights created thereby shall be void and unenforceable'. *Id.* The court decided that, even if this Act applied in this case, 'it is preempted by the PKPA'. *Id*

529. In any event, even if the court was wrong about the DOMA-PKPA relationship, the decision is still correct in the sense that DOMA simply allows but does not require a state to deny recognition to a sister state judgment.[1] However, if the court's view that DOMA does not prevail over the PKPA is correct, then the same logic would suggest that DOMA also does not prevail over the Full Faith and Credit for Child Support Orders Act of 1994 (FFCCSOA). In turn, this would render DOMA inoperative in all cases in which a court has rendered a judgment premised on the validity of a same sex marriage or union and which other states are required to recognize under either the PKPA or the FFCCSOA.

1. However, from the perspective of state law, this decision would have to be reconciled with the Virginia statute reproduced in the previous footnote, *supra*.

530. *Hennefeld* v. *Township of Montclair*[1] is an example of how a willing court can 'accommodate'[2] a civil union partner by according him or her some of the incidents of marriage even though the *lex fori* does not allow such unions. The *Hennefeld* plaintiffs, New Jersey domiciliaries, had entered into both a Vermont civil union and a Canadian same sex marriage. This case involved the question of whether they were entitled to certain property tax benefits that New Jersey law affords spouses.[3] The court found that neither the Canadian marriage nor the Vermont civil union rendered the plaintiff eligible for the requested benefit. However, the court did note that, in the interim, New Jersey had enacted a Domestic Partnership Act (DPA) which accorded domestic partners certain benefits previously reserved for married persons. The court reasoned that, although the DPA did not mention the particular tax benefit, its enumeration of rights was not exclusive and thus it was susceptible to expansive interpretation. Under this reasoning, the court decided to grant requested benefit.

1. 22 N.J. Tax 166 (N.J. Tax Ct. 2005).
2. *See* Hay, 'Recognition of Same Sex Relationships in the United States', 54 *Am. J. Comp. L.* 254, 2006 Supp., 268 (considering this case as an example of 'Angleichung', 'Anpassung', or 'coordination des systèmes').
3. The parties had lived together for 25 years, the last 15 of which they lived in a house they co-owned as tenants by the entirety. One of the plaintiffs was an honourably discharged and 100 per cent disabled veteran. Under a New Jersey tax statute, an honourably discharged 100 per cent disabled veteran is entitled to a property tax exemption on his 'dwelling house'. In applying this statute to veterans who are married, New Jersey assessors have followed the practise of allowing an 100 per cent exemption, even if the veteran had title to less than 100 per cent of the house. In this case, the assessor allowed only a 50 per cent exemption. The plaintiffs challenged this assessment in New Jersey's Tax Court.

531. As this case illustrates, the recognition of foreign same sex marriages or unions and their incidents is entirely discretionary because the Full Faith and Credit clause does not apply to foreign laws or judgments. Thus far, no case has recognized such a marriage or union.

532. *In re Kandu*[1] involved a Canadian same sex marriage between two Washington domiciliaries. The court refused to treat them as spouses under the federal Bankruptcy Code and rejected their argument about comity, citing a 'strong and clear policy'[2] to the contrary. The court noted that, although comity is preferred when the laws of nations are 'in alignment', there is 'no such preference . . . when the laws of a foreign nation are contrary to the sovereign's policy or prejudicial to its interests', and that, in such a case, 'a court must prefer the laws of its own nation'.[3]

1. 315 B.R. 123 (Bankr. W.D. Wash. 2004).
2. *Id.* at 134 note 3.
3. *Id.* at 133.

533. In *Bishop* v. *Oklahoma ex rel. Edmondson*,[1] the court held that the horizontal DOMA has no bearing on foreign marriages or unions. Noting that DOMA refers to same sex relationships that are treated as marriages under the laws of another '*State*', the court found DOMA inapplicable to the parties' Canadian marriage.[2] This conclusion did not mean that the Canadian marriage was entitled to recognition, but rather that the plaintiffs' constitutional challenge against DOMA was misplaced.

1. 447 F.Supp.2d 1239 (N.D. Okla. 2006).
2. *See id.* at 1249 ('Because [DOMA] aims to relieve states of any potential obligation to comply with the Full Faith and Credit Clause, because [it] tracks the language of the Full Faith and Credit Clause, and because [it] was passed pursuant to Congress' authority under the Full Faith and Credit Clause, the Court concludes that use of the word "State" in . . . DOMA (like use of the word "State" in the Full Faith and Credit Clause) was not intended to include foreign countries but instead was intended only to include states within the United States'.).

§4. Divorce

534. American law is rather unique in having 'succeeded' to eliminate the choice-of-law question in divorce cases by merging it into the jurisdictional question – a state that has jurisdiction applies its own law in deciding entitlement to divorce.[1] Until the first part of the 20th century, only the state of the matrimonial domicile (i.e., the spouses' common domicile) had jurisdiction to grant a divorce.[2] Under this regime, it was natural for that state to apply its own substantive law of divorce. Thus, understandably, the choice-of-law question was merged with the jurisdictional question. However, in *Williams* v. *North Carolina [I]*,[3] the Supreme Court held that a state that was not the matrimonial domicile but subsequently became the domicile of only the plaintiff spouse, had jurisdiction to grant a divorce, even in the absence of *in personam* jurisdiction over the defendant spouse ('*ex parte* divorce').[4]

1. In other countries, the question of whether a court has jurisdiction to entertain a divorce action has remained separate from the question of which law that court will apply in granting the divorce. The latter law is usually 'the law that governs the effects of the marriage', which is the law of a state with which *both* spouses are affiliated. In recent years, some countries allow the alternative application of the law of the forum state, but only if both spouses have a sufficient connection with that state. *See* Symeonides, *Private International Law at the End of the Twentieth Century: Progress or Regress?* (The Hague, London, Boston, 2000), pp. 55–56 (discussing rules from Belgium, China, Germany, Holland, Hungary, Italy, Switzerland, and Yugoslavia).
2. *See Atherton* v. *Atherton*, 181 US 155 (1901).
3. 317 US 287 (1942).
4. *Williams [I]* involved two sets of spouses all of whom were domiciled in North Carolina. One spouse from each marriage moved to Nevada and, after arguably establishing a domicile there, sued their stay-at-home spouses for divorce. Since the defendants did not appear in the Nevada proceedings, Nevada did not have *in personam* jurisdiction over them.

535. Although the choice-of-law question was not before the Court in *Williams I*, the Court did state *in dicta* that its decision to grant Nevada jurisdiction also carried with it a permission to apply its divorce law to the merits.[1] Instead of taking the opportunity to detach the two questions now that their separateness became clearer, the Court decided to perpetuate the merger. This decision was hardly the result of inattentiveness or error. The reason the two *Williams I* plaintiffs decided to go to Nevada was because the law of Nevada would grant a divorce while the law of North Carolina, their matrimonial domicile, would not. Therefore, unless Nevada was free to apply its own law, the plaintiffs and others like them would have no incentive to sue there and the migratory divorces movement would not have begun. By allowing Nevada to apply its own law, the Court fuelled that movement and accelerated the process of liberalizing the divorce laws of all other states of the union. Thus, despite the Court's protestations to the contrary, its decision in *Williams I* 'd[id] . . . involve selection of a rule which will encourage . . . the practice of divorce'.[2] If multistate social engineering was not what the Court intended, it is certainly what the Court's decision produced.[3]

1. *See Williams I*, 317 US 287, 296.
2. *See id.* at 302–303.
3. *See, id.* at 312, (Jackson, J., dissenting): 'It is not an exaggeration to say that this decision repeals the divorce laws of all the states and substitutes the law of Nevada as to all marriages one of the parties to which can afford a short trip there'.

536. The Court had another opportunity to detach the choice-of-law question from the jurisdictional question in *Sherrer* v. *Sherrer*,[1] a case in which the plaintiff spouse had lived in the forum state for only ninety-three days. However, the stay-at-home spouse appeared in the divorce proceeding, mounting a lukewarm defence on the merits without contesting either the jurisdiction of the court or its application of forum law. The Supreme Court held that the principle of jurisdictional finality[2] would be impermissibly undermined if spouses were allowed to collaterally attack the divorce judgment in another state. Here again, jurisdictional considerations absorbed or displaced substantive considerations. The fact that such proceedings are not truly adversarial and the parties do not raise, much less litigate, the choice-of-law issue was not viewed by the Court as a sufficient reason to differentiate divorce cases from other cases. Nor did the Court accept Justice Frankfurter's arguments that societal interests beyond and above the parties' interests are implicated in divorce proceedings.[3]

1. 334 US 343 (1948).
2. *See infra* 719.
3. *Sherrer*, 334 US at 362 (Frankfurter, J., dissenting) ('the State of domicile has an independent interest in the marital status of its citizens that neither they nor any other State with which they may have a transitory connection may abrogate against its will. Its interest is not less because both parties to the marital relationship instead of one sought to evade its laws').

537. In *Alton* v. *Alton*,[1] the federal district court for the Virgin Islands did what state courts rarely do. It held that the existence of *in personam* jurisdiction over both spouses, who were Connecticut domiciliaries, did not carry with it the power to divorce them under the law of the forum without actual proof that the plaintiff had acquired a domicile in the forum. The Court of Appeals affirmed over a dissent by Judge Hastie who advanced for the first time the argument of separating choice of law from jurisdiction.[2] Unfortunately, the Supreme Court did not have the opportunity to address Hastie's argument because in the meantime Mr Alton obtained a bilateral divorce in Connecticut, making the case moot.

1. 207 F.2d 667 (3d Cir. 1953).
2. *Id.* at 685 (Hastie, J., dissenting) ('[U]nder correct application of conflict of laws doctrine, and even under the due process clause, it [may be] incumbent upon the Virgin Islands, lacking connection with the subject matter, to apply the divorce law of some state that has such connection, here Connecticut').

538. The practise of merging the choice-of-law question into the jurisdictional question in divorce cases has never been seriously re-examined. This practise was thought to be so deeply imbedded in the American jurisprudence by the time of the Restatement (Second), that its drafters, who rarely opted for inexorable rules, felt confident enough to proclaim that '[t]he local law of the domiciliary state in which the action is brought will be applied to determine the right to divorce'.[1] No qualifications or 'unless' clauses were deemed necessary. Absent is the usual adage that accompanies the vast majority of all other sections of the Restatement which provides that the law designated as applicable is not to be applied 'if another state has a more significant relationship'. Apparently, in the drafter's opinion, no other state can have a more significant relationship than the state of one spouse's domicile, not even a state which was the former matrimonial domicile and continues to be the domicile of the other spouse and of their children.[2]

1. *Restatement (Second)* §285 (1971).
2. The Restatement states that 'the local law of the forum determines the right to a divorce, not because it is the place where the action is brought but because of the peculiar interest which a state has in the marriage status of its domiciliaries'. Restatement (Second) §285 cmt. (a). This is a sound statement when there is only one 'domiciliary' state, but not when, as in *Williams* or *Sherrer*, there are two such states and the forum state is (arguably) the domicile of only the deserting spouse. In such a case, the interest of the forum state 'in the marriage status of its domiciliaries' is 'peculiar' enough but it is not necessarily any more legitimate than the interest of the former matrimonial domicile which continues to be the domicile of the deserted spouse.

539. Any objections to this approach were mooted as, one after the other, the states began liberalizing their divorce laws and adopting 'no-fault' divorce. By merging choice-of-law into jurisdiction, *Williams [I]* fuelled the movement for migratory divorces, which in turn succeeded in eliminating conflicts between the divorce laws of the 50 states. Some of these conflicts may return, albeit on a much smaller scale, with the adoption in some states of the institution of 'covenant marriages' which cannot be dissolved on no-fault grounds.[1]

1. For a discussion of covenant marriages and the attendant conflict-of-laws problems, *see* P. Hay, 'The American "Covenant Marriage" in the Conflict of Laws', 64 *La. L. Rev.* 43, 2003; K. Spaht & S. Symeonides, 'Covenant Marriage and the Law of Conflict of Laws', 32 *Creighton L. Rev.* 1085, 1999.

540. In any event, the American practise in divorce cases is now well settled, as follows. A state is constitutionally free to (and does) apply its own law to grant a divorce, even on a ground not recognized by other states, if that state (1) is the domicile of only one of the spouses and does not have jurisdiction over the other spouse ('*ex parte*' divorce), or (2) is not the domicile of either spouse but has *in personam* jurisdiction over both of them ('bilateral' divorce). In the case of an *ex parte* divorce, the court's power is limited to dissolving the bonds of matrimony by granting a divorce; it does not extend to adjudicating incidents of divorce, such as the right to alimony, support, custody, or dividing the marital property. In order to adjudicate these incidents the court must possess jurisdiction over both spouses. This is the doctrine of 'divisible divorce' enunciated in a series of Supreme Court decisions.[1]

1. *See*, e.g., *Estin* v. *Estin*, 334 US 541 (1948); *Vanderbilt* v. *Vanderbilt*, 354 US 416 (1957); *Simons* v. *Miami Beach First Nat'l Bank*, 381 US 81 (1965).

541. The above discussion is limited to divorces granted in a state of the United States, which for this reason fall within the reach of the Full Faith and Credit clause of the federal Constitution. Since neither this clause nor the principle of jurisdictional finality enunciated in *Sherrer*[1] apply to foreign judgments, the recognition of foreign divorces is entirely discretionary, but subject to due process limits. *Ex parte*, or even bilateral, foreign divorces granted on a jurisdictional basis other than domicile, especially 'quickie' divorces issued by foreign divorce mills during weekend trips to foreign resorts in the Carribean or Mexico, are particularly problematic. Most cases do not recognize these divorces. However, some cases have recognized them or have held that participating parties were estopped from challenging them.[2] Once an American court recognizes a foreign divorce, then the American judgment is entitled to recognition in sister states under the Full Faith and Credit clause.

1. This principle prevents spouses and their privies from collaterally attacking a 'bilateral' divorce granted by a court that had jurisdiction over both spouse.
2. For a thorough discussion of the cases, *see* E. Scoles, P. Hay, P. Borchers & S. Symeonides, *Conflict of Laws* (4th edn, St. Paul, Minn., 2004), pp. 642–662.

§5. Child Support and Custody

542. The practise of merging the choice-of-law and jurisdictional questions is also generally followed in interstate child support or custody cases. As in the case of divorce, the substantive laws of the various states in these two areas differ in detail rather than in basic policy. For this reason, choice of law is rarely a problem in these case. The conflict is almost always about which state has jurisdiction to issue an initial child support or custody decree, or to modify a decree issued in another state. Fortunately, in recent years the enactment of federal statutes as well as uniform laws adopted by all states have removed most of the jurisdictional conflicts that were prevalent in the past.

I. Child Support

543. For interstate child support disputes, the two applicable statutes are the federal Full Faith and Credit for Child Support Orders Act of 1994 (FFCCSOA),[1] and the Uniform Interstate Family Support Act of 2001 (UIFSA).[2] The federal Act requires states to enforce 'according to its terms' a child support order made 'consistently with' the Act by a court of another state.[3] An order is consistent with the Act if it was issued by a court that had jurisdiction under the law of the issuing state (in this case the UIFSA), which in turn must comply with federal due process standards.[4] A state that has issued a child support order consistently with the Act has continuing, exclusive jurisdiction over the order as long as it remains the 'child's home State' or the residence of any individual contestant.[5] Other states must enforce and may not modify the order, unless the issuing state no longer has continuing, exclusive jurisdiction (because it is no longer is the child's State or the residence of any contestant) or all contestants have formally requested the issuing court to allow a court of another state to assume jurisdiction to modify the order.[6]

1. 28 USCA §1738B.
2. This Act, or its predecessor of 1996, have been adopted by all states. Neither this Act, nor the federal Act apply to the foreign-country judgments. Moreover the Uniform Money-Judgments Recognition Act (discussed *infra*, 730) expressly excludes from its scope foreign support decrees. This, however, does not mean that foreign support decrees are not recognized in the United States. Rather it means that their recognition, which is always discretionary, depends on general comity principles. These principles are discussed in Part III, Chapter 2, *infra*.
3. 28 USCA §1738B(a). When the order was issued in the context of a same sex marriage or union, this Act may conflict with DOMA. *See supra* 519–520, 527–529.
4. The UIFSA provides that a state has jurisdiction if it has *in personam* jurisdiction over the defendant under general principles, or: (1) if the defendant: (a) has resided with the child in the forum state or resided there and provided prenatal expenses or support for the child; (b) engaged in sexual intercourse in that state and the child may have been conceived by that act of intercourse; or (c) asserted parentage in the putative father registry maintained in that state; or (2) if the child resides in the forum state as a result of the acts or directives of the defendant. *See* UIFSA §201.
5. 28 USCA §1738B(d). A state is considered the 'child's home State' if the child lived there with a parent or a person acting as parent for at least six consecutive months immediately preceding the filing of the petition or, if the child is less than six months old, if the child lived there from birth. *Id.* at (b).
6. 28 USCA §1738B(e).

544. The federal Act provides that, in issuing or enforcing a support order or, where permitted, modifying such an order, the court 'shall' apply the law of the forum, subject to two exceptions:[1] (1) in 'interpreting' an order issued in another state, the court 'shall' apply the law of the issuing state; and (2) in enforcing arrears under an order, the court 'shall' apply the statute of limitation of either the issuing state or the forum state, whichever provides the longer period of limitation.[2] The repeated use of the verb 'shall' makes clear that these choice-of-law rules are compulsory and thus prevail over contrary rules in state law. The Uniform Act also contains choice-of-law rules, which, although more detailed, are not likely to conflict with the federal Act.[3]

1. 28 USCA §1738B(h). The Uniform Act provides that the court shall apply 'the procedural and substantive law, including the rules on choice of law' of the forum state. UIFSA §303(1) (emphasis added).
2. 28 USCA §1738B(h). For a possible conflict with DOMA, *see supra* 519–520, 527–529.
3. For example, the Uniform Act provides that the law of the issuing state governs the nature, extent, amount, and duration of current payments, the computation and payment of arrearages and accrual of interest, and the existence and satisfaction of other obligations under the support order. *See* UIFSA §604(a). Although some of these issues go beyond 'interpreting' the order, the application of the law of the issuing state is within the spirit of the federal Act.

II. Child Custody

545. The same scheme and interplay between a federal statute and a uniform statute adopted in all states has reduced jurisdictional competition in interstate child custody disputes. The federal Parental Kidnapping Prevention Act of 1980 (PKPA)[1] and the Uniform Child Custody Jurisdiction and Enforcement Act of 1997 (UCCJEA)[2] work together. The federal Act requires states to enforce 'according to its terms', and without modifying, a child custody decree made 'consistently with' the Act by a sister state court.[3]

1. 28 USCA §1738A.
2. By 2007, this Act had been adopted in 47 states. The remaining states adopted its predecessor Uniform Custody Jurisdiction Act (UCCJA).
3. 28 USCA §1738A(a). When the child is the issue of a same-sex marriage or union, this Act may conflict with DOMA. *See supra* 519–520, 527–529.

546. A custody decree is consistent with the Act if it was issued by a court that had jurisdiction under both the law of the issuing state (i.e., the UCCJEA) and the federal Act. Both acts vest primary jurisdiction in the child's 'home state', which is defined as the state in which, at the commencement of the proceeding or immediately before, the child lived with a person acting as parent for at least six consecutive months, or since birth if the child is less than six months old.[1] If no state meets this qualification, then the federal Act authorizes jurisdiction on certain alternative bases, such as in cases of abandoned children or other emergency cases.[2] When a state that has jurisdiction under the Act issues a child custody decree, another state may not modify it unless the issuing state no longer has jurisdiction (or has declined to exercise it) and the second state has jurisdiction under the Act. Neither the federal nor the uniform act address the choice-of-law question. The prevailing American practise in determining custody has been to apply the law of the forum.

1. 28 USCA §1738A(b)(4) and (c)(2)(A).
2. *See* 28 USCA §1738A(c)(2)(B)–(D).

547. The federal Act does not apply to custody decrees issued in foreign countries. However, the uniform Act requires recognition and enforcement of custody decrees issued in a foreign country 'under factual circumstances in substantial conformity with the jurisdictional standards of this [Uniform Act]'.[1] This provision is important in those cases in which the foreign country is not a party to the Hague Convention on the Civil Aspects of International Child Abduction of 1980. This United States is a party to this Convention and has implemented it by enacting the International Child Abduction Remedies Act (ICARA).[2] Because the Convention is well-known internationally, it is unnecessary to discuss it here.

1. UCCJEA §105. The only exception is when the child custody law of a foreign country violates 'fundamental principles of human rights'. *Id.*
2. *See* 42 USC §11601 *et seq.*

§6. Legitimacy and Adoption

548. The status of legitimacy is less important today than it has been in the past. This because of changing social mores and also a series of Supreme Court decisions in the mid-1970s that banned discrimination against illegitimate children with regard to inheritance, support, and other rights. Legitimacy remains legally important to the extent it establishes a presumption of paternity. For example, a child born during the marriage is legitimate and is presumed to be the child of the mother's husband. In this case, the status of legitimacy includes the presumption of paternity; the converse is not true – paternity does not necessarily entail legitimacy. The Restatement (Second) provides that: (1) a child's legitimacy is determined by the law of the state that, with respect to the particular issue, has 'the most significant relationship' to the child and the parent 'under the principles stated in §6'; and that (2) a child will 'usually' be held legitimate if this would be his status under the law of the state where either (a) the parent was domiciled when the child's status of legitimacy is claimed to have been created or (b) the child was domiciled when the parent acknowledged the child as his.[1]

1. *Restatement (Second)* §287.

549. Like most rules affecting status, this alternative-reference rule deliberately favoured legitimacy, precisely because of the (then) serious legal and social consequences of illegitimacy. Following the elimination of most of these consequences, cases began to appear in which the plaintiffs seek not to establish paternity, but to disprove it. One such case is *Hermanson* v. *Hermanson*,[1] in which the child's mother filed a suit in Nevada seeking a judgment that her husband at the time of the child's birth was not the child's father. The child was born during the marriage in California while both spouses were domiciled there. Under the laws of both states, the child was presumed to be the child of the husband, but the presumption was irrebuttable in California and rebuttable in Nevada (the mother's and the child's domicile at the time of the lawsuit). The Nevada court held that the California law was offensive to Nevada's public policy and applied Nevada law.

1. 887 P.2d 1241(Nev. 1994).

550. *Smith* v. *Smith*[1] presented the converse pattern from *Hermanson* – the law of the state of the child's birth and the mother's apparent domicile at the time (Oregon) did not impose a presumption of paternity, but the law of the mother's and child's present domicile (Minnesota) imposed such a presumption, which had become irrebuttable because of that state's statute of limitation. The Minnesota court found that the purposes of the Minnesota presumption was to protect the child as well as the public 'by preventing a child from becoming a public charge' and 'these purposes are served by applying the [Minnesota] presumption'. The court concluded that the application of Minnesota law would further 'the clear statutory purpose of promoting legitimacy' and Minnesota's underlying 'governmental interest'.[2]

1. 1994 WL 149445 (Minn. Ct. App. 1994).
2. *Id.* at *2.

551. In adoption cases, the American practise again merges the choice-of-law question into the jurisdictional question. A state has power to grant an adoption if: (a) it is the domicile of either the adopter or the adoptee; and (b) it has personal jurisdiction over the adopter and either the adoptee or the person having legal custody of the child.[1] According to the Restatement (Second): (1) a court applies its own law in determining whether to grant an adoption; and (2) an adoption granted in a state that has jurisdiction, will 'usually' be given the same effect in another state as is given to adoptions granted by its own courts.[2] Although interstate adoption cases have not occupied the courts for many years, this may change in the near future as adoptions by same sex couples become more common.

1. *Restatement (Second)* §78.
2. *Id.* §289, 290.

Chapter 7. Property, Marital Property and Successions

§1. Property

552. The American law of property is rooted in the common law of England and is better understood in light of its history. American conflicts law, however, departs from the common law distinction between real and personal property and adopts instead a distinction between immovables and movables (chattels). Although the latter distinction generally parallels the former, the term immovables also encompasses certain interests in land such as leaseholds that in other areas of the law usually are regarded as personalty. Whether a thing is a movable or an immovable is determined according to the law of the *situs* of the thing.[1]

1. Basic bibliography for the topics discussed in this Section includes: L. McDougal, R. Felix & R. Whitten, *American Conflicts Law* (5th edn, New York, Ardsley, 2001), pp. 597–630; E. Scoles, P. Hay, P. Borchers & S. Symeonides, *Conflict of Laws* (4th edn, St. Paul, Minn., 2004), pp. 1053–1108; R. Weintraub, *Commentary on the Conflict of Laws* (5th edn, New York, 2006), pp. 542–619.

I. Immovables

553. With respect to immovables, the First Restatement required the application of the law of the state where the immovable is situated (*lex rei sitae*), for almost all issues and virtually without any exceptions. Thus, the law of the *situs* applied to: (1) the substantive and formal validity of a conveyance of an interest in land,[1] the effect and interpretation of the conveyance,[2] and the capacity of the grantor and the grantee;[3] (2) to transfers by operation of law and acquisition through adverse possession or prescription;[4] and (3) to the validity, effect and enforcement of mortgages.[5]

1. *See* American Law Institute, *Restatement of Conflict of Laws* §§215, 217 (1934).
2. *See id.* §§220, 214.
3. *See id.* §§216, 219.
4. *See id.* §§223–224.
5. *See id.* §§225–231.

554. Neither the Restatement (Second) nor judicial practise during and since the conflicts revolution have reduced the dominance of the *situs* rule to an appreciable degree. The Restatement (Second) devotes ten sections to immovables and they all call for the application of the law of the *situs*. The sections cover the validity, effect, and construction of conveyance of an interest in land,[1] equitable conversion of interest in land,[2] transfers by operation of law and acquisition through adverse possession or prescription,[3] the validity, effect, and enforcement of mortgages and liens,[4] and the validity and effect of powers to transfer land.[5] Two of those sections (on adverse possession and mortgages) call for the application of the 'local law' of the *situs*, while the remaining eight authorize the application of 'the law that would be applied by the courts of the *situs*'. The latter phrase is always accompanied by the adage that these courts will 'usually apply their own local law'.[6] In these sections, the Restatement (Second) drafters have subordinated their general preference for an issue-by-issue analysis, opting instead for broad, all-encompassing, and fixed rules. For example, the rule of Section 223, which applies to conveyances of an interest in land, covers formal and substantive validity, as well the capacity of the transferor and transferee.[7]

1. *See* American Law Institute, *Restatement (Second) of Conflict of Laws 2d* §§223–224 (1971).
2. *See id.* §225.
3. *See id.* §§226–227.
4. *See id.* §§228–230.
5. *See id.* §§231–232.
6. *See*, e.g., *id.* §223.
7. *See id.* §223, cmts. a, c–d.

555. The *situs* rule is easy to apply and not as easy to manipulate. Immovables do not move and usually there is little question as to whether a thing is an immovable or where it is situated. It is another question, however, whether the *situs* rule needs to be as broad as in its American version. One of the reasons given for the dominance and breath of the *situs* rule under the traditional approach was the 'power rationale' – the *situs* state has exclusive *de jure* and *de facto* power over land situated within its borders. As Professor Beale put it, '[the] laws [of the *situs*] alone can apply to the land since any contrary provision [by non-*situs* courts or legislatures] would be given no effect by the courts and the executive officers of the state of *situs*'.[1] Statements like these have led some courts to conclude that they do not have jurisdiction to adjudicate disputes involving non-forum land, even when they do apply *situs* law. This conclusion is accurate only with regard to *in rem* jurisdiction, that is jurisdiction to directly affect non-forum land.[2] On the other hand, a court that has *in personam* jurisdiction over the parties may indirectly affect non-forum land by ordering the parties to pay money or to execute the necessary conveyances. Under the Full Faith and Credit clause of the Constitution, such a judgment would be enforceable in the *situs* state,[3] regardless of whether it applied *situs* or non-*situs* law.

1. J. Beale, *A Treatise on the Conflict of Laws* (New York, 1935), vol. 2, pp. 938–939.
2. *See Clarke* v. *Clarke*, 178 US 186 (1900); *Fall* v. *Eastin*, 215 US 1 (1909).
3. *See Durfee* v. *Duke*, 375 US 106 (1963); *Fall* v. *Eastin*, 215 US 1 (1909).

556. In addition to lawyer convenience, the contemporary reasons for the *situs* rule are that it promotes: (1) certainty and clarity of title; (2) the interests of the *situs* state in regulating land situated within its borders; and (3) interstate and international uniformity of result. Indeed, the *situs* state has an interest in ensuring the certainty and integrity of its recording system, protecting good faith purchasers who rely upon the system, and facilitating the task of the title examiner who should not have to interpret foreign laws. The *situs* state also has an interest in ensuring the most efficient, productive, commercially sound, and environmentally prudent utilization of land within its borders and in prescribing rules for adverse possession, boundary disputes, easements, rules against perpetuities, and zoning, or environmental regulations. All of these are good reasons to have *a situs* rule, but whether it is necessary for this rule to cover all issues (such as capacity) in all transactions

involving immovables is quite another question. This question is revisited in the section on successions, a subject in which the dominance and breath of the *situs* rule are more objectionable than here.

II. Movables

557. Despite its shortcomings, the *situs* rule has one undeniable advantage with regard to immovables: it is certain and predictable. The same is not true with regard to movables, which may move or be moved from one state to another. Thus, any choice-of-law rule that is based on *situs* as the exclusive connecting factor must confront the possibility that there may be more than one *situs*, a phenomenon descriptively called *conflit mobile*. Rigid adherence to the law of the first *situs* would ignore the legitimate interest of the second situs in protecting persons who acquire rights in justifiable reliance upon the law of the second situs. Conversely, rigid adherence to the law of the second situs would lead to the divestiture of rights created while the thing was situated in the first *situs*. The conflict between the laws of the two *situses* must be resolved in a way that takes into account the legitimate interests of each *situs*, without frustrating justified party expectations or running afoul of the constitutionally sanctioned principle that the mere movement of a thing from one state to another, without more, should not alter existing rights in that thing.

558. The drafters of the Restatement (Second), aware of these potential complexities and uncertainties, have considerably softened the inexorable *situs* rule of the First Restatement. The Restatement (Second) provides that the validity and effect of a conveyance of an interest in a chattel are determined by the law of the state which, 'with respect to the particular issue', has the 'most significant relationship' to the parties, the chattel and the conveyance 'under the principles stated in §6'.[1] This flexible approach is rendered only slightly more specific by the next sentence stating that, in the absence of an effective choice of law by the parties, 'greater weight will usually be given to the location of the chattel at the time of the conveyance' than to any other contact.[2] However, this rule applies only 'as between the parties to the conveyance'.[3] A separate Restatement section applicable to third parties points to *situs* law in slightly less equivocal terms. It provides that the effect of a conveyance upon a pre-existing interest in a chattel of a person who was not a party to the conveyance will 'usually' be determined by the law that would be applied by the courts of the state where the chattel was at the time of the conveyance, and that these courts would 'usually' apply their own local law.[4] The Restatement abandons its equivocation only in cases of acquisition by adverse possession or prescription, by providing that such acquisition and the nature of the acquired interest are determined by the law of the state where the chattel was at the time the acquisition is claimed to have taken place.[5]

1. *Restatement (Second)* §244.
2. *Id.*
3. *Id.*
4. *Id.* §245.
5. *Id.* §246.

559. Finally, the Restatement addresses the *conflit mobile* problem by providing that interests in a chattel are 'not affected by the mere removal of the chattel to another state', but that such interests 'may be affected by dealings with the chattel in the other state'.[1] Although the Restatement does not explain what exactly can affect such interests, its adoption of the aforementioned distinction between the parties to the conveyance and third parties, and its flexible phrasing of its choice-of-law rules can lead to results rationally accommodating both the interests of the two *situses* and the circumstances of most cases.[2]

1. *Id.* §247. For a recent case following this provision, *see Lurie* v. *Blackwell*, 51 P.3d 846 (Wyo. 2002) (holding that neither the chattel's removal from Missouri to Wyoming nor the owner's subsequent movement to Montana altered his rights in a chattel he acquired in Missouri as tenant by the entirety, even though neither Wyoming nor Montana recognized tenancies by the entirety).
2. For a discussion of these considerations in cases involving stolen works of art or cultural property, *see* S. Symeonides, 'A Choice-of-Law Rule for Conflicts Involving Stolen Cultural Property', 38 *Vand. J. Transnat'l L.* 1177, 2005.

560. The Restatement (Second) contains several additional sections covering intangibles, as well as security interests in movables. Most of these sections are displaced by statutes in the various states, including especially the Uniform Commercial Code (UCC),[1] which has been adopted in all states of the United States. Even a brief description of these fairly complex and detailed rules is beyond the scope of this volume. Suffice it to say that, in contrast to the Restatement and the previous version of the UCC, the current version (effective 2001) shifts the emphasis from the *situs* nexus to the place where the debtor is 'located', which it defines as the debtor's residence for individual debtors, and the place of business for organizations.[2]

1. *See* 9 UCC §§9-301-9-308 (2001).
2. 9 UCC §9-307(b). If the organization has more than one place of business, the debtor is located at its chief executive office. In all cases, however, if the debtor is located in a jurisdiction that does not require information concerning the existence of a nonpossessory security interest to be made generally available in a registration system 'as a condition or result of the security interest's obtaining priority over the rights of a lien creditor', then the debtor is deemed located in the District of Columbia. *Id.* §9-307(c).

§2. Marital Property

I. Substantive Law

561. Although the majority of states of the United States follow the common law system of separate property, eight states follow the Spanish-based system of community property: Arizona, California, Idaho, Louisiana, Nevada, New Mexico, Texas and Washington.[1] In a community-property system, spouses who live under the regime of community property[2] co-own in a 50:50 ratio all property that is acquired by either of them during the marriage and is not classified as the separate property of the acquiring spouse. The definitions of community and separate property vary slightly from state to state but, generally, separate property encompasses property that a spouse owned before marriage and any property a spouse inherits or receives as gift during marriage. Whatever is not classified as separate property is (or is presumed to be), community property, and this includes the earnings of either spouse during marriage. The community-property regime terminates by a judgment of divorce or separation, or with the death of either spouse. Upon termination, the community property is subject to a 50:50 partition at the instance of either spouse or his or her heirs. Because most property is likely to be community property, the separate property of each spouse is in principle free of any claims in favour of the other. For this reason, the separate property is not subject to partition upon divorce, nor to inheritance rights in favour of the surviving spouse upon the death of the owning spouse.

1. Wisconsin also adheres to a form of community property, having adopted the Uniform Marital Property Act in 1983 which approximates the community-property system. *See* 9A U.L.A. 97 (1987).
2. Despite contrary popular belief, not all spouses who live in a community-property state are subject to a community property regime. Rather, that regime (called 'legal regime') applies only to the extent that the spouses have not validly agreed to displace it. Before marriage, prospective spouses are free to opt for a separate-property regime or, within certain limits, to modify the legal regime. During marriage, the spouses may also agree to modify or opt out of the legal regime in certain narrowly defined circumstances. One of those circumstances is when the spouses move to a community-property state.

562. Separate-property states begin with the premise that marriage does not affect the property acquisitions of either spouse. Each spouse owns fully and exclusively any property he or she acquired during the marriage. However, these states exhibit the same concern for protecting the non-acquiring spouse as do community-property states. While community-property states protect the non-earning spouse during the marriage by granting him or her a 50 per cent present proprietary interest in all property classified as community property, separate-property states protect the non-earning spouse through rights such as dower, statutory share, or equitable distribution that materialize at the end of the marriage. For example, upon the death of one spouse, the surviving spouse has a right to 'take against the will' of the deceased spouse a certain 'statutory share' or portion (e.g., one-third or one-fourth) of all the property of the deceased, including, in some cases, property that would be classified as separate property in a community-property state. In cases of divorce, the doctrine of 'equitable distribution' allows a court to give to the non-owning spouse as much of the property of the owning spouse as is 'fair and equitable under the circumstances'. This may in some cases reach or exceed 50 per cent of the property, and it may include property that would be classified as separate property in a community-property state.[1]

1. For the specifics, *see* Symeonides, 'In Search of New Choice-of-Law Solutions to Some Marital Property Problems of Migrant Spouses: A Response to the Critics', 13(3) *Comm. Prop. J.*, 11, 1986, 12–14, 24–25.

II. The Conflicts Problem

563. The increased mobility of the typical American family generates a considerable number of marital-property conflicts. Even when spouses do not move from one state to another, they may live in a separate-property state and acquire immovable property in a community-property state, or *vice versa*. Which law should govern the respective interests of the spouses in such property?[1]

1. Basic bibliography on this topic includes: L. McDougal, R. Felix & R. Whitten, *American Conflicts Law* (5th edn, New York, Ardsley, 2001), pp. 759–780; W. Reppy & C. Samuel, *Community Property in the United States* (6th edn, Durham, N.C., 2004); E. Scoles, P. Hay, P. Borchers & S. Symeonides, *Conflict of Laws* (4th edn, St. Paul, Minn., 2004), pp. 596–626.

564. Civil-law systems focus on the spouses, rather than on the property's location, and generally assign these matters to the law that governs the marital relationship (usually the law of the matrimonial domicile) rather than the law of the *situs* of the property. However, these systems encounter a difficult dilemma in the case of the mobile family and they vacillate between the principles of immutability and mutability of the law governing the matrimonial regime. Some systems take the position that the law governing the regime at the beginning of the marital relationship remains applicable at the end of the relationship, regardless of any intervening change of domicile.[1] Other systems provide that the change of matrimonial domicile brings about a change in the law governing the matrimonial regime, a change that may be partial or total, prospective only or also retrospective.[2] In all instances, these systems recognize the freedom of the spouses to agree on the law governing their property relations.[3] However, as is the case with other choice-of-law agreements, the spouses' agreement may not exceed the public policy limits of the otherwise governing law.

1. *See*, e.g., Peruvian Civ. Code, Art. 2078; Argentine Draft, Art. 24; Austrian PIL codification §19; Greek Civ. Code, Art. 15; Bustamante Code, Art. 187.
2. *See*, e.g., Swiss PIL codification, Art. 55; German EGBGB, Art. 15; Hungarian PIL codification §39; Spanish Civ. Code Art. 9; and Hague Convention on the Law Applicable to Matrimonial Property Regimes, Arts 6–8 (1978).
3. *See*, e.g., Austrian PIL codification, §19; German EGBGB, Art. 15(II); Swiss PIL codification, Arts 52–53; Spanish Civ. Code, Art. 9; Hague Convention on the Law Applicable to Matrimonial Property Regimes, Art. 3.

565. Common-law jurisdictions, including most American states that follow the community-property system, also recognize the spouses' freedom to agree on the governing law, subject to the same public policy limits.[1] However, in contrast to civil-law systems, common-law systems focus *on the property* of the spouses, rather than on the spouses themselves. If the property in question is immovable, then the 'whole law' of the *situs* state governs the respective rights of the spouses.[2] If the property is movable, the applicable law is, in principle, the law of the state in which the acquiring spouse was domiciled *at the time of the acquisition*.[3] The italicized phrase means that when the spouses change their domicile, the movables they acquired in the new domicile will be governed by the law of the new domicile. Indeed, since the early 19th century, American conflicts law adopted the principle of *mutability* of the law governing the property relations of spouses.[4] However, American conflicts law remains divided as to whether this mutability should be prospective only or also retrospective, that is, whether movables the spouses acquired before the change of domicile should be governed by the law of the former or the new domicile.

1. *See*, e.g., *Restatement (Second)* §258(2).
2. *See*, *id.* §§233–234.
3. *See*, *id.* §258.
4. *See Saul* v. *His Creditors*, 5 Mart. (n.s.) 569 (La. 1827).

566. Before exploring this question, it is important to reiterate that the mere change of domicile does not *ipso facto* alter any existing property rights in assets previously acquired.[1] Rather, the question is whether the assets acquired in the former domicile should be subjected (for certain purposes) to the law of the new domicile when a 'critical' and pertinent event (e.g., the termination of the marriage by divorce or death) occurs after the change of domicile. The remainder of this Section discusses the four approaches developed in the United States for answering the above question.[2] To facilitate the explanation of this complex matter, the discussion employs a hypothetical scenario involving a mobile couple, Henry and Wilma.

1. *See* Restatement (Second) §259.
2. For discussions of and citations to cases and other authorities, *see* E. Scoles, P. Hay, P. Borchers & S. Symeonides, *Conflict of Laws* (4th edn, St. Paul, Minn., 2004), pp. 597–626.

III. The Problem of Moving Spouses

A. From a Separate-Property State to a Community-Property State

567. In this scenario, Henry and his wife Wilma lived most of their married lives in state X, a separate-property state. During that time, Henry acquired in his own name movable assets worth a total of 3 million dollars (USD), while Wilma stayed at home raising their children. The law of state X provides that: (1) in the case divorce, Wilma would be entitled to fifty per cent of Henry's USD 3 million under that state's equitable distribution doctrine; and (b) in the case of Henry's death before divorce, Wilma would be entitled to a statutory share of one-third of the USD 3 million. Suppose, however, that the 'critical event' (i.e., the divorce or Henry's death) does not occur while the spouses are domiciled in state X but rather six months after they moved their domicile to state Y, a community-property state. Wilma would then be before a state Y court, either in a divorce or a succession proceeding, asserting her rights or claims to the USD 3 million. Should the court determine these rights by applying the law of the former domicile, state X, or the law of the forum and present domicile, state Y?[1]

1. Similar questions would arise if, with or without a change of domicile to state Y, Henry used the USD 3 million to buy an immovable in state Y. The questions then would be whether Wilma would be entitled to any rights in this immovable and whether this question should be answered under the law of state Y or state X.

1. The Traditional Approach

568. The first approach for answering this problem is referred to hereafter as the 'traditional approach'. Under this approach, the court applies the law of the former domicile (state X) in determining the ownership of the property (i.e., in classifying it as community or separate) and then applies the law of the new domicile (state Y, the forum state), to distribute the property between the spouses. Because state X is a separate-property state, its law probably would not recognize the distinction between separate and community property. Consequently, all USD 3 million would be classified as Henry's separate property. Because state Y is a community-property state – and under its law the separate property of one spouse is, in principle, free of any claims in favour of the other – Wilma will receive nothing out of Henry's three million dollars.[1] To use a proverbial expression, Wilma falls between the cracks of the two systems. She loses, not only the protection of the law of her former domicile (state X), but also the protection that state Y grants to similarly situated wives who were domiciled there throughout the marriage. This approach distorts the common policy of both states in protecting the non-owning spouse, albeit through different means. It is not surprising then that this approach is no longer followed, having been superseded by statutes in most states.

1. For cases applying this approach, *see*, e.g., *In re Thornton's Estate*, 33 P.2d 1 (Cal. 1934), *Stephen* v. *Stephen*, 284 P.2d 158 (Ariz. 1930); *Eggemeyer* v. *Eggemeyer*, 554 S.W.2d 137 (Tex. 1977).

2. The Pure Borrowed-Law Approach

569. The second approach is the 'pure borrowed law approach'. It 'borrows' and applies in its entirety the law of the former domicile (state X), both to classify and to distribute the property. Under this approach, the court would award Wilma USD 1.5 million in a divorce proceeding and USD 1 million in a succession proceeding, that is, exactly the same amounts she would have received in a state X court.[1] This approach produces perfect justice. The only problems with this approach are logistical, especially in cases in which the parties have moved though several states before ending up in the forum state. In such cases, the burden of tracing back the property through the multiple domiciles and ascertaining and applying the laws of all previous domiciles can be considerable.

1. For cases applying this approach, *see*, e.g., *Hughes* v. *Hughes*, 573 P.2d. 1194 (N.M. 1978); *Berle* v. *Berle*, 546 P.2d 407 (Idaho 1976); *Rau* v. *Rau*, 432 P.2d 910 (Ariz. Ct. App. 1967).

3. The Pure Quasi-Community Property Approach

570. The third approach, the pure 'quasi-community approach', compensates too much for the logistical burdens of the previous approach and, moving to the other extreme, applies forum law (state Y), both to classify and to distribute the property. California was the first state to develop this approach, and other community-property states like Texas have followed.[1] California's version is more comprehensive in that, *inter alia*, it applies to both divorce and death cases. For divorce purposes, the California Family Code defines 'quasi-community property' as including 'all real or personal property, wherever situated, . . . acquired . . . by either spouse while domiciled elsewhere which would have been community property if the spouse who acquired the property had been domiciled in [California] at the time of its acquisition'.[2] Upon divorce or legal separation, the court is authorized to treat the quasi-community property as if it were community property and to divide it 'equally' between the spouses.[3] For succession purposes, the California Probate Code defines quasi-community property as including '[a]ll personal property wherever situated, and all real property situated in [California] . . . acquired by a decedent while domiciled elsewhere that would have been the community property of the decedent and the surviving spouse if the decedent had been domiciled in [California] at the time of its acquisition'.[4] If the acquiring spouse dies while domiciled in California,[5] 'one-half of the decedent's quasi-community property belongs to the surviving spouse and the other half belongs to the decedent'.[6]

1. For citations, *see* Symeonides, 'In Search of New Choice-of-Law Solutions to Some Marital Property Problems of Migrant Spouses: A Response to the Critics', 13(3) *Comm. Prop. J.*, 11, 1986, 26. California and Idaho apply this approach to both divorce and succession cases, while Texas and Arizona apply it to divorce cases only.
2. Cal. Fam. Code §4803. Section 5110 of the same Code provides that, unless expressly designated as separate property, 'all real property situated in this state and all personal property wherever situated acquired during the marriage by a married person while domiciled in this state, . . . is community property'.
3. Cal. Fam. Code §§4800, 4800.5.
4. Cal. Prob. Code §66.
5. If the decedent was domiciled outside California at the time of death, California's scheme of quasi-community property is in principle inapplicable. However, §120 of the Probate Code provides that, with regard to California real property that is not classified as community property, the surviving spouse 'has the same right to elect to take a portion of or interest in such property against the will of the decedent as though the property were located in the decedent's domicile at death'.
6. Cal. Prob. Code §101. The same 50:50 ratio applies to community property regardless of whether the decedent spouse was domiciled in California at the time of death. *See id.* §100.

571. Thus, under the above provisions, if state Y were California, the amount that a California court would award Wilma would depend exclusively on how much of the USD 3 million qualified as community property under California's internal law and hence as quasi-community property under the above provisions. If all of the USD 3 million would qualify as community property, then the court will award USD 1.5 million to Wilma, both in case of divorce and in the case of Henry's death. If none of the USD 3 million qualified, then the court will award Wilma nothing. In between these two extremes lie several intermediate possibilities. However, in most of these possibilities Wilma will receive less, or much less, than she would have received in state X. Thus, this approach avoids the logistical problems of the borrowed law approach and, in some cases, reaches the same results by giving Wilma the same percentage she would have received in her previous domicile. In other cases, however, the quasi-community approach can be as unfair as the traditional approach by giving Wilma a much lower percentage.

4. The Louisiana Approach

572. The 1991 Louisiana codification adopted a fourth approach combining the quasi-community and the borrowed-law approaches.[1] Under the Louisiana approach, the state Y court begins with the forum's classification rules. If all the property qualifies as community under those rules, the court treats it as such under the forum's distribution rules and the case ends there.[2] Applied to the above hypothetical, if all of the USD 3 million would be classified as community property under state Y's classification rules, then the court would apply the distribution rules of state Y and award Wilma USD 1.5 million. In this case this approach produces the same result as would the pure quasi-community approach, good or bad.

1. *See* La. Civ. Code Ann. Art. 3526. For an explanation of the rationale and operation of this article and its differences from the pure quasi-community approach, *see* Symeonides, 'In Search of New Choice-of-Law Solutions to Some Marital Property Problems of Migrant Spouses: A Response to the Critics', 13(3) *Comm. Prop. J.*, 11, 1986, 15–23.
2. *See* La. Civ. Code Ann. Art. 3526(1) ('Property that is classified as community property under the law of [the forum] shall be treated as community property under that law').

573. The differences between these two approaches become apparent when some or all of the USD 3 million does not qualify as quasi-community property under state Y law. Then, with regard to the part of the property that does not so qualify, the Louisiana approach authorizes the application of the distribution rules of state X.[1] For example, if none of the USD 3 million qualifies as community property under state Y law, the court will apply the distribution rules of state X and award Wilma USD 1.5 million in a divorce proceeding or USD 1 million in a succession proceeding. In the identical case, Wilma would receive nothing under the pure quasi-community approach.

1. *See* La. Civ. Code Ann. Art. 3526(2) ('Property that is not classified as community property under the law of [the forum] shall be treated as the separate property of the acquiring spouse. However, the other spouse shall be entitled, in value only, to the same rights with regard to this property as would be granted by the law of the state in which the acquiring spouse was domiciled at the time of acquisition').

574. The Louisiana approach adopts the aspirational objectives of the borrowed-law approach but avoids most of its logistical difficulties. It also utilizes the practical advantages of the pure quasi-community approach (application of the forum's classification rules) but avoids its pitfalls (giving Wilma less than she would have received in her former domicile). In divorce cases, the Louisiana approach succeeds in treating Wilma the same way she would have been treated in her former domicile, correcting the problems posed by the pure quasi-community approach. In some death cases, however, the Louisiana approach 'overcorrects' the problem by giving Wilma more than she would have received under the internal laws of either state Y or state X. Thus, if the pure quasi-community approach is guilty of 'under-protecting' Wilma in many divorce and succession cases, the Louisiana approach is guilty of 'over-protecting' Wilma in many succession cases. To be sure, over-protection of the non-owning spouse can be problematic because it comes at the expense of Henry or his heirs. However, unlike under-protection which puts all cards in the hands of the owning spouse, over-protection gives some leverage to the non-owning spouse. In turn, this leverage makes more likely a matrimonial agreement, before or after the change of domicile, or a testamentary arrangement than can equalize the spouses' position.

B. From a Community-Property State to a Separate-Property State

575. Let us now reverse the facts of the original scenario, so that state X, the former domicile, is a community-property state and state Y, the new domicile, is a separate-property state. Everything else remains the same, that is, the marriage is terminated six months after Henry and Wilma moved to state Y, either because of a divorce or because of Henry's death. If the marriage terminates by Henry's death rather than by divorce and state Y is one of the 14 states that have adopted the Uniform Disposition of Community Property Rights at Death Act of 1971 (UDCPRDA),[1] the state Y court will have a clear guidance on how to resolve potential conflicts. This Act applies to 'all personal property, wherever situated' that was acquired 'as community property under the laws of another jurisdiction', and to 'any real property situated in this state' that was acquired through funds that were classified 'as community property under the laws of another jurisdiction'.[2]

1. These states are Alaska, Arkansas, Colorado, Connecticut, Florida, Hawaii, Kentucky, Michigan, Montana, New York, North Carolina, Oregon, Virginia and Wyoming. *See* 8A U.L.A. (West Sup. 2007).
2. UDCPRDA §1.

576. The Act treats this property as if it were community property by equally dividing it between the surviving spouse and the decedent spouse's estate. The Act provides that the surviving spouse's half 'is not subject to testamentary disposition by the decedent or distribution under the laws of succession of this State',[1] and that the decedent's half 'is subject to testamentary disposition or distribution under the laws of succession of this State . . . [and] is not subject to the surviving spouse's right to elect against the will'.[2]

Thus, if under the law of state X, the USD 3 million was classified as community property, then the Act would give Wilma half, without a claim against the other half. If, under the law of state X, the USD 3 million was classified as Henry's separate property, then it would not fall under the scope of this Act, and it would be subject to the general inheritance laws of state Y, including Wilma's possible forced share or 'right to take against [Henry's] will'.[3]

1. *See id.* §3 ('one-half of the property . . . is the property of the surviving spouse and is not subject to testamentary disposition by the decedent or distribution under the laws of succession of this State'.).
2. *Id.* The Act 'does not affect the rights creditors'. *Id.* §6.
3. As good as it is, this Act does not apply to divorce cases. However, the judicially created 'equitable distribution' doctrine gives courts the flexibility of giving to one of the spouses as much of the property of the other spouse as is fair and equitable under the circumstances. One of these circumstances is whether the property was acquired as community property in another state. For a case addressing similar questions, *see In re Marriage of Whelchel*, 476 N.W.2d 104 (Iowa. Ct. App. 1991).

577. The same results would follow if Henry and Wilma never left state X (the community-property state), but Henry used this amount to buy an immovable in his own name in state Y, a separate-property state. If, under state X law, the USD 3 million would be classified as community property, then the Act would be applicable and the immovable would be divided as described above.[1]

1. Although the Act does not apply to divorce cases, courts have reached the same results as provided in the Act. *See Depas* v. *Mayo*, 11 Mo. 314 (1848); *Palmer* v. *Palmer*, 654 So.2d 1 (Miss. 1995).

§3. Successions[1]

I. 'Unity' or 'Scission' of the Estate

578. At a general level, the most pronounced difference between the conflicts laws of the civil-law and common-law traditions on the subject of successions may be synopsized in two words – 'unity' and 'scission' of the estate. Unity of the estate is the operating principle in most civil-law systems.[2] With few exceptions, these systems treat the estate as a single unit to be governed by a single law, regardless of whether the estate consists of movables or immovables or their respective location. The applicable law may be either the law of the last nationality (*lex patriae*) or the last domicile (*lex domicilii*) of the deceased, but it is always his or her personal law.

1. Basic bibliography for the topics discussed in this Section includes: L. McDougal, R. Felix & R. Whitten, *American Conflicts Law* (5th edn, New York, Ardsley, 2001), pp. 649–694; E. Scoles, P. Hay, P. Borchers & S. Symeonides, *Conflict of Laws* (4th edn, St. Paul, Minn., 2004), pp. 1109–1141.
2. For citations and exceptions, *see* Symeonides, 'Exploring the "Dismal Swamp": The Revision of Louisiana's Conflicts Law on Successions', 47 *La. L. Rev.* 1029, 1987, 1035–1036.

579. In contrast, 'scission' has been the operating principle in most common law systems, including the American. These systems differentiate sharply between immovables and movables and assign the former the law of the *situs* (*lex rei sitae*) and the latter to the law of the last domicile of the deceased.

Obviously, the principle of scission means that the succession of a single person may have to be governed by two or more sets of laws. Thus, if a person died domiciled in state X and owned movables and immovables in states Y and Z, her succession will be governed by three different laws: the law of state X for all her movables and the law of states Y and Z respectively for her immovables. Even when the various states differ on issues that pertain to the personal qualities of the individual testator, such as testamentary capacity, this scheme results in treating the same testator as capable in one state and incapable in another. As the great comparatist Ernst Rabel once observed, '[t]hat eight pieces of land need eight different systems of liberty or restraint in testation is bad enough . . . ; but that even the capacity to make a will . . . [is] independent in principle in every jurisdiction where an immovable is found transgresses the borders of tolerable tradition'.[1]

1. Ernst Rabel, *The Conflict of Laws: A Comparative Study* (1958), vol. 4, p. 272.

580. This lack of uniformity in the treatment of a single estate has not troubled common law courts or legislatures. One reason could be that this was the only way to obtain another kind of uniformity which, for historical reasons, was considered more desirable – uniformity of treatment of all immovables within each jurisdiction, regardless of the domicile of the owner or other personal and thus non-stable factors. This preoccupation with land and intrastate uniformity with regard to land may be traced to the feudal conceptions of tenurial ownership of land which prevailed during the period immediately following the Norman conquest in England. In a society that essentially did not recognize individual ownership of land, it was natural that the location of the land, and not the domicile of the tenant, would be the most significant factor. As one author put it, '[t]he feudal lords could not allow the descent of their land to be affected if one of their vassals should acquire a foreign domicile'.[1] It was different with regard to movables which, after all, were susceptible not only to individual ownership but also to movement from one place to another. Their location at a given place at a given time was therefore much less important, if only because it could well be transient. Thus, the domicile of the owner seemed to be a more meaningful connecting factor.

1. Martin Wolff, *Private International Law* (2nd edn 1950), p. 567.

581. Much has changed since those formative years. For instance, substantive common law eventually recognized a concept of individual land ownership encompassing a power of disposition approximating that in the civil law. In fact, the lack of forced heirship in the common law would suggest an even greater power of disposition in the individual owner at death. In both systems, the relative disparity in economic value between movables and immovables has all but disappeared. Yet, despite the disappearance of many substantive-law differences, the conflicts laws of these two worlds have not converged in any appreciable degree. The labels of 'unity' and 'scission' continue to symbolize two quite different conflicts philosophies between the two worlds. Anglo-American conflicts systems continue to maintain a sharp dichotomy between movables and immovables, looking at succession more in terms of the sovereign's power over property than as a means of transmitting personal or familial wealth from one generation to the next. Despite recent injections of what some call 'realism' civil law systems continue to look at succession from the perspective of the society to which the deceased and his family belonged, and to attribute much less significance to the location of his property as such.

II. The Two Restatements

582. Both conflicts Restatements follow the principle of scission faithfully and persistently. The First Restatement assigns all issues of testate and intestate succession of immovables to the whole law of the *situs*[1] and all issues of succession of movables to the whole law of the decedent's last domicile.[2] In typical fashion, the Restatement does not allow exceptions.

The Restatement (Second) abandons its usual equivocation and essentially reproduces the same regime. It calls for the application of 'the law that would be applied by the courts of the *situs*'[3] for immovables, and 'the law that would be applied by the courts of the state where the decedent was domiciled at the time of his death'[4] for movables. The notion of aiming for the state that 'with regard to the particular issue' has 'the most significant relationship' – the two standard phrases found everywhere in the rest of the Restatement – is absent from this chapter of the Restatement. The only flexibility the Restatement (Second) allows is through the repeated statement that the *situs* courts will 'usually'[5] (i.e., perhaps not always) apply their own local law.

1. *See Restatement* §§245–250.
2. *See id.* §§300–310.
3. *See Restatement (Second)* §§236–242.
4. *See id.* §§260–265.
5. *See id.* §§236–239, 241–242, 261–263, 265.

583. The *situs* rule has the same vast scope in the Restatement (Second) as it had in the first Restatement.[1] The rule covers: (1) the formal validity of a testament and its revocation, as well as its substantive validity, including the capacity of the testator and the capacity of devisee;[2] (2) the statutory interest of the surviving spouse and his or her right to take against the will;[3] (3) the right of adopted or illegitimate children to inherit;[4] and (4) all issues of intestate succession.[5]

1. The same is true of the domicile rule for movables in the two Restatements. The rule covers (1) the formal validity of the testament and its revocation, as well as its substantive validity, including the capacity of the testator and the capacity of the devisee (*see id.* §263); (2) the statutory interest of the surviving spouse and his or her right to take against the will (*id.* §265); (3) the right of adopted or illegitimate children to inherit (*see id.* §§261–262) and (d) all issues of intestate succession. (*see id.* §260).
2. *See id.* §239. With regard to the construction of the will, §240 allows the testator to designated the applicable law, but in the absence of such a designation, the will is construed under the law that would be applied by the courts of the *situs*.
3. *See id.* §239.
4. *See id.* §§237–238. The Restatement (Second) does not address the right of children to a 'forced share', apparently because common law states do not grant this right.
5. *See id.* §236.

584. Even if one accepts the need for a *situs* rule, a rule with such a vast scope cannot survive the scrutiny of a modern policy analysis. Indeed, the *situs* state *qua situs* has no interest in regulating matters such as: (a) whether a non-domiciliary has the proper age or mental capacity to make a testament, or whether he was subject to undue influence at the time he made the testament (b) whether children or spouses should be guaranteed a certain minimum share of the decedent's estate (forced heirship, statutory share), or whether illegitimate children can inherit and how much, or whether an adopted child also can inherit from her biological parents. The rules that regulate these matters embody certain societal value judgments that have nothing to do with land utilization or certainty of title – the only legitimate concerns of the *situs* state. If the decedent and all the affected parties are domiciled in one state and the land is situated in another, these value judgments belong to the legislative competence of the latter state.

III. Legislative Interventions

585. At least one state, Louisiana, has succeeded in carving out significant exceptions from the *situs* rule which cover all of the above issues. For example, with regard to testamentary capacity and vices of consent (such as error, duress, or undue influence), the 1991 Louisiana codification adopted a 'validation rule' which upholds the testament if it is valid under the law of the testator's domicile at either the time the testament was made or at the time of death.[1] This rule applies not only to movables but also to all immovables, regardless of their respective *situses*. With regard to movables, this rule differs from the prevailing American rule which mandates the application of the whole law of the state in which the testator was domiciled 'at the time of death',[2] regardless of whether it upholds the testament. The codification also recognizes that Louisiana's unique forced heirship law reflects societal judgments directed at Louisiana families, rather than Louisiana immovables. Consequently, the codification provides that, even when the estate consists of Louisiana immovables, Louisiana's forced heirship law does not apply if the deceased was domiciled outside Louisiana at the time of death and left no forced heirs domiciled in that state at that time.[3] In the converse situation involving a Louisiana decedent and heirs and a non-Louisiana immovable, the codification provides for inclusion of the value of that immovable in calculating the value of the estate and the heirs' forced shares.[4]

1. *See* La. Civ. Code Ann. Art. 3529. Art. 3530 provides that, for both immovables and movables, the capacity or unworthiness of an heir or legatee is determined under the law of the state in which the deceased was domiciled at the time of death. For discussion of the rationale of these articles, *see* Symeonides, 'Exploring the "Dismal Swamp": Revising Louisiana's Conflicts Law on Successions', 47 *La. L. Rev.* 1029, 1987, 1056–1073.
2. *Restatement (Second)* §263.
3. *See* La. Civ. Code Ann. Art. 3533.
4. *See* La. Civ. Code Ann. Art. 3534. For discussion of the rationale of these two articles, *see* Symeonides, 'Exploring the "Dismal Swamp"', *supra* note 1, 1092–1097.

586. Other states have made smaller modifications to the traditional regime. One widespread but rather small-scale modification involves the issue of testamentary formalities. As noted earlier, under the two Restatements and traditional common law, the formal validity of wills was governed by the law of the *situs* with regard to immovables, and by the law of the last domicile of the decedent with respect to movables. This rule, described as being 'unwisely, arbitrarily and unphilosophically' made,[1] has been expanded and liberalized by statutes modelled after the Uniform Wills Act of 1910, which was later replaced by the Uniform Probate Code. These statutes supplement rather than replace the traditional common law rule. They contain 'rules of validation', namely, rules designed to validate the testament by alternative references to the laws of any of the states enumerated therein that would uphold the testament. Under the Uniform Probate Code, these states are the state of making of the testament, or the state where, at the time of the making or at the time of death, the testator was domiciled, resided, or was a national.[2]

1. Rabel, *The Conflict of Laws: A Comparative Study* 290 (1958) vol. 4, p. 290 (*quoting* Phillimore).
2. *See* Unif. Probate Code §2–506. The Code has been adopted the following 17 states: Alaska, Arizona, Colorado, Florida, Hawaii, Idaho, Maine, Michigan, Minnesota, Montana, Nebraska, New Jersey, New Mexico, North Dakota, South Carolina, South Dakota, and Utah. Many other states have adopted similar statutes. *See*, e.g., Cal. Prob. Code §6113; N.Y. Est. Powers & Trusts Law §3–5.1(b) and (c); Wis. Stat. Ann. §853.05. The United States is not a party to the 1961 Hague Convention on the Conflicts of Laws Relating to the Form of Testamentary Dispositions, which is more liberal.

587. The Uniform Probate Code has taken the bolder step of allowing the testator to choose the applicable law, within certain public policy limitations. Sections 2–602 of the Code provides:

> The meaning and legal effect of a disposition in a will shall be determined by the local law of a particular state selected by the testator in his instrument unless the application of that law is contrary to the [forum's] provisions relating to the [surviving spouse's] elective share . . . , the provisions relating to exempt property and allowances . . . , or any other public policy of [the forum] State otherwise applicable to the disposition.[1]

This provision, which does not impose any geographical limits to the testator's choice of law,[2] applies both to movables and immovables and allows the testator's chosen law to determine not only the 'meaning' but also the 'effect' of a disposition. However, the testator's choice of law may not deprive the surviving spouse[3] of certain guaranteed rights or exceed other public policy limitations.

1. Unif. Probate Code §2–602 (1969 version). The 1990 revision of the Code extends this principle beyond wills to all 'governing instruments' *See* Unif. Probate Code §§2–703 (1990 revision).
2. In contrast, the 1989 Hague Convention on the Law Applicable to the Estates of Deceased Persons, which also allows a testator to choose the applicable law, provides that such a choice is effective 'only if at the time of the designation or of his death [the testator] was a national of that State or had his habitual residence there'. *Id.* Art. 5(1). The United States is not a party to this convention. Other systems such as those of Switzerland, Italy, and Quebec, have recently accorded testators limited freedom to choose the applicable law, but have subjected that choice to both geographical and substantive limitations. *See* Symeonides, *Private International Law at the End of the 20th Century: Progress or Regress?* (The Hague, London, Boston, 2000), pp. 56–57.
3. The Uniform Probate Code does not contain a similar express protection for children because, with the exception of Louisiana, most states do not provide for such automatic protection in the form of forced heirship.

588. In contrast, the state of New York has enacted a unilateral rule taking the notion of testator choice a bit too far. Subdivision (h) of Section 3–5.1 of the New York's Estates Powers and Trusts Law (EPTL) provides:

> Whenever a testator, not domiciled in this state at the time of death, provides in his will that he elects to have the disposition of his property situated in this state governed by the laws of this state, the intrinsic validity, including the testator's general capacity, effect, interpretation, revocation or alteration of any such disposition is determined by the local law of this state.[1]

This provision requires the application of New York law even if the testator has never set foot in New York. All that is needed is for the testator to have sent her money to a New York bank and to 'elect' New York law in her testament. From New York's perspective, such an election renders New York law applicable to 'the intrinsic validity, including the testator's general capacity, effect, interpretation, revocation or alteration' of any such testament. This is particularly troublesome when, under the law of her domicile, the testator does not have capacity to 'elect'

New York law, or is not allowed, by election or otherwise, to make dispositions that impinge on the rights of the surviving spouse or the children.

1. N.Y. Est. Powers & Trusts Law §3–5.1(h).

589. In *Wyatt* v. *Fulrath*,[1] the court held that a rather fictitious 'election' of New York law, which was not permitted by the decedent's domicile, resulted in depriving the surviving spouse of protection guaranteed by the law of the marital domicile, Spain.[2] In *Estate of Renard*,[3] a French testator's election of New York law resulted in depriving a child of his forced heirship rights guaranteed by French law. The *Renard* court had no trouble acknowledging that the '[New York] Legislature intended subdivision (h) to permit a decedent . . . to avoid the application of the French law of forced heirship'.[4] The *Wyatt* court spoke of 'honor[ing the foreign citizens'] . . . intentional resort to the protection of our laws and their recognition of the general stability of our Government'.[5] In another case, the court spoke of foreigners who deposit funds in American banks in order to 'evade the currency laws in their native lands or to protect against the fallout from revolutions'.[6] New York may well have an economic interest in attracting bank deposits from citizens of other states or countries and thus preserving the 'general stability' of its financial institutions. However, the pertinent question is whether New York has any affirmative legitimate interest in encouraging foreigners to evade their countries' laws.

1. 211 N.E.2d 637 (N.Y. 1965).
2. In *Wyatt*, two Spanish spouses had deposited funds in a New York joint bank account and had signed a routine bank form stipulating to the application of New York law. Treating this as an 'election' of New York law, the court applied that law, which was contrary to Spanish marital property and succession law.
3. 437 N.Y.S.2d 860 (N.Y.Sur. 1981), *aff'd*, 439 N.E.2d 341 (N.Y. 1982).
4. *Estate of Renard*, 437 N.Y.S.2d at 864.
5. *Wyatt*, 211 N.E.2d at 639.
6. *Neto* v. *Thorner*, 718 F.Supp. 1222, 1226 (S.D.N.Y. 1989).

590. In contrast to *Wyatt*, the testator in *In re Estate of Rhoades*[1] was able to disinherit his surviving spouse by *not* electing to have New York law govern his succession. The testator had died domiciled in Florida and his Florida testament bequeathed his interest in a New York immovable to his first wife. His second wife, also a Florida domiciliary, instituted proceedings in New York, asserting her right of election to 'take against the will'. Under Florida law, a surviving spouse's right to take against the will does not encompass immovables situated outside Florida.

The court held that under New York law this right 'is not available to a spouse of a decedent who was not domiciled in [New York] at the time of death, unless such decedent elects . . . to have the disposition of his property situated in this state governed by the laws of this state'.[2] Because the decedent had not made such an 'election', the surviving spouse had no right to take against his will. The plaintiff argued that this was an 'absurd result [in] that if a spouse wants to disinherit his/her spouse from receiving any property located in New York, he/she can move out of New York State, establish domicile in another state, and then execute a Will in the other state disinheriting a spouse'.[3] The court responded that '[t]his result, however unfortunate, is precisely what New York law allows. . . . [I]t must be assumed that the Legislature intended this result to occur'.[4] Indeed, who said that the Legislature must be reasonable?[5]

1. 607 N.Y.S.2d 893 (N.Y. Sup. Ct. 1994).
2. *Id.* at 894.
3. *Id.*
4. *Id.*
5. For another case of disinherison by non-election, *see Saunders* v. *Saunders*, 796 So.2d 1253 (Fla. Dist. Ct. App. 2001), *rev. denied*, 819 So.2d 139 (Fla. 2002). This case involved a Florida statute providing that, 'when a nonresident decedent . . . provides in her or his will that the testamentary disposition of . . . her or his real property in this state, shall be construed and regulated by the laws of this state, the validity and effect of the dispositions shall be determined by Florida law'. F.S.A. §731.106(2). The *Saunders* decedent, a Colorado domiciliary, did *not* provide in his will for the application of Florida law to his Florida realty. The Florida court held that Colorado law would govern the succession even with regard to the Florida realty, because the statute had displaced the common-law situs rule.

Chapter 8. Statutes of Limitation

§1. Introduction

591. Statutes of limitation function in the same way as statutes establishing what is known as 'liberative' or 'extinctive prescription' in civil law systems. In these systems, the accrual of a liberative prescription period extinguishes the obligation, eliminates the obligee's ability to demand performance, and liberates the obligor from having to perform. In the common law systems, the accrual of the statutory limitation period has exactly the same effect.

The differences between civil-law and common-law systems on this subject go beyond terminology. The majority of civil law systems adopt the premise that, because liberative prescription is a mode of extinction of an obligation, prescription is a substantive matter and as such it is governed by the same law as that which governs the obligation itself.[1] As discussed in this chapter, American conflicts law has never subscribed to this premise, although recently it made a slight move in that direction.[2]

1. *See*, e.g., Swiss Federal Statute on PIL, Art. 148 (1987); Law Amending the Introductory Law to the German Civil Code, Art. 32 (1986); Spanish Civ. Code, Art. 10(10); Hungarian Decree on PIL, Sect. 30(4) (1979); Bustamante Code, Art. 229; Peruvian Civ. Code, Art. 2099; Quebec Civ. Code, Art. 3131.
2. *See infra* 605 (Uniform Act).

592. The issue is very important as a practical matter for attorneys and litigants. Every year, the fate of hundreds of lawsuits hinges on the applicable statute of limitations, be that of the forum state or of another involved state. In multistate cases, the ability of an attorney to correctly predict the court's choice of a statute makes the difference between winning and losing the lawsuit. As the discussion in this chapter illustrates, in many cases such a prediction is not easy. For example, the fact that the suit is filed within the forum's limitation period does not necessarily mean that the plaintiff will win on the issue of time. Occasionally, the converse is also true; the fact that the suit is filed after the expiration of the forum's limitation period does not necessarily mean that the suit will be dismissed as untimely. In both instances – but many more in the first than in the second category – the forum may choose to apply the statute of limitations of another involved state. This chapter discusses how American courts make that choice.[1]

1. Basic bibliography for the topics of this chapter includes: L. McDougal, R. Felix & R. Whitten, *American Conflicts Law* (5th edn, New York, Ardsley, 2001), pp. 425–440; E. Scoles, P. Hay, P. Borchers & S. Symeonides, *Conflict of Laws* (4th edn, St. Paul, Minn., 2004), pp. 129–138; R. Weintraub, *Commentary on the Conflict of Laws* (5th edn, New York, 2006), pp. 63–78.

§2. The Traditional American System

I. The Basic Approach

593. The traditional, and to a great extent current, American approach has been that statutes of limitation are always procedural and thus conflicts between these statutes are always resolved by applying the statute of the forum state.[1] In essence, through this procedural characterization, the traditional approach exempts these statutes from the scrutiny of the choice-of-law process. Codifying this approach, the First Restatement provided as follows:

> §603. If the action is barred by the statute of limitations of the forum, no action can be maintained though the action is not barred in the state where the cause of action arose.
>
> §604. If the action is not barred by the statute of limitations of the forum, an action can be maintained, though the action is barred in the state where the cause of action arose.[2]

Obviously, this approach rewards shopping for the forum that has the longest limitation period. Because in many multistate cases several states may have jurisdiction, a plaintiff who sues in the state with the longest limitation period is automatically guaranteed a victory on the issue of timeliness, even if his lawsuit was untimely in all other involved states.

1. However, for *Erie* purposes, statutes of limitation are considered substantive. *See Guaranty Trust Co.* v. *York*, 326 US 99 (1945). This means that a federal court sitting in diversity must use the forum's statute of limitation, or, in conflicts cases, the statute chosen by the forum's choice-of-law rules. *See supra* 45–48.
2. *Restatement*, §§603–604. The Uniform Statute of Limitations on Foreign Claims Act of 1957 took a more drastic position. It authorized the application of the limitation period of either the forum state or the state where the cause of action 'arose', whichever period was shorter. Its drafters had to withdraw this Act in 1978 because only three states had adopted it (Oklahoma, Pennsylvania and West Virginia).

594. One well-known case involving such a scenario is *Keeton* v. *Hustler Magazine, Inc.*,[1] in which the court applied the forum's unusually long, six-year statute of limitation to an action that was barred by the statutes of all other states of the United States. *Keeton* was a defamation action filed in New Hampshire by a New York plaintiff against a magazine publisher (a resident of Ohio and later California) arising out of a publication five years earlier. By that time, the action would be barred by the statutes of limitation of all other states. New Hampshire's only connection with the case was than one per cent of the magazine's sales occurred there. Under the 'single publication rule', the plaintiff could recover in one action damages for the injuries she suffered in all states.[2] Characterizing New Hampshire's statute of limitation as procedural, the court held that the statute applied in this case, and allowed the plaintiff's action to go forward.

1. 549 A.2d 1187 (N.H. 1988).
2. Although this rule is substantive rather than jurisdictional, it produces almost the opposite results from the rule established by the Court of Justice of the European Communities in *Fiona Shevill* v. *Press Alliance SA*, Case C 68/93, [1995] ECR I – 415, at §33, according to which the state of injury has jurisdiction only with regard to the injury that occurred in that state.

595. To its credit, the court did not simply invoke the traditional mechanical characterization; in fact it acknowledged that 'statutes of limitations do differ from other procedural rules'.[1] However, the court concluded that 'the varied purposes that statutes of limitations are meant to serve justify the application of forum law, and thus the essential treatment of such statutes as procedural rules, in most instances'.[2] After all, the court reasoned, 'the forum . . . is best able to decide when claims are . . . stale . . . and only the forum has a significant interest in insuring that its dockets are not burdened by such claims'.[3] The court concluded that, in any case in which either party is a New Hampshire resident or the cause of action arose in New Hampshire, 'the sum of our . . . interests in applying our own statute, in combination with the benefit of simplification afforded by regular application of our own rule, will tip the choice of law balance in favor of . . . our own limitations period to cases tried here'.[4]

1. *Keeton* 549 A.2d at 1192.
2. *Id.*
3. *Id.*
4. *Id.*

596. The court also asserted that New Hampshire had a certain interest in applying its statute of limitation[1] and that, although other states may have had countervailing interests, the task of assaying those interests was too complex an undertaking.[2] Finally, the court explained why it would reach the same result under Leflar's choice-influencing considerations that the court applies in substantive-law conflicts.[3]

1. *See id.* at 1193 ('Although our own interest in striking an appropriate balance between promoting protection for defendants and legitimate recovery for plaintiffs is less great than it would be if defendants or plaintiff were New Hampshire residents, it is nonetheless substantial . . . because the defendants distributed, in this State, a significant number of libelous publications giving rise to the injuries for which [plaintiff] sues. . . . [O]ur general interest in providing plaintiffs sufficient time to bring suit is enhanced when the injuries for which suit is brought were incurred in this State'.).
2. *See id.* at 1193 ('[F]oreign statutes obviously express what foreign States take to be an appropriate balance among their interests regarding courts, defendants, and plaintiffs. However, it would be nearly impossible for us to discern the weight such States intend to accord these varied interests . . . [and to] embark on the highly uncertain task of discerning precisely what weight a foreign legislature intended to accord the varied interests that statutes of limitations address'.).
3. *See id.* 1194–1198. In an eloquent dissent, Justice David Souter (later of the US Supreme Court) refuted all of the majority's conclusions.

II. Legislative Exceptions: Borrowing Statutes

597. The mechanical character of the traditional approach is problematic as a whole, but it is most deficient in cases like *Keeton* in which the forum has a longer limitation period than the other involved states. For this reason, most criticisms against – and most efforts to improve – the traditional approach have concentrated on this category of cases. As early as the middle of the 19th century, state legislatures recognized the forum-shopping problem this approach encourages and began enacting statutes known as 'borrowing statutes'. By the middle of the 20th century, 38 states had enacted such statutes in one form or another.[1]

1. For citations, *see* Symeonides, 'Louisiana Conflicts Law: Two "Surprises"', 54 *La. L. Rev.* 497, 1994, 532. The only jurisdictions that did *not* enact such a statute are Arkansas, Connecticut, the District of Columbia, Georgia, Maryland, Michigan, New Jersey, New Hampshire, New Mexico, North Dakota, South Carolina, South Dakota and Vermont. In recent years, Ohio and Texas have repealed their borrowing statute.

598. These statutes authorize the 'borrowing' and application of the limitation period of another state. Although they vary in scope and detail, all of these statutes apply only when the forum's limitation period is *longer*, not shorter, than that of the other state. The state whose law is borrowed is typically the state in which the cause of action 'arose', 'accrued', or 'originated'. In identifying that state, many courts continue to employ traditional mechanical formulae, such as the 'last event' rule in torts, even when they sit in states that have abandoned the traditional approach in tort and contract conflicts.[1]

1. *See, e.g., Global Financial Corp.* v. *Triarc Corp.*, 93 N.Y.2d 525, 715 N.E.2d 482 (1999), discussed *infra* 604; *Abraham* v. *Gen. Cas. Co. of Wisconsin*, 576 N.W.2d 46 (Wis. 1998); *Combs* v. *International Ins. Co.*, 354 F.3d 568 (6th Cir. 2004); *Bldg. Erection Services, Inc.* v. *JLG, Inc.*, 376 F.3d 800 (8th Cir. 2004); *Stupak* v. *Hoffman-La Roche, Inc.*, 315 F.Supp.2d 970 (E.D. Wis. 2004); *Shared Communications Servs., Inc.* v. *Goldenberg Rosenthal, LLP.*, 2004 WL 2609546 (S.D.N.Y. 2004); *Stivers* v. *Ellington*, 140 S.W.3d 599 (Ky. Ct. App. 2004); *Sangamon Associates, Ltd.* v. *The Carpenter 1985 Family Partnership, Ltd.*, 2004 WL 2339944 (Mo. Ct. App. 2004); *Levine* v. *Philip Morris Inc.*, 2004 WL 2334287 (N.Y. Sup. Ct. 2004); *Willits* v. *Peabody Coal Co.*, 188 F.3d 510, 1999 WL 701916 (6th Cir. 1999) (decided under Kentucky conflicts law); *Rajala, Donnelly Meiners Jordan Kline P.C.*, 193 F.3d 925 (8th Cir. 1999) (decided under Missouri conflicts law); *Merine* v. *Prudential-Bache Utility Fund, Inc.*, 859 F.Supp. 715 (S.D.N.Y. 1994); *Barsam* v. *Pure Tech International, Inc.*, 864 F.Supp. 1440 (S.D.N.Y. 1994); *Stafford* v. *International Harvester Co.*, 668 F.2d 142, 149 (2d Cir. 1981) (New York conflicts).

599. As noted earlier, these statutes differ in their specifics. For example, although the statutes of 35 out of 38 states encompass all 'actions' or 'causes of action', without regard to whether they arise out of contracts, torts, etc., Wisconsin's statute is confined to personal injury actions and Virginia's and West Virginia's statutes are confined to actions arising from contracts made and to be performed outside the forum state.[1] Moreover, many of these statutes exempt causes of action held by persons who, at the time the action accrued (and in some instances at the time of the filing), were domiciled in the forum state.[2] At least one statute has been interpreted as being applicable only if both parties are non-residents.[3]

1. *See* Symeonides, *supra* 597, at 532–533.
2. *See Huynh* v. *Chase Manhattan Bank*, 465 F.3d 992 (9th Cir. 2006) (California borrowing statute held inapplicable because plaintiffs were domiciled in forum state at time of filing, but not at the time the action accrued); *Flowers* v. *Carville*, 310 F.3d 118 (9th Cir. 2002) (differently worded Nevada statute held applicable because claimant was forum resident at time of filing, though not at time of accrual). For cases involving corporations, *see Paul Fire & Marine Ins. Co.* v. *Paw Paw's Camper City, Inc.*, 346 F.3d 153 (5th Cir. 2003); *Telular Corp.* v. *Mentor Graphics Corp.*, 282 F.Supp.2d 869 (N.D.Ill. 2003).

3. *See Telular Corp.* v. *Mentor Graphics Corp.*, 282 F.Supp.2d 869 (N.D.Ill. 2003) (involving Illinois statute).

600. Borrowing statutes are potent weapons for curtailing forum-shopping, particularly in states that have unusually long limitation periods. The lack of such a statute in New Hampshire deprived the *Keeton* court of a useful weapon. The availability of such a weapon, however, does not always guarantee its use. This point is well illustrated by cases from Mississippi which, like New Hampshire, had a six-year limitation period for tort claims until the early 1990s. These cases exhibit great reluctance to apply Mississippi's borrowing statute, even when it seems to fit a case in all respects.[1]

1. *See*, e.g., *Shewbrooks* v. *A.C. & S., Inc.*, 529 So.2d 557 (Miss. 1988); *Williams* v. *Taylor Machinery, Inc.*, 529 So.2d 606 (Miss. 1988).

III. Judicial Exceptions

601. Courts following the procedural characterization of statutes of limitation have also developed certain exceptions to the *lex fori* rule. One such exception authorizes the court to apply a foreign limitation period that is shorter than the forum's, if the foreign period is conceived or perceived as a condition for the exercise of the right so that the accrual of the period extinguishes the right itself, not just the remedy.[1] The First Restatement recognized this exception by providing that '[i]f by law of the state which has created a right of action, it is made a condition of the right that it shall expire after a certain period of limitation has elapsed, no action begun after the period has elapsed can be maintained in any state'.[2]

1. *See The Harrisburg*, 119 US 199 (1886); *Bournias* v. *Atlantic Maritime Co.*, 220 F.2d 152 (2d Cir. 1955); *Siroonian* v. *Textron, Inc.*, 844 F.2d 289 (5th Cir. 1988); *Shell Oil Co.* v. *Hickman*, 716 F.Supp. 931 (W.D. Va. 1989).
2. *See Restatement* §605.

602. The common example of the application of this exception is a wrongful death action which, not being recognized by the common law, was conferred by statute, ostensibly on the condition that it be brought within the time specified in the statute.[1] Another example is a statute of repose for product manufacturers. These statutes extinguish the victim's action after the passage of a specified number of years from the time the product was marketed, regardless of when the injury occurred. Courts usually characterize these statutes as substantive and thus employ the above exception whenever the foreign statute bars the action.[2]

1. *See Gomez* v. *ITT Educational Serv., Inc.*, 71 S.W.3d 542 (Ark. 2002).
2. *See Baxter* v. *Sturm, Ruger & Co., Inc.*, 644 A.2d 1297 (Conn. 1994); *Cosme* v. *Whitin Mach. Works, Inc.*, 632 N.E.2d 832 (Mass. 1994); *Tanges* v. *Heidelberg N. Am., Inc.*, 93 N.Y.2d 48 (1999).

IV. Current Status

603. In terms of judicial following, the American choice-of-law revolution has made only limited inroads on the traditional approach to statute of limitation conflicts. The majority of states (approximately 30), continue to follow the traditional procedural characterization of limitation periods. These states include New York, the revolution's avant-garde, and many states that have abandoned the traditional approach in tort and contract conflicts.[1]

1. Other examples include New Hampshire (*see Keeton, supra*) and Wisconsin, both of which have abandoned the traditional theory in tort and contract conflicts. In *Abraham* v. *Gen. Cas. Co. of Wisconsin*, 576 N.W.2d 46 (Wis. 1998), the Wisconsin Supreme Court reversed a lower court decision that had applied a 'center of gravity approach' in determining whether a contract cause of action was a 'foreign cause of action' for purposes of applying Wisconsin's borrowing statute. The supreme court held that 'a claim sounding in contract is a "foreign cause of action" when the final significant event giving rise to a suable claim occurs outside the state of Wisconsin'. *Id.* at 53–54. The court reaffirmed its earlier decisions which had adopted a last-event rule in applying the borrowing statute to tort causes of action and had refused to extend to such cases the flexible choice-of-law approach Wisconsin follows with regard to the merits of these actions.

604. The New York Court of Appeals rejected a plea to modernize its approach to limitation conflicts in *Global Financial Corp.* v. *Triarc Corporation.*[1] *Global* involved a contract action brought by a Delaware corporation that had its principal place of business in Pennsylvania. The action would be barred by the statutes of limitations of both Delaware and Pennsylvania but would be timely under New York's six-year statute of limitation. The plaintiff argued that, because the contract was negotiated, executed, substantially performed, and breached in New York, that state's law would be applicable to the merits of the action under New York's 'center of gravity' approach.[2] Consequently, his action 'accrued' in New York rather than elsewhere thus rendering New York's borrowing statute (CPLR 202) inapplicable.

The Court of Appeals rejected the argument by stating that 'there is a significant difference between a choice-of-law question, which is a matter of common law, and this Statute of Limitations issue, which is governed by particular terms of the CPLR'.[3] The court found no evidence that in using the word 'accrued' the New York Legislature intended it to mean anything other than 'the time when, and the place where, the plaintiff first had the right to bring the cause of action'.[4] The court concluded that, '[b]ecause . . . the borrowing statute predate[s] the substantive choice-of-law "interest analysis" test used in tort cases . . . and the . . . "center of gravity" approach used in contract cases . . . , these choice-of-law analyses are inapplicable to the question of statutory construction presented by CPLR 202'.[5] The court noted that the borrowing statute is 'designed to add clarity to the law and to provide the certainty of uniform application to litigants . . . [and] [t]his goal is better served by a rule requiring the single determination . . . than by a rule dependent on a litany of events relevant to the "center of gravity" of a contract dispute'.[6]

1. 715 N.E.2d 482 (N.Y. 1999).
2. *See Zurich Ins. Co.* v. *Shearson Lehman Hutton*, 642 N.E.2d 1065 (N.Y. 1994), discussed *supra* at 172; *Matter of Allstate Ins. Co. [Stolarz]*, 613 N.E.2d 936 (N.Y. 1993).

3. *Global*, 715 N.E.2d at 484.
4. *Id.*
5. *Id.* 485.
6. *Id.* at 485–486. The court then cited with approval cases that held that a cause of action for economic injury such as the one involved here accrues in the state where the plaintiff resides and sustains the economic impact of the loss. In this case, that state would be either Pennsylvania or Delaware but, because the action was barred under the law of both states, it was unnecessary to determine in which of the two the action accrued. Either way, the action was barred under New York's borrowing statute.

§3. Modern Approaches

I. The New Uniform Act

605. In 1982, the Commissioners on Uniform State Laws promulgated a new uniform act,[1] which, somewhat surprisingly, moved to the other end of the spectrum. It adopted the premise that limitation periods are a substantive matter that should be governed by the law of the state on which the claim is 'substantively based' (hereafter *lex causae*).[2] Section 2 of the Uniform Act provides:

> [I]f a claim is substantively based: (1) upon the law of one other state, the limitation period of that state applies; or (2) upon the law of more than one state, the limitation period of one of those states chosen by the law of conflict of laws of th[e forum], applies.[3]

Recognizing that the forum often has important interests in matters of limitation, or that its views on the matter deserve deference in certain cases, the Act makes concessions in favour of the *lex fori*. Section 4 of the Act authorizes resort to the *lex fori* if the limitation period of the *lex causae* is 'substantially different' from the limitation period of the forum state and 'has not afforded a fair opportunity to sue upon, or imposes an unfair burden in defending against, the claim'.[4] Indeed, a foreign limitation period that the *lex fori* considers unduly short may offend the forum's sense of fairness to plaintiffs, despite the fact that a short period reduces the forum courts' workload. Conversely, a foreign limitation period that the *lex fori* considers unduly long, may offend the forum's sense of fairness to defendants, even if the particular defendant is not a domiciliary of the forum state.

1. *See* Uniform Conflict of Laws-Limitations Act, 12 U.L.A. 56 (1988). For an authoritative discussion of the Act by the Chairman of the Drafting Committee, *see* Leflar, 'The New Conflicts–Limitations Act', 35 *Mercer L. Rev.* 461, 1984.
2. Although not directly influenced by the civil law, the new Act coincidentally reflects the civil-law approach of characterizing statutes of limitations as substantive. *See supra* 591.
3. Uniform Act, §2.
4. *Id.* §4.

606. This Act has been adopted by Arkansas, Colorado, Montana, North Dakota, Oregon and Washington.[1] *Cropp* v. *Interstate Distributor Co.*,[2] an Oregon case, is representative of cases decided under the Act. *Cropp* involved the question of how a court identifies the state on whose law the claim is 'substantively based' in applying Section 2 of the Act. *Cropp* arose out of a California traffic accident in which two Oregon domiciliaries had been injured by a truck owned by a Washington corporation and operated by a Nevada driver. Sixteen months after the accident, plaintiffs sued both the owner and the driver of the truck in Oregon. The action would have been timely under Oregon's two-year statute of limitation but not under California's one-year limitation. The plaintiffs charged the defendant driver with 'negligen[ce] in failing to keep a proper lookout, failing to keep his vehicle under control, [and] driving his truck at a speed that was greater than reasonable and prudent under the circumstances'.[3] Correctly perceiving these charges as pertaining to conduct-regulation (although without using this terminology), the court concluded that they had to be governed by the substantive law of California, including its Vehicle Code.[4] Accordingly, the court held that the plaintiffs' claims were 'substantively based' upon California law, and pursuant to the Act, California's one-year statute of limitation was applicable, barring the action.

1. In 1999, Arkansas repealed its earlier adoption of the Act. *See Gomez* v. *ITT Educational Services, Inc.*, 71 S.W.3d 542 (Ark. 2002).
2. 880 P.2d 464 (Or. Ct. App. 1994).
3. *Id.* at 465.
4. *Id.* at 465–566. 'Oregon motor vehicle laws do not define or regulate the operation of motor vehicles in California'. *Id.*

607. In a dissenting opinion, Judge Rossman strongly disputed the majority's conclusion that the plaintiffs' claim was 'substantively based' on California law, contending instead that the state on whose law the claim is substantively based should be identified through a more complete choice-of-law analysis. However, rather than undertaking such an analysis of the *substantive basis* of the claim, the dissent focused primarily on the conflict *between the limitation laws* of the involved states. This analysis led to the conclusion that this was a false conflict in which only Oregon had an interest in applying its statute of limitation. The conclusion was based on the otherwise correct assumptions that: (1) Oregon was interested in applying its two-year limitation for the protection of Oregon plaintiffs; (2) the states in which the two defendants were domiciled, Washington and Nevada, had exhibited no interest in protecting them since both states provided for longer limitations periods than did Oregon and California; and (3) California did not have any interest in applying its one-year limitation, which was intended to protect California courts and California defendants, neither of whom was involved in this case.

608. To the extent that Judge Rossman's analysis focused on the conflicting limitation laws rather than on the potentially conflicting tort laws, the analysis was eminently appropriate. The problem was that – unlike the approaches discussed in the next two sections – both the wording and the background of the Uniform Act make it clear that it does not contemplate a separate analysis of the *statute-of-*

limitation conflict, as opposed to the underlying substantive-law conflict.[1] This is one of the Act's major flaws.

1. Section 2(2) of the Act, *supra* 605, contemplates a (perhaps separate) choice-of-law analysis only when the claim is 'substantively based . . . [u]pon the law of more than one state'.

609. Other cases decided under the Uniform Act, have accepted its single-analysis premise. For example, in *Rice* v. *Dow Chemical Co.*,[1] a products liability case, the court was faced with a conflict between the three-year statute of limitation of the forum, Washington, and the two-year statute of limitation of the state of the injury, Oregon. Finding that the substantive law of Oregon was applicable to the merits of the action, the court concluded, without a separate choice-of-law analysis, that the claim would be 'substantively based' on Oregon law, thus making applicable Oregon's statute of limitation barring the action.[2]

Williams v. *State*[3] involved a wrongful death action filed against the states of Oregon and Washington after the expiration of Oregon's two-year limitation but before the expiration of Washington's three-year limitation. Plaintiff's decedent, an Oregon resident, was killed when his truck collided with the superstructure on the Washington side of a bridge that connects Oregon and Washington.[4] With regard to plaintiff's substantive claims, the Washington court compared the two states' contacts under the Restatement (Second) and found them to be 'nearly equal, although slightly more significant for Washington'.[5] Noting that 'duplicate prizes are not awarded in case of ties',[6] the court opined that Section 145 of the Restatement (Second) 'makes clear that forum law applies in such cases'.[7] The court held that the forum's statute of limitation also applied, noting that, under *Rice*, the limitations issue is '"not subject to conflict of laws methodology" because Washington adopted the Uniform Conflict of Laws-Limitation Act'.[8]

1. 875 P.2d 1213 (1994).
2. For another case decided under the Uniform Act and adopting the same position, *see Hall* v. *Summit Contractors, Inc.*, 156 S.W.3d 175 (Ark. 2004).
3. 885 P.2d 845 (Wash. Ct. App. 1994).
4. The bridge had been constructed and was maintained under agreement by both states, but the side on which the accident had occurred was maintained by Washington.
5. 885 P.2d at 849.
6. *Id.*
7. *Id.* at 850.
8. *Id.* (quoting *Rice, supra*). Without entirely avoiding such an analysis, the court concluded that 'Washington's interests are greater in relation to the statute of limitation issue'. *Id.* Thus, plaintiff's action against the state of Washington was allowed to proceed.

610. Although the Uniform Act is a significant improvement over the traditional *lex fori* approach, the Act falls short in two respects. The first is that, as the above cases illustrate, the Act does not contemplate a separate analysis of the limitation conflict, as opposed to the underlying substantive law conflict. The second is that the Act may have overcorrected the traditional approach by assuming that statutes of limitation are always substantive. Sometimes, this is simply not the case. For example, some statutes of limitation are designed to serve purely procedural interests, such as relieving the courts from the burden of hearing stale claims. When the forum state has such a statute with a shorter period than the foreign statute, then (unless the Section 4 exception is applicable), the Act deprives the forum of the ability to protect those interests.

II. New Judicial Approaches

611. The clearest departure from the traditional approach came in the 1973 decision of the New Jersey Supreme Court in *Heavner* v. *Uniroyal, Inc.*[1] The *Heavner* approach abandons the traditional procedural characterization of limitations issues and instead subjects limitation conflicts to the same choice-of-law *analysis* as other issues in the same case, and without any *a priori* reliance on the *lex fori*. One difference between this approach and the Uniform Act is that, while the Act requires the application of the *same law* state to both the limitation issue and the other issues in the case, the *Heavner* approach simply subjects these two categories of issues to the same choice-of-law *analysis*. Depending on the specifics of a case, this analysis may lead to the same or different laws for the two categories of issues.

1. 305 A.2d 412 (N.J. 1973).

612. Courts in other states, such as California,[1] Rhode Island,[2] Michigan[3] and Indiana,[4] have followed similar approaches. *Gantes* v. *Kason Corporation*[5] is representative of cases decided under the *Heavner* approach. *Gantes* was a wrongful-death action brought by the survivors of a Georgia domiciliary who was killed when struck by a moving part of a machine while working in a chicken processing plant in Georgia. The machine had been manufactured 13 years earlier in New Jersey by a New Jersey based corporation. The action was timely under New Jersey's two-year statute of limitation, but was barred by Georgia's ten-year statute of repose for products liability claims. Applying the Georgia statute, the district court dismissed the action and the intermediate court affirmed. The Supreme Court of New Jersey reversed after an excellent analysis of the interests of the two states.

1. *See* e.g., *Ashland Chemical Co.* v. *Provence*, 181 Cal. Rptr. 340, 341 (Cal Ct. App. 1982); *Ledesma* v. *Lack Steward Produce, Inc.*, 816 F.2d 482 (9th Cir. 1986); *Nelson* v. *Int'l Paint Co.*, 716 F.2d 640 (9th Cir. 1983); *Tomlin* v. *Boeing Co.*, 650 F.2d 1065 (9th Cir. 1981); *Indus. Indemnity Co.* v. *Chapman & Cutler*, 22 F.3d 1346 (5th Cir. 1994) (decided under California conflicts law); *Greer* v. *Academy Equip. Rentals*, 1994 WL 443421 (N.D. Cal. 1994).
2. *See Cribb* v. *Augustin*, 696 A.2d 285 (R.I. 1997) (eclectic approach).
3. *See Sutherland* v. *Kennington Truck Serv., Ltd.*, 562 N.W.2d 466 (Mich. 1997) (*lex fori* approach).
4. *See Nelson* v. *Sandoz Pharm. Corp.*, 288 F.3d 954 (7th Cir. 2002) (decided under Indiana conflicts law; significant contacts approach).
5. 679 A.2d 106 (N.J. 1996).

613. After noting that the Georgia statute had been enacted to protect manufacturers and eliminate stale claims, the court concluded that Georgia had no interest in applying it because Georgia had no contacts with the defendant manufacturer, and its courts were not involved. The victim's Georgia domicile '[did] not implicate the policies of its statute of repose, which is intended only to unburden Georgia courts and to shield Georgia manufacturers'.[1] In fact, the fact that the victim was domiciled in Georgia brought into play that state's general policy 'of fair compensation for injured domiciliaries'.[2] Although Georgia had subordinated that policy in cases in which recovery was sought from a Georgia manufacturer, Georgia had no reason to insist that its general policy be subordinated in a case in which the recovery was sought from a foreign manufacturer. Consequently, the court concluded, the non-application of Georgia law would not undermine Georgia's interest in compensating its injured residents 'because that interest is not actually implicated or compromised by allowing a products-liability action brought by Georgia residents to proceed against a non-Georgia manufacturer'.[3]

1. *Id.* at 114–15.
2. *Id.* at 115.
3. *Id.*

614. In contrast, New Jersey had a 'cognizable and substantial interest in deterrence that would be furthered by the application of its statute of limitations'.[1] The court described the policies embodied in that statute which, as a result of the judicially engrafted discovery rule, is permeated by 'flexible, equitable considerations based on notions of fairness to the parties and the justice in allowing claims to be resolved on their merits'.[2] The court also noted that the goal of torts law in general and products liability law in particular is 'to encourage reasonable conduct, and, conversely, to discourage conduct that creates an unreasonable risk of injury to others'.[3] Because the machine that caused the fatal injury had been 'manufactured in, and placed into the stream of commerce from [New Jersey]',[4] New Jersey had a 'strong interest in encouraging the manufacture and distribution of safe products for the public and, conversely, in deterring the manufacture and distribution of unsafe products within the state'.[5]

1. *Id.* at 113.
2. *Id.* at 110.
3. *Id.* at 111.
4. *Id.*
5. *Id.* at 111–112.

615. The court rejected the lower court's conclusion that this interest in deterrence was outweighed by the possibility of unduly discouraging manufacturing in New Jersey.[1] The court also dismissed the forum-shopping argument because, as shown by the defendant's contacts with the forum, plaintiff was not engaging in forum-shopping in this case.[2]

1. *See id.* at 112.
2. *See id.* at 113: '[T]his State's interest against forum shopping will not be compromised by the application of New Jersey's statute of limitations in the circumstances of this litigation. . . . . In this case, plaintiff does not seek to use New Jersey's court system to litigate a dispute that has only a slight link to New Jersey and where the only plausible reason to select this State is because it is a hospitable forum. This action is materially connected to New Jersey by the fact that the allegedly defective product was manufactured in and then shipped from this State by the defendant-manufacturer'. Justice Garibaldi filed a strong dissent, charging that '[t]he

majority's opinion subjects New Jersey businesses to an increased risk of litigation that would be time-barred in the state where the injured person lives and where the accident occurred, increases forum shopping and further taxes an already overburdened court system, without offering any countervailing benefit to a New Jersey resident or business. *Id.* at 116.

III. The New Revision of the Restatement (Second)

A. The Text

616. In 1988, responding to the above developments, the American Law Institute adopted a revised version of Section 142 of the Restatement (Second), which provides as follows:

> Whether a claim will be maintained against the defence of the statute of limitations is determined under the principles stated in §6. In general, unless the exceptional circumstances of the case make such a result unreasonable:
>
> 1. The forum will apply its own statute of limitations barring the claim.
> 2. The forum will apply its own statute of limitations permitting the claim unless: (a) maintenance of the claim would serve no substantial interest of the forum; and (b) the claim would be barred under the statute of limitations of a state having a more significant relationship to the parties and the occurrence.[1]

Through its cross-reference to Section 6, the first sentence of Section 142 adopts an approach similar to *Heavner* – it instructs the court to choose the law applicable to the limitations issue through the flexible principles of Section 6, and without any *a priori* preference for either the *lex fori* or the *lex causae*.

However, in the interest of judicial economy, the remainder of Section 142 supplements this approach with two presumptive rules favouring the *lex fori*. The rules distinguish between: (a) cases in which the action is barred in the forum state, but not in the other involved state or states (Pattern 1); and (b) cases in which the action is not barred in the forum state but is barred in the other involved state or states (Pattern 2). The burden for rebutting the *lex fori* presumption is intentionally heavier in Pattern 1 (the result must be 'unreasonable') than in Pattern 2 (lack of 'substantial interest').

1. *Restatement (Second)* §142.

B. Representative Cases

617. Thus far, courts in nine states have adopted this section of the Restatement (Second): Arizona,[1] Florida,[2] Idaho,[3] Iowa,[4] Massachusetts,[5] Nebraska[6] Ohio,[7] Texas[8] and West Virginia.[9] The discussion below focuses on three representative cases from these states – *DeLoach* v. *Alfred*,[10] *Washburn* v. *Soper*[11] and *Nierman* v. *Hyatt Corp.*[12] All three cases fall within Pattern 2 in that in all of them the action was timely in the forum state but not in the other involved state. All three cases involved tort actions arising from events in the non-forum state. In the first two cases, the defendant was a forum domiciliary, while in the third case the plaintiff was a forum domiciliary. Thus, these cases represent the most common permutations of this pattern.[13]

1. *See DeLoach* v. *Alfred*, 960 P.2d 628 (Ariz. 1998), discussed *infra* 618.
2. *See Celotex Corp.* v. *Meehan*, 523 So.2d 141 (Fla. 1988); *Fulton County Adm'r* v. *Sullivan*, 753 So.2d 549 (Fla. 1999).
3. *See Dillon* v. *Dillon*, 886 P.2d 777 (Idaho 1994).
4. *See Washburn* v. *Soper*, 319 F.3d 338 (8th Cir. 2003), discussed *infra* 619, (predicting that the Iowa Supreme Court would adopt revised §142 of the Restatement (Second), given the latter court's consistent reliance on the Restatement in other conflicts).
5. *See New England Telephone & Telegraph Co.* v. *Gourdeau Constr. Co., Inc.*, 664, 647 N.E.2d 42 (Mass. 1995).
6. *See Federal Deposit Ins. Corp.* v. *Nordbrock*, 102 F.3d 335 (8th Cir. 1996) (No Supreme Court opinion).
7. *See Resner* v. *Owners Ins. Co.*, 2002 WL 236970 (Ohio Ct. App. 2002).
8. *See Streber* v. *Hunter*, 221 F.3d 701 (5th Cir. 2000) (decided under Texas conflicts law).
9. *See McKinney* v. *Fairchild Int'l, Inc.*, 487 S.E.2d 913 (1997).
10. 960 P.2d 628 (Ariz. 1998).
11. 319 F.3d 338 (8th Cir. 2003), *cert. denied*, 124 S.Ct. 221 (US 2003).
12. 808 N.E.2d 290 (Mass. 2004).
13. In *Jackson* v. *Chandler*, 61 P.3d 17 (Ariz. 2003), an Arizona case, none of the parties were from Arizona but the tort (a three-car collision) occurred in that state and involved California domiciliaries. The action was timely under Arizona's two-year statute of limitations, but not under California's one-year statute. The court noted that, as the domicile of all parties, California had a more significant relationship *to them*, but had a 'less significant relationship *to the occurrence* because the wrongful conduct, the accident, and the injury all occurred in Arizona'. *Id.* at 19 (quoting Section 142(2)(b), emphasis added). The court found that Arizona's interests in allowing the action were both 'substantial' and 'significant'. *Id.* at 21. The court reasoned that, because both the wrongful conduct and the resulting injury had occurred in Arizona, Arizona's interests in 'regulating conduct within the state, deterring wrongful conduct in the state, and providing a forum to adjudicate claims arising from such conduct . . . [were] substantial interests that would be served by entertaining the claim'. *Id.*

618. In *DeLoach* v. *Alfred*,[1] an Arizona case, the tort (a traffic accident) occurred in Tennessee and involved a California plaintiff, an Arizona defendant, and a Tennessee driver. The plaintiff was injured while riding in a car driven by the Arizona defendant when it collided with a car driven by the Tennessee driver. The Tennessee driver was not subject to the court's jurisdiction and, as explained below, this was a significant factor in the court's decision. The action was barred by Tennessee's one-year statute of limitation, but not by Arizona's two-year statute.[2] The lower court applied the Tennessee statute, after finding Arizona to be uninterested and Tennessee to have a more significant relationship because of the involvement of the Tennessee driver. The Arizona Supreme Court reversed, holding that the Arizona statute applied. In particular, the court found that the lower court erred in giving insufficient weight to the presumptive *lex fori* rule of Section 142 and in concluding that Arizona was uninterested and Tennessee had a more significant relationship.

The court found that, because the Tennessee driver was not involved in this litigation, Tennessee had no interest in applying its statute of limitation and that state's relationship with the case was not more significant than Arizona's. The court found that Arizona's longer statute of limitation reflected a deterrence policy of 'holding tortfeasors accountable' and 'requiring [Arizona] citizens to answer for the harm they cause', and that this policy 'extend[ed] to providing a forum for redress against Arizona defendants for their negligent conduct outside the state'.[3] For these reasons, the court concluded that Arizona's interest in the case was 'at least as substantial and as significant as Tennessee's'.[4] Consequently, neither one of the Restatement's exceptions to the presumptive *lex fori* rule was applicable, and the only remaining question was whether applying the *lex fori* would be 'unreasonable' under the circumstances. Comparing this case to *Keeton*,[5] the court concluded that the application of Arizona's statute of limitations was both reasonable and 'entirely consistent with the choice-of-law factors enumerated in Restatement §6'[6] in that it 'protects the justified expectations of the parties'[7] and promotes 'the basic policies underlying tort law – to deter wrongful conduct and compensate victims for their loss'.[8]

1. 960 P.2d 628 (Ariz. 1998).
2. The court did not mention California's statute of limitation.
3. 960 P.2d, at 631–632.
4. *Id.* at 632.
5. *See supra* 594–596.
6. 960 P.2d at 633.
7. *Id.*, (citing Restatement Second §6(2)(d) and referring to the Arizona defendants' 'expectation of being subject to legal action for their tortious conduct for two years under the Arizona statute'.) *See also id.*, 'The only objection to applying the Arizona statute of limitations is from the Arizona residents. In our view, Arizona has a significant interest in applying the Arizona statute of limitations to claims brought in Arizona against Arizona residents'.
8. *Id.*

619. In *Washburn* v. *Soper*,[1] an Iowa case, the defendant was an Iowa domiciliary and the action was timely filed under Iowa law. However, the action was untimely under the law of Illinois, where most of the underlying events occurred. *Washburn* was a legal malpractise claim filed by an Illinois plaintiff against an Iowa attorney who had represented the plaintiff in previous litigation in Illinois. Employing subsection 2 of Section 142, the court dismissed the action under the Illinois statute of limitation, finding that Illinois had a more significant relationship and Iowa had no substantial interest in applying its longer statute of limitations which 'would undermine its interest in protecting resident defendants'.[2] The court recognized that 'Iowa ha[d] an interest in protecting those who retain Iowa attorneys from becoming the victims of professional negligence and in affording parties a 'reasonable time to present their claims' . . . [and] in maintaining the integrity of its bar'.[3] Even so, the court concluded, these interests were not sufficiently 'substantial' in circumstances such as this, where the plaintiffs are Illinois residents, the defendant attorney is licenced in both Iowa and Illinois, the defendant attorney was retained to represent the plaintiffs in Illinois state court proceedings, and these proceedings concerned Illinois residents, Illinois businesses, Illinois trust agreements, and Illinois contracts'.[4]

1. 319 F.3d 338 (8th Cir. 2003), *cert. denied*, 124 S.Ct. 221 (US 2003).
2. *Washburn*, 319 F.3d at 343.
3. *Id.*

4. *Id.* In *Weitz Company, LLC* v. *Travelers Cas. & Sur. Co.*, 266 F.Supp.2d 984 (S.D. Iowa 2003), the action was timely under the statute of limitations of the forum state of Iowa, but not under the statute of Connecticut, where most of the underlying events occurred. However, in contrast to *Washburn* in which the defendant was a forum domiciliary, in *Weitz* it was the plaintiff who was a forum domiciliary. This difference was a sufficient ground on which to distinguish *Washburn* and apply Iowa's longer statute permitting the action.

620. In *Nierman* v. *Hyatt Corp.*,[1] a Massachusetts case, the plaintiff was a domiciliary of the forum state and the defendant was a foreign corporation that owned the Texas hotel in which the plaintiff was injured. The plaintiff's tort action was barred by Texas's two-year statute of limitation, but not by Massachusetts's three-year statute. The plaintiff conceded that Texas had the most significant relationship with regard to other, conduct-regulating, aspects of the case but argued that, in light of plaintiff's domicile in Massachusetts, the latter state had a substantial enough interest to maintain the action.

The Massachusetts court disagreed. It noted that Massachusetts had 'a general interest in having its residents compensated for personal injuries suffered in another State', but concluded that Massachusetts's 'interest in the timeliness of such an action [was not] more compelling than that of Texas'[2] and that Texas had 'the dominant interest in having its own limitations statute enforced'.[3] The court drew support for its decision from a Restatement comment providing that when the plaintiff is domiciled in the forum state and the defendant in the state that has the most significant relationship to the other aspects of the case (e.g., here Texas), 'the forum should entertain the claim only in extreme and unusual circumstances'.[4] In this case, the defendant was not domiciled in Texas, but the defendant 'operate[d] a business there and employ[ed] Texans',[5] and thus came within the protective scope of Texas's statute of limitation.

1. 808 N.E.2d 290 (Mass. 2004).
2. *Id.* at 293.
3. *Id.* at 293–294.
4. *Restatement (Second)* §142 cmt. g.
5. *Nierman*, 808 N.E.2d at 293. The defendant was a Delaware corporation that had its principal place of business in Illinois, and both states' statutes of limitation barred the action. The court reasoned that this fact made this case sufficiently analogous to a case in which the defendant was domiciled in Texas.

621. In both *Nierman* and *DeLoach*, the courts resisted the temptation to favour a forum domiciliary against a foreign domiciliary – the plaintiff in the first case, and the defendant in the second. Although in *Washburn* the result favoured the forum domiciliary, at least the court attempted to explain it (convincingly or not) by emphasizing the other state's contacts.

Nierman presented the direct or 'true conflict' paradigm in that each state's limitation law favoured its own domiciliary.[1] The court's refusal to apply the forum's longer statute for the benefit of a forum plaintiff runs contrary to both modern and traditional decisional trends.

1. *See supra* 181, 275.

622. *DeLoach* and *Washburn* presented the inverse or unprovided-for paradigm in that each state's limitations law favoured the domiciliary of the other state.[1]

Deloach is noteworthy not only because it is a correct and intelligent application of Section 142, but also because it provides a credible articulation of the forum's interest in applying its *longer* statute of limitation in cases in which the defendant is a forum domiciliary and the plaintiff is a foreign domiciliary. In such cases, the fact that the action is timely under the forum's statute negates any procedural interests (such as pruning stale claims from the docket) that are often uncritically invoked in limitation conflicts. After all, the fact that the forum has a longer limitation period means that the claim is not considered stale enough. This means that the interests implicated in the cases of this pattern are *substantive* rather that procedural and that their strength depends on the forum's relationship with the case and the parties.

1. *See id.*

623. In cases like *DeLoach* and *Washburn*, the fact that the plaintiff is not a forum domiciliary may, under Professor Currie's assumptions, suggest the lack of an affirmative interest in providing a forum; but it does not generate an interest in *denying* a forum that is otherwise available to forum domiciliaries. Thus, the plaintiff's 'foreignness' should not be the basis of the court's decision in cases of this pattern. Regarding the defendants, the fact that the forum's statute permitted the action means that the forum had subordinated the policy of affording defendants with repose to the opposite policy of *holding defendants accountable* as the *DeLoach* court concluded. The remaining question is whether this policy is negated by the plaintiff's 'foreignness' (as some courts have held under the pretext of respecting another state's non-existent interest), or whether that policy is unaffected by this factor as the *DeLoach* court held. This is a question which reasonable people may answer differently, as did the two courts in *DeLoach* and *Washburn*. The fact that these two courts reached opposite conclusions is not unusual. The positive aspect of both of these cases, as well as *Nierman*, is that the courts directly confronted the conflicting interests rather than seeking refuge in the artificial characterizations of the traditional method.

IV. The Louisiana and Puerto Rico Codifications

624. The 1991 Louisiana conflicts codification follows an approach that is somewhere between the Uniform Act and the Restatement (Second). Paraphrased, Article 3549 of the codification provides in pertinent part:

1. if the action is untimely under the law of the forum, the action is dismissed unless it would be timely in the state whose law would govern the merits of the action and its maintenance is 'warranted by compelling considerations of remedial justice'; and
2. if the action is timely under the law of the forum, the action shall be maintained unless it would be untimely in the state whose law would govern the merits and its maintenance is 'not warranted by the policies of [the forum] state and its relationship to the parties or the dispute nor by any compelling considerations of remedial justice'.[1]

1. La. Civ. Code Ann. Art. 3549. The article also provides that when the substantive law of the forum governs the merits of an action, then the forum's statute of limitation also applies, whether or not it bars the action. For a discussion of the rationale of this article by its drafter, *see* Symeonides, 'Louisiana Conflicts Law: Two "Surprises"', 54 *La. L. Rev.* 497, 1994, 530–548.

625. This approach suffers from the same flaw as the Uniform Act to the extent it is built around two poles, the *lex fori* and the *lex causae*, that is, the law that governs the other issues in the case, as opposed to the law that should govern the particular issue of limitation. In contrast, the Puerto Rico Draft Code moves closer to the Restatement (Second) by replacing the *lex causae* with the latter law. The Code provides that prescription, and other modes of barring actions by the passage of time, is governed by the law of the state that, under the Code's general approach, 'has the most significant connection *with regard to this issue*'. Nevertheless: (1) an action that is untimely under forum law may not be maintained if, in the circumstances, its maintenance would 'unreasonably burden the administration of justice or would be manifestly unfair to the defendant'; and (2) an action that is timely under the law of the forum may be maintained (even though it is untimely under the law applicable under the above general approach) if the maintenance of the action is 'justified by compelling considerations of remedial justice arising out of the relationship of the parties and the dispute to [the forum]'.[1]

1. Puerto Rico Draft PIL Code Art. 8 (emphasis added). For discussion of this Code by its drafter, *see* Symeonides, 'Revising Puerto Rico's Conflicts Law: A Preview', 28 *Colum. J. Transnat'l L.* 413, 1990, 433–447.

626. *Smith* v. *Odeco (UK), Inc.*[1] was one of the first cases decided under the Louisiana codification. *Smith* involved an action by a British domiciliary for injuries he suffered aboard a US flag vessel (drilling rig) owned by Odeco, while the vessel was engaged in drilling off the territorial waters of Spain. The parties conceded and the court agreed that British law would be applicable to the merits of this action, apparently because the plaintiff was domiciled and had been hired in the United Kingdom and had taken his work orders out of Odeco's office in Scotland. The Louisiana action was filed after the accrual of Louisiana's one-year prescriptive period but before the accrual of the British three-year limitation period. Thus, under Article 3549, the action should be dismissed unless its maintenance is 'warranted by compelling considerations of remedial justice'.

The court held that the 'unless clause' was applicable, allowing the action to proceed, after finding that 'compelling considerations of remedial justice' existed which warranted maintenance of the suit in Louisiana. In support of this finding, the court quoted an example from the Reporter's comments to Article 3549 explaining the application of this exception.[2] The court noted that the plaintiff was blameless in that he had filed the appropriate action in Scotland well within the British three-year limitation period. However, under Scottish law, the Scottish courts did not have jurisdiction over any of the defendants because none of them was either domiciled or had its management and control in the United Kingdom. Instead, all the defendants had their corporate offices in Louisiana. The court concluded that 'Louisiana is the only forum where a suit may be maintained against all the defendants' and that '[i]n the absence of an alternative forum in which there is jurisdiction over all defendants, "compelling considerations of remedial justice" exist which warrant maintenance of this suit in Louisiana'.[3]

1. 615 So.2d 407 (La. Ct. App. 4th Cir. 1993), *writ denied*, 618 So.2d 412 (La. 1993).
2. Reporter's comment (f) to Article 3549, quoted in *Smith*, 615 So.2d at 409. The example refers to cases where 'through no fault of the plaintiff an alternative forum is not available as, for example, when jurisdiction could not be obtained over the defendant in any state other than the forum'.
3. *Smith*, 615 So.2d at 410.

627. In contrast, in *Skyrme* v. *Diamond Offshore (U.S.A.) Inc.*,[1] an alternative forum was available in Brazil, which, '[i]n fact, . . . would be the most convenient forum since the cause of action arose in Brazil, plaintiff reside[d] in Brazil, and the vast majority of the plaintiff's liability and quantum witnesses [were] located in Brazil'.[2] Plaintiff, a British citizen, was employed in Brazil by a Brazilian subsidiary of defendant, a Texas corporation that had its principal place of business in Louisiana. The plaintiff was fired, allegedly without cause, and sued the defendant parent corporation in Louisiana seeking 'moral damages' under Brazilian law. His action was barred under Louisiana law but would have been timely under Brazil's 20-year prescriptive period. The court correctly assumed that Brazilian law would be applicable to the merits of the action but held that the action was barred under Louisiana law. The court properly distinguished *Smith*, *supra*, by noting that unlike the *Smith* plaintiff, the *Skyrme* plaintiff did not carry the burden of showing 'compelling considerations'. In fact, the *Skyrme* 'defendant ha[d] demonstrated that there [were] *no* compelling considerations of remedial justice present which would warrant the maintenance of this action'.[3]

1. 1994 WL 320928 (E.D. La. 1994).
2. *Id.* at *4.
3. *Id.* (emphasis added). The plaintiff had already obtained jurisdiction over the defendant in a Brazilian labour court. Similarly, in *Seagrave* v. *Delta Airlines, Inc.*, 848 F.Supp. 82 (E.D. La. 1994), the court held that the plaintiff had failed to carry his burden of showing that compelling considerations of remedial justice warranted the maintenance of his action in Louisiana. The plaintiff, then a Virginia domiciliary, was injured aboard a Delta airplane on a return flight to Virginia. Approximately 15 months after the injury, he moved to Louisiana and shortly thereafter sued Delta in that state at a time when his action would have been prescribed under Louisiana law but not under Virginia law. The court correctly held that Virginia substantive law would govern the merits of the action and (distinguishing *Smith* and relying on *Skyrme*) held that the action was barred under Louisiana law because there were no 'compelling considerations of remedial justice' to warrant maintaining the action in Louisiana. In fact, the court found that it would have been costlier to try the suit in Louisiana than in Virginia. The court thus ordered the case to be transferred to a federal court in Virginia, pursuant to 28 USC §1404(a).

§4. Supreme Court Cases

628. In *Sun Oil Co.* v. *Wortman*,[1] the US Supreme Court gave its imprimatur to the procedural characterization of statutes of limitations. It held that, simply by being the forum, a state may, without violating the Full Faith and Credit or Due Process clauses of the Constitution, apply its own statute of limitations, even when that state lacks the contacts and interests that, according to the Court's interpretation of the same clauses, are necessary for applying the forum's substantive law to the merits of the case at hand.[2]

Writing for the Court, Justice Scalia looked at the 'historical record' and found that 'the society which adopted the Constitution did not regard statutes of limitations as substantive . . . but rather as procedural restrictions fashioned by each jurisdiction for its own courts'.[3] Seeing no basis for 'updat[ing] our notion of what is sufficiently 'substantive' to require full faith and credit',[4] Scalia held that the forum state 'did not violate the Full Faith and Credit Clause when it applied its own statute of limitations',[5] because '[a] State's interest in regulating the work load of its courts and determining whether a claim is too stale to be adjudicated certainly suffices to give it legislative jurisdiction to control the remedies available in its courts by imposing statutes of limitations'.[6]

1. 486 US 717 (1988).
2. *See supra* 55–62.
3. *Wortman*, 486 US at 725.
4. *Id.* at 728.
5. *Id.* at 729.
6. *Id.* 730.

629. Indeed, if the forum's statute barred the action, this would have been a perfectly plausible conclusion, but in *Wortman* the forum's statute allowed the action (i.e., it did not consider the claim to be 'too stale') and that statute's application would *increase* rather than decrease the forum courts' 'work load'. A state that adopts a longer limitation period subordinates its procedural interests in reducing the court's workload and protecting them from stale claims to the substantive interest of protecting plaintiffs by giving them more time to sue. Thus, the real question in these cases is whether, in the particular circumstances, the application of the forum's longer statute of limitation imposes an unfair burden on the *defendant*, which in turn depends on the defendant's relation with the forum state. Justice Scalia's answer to this question was that the defendant 'could in no way have been unfairly surprised by the application to it of a rule that is as old as the Republic'.[1]

1. *Id.*

630. Whether or not one agrees with *Wortman's* reasoning, what is clear is that its holding simply means that the forum state *may* apply its statute of limitations, not that it must.[1] Also, *Wortman* does not affect the Court's previous holding in *Guaranty Trust Co.* v. *York*,[2] which, for *Erie* purposes, characterized statutes of limitations as *substantive*.

1. *See id.* at 729 ('[W]e do not hold that Kansas must apply its statute of limitations . . . , but only that it may'.).
2. 326 US 99 (1945). In fact, Justice Scalia expressly rejected defendant's plea to adopt *York's* substantive characterization.

631. The latter point has implications for federal courts sitting in diversity, which apply federal procedural law but, under *Erie*, must apply state substantive law.[1] Under *York*, the latter law includes statutes of limitation. In multistate cases,

Klaxon requires the federal court to select the applicable substantive law (including statutes of limitation) through the forum's choice-of-law rules. *Wortman* comes in at this juncture. By granting state courts a constitutional licence to freely apply their own statutes of limitation, *Wortman* also gives the same licence to the federal courts when acting as surrogates for state courts under *Erie*. As *Ferens* v. *John Deere Co.*,[2] illustrates, *Wortman* can also become an effective hunting licence for forum-shopping plaintiffs.

Three years after he was injured in Pennsylvania by a John Deere combine harvester purchased in that state, Albert Ferens and his wife, both Pennsylvania domiciliaries, filed a products liability action against the John Deere Company in federal district court in Mississippi, which at that time had a six-year statute of limitation. The defendant's only connection to Mississippi was the appointment of a local resident agent for service of process as a condition for doing business in that state. Invoking 28 USC §1404(a),[3] the plaintiff sought and obtained an order transferring the case to a federal district court in Pennsylvania, which had a two-year statute of limitation. Deciding before *Wortman*, the transferee court refused to apply Mississippi's limitation period and held that the action was barred under Pennsylvania's two-year statute of limitations. The Third Circuit Court of Appeals affirmed, finding that 'Mississippi's contacts with the parties and the occurrence . . . [were] plainly so insignificant that the application of its law would be arbitrary, fundamen-tally unfair, and therefore unconstitutional'.[4]

In the meantime, the Supreme Court decided *Wortman* and, two weeks later, vacated the Third Circuit judgment and remanded the case for further consideration in light of *Wortman*. On remand, the Third Circuit had to confront the question of whether the case fell within the scope of the Supreme Court's previous decision in *Van Dusen* v. *Barrack*.[5] *Van Dusen* had held that, in a transfer initiated by the defendant under 28 USC §1404(a), the transferee court must apply the same law that would have been applied by the transferee court.[6] The Third Circuit held that *Van Dusen* was inapplicable to this case because the transfer was initiated by the *plaintiff*. Applying Pennsylvania conflicts law, the court held that the action was barred under Pennsylvania's statute of limitation.[7]

1. *See supra* 42–45.
2. 494 US 516 (1990).
3. 28 USC §1404(a) provides that 'for the convenience of parties and witnesses, in the interest of justice', a case may be transferred from one federal district to another district where the action might have been brought.
4. *Ferens* v. *Deere & Co.*, 819 F.2d 423, 427 (3rd Cir. 1987).
5. 376 US 612 (1964).
6. *See supra* 39.
7. *Ferens* v. *Deere & Co.*, 862 F.2d 31 (3rd Cir. 1988).

632. The Supreme Court reversed in a five-to-four decision authored by Justice Kennedy. The Court held that *Van Dusen* did apply to transfers initiated by plaintiffs, and thus the transferee court should have applied '[t]he Mississippi statute of limitations, which *everyone agrees* would [under *Klaxon* and *Wortman*] have applied if the Ferenses had not moved for a transfer'.[1] Justice Kennedy acknowledged that the holding 'may seem too generous because it allows the Ferenses to have both their choice of law and their choice of forum, or even to reward the Ferenses for conduct that seems manipulative'.[2] 'Nevertheless', he explained, the holding was 'doing no more than recognize a forum shopping choice *that already exists*', and allow plaintiffs to 'exercis[e] the opportunities [of transfer] that they already have'.[3] He pointed out that the decision to transfer the case under Section 1404(a) rests with the court rather than with the moving party and that this provision 'also exists for the benefit of witnesses and the interest of justice'.[4]

1. *Ferens* v. *John Deere Co.*, 494 US 516, 526 (1990) (emphasis added).
2. *Id.* at 531.
3. *Id.* 528 (emphasis added).
4. *Id.* at 529. Justice Kennedy noted that, although the application of the transferor law would deprive the defendant of the advantage of 'forcing the Ferenses to litigate in Mississippi or not at all', *id.* at 525, such a deprivation was but a 'slight' loss because the plaintiff 'always can sue in the favorable state court, or sue in diversity and not seek transfer'. *Id.*

633. Justice Scalia, who authored the majority opinion in *Wortman*, filed a strong dissent in *Ferens*, criticizing the majority for enabling the plaintiff 'to have his cake and eat it too – to litigate in the more convenient forum that he desires, but with the law of the distant forum that he desires',[1] and for allowing 'the significant federal judicial policy expressed in *Erie* and *Klaxon* [to be] reduced to a laughingstock'.[2]

1. *Id.* at 537 (Scalia, J., dissenting).
2. *Id.* 536.

634. Justice Scalia astutely described the exploitation of the system by enterprising plaintiffs. However, the blame for the system's deficiencies does not lie in the Court's decision in *Ferens*. The blame and remedy should be sought elsewhere, and most notably in: (1) the current rules of jurisdiction; (2) *Wortman*; and (3) perhaps, in that not-so-sacred cow, *Klaxon*. Surely, the *Ferens* scenario would not have occurred if the current rules of jurisdiction did not allow a state with so minimal and artificial contacts as Mississippi's in *Ferens* to assert jurisdiction over the defendant. Secondly, even with *Klaxon* and *Van Dusen* intact, the *Ferens* scenario would have ended up differently had *Wortman* not issued such an unrestricted licence to any forum to apply its longer limitation period even in the absence of significant contacts with the case. Finally, had it not been for *Klaxon*, the federal district court in Mississippi would not be as inexorably bound to follow the Mississippi Supreme Court's persistent refusal to apply Mississippi's borrowing statute to cases that seem so clearly to fall within its scope,[1] nor would that court be such an attractive place for forum shoppers.

1. *See supra* 600.

§5. Lessons Derived from Comparison

635. In his concurring opinion in *Wortman*, Justice William Brennan said that '[s]tatutes of limitation . . . defy characterization as either purely procedural or purely substantive'.[1] Indeed, it is simplistic to think of statutes of limitation as being always procedural (as did the traditional common-law approach) or always substantive (as does the traditional civil-law approach). A rule of limitation may, and usually does, serve both substantive and procedural objectives and policies.

For instance, a rule that subjects medical malpractise claims to a short limitation period serves substantive objectives by shielding doctors and their insurers from prolonged exposure to liability, but also serves procedural objectives by reducing the number of malpractise actions and thus helps to conserve judicial resources. Similarly, a rule that prohibits anticipatory waivers of the statute of limitation promotes substantive aims by protecting debtors from the coercive power of creditors. At the same time, by preventing the lengthening of the limitation period beyond the time the *lex fori* considers appropriate, this rule serves procedural policies by protecting the courts from the burdens and dangers of adjudicating old claims.

In contrast, a rule that prohibits the parties to certain insurance contracts from shortening a statutory limitation period subordinates the procedural policy of encouraging the early filing of actions to the preferred substantive policy of protecting insureds from the superior bargaining power of insurers. In Brennan's words,

> The statute of limitations a State enacts represents a balance between, on the one hand, its substantive interest in vindicating claims and, on the other hand, a combination of its procedural interest in freeing its courts from adjudicating stale claims and its substantive interest in giving individuals repose from ancient breaches of law. . . . One cannot neatly categorize this complicated temporal balance as either procedural or substantive.[2]

1. 486 US 717, 736 (1988) (Brennan, J., concurring).
2. *Id.*

636. Thus, from the choice-of-law perspective, the automatic application of the *lex fori* to all multistate cases (the traditional common law approach) is as arbitrary as is the automatic application of the *lex causae* (the traditional civil law approach). By exaggerating the procedural function of limitations and ignoring their substantive function, the first approach encourages forum-shopping while ignoring the legitimate interests of other states that may be more intimately related to the parties and their dispute. By overemphasizing the substantive function of limitations, the second approach deprives the forum *qua* forum of the ability to promote its own procedural interests.

For these reasons, it is not surprising that, despite their original differences, both of these approaches have gradually come to recognize the need for concessions in favour of the other and have abandoned their exclusive adherence to a single law. The need for exceptions is perhaps the most important lesson from this experience. In a sense, it is less important which of the two laws (i.e., *lex fori* or *lex causae*) is eventually adopted as the basic rule, as long as it is subjected to appropriate exceptions. The difficult question is therefore not whether exceptions should exist, but which exceptions should be carved out of the basic rule.

637. While reasonable people might disagree on where exactly to draw the lines of compromise, this experience can at least help identify some of the forces generally at work in limitation conflicts. Without a claim to completeness, these forces may be placed in four categories:

1. the procedural and substantive policies embodied in the particular limitation rule of the *lex fori*;
2. the substantive policies embodied in the limitation rule of the *lex causae*;
3. the multistate policy of discouraging forum shopping; and
4. the federally sanctioned policy of providing a forum for causes of action arising under that laws of sister-states.

Obviously, these forces do not appear with the same intensity in all limitation conflicts and usually point in opposite directions. However, they do exist, they cannot be ignored, and they are not susceptible to simplistic recipes.

Chapter 9. Conflicts between Federal Law and Foreign Law

§1. Introduction

638. This chapter discusses how American courts resolve conflicts between US federal law and foreign law. The commonly used phrase to describe this subject is 'extraterritorial reach of federal statutes'. This phrase is accurate to the extent it signifies as explained below, that the methodology employed is primarily unilateralist. However, this phrase is also partly inaccurate because in many cases, the question is not extraterritoriality but rather defining the exact contours of intraterritoriality. Moreover, federal law encompasses not only statutes but also federal common law, although the majority of cases involve statutes, most of which are of a public-law character.

§2. Congressional Power and Its Limits

I. International-Law Limits

639. From the United States' perspective, there is no doubt that Congress has the constitutional power to regulate, or define the legal significance of, events occurring outside the United States. For example, a perusal of Section 8 of Article I of the Constitution reveals several grants of such power, e.g., to 'define and punish Piracies and Felonies committed on the high Seas, and Offenses against the Law of Nations', to 'regulate Commerce with foreign Nations', to provide for copyright and patent protection, and to 'make all Laws which shall be necessary and proper for carrying into Execution . . . all other Powers vested . . . in the Government of the United States'.[1]

1. US Const. Art. 1, §8. Congress's power to regulated foreign commerce is broader than its power over interstate commerce. *See Japan Line Ltd.* v. *County of Los Angeles*, 441 US 434, 445–450 (1979); *Container Corp. of Am.* v. *Franchise Tax Bd.*, 463 US 159 (1983).

640. The reference to the 'Law of Nations' signifies the Framers' respect for international law but alone it does not answer the question of whether, in enacting legislation regulating foreign events or persons, Congress is bound by limits imposed by international law. The Supreme Court's jurisprudence is replete with pronouncements of desired compliance with international law. They include Justice Marshall's 1804 pronouncement in *Charming Betsy* that 'an act of congress ought never to be construed to violate the law of nations if any other possible construction remains',[1] and Justice Gray's statement in *The Paquete Habana*, that '[i]nternational law is part of our law, and must be ascertained and administered by the courts of justice'.[2]

1. *Murray* v. *Schooner Charming Betsy*, 6 US (2 Cranch) 64, 118 (1804).
2. *The Paquete Habana*, 175 US 677, 700 (1900).

641. However, these and numerous other similar pronouncements made through the present are confined to *interpreting* silent or otherwise ambiguous congressional enactments. On the other hand, when the enactment contains language clearly making it applicable to foreign conduct, the prevailing view is that the court must apply it to such conduct, even if that application would violate international law. Judge Learned Hand articulated this view in the *Alcoa* case:

> We are concerned only with whether Congress chose to attach liability to the conduct outside the United States of persons not in allegiance to it. That being so, the only question open is whether Congress intended to impose the liability, and whether our own Constitution permitted it to do so: as a court of the United States, *we cannot look beyond our law.*[1]

1. *United States* v. *Aluminum Co. of Am. (Alcoa)*, 148 F.2d 416, 443 (2d Cir. 1945) (emphasis added).

642. Similarly, the Restatement (Third) of Foreign Relations Law reiterates the principle that international law is 'law of the United States and supreme over the law of the several States'[1] but, as this statement indicates, this is supremacy over state law and not necessarily federal law. In any event, the statement 'is addressed largely to the courts',[2] rather than the President[3] or Congress.[4] Courts are expected to interpret statutes in a way that accommodates both the intent of Congress and the limits of international law. However, if Congress expressed its intent clearly and unambiguously and the latter accommodation is not possible, then international law must yield. Courts 'must give effect to a valid unambiguous congressional mandate, even if such effect would . . . violate international law'.[5] According to the Restatement (Third), '[i]f construction of a statute that accommodates the intent of Congress within the limits of international law is not fairly possible, the statute is nevertheless valid'.[6] Thus, it appears 'well-settled' that, '[i]f Congress enacts legislation in violation of international law, . . . US courts must disregard international law and apply the domestic statute'.[7]

1. American Law Institute, *Restatement (Third) of Foreign Relations Law of the United States* §111(1) (1987) [hereafter referred to as *Restatement (Third)*.
2. *Id.* §111, cmt. c.
3. With regard to the President, the Restatement (Third) states that 'under the President's constitutional authority, as "sole organ of the nation in its external relations" or as Commander in Chief, the President has the power to take various measures including some that might constitute violations of international law by the United States'. *Id.* cmt. c.
4. The Restatement (Third) goes on to explain that: (a) a rule of customary international law 'has no status as law of the United States if the United States is not in fact bound by it', such as when the United States had 'dissociated itself during the process of its formation', *id.* cmt. b; and (b) rules of international law 'are subject to the Bill of Rights and other prohibitions, restrictions, and requirements of the Constitution, and cannot be given effect in violation of them'. *Id.* cmt. a.
5. *CFTC* v. *Nahas*, 738 F.2d 487, 495 (D.C. Cir. 1984).
6. *Restatement (Third)* §403, cmt. g.
7. G. Born & P. Rutledge, *International Civil Litigation in United States Courts* (4th edn, Austin, 2006), p. 576.

II. Constitutional Limits

643. Part I, Chapter 2 discusses the limits that the Constitution imposes on the power of the states of the United States to regulate cases with foreign elements. The question is what limitations the Constitution imposes on the corresponding power of Congress. The Full Faith and Credit clause is clearly inapplicable to international conflicts and does not bind the federal government, but the Due Process clause of the Fifth Amendment binds the federal government, including Congress. Indeed, lower court decisions contain several statements to the effect that, in enacting legislation applicable to foreign events or persons, Congress must remain within the limits of the Due Process clause. For example, in *United States* v. *Greer*, the court said that, '[a]lthough it is clear that Congress has the power to enact statutes that exceed the limits of international law, it may not exceed the limits of the Due Process clause'.[1] In *United States* v. *Davis*, the court said that '[i]n order to apply extraterritorially a federal criminal statute . . . consistently with due process, there must be sufficient nexus between the defendant and the United States so that such application would not be unreasonable or fundamentally unfair'.[2]

1. 956 F.Supp. 531, 535 (D. Vt. 1997).
2. 905 F.2d 245, 248–249 (9th Cir. 1990), *cert. denied*, 498 US 1047 (1991). *See also United States* v. *Juda*, 46 F.3d 961 (9th Cir. 1995), *cert. denied sub nom., Paris* v. *United States*, 514 US 1090, *cert. denied*, 515 US 1169 (1995).

644. These propositions should be self-evident. Nevertheless, no court has ever held unconstitutional under the Due Process clause, a federal statute regulating foreign events or persons. As for the Supreme Court, it has simply intimated that the judicial application of federal law to international conflicts is subject to the restraints of the Due Process clause.[1] In another case involving the President's power to sign executive agreements, the Court stated that 'like every other governmental power, [it] must be exercised in subordination to the applicable provisions of the Constitution'.[2] However, the Supreme Court has never held, and has had no occasion to hold, unconstitutional a federal statute regulating foreign events or persons, or to directly pronounce on the extraterritorial reach of the Due Process clause, to date.

1. *See Lauritzen* v. *Larsen*, 345 US 571, 579 note 7 (1953).
2. *United States* v. *Curtiss-Wright Export Corp.*, 299 US 304, 320 (1936).

645. Even *Rasul* v. *Bush*,[1] a recent Guantanamo case, did no present an opportunity for a direct holding or statement on this issue. The question in *Rasul* was whether aliens held under executive detention in the Guantanamo naval base in Cuba were entitled to a writ of habeas corpus. Although the detainees initially claimed this right as a matter of constitutional law, the issue quickly became one of statutory construction – whether the habeas corpus statute[2] empowered federal courts to hear the petitions of these detainees. The Court answered the question in the affirmative after finding that, functionally and for all practical purposes, the Guantanamo base was subject to US jurisdiction, although subject to nominal Cuban sovereignty.[3] The government invoked the presumption against extraterritoriality, namely that, in the absence of clear contrary expression, congressional legislation is presumed not to have extraterritorial application.[4] The Court's response was that '[w]hatever traction th[at] presumption . . . might have in other contexts, it certainly has no application to the operation of the habeas statute with respect to persons detained within "the territorial jurisdiction" of the United States. By the express terms of its agreements with Cuba, the United States exercises "complete jurisdiction and control" over the Guantanamo Bay Naval Base, and may continue to exercise such control permanently if it so chooses'.[5]

1. 542 US 466 (2004).
2. This statute confers on federal courts, 'within their respective jurisdictions', 28 USC §2241(c)(3), the authority to hear habeas corpus petitions by any person who claims to be held in custody 'in violation of the Constitution or laws or treaties of the United States'. 28 USC §2241(a).
3. The United States occupies this base pursuant to a 1903 lease with Cuba, which gives the United States 'complete jurisdiction and control over and within [the leased area]'. *Rasul*, 542 US at 471. A 1934 treaty with Cuba allows the United States to continue the lease at will.
4. *See EEOC* v. *Arabian Am. Oil Co.*, 499 US 244, 248 (1991), discussed *infra* 684.
5. *Rasul*, 542 US at 480. The Court also noted that, under controlling precedent, the prisoner's presence within the territorial jurisdiction of the court is not an invariable prerequisite to the exercise of jurisdiction under the statute because the writ of habeas corpus 'does not act upon the prisoner who seeks relief, but upon the person who holds him in what is alleged to be unlawful custody'. *Id.* at 478. Consequently federal courts act 'within their respective jurisdiction' under the statute as long as the custodian is within their jurisdiction, even if the prisoner is not. *Id.*

646. In any event, in most cases in which a party urges a court to apply or not to apply a federal statute to foreign events, the question is rarely whether the statute's application will violate international or constitutional law, i.e., whether the statute *can* be so applied. Rather the question is whether the statute *may* or *should* be so applied. The answer depends on congressional intent as evidenced by the statute's language and other factors discussed below.

§3. Statutes Expressly Applicable to Foreign Events or Persons

647. Congress has enacted hundreds of statutes that *expressly* apply to foreign events, foreign persons, or US persons while present or acting abroad. The following are a few examples.

I. Statutes Applicable to US Citizens Present or Acting Abroad

648. Congress has enacted numerous statutes applying to US nationals who live or act abroad. Among these statutes, which are based on the nationality basis of prescriptive jurisdiction, are: (1) the Trading with the Enemy Act of 1917,[1] which applies to '[a]ny individual, wherever located, who is a citizen or resident of the United States';[2] (2) the Logan Act of 1909, which prohibits '[a]ny citizen of the United States, wherever he may be', from contacting foreign governments to affect their policies;[3] (3) the treason statute of 1940, which applies to any person 'owing allegiance to the United States';[4] (4) the selective service law of 1948, which requires 'every male citizen of the United States' to register for military service;[5] and, more recently, (5) the foreign sexual tourism statute, which punishes '[a]ny United States citizen . . . who travels in foreign commerce, and engages in any illicit sexual conduct with another person'.[6]

1. *See* 50 USC App. §5(b).
2. 31 CFR §500.329(a). The Act also applies to any legal person organized under American law or owned or controlled by US citizens, residents, or corporations. *Id.*
3. *See* 18 USC §953.
4. *See* 18 USC §2381 ('Whoever, owing allegiance to the United States, levies war against them or adheres to their enemies, giving them aid and comfort within the United States or elsewhere, is guilty of treason[.]').
5. 50 USC App. §453.
6. 18 USC §2423(c). For a recent application of this statute, *see United States* v. *Strevell*, 185 Fed.Appx. 841, 845 (11th Cir. 2006), *cert. denied*, 127 S.Ct. 692 (US 2006) (noting that 'Congress specifically passed this act to criminalize illicit sexual acts taking place entirely outside the United States. Congress realized the potential effects of domestic harm that come with foreign sex trafficking of minors . . . [and] purposefully passed this statute in order to stop United States citizens from traveling abroad in order to engage in commercial sex acts with minors').

II. Statutes Applicable to US Citizens Injured Abroad

649. Relying on the 'passive personality' principle (the converse of the nationality principle), Congress has enacted several pieces of 'antiterrorist' legislation, including the Anti-Terrorist Act of 1991 (ATA)[1] and the Antiterrorist and Effective Death Penalty Act of 1996 (AEDPA).[2] The ATA provides that '[a]ny national of the United States injured . . . by reason of an act of international terrorism . . . may sue therefor in any appropriate district court of the United States and shall recover threefold the damages he or she sustains . . .'[3] The AEDPA amended the Foreign Sovereign Immunities Act (FSIA) by eliminating the sovereign immunity of certain foreign states (those designated by the US State Department as sponsors of terrorism) in actions filed on behalf of US citizens killed or injured by acts of terrorism sponsored or aided by these states.[4]

1. 18 USC §2333.
2. 18 USC §32.
3. 18 USC §2333(a). For representative cases applying this Act, *see Ungar* v. *Palestine Liberation Org.*, 402 F.3d 274 (1st Cir. 2005).
4. *See* 28 USC §1605(a)(7). For representative cases applying this Act, *see Wyatt* v. *Syrian Arab Republic*, 398 F.Supp.2d 131 (D.D.C. 2005); *Wagner* v. *Islamic Republic of Iran*, 172 F.Supp.2d 128 (D.D.C. 2001); *Flatow* v. *Islamic Republic of Iran*, 999 F.Supp 1 (D.D.C. 1998). The ATA and AEDPA (1) do not create a cause of action, but rather authorize adjudicatory jurisdiction for actions provided by the otherwise applicable substantive law; and (2) do not provide choice-of-law rules through which to select the applicable substantive law, but rather contemplate use of the forum's choice-of-law rules.

III. Statutes Applicable to Foreign Events or Persons

650. The Alien Tort Claims Act (ATCA) and the Torture Victim Protection Act (TVPA) are examples of statutes that expressly apply to foreign events and actors. The ATCA was enacted in 1789, although it has acquired added significance in recent years. It confers on federal district courts original jurisdiction of 'any civil action by an alien for a tort only, committed in violation of the law of nations or a treaty of the United States'.[1] Although ATCA does not expressly create a cause of action, the courts have interpreted it as creating an independent private cause of action for violations of well-established, universally recognized, and obligatory' norms of international law that were understood as such at the time of the statute's enactment.[2] Neither the plaintiff nor the events on which the action is based need have any connection with the United States. As for the defendant, all that is needed is *in personam* jurisdiction, even if it is based on tag jurisdiction.[3]

1. 28 USC §1350. This Act is also known as the Alien Tort Statute (ATS).
2. *See Sosa* v. *Alvarez-Machain*, 542 US 692 (2004), discussed *infra* 691–704.
3. For representative cases involving claims for international law violations in the countries shown in parentheses, *see Sosa* v. *Alvarez-Machain*, 542 US 692 (2004) (Mexico); *Sarei* v. *Rio Tinto*, PLC, 456 F.3d 1069 (9th Cir. 2006) (Papua New Guinea); *Arce* v. *Garcia*, 434 F.3d 1254 (11th Cir. 2006) (El Salvador); *Gonzalez-Vera* v. *Kissinger*, 449 F.3d 1260 (D.C. Cir. 2006), *cert. denied*, 127 S.Ct. 1356 (US 2007) (Chile); *Aldana* v. *Del Monte Fresh Produce, N.A., Inc.*, 416 F.3d 1242 (11th Cir. 2005), *cert. denied*, 127 S.Ct. 596 (2006) (Guatemala); *Kadic* v. *Karadzic*, 70 F.3d 232 (2d Cir. 1995), *cert. denied*, 116 S.Ct. 2524 (1996) (Bosnia); *Filartiga* v. *Pena-Irala*, 630 F.2d 876 (2d Cir. 1980) (Paraguay); *In re Estate of Marcos Human Rights Litig.*, 978 F.2d 493 (2d Cir. 1991), and *Hilao* v. *Estate of Marcos*, 103 F.3d 787 (9th Cir. 1996) (Philippines).

651. The TVPA was enacted in 1992 as a statutory note to the ATCA. It provides that 'an individual who, under actual or apparent authority, or color of law, of any foreign nation (1) subjects an individual to torture . . . or . . . to extrajudicial killing' shall be liable for damages.[1] The TVPA expressly confers a substantive cause of action, but does not itself confer federal jurisdiction. For this reason, plaintiffs often invoke both the ATCA and the TVPA. The courts have held that, once jurisdiction is established under the ATCA, the court also has jurisdiction to hear the plaintiff's TVPA claims. Again, neither the plaintiff nor the events on which the action is based need have any connection with the United States. In fact, the Act contemplates foreign events and defendants acting under colour of *foreign* law, thus excluding defendants who (whether foreign on American) have acted under colour of *United States law*.[2]

1. 28 USC §1350 Note.
2. For representative cases, *see Alvarez-Machain* v. *United States*, 542 US 692 (2004), discussed *infra* 691–704.

652. In *Arar* v. *Ashcroft*,[1] a case involving so-called 'extraordinary rendition',[2] the court erroneously concluded that the plaintiff, an alien, was ineligible for the protection of the TVPA because 'US citizens, and only US citizens, are covered by the TVPA'.[3] The court based this conclusion on a statement from the Congressional Record that does *not* seem to support the conclusion,[4] as well as on cases which held that the TVPA provides a cause of action to US citizens, but did not hold or suggest that it precludes aliens. The court must not have realized that other courts have found the TVPA to be applicable to actions brought by alien plaintiffs.[5] Ultimately, the court based its dismissal on the TVPA requirement that the defendants must have acted under colour of law of 'any foreign nation'. The defendants, who were US officials, argued and the court agreed that 'any "law" under which they were acting in this case would be domestic – not foreign[.]'[6]

1. 414 F.Supp.2d 250 (E.D.N.Y. 2006).
2. This is a typically euphemistic term coined by the CIA to describe its practise of delivering people suspected of terrorist ties or activities to other countries for 'interrogation'. The plaintiff was the victim of such a practise.
3. *Arar*, 414 F.Supp.2d at 263.
4. *See id., quoting* H.R.Rep. No. 102–367, 102d Cong., 2d Sess., at *4 (1991), which states that '[w]hile the Alien Tort Claims Act provides a remedy to aliens only, the TVPA would extend a civil remedy *also* to US citizens who may have been tortured abroad.' (emphasis added). In this author's view, the italicized word suggests that Congress intended to provide a cause of action to *both* US and alien plaintiffs.
5. *See*, e.g., *Arce* v. *Garcia*, 434 F.3d 1254 (11th Cir. 2006); *Gonzalez-Vera* v. *Kissinger*, 449 F.3d 1260 (D.C. Cir. 2006), *cert. denied*, 127 S.Ct. 1356 (US 2007); *Chavez* v. *Carranza*, 407 F. Supp. 2d 925 (W.D. Tenn. 2004); *Doe* v. *Qi*, 349 F.Supp.2d 1258 (N.D. Cal. 2004); *Abiola* v. *Abubakar*, 435 F.Supp.2d 830 (N.D. Ill. 2006), *appeal denied*, 2006 WL 2714831 (N.D. Ill. 20 September 2006); *Bowoto* v. *Chevron Corp.*, 2006 WL 2455752, 2006 WL 2455761 (N.D. Cal. 22 August 2006).
6. *Arar*, 414 F.Supp.2d at 264.

IV. Statutes Applicable to the High Seas

653. Several statutes are expressly applicable to the high seas. They are enacted under the High Seas Clause of the Constitution, which grants Congress the power to 'define and punish Piracies and Felonies committed on the high Seas, and Offences against the Law of Nations'.[1] One such statute is the Maritime Drug Law Enforcement Act ('MDLEA'), which makes it unlawful for any person 'on board a vessel . . . subject to the jurisdiction of the United States' to possess certain drugs with intent distribute.[2] A vessel is 'subject to the jurisdiction of the United States', *inter alia*, if it is: (1) a stateless vessel; or (2) a vessel flying the flag of a foreign country that has consented or waived objection to the enforcement of US law by the United States.[3] Other statutes applicable to the high seas are the Marine Mammals Protection Act,[4] and the Death on the High Seas Act (DOHSA), which applies to deaths caused by acts occurring 'on the high seas beyond a marine league from the shore of any State . . . of the United States'.[5]

1. US Const. Art. I, §8, cl. 10.
2. 46 App. USCA §1903(a).
3. *Id.* at §1903(c). For recent applications of this statute, *see United States* v. *Perlaza*, 439 F.3d 1149 (9th Cir. 2006); *United States* v. *Garcia*, 182 Fed. Appx. 873 (11th Cir. 2006), *cert. denied*, 127 S.Ct. 929 (US 2007); *United States* v. *Ma*, 2006 WL 708559 (S.D.N.Y. 21 March 2006).
4. *See* 15 USC §§1361–1421 (1994); *United States* v. *Mitchell*, 553 F.2d 996 (5th Cir. 1977).
5. 46 USCA app. §761(a) (2002).

V. Statutes Applicable to Aliens while in the US

654. In light of the principle of territoriality, there is nothing unique about a statute that applies to aliens while they are in the United States. However, when the statute applies to the 'internal affairs' of foreign-flag ships, then the statute is worth noting.[1] One such statute is the Seamen's Act of 1915, which governs seamen's wages. In 1920, Congress amended the Act to make it applicable 'to a seaman on a foreign vessel when in a harbor of the United States' and to make '[t]he courts [of the United States] . . . available to the seaman for [its] enforcement'.[2] This amendment was a conspicuous intervention into matters that otherwise clearly belonged to the internal affairs of foreign ships. The stated congressional policy behind this intervention was 'to equalize on foreign vessels the burdens placed by American law . . . upon the American merchant marine, by making such foreign vessels . . . subject to regulations affecting American vessels'.[3]

1. The internal affairs doctrine is discussed *infra* 661–672.
2. 46 USC §10313(I) (2003).
3. Brief for the United States as Amicus Curiae at 4, *Strathearn S.S. Co.* v. *Dillon*, 252 US 348 (1920). *See also* H.R. Rep. No. 645, pt. 1, 62d Cong., 2nd Sess. 7 (1912).

655. In *Strathearn Steamship Co.* v. *Dillon*,[1] the Court upheld the application of the Act to a wage dispute arising out of a British employment contract between a British seaman and the British owner of a British vessel. The Court reasoned that in light of the explicit language of the 1920 amendment, any construction of the Act that would render it inapplicable to foreign vessels or foreign seamen would subvert congressional intent, which was to promote the employment of American seamen by 'plac[ing] American and foreign seamen on an equality of right . . . with equal opportunity to resort to the courts of the United States for the enforcement of the act'.[2]

1. 252 US 348 (1920).
2. *Id.* at 355.

VI. Interpretation

656. As *Dillon* illustrates, when there is clear congressional intent about a statute's applicability to foreign events or persons, the courts' job is simply to apply the statute as written, unless the statute is unconstitutional. From the perspective of choice-of-law methodology, statutes that expressly or impliedly delineate their reach to encompass foreign events or persons are either 'unilateral conflicts rules' or 'spatially conditioned substantive rules'. As such, they legislatively answer the choice-of-law question, leaving little for the courts to do.

In contrast, when a statute does not contain such a delineation, it falls upon the courts to define its potential extraterritorial reach. In so doing, the courts will employ all the resources of statutory construction and interpretation. A related methodological question, which rarely appears on the surface of judicial opinions, is whether this process will be approached from a unilateralist or a multilateralist perspective.[1] As explained below, American courts have vacillated between these two perspectives.

1. Generally speaking, 'multilateralist' approaches are those that purport to select the governing law through predetermined and ostensibly neutral criteria that are in principle indifferent to the

respective claims of the involved states in applying their laws, whereas 'unilateralist' approaches are those in which these claims, especially those of the forum state, are the principal factors in ultimately selecting the governing law. For a discussion of the evolution and contemporary misunderstanding of these concepts, *see* Symeonides, 'Accommodative Unilateralism as a Starting Premise in Choice of Law', in *Balancing of Interests: Liber Amicorum Peter Hay* (2005), p. 417.

§4. Statutes that Are Silent or Ambiguous on Their Territorial Reach

I. Introduction

657. As helpful as they would be, express congressional statements (affirmative or negative) about a statute's intended territorial reach are uncommon, if not rare. Like state statutes, most federal statutes are either silent on the question of their application to foreign cases or contain 'boilerplate language'[1] whose 'literal catholicity',[2] if taken at face value, would make them applicable to any and all activities, territorial or extraterritorial. As Professor Brainerd Currie once observed, '[l]awgivers . . . are accustomed to speak in terms of unqualified generality . . . [using] words like "all," "every," "no," "any," and "whoever"'[3] because 'they ordinarily give no thought to the phenomena that would suggest the need for qualification'.[4] For example, the Jones Act purports to provide a remedy to '[a]ny seaman'[5] who suffers an injury in the course of his employment. Similarly, the Americans with Disabilities Act (ADA) provides that '[n]o individual' shall be discriminated against on the basis of disability by 'any person' who owns or operates a place of 'public accommodation'.[6]

1. *Hartford Fire Ins. Co.* v. *California*, 509 US 764, 813 (1993); *EEOC* v. *Arabian Am. Oil Co.*, 499 US 244, 249 (1991).
2. *Lauritzen* v. *Larsen*, 345 US 571, 576 (1953).
3. B. Currie, *Selected Essays on the Conflict of Laws* (Durham, N.C., 1963), p. 81.
4. *Id.* at 82.
5. 46 USC §688.
6. 42 USC §12182(a).

658. In cases involving such statutes, it falls upon the courts to determine which of the 'any and all' persons or which activities Congress intended to regulate. Courts discharge this task by employing a process of statutory construction 'rather commonplace in a federal system by which courts often have to decide whether "any" or "every" reaches to the limits of the enacting authority's usual scope or is to be applied to foreign events or transactions'.[1]

In discharging this task, the Supreme Court has employed a variety of principles and techniques, developing certain presumptions or canons of construction. Among them are the presumption against extraterritoriality (hereafter territorial presumption), the presumption of intended compliance with international law, the effects doctrine, and the effects doctrine tempered by internationalism. These presumptions are discussed below.

1. *Lauritzen*, 345 US at 578–579.

II. The Territorial Presumption: The Early Version[1]

659. One of the first major cases involving the extraterritorial reach of a federal statute was *The Apollon*,[2] decided by none other than Justice Story, the intellectual father of American conflicts law. Influenced by Huber's views on territorial sovereignty, Story wrote that '[t]he laws of no nation can justly extend beyond its own territory, except so far as regards its own citizens'.[3] Relying on this principle and on the 'law of nations', Story articulated the following presumption: '[H]owever general and comprehensive the phrases used in our municipal laws may be, they must always be restricted in construction, to places and persons, upon whom the legislature have authority and jurisdiction'.[4]

1. From the rich literature on this presumption, *see, inter alia*, Born, 'A Reappraisal of the Extraterritorial Reach of US Law', 24 *Law & Pol'y Int'l Bus.* 1, 1992; Bradley, 'Territorial Intellectual Property Rights in an Age of Globalism', 37 *Va. J. Int'l L.* 505, 1997; Dodge, 'Understanding the Presumption Against Extraterritoriality', 16 *Berkeley J. Int'l L.* 85, 1998; Dodge, 'Extraterritoriality and Conflict-of-Laws Theory: An Argument for Judicial Unilateralism', 39 *Harv. Int'l L.J.* 101, 1998; Gordon, 'United States Extraterritorial Subject Matter Jurisdiction in Securities Fraud Litigation', 10 *Fla. J. Int'l L.* 487, 1996; Kramer, 'Extraterritorial Application of American Law after the Insurance Antitrust Case: A Reply to Professors Lowenfeld and Trimble', 89 *Am. J. Int'l L.* 750, 1995; Lowenfeld, 'Conflict, Balancing of Interests, and the Exercise of Jurisdiction to Prescribe: Reflections on the Insurance Antitrust Case', 89 *Am. J. Int'l. L.* 42, 1995; Turley, '"When in Rome": Multinational Misconduct and the Presumption Against Extraterritoriality', 84 *Nw. U. L. Rev.* 598, 1990; Weintraub, 'The Extraterritorial Application of Antitrust and Securities Laws: An Inquiry into the Utility of a "Choice-of-Law" Approach', 70 *Tex. L. Rev.* 1799, 1992.
2. 22 US (9 Wheat.) 362 (1824).
3. *Id.* at 370.
4. *Id.*

660. This territorial presumption was rigidly applied throughout the 19th century. Justice Holmes reaffirmed it in even stronger terms in *American Banana Co. v. United Fruit Co.*,[1] refusing to apply the Sherman [antitrust] Act to an American company's conduct in Costa Rica. Influenced by the then prevailing choice-of-law doctrine, Holmes said that '[t]he general and almost universal rule is that the character of an act as lawful or unlawful must be determined wholly by the law of the country where the act is done'.[2] Acknowledging that '[t]his principle was carried to an extreme' in certain interstate cases, Holmes concluded that, for a state 'to lay hold of the actor, to treat him according to its own notions rather than those of the place where he did the acts, not only would be unjust, but would be an interference with the authority of another sovereign, contrary to the comity of nations'.[3]

1. 213 US 347 (1909).
2. *Id.* at 356.
3. *Id.*

III. Foreign Ships and Their Internal Affairs

661. The old adage is that a ship is a floating piece of the flag-state's territory. If the adage is 'legally' true, then the question of whether US law applies to foreign ships, even when within US waters, is a question of *extraterritorial* application of US law, which will be answered through the same canons of construction the Court has adopted for such cases, including the presumption against extraterritoriality. Conversely, if the adage is merely a figure of speech,[1] then this becomes a question of straight-forward *territorial* application of US law, because, at the pertinent time, the ship is within US territory.[2] Even under this scenario, however, the application of US law is not automatic, but rather it depends on congressional intent. In determining this intent, the Supreme Court has adopted a canon of construction that appears to preserve much of the old floating-territory fiction. The canon effectively exempts the 'internal affairs' of foreign ships from the reach of American statutes, unless the statute contains a 'clear statement' to the contrary.[3] Thus, whether a US statute applies to foreign ships in US waters ultimately depends on the precise meaning the Court ascribes to these two critical phrases.

1. *See Cunard Steamship Co.* v. *Mellon*, 262 US 100, 123 (1923) ('[T]he statement sometimes made that a merchant ship is a part of the territory of the country whose flag she flies . . . is a figure of speech, a metaphor. . . . It is chiefly applicable to ships on the high seas, where there is no territorial sovereign; and as respects ships in foreign territorial waters it has little application beyond what is affirmatively or tacitly permitted by the local sovereign'.).
2. *See* Restatement (Third) of Foreign Relations §512 (1987) ('[T]he coastal state has the same sovereignty over its territorial sea . . . as it has in respect of its land territory'.). Nevertheless, as explained *infra*, when the application of American law requires permanent, non-removable alterations or additions to the vessel, then such application is both territorial and extraterritorial.
3. *See Spector* v. *Norwegian Cruise Line, Ltd.*, 125 S.Ct. 2169, 2174 (2005) ('Our cases hold that a clear statement of congressional intent is necessary before a general statutory requirement can interfere with matters that concern a foreign-flag vessel's internal affairs and operations[.]'). This canon is analogous, but not identical, to the territorial presumption.

662. The American version of the internal affairs doctrine is traced to the 19th century decision known as the *Wildenhus's Case*.[1] In that case, the Supreme Court restated the general principle that 'when a merchant vessel of one country enters the ports of another . . . , it subjects itself to the law of the place to which it goes'.[2] However, as a matter of international comity, the latter country may choose to 'abstain from interfering with the *internal discipline* of the ship, and the general regulation of *the rights and duties of the officers and crew towards the vessel, or among themselves*'.[3] Most countries have chosen to leave to the flag country 'all matters of discipline, and all things done on board, which affec[t] *only the vessel, or those belonging to her*, and [do] not involve the peace or dignity of the country, or the tranquillity of the port'.[4]

Thus, according to *Wildenhus*, the 'internal affairs' doctrine covers only: (1) matters involving the ship's 'internal discipline;' or (2) other matters that affect 'only the vessel or those belonging to her'. Even with regard to these matters, however, the doctrine does not apply if the particular activity 'affects the peace, dignity, or tranquility of the port'. The *Wildenhus's Case* itself fell within this exception. The case involved a homicide committed aboard a Belgian ship while in an American port. Although the incident occurred below deck and all involved parties and witnesses were Belgian crewmen, the Court found that the incident was of such gravity that, once it became known, it might disturb the peace of the port. For this reason the Court held that the incident fell outside the scope of the internal affairs doctrine and within the reach of American law.

1. *Mali* v. *Keeper of the Common Jail* (*Wildenhus's Case*), 120 US 1 (1887).
2. *Id.* at 11.
3. *Id.* at 12 (emphasis added).
4. *Id.* (emphasis added).

663. The next internal affairs case, *Cunard Steamship Co.* v. *Mellon*,[1] involved the question of whether the 1919 National Prohibition Act (the anti-alcohol statute implementing the Eighteenth Amendment) applied to US ships while outside US territorial waters, and foreign ships within US territorial waters. The Court answered the first question in the negative, reasoning that the Act was 'confined to the physical territory of the United States'[2] and dismissed as a mere 'figure of speech [or] a metaphor' the contention that a merchant ship is a 'part of the territory of the country whose flag she flies.'[3] Then, in addressing whether the Act applied to foreign ships in US waters, the Court noted: 'if it were true that a ship is a part of the territory of the country whose flag she carries, the contention would fail. But, as that is a fiction, we think the contention is right'.[4] The Court held that the Act prohibited foreign ships from serving *or carrying* alcohol in US waters.

1. 262 US 100 (1923).
2. *Id.* at 123.
3. *Id.*
4. *Id.* at 124.

664. The next three internal affairs cases all involved labour disputes affecting foreign ships. In the first case, *Benz* v. *Compania Naviera Hidalgo, S.A.*,[1] the Court ruled that the 1947 Labor Management Relations Act (LMRA)[2] was inapplicable to a dispute arising out of picketing by American unions in support of the striking foreign crewmen of a foreign ship temporarily in an American port. The Court characterized this as a dispute 'aris[ing] on a foreign vessel . . . between a foreign employer and a foreign crew operating under an agreement made abroad under the laws of another nation'.[3] The Court noted the absence of express language declaring the LMRA applicable to foreign ships and crews, but, understanding that such silence did not necessarily imply a negative answer, the Court defined the pertinent question as 'one of intent of the Congress as to the coverage of the Act'.[4] The Court concluded that 'Congress did not fashion [the LMRA] to resolve labor disputes between nationals of other countries operating ships under foreign laws', but rather intended the Act to serve as 'a bill of rights both for American workingmen and for their employers'.[5]

1. 353 US 138 (1957).
2. *See* 29 USC §141.
3. *Benz*, 353 US at 142.
4. *Id.*
5. *Id.* at 143–144.

665. The second labour dispute case was in *McCulloch* v. *Sociedad Nacional de Marineros de Honduras*.[1] Here the Court held that under the National Labor Relations Act (NLRA),[2] the National Labor Relations Board (NLRB) did not have authority to order an election for the unionization of alien seamen recruited in Honduras to serve aboard Honduran-flag ships. The Court rebuffed the Board's effort to distinguish this case from *Benz* on the ground that the *McCulloch* ships were part of a fleet ultimately owned by an American corporation (through foreign subsidiaries) and were frequent visitors to American ports. The Court appeared to reject a balancing-of-contacts test proposed by the Board, but only because the Court concluded that, as in *Benz*, the issue in *McCulloch* was clearly one that fell within the 'internal management and affairs' of 'foreign-flag-vessels manned by alien crews'.[3] The Court also noted that application of the NLRA would cause a 'head-on collision' with the Honduran Labor Code, which prohibited the election proposed by the Board. The Court reasoned that under these circumstances and with the 'possibility of international discord',[4] the NLRA should not apply in the absence of an 'affirmative intention of the Congress clearly expressed'.[5] Finding no such intention, the Court held the NLRA inapplicable.

1. 372 US 10 (1963).
2. *See* 29 USC §151.
3. *McCulloch*, 372 US at 20.
4. *Id.* at 21.
5. *Id.* at 22.

666. Both *Benz* and *McCulloch* involved issues that comprise the very core of a ship's internal affairs, i.e., crew discipline. In contrast, the third case, *Int'l Longshoremen* v. *Ariadne Shipping Co.*,[1] involved the rights of longshoremen who did not belong to the crew or to the vessel. Here, the Court found that the case fell outside the scope of the internal affairs doctrine. The issue in *Ariadne* was whether the NLRA applied to picketing by American longshoremen protesting sub-standard wages paid to them by foreign-flag ships for work in American ports. The Court distinguished *Benz* and *McCulloch* on the ground that *Ariadne* involved 'American residents, who were employed by each foreign ship not to serve as members of its crew but rather to do casual longshore work'.[2] Noting that the longshoremen's 'short-term, irregular and casual connection with the respective vessels plainly belied any involvement on their part with the ships' "internal discipline and order"',[3] the Court held that the NLRA was applicable to the picketing.

1. 397 US 195 (1970).
2. *Id.* at 199.
3. *Id.* at 200.

667. The last case arguably involving the foreign affairs of a foreign ship is *Spector* v. *Norwegian Cruise Line Ltd.*[1] The question in *Spector* was whether Title III of the Americans with Disabilities Act of 1990 (ADA)[2] applies to foreign-flagged ships while in the territorial waters of the United States. Title III prohibits operators of places of 'public accommodation'[3] and 'public transportation services'[4] from discriminating against disabled persons and requires the making of 'reasonable modifications in policies, practices, or procedures' to accommodate the disabled.[5] To this end, Title III also requires removal of 'architectural barriers, and communication barriers that are structural in nature', when such removal is 'readily achievable'.[6]

The ships in question in *Spector* had numerous contacts with the United States. The ships' owner was a Bermuda corporation that had its principal place of business in Florida. Although the ships carried the Bahamian flag, it was admittedly a flag of convenience. The ships operated cruises out of US ports and carried mostly American passengers, including the plaintiffs in this case. The cruises were extensively advertised in the United States and the cruise tickets provided that any disputes between passengers and the cruise operators were to be governed by United States law.

1. 545 US 119 (2005). *Spector* is extensively critiqued in S. Symeonides, 'Cruising in American Waters: *Spector*, Maritime Conflicts, and Choice of Law', 37 J. *Marit. L. & Comm.* 491, 2006. That critique is not repeated here.
2. 42 USC §§12181–1289.
3. 42 USC §12182(a).
4. *Id.* at §12184(a).
5. *Id.* at §§12182(b)(2)(A)(ii), 12184(b)(2)(A).
6. *Id.* at §§12182(b)(2)(A)(iv), 12184(b)(2)(C).

668. Despite the dominance of American contacts and the presence of significant American interests, the Fifth Circuit Court of Appeals held that Title III did not apply to these ships because the court found 'no indication, either in the statutory text or in the ADA's extensive legislative history, that Congress intended Title III to apply to foreign-flagged cruise ships'.[1] The Supreme Court reversed in a six-to-three decision, but the six justices disagreed on the extent to which the ADA applied. Although six justices joined in the judgment of the Court, only two parts of Justice Kennedy's opinion commanded a majority. The rest of the opinion was joined by either two or three justices.

1. *Spector* v. *Norwegian Cruise Line*, 356 F.3d 641, 646 (5th Cir. 2004), *rev'd*, 545 US 119 (2005).

669. Justice Kennedy correctly noted that the purpose of the internal affairs doctrine (and thus the test for employing it) was to presumptively exempt from the reach of US statutes only those activities that do *not* implicate 'the interests of the United States or its citizens', but do implicate 'only the internal order and discipline of the vessel, rather than the peace of the port'.[1] While acknowledging that these two prongs are not mutually exclusive, Kennedy concluded that if moderately construed, the ADA would have a minimal impact on matters claimed to belong to the ship's internal affairs. Kennedy noted that the ADA violations the plaintiffs alleged fell within two categories. The first category consisted of practises such as discriminatory pricing which did not involve the ship's internal affairs but did affect American citizens. He concluded that these practises fell within the territorial scope of the ADA, even in the absence of a clear statement to that effect.[2]

1. *Spector*, 545 US at 130.
2. *See id.* at 133–134. In addition to Justices Stevens and Souter (who joined Justice Kennedy's opinion in all respects), Justices Ginsburg, Breyer, and Thomas seemed to agree with this point, even though they did not formally joined this part of the opinion.

670. The second category of ADA violations *could* fall within the internal affairs doctrine to the extent that they involved certain physical features of the ship's public areas. For example, most of the cabins were not accessible to disabled passengers, and the ships' coamings (the raised edges around the doors) rendered many areas inaccessible to persons with mobility impairment. Justice Kennedy noted that these barriers 'affect the *passengers* as well as the ship and its crew'.[1] This could mean that even if they involved the ship's internal affairs, they could also fall within the *Wildenhus*'s exception insofar as they did not affect '*only* the vessel'.[2] However, Justice Kennedy took a more restrained route. He reasoned that, *if* the ADA did compel removal of these barriers, this would amount to 'a permanent and significant alteration of . . . an element of basic ship design and construction . . . [and] would interfere with the internal affairs of foreign ships . . . [because] it might be impossible for a ship to comply with all the requirements different jurisdictions might impose'.[3] If this were the case, then '[t]he clear statement rule would most likely come into play',[4] meaning that the application of the ADA would have to be grounded on a finding of clear congressional intent.

However, Justice Kennedy concluded that it was unnecessary to answer the above hypothetical at this junction due to the possibility that the ADA might not actually require removal of the above barriers. The ADA requires removal of barriers only when such removal is 'readily achievable'.[5] Kennedy reasoned that 'achievability' should include not only cost or physical difficulty of removal, but also other factors, such as whether the removal would bring the ship into non-compliance with international obligations like those imposed by the International Convention for the Safety of Life at Sea (SOLAS), or otherwise 'pose a direct threat to the health or safety of others'.[6] Kennedy concluded that these were factual questions to be answered by the lower court on remand.

1. *Id.* at 134 (emphasis added).
2. *See supra* 662.
3. *Spector*, 545 US at 135.
4. *Id.*
5. *Id.*
6. *Id.* at 136.

671. Justice Ginsburg, in a concurring opinion joined by Justice Breyer, agreed that the ADA should not be applied to matters involving a foreign ship's internal affairs, but only if such application would create an *actual* conflict with international law. Ginsburg went a step further than Kennedy, reasoning that when there is 'no potential for international discord',[1] and as long as 'there is good reason to apply our own law',[2] US law should apply, even if the matter involves the ship's internal affairs, and even in the absence of a clear statement of congressional intent. Justice Ginsburg concluded that the United States had 'a strong interest in ensuring that US resident cruise passengers enjoy Title III's protections on both domestic and foreign ships' and that, because there was no actual conflict with international legal obligations, there was 'no reason to demand a clearer congressional statement that Title III reaches . . . ships that regularly sail to and from US ports and derive most of their income from US passengers'.[3]

1. *Id.* at 143 (Ginsburg, J., concurring).
2. *Id.* at 145.
3. *Id.*

672. Justice Scalia dissented, reasoning that any structural modifications required by the ADA qualified as 'matters of [the ship's] "internal order"'[1] and that the mere 'possibility'[2] rather than the actuality of international discord triggers the internal affairs canon. In employing this canon, the Court should determine whether Congress '*in fact intended* that its enactment cover foreign-flag ships',[3] as opposed to inferring such intent. In Justice Scalia's view, this determination was an all-or-nothing proposition in the sense that the absence of a clear statement would render the ADA inapplicable to *all* violations alleged by the plaintiffs, including the discriminatory practises that the plurality found not to involve the ship's internal affairs.

1. *Id.* at 152 (Scalia, J., dissenting).
2. *Id.* at 153.
3. *Id.* at 156 (emphasis in original).

IV. Bilateralism: *Lauritzen* and Maritime Conflicts

673. During the same period it was refining the internal affairs doctrine, the Court decided a series of cases delineating the territorial reach of the Jones Act. Enacted in 1920 and speaking in 'literal catholicity', this Act provides a remedy to '[a]ny seaman'[1] who suffers an injury in the course of his employment. Taken literally, the quoted phrase would include foreign seamen injured on foreign vessels in foreign waters, unless courts employ the tools of logical and teleological interpretation to conclude otherwise.

1. 46 USC §688. ('Any seaman who shall suffer personal injury in the course of his employment may maintain an action for damages . . . and in such action all statutes of the United States modifying or extending the common-law right or remedy in cases of personal injury to railway employees shall apply'.).

674. In the first major case to come before the Court, *Uravic* v. *F. Jarka Co.*,[1] the plaintiff was an American seaman (actually a stevedore) who was injured in US waters aboard a German-flag vessel. The Court had no difficulty in holding the Jones Act applicable. In so doing, the Court cited both the *Wildenhus* and *Cunard* cases, reasoning that, because *Uravic* did not involve the ship's internal discipline, there was no reason to apply German law. 'It would be extraordinary', the Court said, 'to apply German law to Americans momentarily on board a private German ship in New York'.[2]

1. 282 US 234 (1931).
2. *Id.* at 240.

675. Next came the landmark case *Lauritzen* v. *Larsen*,[1] involving an action by a Danish seaman for injuries suffered aboard a Danish vessel in Cuban territorial waters. The plaintiff's only connection with the United States was that he had joined the ship in New York, where he signed his employment contract. The contract itself, however, was written in Danish and contained a Danish choice-of-law clause. The Court held that the case fell outside the reach of the Jones Act and was governed by Danish law.

The long-term importance of *Lauritzen* lies in the general methodology the Court articulated for resolving Jones Act conflicts (and by extension most other maritime conflicts). The Court dismissed the plaintiff's argument that, because of 'the literal catholicity of its terminology'[2] (i.e., 'any seaman'), the Jones Act applied to this case.[3] The Court not only rejected subservient reliance on the Act's language, but also avoided any pretence of searching for Congress's *actual* intent in enacting it. Speaking pragmatically, the Court noted that many statutes, including the Jones Act, 'give no evidence that Congress addressed itself to their foreign application'.[4] Lack of evidence, however, hardly means that Congress intended to proscribe their foreign application. Rather, it means that Congress chose to 'leave their application to be judicially determined from context and circumstance' by the courts, which are 'long accustomed to dealing with admiralty problems in reconciling our own with foreign interests and in accommodating the reach of our own laws to those of other maritime nations'.[5]

1. 345 US 571 (1953).
2. *Id.* at 576.
3. *See id.* at 576–577 ('Unless some relationship of one or more of these to our national interest is implied, Congress has extended our law and opened our courts to all alien seafaring men injured anywhere in the world in service of watercraft of every foreign nation – a hand on a Chinese junk, never outside Chinese waters, would not be beyond its literal wording'.).
4. *Id.* at 577.
5. *Id.*

676. The Court then articulated a multifactor test for determining whether the Jones Act applies to maritime torts that have foreign elements. Unlike the 'unilateralist' approach the Court followed in internal-affairs cases, the *Lauritzen* test is a classic multilateralist choice-of-law test. It calls for 'ascertaining and valuing points of contact between the transaction and the states or governments whose competing laws are involved . . . [and] weighing the significance of one or more connecting factors between the shipping transaction regulated and the national interest served by the assertion of authority'.[1] The Court listed seven such connecting factors, one of which was the law of the flag state. The other six were: (1) the place of wrongful act; (2) the allegiance or domicile of the injured; (3) the allegiance of the defendant ship-owner; (4) the place of the contract; (5) the inaccessibility of the foreign forum; and (6) the law of the forum.[2]

1. *Id.* at 582.
2. *See id.* at 583–591.

677. In the next Jones Act case, *Romero* v. *International Terminal Operating Co.*,[1] the plaintiff was a Spanish seaman who was injured aboard a Spanish-flag vessel while in American waters. He sued the Spanish ship-owner under the Jones Act and also under general maritime law. The Court extended the *Lauritzen* test to general-maritime-law cases and held American law inapplicable, despite the fact that the injury occurred in American waters. The emancipation from territoriality was completed.

1. 385 US 354 (1959).

678. *Hellenic Lines Ltd.* v. *Rhoditis*[1] is the last case of the *Lauritzen* trilogy. *Rhoditis* was an action brought by a Greek seaman against a Greek ship-owner for injuries suffered aboard a Greek-flag vessel while in the port of New Orleans. The case was virtually identical to *Romero*, except for one critical difference. The ship-owner, a long-term permanent resident of the United States, had managed his shipping operations out of his offices in the US. Thus, the Court found that he had an American 'base of operations', and this factor – which the Court added to the seven *Lauritzen* factors – tipped the scale in favour of applying the Jones Act.

The Court clarified that the *Lauritzen* test was 'not a mechanical one' and that '[t]he significance of one or more factors must be considered in light of the national interest served by the assertion of Jones Act jurisdiction'.[2] The Court then observed, in language that would aptly describe the *Spector* scenario, that the objective was 'to effectuate the liberal purposes of the Jones Act' while ensuring that ship-owners who draw substantial revenue from commerce with the United States bear their fair share of the concomitant cost. 'We see no reason', said the Court, 'to give the Jones Act a strained construction so that this alien owner, engaged in an extensive business operation in this country, may have an advantage over citizens engaged in the same business by allowing him to escape the obligations and responsibility of a Jones Act employer'.[3]

1. 398 US 306 (1970).
2. *Id.* at 308–309.
3. *Id.* at 310.

679. Although the *Lauritzen-Rhoditis* test was initially designed for cases involving injuries to seamen, lower courts have since extended it to virtually all maritime conflicts, including those involving other torts, collisions, maritime liens, ship mortgages, and limitation of liability.[1] In the meantime, two of the eight *Lauritzen-Rhoditis* factors have attained increased importance, while two others have lost ground. Specifically:

1. The 'base of operations' has emerged as 'the most common, if not the most decisive, basis for applying American law'[2] in maritime conflicts. When the court finds that the ship-owner has such a base in the United States, American law will most likely govern, even if the other factors do not point to American law. This proposition is directly confirmed by the cases that found an American base of operations, and indirectly by those that did not.[3]
2. Another decisive factor is the US citizenship or domicile of the injured seaman. As the *Lauritzen* court stated, the United States 'has a legitimate interest that its nationals and permanent inhabitants be not maimed or disabled from self-support'.[4] For this reason, cases applying American law to actions of American seamen injured aboard foreign vessels are quite numerous, even when the vessel is in foreign waters.[5] The same is true of cases applying American law to the actions of American vacationers injured aboard foreign ships or in foreign resorts in foreign territorial waters.[6]
3. The law-of-the-flag factor has become less important because of the growing use of 'flags of convenience'.[7]

4. The ship owner's 'allegiance' – to the extent it ever existed – has become much less important because of the prevalent practise of vesting ownership in shell corporations chartered by 'countries of convenience'.[8]

1. *See*, e.g., *Carbotrade S.p.A.* v. *Bureau Veritas*, 99 F.3d 86 (2nd Cir. 1996) (dispute between a ship buyer and classification society); *Sealord Marine Co. Ltd.* v. *Am. Bureau of Shipping*, 220 F.Supp.2d 260 (SDNY 2002) (suit against classification society); *Galapagos Corp. Turistica 'Galatours', S.A.* v. *The Panama Canal Comm'n*, 190 F.Supp.2d 900 (E.D. La. 2002) (suit by shipowner against Panama canal company); *and Gund III* v. *Philbrook's Boatyard*, 374 F.Supp.2d. 909 (W.D. Wash. 2005) (dispute between boat owner and boatyard for faulty repairs).
2. E. Scoles, P. Hay, P. Borchers & S. Symeonides, *Conflict of Laws*, (4th edn, St. Paul, Minn., 2004), p. 893.
3. For numerous citations, *see id.* at 893–895.
4. *Lauritzen*, 345 US at 586.
5. For numerous citations, *see* S. Symeonides, 'Cruising in American Waters: *Spector*, Maritime Conflicts, and Choice of Law', 37 J. *Marit. L. & Comm.* 491, 2006, 513.
6. *See id.*
7. *See id.* at 514. In 2004, there was only one cruise ship flying the American flag. *See Spector* v. *Norwegian Cruise Line Ltd.*, Brief for Petitioners, 2004 WL 2803188 at *32.
8. *See Lauritzen*, 345 US at 587 ('[I]t is common knowledge that in recent years a practice has grown, particularly among American shipowners, to avoid stringent shipping laws by seeking foreign registration eagerly offered by some countries. Confronted with such operations, our courts on occasion have pressed beyond the formalities of more or less nominal foreign registration to enforce against American shipowners the obligations which our law places upon them'.); *and Rhoditis*, 398 US at 310 ('If . . . the liberal purposes of the Jones Act are to be effectuated, the facade of the operation must be considered as minor, compared with the real nature of the operation and a cold objective look at the actual operational contacts that this ship and this owner have with the United States'. For a collection of similar case statements, *see* Symeonides, 'Cruising in American Waters', *supra* note 5 at 514.

V. The 'Effects Doctrine': Foreign Conduct with Domestic Effects

680. Many of the old cases that followed the territorial presumption seemed to assume that it was mandated by international law, rather than by self-imposed intra-US constraints. For example, Justice Holmes referred to the 'comity of nations',[1] Justice Marshall to the 'law of nations',[2] Justice Jackson to the 'prevalent doctrines of international law'[3] and Judge Learned Hand to 'limitations customarily observed by nations . . . [that] generally correspond to those fixed by the "Conflict of Laws"'.[4] Indeed, despite the prevailing belief that Congress is free to violate international law if it so chooses, the common assumption has been that Congress does not intend to do so. Consequently, in Justice Marshall's words in *Charming Betsy*, 'an act of congress ought never to be construed to violate the law of nations if any other possible construction remains'.[5]

1. *See supra* 640.
2. *Murray* v. *Schooner Charming Betsy*, 6 US (2 Cranch) 64, 118 (1804).
3. *Lauritzen*, 345 US at 577.
4. *United States* v. *Aluminum Co. of Am. (Alcoa)*, 148 F.2d 416, 443 (2d Cir. 1945).
5. *Murray* v. *Schooner Charming Betsy*, 6 US (2 Cranch) 64, 118 (1804).

681. However, to the extent that the territorial presumption is founded on international law, its foundation has changed since the 19th century. For example, by

1927, the Permanent Court of International Justice held in *The SS Lotus (France* v. *Turkey)*[1] that territoriality was *not* an absolute principle, and essentially validated the 'objective territoriality' principle or 'effects doctrine'. Similarly, conflicts law has undergone an even more drastic transformation which reduced significantly the domain of territoriality as a guiding principle in delineating the spatial operation of laws.[2] In light of these developments, by the middle of the 20th century, the territorial presumption was losing ground to the 'effects doctrine' as courts began to focus on the effects of the conduct at issue, rather than on the place of conduct.

1. P.C.I.J., Ser. A. No. 10 (1927).
2. *See* S. Symeonides, 'Territoriality and Personality in Tort Conflicts', in: T. Einhorn & K. Siehr (eds.), *Intercontinental Cooperation through Private International Law: Essays in Memory of Peter Nygh* (2004), p. 401.

682. The leading case for what is now known as the 'effects doctrine' is *United States* v. *Aluminum Company of America (Alcoa)*,[1] an antitrust case decided by Judge Learned Hand. Historically, however, one of the first articulations of this doctrine was Justice Holmes's statement in *Strassheim* v. *Daily*,[2] that '[a]cts done outside the jurisdiction, but intended to produce and producing detrimental effects within it, justify a state in punishing the cause of harm'.[3]

Relying on *Strassheim* and subsequent cases, Judge Hand stated in 1945 that it was 'settled law' that 'any state may impose liabilities, even upon persons not within its allegiance, for conduct outside its borders that has consequences within its borders which the state reprehends'.[4] He distinguished between two categories of cases involving conduct outside the United States: (a) those in which the conduct was not intended to produce effects in the US but which produced such effects; and (b) those in which the conduct was intended to produce such effects but did not produce them. Judge Hand surmised, without deciding, that Congress probably did not intend either category to be covered by the Sherman Act. He also concluded, however, that when, as in the case at hand, 'both conditions are satisfied'[5] (i.e., when the foreign conduct is intended to produce effects in the United States *and* produces such effects), then the case falls within the reach of the Sherman Act.

1. 148 F.2d 416 (2d Cir. 1945).
2. 221 US 280 (1911).
3. *Id.* at 284.
4. *Alcoa*, 148 F.2d at 443.
5. *Id.* at 444.

683. In *Timberlane Lumber Co.* v. *Bank of America N.T. & S.A.*,[1] the Ninth Circuit moderated the effects doctrine by adding to it an interest-balancing prong, requiring courts to inquire 'whether the interests of, and links to, the United States including the magnitude of the effect on American foreign commerce are sufficiently strong, *vis-à-vis* those of other nations, to justify an assertion of extraterritorial authority'.[2] This inquiry should, *inter alia*, include the following factors:

> [T]he degree of conflict with foreign law or policy, the nationality or allegiance of the parties and [their] locations . . . , the extent to which enforcement by either state can be expected to achieve compliance, the relative significance

of effects on the United States as compared with those elsewhere, the extent to which there is explicit purpose to harm or affect American commerce, [and] the foreseeability of such effect.[3]

By evaluating these factors, a court would identify the 'degree of conflict' and then 'determine whether in the face of it the contacts and interests of the United States are sufficient to support the exercise of extraterritorial jurisdiction'.[4]

1. 549 F.2d 597 (9th Cir. 1976).
2. *Id.* at 613.
3. *Id.* at 614.
4. *Id.* at 614–615.

VI. The Territorial Presumption, Again

684. For several years, the common assumption was that the effects doctrine as amended by *Timberlane* was the prevailing test for resolving these conflicts. However, in the 1991 case *EEOC* v. *Arabian American Oil Co.* (*Aramco*),[1] the Supreme Court returned to the territorial presumption. *Aramco* held that Title VII of the Civil Rights Act of 1964 did not apply to the allegedly discriminatory employment practises of an American employer against an American employee in Saudi Arabia. Characterizing this presumption as a 'longstanding principle of American law' the Court reiterated that 'legislation of Congress, unless a contrary intent appears, is meant to apply only within the territorial jurisdiction of the United States'.[2] The Court thought that this presumption 'serves to protect against unintended clashes between our laws and those of other nations which could result in international discord'.[3] The Court stated:

> We assume that Congress legislates against the backdrop of the presumption against extraterritoriality. Therefore, unless there is the affirmative intention of the Congress clearly expressed, . . . we must presume it is primarily concerned with domestic conditions.[4]

Finding no such affirmative intention, the Court held that the Civil Rights Act did not apply extraterritorially. Congress promptly responded by legislatively overruling *Aramco* and (re)stating its 'affirmative intention' for the very extraterritorial application the *Aramco* Court had rejected.[5]

1. 499 US 244 (1991).
2. *Aramco*, 499 US at 248 (quoting *Foley Bros., Inc.* v. *Filardo*, 336 US 281, 285 (1949)).
3. *Id.*
4. *Id.* (internal quotations omitted).
5. *See* the Civil Rights Act of 1991, 105 Stat. 1077, 42 USCA §2000e(f).

VII. The 'Effects Doctrine', Again

685. In 1993, two years after *Aramco*, the Supreme Court decided three cases, two of which applied the territorial presumption.[1] However, in the third case, *Hartford*

Fire Insurance Company v. *California*,[2] decided only one week after the second case, the Court resurrected the effects doctrine and made *no* mention of the territorial presumption. *Hartford Fire* held that Section 1 of the Sherman Antitrust Act applied to wholly foreign conduct which was intended to, and did, produce a substantial effect within the United States.[3]

The defendants in *Hartford Fire* were British reinsurers accused of conspiring with American insurers to limit coverage of certain pollution risks in North America and, generally, to adversely affect the insurance market in the United States. Supported by the British Government appearing as amicus, the defendants argued: that their London conduct was perfectly consistent with British law and policy; that applying the Sherman Act to that conduct would conflict significantly with British law and the comprehensive regulatory regime that law provided for the London reinsurance market; and, consequently, that US courts should decline to exercise its jurisdiction under the principle of international comity.

1. *See Smith* v. *United States*, 507 US 197 (1993) (decided 8 March 1993), and *Sale* v. *Haitian Ctrs. Council, Inc.*, 509 US 155 (1993) (decided 21 June 1993).
2. 509 US 764 (1993) (decided 28 June 1993).
3. Section 1 of the Sherman Act (15 USCA §1) provides in part that '[e]very contract . . . or conspiracy, in restraint of trade or commerce among the several States, or with foreign nations, is declared to be illegal'.

686. In an opinion written by Justice Souter, the Court held that, because the defendants' London activities were meant to produce, and did in fact produce, substantial effects in the United States, the case fell within the reach of the Sherman Act. In response to the defendants' comity argument, the Court said that, 'even assuming that in a proper case a court may decline to exercise Sherman Act jurisdiction over foreign conduct . . . , international comity would not counsel against exercising jurisdiction'[1] in this case, which did not present a '*true conflict*'[2] between American and British law. By 'true conflict', the Court meant a situation in which one law compels what the other law prohibits, which is a narrower meaning than the quoted term has in the conflicts literature.[3] The fact that conduct is lawful in the foreign state, said the Court, will not, by itself, bar application of the United States antitrust laws, 'even where the foreign state has a strong policy to permit or encourage such conduct'.[4] Because the defendants did not claim that British law required them to act in a way that American law prohibited, or that complying with the laws of both countries was otherwise impossible, there was 'no conflict' and the defendants were perfectly capable of complying with both laws.

1. *Hartford Fire*, 509 US at 799.
2. *Id.* at 798.
3. In the conflicts literature, a true conflict is present whenever each involved state has an interest in applying its law, and that law produces a different outcome. *See supra* 181.
4. 509 US at 799 (citing *Restatement (Third)* §415, cmt. j).

687. Justice Scalia, dissenting, found this assertion of no true conflict between American and British law to be a 'breathtakingly broad proposition', which would bring the Sherman Act and other laws into 'sharp and unnecessary conflict with the legitimate interests of other countries'.[1] He noted that, in the prevailing conflicts lexicon, there is clearly a 'conflict' whenever the two laws provide 'different substantive rules', and that in such a case 'a conflict-of-laws analysis is necessary'.[2]

According to Justice Scalia, such an analysis should encompass two '*independent*' canons of construction: (a) *Aramco*'s territorial presumption; and (b) *Charming Betsy*'s canon that an act of Congress should never be construed to violate the law of nations if any other possible construction remains. Scalia argued that, although in this case the presumption was overcome (as the defendants had conceded), the Court did not satisfy the *Charming Betsy* canon: 'statutes should not be interpreted to regulate foreign persons or conduct if that regulation would conflict with principles of international law'[3] or international comity, which 'includes the choice-of-law principles that . . . are assumed to be incorporated into our substantive laws having extraterritorial reach'.[4] Relying on Section 403 of the Restatement (Third), Justice Scalia concluded that an interpretation of the Sherman Act making it applicable to defendant's London activities would be 'unreasonable'.[5] This is because the defendants were foreign corporations and their activity took place primarily in the United Kingdom, a country which had established a 'comprehensive regulatory scheme governing the London reinsurance markets', and which 'clearly ha[d] a heavy interest in regulating the activity'.[6]

1. *Id.* at 820 (Scalia, J., dissenting).
2. *Id.* at 820–821.
3. *Id.* at 815.
4. *Id.* at 817.
5. *Id* at 818. *See also id.* at 819 ('I think it unimaginable that an assertion of legislative jurisdiction by the United States would be considered reasonable, and therefore it is inappropriate to assume, in the absence of statutory indication to the contrary, that Congress has made such an assertion'.).
6. *Id.* at 819. Since *Hartford Fire*, the Antitrust Division of the US Department of Justice has increased its use of criminal sanctions against foreign companies acting abroad, as well as the severity of the sanctions, especially fines. In 1997 and 1998, 90 per cent of the fines the Division collected were imposed on foreign companies, and in 1999, a year in which the Division collected more fines than in the entire history of the Sherman Act, almost all of the fines were assessed against foreign companies acting abroad. *See* D. Ellis, 'Projecting the Long Arm of the Law: Extraterritorial Criminal Enforcement of US Antitrust Laws in the Global Economy', 1 *Wash. U. Global Stud. L. Rev.* 477, 2002, 478–479.

VIII. The Effects Doctrine Tempered by Internationalism

688. In the 2004 case *F. Hoffman-La Roche Ltd.* v. *Empagran S.A.*,[1] the Supreme Court, in a unanimous decision by Justice Breyer, seemed to take to heart Justice Scalia's insistence on considering the interests of other countries.[2] *Empagran* was a complex case involving the scope of the Foreign Trade Antitrust Improvements Act (FTAIA).[3] Enacted in 1982 as an addendum to the Sherman Act, the FTAIA delineates, and to some extent limits, the extraterritorial reach of the Sherman Act. Simplified and roughly translated, the FTAIA provides that the Sherman Act does not apply to certain anti-competitive non-import activity involving foreign commerce, unless that activity has a direct, substantial, and reasonably foreseeable effect on domestic US commerce. Lower courts have had difficulties with cases in which this activity produces the described adverse effects on *both* domestic *and* foreign commerce. The Sherman Act clearly applies to the domestic injury, but the lower courts have disagreed as to whether or how it also applies to the foreign injury caused by the same conduct. In *Empagran*, the Supreme Court held that the Sherman Act applies to the foreign injury only if that injury is dependent on the domestic injury.

1. 542 US 155 (2004).
2. For another 'internationalist' decision rendered after *Hartford Fire*, *see Vimar Seguros Y Reaseguros, S.A.* v. *M/V Sky Reefer*, 515 US 528 (1995) (enforcing a foreign arbitration clause; discussed *supra* 475–478).
3. *See* 15 USC §6(a).

689. *Empagran* involved several foreign and domestic vitamin sellers who engineered a worldwide price-fixing scheme that artificially raised vitamin prices both in the United States and in several other countries. This part of the case involved only the injuries suffered in those countries, and was based on the factual premise that these injuries were *independent* of any injuries the same conduct caused in the United States.[1] The Court held that under these circumstances, 'a purchaser in the United States could bring a Sherman Act claim under the FTAIA based on domestic injury, but a purchaser in Ecuador could not bring a Sherman Act claim based on foreign harm'.[2]

1. The plaintiffs argued in the alternative that the foreign injury was *dependent* on the domestic injury. *See Empagran*, 542 US at 175 ('because vitamins are fungible and readily transportable, without an adverse domestic effect (i.e., higher prices in the United States), the sellers could not have maintained their international price-fixing arrangement and [plaintiffs] would not have suffered their foreign injury'.) The Court remanded the case to the lower court for addressing the plaintiffs' alternative argument. For the case on remand, *see Empagran S.A.* v. *F. Hoffman-La Roche Ltd.*, 388 F.3d 337 (D.C. Cir. 2004).
2. *Empagran*, 542 US at 159.

690. In addition to the FTAIA's language and history, the Court based its holding on 'principles of prescriptive comity',[1] which suggest that ambiguous statutes should be construed in a way that avoids 'unreasonable interference with the sovereign authority of other nations'.[2] Particularly in 'today's highly interdependent commercial world', courts should seek to reconcile potentially conflicting laws so as to make them 'work together in harmony' and should assume 'that legislators take account of the legitimate sovereign interests of other nations when they write American laws'.[3] One should not impute to Congress motives of 'legal imperialism',[4] said the Court – at least not in *this* case, one might add.

The Court concluded that, although it is reasonable to apply US antitrust laws to foreign anti-competitive conduct that causes domestic antitrust injury, it is '[*not*] reasonable to apply those laws to foreign conduct *insofar as that conduct causes independent foreign harm and that foreign harm alone gives rise to the plaintiff's claim*'.[5] The justification for applying these laws in the latter case 'seems insubstantial', said the court, when compared to the 'serious risk of interference with a foreign nation's ability independently to regulate its own commercial affairs',[6] a risk that was duly brought to the Court's attention by many foreign governments in their *amici* briefs.

1. *Id.* at 169.
2. *Id.* at 164.
3. *Id.*
4. *Id.* at 169.
5. *Id.* at 165.
6. *Id. See also id.* ('Why should American law supplant, for example, Canada's or Great Britain's or Japan's own determination about how best to protect Canadian or British or Japanese customers from anticompetitive conduct engaged in significant part by Canadian or British or Japanese or other foreign companies?')

IX. The 'Headquarters Doctrine': Domestic Conduct with Foreign Effects

691. Two weeks after *Empagran*, the Court decided *Sosa* v. *Alvarez-Machain*,[1] a case involving the converse scenario, that is, domestic conduct that was intended to, and did, produce effects in a foreign country. However, *Sosa* was decided under a different and in some respects peculiar statute, the Federal Tort Claims Act (FTCA) of 1946. Section 1346(b) of the FTCA waives the sovereign immunity of the United States for injuries caused by its employees under circumstances in which the United States would be liable under the law of the 'place where the *act or omission* occurred.'[2] In the majority of cases, the act or omission produces its injurious effects in the same state and for those cases the quoted phrase is nothing but a restatement of the traditional *lex loci delicti* rule. However, this same phrase becomes ambiguous in those cases in which the conduct and the injury occur in different states (cross-border torts). In the first FTCA cross-border case to reach the Supreme Court, *Richards* v. *United States*,[3] the Court interpreted this phrase as referring to the law of the state of *conduct* rather than the state of the resulting injury.[4]

1. 542 US 692 (2004) (decided 24 June 2004).
2. 28 USC §1346(b) (emphasis added).
3. 369 US 1 (1962).
4. *Richards* also found that the quoted phrase referred to the 'whole law' of the conduct state, i.e., including its conflicts law, rather than its internal law.

692. However, because *Richards* was an interstate conflict not involving a foreign country, the Court did not have to consider Section 2680(k) of the FTCA, which contains an exception providing that the waiver of sovereign immunity does not apply to any claim '*arising in a foreign country*'.[1] The next two cases, *United States* v. *Spelar*,[2] and *Smith* v. *United States*,[3] involved foreign torts. However in both cases the conduct and the injury both occurred in the same foreign country, leading to the easy conclusion that the resulting claims had 'aris[en] in a foreign country' and thus the foreign-country exception was applicable.

1. 28 USC §2680(k) (emphasis added).
2. 338 US 217 (1949) (action arising out of the crash of an airplane upon take-off in Nova Scotia).
3. 507 US 197 (1993) (arising from slip-and-fall injury in Antarctica).

693. Following *Richards*, lower courts encountering foreign cross-border torts focused on the place of *conduct*. When the conduct occurred in a foreign country and the injury occurred in the United States, the courts concluded that the claim arose in a foreign country, thus making the foreign-country exception applicable. Conversely, when the critical conduct occurred in the United States and the injury occurred abroad, the courts concluded that the claim arose in the United States, thus rendering the foreign-country exception inapplicable. Most of the cases of the latter pattern relied on, or can be explained by, a doctrine known as the 'headquarters doctrine', which is discussed below.

694. *Sosa* v. *Alvarez-Machain*[1] fell within the latter pattern to the extent that it involved a tort committed partly in the United States and partly abroad. The plaintiff Alvarez-Machain, a Mexican national, was kidnapped in Mexico and brought to the United States where he was prosecuted for allegedly participating in the torture of an American agent of the Drug Enforcement Agency (DEA) in Mexico. The kidnapping was planned in the United States by DEA officers. It was executed in Mexico by Mexican nationals, including defendant Sosa, whom the DEA hired to carry out this plan. Eventually Alvarez was acquitted, after which he brought a tort action against the United States under the FTCA.

1. 542 US 692 (2004).

695. The Ninth Circuit Court of Appeals held for Alvarez, after finding that the FTCA's foreign-country exception was inapplicable.[1] This case fit the headquarters doctrine 'like a glove',[2] said the court, because although the 'operative effect' of Alvarez's kidnapping occurred in Mexico, 'all of the command decisions about the seizure and removal to the United States occurred in California',[3] where DEA agents hired the Mexican kidnapper and gave them 'precise instructions'[4] on how to carry out the kidnapping. The kidnapping was carried out 'pursuant to the plan of the United States government officials' and the injury, Alvarez's false arrest, 'occurred as a direct and intended result of the DEA's plans'.[5]

1. *See Alvarez-Machain* v. *United States*, 266 F.3d 1045 (9th Cir. 2001), and *Alvarez-Machain* v. *United States*, 331 F.3d 604 (9th Cir. 2003).
2. *Alvarez-Machain*, 331 F.3d, at 638.
3. *Alvarez-Machain*, 266 F.3d at 1054.
4. *Alvarez-Machain*, 331 F.3d at 638.
5. *Alvarez-Machain*, 266 F.3d at 1055–1056.

696. In an opinion written by Justice Souter, the Supreme Court reversed, rejecting the headquarters doctrine. Approval of this doctrine, said the Court, would make it a standard part of FTCA litigation in cases involving foreign countries, because 'it will virtually always be possible' to assert that the conduct that caused the foreign injury 'was the consequence of faulty training, selection or supervision ... in the United States'.[1] The headquarters doctrine 'threatens to swallow the foreign country exception whole'[2] because 'even slip-and-fall cases ... can ... be repackaged as headquarters claims based on failure to train, [or] a failure to warn'.[3]

1. *Sosa*, 542 US at 702.
2. *Id.* at 703.
3. *Id.* at 702. Of course, as the courts below found, this was not a case of faulty training or failure to warn, but rather a case of deliberate planning. The foreign injury 'occurred as a direct and

intended result of the DEA's plans', *supra*, hatched in California. The Court must have read these facts differently.

697. Another reason for rejecting the headquarters doctrine was the Court's conclusion that the doctrine is antithetical to the congressional intent embodied in FTCA's foreign-country exception. To reach this conclusion, the Court assumed that Congress must have intended the words 'claim arising in a foreign country' in the foreign-country exception of Section 2680(k) of the FTCA to mean 'a claim *for injury or harm* occurring in a foreign country'.[1] Such intent was likely, the Court surmised, because, at the time of the FTCA's passage, 'the dominant principle in choice of law analysis for tort cases was *lex loci delicti*',[2] which was understood to require the application of the law of the place of injury. Then, assuming that the 'object' of this exception was to avoid the application of foreign law,[3] the Court reasoned that the headquarters doctrine would thwart this object because it would 'displace the exception by recasting claims of foreign injury as claims not arising in a foreign country'.[4] In turn, this would lead to applying foreign law of the place of injury 'in accordance with the choice-of-law rule of the headquarters jurisdiction'.[5] The Court concluded by holding that 'the FTCA's foreign country exception bars all claims based on any injury suffered in a foreign country, regardless of where the tortious act or omission occurred'.[6]

1. *Id.* at 704 (emphasis added).
2. *Id.* at 705.
3. *Id.* at 707. For this conclusion, the Court relied on its 1949 decision in *Spelar*, *supra* 692, which, however, involved a tort in which both the injury and the conduct had occurred in the same foreign country.
4. *Id.* at 708.
5. *Id.* Of course, the headquarters doctrine leads to foreign law only when the headquarters jurisdiction (a state of the United States) follows the traditional *lex loci delicti* rule, or otherwise applies the law of the place of injury. The Court noted that ten states still follow the traditional rule, and that even states that have adopted the modern methodologies tend to apply the law of the place of injury in many cases. The Court also rejected the idea of a 'selective headquarters exception' for cases in which the headquarters jurisdiction would not apply foreign law, because this would produce 'a scheme of federal jurisdiction that would vary from State to State'. *Id.* at 712.
6. *Id.* at 712.

698. Whether the outcome of *Sosa* depended, or should depend, on *actual* congressional intent is a matter on which reasonable minds can differ. However, the legislative history of the FTCA casts doubt on whether Congress intended to tie the foreign-country exception to the place of injury alone.[1] It appears that Congress was thinking in terms of the place of *conduct*, not only in drafting the main rule of Section 1346(b), but also in drafting the foreign-country exception of Section 2680(k) and that in both cases Congress did not consider the possibility of *cross-border* torts – the FTCA 'was passed with . . . garden-variety torts in mind . . . , such . . . as negligence in the operation of vehicles'.[2]

1. In testimony before Congress, the proponent of the foreign-country exception explained that, '[s]ince liability is to be determined by the law of the *situs of the wrongful act or omission* it is wise to restrict the [FTCA] bill to claims arising in this country'. Assistant Attorney General Shea in Hearings on H.R. 5373 *et al.* before the House Committee on the Judiciary, 77th Cong., 2d Sess., 35 (1942) (quoted in *Sosa*), 542 US at 707 (emphasis added).

2. *Sosa*, 542 US at 707 note 4. In *Richards*, the Court found that the legislative history of the FTCA was not helpful in resolving choice-of-law ambiguities, 'except in a negative way', for, as is often the case, 'Congress did not consider choice-of-law problems', or at least those involved in cross-border torts. *Richards*, 369 US at 8. Rather, Congress was preoccupied with typical intra-state torts, like automobile accident cases, in which 'the negligence and the injury normally occur simultaneously and in a single jurisdiction'. *Id.* at 9.

699. If the above is true, then the only certainty is that the foreign-country exception applies to cases like *Spelar* in which *both* the conduct and the injury occurred in a foreign country. Whether the exception also applies to cross-border torts, at least those involving domestic conduct and foreign injury, is a question that FTCA text does not answer. The Court's answer that the exception does apply may be the correct answer, but it should be understood as a *policy choice* rather than as an answer that flows from text or legislative history. Moreover, it is a choice that is not unrelated to the political realities of 2004.

700. Be that as it may, the combined effect of *Richards*, *Spelar*, and *Sosa* is as follows:

1. the United States is amenable to suit for torts in which both the conduct and the injury occurred in the United States. The specifics are governed by the substantive law that is selected under the conflicts law of the state of conduct; and
2. the United States is immune from suit for torts in which both the conduct and the injury (*Spelar*), or only the injury (*Sosa*), occurred in a foreign country.[1]

1. This leaves the cases in which the conduct occurred in a foreign country but the injury occurred in the United States. As noted earlier, lower courts have held that these cases also fall within the scope of the foreign-country exception, and thus outside the waiver of the immunity of the United States because, under *Richards*, the critical contact was the place of *conduct*. These cases must be deemed overruled by *Sosa*'s de-emphasis of the place of conduct and its holding that the foreign-country exception contemplates situations in which the *injury* occurred in a foreign country.

701. *Sosa* also involved a claim under the Alien Tort Statute (ATS)[1] – the plaintiff's tort action against his Mexican kidnapper, Sosa. The Ninth Circuit upheld a judgment for the plaintiff, holding that his right to damages would be governed by American federal common law.[2] The Supreme Court again reversed, holding that the plaintiff did not have an action under the ATS. The Court found that the ATS authorized federal courts to entertain only a 'relatively modest set of actions'[3] that were recognized by both the law of nations and the general American common law of the time of the ATS enactment (in 1789). By focusing on prevailing views and practises of that time, the Court identified three offenses that met both criteria: 'offenses against ambassadors, . . . violations of safe conduct . . . , and individual actions arising out of prize captures and piracy'.[4]

1. 28 USC §1350 (also known as Alien Tort Claims Act (ATCA), discussed *supra* 650).
2. *See Alvarez-Machain* v. *United States*, 266 F.3d 1045 (9th Cir. 2001).
3. *Sosa*, 752 US at 720.
4. *Id.*

702. The Court then rejected Justice Scalia's argument that, by declaring that federal courts had no authority to create 'general' common law, *Erie* had 'close[d] the door to further independent judicial recognition of actionable international norms'.[1] Rather, the Court said, 'the door is still ajar subject to vigilant doorkeeping'.[2] As the doorkeeper, the Court cautioned lower courts to 'not recognize private claims under federal common law for violations of any international law norm with less definite content and acceptance among civilized nations than the historical paradigms familiar when [the ATS] was enacted'.[3] The Court concluded that Alvarez's claim did not meet this standard because his kidnapping was, after all, no more than 'a single illegal detention of less than a day, followed by the transfer of custody to lawful authorities and a prompt arraignment, [and as such it] violates no norm of customary international law so well defined as to support the creation of a federal remedy'.[4]

1. *Id.* at 729.
2. *Id.*
3. *Id.* at 732.
4. *Id.* at 738.

703. Justice Scalia wrote a concurring opinion in order to 'subtract' from the majority opinion 'its reservation of a discretionary power in the Federal Judiciary to create causes of action for the enforcement of international-law-based norms'.[1] After suggesting that, as a matter of original intent, the ATS was not meant to provide *any* private cause of action, Scalia noted that, even if the pre-*Erie* 'general' common law had authorized private actions, *Erie* closed that door. Thus, the question now was not whether to leave the door ajar, but rather whether to open a new door of *federal* common law. After lamenting the phenomenon of 'unelected federal judges . . . usurping [Congress's] lawmaking power by converting what they regard as norms of international law into American law',[2] Scalia criticized the majority for being 'incapable of admitting that some matters – *any* matters – are none of its business' and characterized the majority decision as a victory of the 'Never Say Never Jurisprudence'.[3]

1. *Id.* at 739 (Scalia, J., dissenting).
2. *Id.* at 750.
3. *Id.*

704. This language, as well as the majority's reference to 'ajar doors' and 'vigilant doorkeeping', are already affecting not only the substance – as one should expect – but also the rhetoric of lower court decisions. For example, one court characterized the ATS as 'an area that is so ripe for non-meritorious and blunderbuss suits'[1] and found it necessary to quote a statement by President Bush about overburdening courts with 'ill-founded or politically motivated suits, which have nothing to do with the United States'.[2]

1. *In re South African Apartheid Litig.*, 2004 WL 2722204 at *8 (S.D.N.Y. 2004).
2. *Id.* (quoting Statement of President George H.W. Bush Upon Signing H.R. 2092, 1992 USCCAN 91 (12 March 1992)).

§5. A Few Remarks on Methodology

705. An experienced international litigator and thoughtful academic author has summarized as follows the Court's jurisprudence on the subjects discussed in this chapter as follows:

> [T]he Court's recent approach to the extraterritorial reach of federal legislation leaves much to be desired. With almost haphazard nonchalance, the Court has applied several fundamentally different rules of construction in international cases. One is the traditional *American Banana* rule, revived and applied in *Aramco*, which imposes a strict territoriality presumption on federal legislation. A second is the *Hartford Fire* rule, which looks to the contemporary formulations of *Alcoa*'s effect doctrine. A third is reflected in decisions such as *Lauritzen* . . . , which adopt a multifactor rule of reason approach . . . , which is arguably adopted in [*Empagran*]. Unfortunately, the Court has neither acknowledged the existence of these different approaches, nor provided guidance as to when it will apply one, rather than another. The result is confusion for litigants and lower courts, and arbitrary, unpredictable results.[1]

1. G. Born & P. Rutledge, *International Civil Litigation in United States Courts* (4th edn, Austin, 2006), pp. 658–659.

706. True indeed! The Court has used widely different methodologies, moving from unilateralism to bilateralism and back, perhaps without any awareness of doing so. To be sure, methodological inconsistency is not unprecedented. After all, the cases discussed here span a long period, during which the Court's membership and philosophy changed repeatedly. Even when the composition of the Court was relatively stable, the cases it faced, even when not overtly political, were substantively diverse, despite their common denominator of involving foreign elements. Moreover, one could argue, as some have, that methodology in general, and choice-of-law methodology in particular, does not matter in that it rarely explains a court's choice of law or affects the substantive outcome.[1]

1. *See*, e.g., S. Sterk, 'The Marginal Relevance of Choice of Law Theory', 142 *U. Pa. L. Rev.* 949, 1994.

707. Yet, a common and consistent methodology can be the glue that holds precedents together. Moreover, at least in this area, methodology *can* make a difference. To use a relatively non-political case as an example, had the *Spector* court applied *Lauritzen*'s bilateral approach rather than the unilateralist 'clear statement canon', there would be little doubt that the *Spector* case would fall squarely within the reach of the ADA. To illustrate, suppose that one of the *Spector* passengers (disabled or not) were to sue the shipowner after a slip-and-fall injury that occurred on one of the ships involved in that case. Under established precedents, this hypothetical would fall under the *Lauritzen-Rhoditis* line of cases, leading directly to the application of American law, regardless of whether the injury occurred within US waters, the high seas, or foreign waters. Indeed, in such a case the United States would have more numerous and significant contacts and clearer interests than it had in *Rhoditis*.[1] Moreover, as *Rhoditis* and its progeny indicate, American law would apply even if the plaintiff were a crewman rather than a passenger, at least if the crewman is an American or the injury occurred in US waters.[2] To treat short-term cruise *passengers* differently by denying them the protection available to crewmen makes little sense. The only reason for the disparate treatment is a historical accident – the two categories of cases fall under different lines of precedent.

1. Of the eight *Lauritzen-Rhoditis* factors, only two would point away from American law: the foreign flag (which in *Spector* was a flag of convenience) and the place of the tort, if the tort occurred outside US waters. In every other respect, the case would differ little from a wholly-domestic American case. The *Spector* shipowner had its *principal* place of business, not just *a* base of operations, in the United States. As the Court noted, it was a 'United States-centered venture[ ]' that 'relie[d] upon extensive advertising in the United States to promote its cruises and increase its revenues' and 'serve[d] predominantly United States residents'. Its cruises 'depart[ed] from, and return[ed] to, ports in the United States . . . [and] '[m]ost of the passengers on these cruises [were] United States residents'. *Spector*, 545 US at 126.
2. Interestingly, although the *Rhoditis* line of cases involved disputes between crewmen and shipowners, which could implicate matters of discipline and internal order, the courts have never subjected these cases to the internal affairs doctrine. For this reason, courts were free to resolve these conflicts in a more rational manner, without the artificial restraints of the clear statement canon.

708. The sharp differentiation between the Jones Act cases and cases like *Spector* that arguably implicate the internal affairs doctrine is neither necessary nor easy to defend. The same is true of the dichotomy between cases involving other federal statutes and cases involving federal common law, such as general maritime law. There is no logical reason why some of these cases should be subject to clear statement canons, others to mere presumptions, and others to no presumption at all. In all of these categories, the question is the same: namely, whether the values embodied in American law – legislatively enacted or judicially declared – should be observed in certain cases with foreign elements. This is the primordial choice-of-law question. The answer is often difficult, but the path leading to it should not be completely different depending on historical accidents or the presence of statutes. One hopes that the Court will see fit to merge into a single approach the diverse tests it now employs in cases involving statutes (like the Jones Act, the Sherman Act, or the ADA) and common-law cases.

709. In formulating this approach, the Court will have many choices, including the *Lauritzen* test. While extending the *Lauritzen* test to cases like *Spector* would be a significant improvement over the unilateralist 'clear statement' canon, even the *Lauritzen* test needs updating. One of its problems is that, as Justice Harlan once observed, many lower courts tend to be 'mesmerized by contacts . . . notwithstanding the purported eschewal of a mechanical application of the *Lauritzen* test'.[1] In 1953, when American conflicts law was fixated with simplistic mono-dimensional rules such as the *lex loci delicti*, the *Lauritzen* test was a significant methodological breakthrough, but it was and remains prone to mechanical application. Moreover, because it was designed for personal injury or death cases, the test is ill-suited for other maritime conflicts, and even less so for non-maritime conflicts.

1. *Hellenic Lines* v. *Rhoditis*, 398 US 306, 318 (1970) (Harlan J., dissenting).

710. The good news is that, since *Lauritzen*, American conflicts law has not only broken away from mechanical rules, but has progressed beyond 'contact-counting' as a means of choosing the applicable law. Unfortunately, the Supreme Court has not revisited *Lauritzen*, and has not had the opportunity to take account of the intervening progress.[1] One hopes that, on the next available opportunity, the Court will not only update *Lauritzen* for Jones Act cases, but will also enunciate a new unified approach for all maritime conflicts (if not for all cases with foreign elements) whether or not they involve statutes or common law.

This author lacks the expertise and wisdom necessary for proposing his own approach. Fortunately, however, there is a plethora of good ideas from people who possess both of these attributes. Sections 402 and 403 of the Restatement (Third) of Foreign Relations would be a good start.

1. For suggestions of how to modernize the *Lauritzen* test, *see Neely* v. *Club Med Mgmt. Servs., Inc.*, 63 F.3d 166 (3d Cir. 1995); Symeonides, 'Maritime Conflicts of Law from the Perspective of Modern Choice of Law Methodology', 7 *Marit. Lawyer* 223, 1982.

Part III. Recognition and Enforcement of Foreign Judgments

711. One of the many differences between local and multistate cases is the increased possibility that in multistate cases a judgment may need to be enforced in a state other than the one in which it was rendered. This will be the case if the defeated litigant (judgment debtor) does not comply with the judgment and does not have sufficient assets in the forum state against which the successful litigant (judgment creditor) can execute the judgment. In such a case, the creditor will seek to have the judgment recognized and enforced in another state that has jurisdiction over the debtor and in which the debtor has sufficient assets.

This Part reviews the American practise on recognition of sister-state judgments (Chapter 1) and foreign-country judgments (Chapter 2). The latter chapter is considerably longer, in part because of its interest to foreign readers, but also for an additional reason. The fact that the Full Faith and Credit clause of the federal Constitution applies to sister-state judgments, but not to foreign-country judgments, leaves courts with considerable discretion on how to deal with the latter judgments. In turn, this discretion produces different choices, variations, and nuances, all of which make recognition of foreign judgments a more uncertain and complex subject than the recognition of sister-state judgments.

Chapter 1. Sister State Judgments

§1. The Basic Policies

712. As between the states of the United States, the recognition requirements are prescribed by federal law, primarily the Constitution's Full Faith and Credit clause, which provides that 'Full Faith and Credit shall be given in each State to the . . . judicial Proceedings of every other State'.[1] An implementing statute is only slightly more descriptive. It provides that such proceeding 'shall have the *same* full faith and credit in every court within the United States . . . as they have . . . in the courts of the states . . . from which they are taken'.[2] The statute defines the degree of effect to be accorded the judgment ('same', i.e., no less, and perhaps no more). However, neither the statute nor the clause defines exactly *when* the full faith obligation becomes operable, which proceedings[3] it covers, which conditions must precede recognition, or which exceptions or defences may be interposed. In the absence of a comprehensive federal statute (which Congress is empowered to enact under the second sentence of the clause), these questions are left to the Supreme Court to answer.

1. US Const. Art. IV, §1. The clause refers to 'States' and thus does not apply to judgments of foreign courts, or even US federal courts. A federal statute requires federal courts to enforce state judgments (*see* 28 USCA §1738), and the Supreme Court has held that state courts are required to recognize federal court judgments. Another statute provides that a judgment of one federal district court may be 'registered' in any other federal district and thereby acquire the same effect as a judgment of the latter district. *See* 28 USCA §1963. Basic bibliography for the topics discussed in this chapter includes: L. McDougal, R. Felix & R. Whitten, *American Conflicts Law* (5th edn, New York, Ardsley, 2001), pp. 263–325; E. Scoles, P. Hay, P. Borchers & S. Symeonides, *Conflict of Laws* (4th edn, St. Paul, Minn., 2004), pp. 1257–1307; R. Weintraub, *Commentary on the Conflict of Laws* (5th edn, New York, 2006), pp. 737–759.
2. 28 USCA §1738 (emphasis added).
3. Although both the clause and the statute refer to 'judicial proceedings' rather than to judgments, it is now assumed that they mandate recognition of only final judgments.

713. Judging from the Court's laissez faire attitude in using (or not using) the Full Faith and Credit clause in the choice-of-law area,[1] one might expect a similarly flexible stance with regard to judgments as well. Not so. The Court has aggressively used the Full Faith and Credit clause as a potent unifying instrument mandating recognition of sister state judgments. The Court has repeatedly held that states must recognize an otherwise valid sister-state judgment, even if recognition is contrary to the strong interests, or offensive to a strong public policy, of the recognizing state.

1. *See supra* 78–89.

714. An early and clear example of this principle is *Fauntleroy* v. *Lum.*[1] *Fauntleroy* arose out of a Mississippi gambling contract between Mississippi parties, which would be illegal and unenforceable in Mississippi. The plaintiff obtained a judgment in Missouri and sought enforcement in Mississippi. The Mississippi court refused to enforce it and the US Supreme Court reversed, holding that the Full Faith and Credit clause compelled Mississippi to recognize the judgment. The Court reasoned as follows:

> [W]hether the ruling of the Missouri court . . . was right or wrong, there can be no question that the judgment was conclusive in Missouri on the validity of the cause of action. A judgment is conclusive as to all the *media concludendi*; and it needs no authority to show that it cannot be impeached either in or out of the State by showing that it was based upon a mistake of law. Of course a want of jurisdiction over either the person or the subject-matter might be shown. But as the jurisdiction of the Missouri court is not open to dispute the judgment cannot be impeached in Mississippi even if it went upon a misapprehension of the Mississippi law.[2]

Indeed, Missouri had judicial jurisdiction (albeit 'tag jurisdiction'), but it clearly lacked legislative jurisdiction. Undoubtedly, under the choice-of-law rules of that time, Missouri should have applied Mississippi law. In fact, it would be mandated to do so under the full faith and credit jurisprudence of that time. Instead, Missouri either ignored Mississippi law or applied it incorrectly, and held enforceable a Mississippi contract that was illegal in Mississippi. Nevertheless, the Supreme Court required Mississippi to enforce the Missouri judgment.

1. 210 US 230 (1908).
2. 210 US at 237.

715. Similarly, in *Yarborough* v. *Yarborough*,[1] the Supreme Court held that the Full Faith and Credit clause precluded South Carolina from imposing additional child support payments on a father whose support obligations had been fixed by a Georgia lump-sum judgment. His child later moved to South Carolina, thus generating a strong South Carolina interest in protecting the child. However, the Court rejected the dissent's argument that this interest was a good reason for exempting South Carolina's from its full faith and credit obligation to respect the Georgia judgment.

1. 290 US 202 (1933).

716. Finally, in *Thomas* v. *Washington Gas Light Co.*,[1] the Court allowed a worker who received a worker compensation award in F-1[2] (the state of injury) to receive a supplemental award in F-2 (the state of the employment relationship), thus appearing to create an exception to the principle established in *Yarborough*. Indeed, four justices thought that the interest of F-2 in protecting a worker domiciled and employed there would justify such an exception. However, five justices disagreed. Ultimately, the decision to allow a supplemental award was based on the exceptional nature of worker's compensation cases[3] and a precedent limited only to those cases.[4]

1. 448 US 261 (1980).
2. For the sake of convenience, the abbreviation 'F-1' is used to denote the court that rendered the judgment, and 'F-2' to denote the court which is asked to recognize the judgment.
3. In these cases, the injured worker's choice of initial forum is usually not an educated one nor entirely free from financial pressure, and the initial forum is usually an administrative commission not empowered to apply another state's law.
4. This precedent was *Indus. Comm'n of Wisconsin* v. *McCartin*, 330 US 622 (1947), which allowed a supplemental award unless the first award was based on a statute which in 'unmistakable language' precluded a supplemental award.

717. The message from cases like *Fauntleroy* and *Yarborough* is that the losing litigant's only remedy is to seek direct review of the F-1 judgment to the US Supreme Court – a collateral attack in another state will not work. These cases indicate the Court's willingness to use the Full Faith and Credit clause as an instrument of national uniformity for the free, unimpeded circulation of judgments. Neither the strong interests nor a strong public policy of F-2 are valid defences to recognizing an otherwise valid sister-state judgment. The reason for this sharp difference in how the Court uses the Full Faith and Credit clause in the areas of choice of law and judgment recognition, respectively, is that in the latter area the clause is reinforced by a the national policy of finality embodied in the doctrine of *res judicata*, to which all states adhere. This policy seeks to conserve judicial resources and protect party expectations by prohibiting re-litigation of disputes that have been finally decided in another forum that functions under the same guarantees of impartiality and fairness as the recognizing forum. As the Court noted,

> It is just as important that there should be a place to end as that there should be a place to begin litigation. After a party has his day in court, with opportunity

to present his evidence and his view of the law, a collateral attack upon the decision . . . merely retries the issue previously determined. There is no reason to expect that the second decision will be more satisfactory than the first.[1]

1. *Stoll* v. *Gottlieb*, 305 US 165, 172 (1938).

§2. Requirements for Recognition

718. To be entitled to recognition in F-2 under the Full Faith and Credit clause, the judgment must be 'final' and 'on the merits' as these terms are defined by F-1 law. The F-1 court must have had jurisdiction under its own law, which must also conform to the federal due process requirements.

719. If the F-1 court lacks jurisdiction, the judgment is invalid in F-1. Consequently, the Full Faith and Credit clause does not require, and the Due Process clause prevents, its recognition in other states. Thus, before recognizing a judgment, the F-2 court is free to inquire into the jurisdiction of the F-1 court. This inquiry is precluded, however, if the defendant appeared in F-1 and either litigated or had the opportunity to litigate the jurisdictional issue. In such a case, the jurisdictional findings or assumptions of the F-1 judgment become *res judicata* and are insusceptible to collateral attack in F-2. This is true, not only in cases of *in personam* jurisdiction,[1] but also in cases of *in rem*[2] and status jurisdiction,[3] as well as subject matter jurisdiction.[4] Again the losing litigant's only remedy is to seek review of the F-1 judgment by the US Supreme Court, rather than to collaterally attack the judgment in F-2.

1. *See Baldwin* v. *Iowa State Traveling Men's Ass'n*, 283 US 522 (1931).
2. *See Durfee* v. *Duke*, 375 US 106 (1963).
3. *See Sherrer* v. *Sherrer*, 334 US 343 (1948).
4. *See Aldrich* v. *Aldrich*, 378 US 540 (1964).

720. On the other hand, if the defendant did not appear in F-1, the jurisdictional findings or assumptions of the F-1 court are not *res judicata*. Thus, the defendant, who is now a default judgment debtor, preserves his chances to litigate in F-2 the question of whether the F-1 court had jurisdiction under F-1 and federal law. If it turns out that the F-1 court had jurisdiction after all, the defendant will have lost not only the jurisdictional battle, but also the opportunity to litigate the merits, and the F-1 default judgment will be enforceable against him.

§3. Preclusive Effect of the Judgment

721. The Full Faith and Credit clause and the implementing statute require F-2 to give the F-1 judgment the 'same' effect as it had in F-1. This means, *inter alia*, giving it the same *res judicata* ('claim preclusion') and collateral estoppel ('issue preclusion') effects as it had in F-1. Thus, the judgment will be binding with regard to the same parties (or their privies) as to all issues that were litigated or could have been litigated in F-1.

722. However, while some states adhere to the old rule of mutuality of collateral estoppel, which makes a judgment binding only as between the same parties and their privies, most states adhere to the rule of non-mutuality. Non-mutuality makes the judgment binding *vis-à-vis* certain non-parties if the party estopped had a fair and adequate opportunity to litigate the particular issue. For example, if an air carrier was found negligent for an airplane accident in a trial initiated by one victim, the carrier will be estopped from denying its negligence *vis-à-vis* another victim of the same accident in a different case.

When F-1 adheres to the rule of non-mutuality, F-2 must give the judgment the 'same' (i.e., no less) issue-preclusion effect, even if F-2 adheres to the rule of mutuality. However, if F-1 adheres to the rule of mutuality, then F-2 discharges its full faith and credit obligation by giving the judgment the 'same' (and no more) effect as it had in F-1. Whether F-2 can give the judgment 'more' effect by applying its own non-mutuality rule is not a full faith and credit question but rather a choice-of-law decision which must remain within the due process limits as articulated in *Allstate Ins. Co.* v. *Hague*.[1]

1. *See supra* 82–85. For lower court cases involving this scenario and applying their own non-mutuality rule, *see Finley* v. *Kesling*, 433 N.E.2d 1112 (Ill.App. 1982); *Hart* v. *Am. Airlines*, 304 N.Y.S. 2d 810 (N.Y. Sup. Ct. 1969).

§4. Enforcement and Defences

723. As noted earlier, the forum's strong public policy or other strong interests are not valid defences to recognizing a valid sister-state judgment. Even tax judgments,[1] although not penal judgments,[2] are entitled to recognition under the Full Faith and Credit clause. An allegation that the judgment was obtained by fraud is a valid defence, but only if it would have been a ground for challenging the judgment in F-1 and such challenge was not precluded for other reasons.

1. *See Milwaukee County* v. *M. E. White Co.*, 296 US 268 (1935).
2. *See Huntington* v. *Attrill*, 146 US 657 (1892) (holding that the judgment in question was entitled to recognition because it was not penal).

724. In enforcing the judgment, the judgment creditor is limited to the enforcement mechanisms provided by F-2 law, not F-1 law. For example, if F-1 allows self-help in seizing assets of the judgment debtor but F-2 does not, the judgment creditor may not use self-help in F-2. Similarly, if enforcement of the judgment is barred by the statute of limitations of F-2, but not of F-1, the F-2 court may deny enforcement. The Supreme Court held to that effect in *Watkins* v. *Conway*.[1] However, in *Watkins*, the judgment creditor could revive the judgment in F-1, and then seek enforcement of the revived judgment in F-2. It is unclear whether, in the same situation, F-2 may refuse to enforce a judgment that could not be revived in F-1.

Similarly, it is unclear whether, in the converse situation, F-2 may choose to enforce a judgment that is barred by the statute of limitation of F-1, but not of F-2. The Full Faith and Credit clause is inoperable in this situation. If F-2 chooses to enforce such a judgment under its own law, it should make sure that it has the contacts and interests to sustain the application of that law under *Allstate Ins. Co.* v. *Hague*.[2]

1. 385 US 188 (1966).
2. *See supra* 82–85.

Chapter 2. Foreign-Country Judgments

725. The Full Faith and Credit clause, which plays such an omnipotent role in the recognition of sister-state judgments, does not apply to foreign-country judgments. Thus, recognition of the latter judgments is matter of choice and discretion (or 'international comity'), rather than constitutional compulsion. In turn, this allows for several possible options, ranging from the one extreme of total non-recognition to the other extreme of total full recognition under the same standards governing sister-state judgments. The American practise is somewhere in the middle. However, as this chapter illustrates, the American practise is generally more hospitable to foreign judgments than the practises of most other countries in the world.[1]

1. Basic bibliography for the topics discussed in this chapter includes: E. Scoles, P. Hay, P. Borchers & S. Symeonides, *Conflict of Laws* (4th edn, St. Paul, Minn., 2004), pp. 1308–1343; R. Weintraub, *Commentary on the Conflict of Laws* (5th edn, New York, 2006), pp. 746–759.

§1. *Hilton*: the Starting Point, in the Middle

726. The foundation for the American practise was laid by the Supreme Court in its 19th century decision in *Hilton* v. *Guyot*.[1] *Hilton* involved an action by a French judgment creditor seeking to recognize a French judgment against two American judgment debtors. The Court laid down the general principles as follows:

> [W]here there has been opportunity for a full and fair trial abroad before a court of competent jurisdiction, conducting the trial upon regular proceedings, after due citation or voluntary appearance of the defendant, and under a system of jurisprudence likely to secure an impartial administration of justice between the citizens of its own country and those of other countries, and there is nothing to show either prejudice in the court, or in the system of laws under which it was sitting, or fraud in procuring the judgment, or any other special reason why the comity of this nation should not allow it full effect, the merits of the case should not, in an action brought in this country upon the judgment, be tried afresh. . . .[2]

Ultimately, the Court refused to recognize the French judgment because of lack of reciprocity: a French court in the reverse situation would not have recognized an American judgment without re-examining its merits (*revision au fond*). This part of *Hilton* was sharply criticized, both at the time by the dissenting justices and since then by most commentators. Today, lack of reciprocity as a ground for non-recognition is the exception rather than the rule. As explained later, this may change in the future.[3]

1. 159 US 113 (1895).
2. 159 US at 202–203.
3. *See infra* 733.

727. *Hilton* was a diversity case decided well before *Erie R. Co.* v. *Tompkins*,[1] and *Klaxon Co.* v. *Stentor Electric Mfg. Co.*[2] pronounced that federal courts sitting in diversity must follow the substantive and conflicts law of the forum state. Since *Erie* and *Klaxon*, most federal courts have held that, in the absence of a federal statute or treaty or some other basis for federal jurisdiction (such as admiralty), recognition of foreign country judgments is a matter of state law.[3] Many state courts have also assumed or held that *Hilton*, having enunciated a rule of federal common law, is not binding on the states.[4] In addition, 32 jurisdictions have adopted the Uniform Foreign Money-Judgments Recognitions Act (discussed *infra*) which differs in some respects from *Hilton*.

1. 304 US 64 (1938), discussed *supra* 68–70.
2. 313 US 487 (1941), discussed *supra* 73–75.
3. *See*, e.g., *British Midland Airways Ltd.* v. *Int'l. Travel, Inc.*, 497 F.2d 869 (9th Cir. 1974); *Somportex Ltd.* v. *Philadelphia Chewing Gum Corp.*, 453 F.2d 435 (3d Cir. 1971), *cert. denied*, 405 US 1017 (1972); *Fairchild, Arabatzis & Smith* v. *Prometco*, 470 F.Supp. 610 (S.D.N.Y. 1979).
4. *See*, e.g., *Johnston* v. *Compagnie Generale Transatlantique*, 152 N.E. 121 (N.Y. 1926).

728. As a result of these developments, *Hilton*, though often cited, is rarely dispositive, especially on the issue of reciprocity. Nevertheless, many courts continue to find *Hilton*'s general approach to be persuasive. The general principles enunciated in *Hilton* have formed the foundation of contemporary practise. In summary, as a matter of international comity, American courts recognize final foreign country judgments that meet the requirements for recognizing sister-state judgments, without reviewing the merits.

729. However, the recognition of foreign country judgments is subject to several exceptions and defences that are unavailable with regard to sister-state judgments. For example, recognition may be refused if the judgment does not satisfy American jurisdictional standards, even if it does satisfy the foreign-law standards; if it is a judgment for taxes or penalties; if it offends the recognizing court's public policy; or if it was rendered in a system that does not provide impartial tribunals or does not satisfy certain minimum standards of procedural fairness. These requirements and exceptions are discussed below.

§2. 'Codifications' of Current or Future Practice

730. Before discussing the specific requirements for recognition of foreign country judgments, it would be helpful to briefly describe three documents that prescribe or guide the practise of American courts in this area. The first such document, and the only one that has the status of positive law, is the Uniform Foreign Money-Judgments Recognition Act of 1962, which has been adopted by statute in 32 states,[1] with slight variations from state to state. The Act applies to judgments for the recovery of money 'other than a judgment for taxes, a fine or other penalty, or a judgment for support in matrimonial or family matters'.[2]

1. This Act is referred to hereafter as the 'Uniform Act' and is cited with its acronym UFMJRA. The following states have adopted the Act: Alaska, California, Colorado, Connecticut, Delaware, District of Columbia, Florida, Georgia, Hawaii, Idaho, Illinois, Iowa, Maine, Maryland,

Massachusetts, Michigan, Minnesota, Missouri, Montana, New Jersey, New Mexico, New York, North Carolina, North Dakota, Ohio, Oklahoma, Oregon, Pennsylvania, Texas, Virgin Islands, Virginia and Washington. *See* <nccusl.org/Update/uniformact_factsheets/uniformacts-fs-ufmjra.asp> (last visited 16 June 2007). In 2005, the National Conference of Commissioners on Uniform State Laws proposed a new Act titled 'Uniform Foreign-Country Money Judgments Recognition Act (UFCMJRA). By 2007, this Act was adopted by Idaho and Nevada and was pending before the California and Michigan legislatures. *See* <nccusl.org/Update/uniformact factsheets/uniformacts-fs-ufcmjra.asp> (last visited 6 June 2007). This Act is referred to hereafter only where it differs significantly from the old Act.
2. UFMJRA, §1.

731. The other two documents have only persuasive force. The first is the Restatement (Third) of Foreign Relations,[1] which parallels the Uniform Act in most respects but is not limited to money judgments. Finally, the third document is the most recent and detailed one. It is a draft statute titled Foreign Judgments Recognition and Enforcement Act, which has been proposed by the American Law Institute for enactment by the United States Congress.[2] Although it is doubtful that Congress will adopt this draft, at least in the near future, the draft is expected to exercise considerable influence on American courts.

1. American Law Institute, *Restatement (Third) of Foreign Relations Law of the United States* (1986) (hereafter referred to as '*Restatement (Third)*'). This Restatement has gradually displaced, with regard to this subject, the older Restatement (Second) of Conflict of Laws. The latter Restatement devoted only one section to foreign country judgments, which states laconically that '[a] valid judgment rendered in a foreign nation after a fair trial in a contested proceeding will be recognized in the United States'. American Law Institute, *Restatement (Second): Conflict of Laws* 2d §98 (1971). A foreign trial is considered fair if it meets the standards enunciated in *Hilton* (*see id.* §98 cmt. c), and valid if it meets the standards for a valid sister-state judgment. *See id.* cmt. a, which refers to §92. (This section requires *in personam* and subject matter jurisdiction, reasonable notice and opportunity to be heard, and 'compliance with such requirements of the state of rendition as are necessary for the valid exercise of power by the court'.). Indeed, the Restatement (Second) subscribes to the view that, '[i]n most respects', foreign judgments that meet this standard 'will be accorded the same degree of recognition to which sister State judgments are entitled . . . because the public interest requires that there be an end to litigation'. *Id.* §98 cmt. b. However, this statement is modified by a public policy exception and an exception regarding governmental claims. *Id.* §98 cmt. g.
2. American Law Institute, *Recognition and Enforcement of Foreign Judgments: Analysis and Proposed Federal Statute* (2006) (hereafter referred to as 'REFJA' or 'proposed statute'). For an excellent discussion of the general subject by the two ALI Reporters, *See* L. Silberman & A. Lowenfeld, 'A Different Challenge for the ALI: Herein of Foreign Country Judgments, an International Treaty, and an American Statute', 75 *Ind. L.J.* 635, 2000.

§3. Reciprocity

732. The Uniform Act departed from *Hilton's* holding that lack of reciprocity is a ground for refusing to recognize an otherwise valid foreign country judgment. Many courts have held likewise.[1] The Restatement (Third) also disapproves of this ground for non-recognition.[2]

1. *See*, e.g., *Chabert* v. *Bacquie*, 694 So.2d 8052 (Fla. Ct. App. 1997); *Bank of Montreal* v. *Kough*, 612 F.2d 467 (9th Cir. 1980); *Hunt* v. *BP Exploration Co. (Libya) Ltd.*, 492 F. Supp. 885 (N.D. Tex. 1980); *Nicol* v. *Tanner*, 256 N.W.2d 796 (Minn. 1976); *Somportex Ltd.* v.

Philadelphia Chewing Gum Corp., 453 F.2d 435 (3d Cir. 1971), *cert. denied*, 405 US 1017 (1972); *Johnston* v. *Compagnie Generale Transatlantique*, 152 N.E. 121 (N.Y. 1926); *Hilkmann* v. *Hilkmann*, 858 A.2d 58 (Pa. 2004).

2. *See Restatement (Third)* §481 cmt. d.

733. However, eight of the states that adopted the Uniform Act did add lack of reciprocity as either a discretionary or a mandatory ground for non-recognition.[1] Moreover, the proposed federal statute would make lack of reciprocity a mandatory ground for non-recognition, in both state and federal courts. The statute provides that the foreign judgment 'shall not' be recognized if the court finds that 'comparable' American judgments would not be recognized in the foreign country.[2] The statute defines 'comparable' judgments through several illustrative presumptions[3] and places on the judgment debtor the burden of proving lack of reciprocity.[4] The stated rationale of the reciprocity requirement is 'not to make it more difficult to secure recognition and enforcement of foreign judgments, but rather to create an incentive to foreign countries to commit to recognition and enforcement of judgments rendered in the United States'.[5] The proposed statute would authorize the US Secretary of State to negotiate agreements with foreign countries setting forth reciprocal recognition practises. The existence of such an agreement covering the judgment in question would satisfy the reciprocity requirement, although the lack of an agreement would not necessarily negate it.

1. These states are Florida, Georgia, Idaho, Massachusetts, North Carolina, Ohio and Texas. In Georgia and Massachusetts, reciprocity is a mandatory ground for non-recognition, while in the other states it is discretionary. New Hampshire has a reciprocity provision that is confined to Canadian judgments. *See* N.H. Rev. Stat. Ann. §524:11.
2. REFJA §7(a).
3. *See id.* §7(c)–(e).
4. *See id.* §7(b).
5. *Id.* §7 cmt. b.

§4. Jurisdiction

I. Jurisdictional Bases

734. As *Hilton* proclaimed, 'in order to be entitled to any effect', a foreign judgment 'must have been rendered by a court having jurisdiction of the cause'.[1] Indeed, this is a universal principle. No country will recognize a judgment rendered by a court that did not have jurisdiction over the judgment debtor.

As noted in the previous chapter, with regard to sister-state judgments, the jurisdiction of the rendering court (F-1) is judged by F-1 law, which necessarily incorporates federal due process standards. Here, however, the F-1 court is a foreign court that is not subject to similar super-arching and shared standards. This raises the question of whether the F-1 court's jurisdiction should be judged by: (1) the foreign country's standards; (2) American state and/or federal standards; or (3) a combination of the foreign and American standards.

1. *Hilton*, 159 US at 166–167. The statement applies to territorial (or 'personal') jurisdiction. Regarding lack of subject-matter jurisdiction, the UFMJRA treats it as a mandatory ground of

non-recognition (*see* Section 4(a)), while both the Restatement (Third) and the REFJA treat it as a discretionary ground of non-recognition.

735. The Uniform Act answers this question obliquely. It provides that a foreign judgment 'shall not' be recognized 'if the foreign court did not have personal jurisdiction over the defendant',[1] and that the judgment 'shall not'[2] be refused recognition on jurisdictional grounds, if the defendant:

> (1) was served personally in the foreign state;[3] (2) voluntarily appeared in the proceedings, other than for the purpose of protecting property seized or threatened with seizure in the proceedings or of contesting the jurisdiction of the court over him; (3) prior to the commencement of the proceedings had agreed to submit to the jurisdiction of the foreign court with respect to the subject matter involved;[4] (4) was domiciled in the foreign state when the proceedings were instituted, or, being a body corporate had its principal place of business, was incorporated, or had otherwise acquired corporate status, in the foreign state; (5) had a business office in the foreign state and the proceedings in the foreign court involved a cause of action arising out of business done by the defendant through that office in the foreign state; or (6) operated a motor vehicle or air plane in the foreign state and the proceedings involved a cause of action arising out of such operation.[5]

The above non-exclusive list[6] sums up most of the permissible jurisdictional bases under American law but says nothing about whether the judgment must also meet the jurisdictional standards of the foreign court. The Restatement (Third) answers this question by providing that the foreign court must have had jurisdiction 'in accordance with the law of the rendering state *and* with the rules set forth in §421'.[7] Section 421 purports to restate or to enunciate standards of jurisdiction that are 'similar to those developed under the due process clause of the United States Constitution'.[8]

1. UFMJRA, §4(a).
2. *Id.* §5(a).
3. UFMJRA, §4(b) provides that the judgment 'need not' be recognized if jurisdiction was based only on personal service and the foreign court was a 'seriously inconvenient' forum.
4. UFMJRA, §4(b) provides that the judgment 'need not' be recognized if the foreign proceeding was 'contrary to an agreement between the parties under which the dispute in question was to be determined otherwise than by proceedings in that foreign court'.
5. UFMJRA, §5(a).
6. Section 5(b) of the Uniform Act expressly permits recognition of a judgment rendered on jurisdictional bases other than those listed above.
7. *Restatement (Third)* §482 (emphasis added).
8. *Restatement (Third)* §421 Reporter's note 1. However, having been drafted before *Burnham* v. *Super. Ct. of California*, 495 US 604 (1990) (discussed *supra* 37), Section 421 specifically disapproves of 'tag jurisdiction', i.e., jurisdiction based exclusively on service of process on a person only transitorily present in the forum state.

736. The proposed federal statute takes a different approach by listing the 'unacceptable' jurisdictional bases. It provides that a foreign judgment *shall not* be recognized if it was rendered on a jurisdictional basis that is 'unacceptable under §6'.[1] Section 6 lists the following as 'unacceptable' bases of jurisdiction:

(1) (Except in admiralty cases) the presence in the forum state of property belonging to the defendant, when the claim does not assert an interest in or is otherwise unrelated to the property; (2) the plaintiff's nationality, domicile, residence or incorporation; (3) tag jurisdiction, unless 'no other appropriate forum was reasonably available', and (4) any other basis that is regarded as 'unreasonable or unfair given the nature of the claim or the identity of the parties'.[2]

This negative provision leaves open the question of which jurisdictional bases *are* acceptable. The Reporter's Comments state that, 'in general, any basis of jurisdiction that would meet the requirements of due process if asserted in an action in the United States will meet the requirements of jurisdiction for recognition'.[3]

1. REFJA, §5(a).
2. REFJA, §6(a). Section 6 also provides that a jurisdictional basis is not regarded as unreasonable or unfair 'solely' because it is not permissible under American law.
3. REFJA, §5, cmt e.

737. If the F-1 court asserts a basis of jurisdiction that is available under its law but unacceptable by American standards, recognition is not necessarily precluded. The F-2 court may inquire into whether factually there was another jurisdictional basis that would be acceptable by American standards. If so, the judgment would satisfy the jurisdictional requirements for recognition in the United States. For example, if, in an action arising from a traffic accident caused by the defendant in France, the French court based its jurisdiction on the plaintiff's nationality, the judgment would satisfy the jurisdictional requirements for recognition in the United States because operating a vehicle within the forum's territory is a ground for specific jurisdiction under American law.[1]

1. REFJA. §6(b) specifically provides to this effect, but the same solution should prevail under the Uniform Act.

II. Default Judgments

738. If the defendant did not appear in the foreign proceeding in F-1 (and did not otherwise waive the right to contest the foreign court's jurisdiction), then the defendant may challenge the rendering court's jurisdiction in the recognition proceeding in F-2. However, this opportunity does not guarantee a victory. If F-2 determines that F-1 had jurisdiction under both its own law and American standards, then F-2 will most likely recognize the default judgment. Many cases have held to this effect,[1] and both the Restatement (Third)[2] and the proposed federal statute[3] endorse this practise as well.

1. *See*, e.g., *Chabert* v. *Bacquie*, 694 So.2d 805 (Fla. Ct. App. 1997); *John Sanderson & Co. (Wool) Pty. Ltd.* v. *Ludlow Jute Co., Ltd.*, 569 F.2d 696 (1st Cir. 1978); *Bank of Montreal* v. *Kough*, 612 F.2d 467 (9th Cir. 1980); *Tahan* v. *Hodgson*, 662 F.2d 862 (D.C. Cir. 1981); *Porisini* v. *Petricca*, 90 A.D.2d 949, 456 N.Y.S.2d 888 (4th Dept. 1982).
2. *See Restatement (Third)* §481 Rptr's note 4 ('If jurisdiction of the foreign court over a resident of the United States was based on concepts similar to those of longarm jurisdiction in the

United States . . . , a default judgment so rendered will be recognized in the United States-provided defendant received adequate notice'.).

3. Section 3(b) of the proposed REFJA provides that a foreign default judgment is entitled to recognition if the foreign court had jurisdiction on a basis which the foreign law permits and which is not one of the 'unacceptable' bases as defined in Section 6.

III. Contested Proceedings

739. In contrast, when the defendant appears in the F-1 court and unsuccessfully challenges or fails to challenge its jurisdiction, the practise of American courts differs depending on whether the F-1 court is a sister-state court or a foreign court. In the former case, the defendant will be barred from re-litigating the jurisdictional issue in F-2.[1] In the latter case, the answer is not uniform. While some courts have assumed or held that the defendant is precluded from challenging the jurisdiction of the foreign court,[2] none of these cases involved a jurisdictional basis that would be impermissible by American standards. The Restatement (Third) addresses this possibility. It provides that the defendant is generally precluded, '*unless the proceeding in the foreign court was manifestly unfair or the asserted basis for jurisdiction clearly untenable*'.[3]

1. *See supra* 719.
2. *See*, e.g., *Sprague & Rhodes Commodity Corp.* v. *Instituto Mexicano Del Café*, 566 F.2d 861 (2d Cir. 1977); *Somportex Ltd.* v. *Philadelphia Chewing Gum Corp.*, 453 F.2d 435 (3d Cir. 1971), *cert. denied*, 405 US 1017 (1972). *But see Nippon Emo-Trans Co., Ltd.* v. *Emo-Trans, Inc.*, 744 F.Supp. 1215 (E.D.N.Y. 1990).
3. *Restatement (Third)* §481 cmt. i. (emphasis added).

740. The proposed federal statute states this proposition more directly: 'An appearance by the defendant in the state of origin, or an unsuccessful objection to the jurisdiction of the rendering court, does not deprive the defendant of the right to resist recognition under this section', which lists the 'unacceptable' bases of jurisdiction.[1] Thus, if the defendant can prove that the jurisdictional basis asserted by the F-1 court is unacceptable by American standards, then – regardless of whether that basis satisfied the F-1 standard – the judgment will be denied recognition on this ground.

1. REFJA §6(c). *See also id.* §4(b) (giving preclusive effect to the F-1's factual findings); *id.* §4(c) (providing that a defendant who appeared in F-1 but did not challenge its jurisdiction will be precluded in F-2 from challenging F-1's jurisdiction under F-1 law, but will be allowed to show if such jurisdiction was unacceptable by US standards).

§5. Procedural Fairness

I. Fairness of Foreign Courts or Proceedings

741. Procedural fairness may be lacking because of endemic defects in the entire judicial system of the foreign country or in the procedures generally employed by its courts. Examples from history are the treatment of Jews in Nazi Germany or of Blacks in South Africa during the apartheid regime. Procedural fairness may also be lacking because of defects in the particular foreign court or the proceeding that produced the judgment in question, such as bribery or corruption of a particular judge or undue external influence on the proceeding.[1]

1. *See*, e.g., *Films by Jove, Inc.* v. *Berov*, 250 F.Supp. 2d 156 (E.D.N.Y. 2003) (finding that a certain Russian decision 'was strongly influenced, if not coerced, by the efforts of various Russian officials seeking to promote "state interests"'. *Id.* at 216.

742. One of the essential requirements for recognition of a foreign judgment is the requirement of a 'fair trial', a 'regular proceeding', conducted 'under a system of jurisprudence likely to secure an impartial administration of justice'.[1] When the judgment is from a sister-state court, this requirement is part and parcel of the requirement for a 'valid' judgment because that court is bound by the fairness guarantees of the federal due process clause. If a judgment does not meet these guarantees, the judgment will be invalid in F-1 and thus not entitled to recognition in F-2. However, in the case of foreign country judgments, there is no automatic assurance that the foreign court will operate under similar guarantees. This is why procedural fairness is a legitimate criterion for recognizing a foreign country judgment.

1. *Hilton*, 159 US at 202.

743. The Uniform Act, the Restatement (Third), and the proposed federal statute, all prohibit recognition of a foreign judgment rendered 'under a system which does not provide impartial tribunals or procedures compatible with the requirements of due process of law'.[1] The proposed statute also prohibits recognition of a judgment rendered 'in circumstances that raise substantial justifiable doubt about the integrity of the rendering court with regard to the judgment in question'.[2] The Uniform Act does not address this particular defect, but the revised Uniform Act of 2005 added two grounds for discretionary non-recognition. It provides that a foreign judgment 'need not' be recognized if: 'the judgment was rendered in circumstances that raise substantial doubt about the integrity of the rendering court with respect to the judgment; or . . . the specific proceeding . . . leading to the judgment was not compatible with the requirements of due process of law.[3]

1. UFMJRA §4(a); *Restatement (Third)* §482(1)(a). The proposed REFJA §5(a)(i) uses more generic terms ('procedures compatible with fundamental principles of fairness'.). *Id.*
2. REFJA, §5(a)(ii).
3. Uniform Foreign-Country Money Judgments Recognition Act (UFCMJRA), §4(c)(7)(8).

744. Cases refusing to recognize a foreign judgment because of endemic corruption or the lack of impartial tribunals in a foreign country are rare. One such case is *Bridgeway Corp.* v. *Citibank*,[1] which involved a Liberian judgment rendered while Liberia was going through a vicious civil war. The court upheld the lower court decision denying recognition after finding that, during the period in question, the Liberian judicial system was in disarray and that the members of the Supreme Court were beholden to the warlords who had appointed them.

1. 201 F. 3d 134 (2d Cir. 2000).

745. In *Bank Melli Iran* v. *Pahlavi*,[1] the issue was whether a particular defendant, the sister of the former Shah of Iran, could have received a fair trial in Iran in the period following the overthrow of the Shah. Quoting *Hilton*, the court found that Iran did not have 'a "system of jurisprudence likely to secure an impartial administration of justice"'.[2] Citing evidence that the court requested *sua sponte* from the US State Department, the court found that Iranian trials were 'highly politicized' and 'rarely held in public', and that the Iranian government 'd[id] not believe in the independence of the judiciary'.[3] The court concluded that the defendant 'could not expect fair treatment from the courts of Iran, could not personally appear before those courts, could not obtain proper legal representation in Iran, and could not even obtain local witnesses on her behalf'.[4]

1. 58 F.3d 1406 (9th Cir. 1995).
2. *Id.* at 1413 (quoting *Hilton*).
3. *Id.* at 1412. The court continued, stating that, in Iran, judges were 'subject to continuing scrutiny and threat of sanction and cannot be expected to be completely impartial toward US citizens', that attorneys were 'officially discouraged from representing politically undesirable interests', and that witnesses were 'likely to be subject to the same risks as lawyers'. *Id.* The court concluded that, although these findings concerned US citizens, they also applied to defendant ('those with close ties to the Shah's regime') because 'much of the hostility to United States citizens stemmed from this country's connection to the Shah's regime'. *Id.*
4. *Id.* at 1413. In an earlier unrelated case, this defendant sought and obtained a *forum non conveniens* dismissal after arguing that the claim against her 'would more properly be tried in Iran'. *Id.*

746. *Cooley* v. *Weinberger*[1] also involved an Iranian judgment, but one rendered during the Shah's regime. The defendant, a US citizen living in Iran, was convicted by an Iranian court which found her guilty of killing her husband. Following an amnesty from the Shah, the defendant returned to the United States and filed for social security benefits based on her husband's contributions. Her eligibility for those benefits depended on the validity of her Iranian conviction. She claimed that her Iranian trial suffered from serious shortcomings which impeded her ability to defend herself, and that the prosecution did not prove her guilty beyond a reasonable doubt. The lower court disagreed with most of her factual contentions and concluded that the evidence reflected 'a legitimate legal process, although procedurally and substantially different from the United States federal system'.[2] The Court of Appeals affirmed, stating: 'The fact that Iranian procedures may not be consistent with due process protections guaranteed in United States criminal proceedings will not in itself prevent effect being given a judgment rendered in Iran in accord with Iranian law'.[3]

1. 518 F.2d 1151 (10th Cir. 1975).
2. *Id.* at 1155.
3. *Id.*

747. Indeed, although the use of the phrase 'due process' in the Uniform Act implies use of American standards, the word 'compatible' tempers that implication. Political biases aside, what is expected is not 100 per cent conformity, but rather substantial compliance with a certain international minimum standard of procedural fairness.[1] Indeed, since the time of *Hilton*, cases that find a foreign tribunal to be partial, or a foreign proceeding to be unacceptably irregular, are rare. The majority of cases apply a lenient standard for judging the fairness of foreign proceedings.

1. In *Society of Lloyd's* v. *Aschenden*, 233 F.3d 473 (7th Cir. 2000), Judge Posner said 'We'll call this the "international concept of due process" to distinguish it from the complex concept that has emerged from American case law'. *Id.* at 477.

748. *Hilton* itself laid the foundation for this standard. Although it employed universal terms, such as impartiality, regularity, and fairness, the *Hilton* Court made it clear that the laws and regular practise of the foreign country are an essential, though not determinative, element in judging the fairness of the foreign proceeding. In *Hilton* itself, the Court took note of the defendant's assertions that the French court admitted into evidence documents that would be inadmissible under American law, allowed the plaintiff to testify without being under oath, did not allow his cross-examination, and generally did not follow 'safeguards which are by our law considered essential to secure honesty and to detect fraud in a witness.[1] Nevertheless, the Court concluded that, because 'the practice followed and the method of examining witnesses were *according to the laws of France*', the Court would not hold that the difference in procedure was in and 'of itself, a sufficient ground for impeaching the foreign judgment'.[2]

1. *Hilton*, 159 US at 204.
2. *Id.* at 205 (emphasis added).

749. Most courts have followed *Hilton's* approach. In *British Midland Airways Ltd.* v. *International Travel, Inc.*, the court declared that only an 'outrageous departure' from due process standards would prevent recognition.[1] In *Panama Processes S.A.* v. *Cities Service Co.*,[2] the judgment-debtor complained that 'in Brazil: (1) no witnesses of any party may be subpoenaed; (2) testimony of corporate employees is inadmissible; (3) there is no available process for requiring testimony of indispensable US witnesses; (4) there is no right of cross-examination; and (5) the parties may neither conduct pre-trial discovery nor subpoena documents'.[3] The court responded:

> This argument, rather than having its basis in a denial of due process, actually rests on the procedural differences between United States and Brazilian courts. Although Brazilian norms of procedure differ from ours, that is not a basis for their condemnation as falling short of the minimum due process standards in the Anglo-American sense.[4]

In *Tonga Air Services, Ltd.* v. *Fowler*, the court observed:

> [T]he public policy of the state of Washington is not violated simply because there is a difference between the laws of a foreign state and this state. The laws and legal systems of different nations reflect historic and cultural diversity of their people. These laws and systems are designed to meet the needs of those people. Accordingly, differences of systems and of issues addressed by laws rationally exist between nations.[5]

The court held, *inter alia*, that certain 'irregularities' in the foreign proceeding, such as the lack of a verbatim trial record and the fact that the judgment-debtor was not allowed to present certain documentary evidence, were inconsequential.[6]

1. 497 F.2d 869, 871 (9th Cir. 1974).
2. 796 P.2d 276 (Okla. 1990).
3. *Id.* at 285.
4. *Id.* at 286.
5. 826 P.2d 204, 214 (Wash. 1992).
6. *See also Ingersoll Mill. Mach. Co.* v. *Granger*, 631 F.Supp. 314 (N.D.Ill. 1986), *aff'd*, 833 F.2d 680 (7th Cir. 1987); A. von Mehren, 'Recognition and Enforcement of Foreign Judgments: General Theory and the Role of Jurisdictional Requirements', 167 *Recueil des Cours* 9, 1980, 38 ('In principle, all procedural systems should be viewed as a whole; weakness in one department may well be offset by strength in another. Furthermore, one must be cautious in evaluating other systems: too often the unfamiliar is equated with the unjust'.).

750. In *Brennan* v. *University of Kansas*,[1] one litigant argued that a search and seizure conducted in Italy according to Italian procedures violated his Fourth and Fourteenth Amendment rights under the US Constitution and hence should not be recognized by United States courts. The court rejected this argument, reasoning that the amendments did not have extraterritorial effect, and noting that the search was conducted lawfully under Italian law and its execution was not 'so shocking to the forum community that it cannot be countenanced'.[2]

1. 451 F.2d 1287 (10th Cir. 1971).
2. *Id.* at 1289.

751. In *CIBC Mellon Trust Co.* v. *Mora Hotel Corp. N.V.*,[1] judgment creditors sought to enforce an English judgment by attaching defendant's 30 million US dollars (USD) hotel in New York. The judgment debtors, the defendants in both cases, objected on the ground that the English proceeding was incompatible with the due process standards because the English court employed the inherently coercive power of *Mareva* preliminary injunctions[2] threatening to freeze the defendants' assets on a worldwide basis unless the defendants complied with the court's discovery orders. The New York court acknowledged its previous expression of concern regarding 'the power and potential commercial disruption of *Mareva* orders',[3] but concluded that 'the use of this device, standing alone, does not render the English *system* as a whole incompatible with our notions of due process'.[4] The court noted that the Uniform Act 'does not demand that the foreign tribunal's procedures exactly match those of New York. Rather, the [Act] is satisfied if the foreign court's procedures are "compatible with the requirements of due process of law"'.[5] After reciting the usual platitudes about the impartiality of the English legal system,[6] the court reiterated that 'the relevant inquiry . . . is the overall fairness of England's legal "system," which is beyond dispute'.[7]

1. 792 N.E.2d 155 (N.Y. 2003), *cert. denied*, 124 S.Ct. 399 (US 2003).
2. *See Mareva Cia. Naviera S.A.* v. *Int'l Bulkcarriers S.A.*, 2 Lloyd's Rep 509 (1975).
3. *CIBC Mellon*, 792 N.E.2d at 159–160. (citing *Credit Agricole Indosuez* v. *Rossiyskiy Kredit Bank*, 94 N.Y.2d 541, 550–551 (NY 2000)).
4. *Id.* at 160.
5. *Id.*

6. *See id.* ('Moreover, "[c]onsidering that our own jurisprudence is based on England's, a defendant sued on an English judgment will rarely be in a position to defeat it with such a showing," ' and 'any suggestion that (England's) system of courts does not provide impartial tribunals or procedures compatible with the requirements of due process of law' borders on the risible' (quoted sources omitted).
7. *Id.*

752. Actually, this was *not* the 'relevant inquiry'. The defendant's objection was directed against a particular foreign procedure, not against the foreign system as a whole. If that procedure was incompatible with due process, then it is no consolation for that defendant to be told that the foreign system renders perfect justice to all other defendants. In this sense, the numerous recent cases that refused to recognize English libel judgments[1] are not an indictment of the English legal system as a whole. Rather they suggest that the relevant inquiry is very rarely the fairness of the entire system but more often the fairness of a particular procedural or substantive rule.[2] Ultimately, the *CIBC Mellon* court did offer a more relevant, case-specific conclusion, that the defendants were 'given ample notice and numerous opportunities to present their defence in England',[3] and they elected to forego these opportunities.

1. *See infra* 761.
2. While it is true that the libel cases based the non-recognition on the public policy exception (*see infra* 758–762), that exception often overlaps with the unfair-procedures exception.
3. *CIBC Mellon*, 792 N.E.2d at 160.

753. Finally, in *Society of Lloyd's* v. *Mullin*,[1] one of many similar cases in recent years recognizing English judgments in favour of the Lloyd's of London,[2] the court again misread the judgment debtor's challenge. The debtor argued that the English court's procedures were incompatible with due process because the judgment ordered enforcement of a 'pay-now-sue-later' clause in a reinsurance contract that prohibited certain defences and counterclaims in the English proceeding. The Pennsylvania court rejected the debtor's argument after assuming that, under the Uniform Act, the court 'must restrict its inquiry to a panoramic examination of the English judiciary, i.e., the English "system" ',[3] rather than examine the specifics of the particular proceeding. Finding that 'the integrity and fairness of the English courts are not open to doubt',[4] the court rejected the debtor's challenge.

1. 255 F.Supp.2d 468 (E.D. Pa. 2003).
2. *See*, e.g., *Society of Lloyd's* v. *Turner*, 303 F.3d 325 (5th Cir. 2002); *Society of Lloyd's* v. *Ashenden*, 233 F.3d 473 (7th Cir. 2000); *Society of Lloyds* v. *Hudson*, 276 F.Supp.2d 110 (D. Nev. 2003); *Society of Lloyds* v. *Webb*, 156 F.Supp.2d 632 (N.D.Tex. 2001), *aff'd*, 303 F.3d 325 (5th Cir. 2002); *Society of Lloyd's* v. *Grace*, 718 N.Y.S.2d 327 (NY App. Div. 2000).
3. 255 F.Supp.2d at 472.
4. *Id.* (internal quotations omitted).

II. Judgment Obtained or Tainted by Fraud

754. The older literature and case law distinguished between 'extrinsic' and 'intrinsic' fraud. Although the distinction is less than clear, 'extrinsic fraud' is usually defined as fraud that prevented the judgment debtor from having the opportunity to present his case fully to the foreign court (such as a default judgment based on a false affidavit that the defendant had been duly served). In contrast, 'intrinsic fraud' is defined as fraud committed in the proceeding, such as the use of perjured testimony or falsified documents, which could have been addressed by the foreign court.[1] With regard to sister-state judgments, either type of fraud is a defence to recognition, but *only* if it would have been a ground for challenging the judgment in F-1 and such challenge was not precluded by other factors.

1. *See John Sanderson & Co.* v. *Ludlow Jute Co.*, 569 F.2d 696 (1st Cir. 1978); *Fairchild, Arabatzis & Smith, Inc.* v. *Prometco (Produce & Metals) Co.*, 470 F.Supp. 610, 615 (S.D.N.Y. 1979).

755. With regard to foreign country judgments, either type of fraud is a ground for non-recognition, *regardless* of whether it would also be a ground for challenging the judgment in F-1. The difference is that here non-recognition is mandated in some instances and is discretionary in others. Under both the Uniform Act and the Restatement (Third), either type of fraud is a discretionary ground for non-recognition.[1] In contrast, the proposed federal statute addresses only extrinsic fraud and makes it a ground for mandatory non-recognition.[2] The revised Uniform Act also addresses only extrinsic fraud, but makes it a ground for discretionary non-recognition.[3]

1. *See* UFMJRA §4(b)(2); *Restatement (Third)*, §482(2)(c). For cases holding that fraud of either type will defeat a foreign judgment, *see*, e.g., *Bandai Am., Inc.* v. *Bally Midway Mfg. Co.*, 775 F.2d 70, 73 (3d Cir. 1985), *cert. denied*, 475 US 1047 (1986). For a case denying recognition to a Bolivian judgment on the basis of fraud that was probably more intrinsic than extrinsic (failure to reveal the existence of a critical document that would be fatal to the judgment creditor's claim), *see De la Mata* v. *American Life Ins. Co.*, 771 F.Supp. 1375 (D.Del. 1991).
2. *See* REFJA §5(a)(v).
3. *See* UFCMJRA §4(b)(2).

III. Notice Requirements

756. Lack of timely and adequate notice is a subspecies of lack of procedural fairness that may defeat recognition of a foreign judgment. Under both the Uniform Act and the Restatement (Third), failure to give notice to the defendant 'in sufficient time to enable him to defend' is a discretionary ground for non-recognition of the foreign judgment.[1] However, the better view is that the court's discretion is limited to determining whether the notice was sufficient to meet due process standards. If those standards are not met, then non-recognition ought to be mandatory.[2] The proposed federal statute directly adopts this view by making lack of timely and adequate notice a mandatory ground for non-recognition.[3]

1. *See* UFMJRA §4(b)(1); *Restatement (Third)* §482(2)(b). For cases denying recognition on this ground, *see Koster* v. *Automark Indus.*, 640 F.2d 77 (7th Cir. 1981); *Ma* v. *Continental Bank, N.A.*, 905 F.2d 1073, 1076 (7th Cir.), *cert. denied*, 498 US 967 (1990); *De la Mata* v. *American Life Ins. Co.*, 771 F.Supp. 1375 (D.Del. 1991); *Bank of Montreal* v. *Kough*, 612 F.2d 467 (9th Cir. 1980); *Boivin* v. *Talcott*, 102 F.Supp. 979 (N.D. Ohio 1951).

2. *Cf. Ackermann* v. *Levine*, 788 F.2d 830, (2d Cir. 1986); *Ma* v. *Cont'l. Bank, N.A.*, 905 F.2d 1073 (7th Cir. 1990), *cert. denied*, 498 US 967 (1990); *Koster* v. *Automark Indus.*, 640 F.2d 77 (7th Cir. 1981).
3. *See* REFJA §5(a)(iv).

757. Besides being timely, the notice must also be adequate, that is, it must be 'reasonably calculated . . . to apprise interested parties of the pendency of the action and afford them an opportunity to present their objections'.[1] If this requirement has not been met, the judgment will not be recognized.[2] Conversely, if the notice complies with this requirement, the notice is effective, even if the defendant did not actually see or understand it.[3]

1. *Mullane* v. *Central Hanover Bank & Trust Co.*, 339 US 306, 314–315 (1950).
2. *See*, e.g., *De La Mata* v. *Am. Life Ins. Co.*, 771 F.Supp. 1375 (D.Del. 1991), *aff'd*, 961 F.2d 208 (3d Cir. 1992) (denying recognition to Bolivian default judgment because purported service on insurer through its former agent did not provide notice or opportunity to defend); *Choi* v. *Kim*, 50 F.3d 244 (3d Cir. 1995) (denying recognition to South Korean default judgment because a confession of judgment pursuant to 'compulsory execution' clause in notarial deed was not adequate notice); *Int'l. Transactions Ltd.* v. *Embotelladora Agral Regiomontana*, 347 F.3d 589 (9th Cir. 2003).
3. *See Roy* v. *Buckley*, 698 A.2d 497 (Me. 1997) (recognizing Canadian judgment in which notice was sent by registered mail that defendant refused); *Tahan* v. *Hodgson*, 662 F.2d 862 (D.C.Cir. 1981) (recognizing an Israeli judgment, even though the notice served on an American in Israel was written in Hebrew: 'Even if defendant were unable to read Hebrew, he should have surmised that the papers being served on him were legal in nature, and that he could ignore them only at his peril'. *Id.* at 865). *But see Julen* v. *Larson*, 101 Cal.Rptr. 796 (Cal. Ct. App. 1972) (denying recognition to German judgment because notice served on defendant in Germany and written in German was inadequate).

§6. Substantive Defences

I. The Public Policy Exception

758. As noted in the preceding chapter,[1] the fact that a sister-state judgment or the underlying cause of action is repugnant to the public policy of the state in which recognition is sought is not a ground for denying recognition. In contrast, for reasons too obvious to need elaboration, public policy is a major and frequently invoked defence to recognition of foreign country judgments. This is true not only in the United States but also in virtually any other country in the world, although the precise parameters of public policy differ from country to country.

1. *See supra* 714–717.

759. Although *Hilton* did not explicitly articulate a public policy exception, the fact that the Court based the entire question of recognizing foreign country judgments on international comity left no doubt that such an exception was available. Subsequent cases have recognized this exception, as do the three documents under discussion here. The Uniform Act and the Restatement (Third) provide that repugnancy to the forum's public policy is a discretionary ground for non-recognition, while the proposed federal statute makes it a mandatory ground. The three documents differ in the following respects:

1. under the Uniform Act, the public policy exception becomes operable if the '*cause of action*' on which the foreign judgment is based is repugnant to the public policy of the forum '*state*;'[1]
2. in contrast, under the Restatement (Third), the exception is applicable if *either* the cause of action on which the judgment was based, *or* '*the judgment itself*', is repugnant to the public policy 'of the *United States*' or of the forum state;[2]
3. finally, under the proposed federal statute, the exception operates in the same way as under the Restatement, except that: (a) it is mandatory; and (b) it is not tied to the forum state as such, but rather to any 'state of the United States when the relevant legal interest, right, or policy is regulated by state law'.[3]

1. UFMJRA §4(b)(3). For cases that upheld the foreign judgment because the *cause of action* did not offend the forum's public policy (even though the judgment itself arguably might), *see* *Southwest Livestock & Trucking Co.* v. *Hargrove*, 169 F.3d 317 (5th Cir. 1999) (recognizing Mexican judgment on promissory note with interest rate of forty-eight per cent because cause of action to collect on promissory note did not violate public policy); *Society of Lloyd's* v. *Turner*, 3003 F.3d 325 (5th Cir. 2002) (rejecting argument that standard for establishing elements of breach of contract violated public policy because cause of action for breach of contract itself was not contrary to state public policy); *Guinness PLC* v. *Ward*, 955 F.2d 875 (4th Cir. 1992). The revised Uniform Act of 2005, expressly disapproves of these cases. *See* UFCMJRA §4(c)(3), cmt. 8.
2. *Restatement (Third)* §482(2)(d). The revised Uniform Act adopted the position of the Restatement (Third). *See* UFCMJRA §4(c)(3).
3. REFJA §5(a)(vi). The accompanying official comments explain this provision as follows: 'In those areas where regulation is a function of state law, the public policy is to be determined by reference to the state with the predominant interest in the events and the parties in question. Thus, it should not matter in which court recognition or enforcement is sought'. *Id.* cmt. h.

760. Despite these differences, all three documents as well as the courts adopt a very high threshold for employing the public policy exception. For example, the fact that the foreign court applied a different law or denied or granted a different remedy than the recognizing court would is not sufficient to trigger the public policy exception.[1] Courts have repeatedly stated that the public policy exception operates: 'only in those unusual cases where the foreign judgment is "repugnant to fundamental notions of what is decent and just in the State where enforcement is sought"';[2] or when the judgment '"tends clearly" to undermine the public interest, the public confidence in the administration of the law, or security for individual rights of personal liberty or of private property',[3] or undermines 'that sense of security for individual rights, whether of personal liberty or of private property, which any citizen ought to feel'.[4]

1. *See*, e.g., *Society of Lloyd's* v. *Mullin*, 255 F.Supp.2d 468 (E.D. Pa. 2003) (rejecting debtor's argument that English judgment violated Pennsylvania's public policy by enforcing a claim that Pennsylvania would not enforce; noting that such differences do not trigger the public policy exception, unless they 'present a substantial risk to fundamental public values against which only nonrecognition of the judgment can protect'. *Id.* at 475); *Neporany* v. *Kir*, 173 N.Y.S.2d 146 (N.Y.A.D. 1958) (recognizing a Quebec judgment based on claim for seduction and criminal conversation, although New York had abolished this cause of action); *Spann* v. *Compania Mexicana Radiodifusora Fronteriza*, 41 F.Supp. 907 (N.D. Tex. 1941), *aff'd*, 131 F.2d 609 (5th Cir. 1942) (recognizing Mexican judgment awarding costs and attorney fees against unsuccessful plaintiff, although forum law would not award them); *In re Hashim*, 213 F.3d 1169 (9th Cir. 2000) (same issues and result with regard to an English judgment awarding attorney fees and costs).

2. *McCord* v. *Jet Spray Intern. Corp.*, 874 F.Supp. 436 (D.Mass. 1994) (quoting *Tahan* v. *Hodgson*, 662 F.2d 862 at 864 (D.C. Cir. 1981)).
3. *Ackermann* v. *Levine*, 788 F.2d 830, 841 (2d Cir. 1986) (quoting *Somportex* v. *Philadelphia Chewing Gum*, 453 F.2d 435, 443 (3d Cir. 1971), *cert. denied*, 405 US 1017 (1972)).
4. *Hunt* v. *BP Exploration Co. (Libya) Ltd.*, 492 F. Supp. 885, 901 (N.D. Tex. 1980).

761. In recent years, several cases have invoked the public policy exception to deny recognition to foreign libel judgments rendered under laws that did not protect freedom of speech to the same extent as the First Amendment of the US Constitution. For example, in *Bachchan* v. *India Abroad Publications Inc.*,[1] a New York court refused to recognize an English libel judgment against a foreign publisher operating in New York, who approved in New York a libellous story published in New York, England, and India. In *Telnikoff* v. *Matusevitch*,[2] a Maryland court also refused on public policy grounds to enforce an English libel judgment, even though neither the parties nor the publication had any pertinent connection with the United States.

1. 585 N.Y.S.2d 661 (N.Y. Sup. Ct. 1992).
2. 702 A.2d 230 (Md. 1997). *See also Matusevitch* v. *Telnikoff*, 877 F.Supp. 1 (D.D.C. 1995); *Abdullah* v. *Sheridan Square Press, Inc.*, 1994 WL 419847 (S.D.N.Y. 1994).

762. *Yahoo! Inc.* v. *La Ligue Contre Le Racisme et L'Antisemitisme*[1] involved two interim orders obtained by two French plaintiffs against Yahoo!, a California internet service provider. The orders required Yahoo! to remove from its auction website Nazi memorabilia or to prevent access to it from French territory. The district court held, on First Amendment grounds, that the French orders were unenforceable in the United States. Ultimately, the Ninth Circuit Court of Appeals sitting *en banc* reversed this decision on other grounds.[2] However, the court agreed that the First Amendment would preclude recognition of a foreign judgment that imposed restrictions on speech in the United States. Three of the panel's eleven judges found that, in its present phase, this case did not implicate the First Amendment because the French orders did not purport to restrict access by internet users in the United States and Yahoo! did not have a First Amendment interest in enabling internet users in France to violate French criminal law.

1. 169 F.Supp.2d 1181 (N.D. Cal. 2001).
2. *See* 433 F.3d 1199 (9th Cir. 2006), *cert. denied*, *La Ligue Contre le Racisme et l'Antisemitisme* v. *Yahoo!, Inc.*, 126 S.Ct. 2332 (US 2006).

II. Penal Judgments

763. Even before deciding *Hilton*, the US Supreme Court held, in *Huntington* v. *Attrill*,[1] that judgments that are 'penal in the international sense' are not entitled to recognition. This principle holds true today, even as among the states of the United States. All three documents under discussion here provide that American courts need not enforce foreign country judgments imposing fines or penalties.[2] The Restatement (Third) considers a judgment to be penal if it is 'a judgment in favour of a foreign state or one of its subdivisions, and [is] primarily punitive rather than compensatory in character'.[3] Most courts employ a similar definition.[4]

1. 146 US 657 (1892).
2. *See* UFMJRA §1(2); *Restatement (Third)* §483; REFJA §2(b)(i).
3. *Restatement (Third)* §483 cmt. b.
4. *See*, e.g., *Chase Manhattan Bank, N.A.* v. *Hoffman*, 665 F.Supp. 73 (D. Mass. 1987) (recognizing a Belgian judgment awarding restitution in the context of a criminal proceeding).

764. The above principle means only that the court does not *enforce* a foreign penal judgment. The court may choose – or may be required by statute – to *recognize* foreign convictions for purposes other than enforcement, such as determining whether a person is a multiple offender or a convicted felon ineligible for certain benefits, such as naturalization or admission to the United States.

In *Small* v. *United States*,[1] the question was whether a provision of the US Criminal Code that prohibits the possession of firearms by persons convicted 'in any court'[2] and sentenced to more than a year imprisonment encompassed convictions in a foreign country.[3] The Supreme Court answered this question in the negative. Invoking the 'commonsense notion that Congress generally legislates with domestic concerns in mind',[4] the Court surmised that, in using the words 'any court', Congress did not contemplate *foreign* courts, because 'foreign convictions differ from domestic convictions in important ways'.[5] For example, besides the fact that the applicable foreign laws may prohibit conduct that US law permits or punishes much less severely,[6] some foreign convictions may result from proceeding that are 'inconsistent with an American understanding of fairness'.[7] The Court reasoned that, although these differences alone were not determinative, they tipped the scales in cases such as this, in which 'Congress likely did not consider the matter and where other indicia of intent are in approximate balance'.[8] The Court concluded that it was reasonable to adopt an assumption that Congress intended the phrase 'convicted in any court' to apply 'domestically, not extraterritorially'.[9]

1. 125 S.Ct. 1752 (US 2005).
2. 18 USC §922(g)(1) (2005).
3. The defendant in *Small* was convicted by a Japanese court for smuggling ten firearms into Japan and was sentenced to five years imprisonment. Two years later, he was paroled and returned to the United States where, one week after completing parole for his Japanese conviction, he was arrested in possession of two other firearms.
4. *Small*, 125 S.Ct. at 1755 (1993).
5. *Id.* 1755.
6. *See id.* 1755–1756 (citing examples from the Soviet Union, Cuba, and Singapore).
7. *Id.* at 1755.
8. *Id.* at 1756.
9. *Id.*

III. Tax and Fiscal Judgments

765. The recognition of foreign tax or fiscal judgments is discretionary in theory,[1] but rare in practise, unless of course a treaty provides otherwise. A tax judgment is defined as 'a judgment in favour of a foreign state or one of its subdivisions based on a claim for an assessment of a tax, whether imposed in respect of income, property, transfer of wealth, or transactions in the taxing state'.[2] In *Her Majesty the Queen in Right of the Province of British-Columbia* v. *Gilbertson*,[3] the court refused to recognize a Canadian judgment involving a logging tax assessed against US citizens who had engaged in lumber operations in Canada. The court expressed its misgivings about the soundness of the rule that precluded enforcement of foreign tax judgments but, like other courts, concluded that the rule was 'firmly embedded in the law'.[4]

1. *See* UFMJRA §1(2); *Restatement (Third)* §483; REFJA §2(b)(i).
2. *Restatement (Third)* §483, cmt. c. 'Judgments arising out of failure to pay license fees or for violation of exchange controls or similar laws are not tax judgments, but they may be treated similarly'. *Id.*
3. 597 F.2d 1161 (9th Cir. 1979).
4. *Id.* at 1165.

IV. Inconsistent Judgments

766. The Uniform Act, the Restatement (Third), and the proposed federal statute all provide that a foreign country judgment 'need not' be recognized if it conflicts with another foreign country judgment that is entitled to recognition.[1] The decision as to which of the two conflicting judgments will be recognized, if any, depends on several factors. Among these factors are which lawsuit was first filed and which judgment was rendered first, whether the one judgment was brought to the other court's attention and whether that court denied recognition under standards similar to the American standards.[2] In *Byblos Bank Europe, S.A.* v. *Syrketi*,[3] the court was asked to recognize a Belgian judgment that conflicted with a prior Turkish judgment. The Belgian judgment creditor invoked the last-in-time rule, which applies to sister-state judgments.[4] The court found that rule inapplicable because the then applicable Belgian law required a *de novo* review of the underlying claim without any deference to the Turkish judgment and thus precluded the Turkish judgment creditor from asserting the *res judicata* effects of the Turkish judgment in the Belgian court.

1. *See* UFMJRA §4(b)(4); *Restatement (Third)* §482(2)(e); REFJA §5(c)(ii). If the other judgment is that of a sister-state, then the Full Faith and Credit clause becomes applicable and precludes recognition of the foreign country judgment.
2. *See* REFJA §5 cmt. j.
3. 819 N.Y.S.2d 412 (N.Y.Sup.Ct. 2006), *aff'd*, 837 N.Y.S.2d 54, 2007 WL 1531795 (N.Y.A.D. 1 Dept. 29 May 2007).
4. *See Treinies* v. *Sunshine Mining Co.*, 308 US 66 (1939).

V. Other Defences

767. In addition to the above grounds for non-recognition, an American court may refuse to recognize a foreign judgment if it resulted from a proceeding that was undertaken in violation of an exclusive choice-of-forum or arbitration agreement[1] or was initiated after commencement of a proceeding in an American court on the same subject between the same parties.[2] Recognition may also be denied if the foreign court employed devices such as antisuit injunctions or restraining orders designed to 'frustrat[e] the claimant's opportunity to have the claim adjudicated in a more appropriate court in the United States'.[3]

1. *See* UFMJRA §4(b)(6); *Restatement (Third)* §482(2)(f); REFJA §5(b)(i).
2. *See* REFJA §5(c)(iii).
3. REFJA §5(c)(iv). For the converse situation in which an action is filed in the United States after an action on the same subject and involving the same parties was filed in another country, *see id.* §11 (requiring stay of proceeding under certain conditions).

§7. Arbitral Awards

768. Like more than 130 other countries, the United States is party to the United Nations Convention on the Recognition and Enforcement of Foreign Arbitral Awards of 1958 ('New York Convention').[1] Because the Convention is widely known outside the United States, this Section assumes the reader's familiarity with it and discusses only a few aspects of its application in the United States.

According to Article I, the Convention applies to 'non-domestic' awards rendered outside the United States. The implementing federal statute confines the Convention to awards arising out of 'commercial' relationships and exempts from its scope awards arising from 'a relationship which is entirely between citizens of the United States . . . unless that relationship involves property located abroad, envisages performance or enforcement abroad, or has some other reasonable relation with one or more foreign states'.[2]

1. *See* 21 UST 2517, 330 UNTS 3. In addition, the United States is a party to the Inter-American Convention on International Commercial Arbitration of 1975 (*see* 14 I.L.M. 336 (1975)) known as 'Panama Convention', and the Convention on the Settlement of Investment Disputes Between States and Nationals of Other States of 1965 (*see* 17 UST 1270, 575 UNTS 159).
2. 9 USCA §202 (2007).

769. The same statute defines the Convention's substantive scope by limiting it to arbitration agreements or awards arising out of a 'legal relationship . . . which is considered as commercial, *including a transaction, contract, or agreement described in Section 2 of* [*the FAA*]'.[1] The italicized cross-reference to Section 2 (but not Section 1) of the Federal Arbitration Act (FAA) makes the Convention applicable not only to all consumer contracts (like the FAA), but also to *all* employment contracts, including those involving transportation workers (unlike the FAA). Unlike most other countries which do not enforce *pre-dispute* arbitration clauses in consumer and employment contracts, the FAA does not make this distinction and thus holds these clauses enforceable. As a knowledgeable commentator observed, this feature of American law is 'unique, or at least highly unusual, compared to the rest of the world'.[2]

1. *Id.*
2. Drahozal, 'New Experiences of International Arbitration in the United States', 54 *Am. J. Comp. L.* 233, 2006 Supp., 233. *See also* Drahozal & Friel, 'A Comparative View of Consumer Arbitration', 71 *Arb.* 131, 2005.

770. Article III of the Convention requires each contracting state to recognize and enforce arbitral awards that fall within the Convention's scope without imposing 'substantially more onerous conditions . . . than are imposed on the recognition or enforcement of domestic arbitral awards'.[1] Article V sets forth seven permissible exceptions or defences to recognition, including a public policy exception. The fact that Article V's enumeration is not accompanied by words suggesting its exclusivity, coupled with a comparison with Article III, leaves room for argument that a contracting state may impose additional exceptions to recognition, as long as it does likewise with regard to domestic awards.

Nevertheless, American courts have taken the position that the enumeration of exceptions in Article V is exclusive.[2] This position has been influenced by the categorical, though not necessarily conclusive, language of the implementing statute, which mandates recognition of awards falling within the Convention's scope 'unless [the court] finds one of the grounds for refusal or deferral of recognition or enforcement of the award specified in the said Convention'.[3] This issue has practical relevance because, in scrutinizing domestic arbitral awards, American courts have developed a special exception to the recognition of domestic arbitral awards known as 'manifest disregard of the law',[4] which is not included in Article V of the Convention. Although some early cases held that this exception also applied to foreign awards, the prevailing view is to the contrary.[5]

1. New York Convention Art. III.
2. *See*, e.g., *Yusuf Ahmed Alghanim & Sons* v. *Toys 'R' Us, Inc.*, 126 F.3d 15 (2nd Cir. 1997), *cert. denied*, 522 US 1111 (1997); *Parsons & Whittemore Overseas Co., Inc.* v. *Societé Generale De L'Industrie Du Papier (RAKTA)*, 508 F.2d 969 (2nd Cir. 1974); *Brandeis Intsel Ltd.* v. *Calabrian Chemicals Corp.*, 656 F.Supp. 160 (S.D.N.Y. 1987); *Admart AG* v. *Stephen and Mary Birch Foundation, Inc.*, 457 F.3d 302 (3d Cir. 2006).
3. 9 USCA §207.
4. For citations and discussion, *see* Hayford, 'Reigning in the Manifest Disregard of the Law Standard: The Key to Stabilizing the Law of Commercial Arbitration', 1999 *J. Disp. Resol.* 117, 1999.
5. *See*, e.g., *Yusuf Ahmed Alghanim & Sons* v. *Toys 'R' Us, Inc.*, 126 F.3d 15 (2nd Cir. 1997), *cert. denied*, 522 US 1111 (1997); *Int'l. Standard Elec. Corp.* v. *Bridas Sociedad Anonima Petrolera, Indus. Y Comercial*, 745 F.Supp. 172 (S.D.N.Y. 1990); *M & C Corp.* v. *Erwin Behr GmbH & Co., KG.*, 87 F.3d 844 (6th Cir. 1996); *Indus. Risk Insurers* v. *M.A.N. Gutehoffnungshutte GmbH*, 141 F.3d 1434 (11th Cir. 1998), *cert. denied*, 525 US 1068 (1998).

771. As in other countries, the threshold for applying the public policy exception is very high. American courts have held that the public policy defence is 'to be applied only where enforcement would violate the forum state's most basic notions of morality and justice', and that '[t]he general pro-enforcement bias informing the convention . . . points to a narrow reading of the public policy defence'.[1]

1. *Karaha Bodas Co., L.L.C.* v. *Perusahaan Pertambangan Minyak Dan Gas Bumi Negara*, 364 F.3d 274, 306 (5th Cir. 2004), *cert. denied, PT Pertamina (Persero)* v. *Karaha Bodas Co., L.L.C.*, 543 US 917 (2004). *See also Encyclopaedia Universalis S.A.* v. *Encyclopaedia Britannica, Inc.*, 403 F.3d 85 (2nd Cir. 2005); *M & C Corp.* v. *Erwin Behr GmbH & Co., KG.*, 87 F.3d 844 (6th Cir. 1996); *Parsons & Whittemore Overseas Co., Inc.* v. *Societé Generale De L'Industrie Du Papier (RAKTA)*, 508 F.2d 969 (2nd Cir. 1974); *Karen Maritime Ltd.* v. *Omar Intern., Inc.*, 322 F.Supp.2d 224 (E.D.N.Y. 2004); *Coutinho Caro & Co. USA, Inc.* v. *Marcus Trading, Inc.*, 2000 WL 435566 (D. Conn. 2000).

772. In *Karaha Bodas Co., L.L.C.* v. *Perusahaan Pertambangan Minyak Dan Gas Bumi Negara*,[1] the plaintiff sought the enforcement of a Swiss arbitral award.

The defendant, a company owned by the Indonesian government, objected on the ground, *inter alia*, that an Indonesian court had annulled the Swiss award. The New York Convention provides that only a court in a country with 'primary jurisdiction' over an arbitral award may annul that award, and that courts in other countries have 'secondary jurisdiction' to decide whether the award may be enforced in those countries. The country that has primary jurisdiction is 'the country in which, or under the law of which, th[e] award was made'.[2] The defendant argued that this provision permits more than one country to have primary jurisdiction, namely, either the country in which the award was made (Switzerland) or the country under the law of which the award was made. The defendant argued that, in this case, the latter country was Indonesia because the arbitration agreement contained a choice-of-law clause designating Indonesian law as the governing law.

The court rejected the argument, reasoning that, when it speaks of 'the country . . . under the law of which, th[e] award was made', the Convention contemplates the procedural law the arbitrators should follow, not the substantive law. In this case, that was Swiss procedural law because the parties had chosen Switzerland as the site of the arbitration and that choice 'presumptively designated Swiss procedural law as the *lex arbitri*, in the absence of any express statement making another country's procedural law applicable'.[3] Thus, the court concluded, 'both of the New York Convention criteria for the country with primary jurisdiction point to Switzerland – and only to Switzerland. The Award was made in Switzerland and was made under Swiss procedural law'.[4] Consequently, only Swiss courts had jurisdiction to annul the award and, because they refused to do so despite defendant's efforts, the award was enforceable in the United States.

1. 364 F.3d 274 (5th Cir. 2004), *cert. denied*, PT Pertamina (Persero) v. Karaha Bodas Co., L.L.C., 543 US 917 (2004).
2. New York Convention, Art. V(e), 9 USCA §201.
3. *Karaha Bodas*, 364 F.3d at 309–310.
4. *Id.* at 309.

Table of Cases

(References are to paragraphs, not pages)

Index

(References are to paragraphs, not pages)

Index

Index

Index